Essentials of Digital Pho

Essentials of Digital Photography

Akira Kasai and Russell Sparkman
Elizabeth Hurley, Translator

New Riders Publishing, Indianapolis, Indiana

Product Development Specialist
John Kane

Senior Editors
Sarah Kearns, Suzanne Snyder

Project Editor
Cliff Shubs

Copy Editors
Amy Bezek, Dayna Isley, Michelle Warren

Technical Editor
Bob Schaffel

Software Specialist
Steve Flatt

Assistant Marketing Manager
Gretchen Schlesinger

Acquisitions Coordinator
Stacey Beheler

Administrative Coordinator
Karen Opal

Manufacturing Coordinator
Brook Farling

Photographs
Akira Kasai, Russell Sparkman, Yumiko Kasai

Illustrations
Kazuo Akai, Akira Kasai

Cover Design and Production
Nathan Clement

Book Designer
Sandra Schroeder

Original Cover Design
Hirokazu Mukai

Original Book Design
Akira Kasai

Director of Production
Larry Klein

Production Team Supervisors
Laurie Casey, Joe Millay

Graphics Image Specialists
Wil Cruz, Brad Dixon, Sadie Crawford, Tammy Graham

Production Analysts
Dan Harris, Erich J. Richter

Production Team
Kim Cofer
Diana Groth
Mary Hunt
Malinda Kuhn

Indexer
Joe Long

Essentials of Digital Photography

By Akira Kasai and Russell Sparkman. Elizabeth Hurley, translator.

Published by:
New Riders Publishing
201 West 103rd Street
Indianapolis, IN 46290 USA

Printed in the United States of America 1 2 3 4 5 6 7 8 9 0

Library of Congress Cataloging-in-Publication Data

CIP data available upon request

ISBN: 1-56205-762-6

Warning and Disclaimer

This book is designed to provide information about various imaging software and computer hardware. Every effort has been made to make this book as complete and as accurate as possible, but no warranty or fitness is implied.

The information is provided on an "as is" basis. The authors and New Riders Publishing shall have neither liability nor responsibility to any person or entity with respect to any loss or damages arising from the information contained in this book or from the use of the disks or programs that may accompany it.

The publisher, the authors and companies who supplied the demo software shall have neither liability nor responsibility to any person or entity with respect to any loss or damages arising from inserting this CD-ROM into a computer or handling any of the files contained on this CD-ROM.

Copyrights

The authors hold all copyrights and related rights to all of the digital image data contained on the CD-ROM accompanying *Essentials of Digital Photography* (hereafter, "the images").

In addition, the companies who provided the demo software on this CD-ROM and all accompanying files own all copyrights and intellectual property rights to this software and related files.

Anyone who wishes to use any of the materials on this CD-ROM in ways other than those expressly permitted by the authors and companies who hold the copyrights (hereafter, "copyright holders"), must personally request permission in writing from the copyright holders and receive that permission in writing from the copyright holders.

The copyright holders will permit the following uses of the images and materials.

1. To understand the material contained in the book, *Essentials of Digital Photography*.
2. Secondary changes to the images and the materials "not for the purposes of publication."

The copyright holders forbid the following uses of the images and materials.

1. Offset printing, hard copy output, display on display devices or any type of visual display of the images, as well as secondary changes to the images for the purpose of profit.
2. Hard copy output, display on display devices or any type of visual display of the images, as well as secondary changes to the images at seminars, presentations or instruction venues.
3. Copying of the images in the book, *Essentials of Digital Photography*, by more than one reader on more than one hard disk on more than one computer.

Publisher *Don Fowley*
Associate Publisher *David Dwyer*
Marketing Manager *Mary Foote*
Managing Editor *Carla Hall*
Director of Development *Kezia Endsley*

About the Authors

Russell Sparkman

Russell Sparkman is originally from Boston, MA, where he worked as the staff photographer at Northeastern University. He became interested in digital imaging after taking a five-day Photoshop course at the Center for Creative Imaging in Camden, Maine, in early 1992. In the summer of 1993, Sparkman moved to Nagoya, Japan.

He is an internationally recognized artist whose artwork has been published in numerous computer art and design-related magazines and books, including *Photo: Electronic Imaging* (America), *Computer Artist* (America), *Mac Art and Design* (Sweden), *Superdesigning* (Japan), *Step-By-Step Electronic Design* (Japan), *Idn* (Hong Kong), and the *Photoshop WOW* book. In addition, Sparkman is one of the featured artists in the gallery section of the Adobe Photoshop 4.0 CD-ROM. His stock photography and digital artwork are represented by Photonica (Tokyo) and Image (Nagoya).

Mr. Sparkman is also highly regarded as an author about digital imaging. He is a co-author of *Adobe Photoshop A to Z II* (BNN) and *Adobe Photoshop A to Z III* (BNN), as well as the author of *Collage Design* (Graphic-sha).

He has been a speaker and presenter for Adobe Systems at the Adobe Fair (1994) and the PowerDTP Seminar (1994). In November 1995, Sparkman toured eight Southeast Asian countries co-presenting seminars about digital photography for Kodak/Asia Pacific. In 1996, Mr. Sparkman helped introduce the new features of Photoshop 4.0 at the Seybold Seminars in Tokyo.

In addition to his work as a creative artist and author, Sparkman is a consultant in the field of digital imaging, including a project to design and implement a digital photo studio for one of Japan's largest auto manufacturers. Sparkman is also regularly called upon to use and analyze beta versions of digital imaging software and hardware.

Mr. Sparkman is the Japan representative of the *Future Image Report*, a monthly market analysis report about digital photography.

Telephone (052) 703-6305
Fax (052) 703-6986
e-mail #1: VFE04663@niftyserve.or.jp
e-mail #2: rspark@tcp-ip.or.jp

Sparkman Comment

We've all known someone in our life—perhaps a grandparent, perhaps an elderly friend—who can reflect on the past and remember a time when there wasn't such a thing as a TVs, telephones, or cars. Often, I've wondered how these people felt as they watched these new technologies emerge and quickly become common life-changing tools.

But I needn't wonder any longer. As the 21st Century approaches, we are witnessing numerous cases of change to society being brought about by digital technology, especially with the emergence of desktop publishing and the Internet. At the same time, digital technology is also having a tremendous impact on photography. Without question, the way we create and use photographs in the future is going to be very different from what it is today.

My first introduction to this change came in early 1992 when I decided to attend a Photoshop workshop, taught by Katrin Eismann, at the Kodak Center for Creative Imaging in Camden, Maine. During the course of the workshop, I was continually amazed at the almost magical sensation of scanning and manipulating photos on the Macintosh computer. By the end of the five-day workshop, I was convinced that the future of photography was to be digital.

Part of my convictions about photography in the digital age was the realization that new types, and uses, of the photographic image would be invented. However, my enthusiasm was soon tempered by the discovery that even though new and exciting directions in photography were just over the digital horizon, the technology was having the curious side effect of homogenizing the digital photograph. My own artwork was (and still is) no exception.

The homogenization of digital images, I realized, is the result of electronic imaging becoming available to vast numbers of people through easy-to-use software and computers. Although these tools seem to bring an infinite amount of potential to the art of photography, the truth is that currently there is a lot of similarity of images and style. This is due to the fact that for the first time in graphic arts history photographers, designers, and illustrators are all using the exact same systems (for example, Macintosh computers, Adobe Photoshop, and royalty-free photography) as part of their creative tool

continues

set. It's as if the designer's pens, the illustrator's paints, and the photographer's film have all been distilled into one little magic paint-by-numbers kit. The result is that there is a tendency for many computer-manipulated photographs to have an overwhelmingly uniform appearance.

This means that photographers who adapt digital imaging and digital photography methods must strive to create photographic artwork that's different from the type of artwork created by illustrators and designers using this shared set of digital tools. And the way that photographers can separate themselves from the masses is to remember why they're photographers in the first place—they find magic in using cameras, lighting, and other tools of photography to create artwork. And by combining imaginative lighting and camera techniques with the power of digital imaging, photographers are ideally suited to push the photograph beyond the boundaries of imagination.

Digital cameras, scanners, desktop computers, Photoshop, and Live Picture—these are the tools that are revolutionizing photography. From these tools a new definition of the photographic image is emerging. It's history taking place. And when we're old and gray (or older and grayer!), we'll look back on a time when the word "digital" had more to do with fingers and toes than photography, and film was the only way to take a photo, and we'll be able to say that we were there.

Akira Kasai

Akira Kasai was born in 1955 and resides in Kyoto, Japan. He is currently the president of InfoArts Co., Limited, and is a photographer and member of the Kansai DTP Association. He attended Kyushu University where he majored in photography with a specialization in documentary photography, and graduated with a degree in Fine Arts in 1978. In 1980 he received his Masters from Kyushu University, specializing in the history of photography. He is currently a guest lecturer in the Fine Arts department at Kyushu University, specializing in photographic technology.

As a student Kasai worked as a staff photographer in an architecture firm and a commercial photography studio. During this period, he also freelanced doing underwater photography and conventional color photo compositing.

After graduating, Kasai was hired by Dainippon Screen Mfg. Co. and served as an instructor of high-end scanning and prepress systems. While working for Screen in Singapore, he traveled widely, photographing in India, Sri Lanka, Nepal, and Indonesia. In 1987 he moved into design production and became a director of technology. DTP had just been introduced into Japan at that time, and Kasai became responsible for redesigning the traditional workflow and integrating new systems.

In 1994, Kasai established his own company, Info Arts. Info Arts offers a wide range of services from multimedia and software interface design, to high-end digital photo processing, MIDI, and audio processing, such as digital recording, as well as consultation for digital image processing and software development.

Kasai has co-authored *Adobe Photoshop A to Z II* and *Adobe Photoshop A to Z III* (BNN) and edited *How to Check and Correct Color Proofs* (Genkosha). He was a co-author of the Printing *Guide for Creators 5 & 6* (Genkosha) and a regular contributor to *SuperDesigning* magazine (Genkosha).

Kasai provided technical support for the establishment of the Shiseido Design & Prepress In-house Plant and has taught extensively, giving seminars sponsored by the Japan Printing Academy, the Too Corporation, JAGAT, Heidelberg PMT, Fuji Xerox, and the Kansai DTP Association. He has also been a speaker at Seybold Boston and Seybold Tokyo and has provided digital image technical support for the Indonesia Newspaper Publishing Association.

Kasai Comment

At the beginning of his comments, my co-author, Russell Sparkman, spoke of grandparents and older friends reflecting on a past without modern conveniences such as telephones and cars. When I first read that comment, I realized I fit his description of "older friend."

When I was in third grade, I used my first camera, an Olympus Pen D half-frame format manual camera with an integrated exposure meter and EV value control. The first photographs I ever took were of a waterfall, the first at F4 for $\frac{1}{500}$ second and the second at F22 for $\frac{1}{15}$ second (my father taught me how to take them). When the black-and-white photographs came back from processing, the first photograph stopped the motion of the flowing water and in the second, the water was blurred. It was an exhilarating experience to see the differences, and I was immediately hooked on photography.

The first time I was involved with anything related to digital photography was during graduate school. I was working in a photography studio at a prepress trade shop where we made CMY color separations and output continuous tone black-and-white films using a Crosfield MagnaScan 460. We brought the separation films to a color processing lab and made three exposures onto a sheet of photographic paper using C, M, and Y light in order to create color prints. The resulting prints were very sharp, with excellent flesh tones. I was amazed at how dramatically different the colors were from colors obtained using E4 process color reversal positive film. That was in 1978.

These two experiences were critical in shaping my interest in the technical aspect of photography. Although photography is a means of artistic expression, it is also valuable for simply recording information. Technology is the common thread running through both of these aspects of photography.

When photography first reached Japan, it was called "exposure technology." The term "light images" was also used. It is only in the present day that we have come to use the word "photograph." In Japanese, the term "photograph" is created by combining two characters, one for "reality" and the other for "copy," and I believe the word itself has served to narrow the enjoyment and appreciation of photography. In English, the word comes from "photo," which means "light" and "graph," which means "picture," and this seems like a better etymology of the word. In Japanese, with the spread of computer technology, we are going back to our beginnings and calling photographs "images" and "exposures" once again.

Another side of this is that it is becoming increasingly difficult to distinguish between what is reality and what is not with digital photography techniques. With digital methods, photographs of subjects that seem real but are not are becoming increasingly common.

We have written this book with the intention of introducing new photography techniques. However, we don't want you simply to learn the image processing techniques associated with using digital cameras and stop there. We hope that the material in this book will make you think about other issues, such as how well we really need to reproduce tonality and fine detail in photographs. Finally, we would like you to think about the direction photography is going to go from here (regardless of whether you think it is good or bad...).

Trademark Acknowledgments

Acknowledgments

Our thanks to...

We would like to express our thanks to the following companies and individuals for their cooperation in making this book a reality. We received many valuable suggestions at the planning and preparatory stages, as well as help with arrangements for many aspects of initial production, including equipment loans, software, artwork, and models. Materials, including documentation and close-up photography, technical advice and editing, and a variety of experiments using equipment we do not own were graciously provided throughout the project.

We could not have written a single page without the help of everyone mentioned here. We hope that we will be able to continue to work together and learn from each other as digital photography develops and matures.

Finally, we would like to thank our families for putting up with our long absence from family life during the writing of the original Japanese version of the book and then, once again, during the translation and editing of the English version. We are extremely grateful for their personal sacrifice and invaluable behind-the-scenes support, without which we never could have survived these tasks.

In America (in alphabetical order)

Pyiah Alexander, Aladdin Systems

RoseAnn Alspektor, Valis Group

Michael Brown

Anne Cutting

Andy Darlow

John Derry, Fractal Design

James Dunn

Eileen Ebner, McClean Public Relations

Katrin Eismann, Praxis.Digital Solutions

Alexis Gerard, Future Image, Inc.

Tom Hale, Macromedia

John Harcourt, Nikon, Inc.

David Hazlett, Kodak

Peter Hogg, The Digital Pond

Elizabeth Hurley

John Kane, New Riders

John Lund, TeamDigital

Michael Mayer

John McIntosh, Praxis. Digital Solutions

Nancy Miller, Canto Software, Inc.

Heather Moore, Live Picture

Brigitte Ozzello

Frank Petronio

Bob Schaffel

Jeff Schewe

Cliff Shubs, New Riders

Andrew Yonemoto, Minolta

Alex Wayne

In Japan (in alphabetical order)

Kazuo Akai, InfoArts

Andy Boone

Etsuro Endo

Kyoko Funabiki

Hiroyuki Hayakawa, Hayakawa Studio

Hiroshi Hirayama, Marubeni Electronics

Ichiro Hirose, Agosto

Katsuhiko Iida, Seiko Epson Corp.

Shyuichi Ichinose, Seiko Epson Corp.

Yasuo Inoue, Fuji Photo Film

Akira Ishihara, Agai Trading Co.

Shinkichi Kasai, Mascot

Yumiko Kasai, La Bit

Kohei Koie, Janac Corporation

Yoshinori Kaizu

Takeshi Kato, Nihon Scitex

Yoshihiro Kishida, Dainippon Screen

Gary Lynch, Shriro Trading Co.

Shinichi Miyamoto, Shashin Kagaku

Hirokazu Mukai

Tsuyoshi Narumiya, Konica Color Kansai

Tommy O'Gara

Tokiko Oda, InfoArts

Kouzou Okada, K.K. Central Graphic Center

Ichiro Onishi, Koyosha Graphics

Tomihiro Oue, Nihon Kodak Osaka

Joji Sakaguchi, Macromedia, Japan

Masayuki Shimotori, Carrot

Guy Sparkman

Maia Sparkman

Noriko Sparkman

Mariko Sumita

Katsunori Tanaka, Adobe Systems Co., Ltd

Hideaki Tobe, Shriro Trading Co.

Tony Torres, Moo Multimedia

Akihiro Usuki, Interprog

Tadashi Yoshida, Shriro Trading Co.

Contents at a Glance

Table of Contents

3 Correcting Photographs 3–1

5 Digital Exposures and Follow-Up Processing 5–1

6 Digital Photomontages 6–1

Preface

We first began planning this book in the summer of 1995. Because new digital cameras were appearing on the market every day, our first thought was to write a book called *How to Use Digital Cameras*. We thought we would touch briefly upon Photoshop, Live Picture, and other image-manipulation software, and then introduce the many kinds of artwork that can be created using digital cameras.

We considered a number of different approaches and at some point realized that it wasn't digital cameras, but digital photography, that we wanted to write about. They are not the same thing.

A digital camera is no more than an input device. With a digital camera alone, you cannot expect to create something original and bring it to final production. Just as in conventional photography, where we take a picture, develop it, and enlarge it, digital photography requires a series of steps that comprise the digital workflow.

Even if we had chosen to write a simple introduction to digital cameras, they were evolving so rapidly that our information would have become outdated while the writing was still in progress. We decided instead to provide an examination of the essence of digital photography, the aspect of digital photography that does not depend on advances in technology.

It was only after this arduous process of thinking and rethinking that we began writing in the summer of 1996. Every day we were drawn to the latest cameras and the newest software. Through a lengthy trial-and-error process, we finally decided what to include in the book. We touch upon some high-end digital cameras in this book, and we take pride in the fact that we have provided a thorough explanation of how to take what has been traditionally known as a "photograph" by using digital techniques. We do not, however, provide an introduction to compact digital cameras because there are too many of them and new ones appear all the time. As image input devices for digital photography, compact digital cameras are essentially the same as high-end digital cameras. We therefore have confidence that this book will prove very useful to compact digital camera users, too.

Adobe Photoshop is, of course, the primary software product that we use throughout this book. We do, however, look at other software, such as LivePicture and Painter, to provide contrast to Photoshop. As a whole, we have deliberately avoided giving detailed explanations about the operation of the various software products. Ultimately our purpose is to present what we consider to be the essence of digital photography.

Throughout the text, we contrast digital photography with photography as it has been universally known up to the present. For issues that require an entirely new way of thinking, we provide several different points of view.

We could not have written this book without the help and cooperation of the many people whose names appear in the Front Matter. We would like to take this opportunity to express our warmest thanks to them all.

Akira Kasai
Russell Sparkman
January, 1997

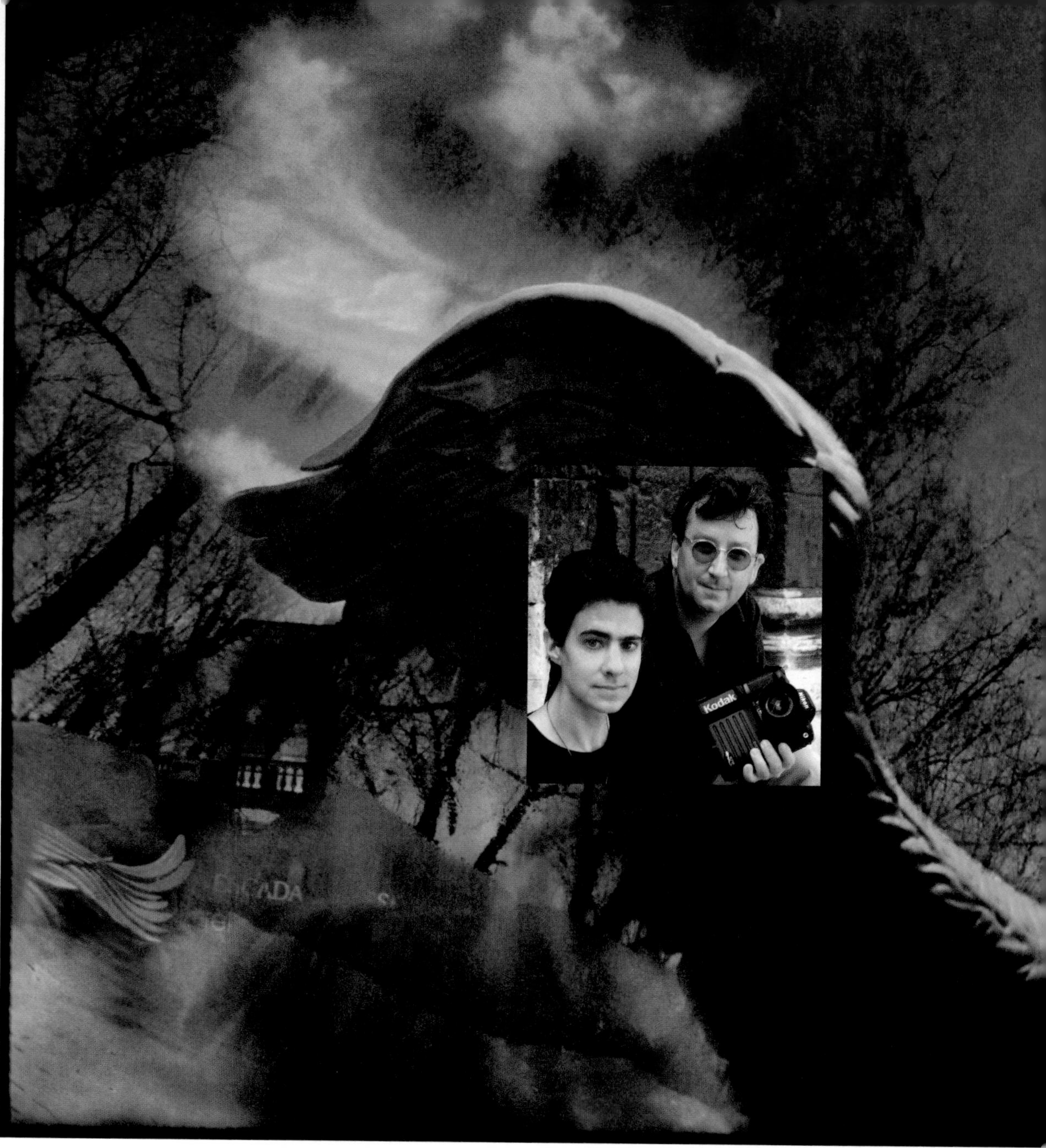
Kodak

Essentials of Digital Photography

The history of photography is punctuated by periods of evolution in photographic imaging technologies that have not only altered the aesthetic possibilities but also the cultural significance of the medium itself. When historians look back on the emergence of digital photography, events in 1991 will be viewed as such a turning point in the history of photography.

That was the year that the Kodak Center for Creative Imaging opened in Camden, Maine. The Center provided a unique educational setting where photographers and graphic artists could explore the creative use of the latest technologies. It was an extraordinary environment where, in just a single visit, photographers' perceptions of photography were fundamentally changed upon the realization of an entirely new set of imaging tools and creative options.

The new tools included the Apple Macintosh computer, Adobe Photoshop 1.5, the Kodak Digital Camera System DCS 100, and the Kodak XLS 7700 Thermal Dye Sublimation Printer. Reactions to demonstrations of these tools were consistently the same—eyes opened wide and jaws dropped in amazement. Many photographers became instant believers, eagerly embracing the new technology. It's safe to say that with those tools, the Center became the place where people started referring to "photography" as "imaging," and photographers began calling themselves "imaging artists" and "digital photographers."

This shift in definitions was further assisted by the rapid, seemingly sudden change in the availability and affordable costs of digital imaging technology. Instead of abating, the pace of these changes continues to gain momentum. In the face of such overwhelming change, the greatest challenge we face today as visual artists is how to rationally incorporate tools into the traditional photographer's toolbox.

A "hybrid" approach of using digital imaging tools side-by-side with traditional silver halide materials is often the easiest, most effective way to begin working with the digital imaging process. To do this well, it's critical to identify the strengths and weaknesses of each technology in terms of cost, quality, and efficiency. For this learning process to succeed, photographers need objective resources that are relevant to both the photochemical and photo-electronic mediums. *Essentials of Digital Photography* is such a resource.

Written by photographers for photographers, *Essentials of Digital Photography* explains key concepts about digital photography by using an approach that is independent of changes in specific imaging software and hardware. As a result, this professional workbook and tutorial explains not only what photographers need to know to apply their traditional photographic skills to digital imaging tools today, but for years to come.

John McIntosh
Director of Technology Programs/
American Film Institute

Katrin Eismann
Photo Imaging Artist/PRAXIS. Digital Solutions

chapter 1

Digital Photo Gallery

In this chapter we would like to introduce you to digital photography artwork created by the authors and their friends. Information about how these photographs were created will appear in Chapter 6 and Chapter 10.

01 1
Digital Photo Gallery

Andy Darlow

■ Allison 3, Part 1

Sinar P2/60 mm Sinnaron lens/Leaf DCB/Adobe Photoshop 3.0.5/Self-promotion for photographer and model

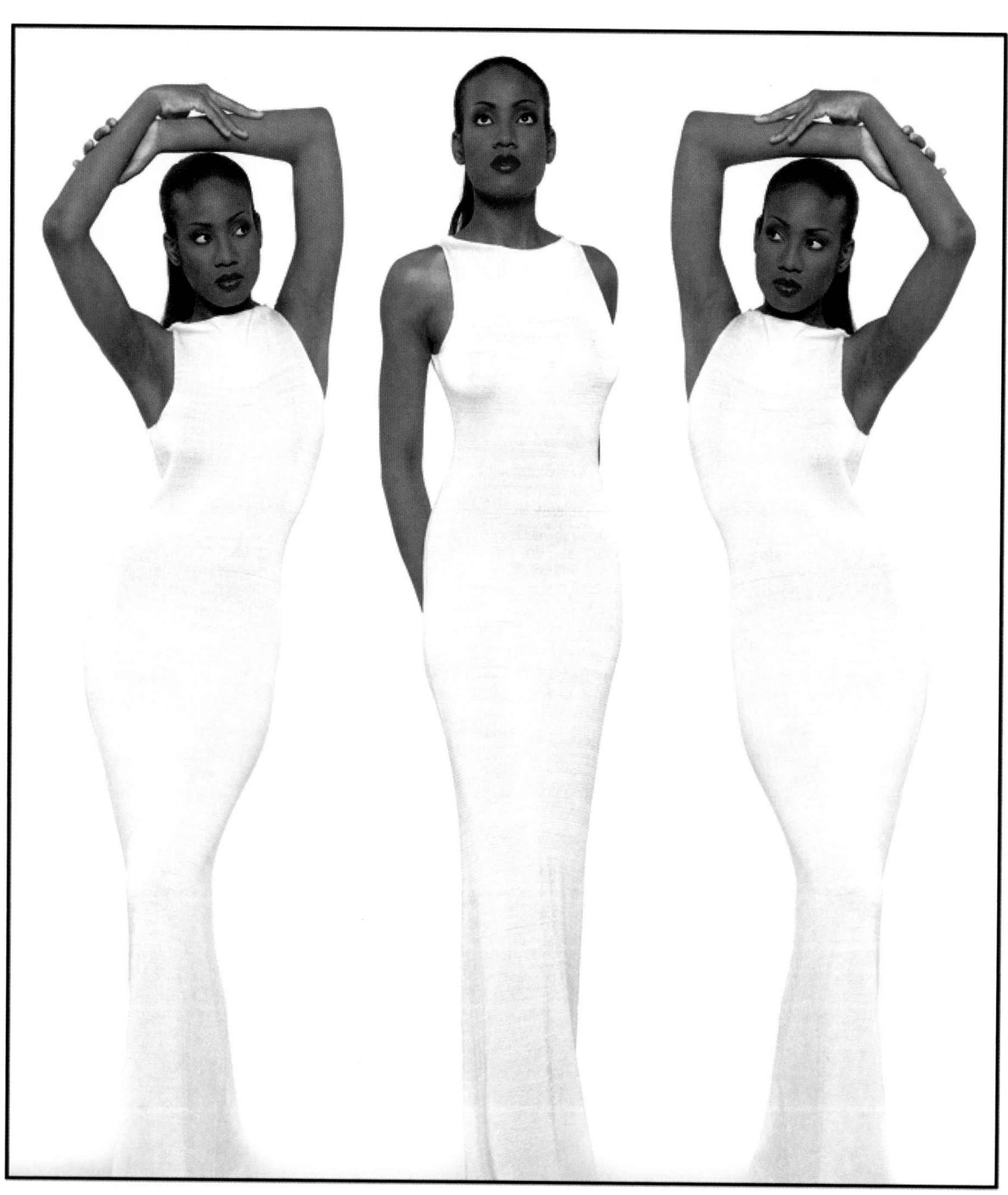

Ann E. Cutting

■ Webmaster

Still Life Objects—4×5 View Camera with 210 mm lens; U.S. Capitol Building Photo—stock photo/Adobe Photoshop 3.0/Cover illustration for *Webmaster Magazine*

Jeff Schewe

■ Barkman

4×5 Sinar/Kodak EPP film/Adobe Photoshop, Live Picture, and Valis Group's MetaFlo/Used in an advertisement

■ Hip Hog

4×5 Sinar/Kodak EPP film/Adobe Photoshop 2.5/Used in a poster

■ Globe on Hands

4×5 Sinar/Kodak EPP film/Adobe Photoshop 3.0/Used in a corporate brochure

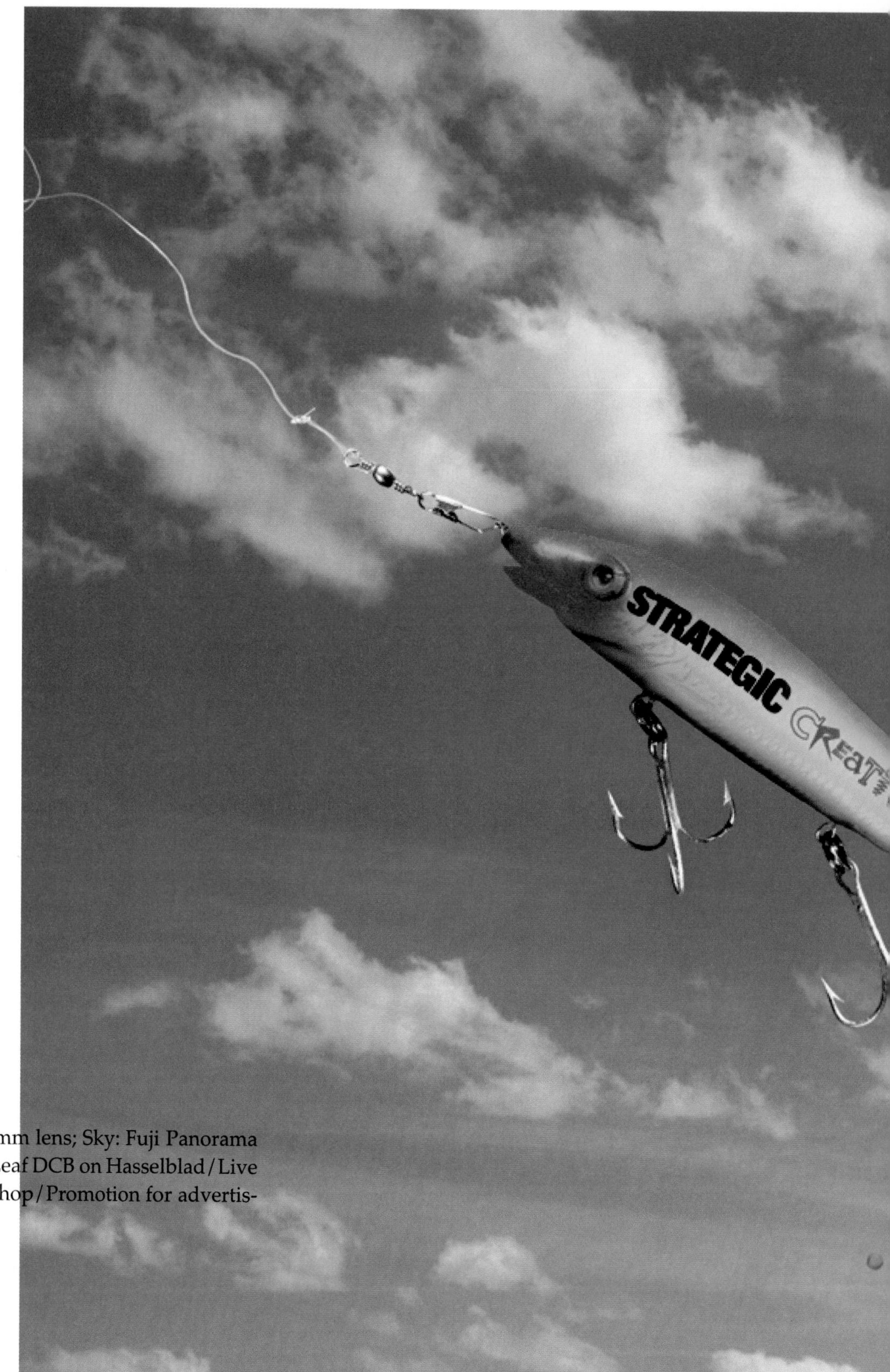

John Lund

■ The Lure

Man: Hasselblad with 90 mm lens; Sky: Fuji Panorama Camera; Fishline / Water: Leaf DCB on Hasselblad / Live Picture and Adobe Photoshop / Promotion for advertising agency

Michael Brown

■ 1997 Pathfinder—Bryce Canyon

Toyo 4×5 / Vehicle: 400 mm Scneider f5.6; Landscape: 360 mm Schneider f6.8 / Kodak Ektachrome 6117 / Adobe Photoshop / Public Relations and Regional Advertising

Russell Sparkman

■ The Dr. Martens Kids Boot

Leaf DCB II on Hasselblad 553elx / Adobe Photoshop 4.0 and Fractal Design Painter 4 / Digital photography demonstration for book

■ Blue Smoke

Leaf DCB II on Hassleblad 553 elx / Adobe Photoshop 4.0 / Self-promotion for photographer and model

"Blue Smoke" was created by using the Leaf DCB II as a single-shot, black-and-white camera. The model and incense smoke were photographed separately, and then composited together in Photoshop. The highlight behind the model's head was added onto a layer below the layer of the model. A top layer of the original photograph was blurred with the Gaussian Blur filter and then erased to show only the face as a sharp point in the image. The final image was tinted blue with the Hue / Saturation Adjustment layer.

Akira Kasai

■ Cocktail Glass

Nikon E2 / Tokina 28–70 mm lens / Adobe Photoshop 3.0 / Multimedia title illustration / Manipulated multiple layers of the same image to create back-lit effect on the glass

■ Spirits

Nikon E2 / Nikkor 103 mm macro lens / Adobe Photoshop 3.0 / Multimedia title illustration / Created shallow depth of field effect in Photoshop to enhance cocktail bar atmosphere

chapter 2

Digital Photography Basics

02 1

What is Digital Photography?

Our Definition of Digital Photography

When did the term "digital photography" first come into use?

For the average person not concerned with scientific research, the origins of the universe, or the military, the term "digital photography" first appeared after Adobe Photoshop was released in 1990. There is still no set definition to which everyone agrees, so we would like to spend some time defining the term as it is used throughout this book. "Digital photography" is used in the following cases:

- When photographs are taken without using film, using a digital camera.
- When existing images, on film or photographic paper, are scanned to create digital image data.
- When the digital image data is processed on a computer.
- When some type of hard copy output is generated from the final digital image data. The hard copy can be an offset print, a color film recording, an inkjet print, or some other format.

Conversely, are there things that seem like digital photography that really are not? The rule of thumb is "does the subject actually exist in the real world?" This is to say that we focus only on subjects in the outside world that have been composed through a lens and exposed, then digitally input, electronically processed, and output. Anything else, such as painting on an empty canvas with a brush or processing that painting using either digital or analog photographic methods, isn't considered digital photography in this book.

Digital Photography and Analog Photography

In contrast to digital photography, there is "analog photography." This term has not been clearly defined either because up until now there has been no need to do so. However, we assume that most of our readers are people who are interested in or are in the business of what has been traditionally known as "photography," which is to say *analog* photography.

For these readers we have provided a summary chart on the following page showing the differences between silver halide photography—which we are taking as representative of analog photography—and digital photography. There are other kinds of analog photography than silver halide photography, but for our purposes, the sole focus remains on silver halide photography. The chart includes some technical terminology, but should prove useful for anyone interested.

Methods of Digital Photography

When we limit ourselves to motifs that are the essence of something in the external world composed through the lens of a camera, categorizing the photography method used as either digital or analog should have little bearing on the quality of the artwork created. For example, many great photographic images have been created using only digital methods, such as special effect filters, to create imagery that could not have been created any other way. In other cases, digital photography was only one of many techniques, including film-based photography, used to create the image. Asking whether the photograph is analog or digital is as futile as asking which is better—using automatic or manual exposure on your single lens reflex camera. Ultimately, achieving the goal of creating a great piece of photographic artwork is more important than whether the image was processed digitally. Given these issues, we have tried particularly hard in this book to narrow the gap between analog and digital photography by introducing digital photography tips and techniques that correspond to traditional tricks of the trade, such as dodging, burning, and masking.

Silver Halide Photography and Digital Photography Compared

Some basic assumptions: We understand that there are many applications for both silver halide photography and digital photography. For the purpose of comparison, we've considered indoor and outdoor compositions of typical subjects, such as people, scenery, and still life objects. The following chart presents a subjective comparison of the two types of photography and includes a variety of attributes for each type.

	Attributes	Silver Halide Photography	Digital Photography
General	Resolution of detail	Depends on physical size of photosensitive material and properties of emulsion. Opinion differs; as yet undetermined.	Depends on number of light sensors. Opinion differs depending on type of CCD, number of cells, method of image generation after sampling.
	Color reproduction	Depends largely on properties of photosensitive material and emulsion. Feeling is more important than accuracy.	Optically and electronically faithful to color of subject. If profiles are made of device characteristics, possible to accurately reproduce subject color by colorimetry.
	Speed of results	Maximum possible exposure speed is 20 frames per second. Except with instant cameras, hours, if not days, required to produce film or prints post-photography.	Time lag exists while data is stored to memory, so maximum speed is several frames per second. Post-photography system, including monitor proofing and hard copy printer output, much faster than silver halide photography.
	Convenience	Film loading and unloading requires time. However, camera operation and convenience have been perfected over time.	Proficiency in personal computers required. Technology evolving so operability steadily improving. Convenience still inadequate.
	Creative possibilities	If not using own darkroom, high dependence on outside labs limits creativity involving image enhancement.	Many possibilities: straight photography, photomontage, distortion, all types of image enhancement, scanning of silver halide photos. Easy to move into virtual 3D and video.
	Final image quality	Good image quality up to 20 times original size. Above this, images deteriorate and become grainy proportional to amount of enlargement.	Image data can tolerate being enlarged by interpolation up to four times original size. Further interpolation causes loss in quality but isn't due to graininess. Information about techniques for maintaining image quality is late in coming, giving mistaken impression that silver halide photography is better.
	Cost	High running costs for film and developing. Fixed costs for cameras and other equipment relatively low. High compatibility between equipment.	Running costs extremely low. Initial investments in cameras, computers, scanners, memory, printers, and so forth, many times higher than that required for equivalent setup for silver halide photography. Also, numerous incompatibility issues between light source and camera types.
Interaction of camera and photosensitive material	Photographing subjects in motion	High speed photography up to many thousandths of a second.	Depending on the camera, only completely still subjects can be taken. However, there are cameras that can capture moving subjects equivalent in quality to silver halide cameras.
	Time exposures	Only limitation is reciprocity failure of the photosensitive material.	If CCD pellucid elements are cooled, time exposures in excess of one second are possible, but sensor element sensitivity produces electronic noise.
	Speedlight exposure	Few limitations except for synchronization of focal plane shutter.	Depends on type of camera. Same capabilities as silver halide cameras that use speedlights. Cannot be used with incompatible devices.
	Exposure using special light sources	Depends on characteristics of photosensitive material. Many restrictions exist.	Electronically optimized light sensor systems provide many possibilities.
	Exposure under special environmental conditions	Limits at high and low temperatures.	Except for a few cases, little temperature dependence; however, necessary to insure stable power supply, especially in cold environments.
	Latitude	With average film, can record images up to a maximum 9 stop luminance range (with special film processing).	Limit with digital cameras is 6 stops. For scanned silver halide images, possible to adjust with image manipulation software to widen latitude.
	Camera body	As a tool, has greatly improved over time. Overall compact.	Not standardized since have just arrived on the market. Still in prototype design stages. Great dependence on power supplies. Trend toward becoming relatively large.
	Lenses	Wide variety available. Little compatibility among lens mounts, and so on.	Same as for silver halide camera lenses, but because CCD arrays are small, limits exist on permissible field of view. Some cameras require dedicated lenses or low pass optics.
	Shutters	Physically block light.	Two systems available, one that physically blocks the light and one that electronically controls data capture.
	Finders	Optical viewers most popular.	Two types available: optical viewers and LCD panels. In practical studio use, monitor also acts as viewfinder.
Image manipulation	Developing	Tightly controlled chemical processing required for color.	Chemical processing not required.
	Brightness/color adjustment	Depends on amount of exposure during exposure and enlargement as well as on photosensitive material properties.	Much better range than for silver halide photography when adjusting properly exposed images.
	Enlarging	No optical limitations. In actual practice, 30–50%.	In actual practice, four times, with interpolated enlargement. Ten times possible with extraordinary measures.
	Use in commercial applications	Standardization progressing; wide range of applicability.	Not standardized; depends on printing companies. Quality relatively high.
	High volume	Relatively low.	Overall high productivity for proofing, data management, delivery to post-processing. Industry expertise not established, not yet evaluated.
Other	Credibility	High credibility.	Low credibility since no traces of tampering remain after post-exposure processing.
	Durability	Deteriorate over time.	Theoretically digital data does not deteriorate. Hard copies not as durable as silver halide photography prints.

02 2

The First Step—Monitor Calibration

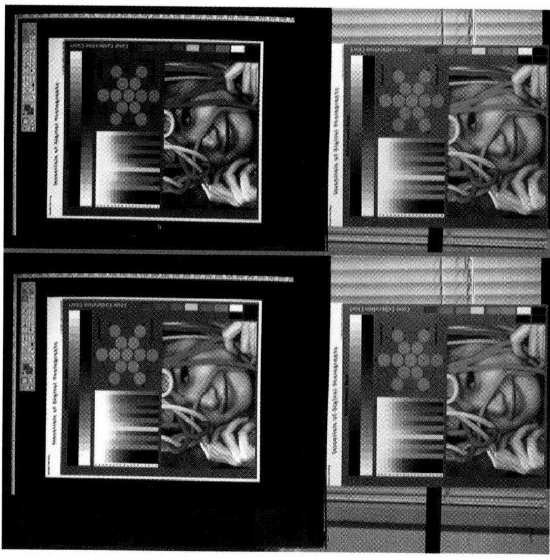

Top: Monitor display of Color Calibration Chart, before calibration, photographed alongside printed version from back of book.

The display of the calibrated monitor matches the print output much better than the display of the uncalibrated monitor.

Bottom: Monitor display of Color Calibration Chart, after calibration, photographed alongside printed version from back of book.

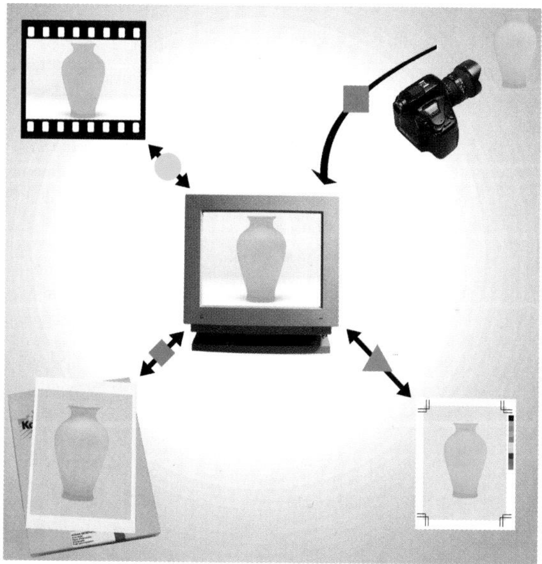

The Importance of Monitor Calibration

To generate the best possible pictures using digital photography, you must always adjust your monitor. The process of matching the color and gray balance of the monitor to original or final artwork is called *monitor calibration*. When the brightness and color of the image you see on your monitor is different from your original color reversal film or the final artwork output you generated from that data, it's hard to have confidence in the quality of the artwork you're creating. In essence, you're working blind.

Monitor calibration is much the same as standardizing the color temperature and luminance of the lightbox through which you view color reversal film. For example, if the lightbox has a red bias and is too bright, you might look at a very blue biased underexposed frame and think it's okay. If the same consideration isn't given to how a monitor's display characteristics can affect the visual interpretation of image data, your results will be disappointing. This could certainly lead you to conclude that the quality of digital photography is poor in comparison to analog photography.

To help prevent these kinds of problems, it's important to optimize your monitor's display characteristics. After that, it's important to use the same procedures to calibrate all of the other monitors in your workplace, and any other monitors where people may be viewing your work.

What Are We Matching to What?

In the world of desktop publishing, when we design a piece of artwork on the computer and go through the steps of having it printed as hard copy output, we need a process to insure consistency of color from one step to the next. This process, called color matching, is a process that includes profiling the color characteristics of a number of devices from input (scanners) to proofing (desktop printers/monitors) to output (film/printing press). Monitor calibration plays a central role in this process.

As a digital photographer, the monitor is the canvas upon which you create your artwork. To insure image quality, you might think that all you need to do is match the color and brightness of your own monitor to one form of final output. But unfortunately, it's more complicated than that, since there are many different ways that a digital photograph can be output. For example, you might output the same image to both CMYK films (meaning four-color offset printing) and to a color film recorder for 4×5-inch Ektachrome film output.

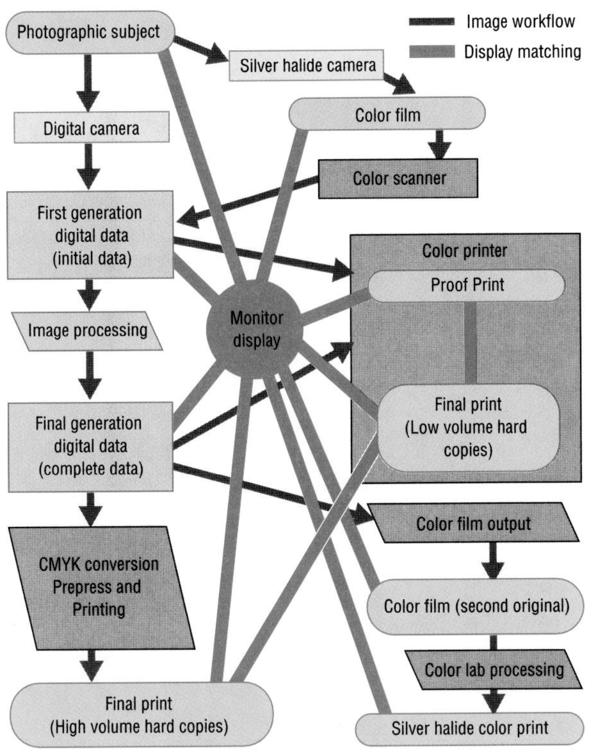

Color matching to the monitor display may be required often. It's impossible to make everything match, but at least one match should be possible.

Color viewing environment	
Room lighting	If the ambient light around the monitor is too bright, there will be a loss in monitor contrast. Bightness should be set to a level where you can read text comfortably.
Room color	If there are brightly painted pieces of furniture or walls in the room, the reflection off their surfaces can generate tints on the monitor or hard copy or cause optical illusions to the human eye. Rooms should be neutral gray or white.
Lighting for viewing original or final artwork	The light source illuminating your photography or other hard copy must have a color temperature of 5,000K (5,500K or 6,500K are also possible). Also, the light source luminance and distance must be adjusted so that the white of the paper and the white on the monitor are the same.
Monitor hood	Attach a large monitor hood (depth of at least 30 cm) to your monitor. Make sure the monitor is completely shielded from stray light.

If you output two sheets of film, you may file one sheet away in your stock photo library as an archived original. At the same time, you might make arrangements to lend the other sheet to a client who wishes to use the film to make a large, photographic display print. At this point the issue of which version of the image is the original and which is the final form becomes murky—is it the monitor display, the CMYK output, the Ektachrome output, or the photographic display print? Because of the different characteristics of these output devices, as well as the way the human eye perceives color, it's complicated to say definitively what is supposed to match to what.

For photographers shooting silver halide color reversal film, this has never been a big issue because the film itself has been the original piece of art. It's always been a fairly simple matter to tell a printer or a photo lab to match color, and so on, to the original. But as a digital photographer, once you begin to scan your photographs and make your own digital photo library, output from the data becomes a complicated issue. Upon which original do you base decisions about color? The film? The original scan? Or the slightly manipulated version of the scan?

As you can see, there can be a lot of confusion concerning which is the original color, which is the intermediate color (monitor display, hard copy proofs) and which is the final color in digital photography. The problem is further intensified by a wide variety of display and output media types, from monitors to film to paper. In the diagram to the left, we illustrate typical relationships between these different media, as well as the central role of the monitor to these relationships.

A Minimum Level of Calibration

As has been described previously, there are many different relationships between "originals" and "final results" when you do color matching, and as we will discuss later, due to limitations in color gamut for different media, it's not possible to make everything match.

For the moment, we would like to describe what we think is the minimum level of calibration that you should maintain. It takes some time, but if you seriously intend to do digital photography, we urge you to take the time to follow these steps carefully.

Room Illumination

You must be very careful about the work environment where you set up your computer and monitor. Try to maintain conditions as close as possible to the ideal conditions shown in the chart to the left.

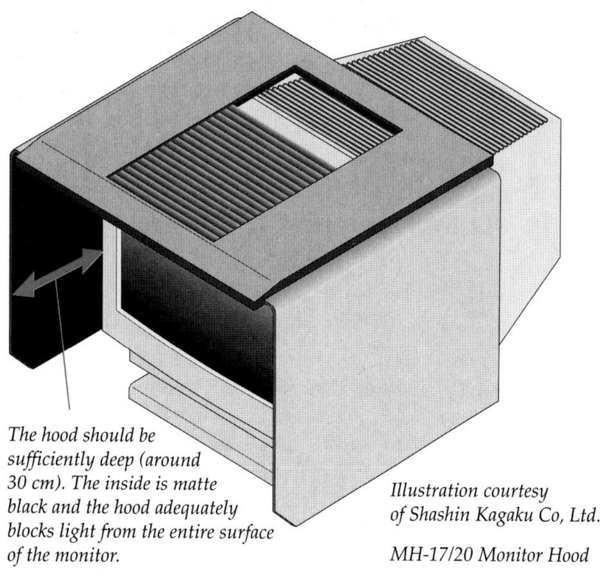

The hood should be sufficiently deep (around 30 cm). The inside is matte black and the hood adequately blocks light from the entire surface of the monitor.

Illustration courtesy of Shashin Kagaku Co, Ltd.

MH-17/20 Monitor Hood

Setting the Signal the Computer Sends to the Monitor

If you intend to do serious digital photography, you must set the video signal so that the number of colors on your monitor is at least 32,000. If possible, 16 million colors—full color—is best. After setting the number of colors on the monitor, it's important to take steps to adjust the characteristics of the color signal that the computer is sending to the monitor. These steps are described below, based on a current Macintosh computer running System 7.5.5 or newer. Some of these steps may not apply to older Macintosh operating systems, older monitors, or to the control panels of some video cards.

STEPS

1. If you already have the Gamma control panel that comes with Photoshop installed in the Control Panels folder, turn it off.

2. Go to the Apple Menu, select Control Panels, choose the Monitors and Sound control panel, and then select Mac Standard Gamma in the Gamma field of the dialog box.

NOTE

■ If a video board is connected between the computer and the monitor, it may be impossible to do this step. If this is the case, follow the instructions in the video board manual and set the monitor gamma to 1.8.

■ If you select Mac Standard Gamma, the midtones are slightly brighter than when Uncorrected Gamma is selected.

■ If you select Uncorrected Gamma, the entire display is darker than when Mac Standard Gamma is selected. When you select Uncorrected Gamma, the monitor displays images with its original display characteristics. The resulting change of brightness in the midtones (called *tonal response*, or *gamma*) is a contrasty display. If you look carefully, the shadows are too dark and the differences in density are more difficult to see (this is the standard display characteristic of a Windows system).

■ Just because you're brightening or darkening the video signal that the Macintosh sends to the monitor when you select Mac Standard Gamma doesn't mean that you're adjusting the monitor characteristics themselves to be brighter or darker. Other steps, which we will explain, are required to fine tune the monitor characteristics.

■ On a Windows machine, the function that enables you to make these adjustments is in the software that comes with the graphics board, so adjustment techniques may vary. However, techniques similar to ours can be done in the Windows version of Photoshop (in the Monitor Setup dialog box), so Windows users can move to the next step, adjusting the black point.

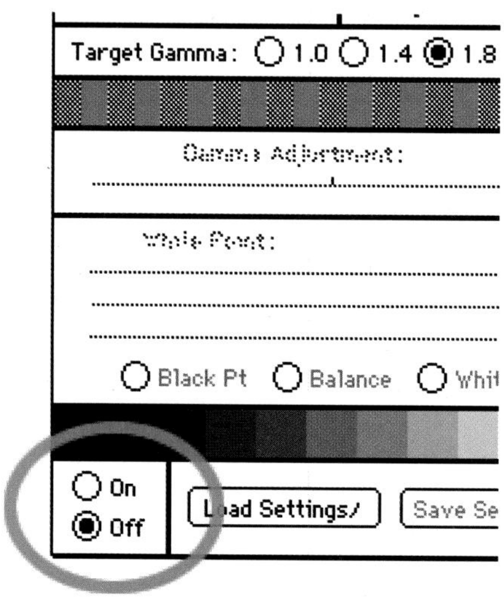

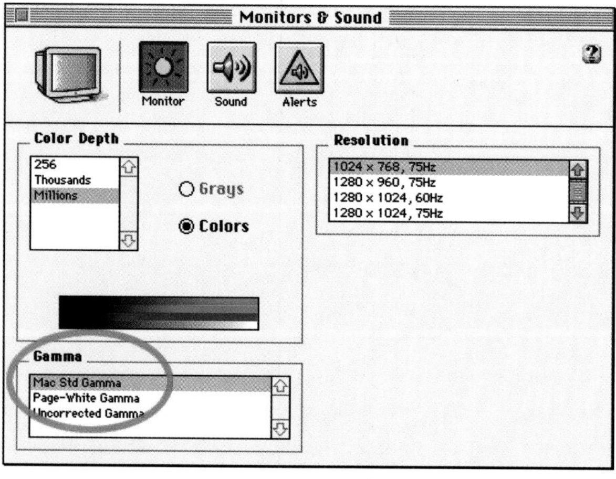

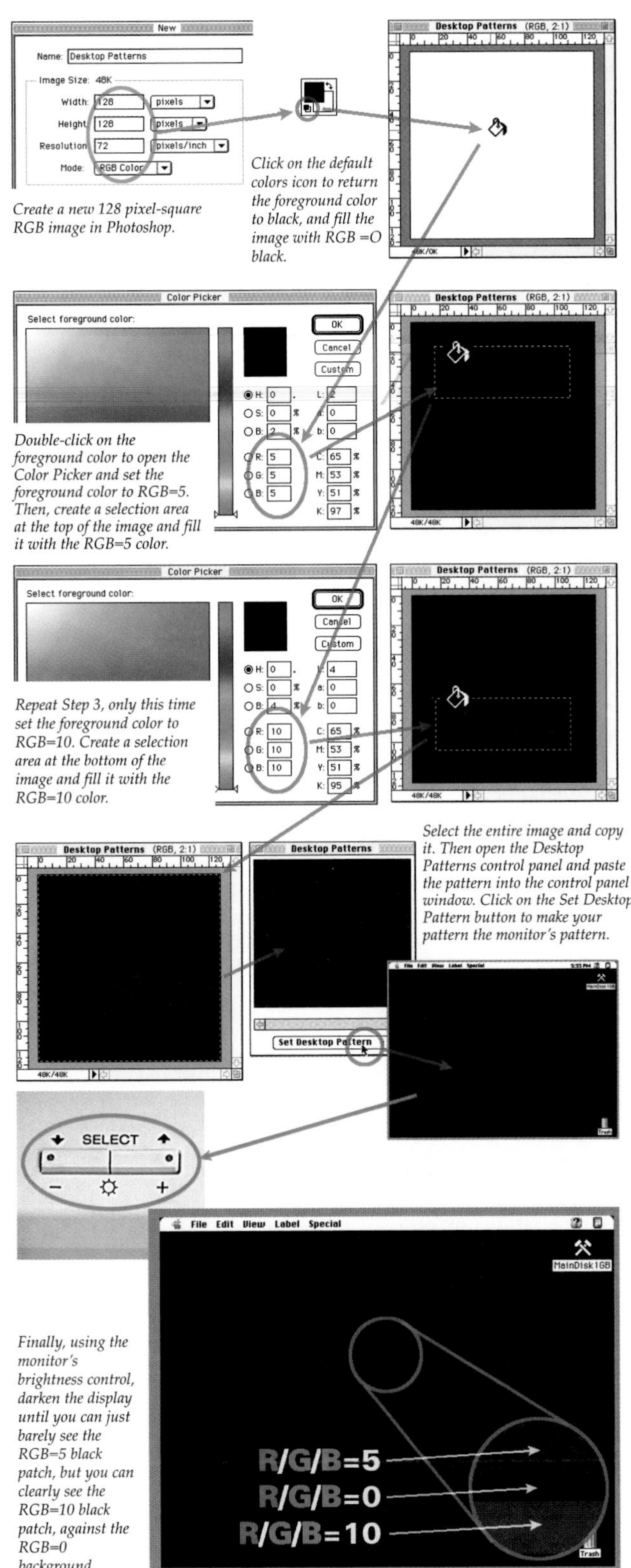

Create a new 128 pixel-square RGB image in Photoshop.

Click on the default colors icon to return the foreground color to black, and fill the image with RGB =O black.

Double-click on the foreground color to open the Color Picker and set the foreground color to RGB=5. Then, create a selection area at the top of the image and fill it with the RGB=5 color.

Repeat Step 3, only this time set the foreground color to RGB=10. Create a selection area at the bottom of the image and fill it with the RGB=10 color.

Select the entire image and copy it. Then open the Desktop Patterns control panel and paste the pattern into the control panel window. Click on the Set Desktop Pattern button to make your pattern the monitor's pattern.

Finally, using the monitor's brightness control, darken the display until you can just barely see the RGB=5 black patch, but you can clearly see the RGB=10 black patch, against the RGB=0 background.

Calibrating Your Monitor—Step 1: Adjusting the Black Point

After you standardize the signal that the computer sends to the monitor, the next step is to adjust the density of the black that is displayed on your monitor hardware. This may seem slightly complicated at first, so we recommend that you carefully study the procedure shown at the left.

NOTE

A similar pattern to the Desktop Pattern described at left can be found on the CD-ROM in the MonitorCalib folder. The file is called EDP_DeskTopPattern. In addition to the RGB = 5 and the RGB = 10 color patches, the pattern on the CD-ROM has 3 additional patches. The upper patch is a warm gray, the middle patch is a neutral gray and the lower patch is a cool gray. How to use these additional patches is explained on page 2-9, "Calibrating Your Monitor—Step 3: Adjusting the Midtones."

Calibrating Your Monitor—Step 2: Adjusting the White Point

Recently, more monitor manufacturers have added the capability to adjust the white point with a software-based contrast control that enables you to adjust the Red, Green, and Blue beams individually. Here we will show how to adjust this type of monitor so that its "pure white" is the white of photographic paper, printing paper, or the backlit surface of a lightbox. If your monitor does not have a mechanism for adjusting individual RGB contrast, please see the discussion about using the Gamma control panel in the section, "Adjusting the Midtones."

Select 5000K daylight fluorescent bulbs, such as the one shown here, for your imaging studio environment. If you're in doubt about exactly what type to use, ask your local printer or prepress house for a recommendation.

Light source color rendering properties assessment card.

Contrast adjustment control.

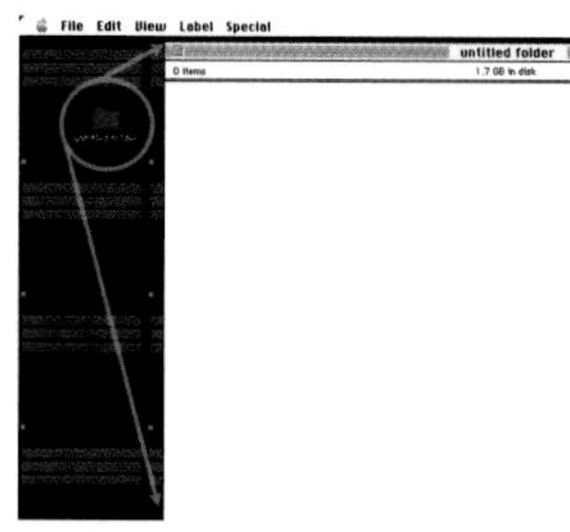

Open a large empty folder window.

STEPS

1. First, place a reference white next to your monitor.

■ Because the color temperature of most lightboxes is adjusted to a standard 5,000K you will need to lower the brightness of the monitor if you're using a 5,000K lightbox for photographs as your reference.

■ If you're using printing paper or photographic paper as your reference, select a sheet with a non-reflective matte finish, place a sheet of black paper underneath it, and shine a 5,000K light on it.

2. Set the monitor contrast adjustment control to maximum. Depending on the type of monitor, white areas occasionally become too bright when the contrast adjustment is set to maximum. On the Macintosh desktop, you can see when this has happened by looking at a folder icon. If the white is too bright, the contrasting densities that make the icon look like a three-dimensional folder disappear. To adjust this, set the monitor contrast to the setting immediately preceding the setting that caused the white to blow out.

NOTE

■ Most people are not going to have the perfect 5,000K viewing environment for comparing a reference white to their monitor. Therefore, a work-around for creating a simulated 5,000K environment is to turn on a combination of daylight fluorescent and tungsten bulbs. While not an absolutely perfect solution, this does create a fairly neutral environment. Another solution is to shine an inverter type desk lamp with a 4,700K fluorescent bulb, which is close enough to 5,000K, onto the reference white.

■ It's best to use fluorescent bulbs manufactured for color rendering assessment, available from all fluorescent bulb manufacturers.

■ A recommended way to check whether your light is 5,000K is to use a light source color rendering properties assessment card (such as the Kodak Color Viewing Light Selector card) to check your light source. Measuring the actual color temperature using a color temperature meter is another method.

■ If your illumination is too bright, you can decrease its intensity with something like a piece of tracing paper, but usually adding a diffuser to a light source decreases the color temperature. If you want to further decrease the intensity, we recommend adding strips of non-flammable black tape (a type of tape commonly found in photo studios) down the length of your fluorescent bulbs.

3. Open an empty folder window and resize it to fill the entire screen.

4. Turn to the back of this book, cut out the gray reference card and then cut out the two holes in the card. Hold the card so that empty folder window on the monitor display can be viewed through one cut-out and the reference white can be viewed through the other, as shown in the illustration to the left.

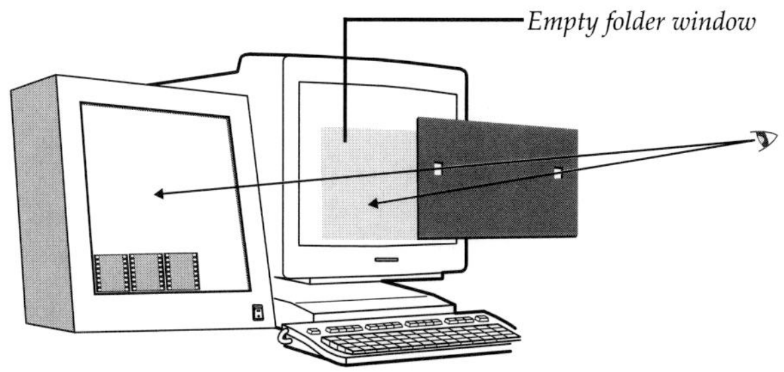

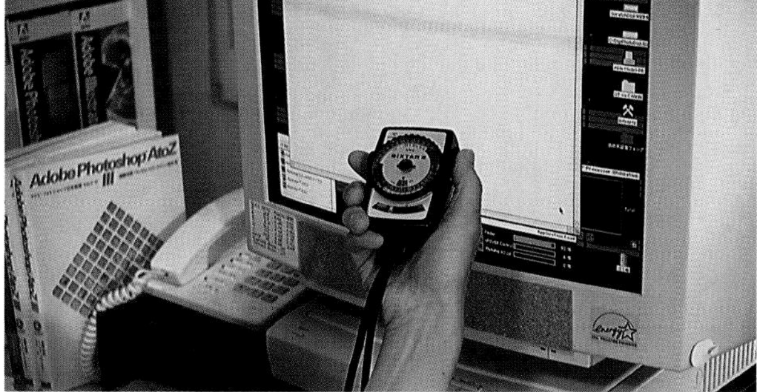

Measure both whites (the empty folder on the monitor and the reference white) with a reflected-light meter and make the luminance as close as possible. We have learned from experience that a difference of 1 EV is acceptable. If you're using a digital meter, your readings may be erratic, so you should make at least five measurements and take an average.

Some monitors, such as the Sony Multiscan series of monitors, have built-in color temperature controls.

5. Using the same monitor contrast adjustment control you used for Step 2, lower the monitor contrast adjustment control to the point where the brightness of the desktop white and the brightness of the reference white look the same. Because making them look exactly the same is usually difficult, it's better for the monitor to look just slightly brighter, rather than darker, than the reference white.

NOTE

■ At this stage, if the reference white appears brighter than the monitor, your illumination is too strong. The majority of light sources that follow standard ratings for evaluating print are too strong. They don't have to be exactly the same, but if the illumination is much too bright, decrease the intensity by using the methods described earlier.

■ Even if the illumination is too strong, you can still calibrate your monitor. However, since your eyes have to re-adjust between two different intensities of light each time you look at the monitor and then at your original or final artwork, you may experience eye fatigue.

6. Start the monitor's built in RGB individual contrast adjustment control. This control varies from monitor to monitor, but usually has some type of slider, as shown to the left. By using the same viewing method described in step 4, adjust the individual RGB sliders so that the monitor white and the reference paper white are the same. Monitors usually have a bluish tint, but you can remove this by slightly decreasing the G and the B. If your monitor doesn't have a built-in RGB contrast adjustment control, see "Calibrating Your Monitor—Step 3: Adjusting the Midtones" for instructions about how to use the Gamma control panel to match a monitor white to a reference white.

NOTE

If you have a color temperature meter for photographers, you can use it to measure the color temperature of the reference white and the monitor white. Use the color temperature meter like a reflective meter by holding the meter close to the areas you're trying to measure. A difference of up to 300K is acceptable. Reference whites, such as paper, often have a slightly yellowish tint and a relatively low color temperature of 4,700K. To keep your reference white at 5,000K, therefore, it's a good idea to use a light source that is around 5,500K.

The steps taken to this point should give you a monitor with an ideal RGB display. The black should be just dark enough so that you can distinguish the differences in density between pure black and slightly brighter shadows. The white should be nearly equivalent to the white areas on a piece of color reversal film as viewed on a lightbox, or the white of an unexposed, fixed sheet of photographic print paper.

Calibrating Your Monitor—Step 3: Adjusting the Midtones

After completing the black point and white point adjustments, what remains to be done is an adjustment of the midtones.Under normal circumstances we shouldn't need to do anything more because we have already created nearly neutral monitor gamma using the above steps. But sometimes after following the preceding steps, the midtones can have a color cast. You can adjust the color cast in midtones using Adobe Photoshop's Gamma control panel. Before you can use the Gamma control panel, however, you must install it in your system folder.

After installing Photoshop the Gamma control panel can be found inside the Calibration folder, which is located inside the Goodies folder. In order to use the Gamma Control Panel, put it into the Control Panels folder inside your System folder and restart your computer.

■ Open the Gamma control panel and if it's turned off, turn it on. If you are following our method, be sure the Gamma Adjustment slider is set to zero (see A in the

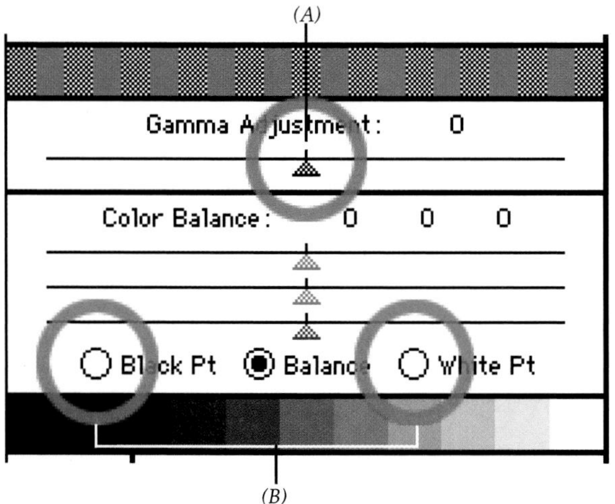

illustration above). Because of the black and white point (brightness and contrast) adjustments you made in previous steps, you've already established an ideal gamma for your monitor. This means that you should not try to make the alternating gray patches of the Gamma control panel appear as one continous gray, as recommended in the Photoshop Users Guide. If you move the Gamma Adjustment slider to try to make the gamma strip look like one continous gray, you will nullify your previous adjustments.

■ Be sure that the RGB values for the black point are set to 0 (all 3 sliders should be all the way to the left) and the white point are set to 255 (all 3 sliders should be all the way to the right). Because you have already adjusted the monitor's gray balance using your monitor's built in RGB contrast adjustment control, you do not need to use the Gamma control panel's Black Pt and White Pt radio buttons (see B in the illustration at the top of the page). However, if your monitor doesn't have a built in software-based RGB contrast adjustment control, you can use the Gamma control panel to adjust the white point. In this case, select the While Pt radio button and use the RGB sliders to match the color of the monitor white to

Luminance values for white point and gray balance at various gamma settings

Gamma setting	White point		Gray balance		White point & gray balance
	EV value	Y value	EV value	Y value	EV value
1.00	10.5	85.9	8.7	7.45	1.8 Stop difference
1.40	10.5	86.1	7.8	2.91	2.7 Stop difference
1.80	10.6	86.9	6.7	1.19	3.9 Stop difference
2.00	10.7	87.1	6.0	0.81	4.7 Stop difference
2.20	10.8	87.2	5.8	1.07	5.0 Stop difference

Measurements were taken in the dark. The gray area measured was an RGB = 25 gray. After setting the gamma, we set the white point luminance. The EV was measured using a Sekonix Dual Spot F. We took an average of 5 different measurements (at ISO 800). We used a Minolta CS-100 colorimeter to measure the Y value. If the difference in luminance between the white point and the gray balance is approximately 4 stops, the monitor gamma is close to 1.8.

your reference white using the same procedures described in step 6 (see page 2-7) of "Calibrating Your Monitor—Step 2: Adjusting the White Point."

■ Next, turn on only the Balance radio button and adjust the RGB sliders to neutralize any tint, or color, that appears in the midtones of the grayscale at the bottom of the Gamma control panel. Also, if you are using the EDP_DeskTopPattern mentioned on page 2-7 as a desktop pattern, you can use it as a reference for neutralizing midtones. If your monitor's midtones are neutral, the top bar of the pattern will display correctly as a warm gray, the middle bar will be neutral gray and the bottom bar will be cool gray. However, if your monitor midtones are too cool, then the top bar will become neutral. If your monitor midtones are too warm, then the bottom bar will become gray. To correct either instance, add or subtract RGB values accordingly.

NOTE

■ Be sure to leave the Target Gamma setting on the standard setting of 1.8.

■ In the Windows version of Photoshop, these gamma adjustments are done with the Calibrate dialog box, which you open by pressing the Calibrate button under File, Color Settings, Monitor Setup. In principle, this is exactly the same operation, so please refer to Chapter 2 in your Photoshop manual, "Calibrating Your System."

■ After we made the black point and the white point adjustments we used a spot meter to confirm that our monitor gamma was 1.8. We did this by first measuring, in a darkened room, a white point (an open folder) and then a gray point. The gray point was a gray Photoshop file in which all levels were 25 (R=25, G=25, and B=25). We took an average of 5 different measurements of each point (at ISO 800). The white was approximately 10.6 EV and the gray point was approximately 6.7 EV. The difference of 3.9 EV indicates a 1.8 gamma. These numbers are universal and can be used as a reference!

■ We've calculated the difference in EV values of the white point and gray point for various Gamma settings of 1.0, 1.4, 1.8, and 2.2 and listed them in the table to the left. Also, we've noted in the file "RGBchart.tif" in the CD-ROM in the back of the book the 25 gray and 255 white area of a grayscale. You can measure these with your spot meter to calculate the Gamma. It's necessary, when taking the readings, to enlarge each area as much as possible. While the spot meter isn't the most precise method for measuring the monitor's gamma, it is adequate for our purposes here.

A difference in luminance between the white point and the gray point of approximately 4 stops indicates a monitor gamma that's close to 1.8 (shown in blue). Differences in EV for additional gamma settings are also shown.

Adjusting Your Monitor for Offset Presses and Color Printers

From here we will look at color calibration for images that need to be converted into CMYK mode data. You're using Photoshop for calibration. You convert RGB mode images into CMYK mode images in order to output on a four-color color printing press or when you want to output CMYK data from a desktop color printer.

If you do not need to worry about offset printing, or if you're using your own color printer to output RGB data (that is, when you don't need to convert RGB into CMYK data), it's not always necessary to use the procedure described in the following section.

Telling Photoshop about Your Monitor Display Parameters

If you give Photoshop information about the color you see on your monitor, Photoshop can simulate in the monitor's RGB color space what the RGB and CMYK image conversion, as well as your final hard copy CMYK output, will look like.

To provide Photoshop with this information, select Monitor Setup under Color Settings and make the following settings in the Monitor Setup dialog box.

STEPS

1. Select your monitor from the pop-up menu in the Monitor field. If you don't find your monitor, leave the setting at Default and proceed with steps 2, 3, and 4.

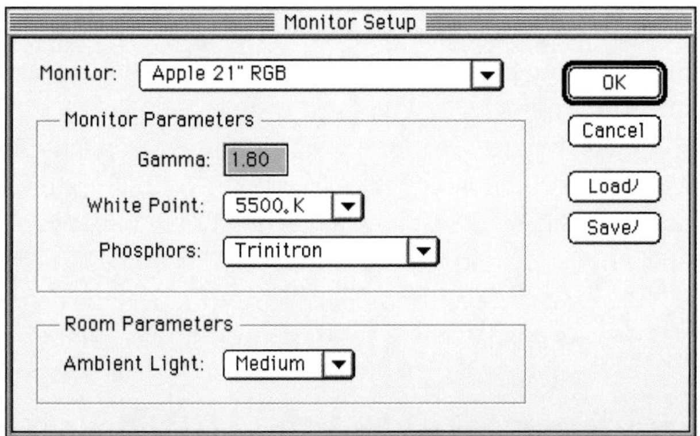

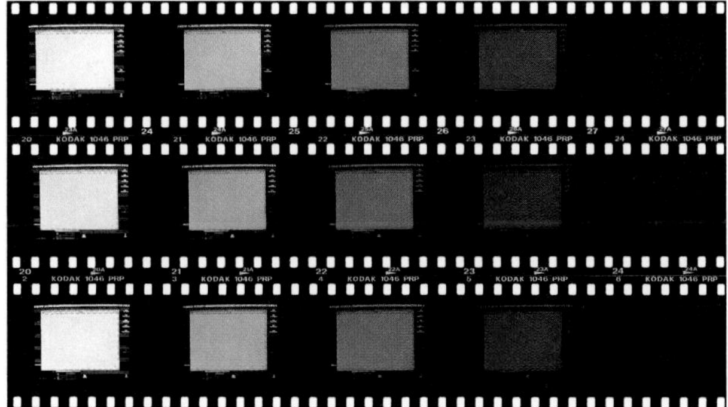

Top series: Monitor white is set to 5,500K. Middle series: 6,500K. Bottom series: 7,500K.

Bracketed exposures, sequentially reduced by $^{2}/_{3}$ stop, starting from the left.

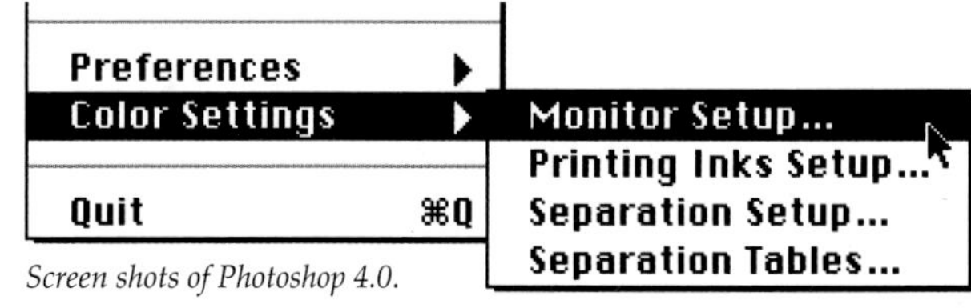

Screen shots of Photoshop 4.0.

2. Enter 1.8 in the Gamma field. This value is the same as when you select Mac Standard Gamma in the Monitors and Sound control panel, previously described in "Setting the Signal the Computer Sends to the Monitor."

As was explained previously, the sliders in the Gamma control panel device should always be set to their default levels of 0 for Gamma Adjustment, RGB = 0 for the Black Pt, and RGB = 255 for the White Pt. The exceptions are when you've used the White Pt option to match a monitor white to a reference white, and/or used the Balance radio button to make a midtone color balance adjustment (both of which were explained on page 2-10).

3. If an appropriate color temperature is listed in the White Point pop-up menu, select it. Or if you wish to use custom settings, please refer to the chart on page 2-12 for custom x and y values for different color temperatures. These x and y values are universal.

NOTE

If you used the method described in "Calibrating Your Monitor—Step 2: Adjusting the White Point," your monitor's color temperature should already be about 5,000K +/- 300K. If you have a color temperature meter you can confirm this by facing the meter close to a monitor displaying an open, white folder and taking a reading. However, if you don't have a color temperature meter, you can use daylight film to confirm the color temperature using the following technique.

In a darkened room, take bracketed exposures of an open, white folder on your monitor. On monitors with color temperature between 4,700K and 5,500K there will not be a bluish tint to the white on the 1 to 1 $^{1}/_{2}$ stop underexposed frames. When the color temperature is over 6,000K, the underexposed frames will have a strong bluish tint in the white. If your color temperature is below 4,500K, the underexposed frames will have a strong reddish tint in the white.

4. The Phosphors field in the Monitor Setup dialog box is where you enter the type of red, green, and blue phosphors that are coated on the inner surface of your monitor picture tube. If the phosphor set on your monitor is in the pop-up menu, select it.

NOTE

■ The manufacturer names in the pop-up menu are not monitor manufacturer names, but manufacturers who supply monitor CRT tubes. For example, Apple monitors use Trinitron tubes, so select "Trinitron" if you have an Apple monitor. Check with your dealer, your monitor's manufacturer, or monitor's users guide that came with your monitor to determine which CRT tube is in your monitor.

● If you have access to a transmissive colorimeter, you can determine your own custom Phosphors settings. Open the RGBchart.tif file in the MonitorCalib folder on the CD-ROM in the back of the book, measure each of the R, G, and B areas and record their respective x and y chromaticity values. Then select Custom in the Phosphors pop-up menu and enter the x and y coordinates for R, G, and B.

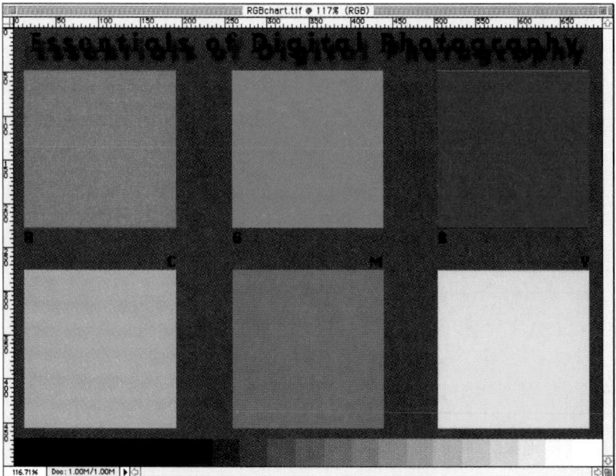

Actual RGB Chromaticity coordinate values for our monitors

Monitor	RGB chromaticity coordinates	x value	y value
Sony GDM2000TC & Multiscan 17sf II	Red	0.616	0.343
	Green	0.280	0.595
	Blue	0.144	0.062
Nanao Flexascan 56T & T567	Red	0.617	0.345
	Green	0.277	0.587
	Blue	0.146	0.064
Mitsubishi DiamondTron 17GX II	Red	0.618	0.346
	Green	0.291	0.597
	Blue	0.145	0.069

Standard chromaticity coordinate values for different white point color temperatures

Measured color temperature	x value	y value
4500K	0.361	0.368
5000K	0.345	0.355
5500K	0.340	0.350
6000K	0.332	0.340
6500K	0.312	0.330
7000K	0.305	0.323
7500K	0.300	0.317

We measured the color temperature of the monitor surface (empty folder window) using a color temperature meter for photography. Refer to this chart if you're entering x and y values in the Monitor Setup dialog box in Photoshop.

■ For your reference, we listed the phosphor values for all the monitors in our work environment in a chart. The values in this chart show the particular characteristics of each monitor. The differences were very slight except in the case of monitors that had been used for a long time.

5. Because you have already adjusted the brightness of your monitor white to match a reference white that should have had a similar brightness to the monitor, you should select the Medium setting in the Ambient Light pop-up menu.

Telling Photoshop about the Color Characteristics of Your Hard Copy

In the previous section, you told Photoshop about the color characteristics of your monitor display. This enabled Photoshop to understand what color you were seeing when it sent image data to your monitor. The next step is to tell Photoshop about the color characteristics of your color hard copies—offset prints or color printer output—so it knows how the colors for your image data are being produced.

In order to do this with the most accuracy for your printing conditions, you must use a colorimeter that can express the colors from your hard copy in terms of xyY or L*a*b color space. However, because most people don't have a colorimeter, we've prepared the following technique, based on the Color Calibration Chart in the back of the book for visually adjusting a CMYK environment for your monitor. Although not as accurate as the colorimeter, the results will be better than an "in the ballbark" level of calibration.

STEPS

1. Open to the printed Color Calibration Chart in the back of the book and place it under proper (5,000K) viewing light in a position next to your monitor.

2. Copy the MonitorCalib folder from the accompanying CD-ROM onto your hard disk.

3. Start Photoshop and open the MonitorCalibCMYK.tif file from the folder you just copied. Please note that this is a 26MB file and will require approximately 90–100MB of free disk space to perform this procedure.

4. Choose File, Color Settings, Printing Inks Setup to open the Printing Inks Setup dialog box. Click on the Load button and load the Sample Ink Setting ink preferences

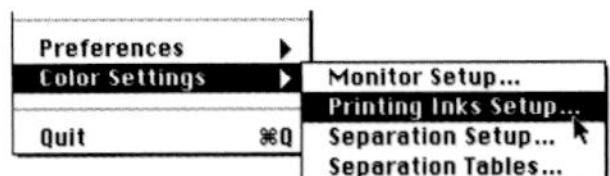

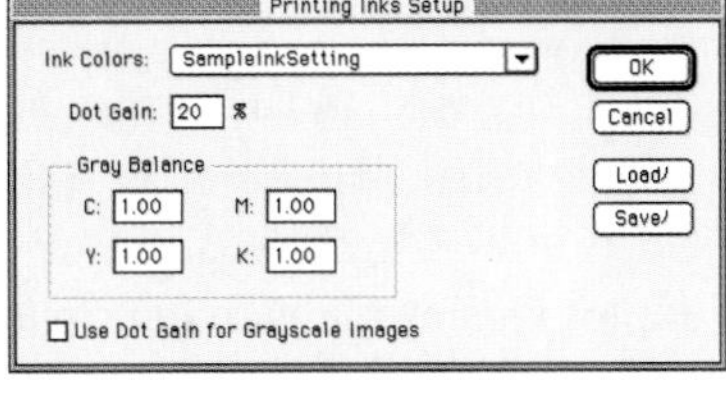

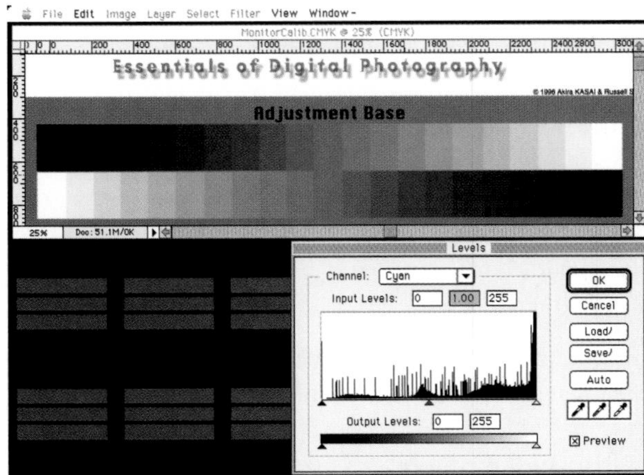

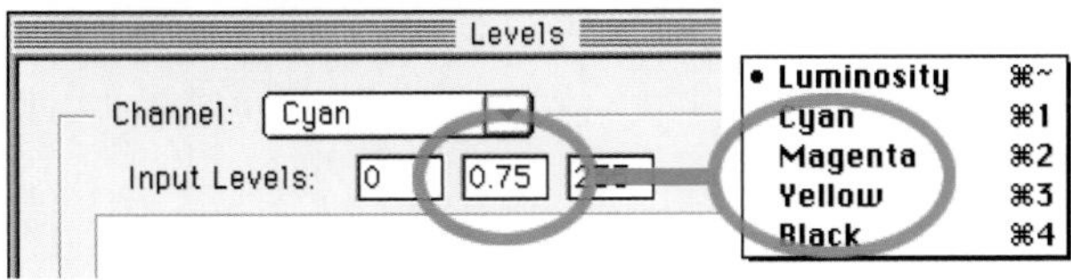

file from the MonitorCalib folder. Immediately after you have loaded this file, the fields in the Printing Inks Setup dialog box show the values that appear in the illustration above.

5. Click OK to close the dialog box and colors in the open image should change immediately. Next, we will match the colors on the monitor to the colors on the print.

6. Resize the window so you're only able to see the Adjustment Base grayscale at the top of the image. Move this window so it's in the upper half of your monitor screen. For the following steps, it's helpful to have a neutral desktop pattern that doesn't interfere with your color perception. We recommend creating a new, neutral gray desktop pattern or using the one you created following the steps in "Calibrating Your Monitor—Step 1: Adjusting the Black Point."

7. Choose Image, Adjust, Levels to open the Levels dialog box. Move the dialog box so it's in the lower half of your screen.

8. Turn the Preview check box on.

9. Compare the monitor display version of the Adjustment Base grayscale midtones with the printed version. You should see a color cast in the midtones of the monitor display version. If so, take turns selecting the individual Cyan (C), Magenta (M), and Yellow (Y) channels from the Channel menu and drag the midtone slider under the histogram (the middle slider is the gray levels slider) to the right or left to adjust the midtones. If the midtones look a little reddish, for example, select the Cyan channel and move the gray levels slider to the right. This increases the amount of Cyan and neutralizes the reddish tint. Use the same procedure with the Magenta and Yellow channels until the grayscale on your screen matches the grayscale on the print as closely as possible. Expect this process to take some trial and error before you get the screen version of the grayscale close to the printed version.

10. After you have finished adjusting all the channels, write down the gamma values for each of the C, M, and Y channels. The gamma values must be between 0.5 and 2.0.

11. Click on Cancel (*Important—do not click on OK!*) in the Levels dialog box and any changes you have made will be discarded. The point here is to use the Levels dialog box only as a tool for determining settings, not for applying changes to the image data.

12. Choose File, Color Settings, Printing Inks Setup again to open the Printing Inks Setup dialog box.

13. Take the gamma values you noted in step 10 and enter them into their respective Gray Balance fields in the Printing Inks Setup dialog box. Then determine the value for Black (K) by taking the average of the C, M, and Y values. Enter this value into the K Gray Balance field.

14. As you click OK in the Printing Inks Setup dialog box watch the Adjustment Base grayscale on your monitor. It will change to reflect the correction you determined

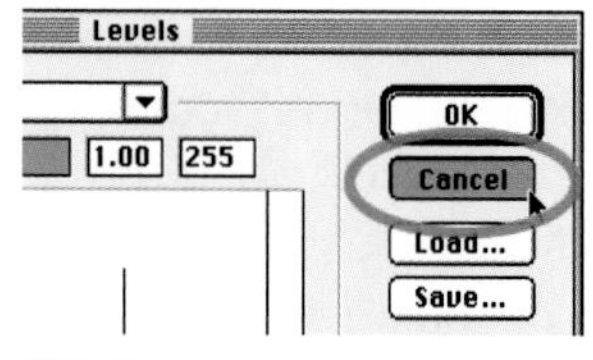

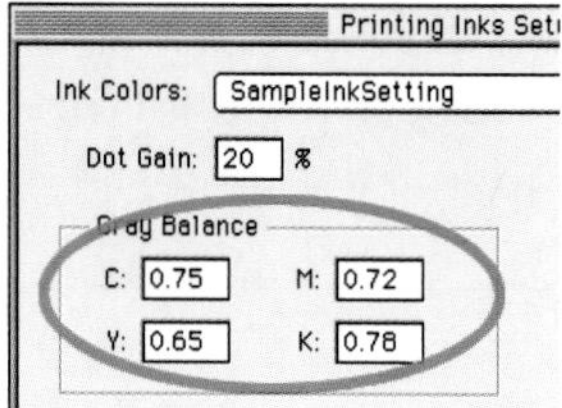

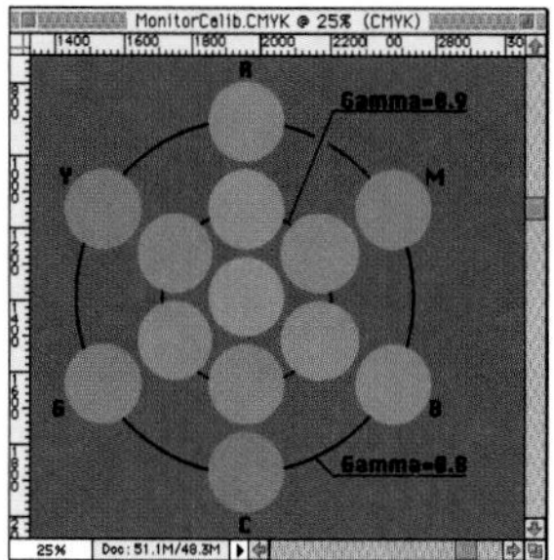

Gray Comparison Chart.

in steps 9–11. However, you haven't actually changed the image data itself. Instead, you've told Photoshop how to change the display of the data so that it matches the printed version.

NOTE

■ It's important to remember that changing the Gray Balance values in the Printing Inks Setup dialog box doesn't affect the display until *after* you press OK.

■ It's helpful to repeat the monitor black point, white point, and midtone adjustments, as well as the Printing Inks Setup Gray Balance adjustment once or twice after the first pass. However, if any values are not 1.0 in the Printing Inks Setup Gray Balance, multiply the new value times the old value and use the result.

15. After Step 14, your monitor is calibrated to one type of printed output (in this case, the CMYK version of the Color Calibration Chart from the back of the book). Although no further adjustments are necessary, some additional fine tuning can be done using the Gray Comparison chart (the portion of the Color Calibration Chart with circles on it). Begin this optional adjustment by opening your image window so it appears as shown in the illustration, with just the Gray Comparison chart displayed.

16. Next, you make adjustments to the Printing Inks Setup Gray Balance fields by studying the circles-to-gray background relationships on the hard copy and then trying to establish similar circles-to-gray background relationships on the monitor copy (as described in the sidebar to the left).

NOTE

The monitor calibration chart found at the end of the book and the resulting Sample Ink Setting for the Printing Inks Setup dialog box are based on the printing conditions of the printer who produced this book. You should create your own Printing Inks Setup settings to reflect the conditions of your own, or your client's, printer.

■ To match your monitor display to output from your printing company, you should have your printer print the MonitorCalibCMYK.tif file found on the CD-ROM. Then, using a colorimeter, measure the L*a*b* or Yxy values of the C, M, Y, M+Y, C+Y, C+M, and C+M+Y patches on the hard copy. Enter these values into a Custom Printing Inks Setup setting, and save the settting. You can use the same process to calibrate your monitor to a CMYK proofing device.

■ If you don't have a colorimeter, load the SWOP (Coated) setting (Photoshop's default setting) and use the average values for American standard printing conditions. You can also use the available profiles in Ink Colors in the Printing Inks Setup dialog box in Photoshop.

How to Use the Gray Comparison Chart

1. Look at the hard copy version of the Gray Comparison chart and determine the relationship between its center gray circle and its gray square background. For example, is the circle darker or lighter than the background? Then adjust the K value of the Gray Balance fields in the Printing Inks Setup dialog box so that the monitor version of the center circle and background have the same relationship.

For example, if your hard copy's gray background is darker than its own center gray circle, but your monitor's gray background is lighter than its own center gray circle, reduce the K value in the Printing Inks Setup Gray Balance field by about 0.05. Click on OK and check the result. Keep adjusting this value until the monitor's gray background is darker than its center circle, in the same way that the hard copy's gray background is darker than its center circle.

2. On the hard copy, note the position of the tinted circle that most closely matches, or blends into, the gray background. Then look at the exact same circle on the monitor display. If the monitor's circle doesn't have the same relationship to its background that the hard copy version has (meaning it doesn't match its own background), adjust the appropriate C, M, or Y Gray Balance value until it does have the same relationship.

Assume, for example, that the R (red) gray circle on the Gamma = 0.9 line on the hard copy matches its background, but the same R gray circle on the monitor doesn't match its background. To make the monitor's R circle match its background, you need to make a correction to the Printing Inks Setup Gray Balance C value (cyan value, the complement of red) by multiplying the current Gray Balance value for C by 0.9 (for example 0.8×0.9 = .72). Enter this new value in the C field, click OK and check the result. You can tweak the C value up or down in .05 increments until the monitor's R circle matches, or blends, into the background. You can also determine incremental changes by using the Levels dialog box, as described in steps 7–11. In this case, the gray level values determined by repeating steps 7–11 need to be multiplied by the current Gray Balance values to arrive at a new Gray Balance value.

3. In order to account for variations in perception of tone and color, and so on, repeat steps 1 and 2 one or two more times. This has the effect of averaging out your fine tune adjustments, making for a more dependable result.

Complete Color Calibration Steps

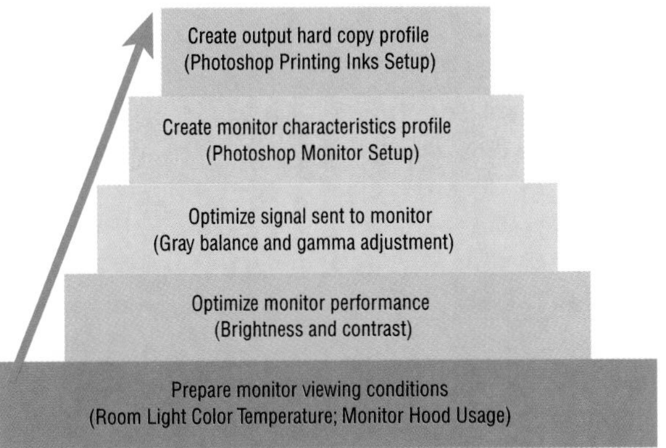

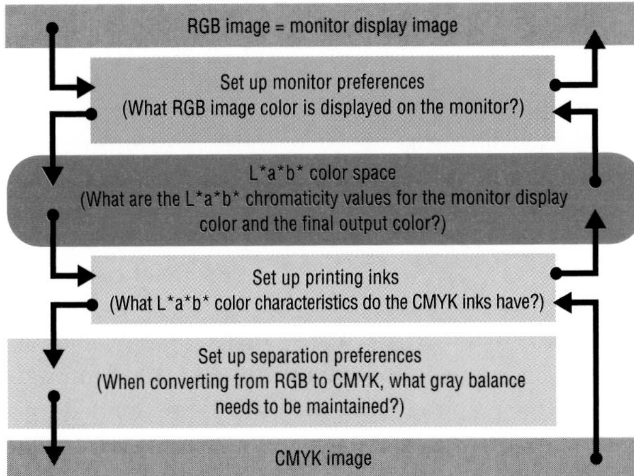

What Did We Accomplish with These Procedures?

This series of operations accomplished the following:

- We adjusted the external monitor viewing environment—the brightness and color of the room, the hood on the monitor.
- We optimized the monitor display characteristics—brightness adjustment (black point), contrast adjustment (white point).
- We set the quality of the signal the computer sends to the monitor—gray balance (gamma) adjustment.
- We made Photoshop aware of the basic display characteristics of the monitor—Monitor Setup.
- We made Photoshop aware of the color characteristics of the final output (color print)—Printing Inks Setup.

After you do all the previous steps, Photoshop is aware of how you see color on your monitor when it sends out image signals. At the same time, Photoshop is aware of what colors you see on the same image when it's printed. This means that Photoshop is able to interpret the difference between the image data itself, the data as it appears on your monitor, and the data as it appears in print. Photoshop converts the CMYK image data into an RGB signal for monitor display so you can make further adjustments if necessary. When you look at the resulting CMYK data, it should look similar to a hard copy version of the image placed next to your monitor.

These adjustment procedures also ensure that you have used the optimal parameter settings when converting from RGB image to CMYK. Following conversion, areas of the original RGB image whose colors are outside the printing range of CMYK inks can be seen in the monitor CMYK preview just as they will be printed.

We have taken considerable time with monitor calibration, but if you make the proper adjustments, you can trust your monitor, eliminate guesswork, and minimize readjustments on your final output.

NOTE

Unlike with CMYK Color mode images, Photoshop doesn't change the display of RGB image data based on settings in the Printing Inks Setup dialog box. However, the View, CMYK Preview menu option does. This means that you can create and use Printing Inks Setup settings that match the RGB data on your monitor to the characteristics of hard copy generated on an RGB output device, such as a film recorder or RGB color printer.

- Start by reproducing the CompColorRGB.tif file (located in the CD-ROM's PrintTest folder) on your RGB output device. Then, with the View, CMYK Preview function turned on, follow the steps in "Telling Photoshop about the Color Characteristics of Your Hard Copy" to create custom Printing Inks Setup settings that will match the display of an image in RGB Color mode with hard copy from an RGB output device. Afterward, toggle the View, CMYK Preview function between on and off to see the preview effect on the RGB data. Don't forget to reload previously saved CMYK Printing Inks Setup settings when you go back to working on a CMYK project.

02 3

Light, Color, and the Human Eye

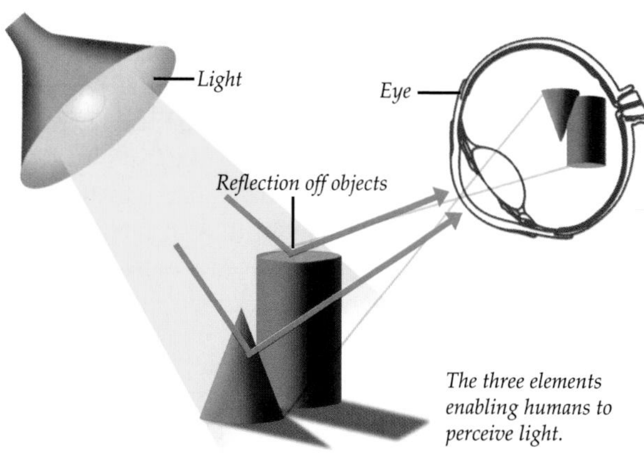

The three elements enabling humans to perceive light.

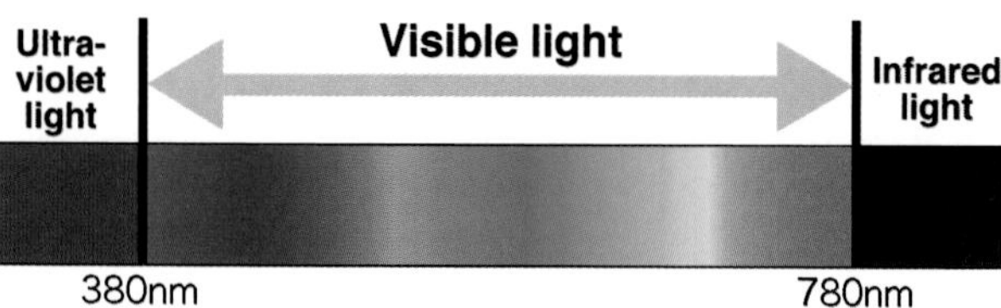

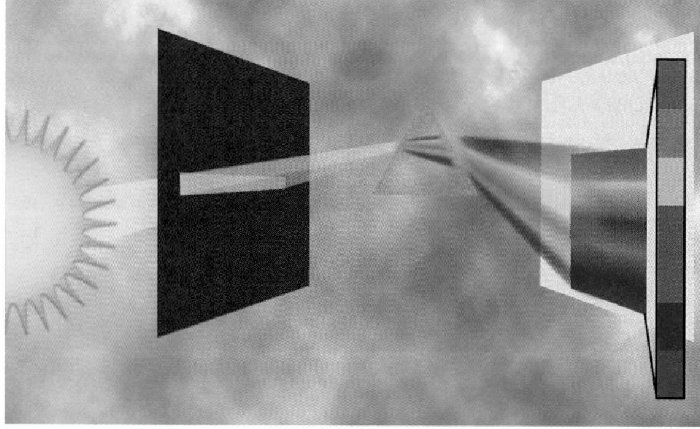

How Do We See Color?

To express an idea or vision using digital photography, we make use of computers—extremely logical machines—to manipulate color and tone information. To make the best use of our computers, we need to understand a little more about natural science. While this may not directly relate to digital photography, some knowledge of color and light is useful for digital image processing (please allow for the fact that we are not experts in color science and the psychology of vision).

Physical Qualities of Light

How do human beings perceive color? When light shines on an object, the object absorbs (or radiates, as is the case with fluorescent colors) part of that light and reflects part of that light back into the human eye. The result is that it looks to us like the object has color. If there were no light, we wouldn't be able to see color, and thus would not be able to visually sense that objects exist. Color exists because of a combination of three things. First, light exists. Second, objects reflect or absorb that light. And third, humans can perceive the color of light.

Just like radio or X-rays, light is a type of electromagnetic radiation that may be described using the wave as a model for its propagation. It's classified into three types depending on the range of wavelengths: ultra-violet light, visible light, and infrared light. The range of wavelengths that humans can perceive is from 380 to 720 nanometers and is equal to one billionth of a meter.

White light is comprised of all the wavelengths that are visible to the human eye. We see objects the most naturally under white light. If you shine white light through a prism, the resultant light can be roughly divided into seven colors, as shown in the illustration. Even if you shine one of these seven divisions of light through a prism again, you cannot break it up into smaller components. We call these minimum units of light *spectral light*.

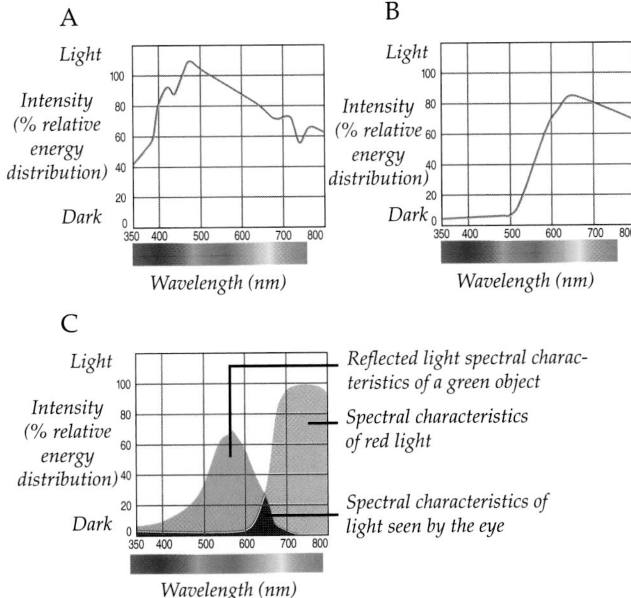

If you compare the grayscale values of a red car under daylight illumination with the grayscale values of the same red car under orange lights (such as tunnel illumination), the tunnel version would look lighter.

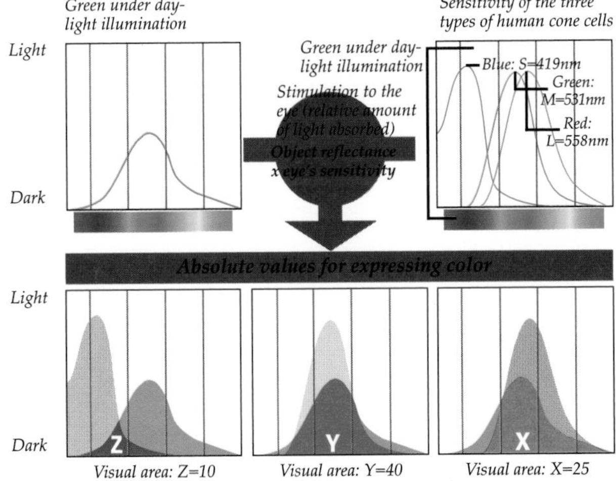

This illustration provides a schematic representation of vision and color.

We can measure the intensity of white light reflected from an object, plot the energy (intensity) of its spectral components, and thus understand what color that object is. For example, the energy of the spectral light from a standard white (D65) illuminant is distributed as shown in illustration A, and the spectral light energy reflected from a red object (red cloth, in this case) is distributed as shown in illustration B.

However, if we shine light other than white light at a colored object, there may be no energy reflected. Illustration C, at left, shows the spectral light energy configuration of a white light source (in green) being reflected off of a green object. The spectral light energy configuration of a red light source is shown in red. The intersection of the two represents the few wavelengths from the red source light which can be reflected by the green object. This means the object would appear black under a red light source, as if there were no light. This is the same phenomenon that makes a red car passing through a tunnel with orange illumination look lighter in comparison to a blue or green car, which would look black. Or imagine what a black-and-white photograph looks like when you enlarge it in a darkroom under safelights.

So a very close relationship exists between the quality of the illuminant and the color of the object we see. If the illuminant changes, the color of the object looks different to us. This is why we spent so much time at the beginning of the book discussing monitor calibration.

The Eye as Light Sensor

The human eye contains two types of cells that respond to light. The first type of cell is called the *rod cell*. These cells are mainly concerned with night vision and are able to respond to minute changes in light and darkness. However, they are not able to distinguish differences in spectral light. We can think of them as ultrasensitive monochrome receptors.

The second type of eye cell is the *cone cell*. Three different types of cone cells exist, and each type responds particularly well to red, green, or blue spectral light. The brain receives different information depending on which cone cells have been stimulated, and this gives us the sense of color. However, cone cells stop responding when they reach certain limits of energy. The cone cells have highly accurate color rendition, but like color film, they have minimum and maximum limits to which they can accurately reproduce color.

American blue?

Bali blue?

Japan blue?

If we created our own names for the blues we have seen in Bali, or in California, or on a clear fall day in Japan, what would they be...

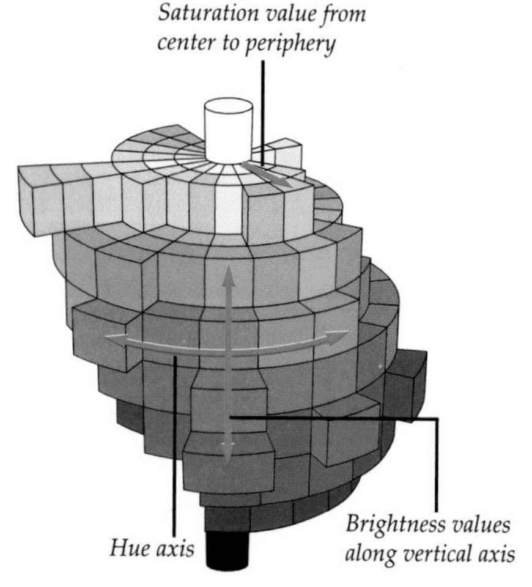

Quantifying Color

The quantification of color has a direct relationship to digital photography. Quantification is necessary for both you and the computer to be speaking the same language when you talk about color. For example, it's important to understand that L* = 50/ a* = -30/b* = +15 means a dark blue-green to the computer. Because color is fundamentally something that we see with our eyes, however, you don't always have to rely on reading colors by number. This is another reason why monitor calibration is so important.

Communicating about Color

We've always used names to express the colors we see in the world around us. For example, the word "blue" conjures up a color in everyone's mind. But there are many types of blue, such as "horizon blue," "cobalt blue," or "celestial blue," so the word blue can mean different things between individuals—or even between cultures.

For example, in Japan (where this book was first published) the word for pink is *momo-iro,* purple is *murasaki,* blue is *aoi,* and green is *midori.* How do we know that these Japanese words refer to the same color referred to by the English word? The blue sky that we see directly above us in California is different from the blue in the same part of the sky in Japan. So we can image that an American word for blue sky, such as "celestial blue," describes a different blue than the Japanese word for blue sky.

This problem of how to describe colors between individuals and cultures is the same problem that exists when we try to use computers to describe colors. The only consistent way, then, of communicating colors is to characterize them numerically.

One painter who devised a well-known system for characterizing color was Albert Munsell (1858–1918). He created the Munsell System, which is still used today in many fields (see the illustration).

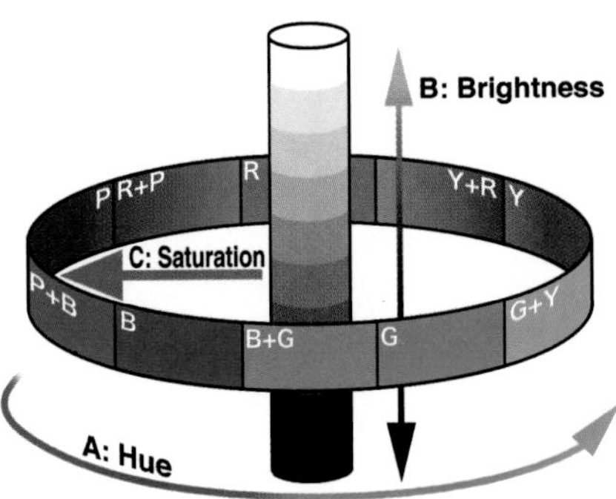

Munsell System

Characterizing Color Numerically

The Munsell System characterizes colors as follows:

- Hues are divided into 10 categories: Red / YellowRed / Yellow / GreenYellow / Green / BlueGreen / Blue / PurpleBlue / Purple / RedPurple (see A in the illustration).
- Each of the 10 hue categories can be further divided into 10 levels of brightness (see B in the illustration).
- Each of the 10 hue categories can be further divided into 10 levels of saturation (hue intensity) (see C in the illustration).

A blue-green color would be characterized in the Munsell System as BG=7/2, where *BG* stands for blue-green, 7 expresses a high level of brightness, and 2 indicates a nearly gray color.

The Munsell System isn't the only system for characterizing color numerically. In the world of photography, we use color compensating (CC) filters to alter the color of light used to expose or view color images. If a photographer sees the term "CC-R05 + CC-Y10" he or she can easily imagine a light orange color. Similarly, "CC-05M + CC-15Y" is a typical combination that creates a light orange color.

In printing, we characterize color in terms of halftone dot percentages. The color characterized by "C = 55/M = 43/Y = 43/K = 10" would be understood as a relatively dark neutral gray by a printing expert. Conversely, a photographer might ask why the color is gray, if the values for C, M, and Y are different. We will go into this further on.

CC filters, familiar to photographers, are one method of characterizing color numerically.

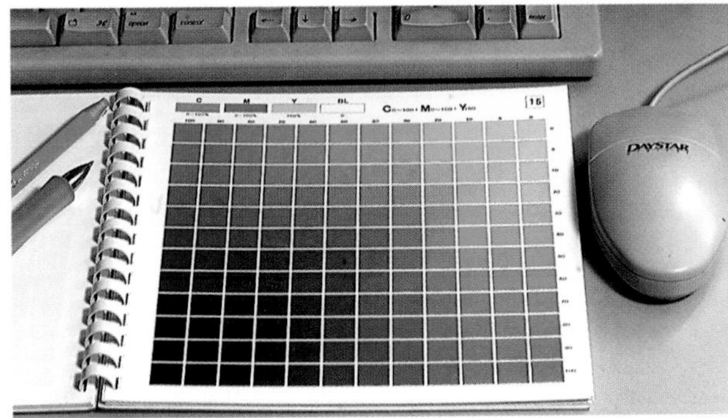

Color chart for printing inks.

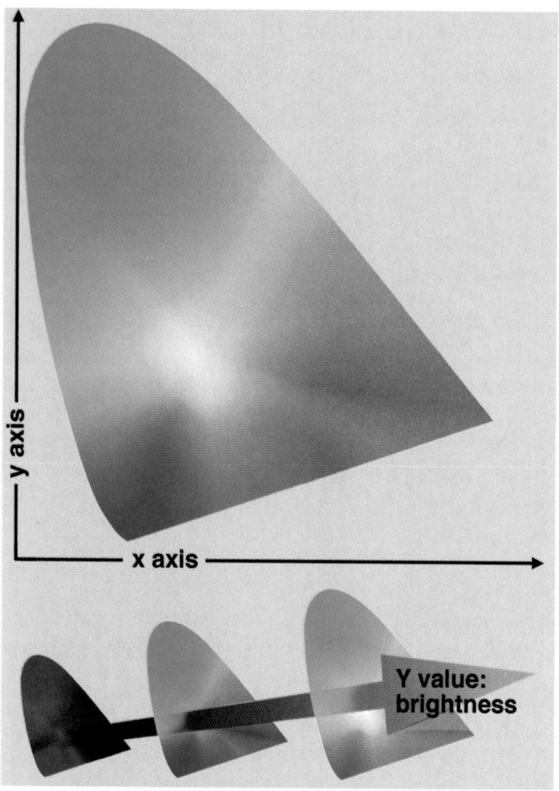

In the xyY color model, only two (hue and saturation) of the three aspects of color (X, Y, Z) are used to form a two-dimensional model (the z value is 1-x-y). However, this does not take into account the intensity of the light, so a third value, Y, is used to express luminance.

The color system that has become standard in all types of industry as well as scientific research is the CIE xyY (or Yxy) color space, also called the "xy ratio" system (see the illustration to the left). Because it calculates color mathematically, color scientists find it convenient for characterizing color. However, even if we take a color and express it numerically, let's say an x = 0.5227 y = 0.3685 Y = 63.21 orange, people's perceptions of it differ greatly. At least Y, the value that expresses the luminance of a color, can vary from 0 to 100, so the Y = 63.21 value above indicates a color that is neither bright or dark, but falls in the middle.

NOTE

This xyY color model is used in the deeper levels of the Printing Inks Setup and the Monitor Setup dialog boxes in Adobe Photoshop, the software most used by digital photographers. Color temperature, a concept familiar to photographers, is also defined in this xyY model.

Other methods of expressing color numerically are also used to control computer color. Here we show how Photoshop uses the most common of these methods.

Systems for numerically controlling color on the computer

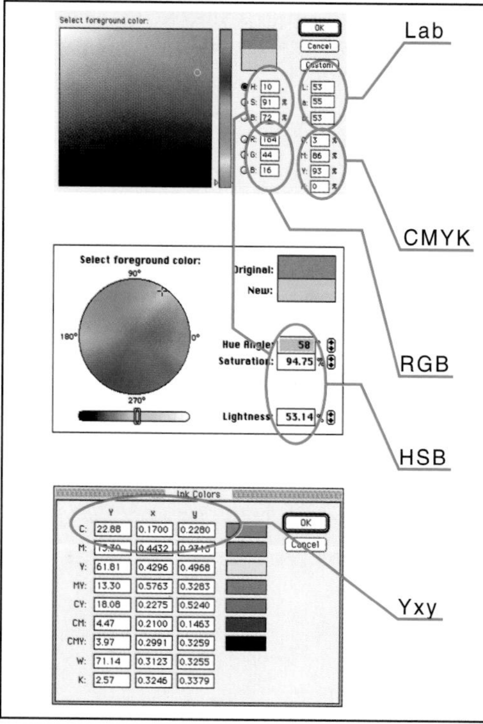

Lab

This is properly written as "L*a*b*". The L* value indicates the brightness, and the larger the number, the brighter the color. As the a* value decreases, the color becomes more green, and as it increases, the color becomes more magenta. This expresses the complementary relationship between green and magenta. As the b* value decreases, the color becomes more blue, and as it increases, the color becomes more yellow. This expresses the complementary relationship between blue and yellow. When a* and b* both equal zero, the color is gray.

CMYK

The CMYK system expresses quantities of printing ink. The values are expressed in percentages from 0 to 100 for each of the four inks, and indicate the percentage of the halftone dot surface area covered by that ink on a piece of white paper.

RGB

The RGB system expresses quantities of light. A value of 0 indicates that there is no light, and a value of 255 indicates that the quantity of light is at the maximum. Therefore, when R, G, and B each equal 255, we see pure white, meaning there is no color.

HSB

HSB (hue, saturation, brightness). Hue indicates the different wavelengths of radiant energy that we perceive, such as red or blue. Saturation indicates the purity of a color, and brightness indicates how light or dark a color is. Hue values range from 0° to 360°. At 30°, neighboring colors are evenly balanced. Complementary colors are at 180° from each other.

Yxy

This system expresses the position of a color in CIE color coordinates. Y indicates brightness, and xy indicates hue and saturation respectively. This is an extremely technical method of measuring color and is difficult to use if you're not a specialist. It appears in Photoshop only in the Printing Inks Setup dialog box.

02 4

Recording and Reproducing Color and Tonality

Georg Brander Camera Obscura (1769)

Adapted from The History of Photography *by H & A Gernsheim*

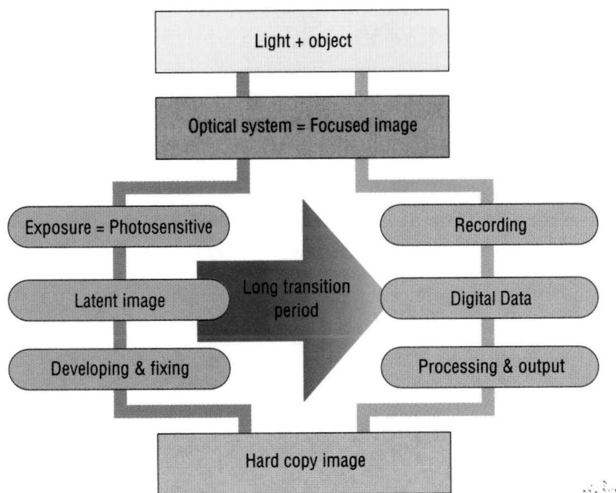

External Visual Recording Methods

Let's examine the various elements of photographic technology. First, the core technology of the "black box," including shutters and finders, and the optical technology, namely the lens system, have been combined to form the modern camera (now we can add electronics and computer technology to these). Even before 1830, when photographic technology was invented, a device called the *camera obscura* enabled an object to be focused through a lens on a piece of ground glass and then projected onto a piece of white paper and copied by hand.

However, the biggest difference before and after the invention of photographic technology was actually not the camera, but the photosensitive materials. The significant advancements were in the field of chemistry. The "invention of photographic technology" can be said to be nearly synonymous with the "chemistry of exposure and fixing of the optical image."

When the camera was invented, silver was already in use in photographic technology. A well-polished copper plate was coated with silver, chemically processed to change the silver into silver iodide, and put into the camera. After 10–15 minutes of exposure, it was oxidized with mercury vapor and developed—processes we now call exposure and developing. Of course, even before the invention of the camera, chemical materials that changed color or hardened when light was shone on them had been discovered and invented, but they were not as good as silver plates in terms of sensitivity. And of course developing, which could amplify the effect of light and make images distinct and clear, had not yet been invented.

Soon after this, the process of stabilizing a photographic image, called *fixing*, was invented. So in the 160 years since then, photographic materials have evolved from collodion wet plates and dry glass plates to film, but overall the path to silver halide photography has not really seen any significant qualitative changes.

However, it's fair to say that photographic materials and silver halide photography are currently facing a period of transition. New photographic methods are dramatically evolving and growing in popularity. Images are now captured with light sensors and converted into digital signals that are digitally recorded, displayed on the monitor, and then printed on paper and film (*imaged* would be a more accurate term).

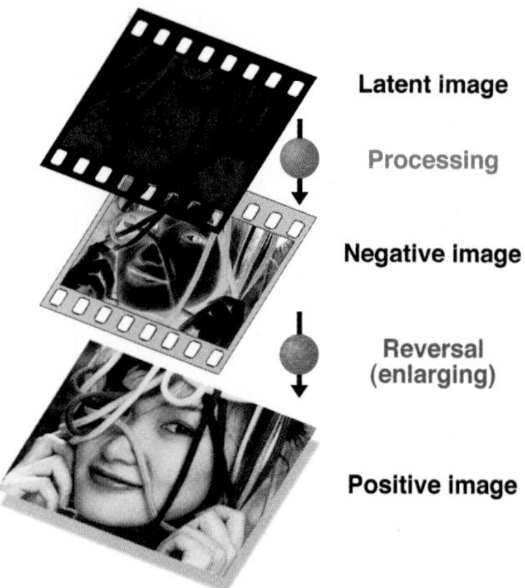

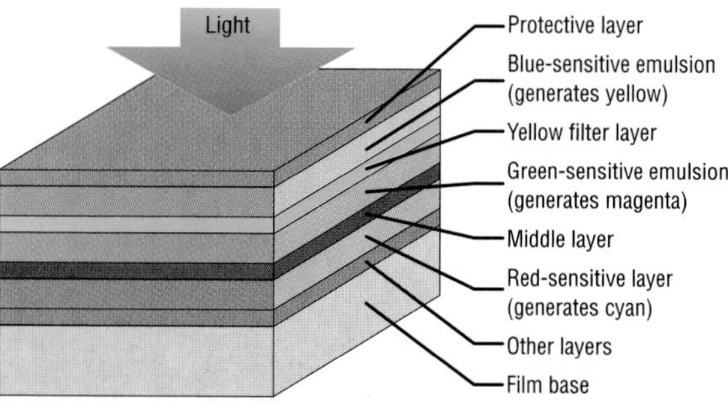

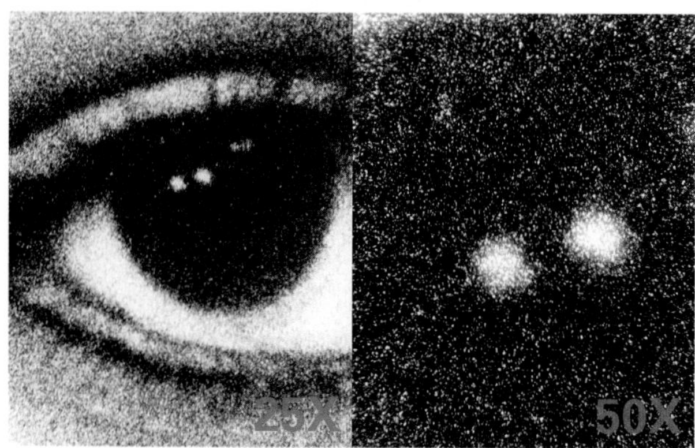

Photographs courtesy of Fuji Photographic Film.

Silver Halide Photosensitive Material

Silver halide photosensitive materials are film or paper coated with an emulsion containing light-sensitive silver halide mixed with gelatin. When the light used to focus the image with the lens hits the surface of the silver halide photosensitive material (we are omitting some complicated intermediate steps), an image we cannot see, called a latent image, is formed. Then this exposed photosensitive material is developed so the latent image becomes visible.

The image becomes visible because the silver halide changes into metallic silver, and depending on the amount of light (luminance of the photographic subject), the density of the tiny grains of metallic silver changes. Bright areas have many silver grains, and dark areas have few. The film is then fixed to prevent any further chemical changes.

This process will generate a photograph, but this isn't all there is to it. We have generated a negative, which means that the light and dark areas on the image are the opposite of how they were on the subject. So we use an enlarger (or a contact printer) and repeat the same process to create a positive image.

If we are using color reversal film, there are basically three emulsion layers, as shown to the left. The first layer is sensitive to blue light, the second is sensitive to green light, and the third is sensitive to red light. Because areas that receive more light become darker, the metallic silver areas that have not been chemically changed appear as color dyes after developing. The first blue emulsion layer generates yellow (the complement of blue), the second green emulsion layer generates magenta (the complement of green) and the third red emulsion layer generates cyan (the complement of red).

For black-and-white photography, the image appears as different densities of extremely fine silver grains caused by variations in light exposure. For color photography, the image appears as densities of the color dyes. The grains are as tiny as a single micron (one thousandth of a millimeter), so we are not able to see them with the naked eye at normal viewing distance.

Continuous-tone and Dot Coverage Method

When we physically display images on paper and film, or on a monitor, you can reproduce differences in tonality in two ways. The first method is the continuous-tone method, and the second is called the *dot coverage method*.

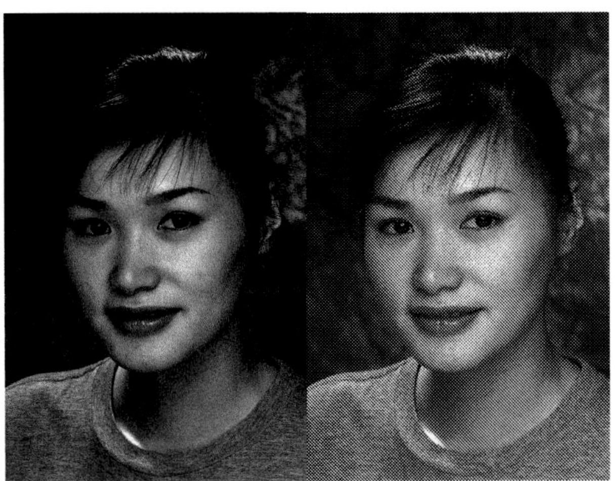

If the grains are randomly arranged, we perceive coarse graininess (left). If the grains are uniformly arranged, even large grains will not give the appearance of excessive graininess (right).

Grains are distributed throughout the depth of the emulsion.

Kodak XLS8300 dye sublimation printer.

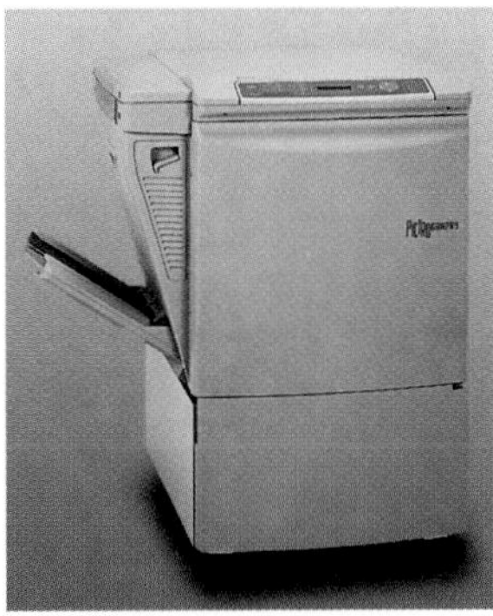

Fuji Photographic Film Pictrograph (silver halide system).

Photograph Graininess and Tonality: Generating Continuous Tones

Whether a photograph is black and white or in color, it has tonality (density). Dark areas of the image have a high density and light areas have a low density. As we explained earlier, the density of the metallic silver or color dye grains makes an image appear on paper or film. When photographs are enlarged, a phenomenon called *graininess* occurs. This isn't because we can see each individual grain, but rather because neighboring grains are nonuniformly distributed, making them stand out. We call this *excessive graininess.*

However, whether a silver halide photograph is grainy or not, the density changes (we call this *tonality*) give it continuous tones, which appear because of the grains deep within the emulsion. We call reproducing images through tonal changes the *continuous-tone method.*

Photography isn't the only system that reproduces tonality through continuous tone. The majority of dye sublimation color printers do as well. On the surface of a dye sublimation print, you cannot see the coarseness and fineness of the grains. This is because the color dyes penetrate the surface of the paper, and the changes in the densities of the dyes reproduce tonality. Silver halide color prints reproduce tonality in this same way.

Digital photography artwork that is output as hard copies can look the same as silver halide prints. Using a dye sublimation printer or a printer that uses silver halide photosensitive material is best.

Conventional gravure printing also creates continuous-tone output by continuously varying the thickness with which the ink is laid on the paper. (We cannot illustrate this in this book because it was printed using offset, not gravure, printing.)

Halftoning method. *Diameter changes, pitch remains constant*

Reproducing Tonal Range Through Offset Printing: Halftoning

Another way to reproduce tonality is the dot coverage method. Dot coverage does not reproduce tonality through changes in the density of dye on paper like the continuous-tone method discussed earlier. Instead, tonality on the paper surface is reproduced by how much of the paper area is occupied by small dots of colorant that have a fixed density. Two types of dot coverage exist: halftoning and dithering.

Halftoning reproduces tonality by varying the diameter of halftone dots that are placed in regular intervals on the paper. This method is used in offset printing like that used to produce this book, as well as in electronic imaging products such as laser printers. The advantage of halftone printing is that graininess can be controlled through evenly spaced groups of dots, enabling beautiful, smooth tonal reproduction. However, the disadvantage is that in order to distribute varying sized halftone dots with precise uniformity, you must have very precise output devices.

Dithering method. *Diameter remains constant, pitch changes*

Inkjet Printer Tonality: Dithering

Another dot coverage method is dithering, one of today's most popular methods for reproducing tonal range. Generally, all inkjet and thermal printers use dithering. Even some offset printing is done using a type of dithering called FM dot coverage (or stochastic screening).

Unlike halftoning, the size of the dot is fixed, and the distance between the dots is variable, which means that the changes in dot frequency on the paper enables the reproduction of tonal range.

Seiko Epson MJ5100C Inkjet Printer.

Color printers that use dithering are both simple in design and inexpensive, but by and large the results are grainy, particularly in bright highlight areas. More recently, manufacturers have improved their technology and are offering printers that can adequately change the density of the clusters of tiny dots. The result is that on average, distinguishing between printer output and a photograph in terms of graininess and range of tonal reproduction is not possible.

Converting Light into Electronic Signals

After the method of numerically characterizing color is decided, it's very simple for a computer to handle high-speed calculations and recording. However, originally color is something that is reflected off or absorbed by objects. It then hits the rod cells in our eyes that, when stimulated, generate a chemical that is sent to the brain, whereupon we "see" it. Just as the light stimulus generates chemicals in the brain, in a computer, light energy must be converted into a digital signal in order for the computer to be able to manipulate it.

Camera Exposure Meters

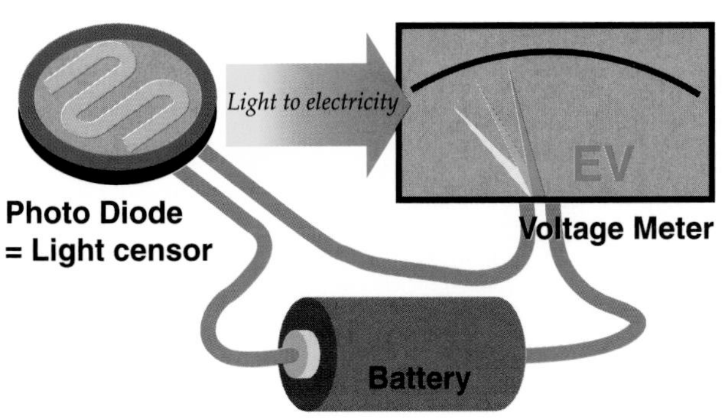

How an exposure meter works: light is converted into voltage changes.

Because photographers have experience using various types of exposure meters, they are already familiar with the result of converting light into electronic signals. When an exposure reading is made, a voltage meter measures the voltage resulting from the conversion of light to an electrical current. In bright situations where there is a lot of light, there is a higher electrical current, resulting in a higher EV value reading on the exposure meter. Conversely, if it's dark, the EV values are low.

Digitally recording images uses the same principle. However, with images, we work with extremely small units, and we can think of it as shining a spot meter from corner to corner of the image surface and sending those signals to the computer.

CCD for a compact digital camera.

Photograph courtesy of Seiko Epson.

CCD Light Sensors

We call devices that convert light into electricity *light sensors*. Many different types of light sensors exist, but the most familiar to photographers is the CCD.

CCD stands for charge coupled device. You can imagine the structure of a CCD as an array of thousands or millions of exposure meter light sensors. But if an electrical line ran from each light sensor, it would be very difficult to connect them all to the computer. To solve this problem, the CCD is designed so that all the light sensors are lined up in a row and each sends its electrical signal one at a time along a single electrical line. Sending the electrical signal one at a time means that there is a lag between when the first signal is sent and when the last signal is sent. To eliminate the lag time, the signals (separate from the light sensors) are all held inside the CCD, and a timing signal is used to send the signals all at once to the outside. Of course, this time lapse is too small for us to perceive. All the signals are sent from the light sensors in a matter of milliseconds, as shown in the illustration to the left.

Image density=Variation in amount of light

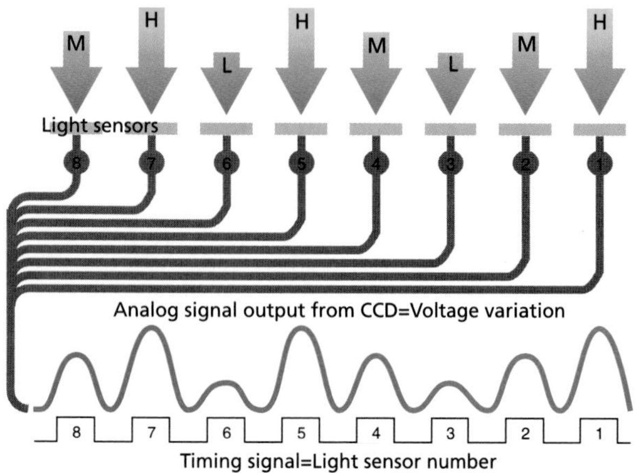

Types of CCDs

Linear arrays: Several thousand light sensors are arranged in a single line and detect light line by line. As the array moves across the surface of the image, the variation in the amount of light (the image) is detected.

Array arrays (Imagers): Several hundred to several thousand light sensors are arranged in a matrix. The array remains stationary and the variation in the amount of light (the image) is scanned.

CCDs were originally used in video cameras. More recently they have been incorporated into digital cameras and are familiar to photographers doing still photography. CCDs are also used in scanners. All these CCDs, whether for scanners, video cameras, or digital cameras, operate using essentially the same principle. However, there are actually two different types—linear arrays and area arrays—as shown in the illustration to the left.

Photomultipliers

Photomultiplier. The light sensor is the striped metal grid on the right side. Photo courtesy of Dainippon Screen Mfg. Co., Ltd.

CCDs became popular in the early 1980s, but scanners had been in use before then. Between the time when scanners were still expensive and the present day, the light sensors that provided the best performance were photomultipliers.

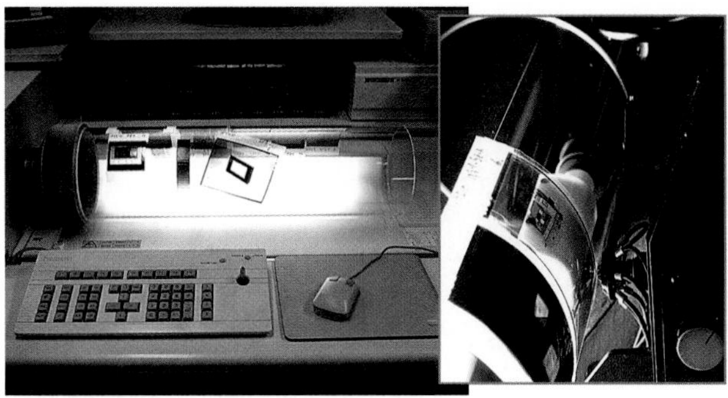

A high-end drum scanner in a commercial prepress shop. These scanners are capable of scanning hundreds of photographs a day, converting them into digital data. This is a Dainippon Screen SG-747. Photograph courtesy of Shashin Kagaku Co., Ltd.

Photomultipliers are cylindrical glass vacuum tubes about 20 mm in length and 10 mm in diameter. When light hits the grid area inside the glass tube, electrons in the tube are excited, and the energy is amplified hundreds of thousands of times. The movement of electrons is converted into an electrical current outside the tube and then transmitted.

The advantage of photomultipliers is that they are extremely sensitive to light and generate very little noise. They are capable of responding to the brightness of even a single star in the night sky. Even today, 100 percent of drum scanners for prepress use photomultiplier tubes (see also Chapter 4, page 4-2). Photomultipliers are also indispensable light sensors for all kinds of professional fields, from medicine to astronomy to broadcasting.

In digital photography as well, to output the very best artwork, photographers use scanners with photomultipliers rather than scanners with CCDs to digitize their photographs. For example, a scanner with photomultiplier tubes can more accurately capture the shadow detail on a low key piece of artwork on color reversal film.

Converting Electronic Signals Back into Light

After the light from the light sensors has been converted into electrical signals, those variations in voltage must be converted into digital signals. We call this *analog to digital conversion* (A/D conversion). This converted signal can then be manipulated by the computer in many different ways, but if you want to view your image right away, the signal must be converted for monitor display.

Monitors emit light of varying intensities from electron guns in the back of the glass picture tube, which enables us to view the picture with our eyes. Also, after the digital artwork is finished, it's usually output as a hard copy.

In both of these cases, the digital signal is converted back into an analog signal (D/A conversion). In both monitors and printers, the electrical signal generates light, or in the case of some devices, heat or static electricity, and this generates the image we see.

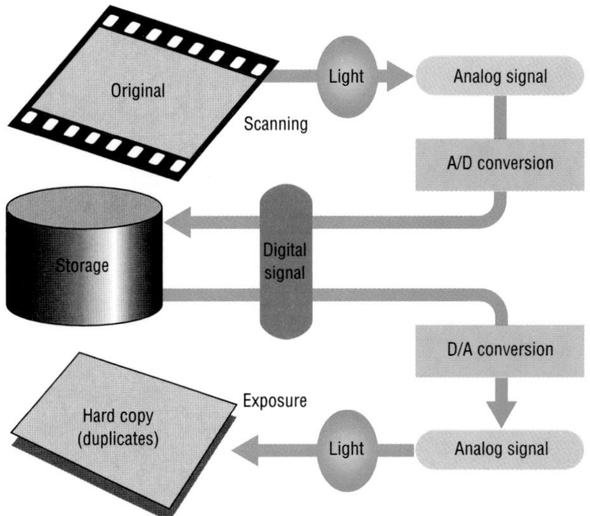

The cycle for a digital photograph: light-analog-digital-analog-light

In digital photography, photosensitivity and storage are separate.

Photographic processes using silver halide photosensitive materials reproduce artwork using photochemistry, and the silver halide film performs the double task of being light sensor and image recorder. In contrast, the light sensors used in digital photographic processes do not both record and store image information. The information resulting from A/D conversion must be stored on a hard disk or some other storage medium. This can be considered a major technological difference between silver halide photography and digital photography.

02 5

Recording and Output Devices

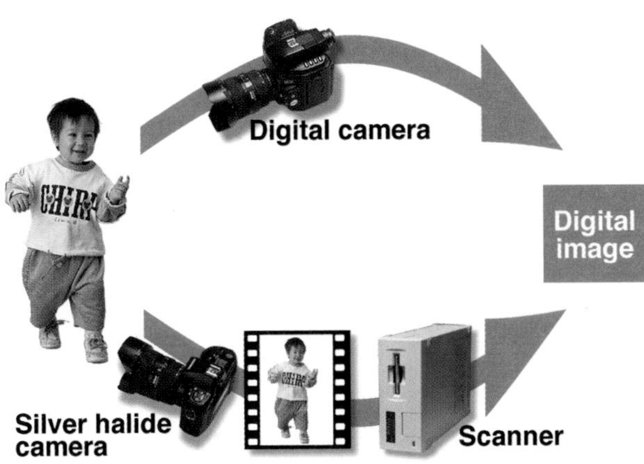

Structure of a digital camera. (Conceptual photograph)

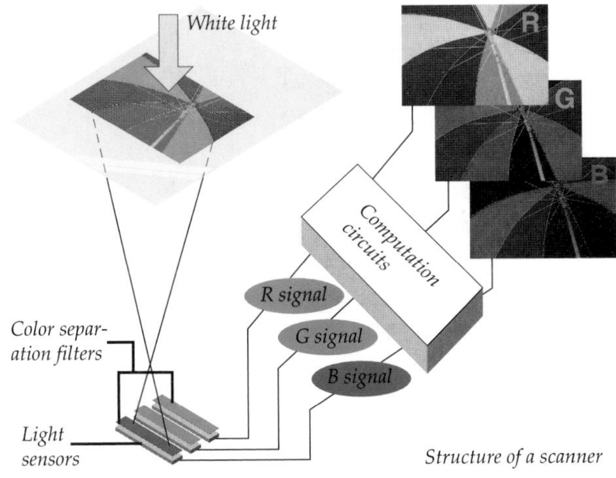

Structure of a scanner

Input and Output

Let's imagine a video image, the predecessor of the digital image. Both capturing the world around you with a video camera and taping a TV program using a VCR can be called *recording*. Likewise, enjoying the recorded images on a television can be called *playback*.

In digital photography, we have the same concepts of recording and playback, but we call them *input* and *output*. From here on, we shall use the terms input and output.

Essentially, two ways exist to digitize the world around us. The first is to use a digital camera. If you use a digital camera, you don't have to use silver halide film. Therefore, all the associated processes, as well as enlarging and printing, also become unnecessary. The other way is to use silver halide film and a scanner. If you do this, you have to process your film, enlarge it, and make a print from it. Then you have to use a scanner to digitize the processed silver halide film.

Digital Cameras

There are many different types of digital cameras, which are introduced on page 2-40. What is common to all of them is that they have camera bodies similar in structure to that of silver halide cameras, the CCDs are positioned on what would be the film plane (focal plane where the image is focused) on a conventional camera, and they digitize images.

Scanners

A *scanner* is a device that converts light into electrical signals and then digitizes those signals. Color scanners have RGB filters attached to their light sources or light sensors so that the light reflected off an original or that passes through a transparency is separated into three components—R, G, and B. We call this process of separating light into its three RGB components a form of *color separation*.

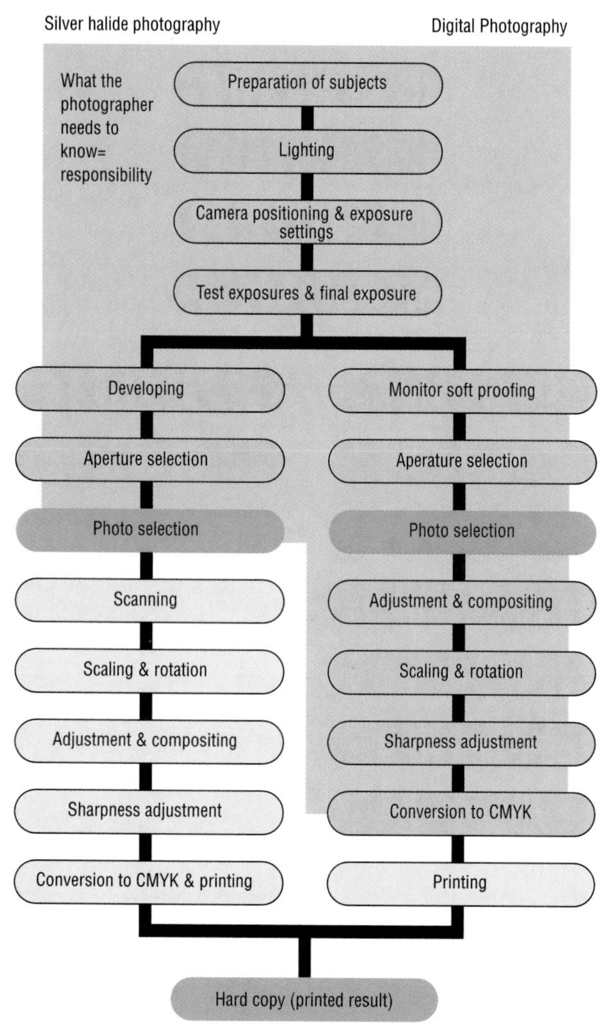

Digital Output Devices for Appreciating the Final Artwork

It's possible to appreciate digital artwork on a monitor, but usually we output some type of hard copy. By *hard copy* we mean offset prints, output from color printers, or output onto color reversal film.

Until now, in advertising photography, a photographer's responsibility was to present the client with the artwork on color reversal film; the photographer usually didn't participate to any great extent in the processes that followed, such as printing. But now as digital photography methods are incorporated into the advertising workflow, like it or not, photographers have to be involved up through the last phase of output, printing.

Artists and amateur photographers have to maintain control over the final result when they create their artwork, just as they have always had to. For color photography, now that artists no longer need to rely upon a lab for their results, they have more creative freedom than they have had in the past.

For simple snapshots or mementos, until now you have had to expose a color negative, have it printed at a one-hour lab on photo-album-size paper, and that would be the end of it. But with digital photography, few shops will make this type of photo album size print for you, so you have to have it printed yourself.

No matter what level of digital photography you're doing, you need to know something about output devices. Think of it as similar to when black-and-white photography was so popular, and we all buried ourselves in our darkrooms and created our artwork. It's the same kind of feeling. We could say that we have a "brightroom" not a darkroom, for our computer work.

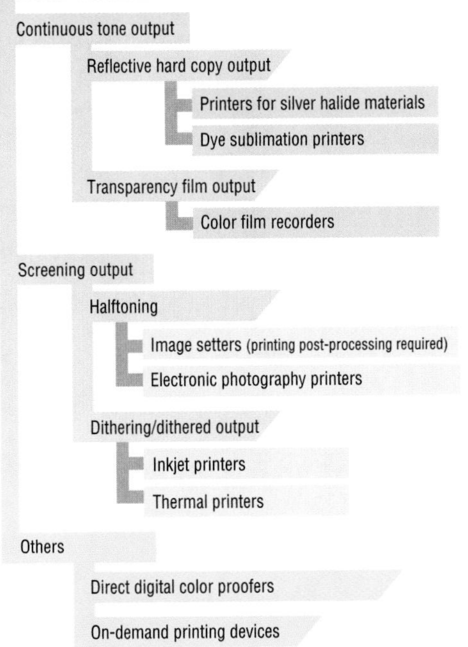

Types of Output Devices

Output devices for digital photography can be classified as shown in the illustration. To output continuous-tone output, electronic scans or photographic prints are used as second-generation originals. Transparencies produced from silver halide film recorders, for example, are very high-quality second-generation originals.

The quality of hard copy output using the dot coverage method is excellent. Output costs are low and large format output is possible, so prints can be used for anything from presentations to exhibitions. If you use an imagesetter to output four pieces of film or use digital printers for on-demand printing, however, the cost increases if you need more than a few hundred copies.

02 6

The Language of Digital Imaging

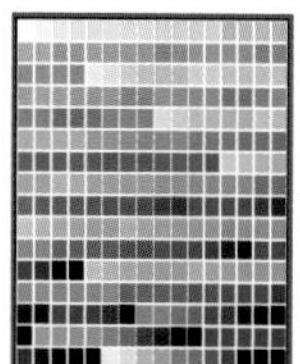

Indexed color: all together, there are 256 CMY (or RGB) distinct colors. Each color is assigned to one pixel.

Dithered color: only one distinct color exists for each of the CMY (or RGB) colors, and the image is reproduced by means of groups of tiny dots in varying densities.

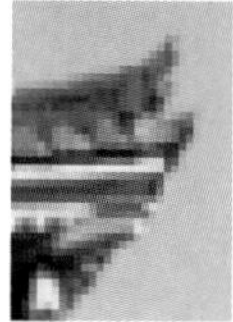

Full color: there are 256 levels of gradation, and the image can be reproduced in 256×256×256 or 16.7 million colors.

Raster Images

We call digital photography images *raster* images. The word "raster" means scanning line. Just like on a television, an image whose brightness and color can be controlled by scanning line is called a raster image.

Types of Raster Images

Several types of digital data raster images exist.

- Indexed color (256 colors)
- Dithered color (each RGB or CMY color on or off)
- Full color (16,777,216 colors)

In digital photography, the majority of images are in full color.

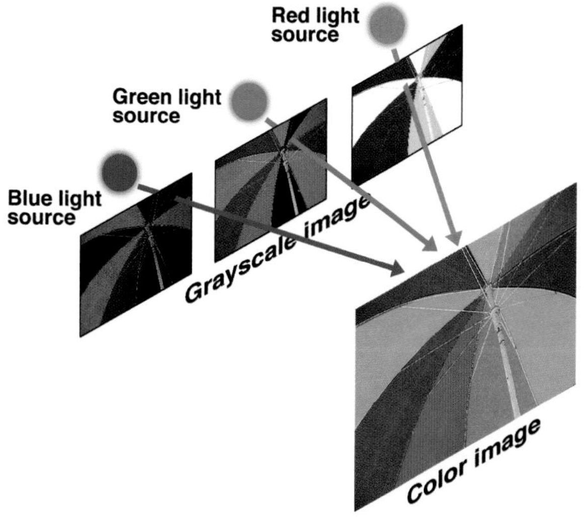

RGB Raster Images

We can perceive images on color reversal film or color photographs because when viewed from a distance, we see a mixture of cyan (C), magenta (M), and yellow (Y) dye colorants on their surfaces. When we understand how light sensitive material is exposed, however, we realize that the photosensitive material responds not to CMY color light, but to RGB color light.

Digital cameras and color scanners respond to the varying amounts of RGB light, generating three types of achromatic information that are recorded separately. We call data that has been acquired this way *RGB raster data*. We call them *RGB images* in this book.

CMYK Raster Images

An RGB raster image is generated by recording the amounts of the three primary colors of light, but, if you want to output hard copy color prints of this image from a computer, you have to use CMYK image data. Particularly when you make color offset prints, black ink is added to the CMY inks in order to deepen the dark areas of the image, so you need raster data with density information for all four CMYK colors, as shown to the left. This raster image data converted especially for color printing is called a *CMYK raster image*. We call them *CMYK images* in this book.

Composite

Photoshop Channels Palette

Raster Image Channels

When we work with RGB and CMYK images on the computer, we handle each color in monochrome images called *channels*. An RGB image has three channels of color information, and a CMYK image has four channels of color information. During display or output, these channels are layered on top of one another to create the color image. Photoshop has a *composite channel* to display all the channels layered on top of each another.

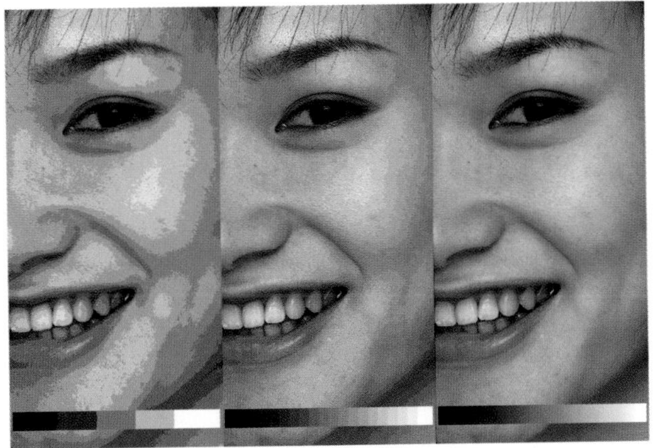

5 levels 20 levels 256 levels

Levels

We call changes in lightness or darkness *levels* or *shades of gray*. Different raster image data systems produce different numbers of levels, which are called the *number of levels*.

The number of levels expresses the range of discrete tone steps between the lightest and the darkness points on an image. The number of available levels affects the rendering of the image—the more the better. Most systems currently in use render 256 levels. Newer systems for image input, such as digital cameras, can record 1,024, 4,096, or 16,384 levels.

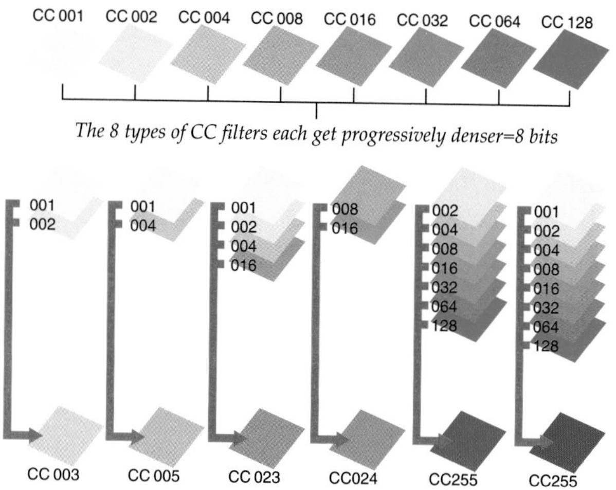

The 8 types of CC filters each get progressively denser=8 bits

If all 8 CC filters are added together, we can reproduce a range of tones from 1 to 255, or 256 tones if we include zero.

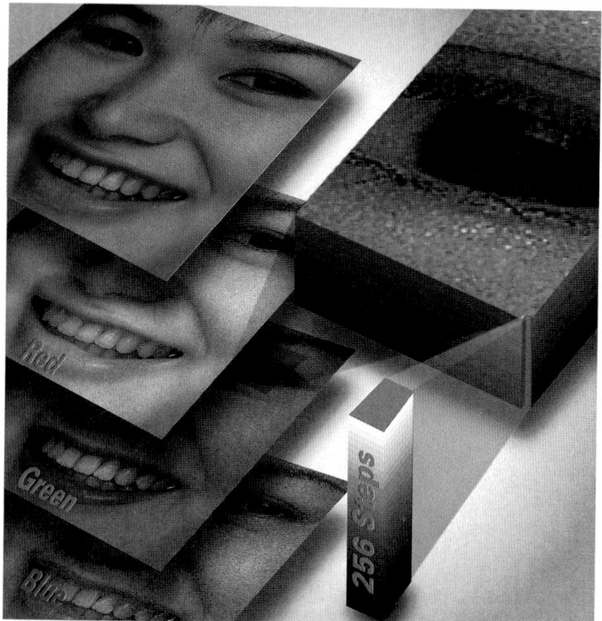

In an RGB 24-bit image, each pixel channel can reproduce up to 256 levels, depending on the brightness.

24-bit Images

Computers use a binary system, which means that values can only be expressed by means of a zero or one, called a bit. In imaging, a 1-bit image means that a pixel is either a one or a zero, black or white. Adding more bit choices increases the number of potential combinations, meaning an increase in tonal values. A grayscale image is an 8-bit image, meaning there can be a total of 256 combintion of ones and zero (2^8), or 256 levels of tone.

Because an RGB image is made up of three 256-level images, we call it a *24-bit image*. More accurately, we should call it an *RGB 24-bit image* to distinguish it from CMYK and monochrome images.

Similarly, an image with 1,024 steps for each color is a *30-bit image* (10 bits for each RGB color), an image with 4,096 steps for each color is a *36-bit image* (12 bits for each RGB color), and an image with 16,384 steps for each color is a *42-bit image* (14 bits for each RGB color).

Photoshop mainly handles RGB 24-bit images and CMYK 32-bit images (both with 256 levels per channel), but with changes in brightness and cropping, some sections of images can be rendered with 65,536 steps (16 bits) per color for 48-bit color. Please see Part 5, "Digital Exposures," for details.

NOTE

PICT format images on the Macintosh are 32-bit images, but 8 bits are used for an additional alpha channel. The images themselves are actually 24-bit images.

Quantity of Information and Resolution

Rasters, or scanning lines, are thought of differently in televisions than they are with digital cameras. In television or video, the number of vertical scanning lines is fixed at around 500. No matter how big the television, the same number of scanning lines always exists. But in digital photography, the number of scanning lines can be freely determined by the artist.

On less expensive digital cameras, the short dimension has around 400 scanning lines, but on high-end models there can be 1,000 to 2,000, and on studio cameras there are 4,000 to 8,000. The quality of the image depends on this number of scanning lines. The more lines there are, the more information. The quality of a silver halide photograph is similarly impacted by the size of the image—since the density of the silver (dye) in the emulsion is fixed, the larger the format—from half-frame, to 35 mm, to 6×4.5 cm, to 6×6 cm, to 4×5 inches, to 8×10 inches—the more detailed the picture.

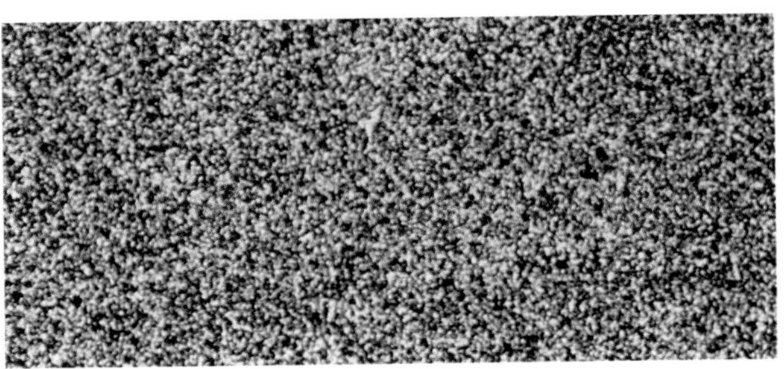

Silver halide film grains. *Courtesy of Fuji Photographic Films.*

Silver Halide Film Grains

Silver halide film contains many grains of silver. If we view these grains under a microscope after processing, the light areas have only a scattering of grains, and dark areas have a high concentration of grains. In addition, the grains are different sizes and are not arranged uniformly.

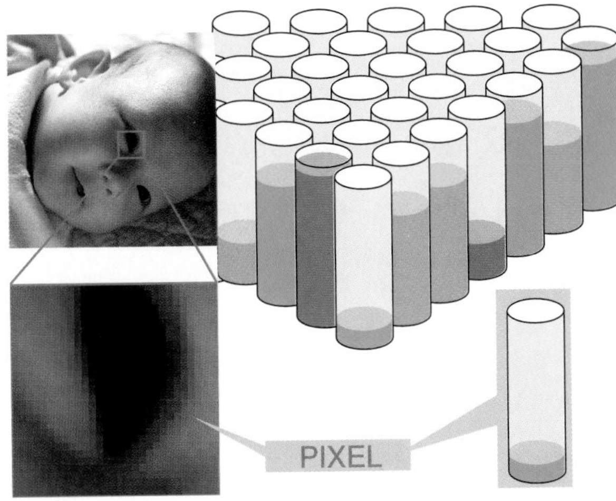

To understand the concept of a pixel, imagine glass tubes filled with different amounts of different colors. We can think of an image created by the horizontal and vertical arrangement of these pixels.

Digital Image Grains: Pixels

Raster images have something analogous to grains for rendering brightness. A raster image is created with a fine grid pattern, and we call a single square in this grid a *pixel* (the word is derived from "picture element" or "picture cell"). A pixel is the smallest unit of a raster image, and therefore corresponds to a grain of silver in a silver halide image. Unlike silver halide grains, pixels are uniform in size and are arranged uniformly.

The Number of Pixels on a Digital Camera

Most digital cameras have a fixed number of pixels on their imaging surface. For example, the popular Kodak DC50 has 756×504 pixels, the Olympus D300L has 1,024×768 pixels, the Nikon E2 (Fujitsu DS505) has 1,000×1,200 pixels, and the Kodak DCS460 has 2,000×3,000 pixels. We multiply the horizontal times the vertical number of pixels to determine the amount of information the camera can capture, and this is known as the *resolution*.

Resolution

When you make an exposure with a digital camera or scan a silver halide photograph and output a hard copy of it with any type of printer, you're only uniformly mapping all the pixels onto the page. We call this arrangement of pixels *resolution*. When used to refer to photographic film or lens characteristics, the term resolution usually describes "resolving power," or the ability to hold fine detail in a photograph. However, for digital images, the term resolution means "the amount of information in the image."

A simulation of different image resolutions.

Image Resolution

The more pixels there are, the more accurately the detailed areas of a picture can be reproduced. The more accurately the image can be reproduced, the more it can be enlarged without deterioration in quality.

We express the number of pixels in image data in terms of *pixels per inch* (ppi). Ppi is sometimes referred to as "dpi." However, dpi (dots per inch) is more appropriately used when referring to spots per inch output on an imagesetter or other printing device. When talking about the size or resolution of an image, "ppi" is the term used in this book.

We also use the term "image resolution" to distinguish from "image input resolution" and "output device resolution," which is discussed next.

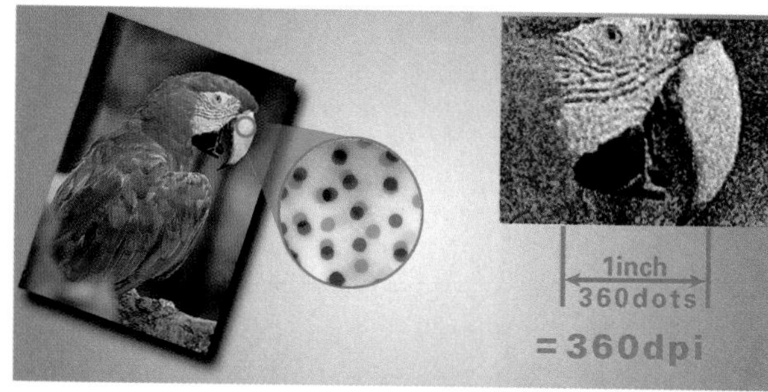

Output resolution of an inkjet printer.

Output Device Resolution

All output devices, such as color printers, have a fixed density of scanning lines. We call this *output device resolution*, and it's expressed in dots per inch (dpi). Output device resolution is sometimes referred to as "output recording density."

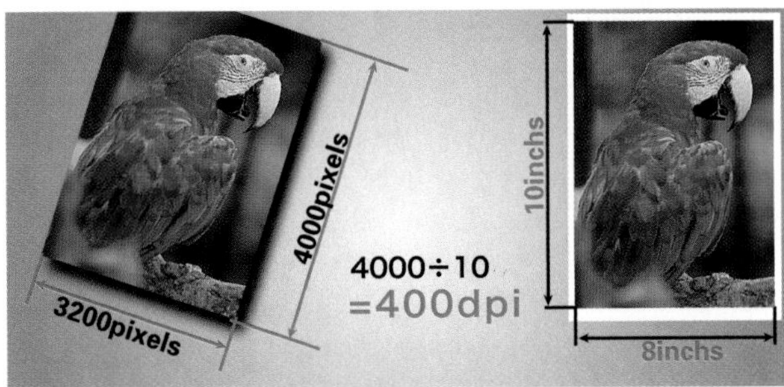

The number of pixels required for output on a dye sublimation printer.

The Number of Pixels Required for Output on a Continuous-tone Printer

To output hard copies from continuous-tone printers such as dye sublimation printers or silver halide film recorders, you must determine the image resolution required from the output device resolution. For example, if a dye sublimation printer is capable of generating 400 marks per inch (400 dpi) to reproduce different densities, and the output size is 8×10-inches, the number of pixels required is 8×400 = 3,200 pixels for the 8-inch short dimension and 10×400 = 4,000 pixels for the 10-inch long dimension.

Output Device Resolution for the Dot Coverage Method

For output devices that use dot coverage methods, such as inkjet printers and imagesetters, different density levels are created by varying the size or the frequency of the dots to reproduce the pixels in the image data. The output device resolution is higher than the image resolution required for screened output, so output devices reproduce pixels with many smaller marks, or dots.

Imagesetter Halftone Screen Rulings

We call the frequency of halftone dots the *screen ruling*. An average offset color print has 150 to 175 halftone dots per inch. The number of lines of halftone dots is expressed as *lines per inch* (lpi).

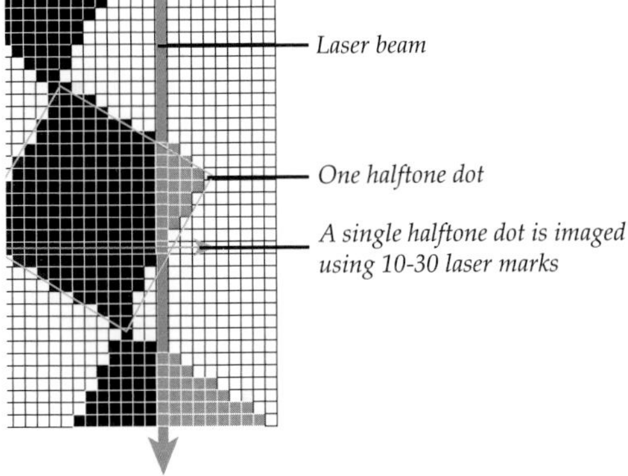

Imagesetter Output Device Resolution

Halftone dots are usually created by grouping laser marks into a square cell whose dimension on medium and high resolution output devices varies from 10 to 30 laser marks along one side. If each halftone dot on a 150 lpi screen is created using 20 laser marks, it's necessary to use an output device with a laser beam whose recording density is fine enough to create an output device resolution of 3,000 (150 lpi×20) dpi.

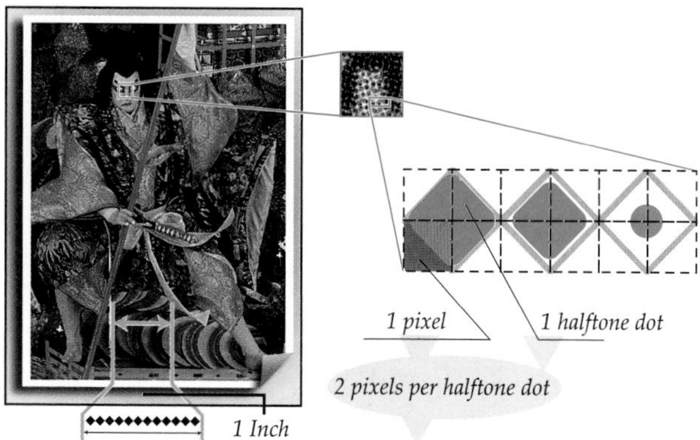

150 halftone dots = 150 lpi×2 = image resolution (ppi).

Required Number of Pixels for Imagesetter Output

For halftone image output on an average imagesetter, one halftone dot corresponds to 2×2 pixels. If only one pixel is assigned to one halftone dot, it's not possible to reproduce a wide enough range of tones, and the image will not be sharp. If we are printing at 150 lpi, where one inch contains 150 halftone dots (150 lpi is a standard screen ruling for commercial printing), we need 150×2 = 300 pixels per inch (ppi).

Required Number of Pixels for Inkjet Printer Output

Inkjet printers use a dot coverage method called *dithering*. On average, for dithered output, the output device resolution is 3 dots per pixel to obtain acceptable image quality. If the image resolution is exactly the same as the output device resolution for highly detailed images with a lot of contrast, it's possible to obtain very rich, detailed hard copy reproductions.

If you're using an inkjet printer with an output resolution of 720 marks, or dots, per inch (dpi) and if you maintain the 3 to 1 dot to pixel ratio, for example, you will need 720÷3 = 240 pixels per inch.

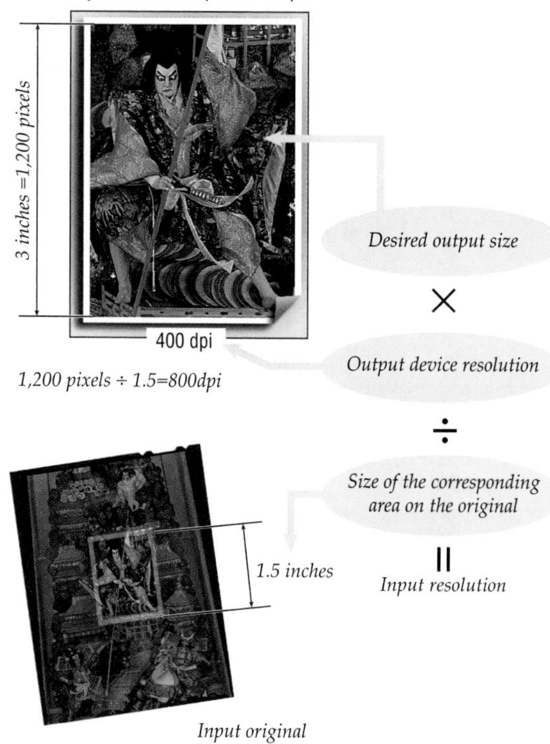

Input Resolution

When you scan photographs, you have to determine at what frequency you should divide your original into pixels. We call this the *input image resolution, scan line density*, or *sampling pitch*, and it's expressed in dots per inch (dpi), the same as for the output device resolution.

To determine the input image resolution, first measure the area on your original image that you want to output in inches. Then decide what your final output size will be. From these you can determine how many pixels you will need to output that area using a particular output device.

For example, on the 400 dpi dye sublimation printer discussed earlier, for continuous-tone output, the output device resolution and the image resolution are the same. To output a portion of that image with a finished size of 3 inches, therefore, 3×400 = 1,200 pixels are needed in that 3-inch finished piece of artwork. The area on the original that corresponds to the area that we wish to output is 1.5 inches. So if we divide 1,200 by 1.5, we get 800 dpi as our input image resolution.

If we were using a 720 dpi inkjet printer, we would need one third this image resolution (240 ppi), so to output a portion of that image with a finished size of 3 inches, 3×240 = 720 pixels will be needed in that 3-inch finished piece of artwork. As in the previous example, the area on the original that corresponds to the area that we wish to output is 1.5 inches. So if we divide 720 by 1.5, we get 480 dpi as our input image resolution.

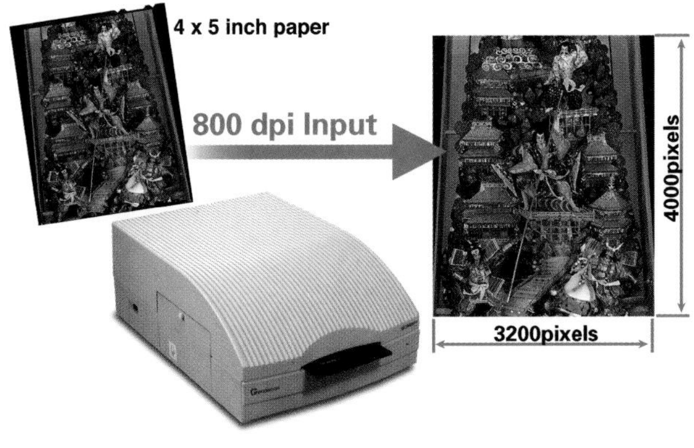

Image Interpolation

After we have input our raster image, the pixel count for the area that we are going to output is fixed. If we scan a 4×5-inch photograph at 800 dpi, for example, the short 4-inch dimension has 4×800 = 3,200 pixels, and the long 5-inch dimension has 5×800 = 4,000 pixels.

As we have said before, digital cameras are capable of capturing only a fixed number of pixels with their CCD sensors, so the total pixel count is determined immediately after exposure. As we have just seen, however, the total number of pixels required for our output image (per 1-inch area) on a particular output device is fixed, so there may be times when we have to adjust the number of pixels by adding (enlarging) or removing (reducing) the number of pixels we have input to obtain the final output size. We call this type of processing *interpolation*.

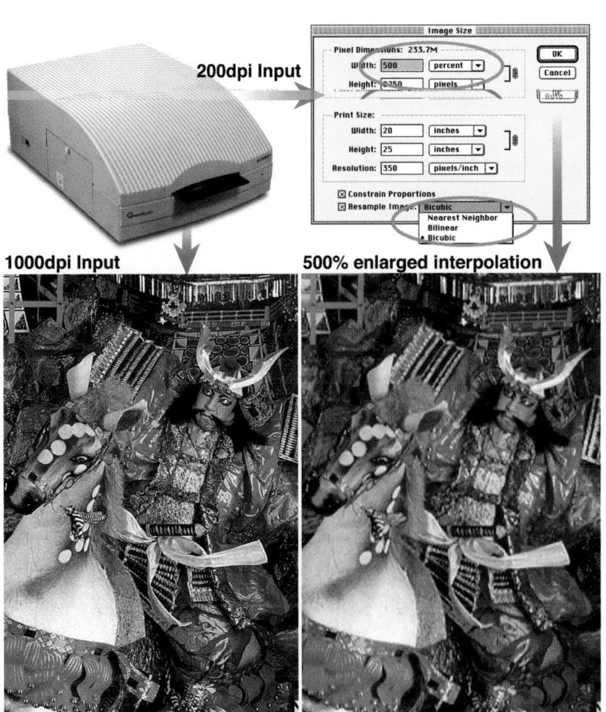

If we compare output using the number of pixels determined at scanning time with output using interpolation (enlarged), we can see the difference in image quality.

Interpolation causes the quality of images to deteriorate. When you have an insufficient number of pixels, you add new pixels, using existing pixels as a reference (called upsampling). Or if you need to take out excess pixels, you remove pixels that are actually in the data (called downsampling). If you compare images before and after interpolation, the interpolated images look enlarged or reduced because a different number of pixels is being displayed in a given area; therefore, interpolation is a type of scaling.

You can do interpolation in many ways. In Photoshop these methods are called *nearest neighbor*, *bilinear*, and *bicubic* interpolation. Please see Section 7 for details.

02 7

An Overview of Digital Cameras for 1997 (October, 1996)

The majority of popular, less expensive cameras available on the market are fast one-shot cameras. The name plate on the Nikon E2 is covered (far right) to prevent the name from reflecting off the glass when we use the camera for copy work.

The BigShot 4000, announced at the Tokyo '96 Seybold Seminars. It was still a slow three-shot camera at that time. The technology for changing the high-speed RGB filters on the front of the lens requires further development.

Classifying Digital Cameras

Digital cameras can be divided into two groups: one-shot cameras and three-shot cameras. Both one-shot and three-shot cameras can be further divided into fast and slow cameras. These groups differ from each other in terms of their CCD technology, and the distinctions between them are changing as digital camera technology evolves. As recently as a year ago, for example, the "fast three-shot camera" did not even exist.

Fast One-Shot Cameras

Short exposure, single-shot cameras are exactly the same as average point-and-shoot cameras. Strobe lights can be used for exposure, and with a few exceptions, all these cameras are capable of time exposures. Lately there has been a great increase in the number of cameras for taking snapshots, and they are all fast one-shot cameras. The Kodak DCS series, the Nikon E2 (Fujitsu DS505), the Minolta RD175, the ActionCam from Agfa, and the Polaroid PDC2000 series can be used for professional work.

Most of these cameras have their own camera body, and only the Kodak DCS series is also available as camera backs for silver halide cameras like the Hasselblad or the Mamiya 67.

Fast Three-Shot Cameras

The Dicomed BigShot 4000 uses a color image input system that takes three exposures nearly instantaneously—at several thousandths of a second (at press time, this technology was still in development). Liquid crystal RGB filters are directly in front of the camera lens, and when you press the shutter, they rotate at high speed as the three exposures are taken. The new technology on this camera has received considerable attention.

Artist's conceptual drawing of a scan type digital camera with a linear CCD array, attached to a 4×5 view camera.

Slow One-Shot Cameras

Slow one-shot, or scan type, digital cameras require several seconds to several minutes for exposure. For a studio photographer, long exposures are not uncommon. Generally, when silver halide cameras are used for long exposure times, changes in illumination during exposure don't create a big problem (think of open bulb techniques that combine strobe and tungsten illumination, for example). But on scan type digital cameras, the illumination cannot change during exposure, not even for a moment. This is because the CCDs on the image plane are not all recording the image at the moment the illumination changes. If the illumination changes, or turns off, during exposure, the resulting image has the same type of flaw as using strobe lights out of synch on a focal plane shutter camera—only one portion of the image shows the change in illumination.

There are two major types of slow, one-shot cameras: scanning cameras with linear array CCDs, and scanning cameras with area array CCDs. There are two major types, scanning cameras with linear CCD arrays, and scanning cameras with area CCD arrays.

Scanning cameras with linear CCD arrays attach as camera backs to 4×5-inch view cameras and 120 mm film format cameras. When you press the shutter button, the linear CCD array scans across the image just like a scanner, and the exposure is finished in a matter of minutes.

The second type, scanning cameras with area CCD arrays, are similar to linear CCD arrays. Instead of a moving linear CCD, however, these cameras use a moving CCD array in which the array shifts across and down in one micron increments. Current designs of this style of camera often look more like a convenience store security camera than a professional photo studio camera.

Both types of cameras provide a tremendous amount of information (which is to say, a lot of pixels) and very high quality images. They can be used for shooting catalog photography, as well as photography requiring high quality, advanced lighting and camera techniques, such as car photography.

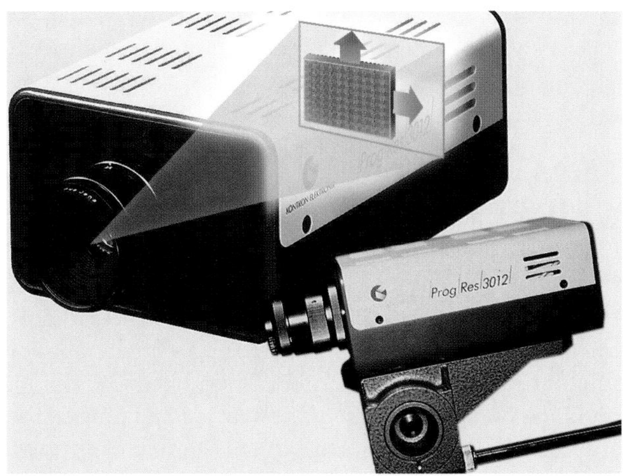

Area CCD array that shifts up and down, then left and right during exposure.

The Kontron ProgRess 3012. This camera provides startlingly high quality images.

Courtesy of Shriro Trading

Scitex Leaf DCBII. *Courtesy of Shriro Trading*

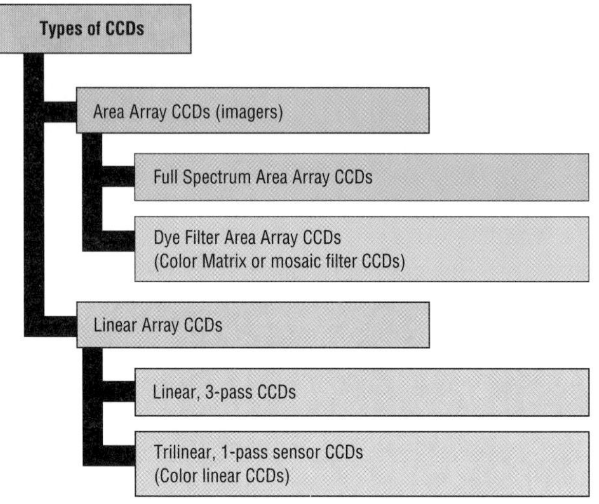

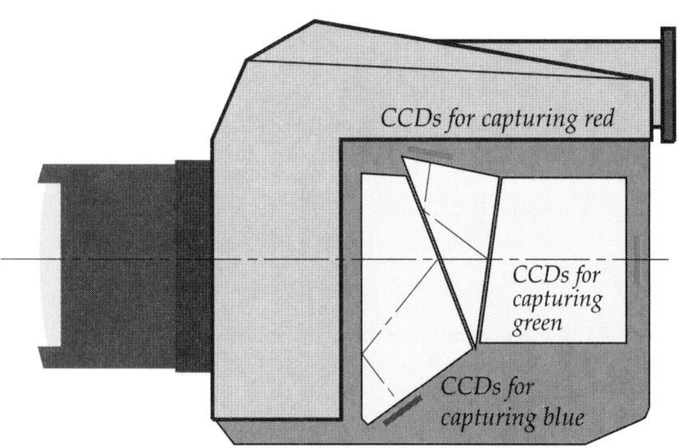

Illustration of a digital camera using three separate, full spectrum CCDs with three color filters. This style camera is designed for professional photographers, but given current CCD technology, is very large and expensive.

Slow Three-Shot Cameras

Slow three-shot type cameras take three exposures in several seconds. Two representative cameras in this class are the Scitex Leaf DCB and the Dainippon Screen (Megavision) Fotex. An RGB filter wheel is mounted in front of the CCD array and rotates with each exposure. The filter wheel is external—in front of the lens—on the Leaf. It's internal—in front of the CCD—on the Fotex. It's possible to synchronize strobe lights to flash as the filters rotate.

These cameras are relatively compact and can be attached as backs to existing film-based cameras. They provide a lot of high quality image information and are widely used in commercial photography.

Types of Digital Camera CCDs

Two types of CCDs exist for digital cameras: Area Array CCDs and Linear Array CCDs. Each CCD type has subtypes. The Area Array CCD comes in two flavors: a Full Spectrum Area Array or a Dye Filter Area Array. The Linear Array CCD is either a Linear Array, 3-pass CCD or a Trilinear Array, 1-Pass CCD.

On Area Array CCDs, the light sensors are arranged in a horizontal and vertical matrix, just as they are in an average video camera. On Linear Array CCDs, the light sensors are arranged in single rows, the same as in typical desktop scanners.

Full Spectrum CCDs

Full Spectrum CCDs (or Plain Area Array CCDs) do not have RGB filters coated on their surface. This means that they take monochrome, not color, exposures. Full Spectrum CCDs are used in the fast three-shot and the slow one-shot cameras discussed earlier. To create a color photograph with this type of CCD, separate Red, Green, and Blue filters are positioned one at a time between the subject and the CCD during three separate exposures. This creates three separate monochrome images that, when combined to make a composite RGB image file, result in a color photograph.

When used with RGB filters, this type of CCD provides excellent image quality with clear, sharp color. At our current level of technology, 2,000×2,000 pixel arrays are the most common, with larger 4,000×4,000 pixel arrays in development or soon to be released. Many of the photographs in this book were taken with the Scitex Leaf DCBII, a full spectrum array, three-shot type camera back, mounted on a Hasselblad camera.

NOTE

Area array CCDs with the light sensors arranged in a horizontal and vertical matrix are frequently referred to as *imagers*.

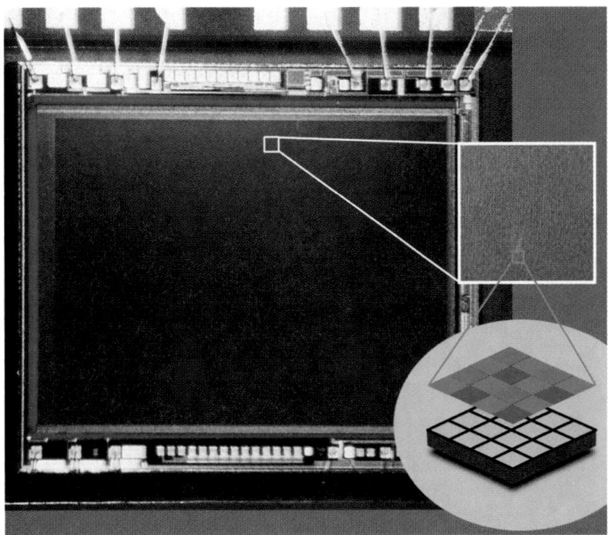

Courtesy of Seiko Epson

Dye Filter Area Array CCDs.

Left: Example of "rainbow" colored artifacts on pictures taken with cameras using Dye Filter Area Array CCDs. The effect is particularly noticeable in the word "Jaboulet" on the enlarged view of the wine label.

Right: Example of blurring removed using image enhancement. See Chapter 5, "Digital Exposures and Follow-Up Processing," for details.

Photo courtesy of Hiroyuki Hayakawa and Michio Abe

Dye Filter Area Array CCDs

On Dye Filter Array CCDs (or Color Matrix Array CCDs) each light sensor is individually coated with a Red, Green, or Blue filter coating. This type of CCD is used in fast one-shot cameras and some slow one-shot cameras.

The advantage of this type of CCD is that all the RGB color information is being captured on a single CCD array. However, each CCD sensor is only capable of capturing a single color. The Red filter light sensors cannot capture Green and Blue color information, the Green filter light sensors cannot capture Red and Blue color information, and the Blue filter light sensors cannot capture Red and Green. As a consequence, the full color image is created through a process of interpolation (this process takes place through the camera's software and is transparent to the user). As a consequence, "rainbow" colored artifacts that can affect the image quality often occur.

This book contains many pictures taken with the Kodak DCS-460 and DCS-465 (with a Hasselblad body) as well as the Nikon E2 and other compact cameras using this type of CCD array.

Linear Array, Three-Pass CCDs

A Linear Array is a single line of CCDs. The array moves across the image, recording an image as it moves. If only one scan pass is made, the resulting image is monotone. But a color image can be created by placing individual Red, Green, and Blue filters over the CCD in three separate passes, similar to the method used by the three-shot digital camera back. This type of CCD is most commonly used in low-end flatbed scanners and is not found in digital cameras.

Trilinear One-Pass CCDs

Trilinear one-pass CCDs contain three parallel rows of sensors on one array, one row each for Red, Green, and Blue. The array moves slowly across the image, capturing the image as it moves. Although cameras employing this type of CCD are called digital cameras, they could more accurately be called 3D scanners!

This type of CCD array uses an enormous number of light sensors in each row—5,000 to 10,000—enabling it to capture much image information. In terms of image detail, the results are strikingly close to 8×10 film.

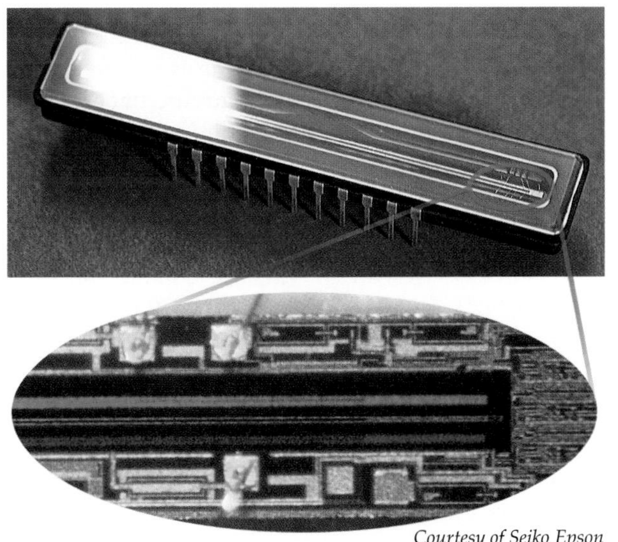

Courtesy of Seiko Epson

chapter 3

Correcting Photographs

02 1

Brightness and Contrast

Long before most edits, and certainly before any compositing is done, the characteristics of the images have to be adjusted. The objective when adjusting individual images is to make each one look as good as it can when it's output, either as a straight photograph or as part of a photomontage. The process of correcting and adjusting your digital photographs begins by analyzing and evaluating the brightness and contrast of each image.

Image with correct contrast and brightness

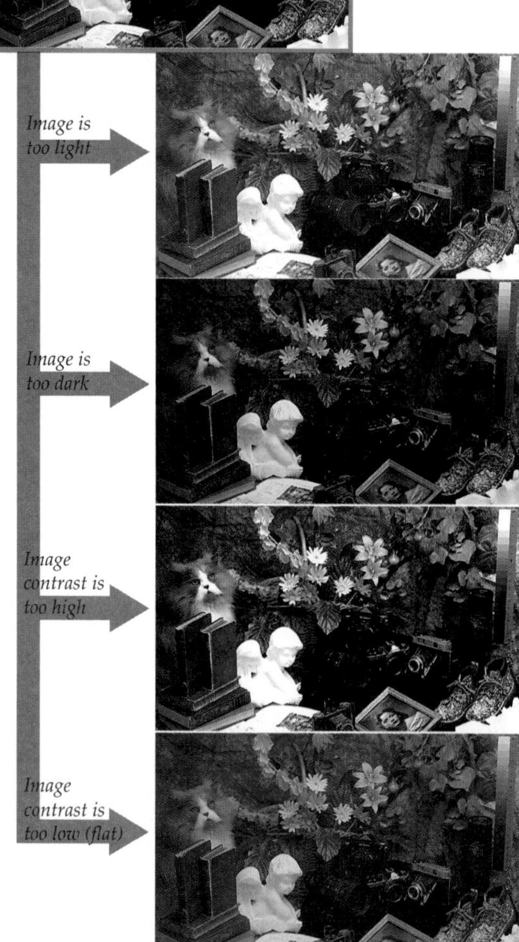
Image is too light
Image is too dark
Image contrast is too high
Image contrast is too low (flat)

Images That Are Too Light or Too Dark

When you compare images on your monitor that are too light or too dark with images that have the appropriate brightness, you should notice several attributes:

■ Images that are too light

• Highlights show little tonal variation, meaning that whites look blown out.

• Pure blacks in shadows look gray (too light) and flat.

• Pure color areas look pale and show little tonal variation.

■ Images that are too dark

• Highlights are dark and muddy.

• Shadows show little tonal variation and blacks are blocked up (show no detail).

• Pure (saturated) color areas are muddy and lack saturation.

Images with High Contrast and Low Contrast

Contrast can be described as the extent of the differences between light and dark tones from the highlights to the shadows.

When a sharp transition appears between the light and dark tones, we say that the contrast is high (contrasty). When very little variation appears between the light and dark tones, we say that the contrast is low (flat). When you view high and low contrast images, you should notice the following attributes:

■ High contrast images

• Highlights show little tonal variation, meaning that whites are blown out.

• Shadows show little tonal variation, meaning that blacks are blocked up.

• Pure color areas look vivid but show little tonal variation.

■ Low contrast images

• Highlights are dark and muddy.

• Pure blacks in shadows look gray (too light) and flat.

• Pure color areas look pale and show little tonal variation.

03 2

Underexposure and Overexposure

Histograms

Each channel in a digital photograph is divided into 256 steps of brightness. These steps are called *levels* or *tones.*

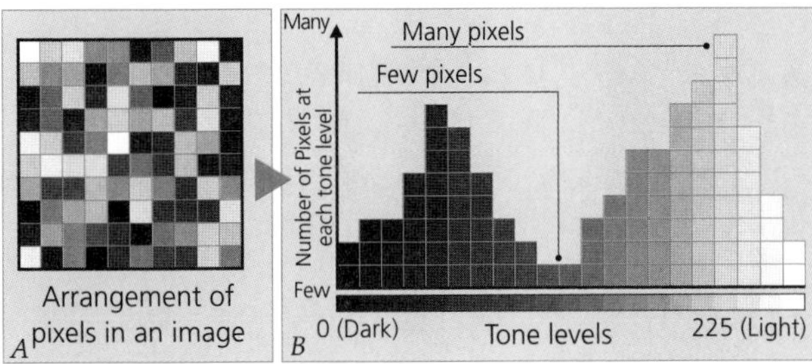

Standard

High key

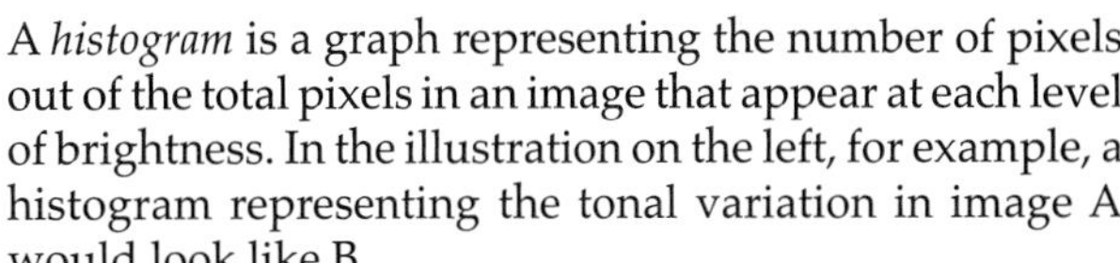

A *histogram* is a graph representing the number of pixels out of the total pixels in an image that appear at each level of brightness. In the illustration on the left, for example, a histogram representing the tonal variation in image A would look like B.

A histogram shows you the tonal range of your original image. In Photoshop, you see a histogram of the active image either by selecting the Image, Histogram or Image, Adjust, Levels menu options.

The vertical lines of the histogram represent the number of pixels at each level of brightness in the image (there are 256 levels of brightness, so the histogram can have 256 vertical lines, one for each brightness level). We call this range of tonality in an image the *dynamic range*. The wider the histogram, the greater the dynamic range of the image, and the greater the dynamic range the more the image can be adjusted without quality degradation. Peaks in the histogram indicate a concentration of a particular range of tones.

A histogram can tell you a lot about the special characteristics of an image, as explained in the following:

1. A histogram with uniform peaks and wide tonal range: Standard image = image with maximum dynamic range.

2. A histogram with peaks concentrated on the right: Overexposed image = image that is too bright or is a high key image.

3. A histogram with peaks concentrated on the left: Underexposed image = image that is too dark or is a low key image.

4. A histogram with peaks concentrated in the center and none on either the right or left: flat or dull image with little or no contrast.

5. A histogram with vertical lines spread out in intervals, resembling the teeth of a comb: image with tone jumps (a lack of smooth tonal gradation).

NOTE

To determine the optimal exposure for a digital camera, take a series of bracketed exposures of a subject that has both highlights and shadows. Look at a histogram of each of the images and select the one that shows the maximum range of tones. It is important to select a frame where the levels from 240 to 255 do not appear to run off the graph vertically, which would indicate that a large number of highlight value pixels in the image are blown out.

Low key

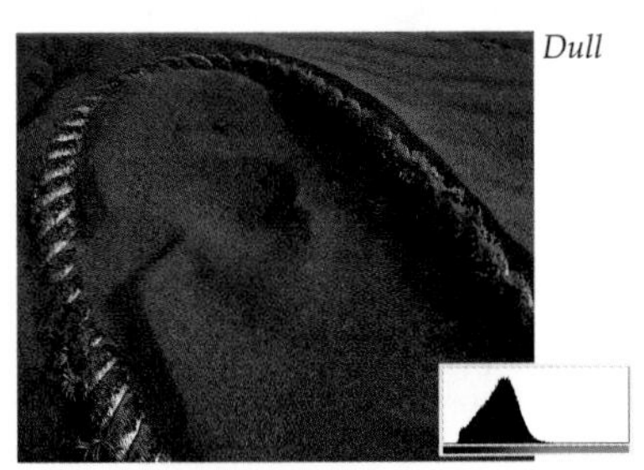

Dull

Tone jumps

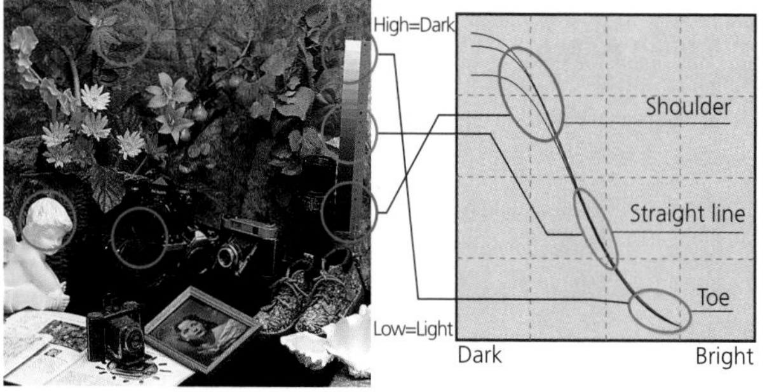

Photograph Characteristic Curves

Photographs have measurable qualities that are called gradient characteristics. *Gradient characteristics* refer to how the variation in brightness between the subject's highlights and shadows (otherwise known as *subject luminance*) is reproduced as density on the photograph. Graphs of gradient characteristics are called *characteristic curves*.

Characteristic curves vary greatly depending on whether the photosensitive material is a negative or a positive. However, they basically look like the curve shown in the illustrations on the left. Here we've used color reversal film for purposes of explanation. The shape of the curve would be reversed for negative film.

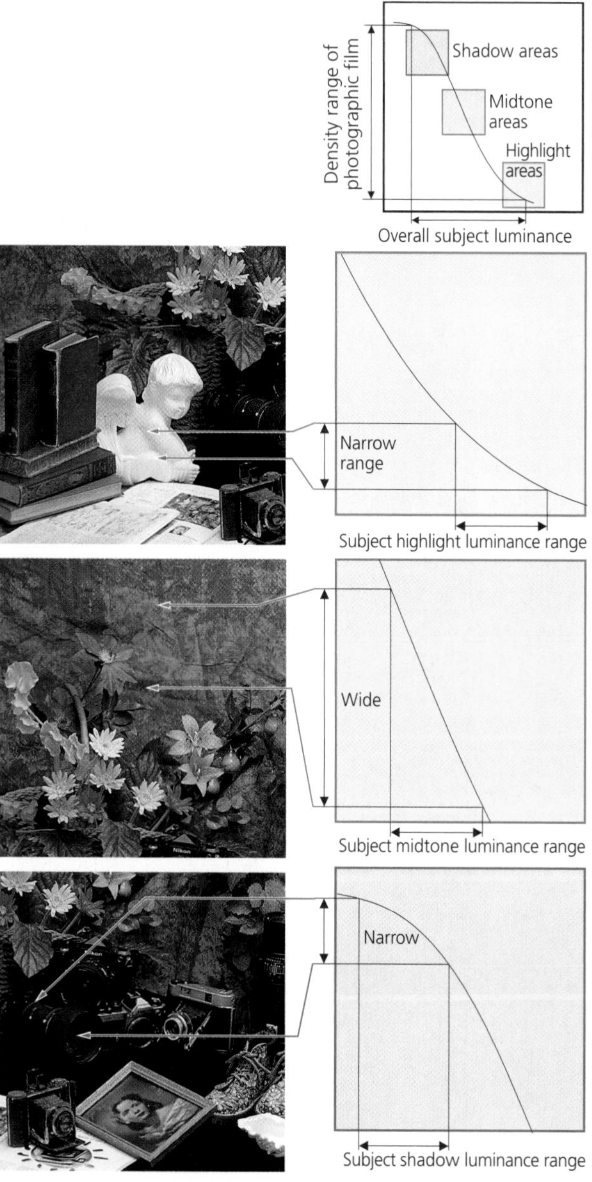

Curve Parts: Toe, Straight Line, and Shoulder

Characteristic curves have three parts: the toe, the straight line, and the shoulder. The *toe* represents how the variation in brightness within the high luminance areas of the subject (highlights) is reproduced on film.

The *straight line* represents the relationship between the middle brightness tones in the subject (middle tone areas) and the finished photograph.

The *shoulder* is the opposite of the toe. It represents how the variation in brightness within the low luminance areas of the subject (shadows) is reproduced on film.

Interpreting these three parts of the characteristic curve can tell us important information about an image. In this case, the curve is describing a subject which has very little contrast in both the highlights and the shadows:

- The light areas of the subject show little density variation (or a narrow density range) on film in proportion to the variation in the subject luminance.
- The midtone areas of the subject show density variation (wide density range) on film roughly proportional to the variation in the subject brightness.
- The dark areas of the subject show little density variation (narrow density range) on film in proportion to the variation in the subject brightness.

Because of the existence of gradient characteristics, photographic media is capable of reproducing likenesses of subjects with photographic quality. The characteristic curves that describe the gradient can also be used to tell us about the "response" to different amounts of exposure of different film types, particularly by evaluating the changes in the toe portion of the curve (for color reversal film).

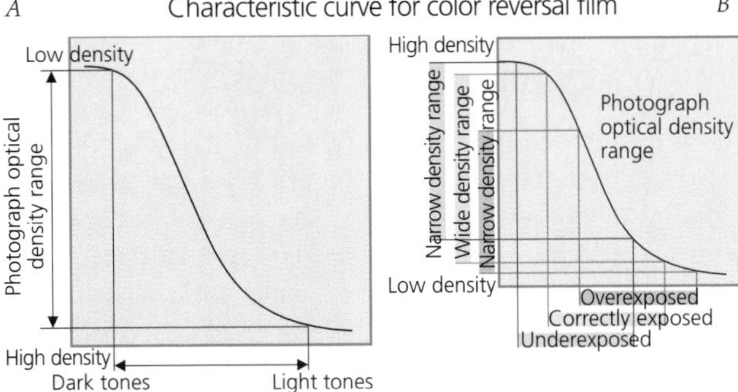

Characteristic Curves for Overexposed and Underexposed Photographs

Incorrectly exposed photographs can be either too light or too dark. Therefore, it's not surprising that to correct these kinds of photographs using digital imaging processes, you have to understand the principle characteristic of light and dark photographs. You can achieve this understanding by studying the relationships between the subject luminance range and the optical density range.

We call the range of tones in the subject from the lightest highlight to the darkest shadow the *subject luminance range*, as shown on the horizontal axis in illustration A. As long as the same subject is photographed under the same lighting conditions, the subject luminance range always remains constant.

The range of density values when the subject luminance range is reproduced on film is called the *optical density range* of the photograph, as shown on the vertical axis in illustration A.

When the photograph is overexposed or underexposed, the optical density range of the original photograph changes, even though the subject luminance range remains constant (see illustration B).

The characteristic curve that represents normal, overexposed, or underexposed photographs is called the *S-curve.*

When a photograph is overexposed or underexposed, the width of the subject luminance range stays the same along the S-curve, but the subject luminance range shifts to the right or left along the S-curve, as shown on the horizontal axis in illustration B. This means that the amount of light hitting the film emulsion has changed.

So what is happening when you slightly overexpose or underexpose your photographs? They will look a bit too light or a bit too dark. But whether they are overexposed or underexposed, the same thing is happening—the optical density ranges of the original photographs (vertical axis in illustration B) are being shortened (narrowed) in comparison to originals with the correct exposure. If the level of overexposure is high, the whites in the highlights are blown out. If you seriously underexpose a photograph, the shadows will be so dark that the detail will be lost. The range of overexposed and underexposed photographs shown in photographs C through G illustrate the results of over- and underexposing a photograph.

C

D

E

F

G

NOTE

Although all photographers are familiar with over- and underexposed photographs, this review has been provided in order to introduce characteristic curves as a background for discussing tone curve adjustments in the digital world of photography. Understanding the nature of tone curves will enable you to achieve excellent, predictable results when correcting digital photos, particularly when scanning and correcting color reversal films. The basics of tone curve adjustments are discussed in section 3.5.

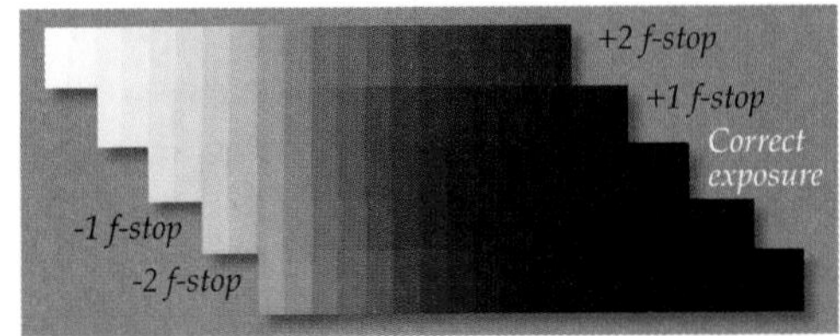

The grayscales for photographs C–G have been arranged so their densities line up. Compare the highlights and shadows of the grayscales from the correctly exposed frame with those from over and underexposed frames.

03 3

Real World Corrections

Correcting Highlights and Shadows

To correct digital images that are photographs of real world subject matter, the first step is to look carefully at the contents or theme of the picture and decide how you want the highlights and shadows to look (that is, do you want the photos to look realistic, high key, and so forth). In particular, the way you correct the highlights dramatically alters the impression of your photograph.

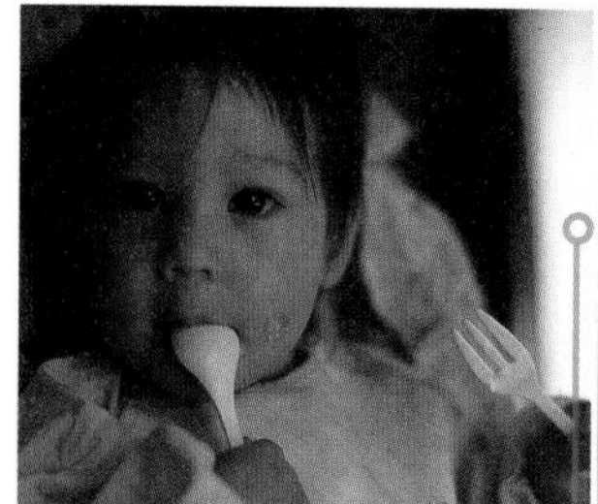

This is not the highlight

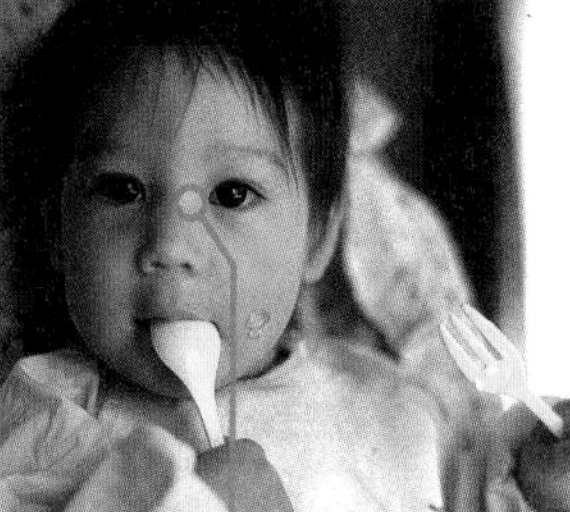

H (R=245 G=176 B=150)

Highlights

When you use something like a color printer, a press, or a monitor to print or display an image, the purest possible white areas of the image are the color of the paper or the monitor signal at maximum. However, proper highlights in digital images should not be the pure whites of these ouput options. Because highlights can be reflected into a camera lens by many types of materials, highlight levels will vary when the photographs are digitized (scanned or captured with a digital camera). But in all cases, the highlights should be slightly darker than the output medium's maximum white.

NOTE

Some photographs may appear not to have any white highlights. In the case where the photo is comprised of only light or pale colors, the brightest of these can be considered the highlight color.

■ Shiny areas on a camera body

No tonal variation appears within these shiny areas, which causes us to perceive them as shiny. Rather than highlights, they are called *specular highlights* (SH), or *catchlights*. In this case, the highlights (H) are along the borderline between the shiny and non-shiny areas. If a metallic object, such as this camera body, doesn't have at least a tiny amount of tonality between the specular highlight and the darker tones of gray, it won't look convincingly metallic.

■ Background for a human subject

This photograph of a child was taken against the background of a window. The dazzlingly bright sky you can see through the window is the specular highlight area. But the actual highlight of the photo would be considered the red channel area along the bridge of the child's nose, as identified in the caption.

Shadows

You can think about shadows similarly to the way you think about highlights. In this case, shadows are not simply the pure black areas of an image (just as highlights are not purely white areas). For example, in printing, pure blacks are created by laying down 100 percent printing ink or color printer colorant so that you cannot distinguish any tonality. Shadows are not this level of pure black. Instead, the deepest shadows in a photograph are a color, or colors, which are just dark enough to allow one to barely perceive detail in the image.

In practice, you choose shadow areas by studying parts of the image that have a lot of black but show a small amount of detail. Keep in mind that if the RGB values in those areas are less than 10 each, they will appear as pure

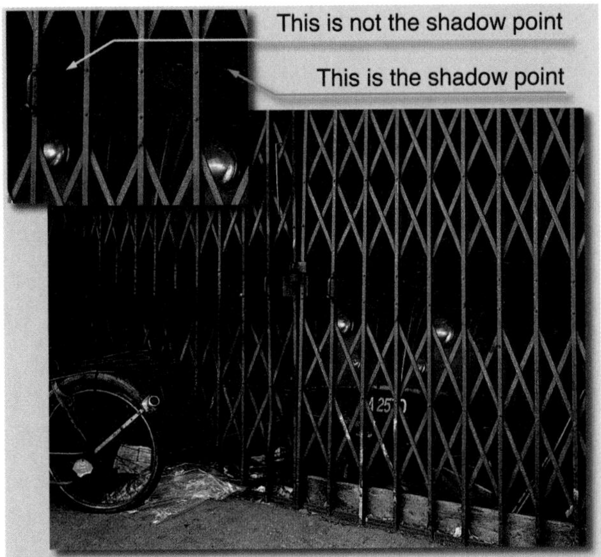
This is not the shadow point
This is the shadow point

black (or be unpredictable) on press or color printer output. Because influences such as monitor brightness (see Monitor Calibration on pages 2-4 through 2-14) can affect the way you visually analyze an image, the best method for confirming shadow and highlight values is with the Info palette, as described below.

First Check the Highlights and the Shadows

Before beginning your image correction, always carefully check the original film first, if it's available. If it is on color reversal film, use a large loupe that's at least 5× magnification and carefully study the original. This means determine where the highlights, specular highlights, and shadows are and determine their levels values.

Photoshop users (as well as users of other imaging applications) can make individual choices about how they want their images to look, particularly when determining the highlight and shadow values. For reasons of quality reproduction, however, it's a good idea to understand these qualities by numerical values, especially the highlights. To view the numerical values of highlights and shadows, refer to the Info palette (Window, Show Info). In the sidebar to the left are standard values that can be measured from the Info palette for both highlights and shadows. It is a good idea to learn them for determining the brightness of your images.

© Russ Sparkman

Please consider the following points anytime you look at a photograph on your computer. If your images don't meet the following criteria, it may be due to a scanning problem. If so, make the scan again. If you took the photograph with a **digital camera**, it could be that you have an exposure problem. If you have taken a series of bracketed exposures, choose another frame.

■ Determining Numerical Values for the Highlight Point

• If the RGB levels for the Highlight point are all between **200–250**, you will be able to make satisfactory corrections.

• If the RGB levels for the Highlight point are all **above 251**, that is, **close to 255**, there may be a loss of differentiation between the highlights and the specular highlights if you correct the image to make it significantly darker.

• If the RGB levels for the Highlight point are all **below 200**, that is, dark enough to be close to the midtones, you may cause tone jumps in areas that require smooth tone transitions when you lighten the overall image, such as in flesh tones.

• If the RGB levels for the Highlight point are all **255**, you cannot make that point any brighter. You can make it darker, but different places that ought to be brighter than that point cannot get any more saturated than 255, so you won't get the result you hope for.

• If **one or two** of the RGB levels for the Highlight point is **255**, you cannot make the channels that are 255 any brighter than they already are. You can make them darker, but the specular highlight channel that is not 255 may cause a color cast in that area.

■ Determining Numerical Values for the Shadow Point

• If the RGB levels for the Shadow point are all between **5–30**, you will be able to make satisfactory corrections.

• If the RGB levels for the Shadow point are all **below 5**, that is, **close to 0**, a loss of subtle differentiation between the shadows and the deepest shadows may occur if you correct the image to make it significantly lighter.

• If the RGB levels for the Shadow point are **all 0**, you cannot make that point any darker. You can make it lighter, but different places that ought to be darker than that point cannot get any more saturated than 0, so all the shadows will only lose depth and you will not be able to recover the loss of detail in the shadow area.

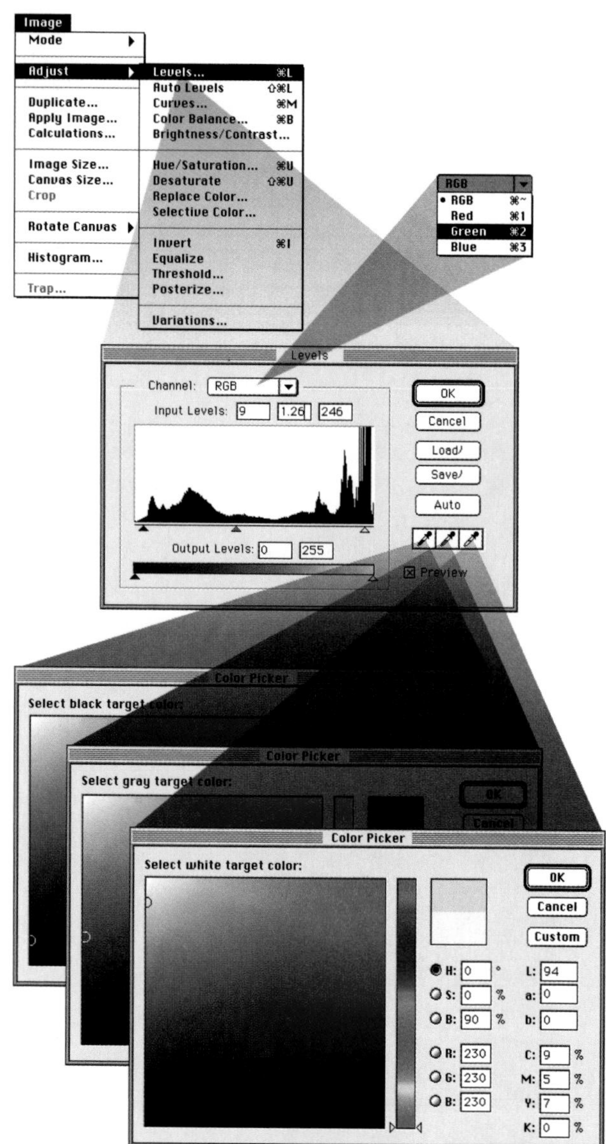

NOTE

After setting values for either the White Point or the Black Point in the Color Picker, it's possible to change the value while maintaining a white or black target color just by entering a single value into either the B field of HSB or the L field of L*a*b*.

Adjusting Highlights and Shadows with Levels

The Levels dialog box in Photoshop (as well as similar functions in other imaging applications) is a fairly easy, straightforward means of correcting highlight and shadow values, as long as images are no more than slightly underexposed or overexposed. Use Image, Adjust, Levels to open the Levels dialog box, which will include a histogram and several slider controls.

■ The ▲ slider under the histogram

This slider (the shadow point slider) is used to adjust the shadow areas. If you slide it to the right, the dark areas of the image become darker.

■ The △ slider under the histogram

This slider (the highlight point slider) is used to adjust the highlight areas. If you slide it to the left, the light areas of the image become lighter.

■ The Output Levels ▲ slider

This slider is used to adjust the dark areas of the image. If you move the slider to the right, the dark areas of the image become lighter.

■ The Output Levels △ slider

This slider is used to adjust the light areas of the image. If you move the slider to the left, the light areas of the image become darker.

■ Channel pop-up menu

When you open the Levels dialog box, the Channel is set to RGB (or composite) mode, which means that all the image channels except the alpha channel are adjusted simultaneously. If you want to adjust each of the channels individually, select each channel from the Channel pop-up menu.

■ Highlight eyedropper

The Highlight eyedropper enables you to select which area of the image will be white. If you double-click on the Highlight eyedropper icon, the Color Picker (white target color) dialog box is displayed. Here you can enter numerical RGB values for your target white. In general, the values for the brightest highlight range are 243–248; the same number should be entered for all three RGB values (for example, R = 243, G = 243, and B = 243). After you have made your entries, close the dialog box and move the pointer into the image. The pointer becomes the Highlight eyedropper. Click on the area of the image you wish to be changed to the white color you specified in the Color Picker.

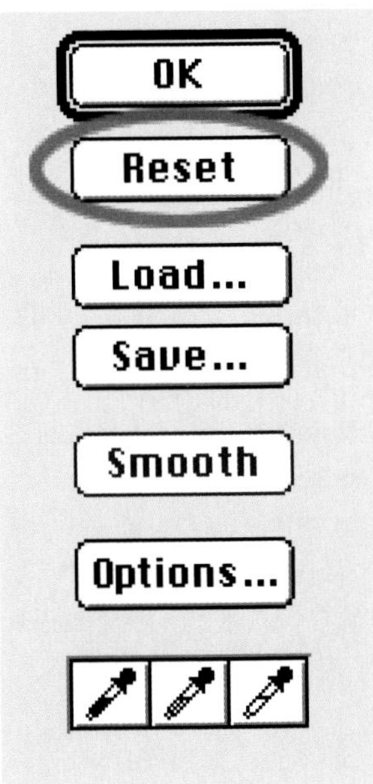

■ Shadow eyedropper

The Shadow eyedropper enables you to set which area of the image will be black. If you double-click on the Shadow (black target color) eyedropper icon, the Color Picker dialog box is displayed. Here you can enter RGB numerical values for your target black. In general, the values for the darkest Shadow values range from 8 to 25 for all three RGB values. After you have made your entries, just as with the Highlight eyedropper, click on the area of the image you wish to set as the shadow point, and it will become the color you specified.

■ Reset button

If you want to return your image to what it looked like before you made adjustments with the Levels sliders and Highlight and Shadow eyedroppers, hold the Option key while the Levels dialog box is still displayed and the Cancel button becomes a Reset button. Click on Reset to return to the pre-adjusted stage.

NOTE

■ Before using the Highlight and Shadow eyedroppers, set the Sample Size to 3×3 Average or 5×5 Average in the Eyedropper Options palette. This way the levels values for either the 9 (for 3×3) or 25 (for 5×5) pixels surrounding the point selected with the eyedropper are averaged and used as the reference value for correction. This is very important, especially when you are working with enlarged 35 mm film that is very grainy. With this type of film, even a very small difference in the eyedropper position can produce a very different correction effect.

■ If you make adjustments by repeatedly applying the Levels command directly to an image layer, the quality of your image will deteriorate. Try as much as possible to make all your corrections at one time. Or, in Photoshop 4.0, use the Adjustment Layer feature, which is explained next.

■ In Photoshop 4.0, you can use the Levels dialog box by selecting Layers, New, Adjustment Layer and then selecting Levels as the type of layer. This function enables you to make your levels corrections by using a separate layer that applies the adjustment to all underlying layers without actually altering the pixels of those layers. You can change the correction parameters in this special layer as many times as you like and not worry about the quality of your image deteriorating through repeated corrections, as you do in Photoshop 3.0.

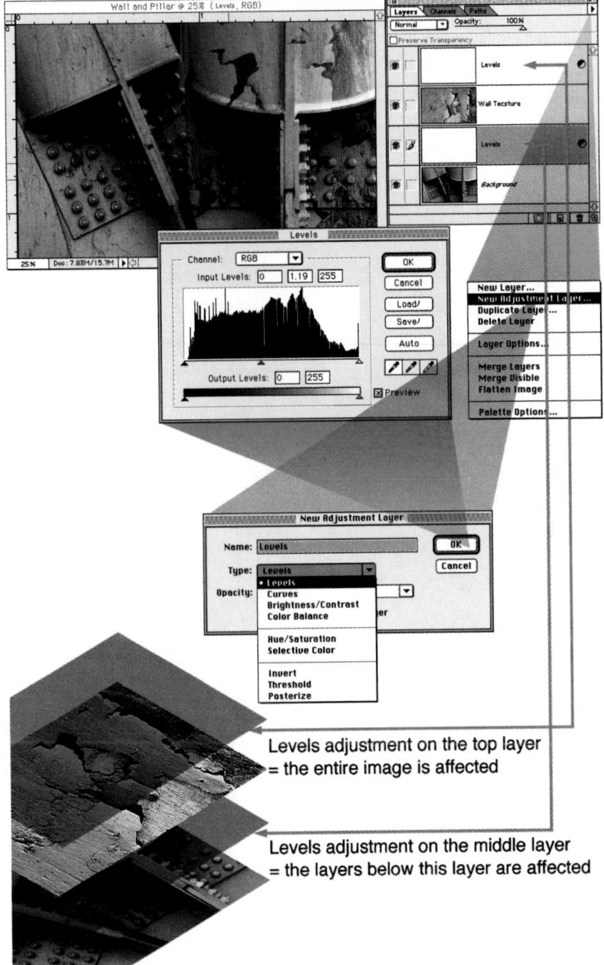

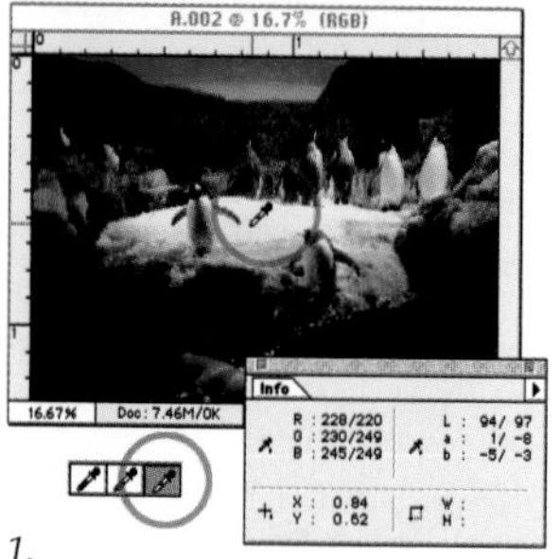

1.

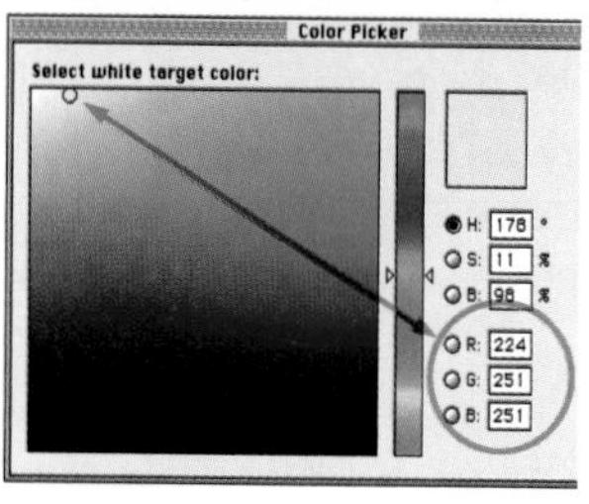

2.

3.

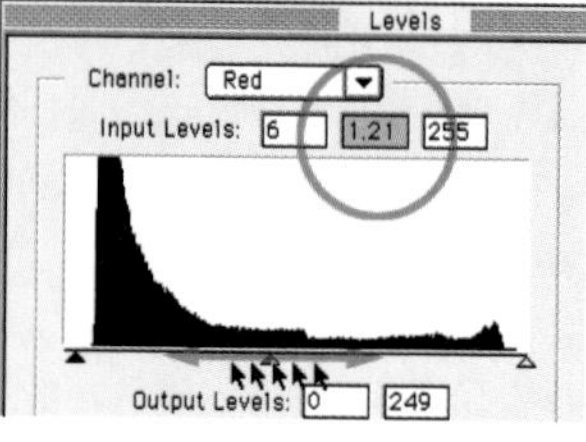

4.

Real World Levels Adjustments

A typical Levels adjustment of a scan is demonstrated at left.

1. The Levels dialog was opened and the Highlight eyedropper was selected. The eyedropper was moved over an image highlight. The Info palette reading indicated the highlights were less than approximately RGB=230, which was too low for the highlight value.

2. The Highlight eye dropper icon was double-clicked to open the "Select white target color" Color Picker. Set highlight values. This time, however, instead of selecting the same highlight value for all three RGB values, R was set at 245, whereas G and B were each set at 251. Instead of a neutral highlight, this created slightly cyan highlight.

3. The Shadow eyedropper tool, with RGB=10 values set in the "Select black target color" Color Picker, was used to set the shadows.

4. The gamma slider was used to adjust the midtone values.

High Key and Low Key

Adjusting an image in Photoshop by referring to the Levels histogram makes it easy to make your images high key or low key, or to correct images that are too high key or too low key.

For example, if you want to make an image low key, move the ▲ slider under the histogram toward the center so that it is inside the peaks that represent the darkest shadows. When you want to make an image high key, move the △ slider under the histogram toward the center so that it is inside the peaks that represent the lightest highlights. In both cases, the pixels in the peaks that fall outside the slider triangle are eliminated, creating typical low key, or high key histograms (shown as the light gray histograms).

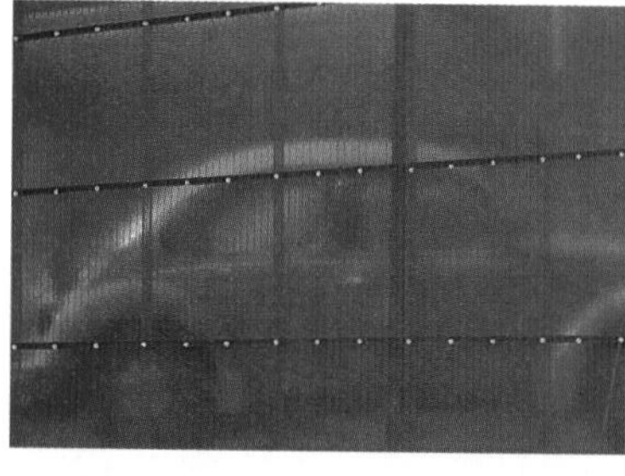

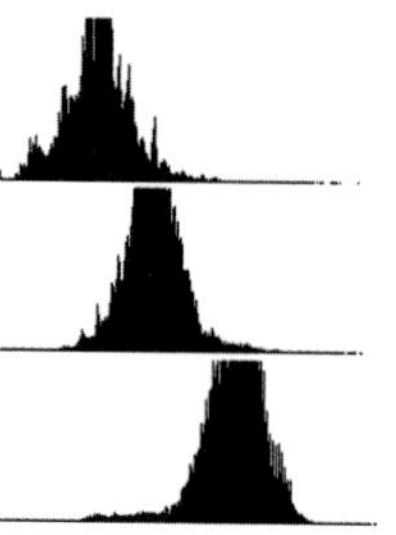

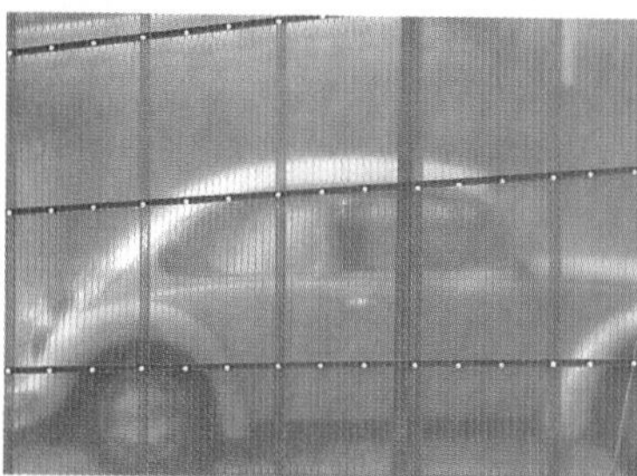

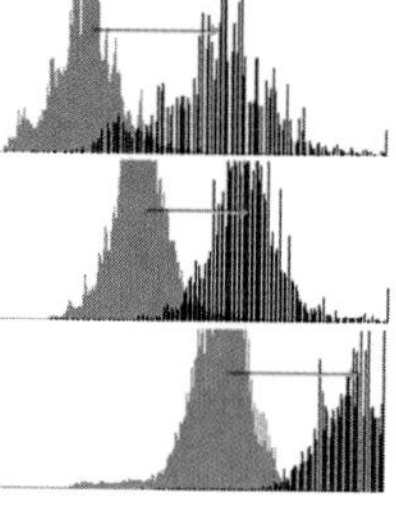

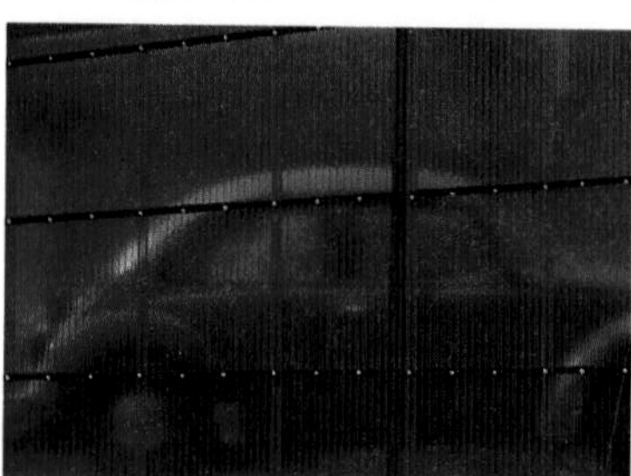

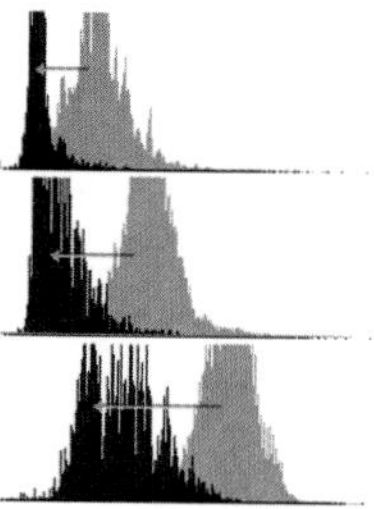

NOTE

Histograms for images that have been made high key or low key do not show evenly distributed peaks, but rather look like the histograms shown below, with the peaks concentrated in one area of the image.

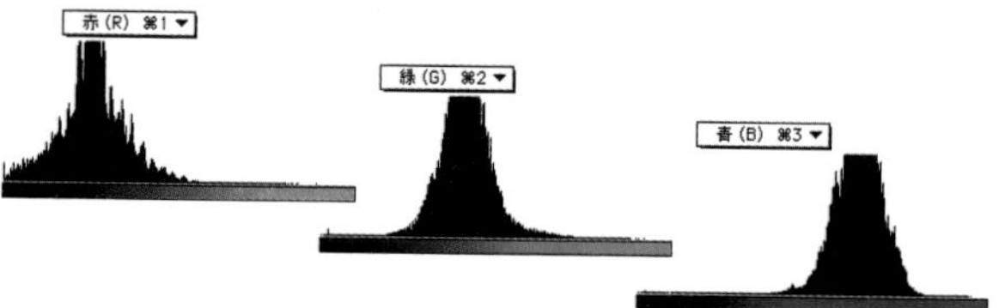

03 4

Color Balance

When we say, "the color balance doesn't look right," we mean one of two things. Either the entire image is leaning toward a particular color, called a *color cast*, or specific colors within the image do not have the right colors. This can be caused by many factors, including the characteristics of the digital camera, the type of light source and film combination used or the even the scanner setup.

The first step for optimizing color balance is to correct any color cast that may exist in the image. After that, make adjustments to specific, or localized, regions of color you want to change.

■ Practical examples of color cast originals

Photograph taken on a cloudy, rainy day. Normal daylight film is designed so that the color on pictures taken on bright days or under strobe lights will be reproduced correctly. If daylight film is used on cloudy or rainy days, the pictures have a bluish (cool) cast.

Photograph taken in artificial light. Except for pictures taken using strobe lights or light sources for color evaluation, artificial lights cause the picture to take on the color cast of the bulbs used. Fluorescent and mercury bulbs produce a green cast, and incandescent light bulbs produce an orange cast, as in this example.

Photograph of a distant view. Even in a photograph taken on a clear day, if the view is distant, the effect of ultraviolet rays will give it a bluish cast.

Photograph taken of shadows on a clear day. If you take pictures under the trees on a beautiful clear day, the picture will have a bluish (cool) cast because of the large amount of light from the sky.

Photograph taken at sunrise or sunset. If you take pictures at sunrise or sunset with normal color film, they will have a strong orange (warm) cast.

Photograph taken with strong and weak colors next to each other. If you take pictures of a subject against red signs or yellow walls, the light reflected off those colors will affect the colors of the main subject.

Photograph that has changed over time. Photographs may acquire a color cast after five or ten years have passed. On normal film, the cyan dye fades, leaving the photograph with a reddish-brown cast.

Photograph resulting from chemical accident. Undeveloped film that is exposed to volatile gases or film that has altered due to developing or other chemical processing may acquire a color cast. Undeveloped film that has repeatedly passed through security equipment at airports may also display a color cast after developing.

Original

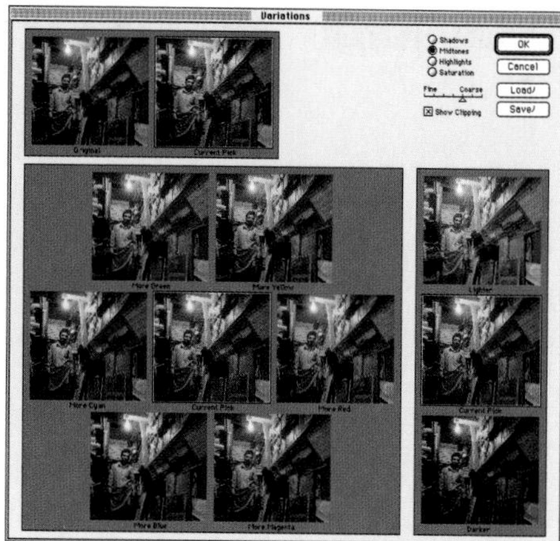

Variations command

Final

Original

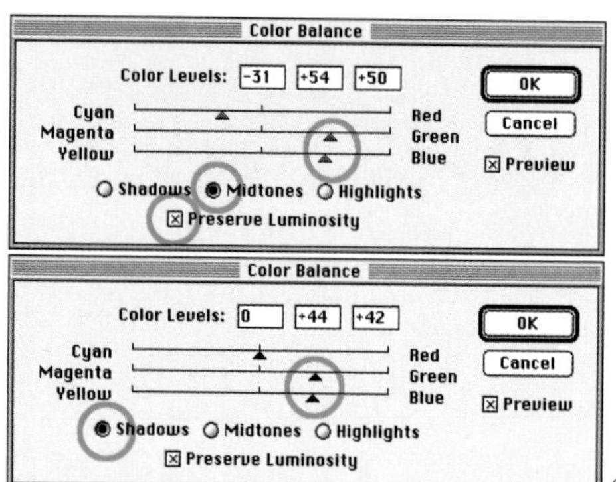

Color Balance command (RGB Color mode)

Final

Original

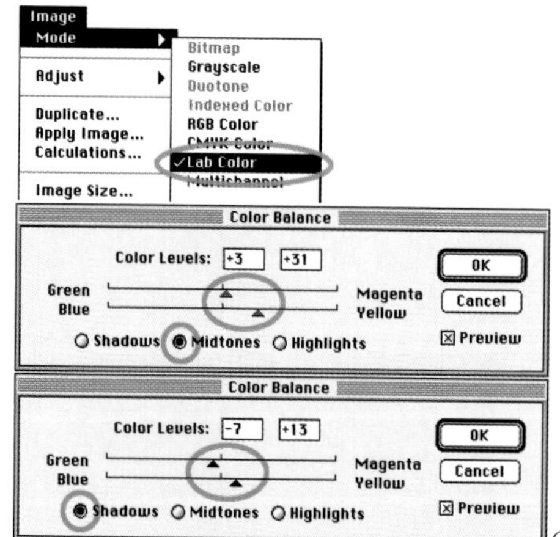

Color Balance command (Lab Color mode)

Final

03 5

Tone Curve Adjustments

Photographic Quality Corrections

As we have seen, highlight and shadow targets can be easily set using Photoshop's Levels command. In addition to adjusting the highlights and shadows in a digital photograph, however, you often have to subtly adjust the image contrast and control the characteristics of the midtones.

It's possible to make some adjustments to the image contrast and the midtone characteristics by using the center gray slider under the histogram in the Levels dialog box. Compared to adjustments made using tone curves, however, this Levels function doesn't give you much control over just how much or even where your adjustment will be made.

The Curves command in Photoshop (and similar commands in other applications) is a tool that provides precise control for tone and color adjustment by employing the use of a linear tone curve. This enables you to make a wide range of adjustments, from global adjustments of the entire image to very specific, localized adjustments of highlights, midtones, and shadows. You can make the following image corrections using tone curves:

- Highlight and shadow tone adjustment (similar to the Levels function)
- Adjustment to only specular highlights or deep shadows, leaving other areas unchanged
- Adjustment of the contrast, while leaving the highlight and shadow levels values as they are
- Separate adjustment of tone range in light areas only or dark areas only
- Fine-tune adjustments to gray balance
- Color cast correction
- Precise adjustment to areas of specific tone and color, like flesh tones
- Solarization effects

Being able to effectively manipulate tone curves is essential for photographers who wish to create artwork with their own unique look and feel. From here on we look at tone curves in more detail.

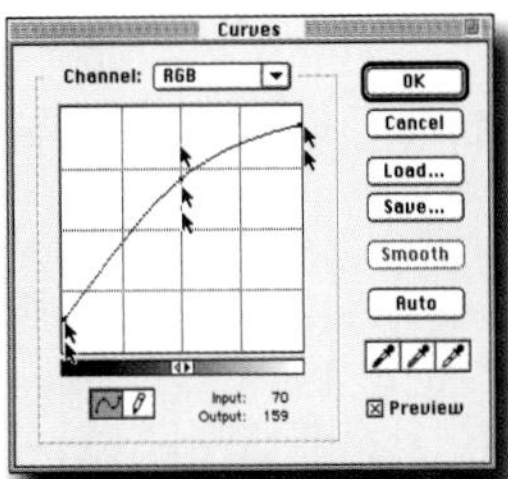

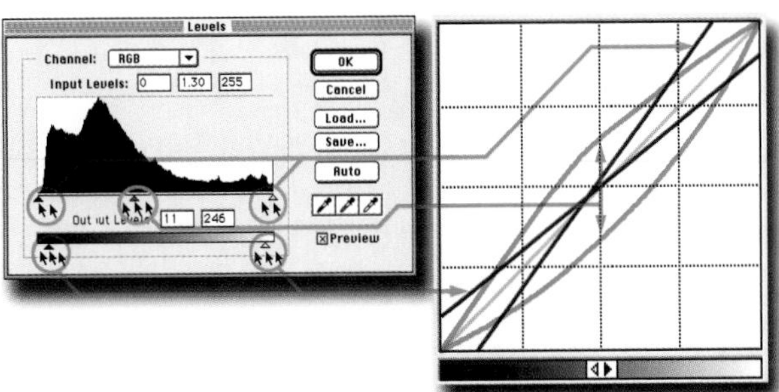

The relationship between levels adjustment and tone curves

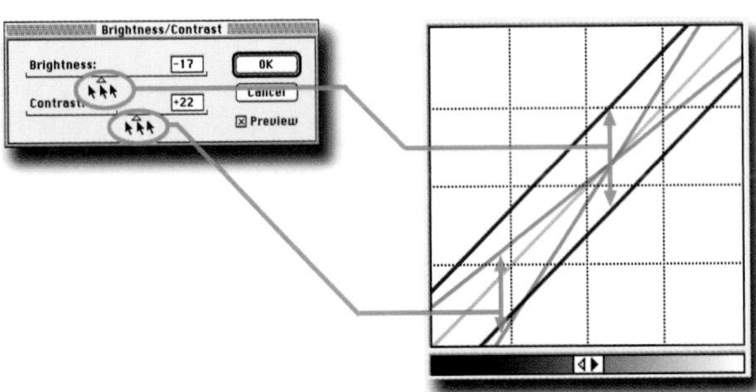

The relationship between brightness and contrast adjustment and tone curves

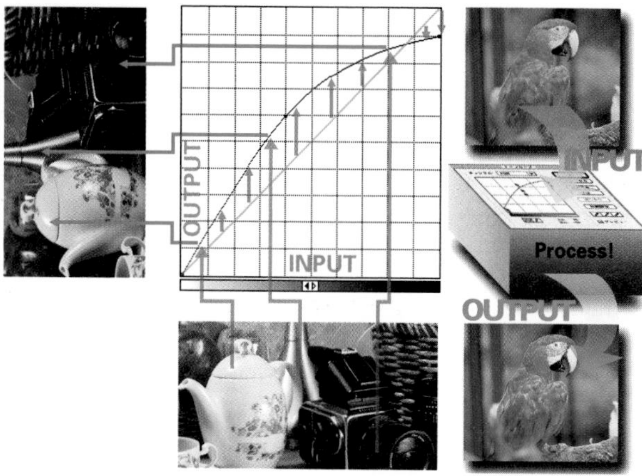

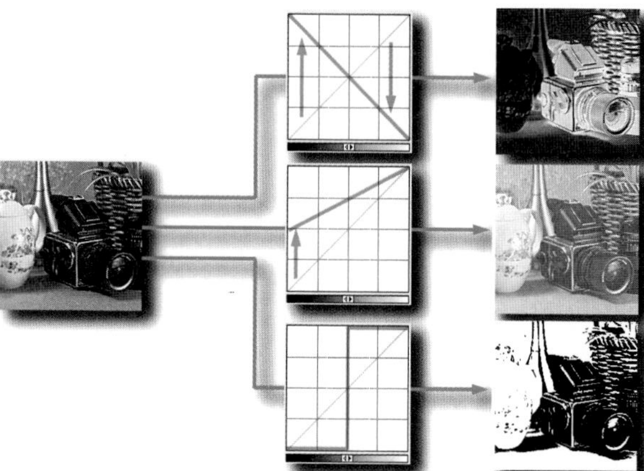

Tone Curves Express the Relationship Between the Original and the Result

A *tone curve* plots a graph of the original image before correction (X axis) versus the result after correction (Y axis). The default curve that appears immediately after you open the Curves dialog box is an upward 45 degree line that represents what we call a "linear" relationship between the image before and after correction. In a linear relationship, there is no change before and after correction, meaning that no correction has been done.

■ The horizontal axis represents the variation in levels, from 0 (pure black) to 255 (pure white) in the image before correction.

■ The vertical axis represents the variation in levels, from 0 (pure black) to 255 (pure white) in the image after correction.

Significantly altering the angle of the graph creates noticeable differences in the image. For example, reversing the linear relationship to a downward sloping 45 degree angle creates a negative version of the image. Or if the angle of the graph approaches horizontal, the contrast in the image weakens. If it becomes completely horizontal, all tonal variation is lost and the image is simply one color.

On the other hand, as the angle of the graph approaches vertical, the image contrast becomes stronger. If it becomes completely vertical, the line marks the boundary between pure white and pure black. In the case of a color image, where the levels for a particular place in the image are not exactly the same in each channel, one color will be stronger than another.

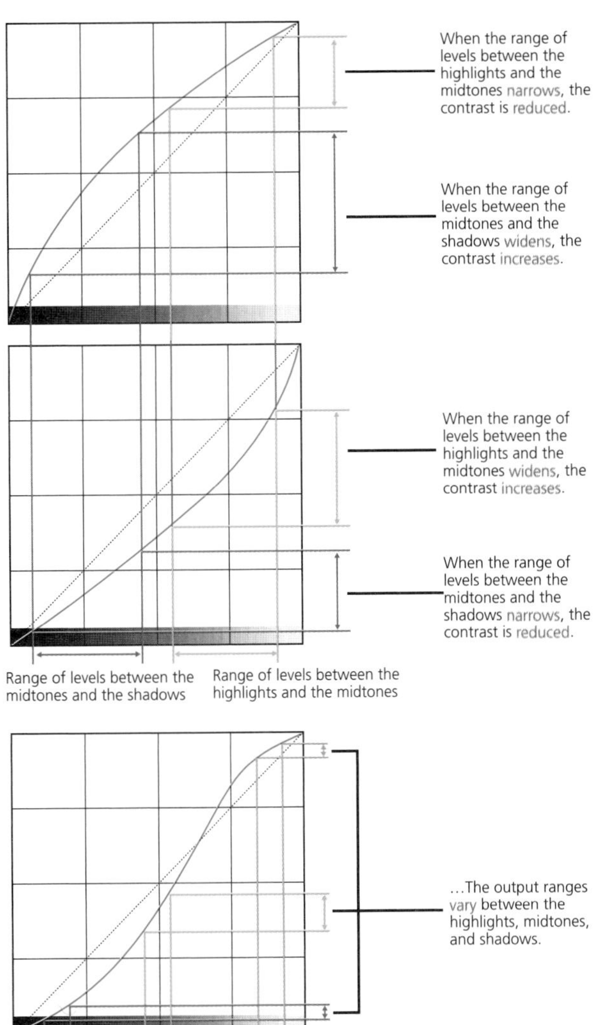
When the range of levels between the highlights and the midtones narrows, the contrast is reduced.
When the range of levels between the midtones and the shadows widens, the contrast increases.
When the range of levels between the highlights and the midtones widens, the contrast increases.
When the range of levels between the midtones and the shadows narrows, the contrast is reduced.
Range of levels between the midtones and the shadows
Range of levels between the highlights and the midtones
...The output ranges vary between the highlights, midtones, and shadows.
Even if the input axis ranges are the same...

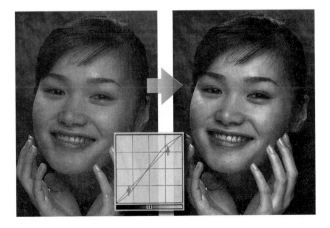

Graph Curves

Graphs don't change only by changing the angle of straight lines. They can also become curves by adding control points in different places on the line.

By changing the shape of the curve using control points, you can adjust the brightness and feeling of the tonal range for almost any image. In Brightness mode (to be discussed further on), for example, if you change the line so it curves above the 45 degree line, the variation in brightness increases between the shadows and the midtones and falls off from the midtones to the highlights. Conversely, if you change the line so it curves below the 45 degree straight line, the variation in brightness decreases between the shadows and the midtones and increases from the midtones to the highlights.

Moving One Point Means Changing the Distance Between Two Points

As you acquire expertise in adjusting tone curves, you will see that it is not a matter of moving specific points. Rather it is a matter of how you can affect the relationship between ranges on the horizontal and vertical axes by changing the slope and shape of the curves.

For example, with tone curves like the S-curve on the left, the range for the highlights on the horizontal axis becomes narrower on the vertical axis, and the shadows also become narrower on the vertical axis. But the range for the midtones on the vertical axis is wider than the range on the horizontal axis. The result is that the highlights and shadows become flatter while the midtones show more contrast. The image corrected with this curve shows stronger midtones in the background and in the flesh tones.

Conversely, in a tone curve shaped like a reverse S-curve, the range of the midtones on the vertical axis becomes narrower than the range on the horizontal axis, and the range for the highlights and shadows becomes wider along the vertical axis. This results in an image with less contrast in the midtones and more vivid highlights and shadows.

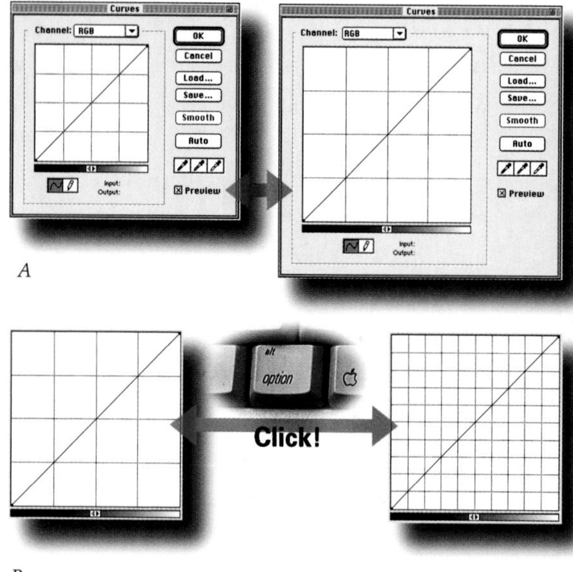

A

B

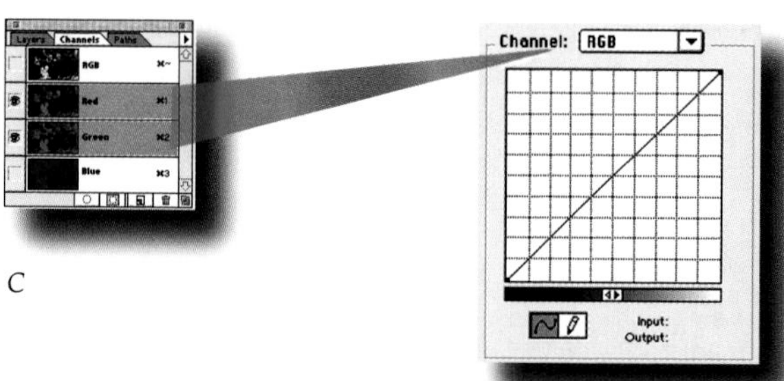

C

By Shift-clicking multiple channels in the Channels palette prior to opening the Curves dialog box, you can also use the Channel pop-up menu like this.

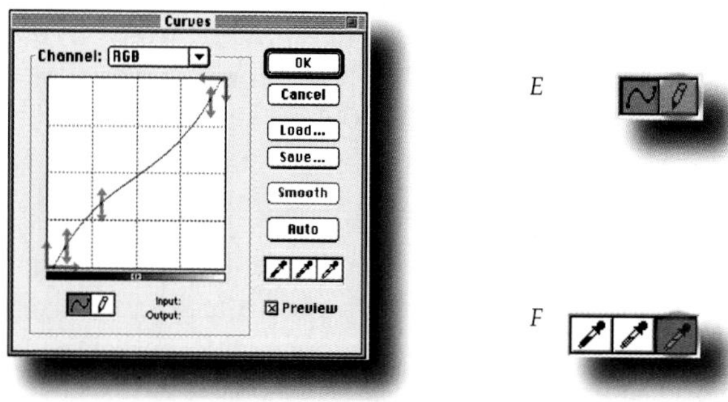

Control points

D

E

F

The Curves Dialog Box

The Curves dialog box has the following features:

■ Dialog box resize button

If you click on the resize button, shown in (A) to the left, the Curves dialog box becomes larger. If you click on it again, the box returns to its original size. This feature is convenient for drawing more fine-tuned graphs. Also, if you Option-click anywhere inside the graph itself, you can make the grid finer (B).

■ Channel pop-up menu (C)

The Channel menu enables you to adjust all the RGB or CMYK channels at one time or select and adjust each channel separately.

■ Control points

Two black points, called *control points*, are in the bottom-left corner and the upper-right corner of the graph (D). You can add as many control points as you wish by clicking on the tone curve line. Dragging the control points to different positions changes the shape of the tone curve. To delete a control point, click on it and drag it outside the graph.

NOTE

The control points are available only when the Custom Map icon, to the left of the Pencil icon, is selected.

■ Pencil icon

Use the Pencil icon when you want to draw your own custom curves (E right). When you select the pencil, you can draw a curve with the pencil that appears over the graph. By Shift-clicking on the graph, you can connect the previous point to the point you are now adding. This feature is convenient only when you want to adjust the specular highlights and the deep shadows.

■ Custom Map icon

Click on the Custom Map icon to generate control points on the tone curve you have drawn with the pencil (E left).

■ Highlight eyedropper

The Highlight eyedropper enables you to select which area of the image will be white (F far right). If you double-click on the Highlight eyedropper icon, the Color Picker's white target color dialog box displays. Here you can enter RGB (or CMYK) numerical values for your target Highlight color.

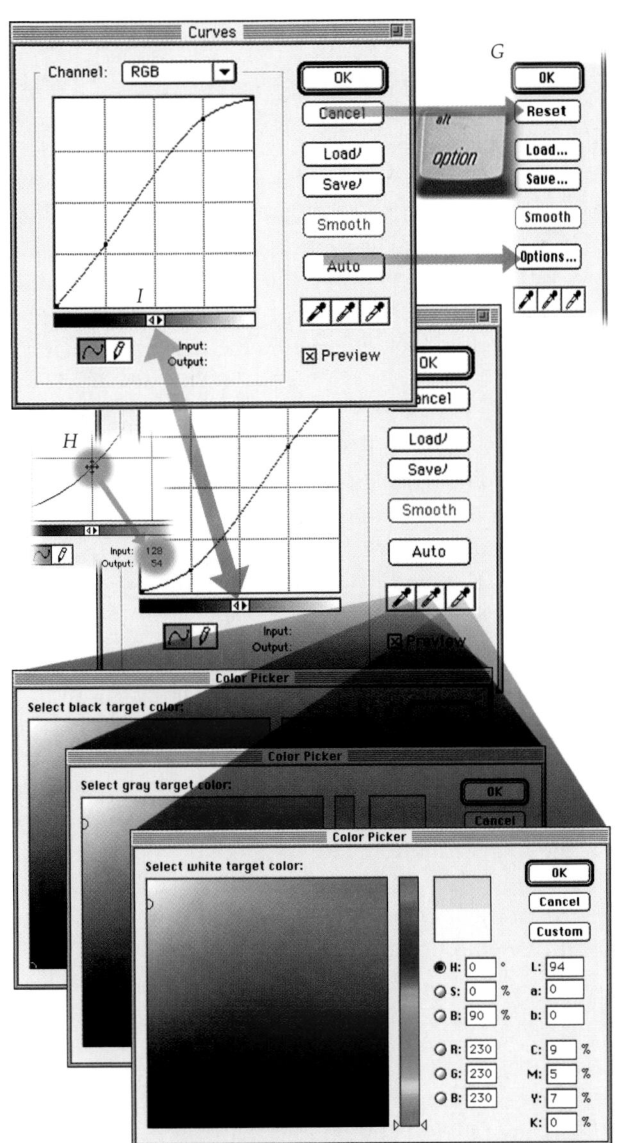

■ Shadow eyedropper

The Shadow eyedropper enables you to select which area of the image will be black (F left, on the previous page). If you double-click on the Shadow eyedropper icon, the Color Picker's black target color dialog box displays. Here you can enter RGB (or CMYK) numerical values for your target Shadow color.

■ Midpoint eyedropper

The Midpoint eyedropper enables you to select the area of the image which will become the midtone color (F center, on the previous page). If you double-click on the Midpoint eyedropper icon, the Color Picker's gray target color dialog box displays. Here you can enter RGB (or CMYK) numerical values for your target Midpoint color.

■ Reset

If you press on the Option key, the Cancel button changes to a Reset button (G). Click on this if you want to return your image to what it was before you made corrections with the Curves adjustment sliders or the eyedroppers.

■ Input and Output fields

The Input and Output fields show you the levels values (or halftone percentages) for the pointer location in the tone curve field (H). The input value (X axis) is the value before adjustment and the output value (Y axis) is the value after adjustment.

■ Brightness mode and percentage mode

The graph axes can be switched between displaying brightness values (= amount of light) from 0 (dark) to 255 (bright), and displaying halftone dot percentage values (= amount of ink) from 0% (white) to 100% (all ink) (I). We recommend using the default Brightness mode. In particular, please note that using Percentage mode to correct gray balance requires considerable knowledge of prepress.

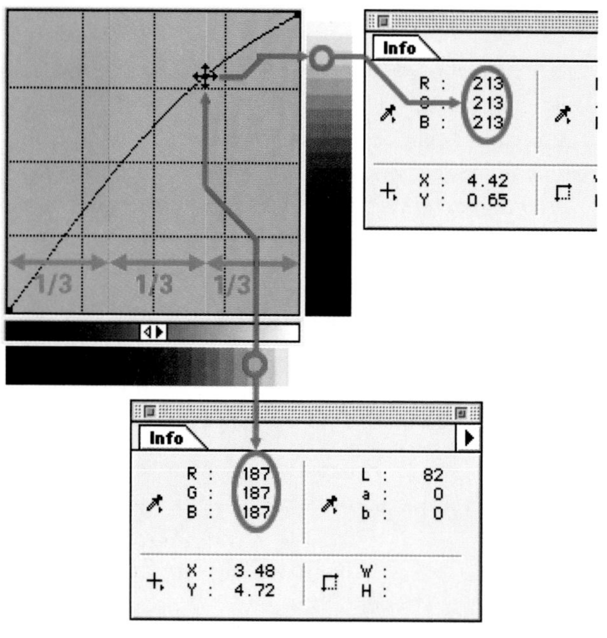

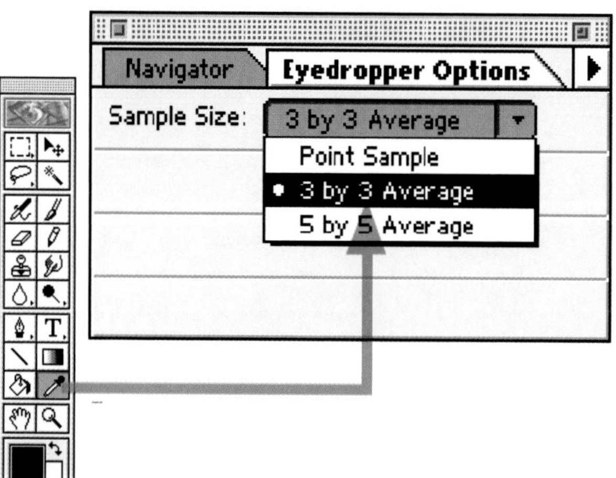

The Center of the Graph Does Not Represent the Midtones

At first you might think that the midtones would be centered right at the center of the graph (RGB=128 or CMYK =50 percent), but this is not the case. Because the human eye is more sensitive to differences between highlight and the midtones, basic midtone adjustments are made by dividing the X axis into thirds or quarters and adding control points to the curve within a ⅓ or ¼ area below the highlights (as shown in the illustration at left).

Basic Operations: Some Basic Procedures

While there isn't one set way to adjust tone curves, there are recommended techniques to follow, which we introduce here. For the following explanation, we have set the mode to Brightness mode so the far left of the X axis represents the shadows and the far right represents the highlights.

● You can find this image, Photo001.tif, in the Tone Curve Study folder on the accompanying CD-ROM.

STEPS

1. The first step is to analyze the photograph (study the original film version if you're working from a scan). Look at the image carefully and determine where the highlight and shadow points should be. Also, if there is a place on the image that you want to appear as neutral gray, you should also note where that is. Make notes, draw sketches, and so on as a guide for making consistently repeatable corrections.

2. Double-click on the Eyedropper tool in the Tools palette and set the Sample Size to 3×3 Average or 5×5 Average in the Eyedropper Options dialog box.

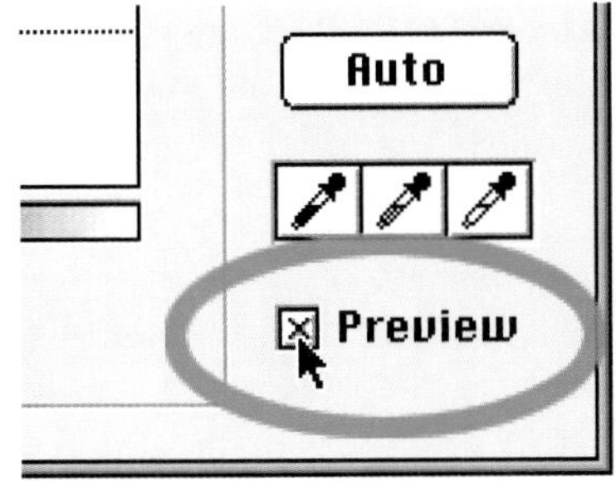

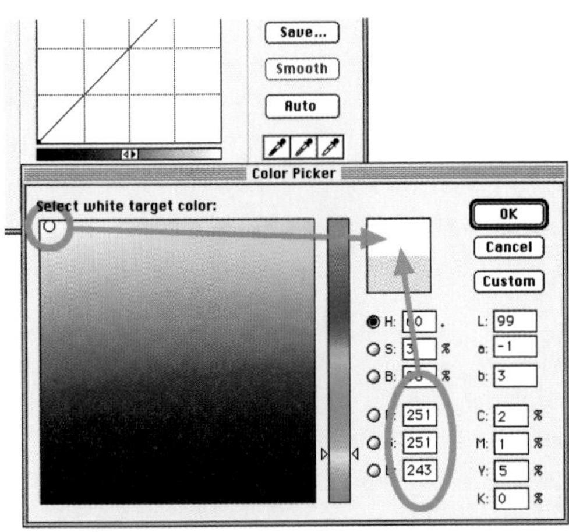

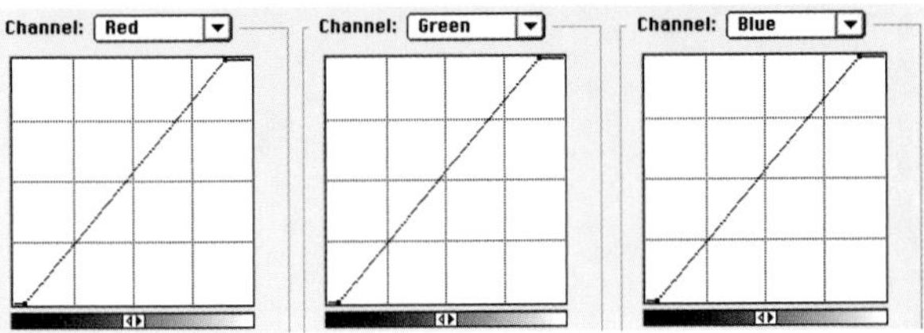

3. Open the Curves dialog box and turn the Preview on.

4. Double-click on the Highlight eyedropper icon and select the color you want to use as the highlight color from the Color Picker or enter numerical values for it. Enter values between 243 and 248 for each of the RGB values in order to select a pure white that will not be blown out in reproduction.

5. Click on OK in the Color Picker and return to the Curves dialog box. Double-click on the Shadow eyedropper icon and set the shadow color, as in step 4. Enter RGB values between 8 and 15 to select a pure black that will be reproduced without blocking up.

6. As in step 4, double-click on the Midtone eyedropper and enter 127 for each of the RGB values to set a neutral gray. If you prefer a warmer or cooler gray, you can make that adjustment by increasing the value in either the R channel of the Color Picker (makes the gray warmer) or increasing the value in the B channel of the Color Picker (makes the gray cooler).

7. The previous steps preset the brightness and color values for the Highlight, Shadow, and Midpoint eyedropper tools. After adjusting the Midtone values, click on OK in the Color Picker and return to the Curves dialog box.

8. Click on the Highlight eyedropper, move the cursor inside the image to the highlight point you identified in step 1, and click. You should be able to see the entire color of the image change (circle 1 in the image on the left).

9. Next, click on the Shadow eyedropper, move the cursor to the Shadow point in the image, and click (circle 2 in the image on the left).

10. Click on the Midtone eyedropper and then click on the neutral gray in the image (circle 3 in the image on the left).

11. Through the previous steps, we have set an optimal highlight and shadow point as well as a neutral gray balance for the image. However, the linear curve of the RGB composite channel is unchanged. What's happened? If you look at the tone curves for the individual channels, you'll see that the adjustment was made to the individual channels. At this point, if you feel that you have overcorrected your image, you can adjust the highlight, midtone, and shadow points of each channel's tone curves so that they're closer to the original linear curve. If you don't feel the corrections were enough, adjust in the other direction (away from the original linear curve).

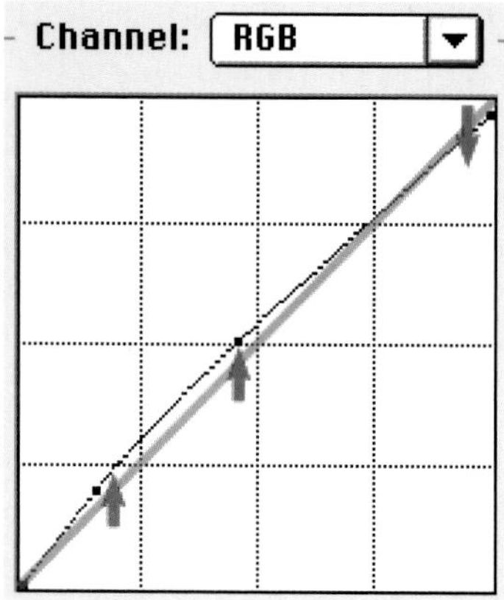

12. Finally, display the composite RGB channel and create two control points in the middle of the tone curve (shown to the left) to adjust the tonal range of the midtones.

13. Click OK after you are finished.

NOTE

■ If you make repeated adjustments using the Curves command, the quality of your image will deteriorate. Try as much as possible to make all your corrections at one time.

If you don't like the results of your corrections after you are finished, press Command-Z to undo it and return the image to what it was before you started. Then, while holding down the Option key, choose Image, Adjust, Curves again. The tone curve you applied previously is available and active again, and you can continue making corrections where you left off. This tip works with most of the Image, Adjust menu commands.

■ A higher quality Curves adjustment can be made by selecting the Mode, 16-bits/Channel option. By giving more bits of information to use in the adjustment, the amount of image deterioration is minimized, especially if you have to make a repeated adjustment. After the adjustment is made, switch the image back using the Mode, 8-bits/Channel option.

■ In Photoshop 4.0, you can use the Curves dialog box by selecting Layers, New, Adjustment Layer and then selecting Curves as the type of layer. This function enables you to make your Curves corrections using a separate layer that applies the adjustment to all underlying layers without actually altering the pixels of those layers. You can change the correction parameters in this special layer as many times as you like and not worry about the quality of your image deteriorating through repeated corrections, as you do in Photoshop 3.0. (See a description of this function with respect to Levels corrections in Chapter 9-9.)

Before tone curve corrections

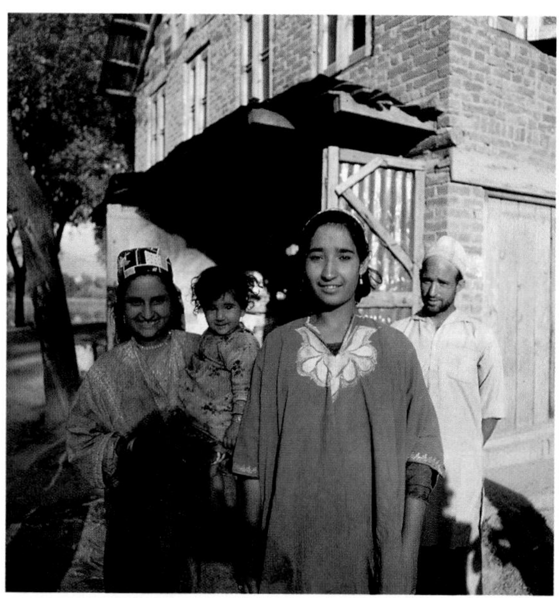
After tone curve corrections

A Practical Example of Tone Curve Adjustments

Tone curve adjustments are not done by blindly moving the curve around and seeing the results on the monitor. If you remember that the graph represents the relationship between the original image (horizontal axis) and the result (vertical axis), you can approach the use of the Curves function methodically and more successfully. Let's look at the application of tone curve adjustments for several images and analyze the results of the adjustments.

Original

Emphasizing Highlights

● The image used in this example is the Photo002.tif image in the Tone Curve Study folder on the accompanying CD-ROM.

To emphasize the highlights in metals like gold and silver, or to emphasize details in white cloth, you have to slightly increase the tonality in the quarter tones of the graph. You do this by adjusting the tone curve after selecting a target white value.

Image adjusted so the highlights are slightly blown out but are emphasized by darkening the midtones.

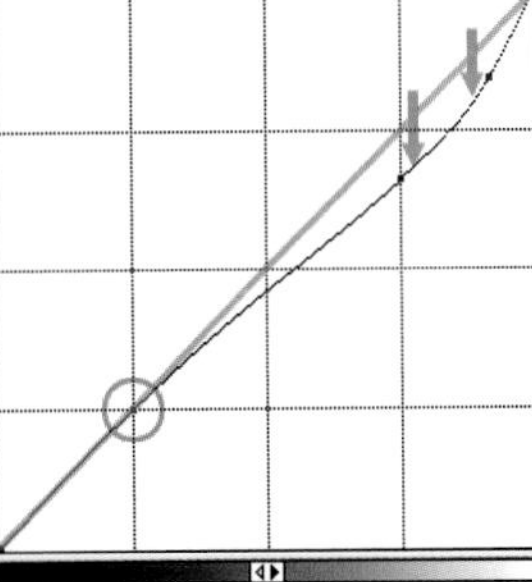

Image adjusted so the highlights are not blown out, but the tonal variation in the area from the highlights to slightly darker region is increased.

Before correction

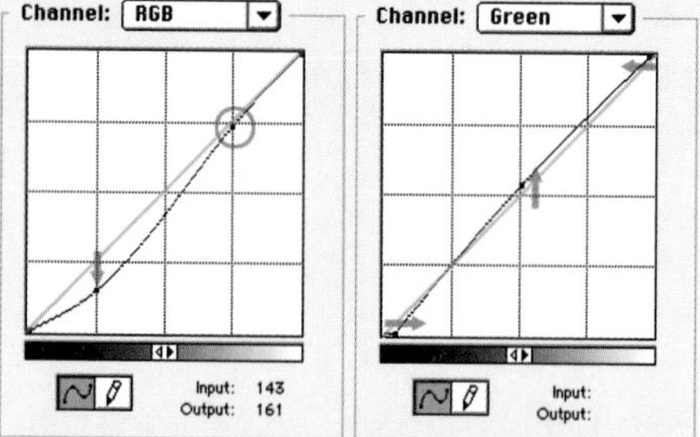

After correction

Controlling the Midtones

● The images used in this example are the Photo003.tif and the Photo004.tif images in the Tone Curve Study folder on the accompanying CD-ROM.

To successfully bring out dull scenery with no contrast or the subtle detail in flat walls, you have to darken the ¾ tones of the graph. This widens the tonal variation in the midtones between the ¼ and the ½ tones, with the effect of bringing out the detail.

Fundamentally, this kind of adjustment (adding contrast) is done by leaving the control points in the bottom-left and the top-right corners fixed and increasing the slope of the curve in the midtones, as shown in the figures at the bottom of the page (Photo004.tif on the CD). This type of S-shaped tone curve is a basic curve for acquiring contrast. This curve shape, for example, is a good adjustment for adding punch to photographs that are going to be used on the World Wide Web.

Before correction

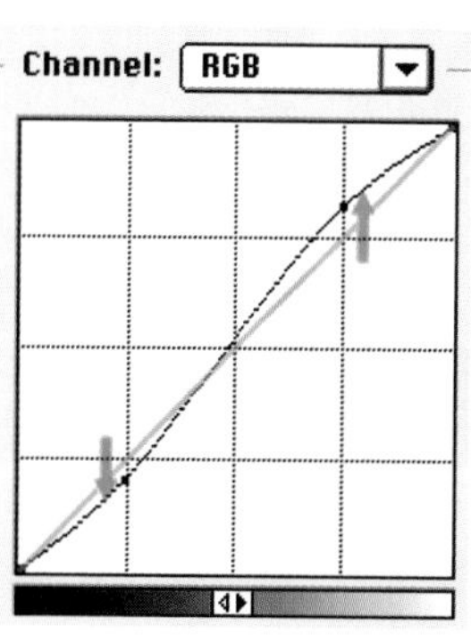

After correction

Left: Original

Lower left: To decrease the color that was too strong (cyan), we widened the curve in the R channel.

Lower right: To increase the color that was lacking (red), we adjusted the G and B channels. After that we adjusted the composite RGB curve as shown below in order to increase the area of bright tones.

Flesh Tones

● The image used in this example is the Photo005.tif image in the Tone Curve Study folder on the accompanying CD-ROM.

When flesh tones appear too red or bluish, consider the following two techniques for correcting them:

■ Add color where it is lacking.

■ Decrease color where there is too much.

Without experience it is difficult to understand how to determine which method is better, so let's try both.

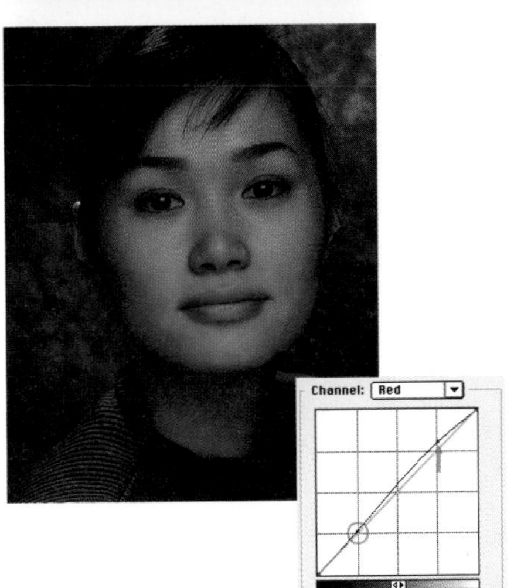

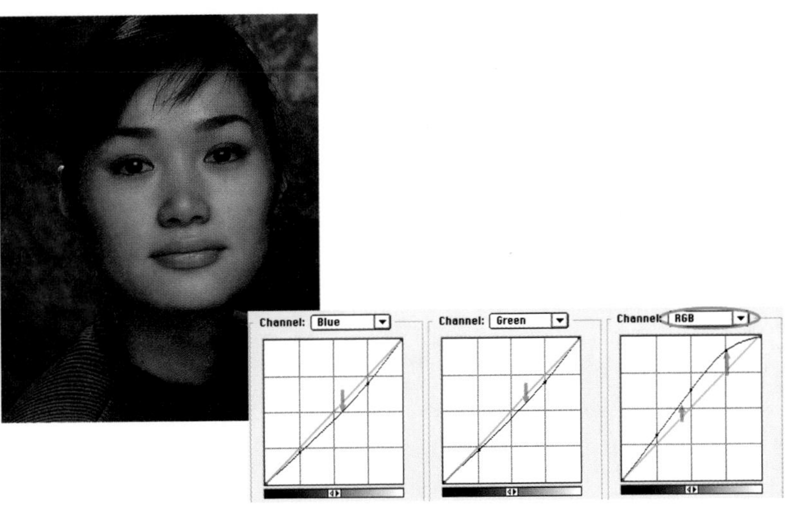

Before correction

After correction

PhotoDisc Library image

The idea behind correcting the flesh tones on this image was basically the same as for the image above, but in this case, the main adjustment was done by moving the control point in the bottom-left corner of the graph.

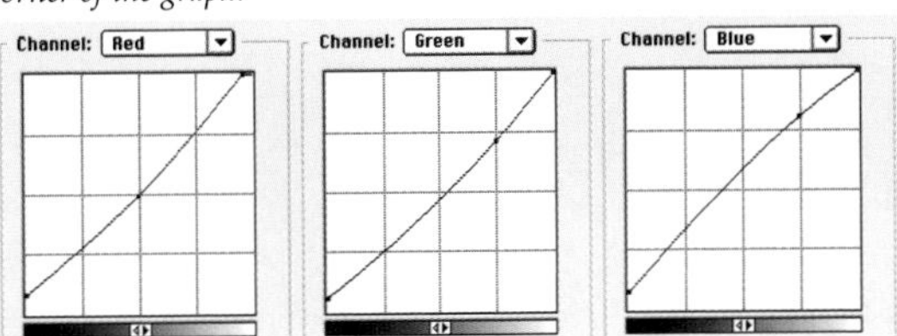

Before correction

Giving the Blacks Depth

● The image used in this example is the Photo006.tif image in the Tone Curve Study folder on the accompanying CD-ROM.

To bring out a feeling of depth in images like this one with backlighting, or pictures of cameras, audio equipment, dark sculptures, or dark cloth, you have to darken the ½ tones of the image and then lighten the highlights that have been darkened by the first correction as necessary.

After correction

Channel: RGB

Correcting Color Cast

● The image used in this example is the Photo007.tif image in the Tone Curve Study folder on the accompanying CD-ROM.

Images with very strong color cast must be corrected channel by channel. We begin by taking a look at the characteristics of the individual channels.

In most cases, the channel with the color cast has very dark tonality or the channel with the color that is the opposite of the color cast is very bright. In the former case, we adjust the midtones in the channel that is very dark. In the latter case, we darken the midtones in the channel that is very bright.

Before correction

After correction

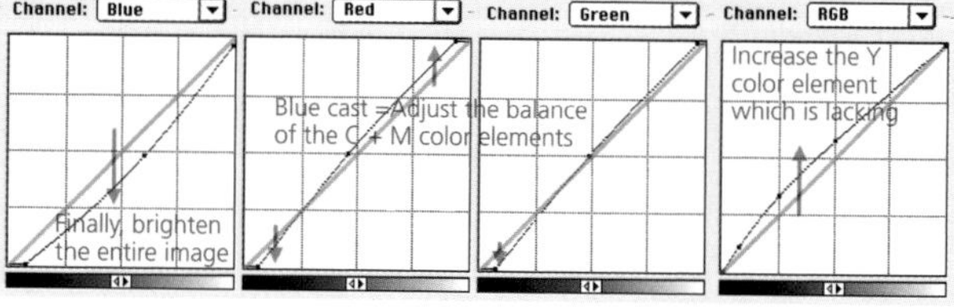

Emphasizing Specular Highlights

To intentionally blow out subtle catchlights (specular highlights) that are just brighter than the highlights but not yet blown out, use the pencil pointer to draw in the area of the curve that is brighter than the highlights.

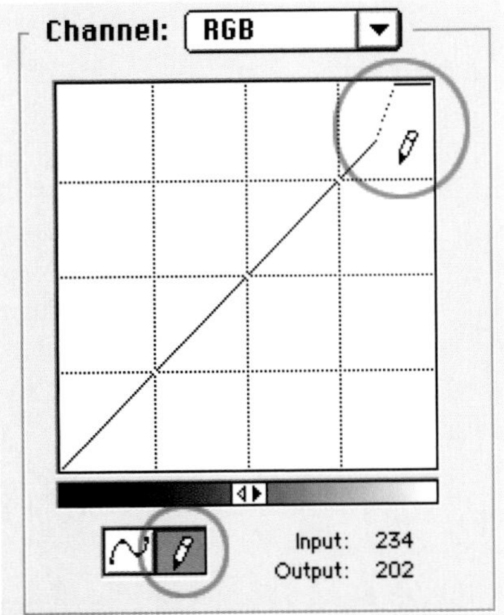

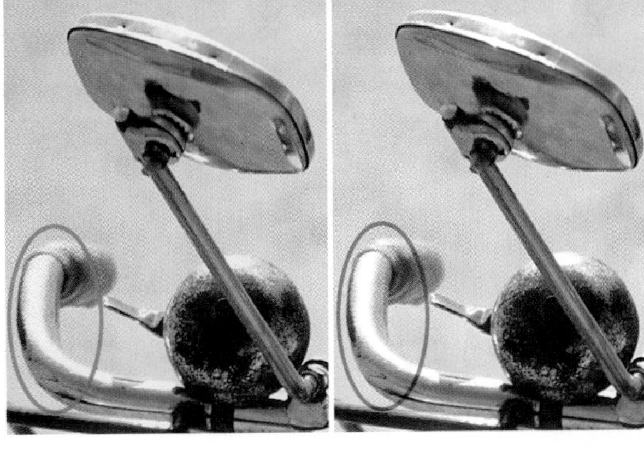

Left: Before correction

Right: After correction

Overexposed image corrected

Correcting Overexposed and Underexposed Photographs

By creating tone curves like the ones shown to the left, you can make overexposed or underexposed photographs appear as if they have nearly the correct exposure. While the samples shown here were done in Photoshop after the photos were scanned, it's possible (and highly recommended in most cases) to do this adjustment at the scanning stage. If you do make this adjustment while scanning, any post-scanning adjustments will produce different tone curves than the ones shown in these illustrations. When making the adjustments in Photoshop, it's best to start with the eyedropper functions to adjust the highlights and shadows before using tone curves to make manual adjustments.

NOTE

When the Curves box is open, you can click and drag the pointer inside the image to see where various tones in the image are represented along the tone curve. This is indicated by a small circle that appears on the diagonal line of the curve, and which makes it easy to find specific points along the curve to adjust. In the case of correcting color tone, however, this is not very useful unless you are displaying individual channels. If you are displaying the RGB composite channel, you won't know which RGB levels values are being referenced (see the following figures). When setting highlight and shadow points, however, it's necessary to make those measurement in the RGB composite mode.

Underexposed image corrected

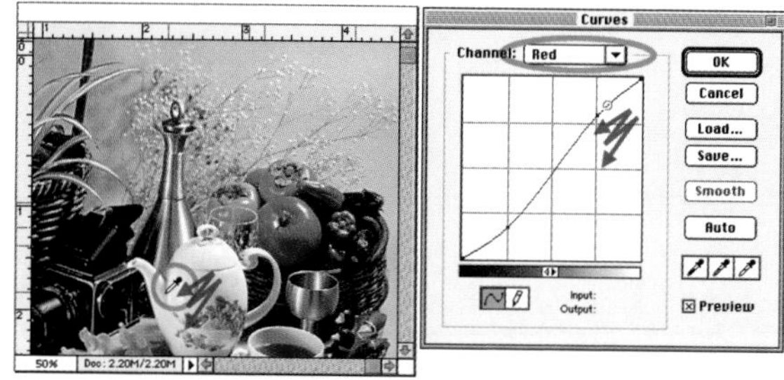

Photograph with correct exposure (reference)

03 6

Selective Color Correction

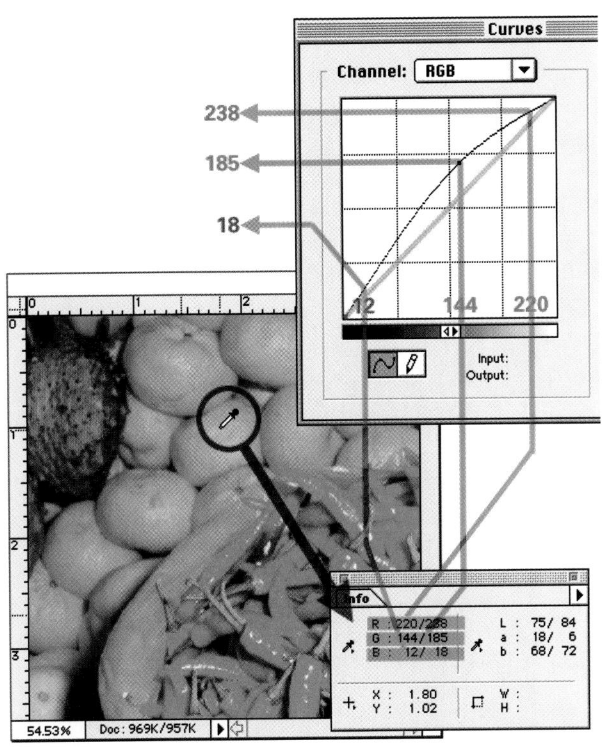

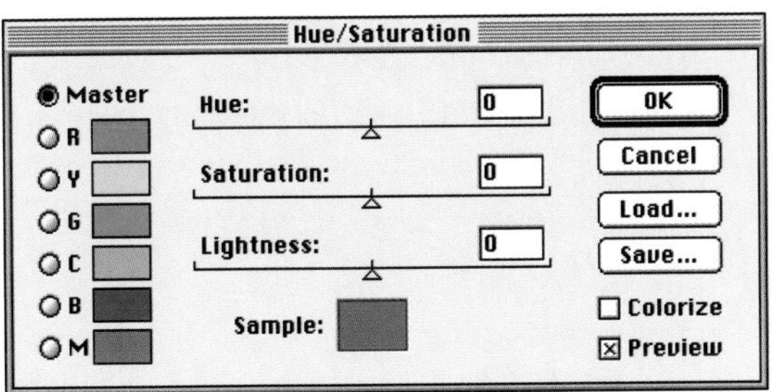

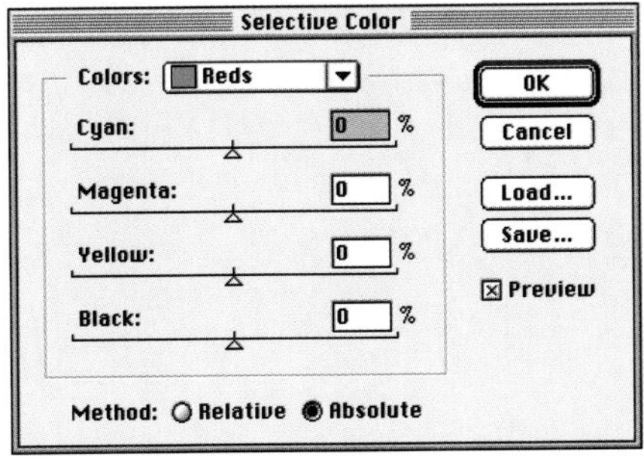

Changing Dark Colors using Tone Curves

When you adjust images using the Curves dialog box, you can change the brightness or contrast of the entire image. At the same time, however, you end up changing some of the image's colors.

Consider the color orange. In RGB mode, you create orange when you use mostly red, a little green, and almost no blue. For example, R = 220, G = 144, and B = 12 make a typical orange color (in a CMYK image, orange is created when you use a lot of M and Y ink, particularly Y). Now, if you were to raise the curve at the ⅓ tones of the composite channel, the before and after values would match the ones in the illustration. In this case, the R tones close to 255 and the B tones close to 0 haven't changed very much. Whereas the midtones were increased considerably, the areas of the curve near the bottom-left and upper-right origin hardly changed at all. However, the increase in the midtones caused a substantial increase to the G tones in the center of the graph.

You can see that in order to adjust the R or the B on an orange color with a midrange brightness, you have to make a large adjustment to your curve. Unfortunately, if the amount of adjustment has to be large, this will have an effect on the other colors in the image.

To get around this problem, Photoshop offers two commands that enable you to correct specific colors without affecting the other colors of the image.

■ Hue, saturation, and brightness controls

The Hue/Saturation command enables you to adjust the hue, saturation, and brightness for all the colors in the image at once or individually, which is convenient for making intuitive changes to an image as you view it on the monitor. Adjusting individual channels is not possible, however, because one slider affects all the channels (except K).

■ Selective color

The Selective Color command enables you to adjust the individual color components in all the channels for any color in an image. This is similar to the Hue/Saturation command except that its functionality is more similar to color correction, as it is known in the prepress industry. Selective Color is useful for making corrections when you need to precisely control CMYK ink quantities. However, this control is not geared toward intuitive corrections.

We call this type of correction where specific colors rather than all the colors in an image are corrected "selective color correction."

Before correction

After correction

Real World Hue and Saturation Corrections

When you actually use the Hue/Saturation command, you almost always use a combination of the Hue, Saturation, and Lightness sliders. For example, this photograph was slightly overexposed by ⅔ of a stop in order not to lose the tonality in the people in the shadows under the trees. As a consequence, the color in the building in the background is too light. If you darken it using a tone curve, the shadows under the trees also become darker. Here is where you would use the Hue/Saturation command to darken only the red and green to blue-green tones, leaving the people and the bark of the tree unchanged.

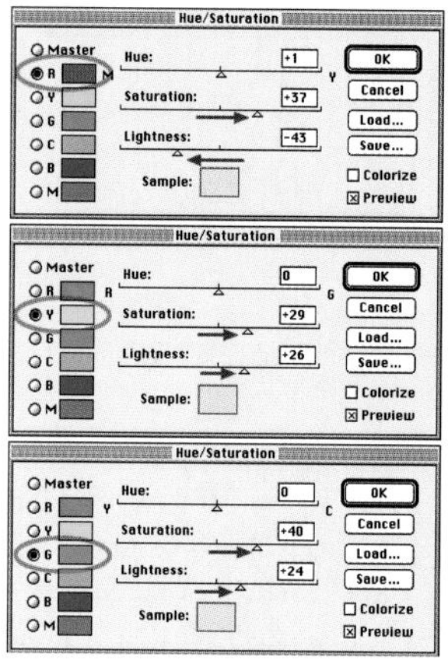

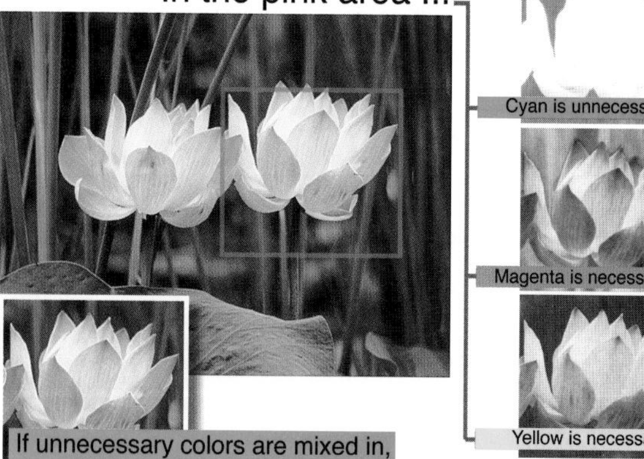

Wanted and Unwanted Colors

Pure colors are made of either a single color or two colors. The substractive primaries—C, M, and Y—are made up of a single color. The additive primaries—R,G, and B— are made up of two colors.

In a CMYK mode image, for example, red (R) is made up of M and Y. In this case we call the M and Y channels *wanted color channels*. When the color produced by one channel (in this case, C) makes the color of other channels (in this case M and Y) less vivid, the channel causing the problem is called the *unwanted color channel*.

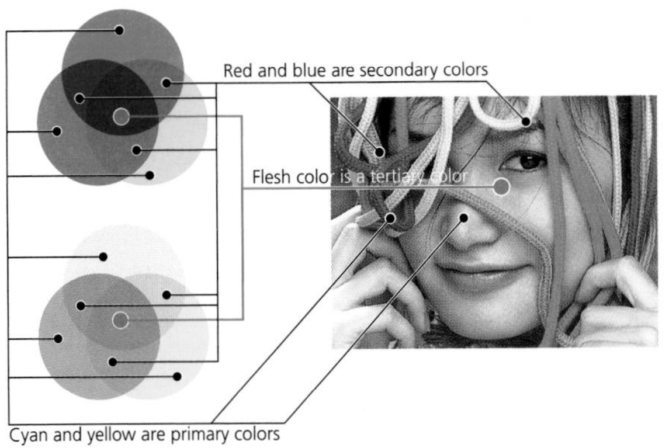

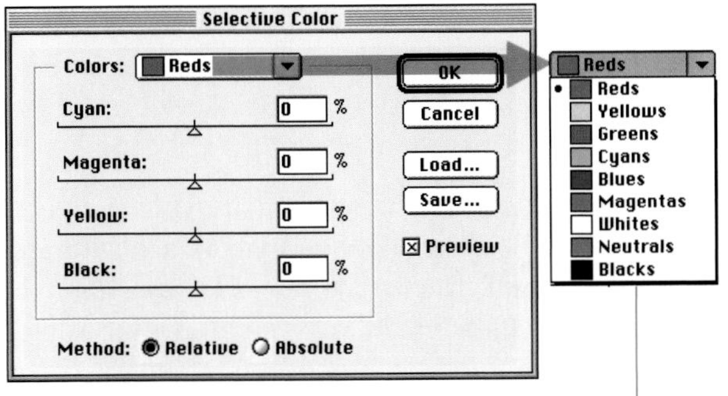

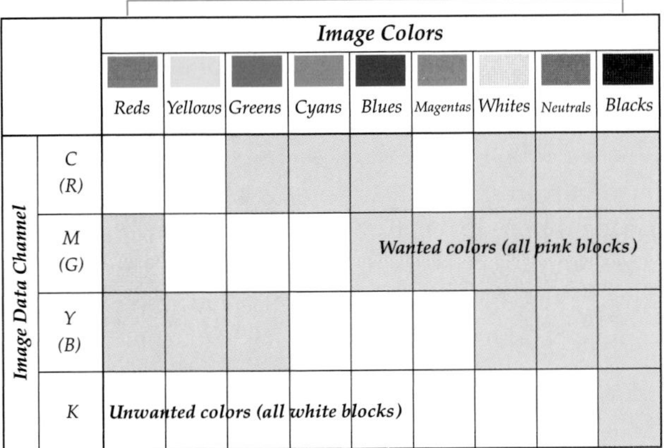

Image Colors
Reds
Yellows
Greens
Cyans
Blues
Magentas
Whites
Neutrals
Blacks
Image Data Channel
C (R)
M (G)
Y (B)
K
Wanted colors (all pink blocks)
Unwanted colors (all white blocks)

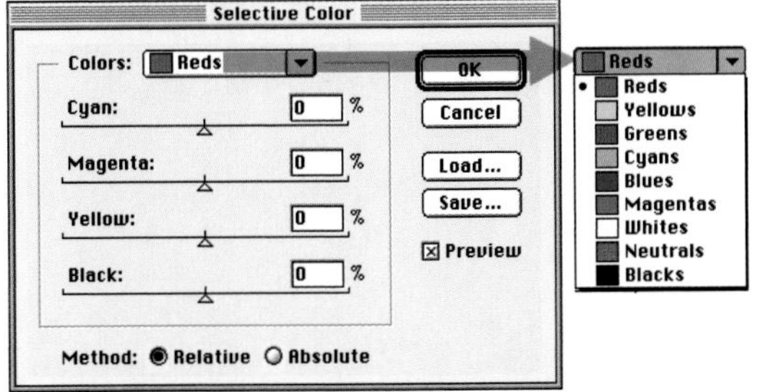

Primary, Secondary, and Tertiary Colors

All colors are classified as either primary, secondary, or tertiary.

■ *Primary colors* can be reproduced by using a single cyan (C), magenta (M), or yellow (Y) color.

■ *Secondary colors* can be reproduced using any two colors among cyan (C), magenta (M), and yellow (Y).

■ *Tertiary colors* can be reproduced by mixing cyan (C), magenta (M), or yellow (Y).

Cyan in Cyan?

In high-end prepress systems, there are terms for colors such as "cyan in cyan (CinC)," "magenta in green (MinG)," and "yellow in red (YinR)." They each have the following meanings:

■ CinC: Cyan areas in the original are created with C channel color components / elements.

■ MinG: Green areas in the original are created with M channel color components / elements.

■ YinR: Red areas in the original are created with Y channel color components / elements.

For example, if you select Greens from the Colors pop-up menu in the Selective Color dialog box and adjust the yellow (Y) slider, this would be a yellow in green adjustment. Wanted and unwanted colors, described earlier, are shown in the chart on the left.

The Selective Color Command

The Selective Color command has almost the same purpose as the Hue / Saturation command, but it is more targeted to the prepress industry. This command groups colors into nine groups and enables you to increase or decrease their CMYK color components. Those groups are: reds, yellows, greens, cyans, blues, magentas, whites, neutrals, and blacks.

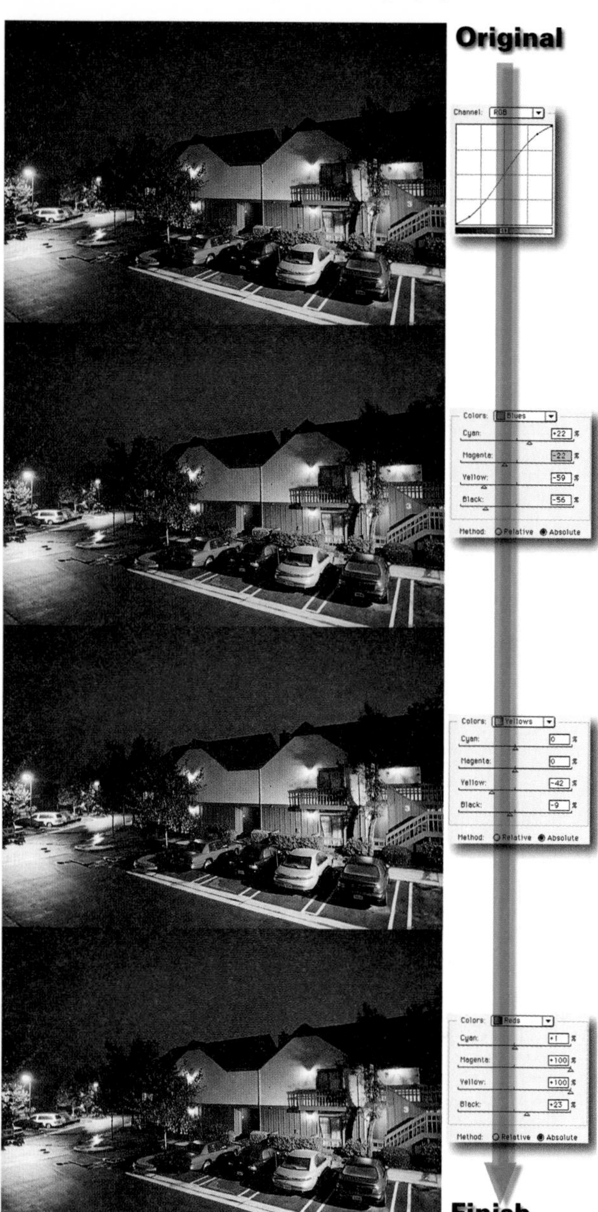

Color Correcting Photographs with Multiple Light Sources

Adjusting photographs like the one shown on the left—with mercury bulbs shining in the foreground and the natural light of the night sky in the background—is very difficult using just tone curves. In this case, we corrected the photograph by using Photoshop's Selective Color command.

First, we looked at the photograph and decided which colors to adjust. Because the photograph was going to require a relatively complicated adjustment, we planned the operations carefully.

In this photograph, we saw that three main colors were present, the dark blue of the sky, the yellow in the foreground, and the relatively minor (not a lot of surface area), but important, catchlights of the red car.

We began by adjusting the colors that made an overall impression on the eye and covered a relatively wide area of the photograph. The first step was to strengthen the contrast in the already contrasty night sky by using a tone curve. The color contrast in this photograph was created with the two complementary colors—blue and yellow. We predicted that replacing the blue and yellow with a neutral color would make the photograph appear as if there wasn't enough contrast.

The second step and the rest of the corrections were done using the Selective Color command. We selected Blues from the pop-up menu and removed the magenta (channel) components using the settings shown in the illustration. We then selected Yellows and removed the yellow (channel) components.

Finally, we selected Reds and increased the magenta and yellow (channel) components and at the same time increased the black (channel) components to strengthen the rich red in the car. This was in order to make the black channel (including the magenta and yellow components) components in the dark red even richer.

Because this dialog box also includes four sliders for CMYK image channels, you can use this for RGB images with no difficulty. However, you have to think in terms of CMYK....

Original

Dividing Vivid Colors

If you look at the red in this macaw's wings, you will notice that there are pure red and orange areas.

First, we turned on the Relative button in the Selective Color dialog box and increased the magenta component in the reds. This adjusted the pure red areas so the red and magenta colors were completely saturated (couldn't get any more red). After this, we slightly brightened the three-quarter tones in the G channel using the Curves command, which strengthened the distinction between the vivid reds in the feathers.

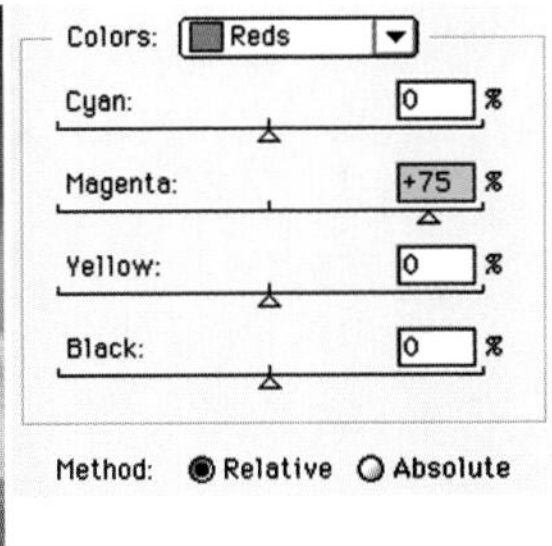

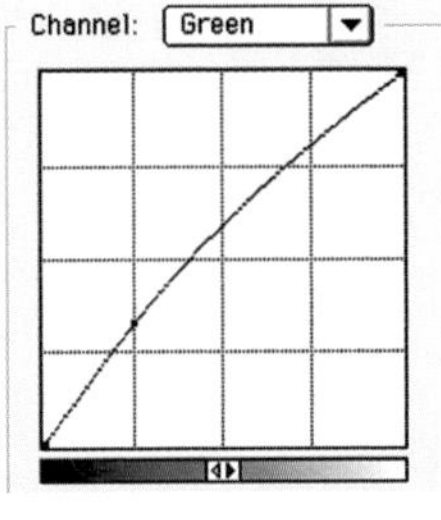

After correction

Adjusting Gray and Black "Colors"

Before correction

Black and white are both considered colors. With Photoshop's unique color computation capabilities, neutral gray colors like charcoal or black can also be selectively adjusted.

Here too, we used the Selective Color command. This is particularly effective where, as in this case, you have scanned a dark photograph on a scanner, and there isn't enough tonal range in the shadows.

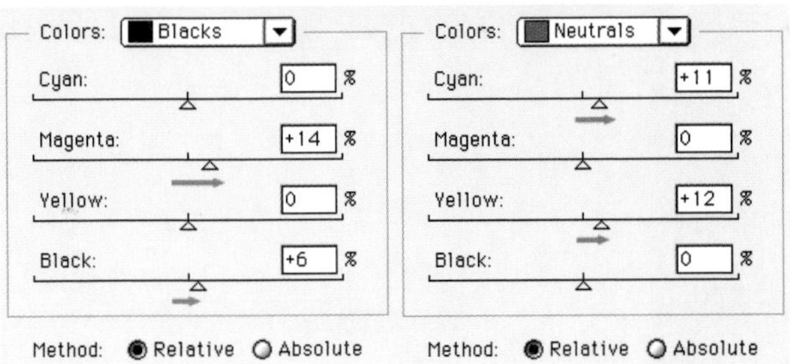

After correction

03 7

Practical Correction Techniques

Color Correction Tricks

Tone curve and levels adjustment as well as selective color correction are all, in and of themselves, conservative techniques. If you combine them with the use of layers or channel swapping, however, you can greatly improve flawed images while minimizing the amount of image deterioration as much as possible. Here we introduce a few of these techniques.

Correcting Uneven Lighting

This photograph was taken with a clip-on strobe light. The area in the back of the image is too dark because there wasn't enough light from the strobe.

We created a blurred mask in the shape of the background (excluding the foreground subjects) using the alpha channel (mask channel #4) and, after making this alpha channel into a selection area, applied a tone curve to it. This left the foreground as it was and brightened only the dark subjects in the back of the picture.

Before correction

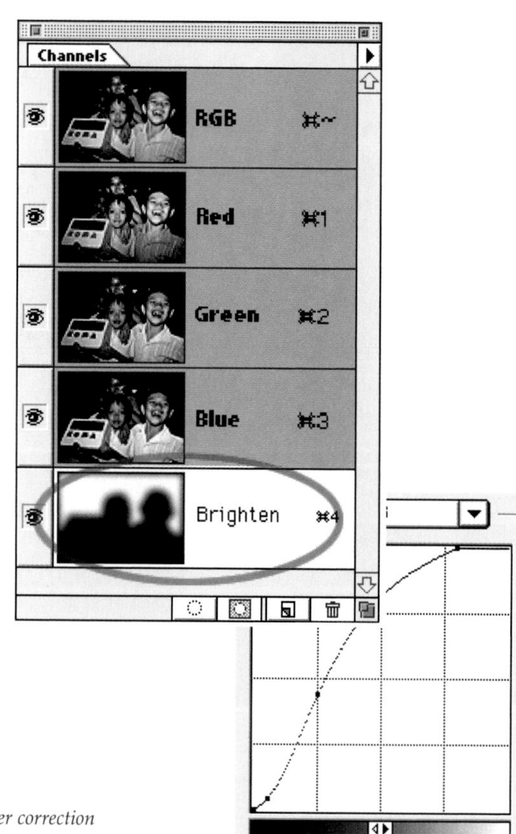

After correction

Precision Hue and Brightness Corrections using Layers, Masks, and Blending Modes

The lighting for the foreground of this photograph was daylight on a cloudy day, and the back was lit with an incandescent light bulb inside a red tent.

We could have adjusted this picture by using the method described on the previous page, but in this case, when we looked at just the Curves layer, we thought that only the very top of the red tent was lacking in vividness.

Before correction

So we decided to make another layer containing the same image and blend the two together using the Screen layers mode. In addition, we added a layer mask containing a front to back gradient to the top layer to make the image blended with Screen mode more striking.

This should have been enough. But by using the new Adjustment Layer function in Photoshop 4.0, we were able to selectively apply a Curves adjustment through a back to front gradient mask to make the changes in the image even more dramatic.

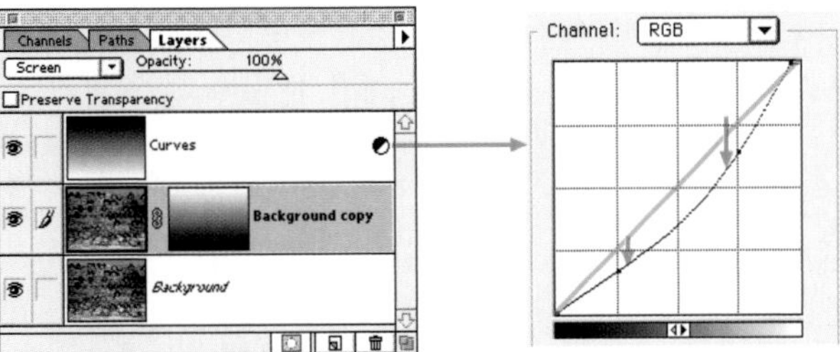

By using these masks, we were able to make corrections that slightly darkened the midtones in the entire blended image. In the final image, the tones in the front that were too bright became just right, and the color in the back stayed bright but became more vivid.

After correction

Before correction

Restoring Shadow Detail with Channel Swapping

This is a photograph with almost no detail in the shadows. But if you look at each individual RGB channel, you can see that some detail remains.

We decided to use the following procedure to take the tonality in the R channel and place it in the G and B channels.

First, we used the Magic Wand to select only the shadow areas, using the settings shown in illustration A. Because it isn't always possible to successfully make the selection in one try, you may have to modify the selection area. This isn't shown in the illustrations, but the selection in this photograph had to be modified.

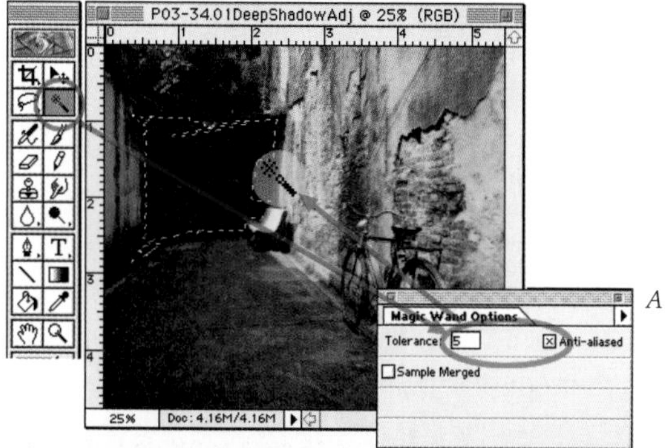

A

You can also save the selection in the alpha channel and blur the edges of the selection as necessary. In fact, it's a good idea to save the selection as an alpha channel so that if it's deselected it can be easily reloaded for use. This selection plays an important role in properly lining up the paste steps explained in the next paragraph.

With the selection loaded, we made only the R channel active in the Channels palette and copied the image information in that channel. Then we made only the G palette channel active in the Channels palette, and while the selection from the original R channel was still active, used the Paste Into command. This process precisely placed the info from the R channel into the exact same position in the G channel. We repeated the process with the B channel, which made the shadow area completely gray.

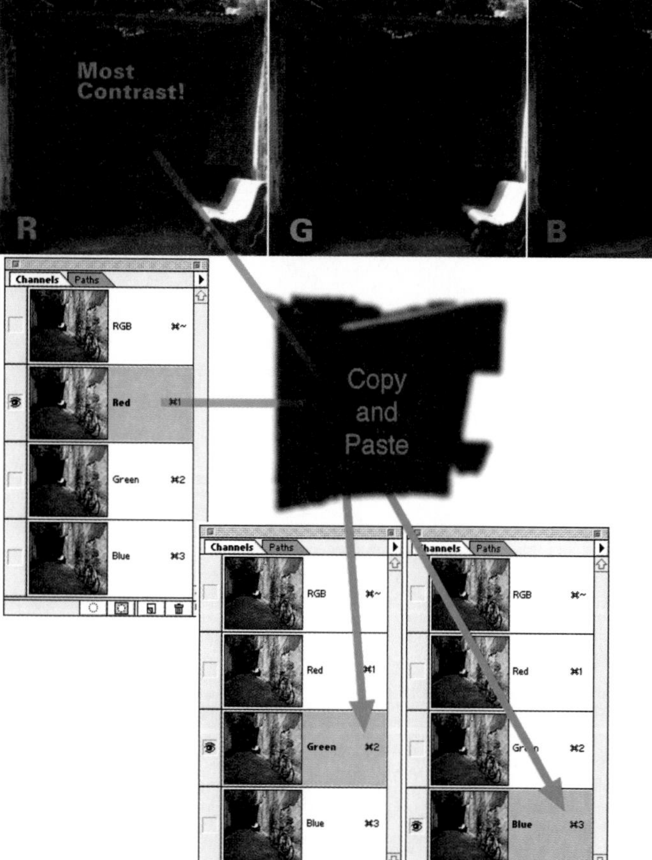

Finally we used the Curves and Color Balance commands to make the grays match their surrounding colors.

An important point to remember is to not delete the selection until the work is completely finished. However, as a good precaution, save the selection as an alpha channel so that if it's deselected it can be easily reloaded for use. This selection plays an important role in properly lining up the paste steps and tone adjustments required in this technique.

After correction

Emphasizing Highlight Detail

Photograph A is fairly overexposed (the shadows influenced the light reading at the time of exposure).

However, we thought it would look nice if we could leave the bright sunlit background as it was, but try to give the photograph a little more depth by darkening tones of the foreground.

A

B

C

We began by duplicating the layer so we had a two-layer image with exactly the same image in both layers, perfectly lined up one above the other. Next, we chose the Multiply blend mode and blended the layers to create the image with the correct exposure (B).

By doing this, however, we lost the brightness of the original background.

To recover the background, we used a technique called a *layer mask*. First we took our two-layer image and added a mask to the top layer. We looked at the individual RGB channels for the original image and made the channel with the most contrast (the G channel in this case) active. Then we loaded a selection from the channel and copied it.

We pasted this into the alpha channel for layer masks in the Channels palette. Then we used Image, Adjust, Invert to invert the tones in this alpha channel. Next, we experimented with two blend modes, Multiply or Color Burn (which is a new Blend Mode in Photoshop 4.0), to achieve the look we wanted. Finally, we adjusted the opacity slider to the correct opacity to complete the image.

By inverting the tonality in the layer mask we were able to make the light areas of the mask dark (that is, the masked area). As a result, the Multiply or Color Burn blends could not have much effect on the background, resulting in only the dark areas, like the people (which were fairly overexposed), looking darker than they had originally.

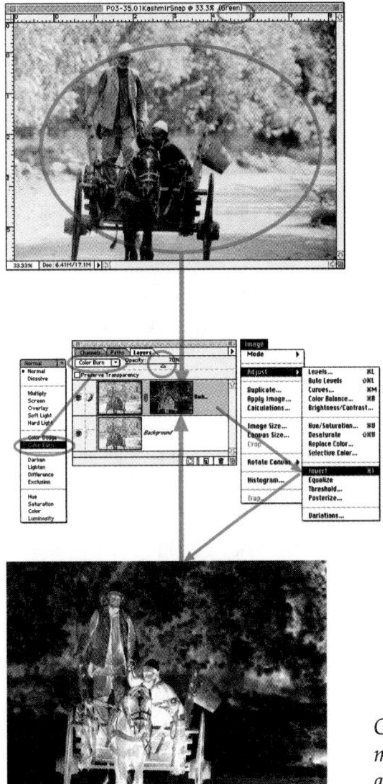

Copy the channel that has the most contrast and paste it into the alpha channel for layer masks.

A

Making a Monochrome Image from a Color Image

One way to make a monochrome image from a color image is to select Grayscale command from the Mode menu, but there are times when this results in an image that lacks depth (A).

On the other hand, other methods give us very dramatic results. Here we selected Split Channels from the Channel palette Options menu in order to split the RGB image into three monochrome images. Then we placed the R channel image in a layer over the G channel image and blended the layers by using the Hard Light command, as shown in the illustration.

This created a composite monochrome image from the R and G images (B).

It was also effective to add a layer mask to the R layer by using data from channel B (C).

NOTE

This blending method enables you to achieve the same effects as you would if you used Y, O, or G filters when taking black-and-white photographs.

B

C

03 8

Techniques for Retouching Highlights

A

B

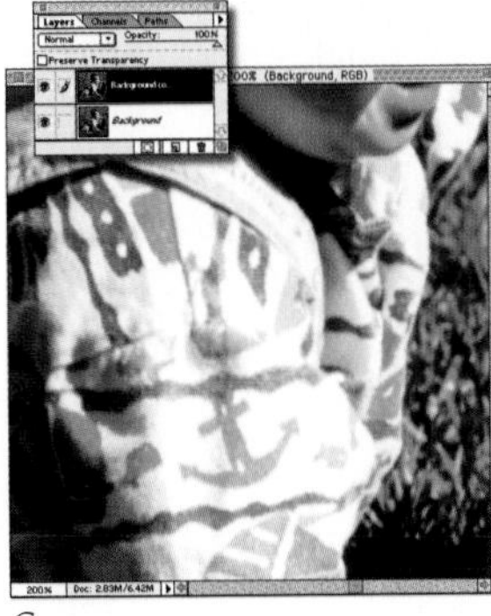
C

D

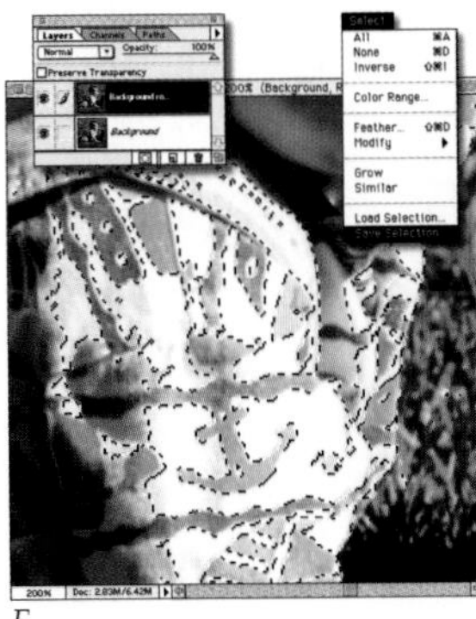
E

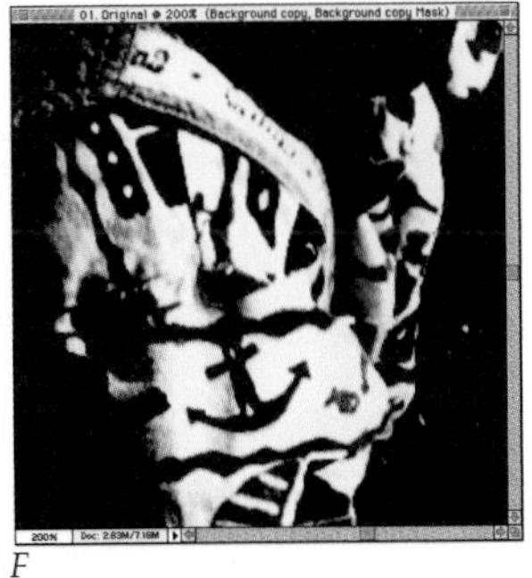
F

Original

STEPS

1. In the original of this scanned image, the highlights on the child's shirt were too bright, causing a loss of texture detail. Here we introduce you to techniques for slightly darkening only the highlights and for adding texture detail.

2. We used the eyedropper to check the values in the brightest color area (A) using the Info palette (B) and determined they were R = 251, G = 250, and B = 248. The purpose of the retouching was to bring these values down to around 240.

3. Next, we duplicated the Background layer (C) and selected only the whites in the child's shirt using the Color Range dialog box (D).

4. Then we used the Save Selection command to save the selection as a layer mask (E). When all the other layers were not displayed, we could see the white areas of the image that separated from the rest of the image with the mask (F).

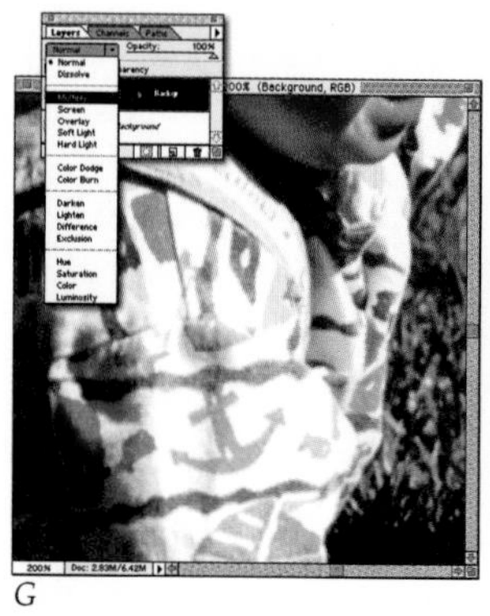

G

H

5. Then, with the top layer selected, we used the Multiply command in the layers palette (G). Next, we used the Add Noise filter to add a small amount of Monochromatic noise to the selection. This gave the white areas a small amount of texture (H).

6. At this point we were finished, so we went back to step 2 and used the eyedropper to measure the same highlight area once again (I). The values shown in the Info palette this time were R = 242, G = 240, and B = 236 (J).

7. If you compare the detail in the highlight areas in the original and the retouched image, you notice that the new version of the image shows more texture detail (K).

I

Info | Options

R : 242 C : 7%
G : 240 M : 4%
B : 236 Y : 7%
K : 0%

X : 0.50 W :
Y : 0.42 H :

J

K

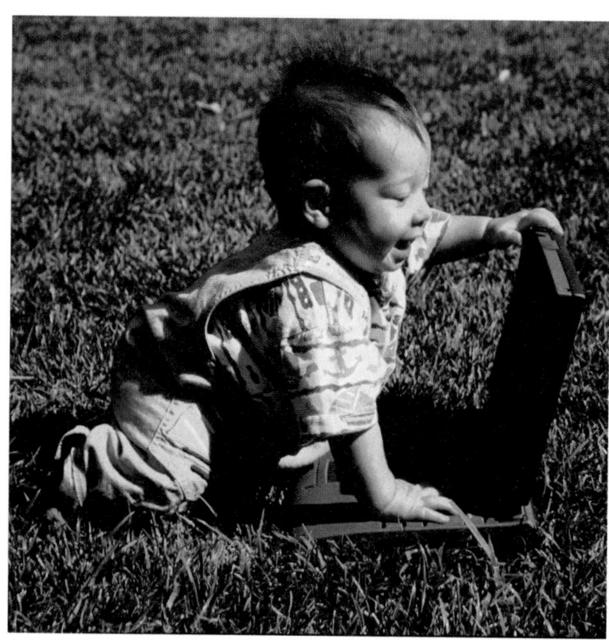

Finished image

03 9

Techniques for Retouching Portraits

Original

STEPS

1. The purpose of this retouching task was to smooth out the skin tones, brighten the area around the eyes, and remove the shadows from under the eyes. This kind of work is often necessary in portrait or fashion photography. In this case, the subject wasn't wearing any make-up and the lighting was not appropriate for taking a portrait picture, so retouching was required to create a more attractive photograph.

2. First, we created a duplicate layer of the portrait and applied the Gaussian Blur filter to it.

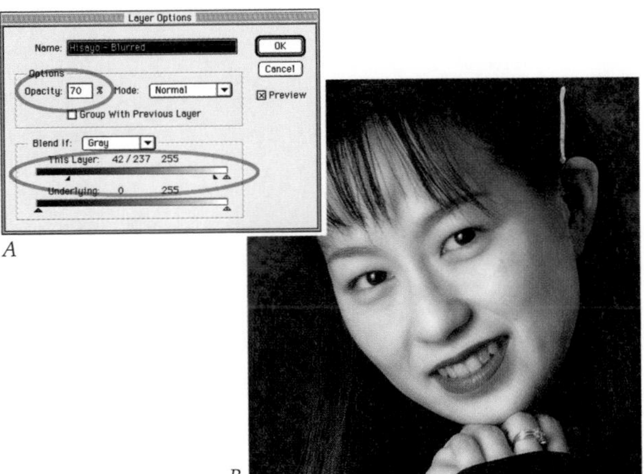

A

B

3. Next, we set the opacity of the blurred layer to 70% and opened the Layer Options dialog box. While holding the Option key, we placed the pointer on the slider in the This Layer field to split the slider in two (A). By moving the split slider from left to right, we gradually revealed the dark tones in the bottom layer (see page 9–29 for more information). This caused the sharp details of the eyes and hair to display through the blurred upper layer while leaving the flesh tones smooth (B).

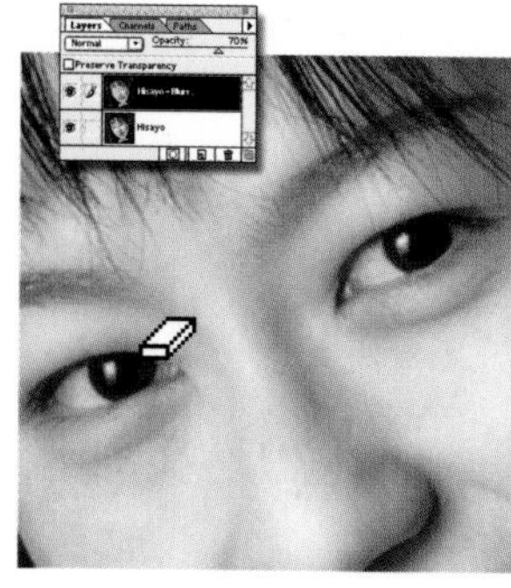

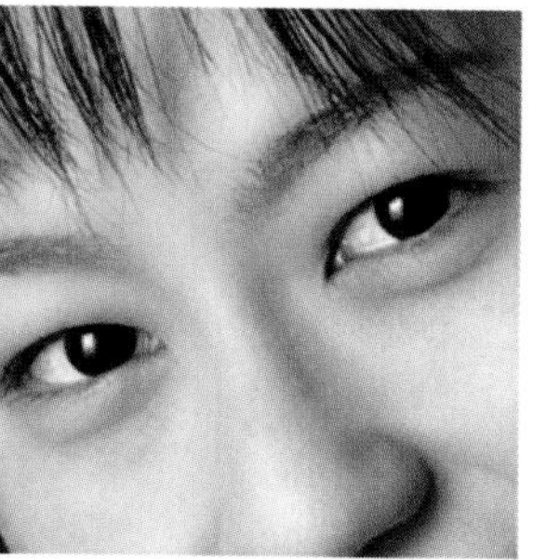

4. To make the eyes even sharper, we erased the area around the eyes in the upper blurred layer with the Eraser tool.

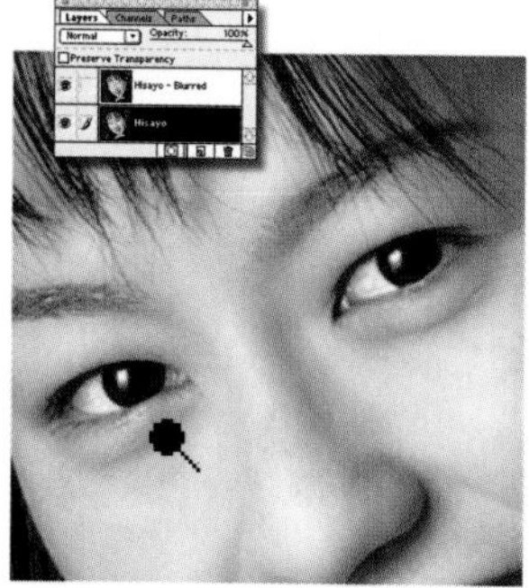

5. Then to remove the shadows under the eyes in the bottom layer, we used the Dodge tool. This tool was also used to whiten the eyes and the teeth.

Finish 1

6. If you compare the retouched image to the original photograph, you can see it looks much better.

7. If you blur different areas of a portrait, it gives the image a more romantic feel or a look of high fashion. So we opened this image in Live Picture and used a brush on the Blur layer to blur the area around the face.

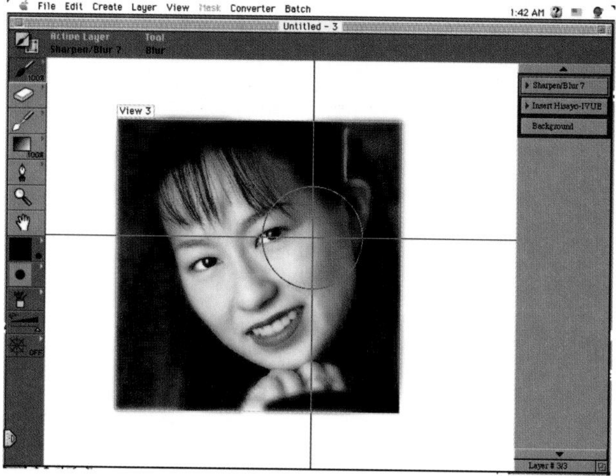

Finish 2

8. Blurring around the face had the effect of softening the background, which resulted in emphasizing the face and the eyes of the subject even further.

03 10

Restoring Damaged Photographs

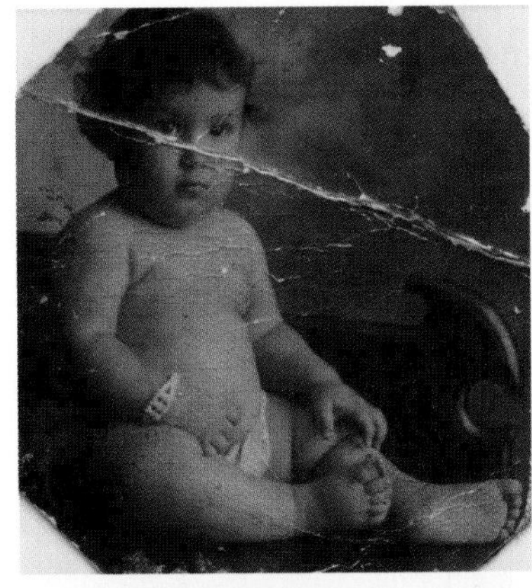

1. Restoring photographs like this one from 60 years ago is also part of the retouching work that can be done with digital photography.

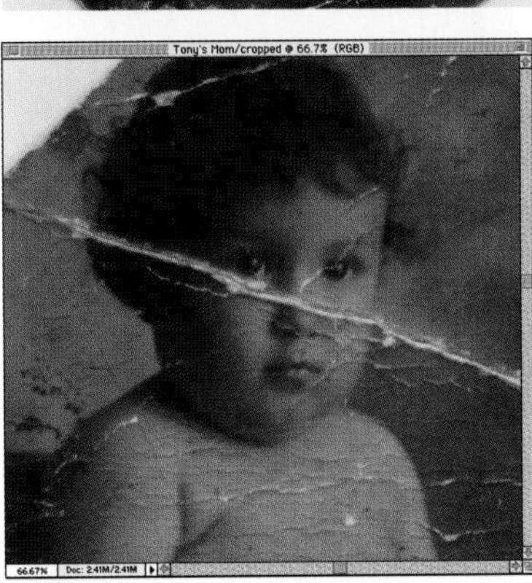

2. Before beginning the image retouching work, it is a good idea to set a goal. In this case, for example, rather than restoring the entire image, which would take a considerable amount of time, we decided to restore only one area of the photograph.

3. This photograph had small cracks all over the entire surface and was not in good condition. Because we would be using cloning techniques to copy pixels from one area of the photograph to another, the first step was to remove these cracks. We applied a small amount of Gaussian Blur filter to soften or remove the cracks.

4. When using the Rubber Stamp tool, it is easier to work on the image if you zoom in on it. When you are working on long crack lines, you have to work back and forth, moving pixels from both sides of the crack (A). For repairing wrinkles or holes, sampling should be done using a circular pattern (B).

5. Every now and then we zoomed out to check the progress of our work. As shown on the left, we could compare the original to the restored version with the left side of the face repaired.

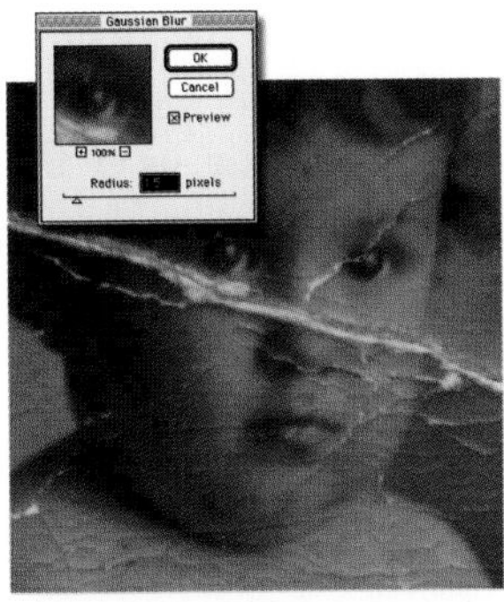

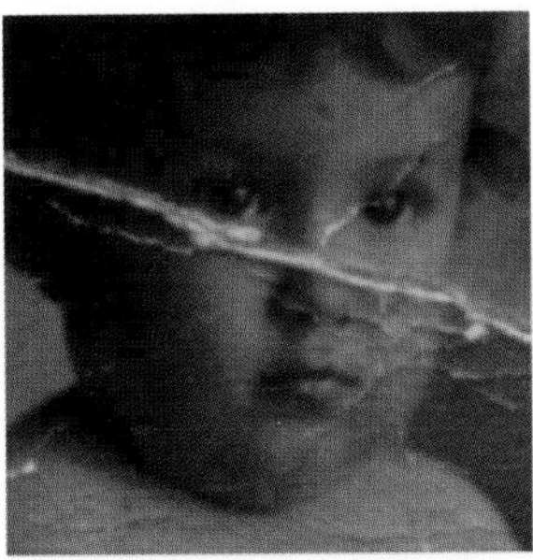

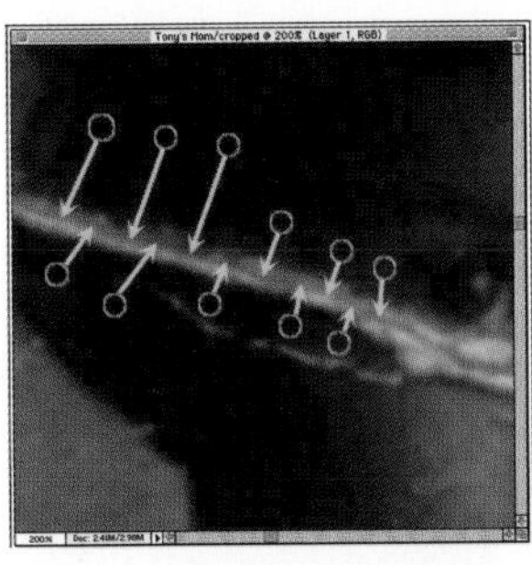

A

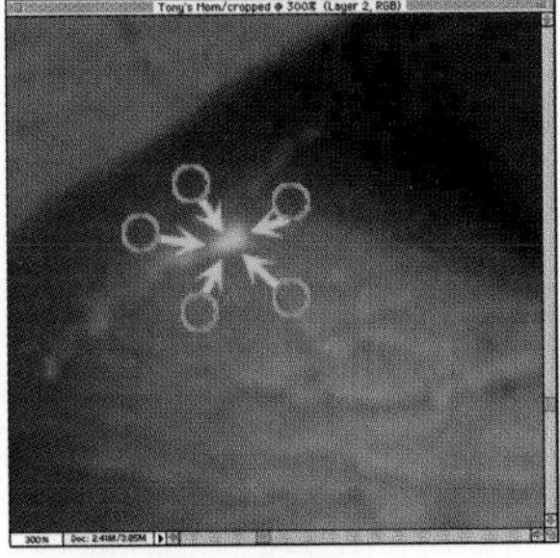

B

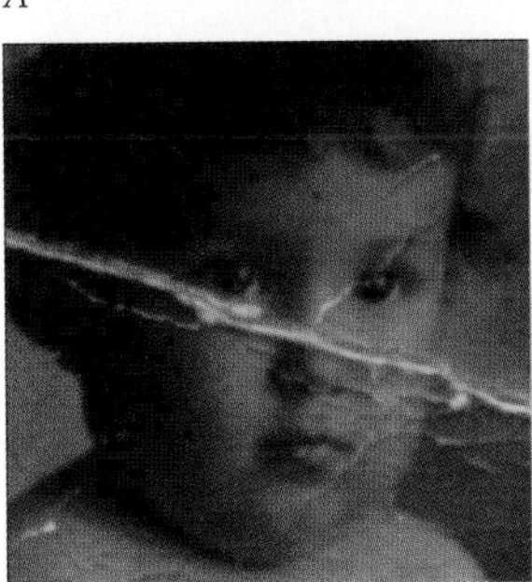

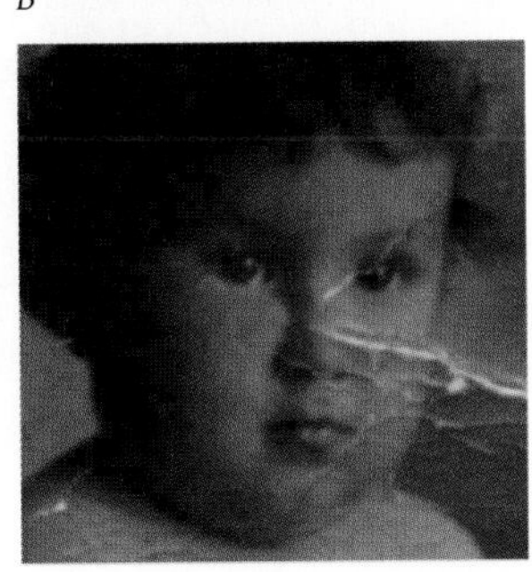

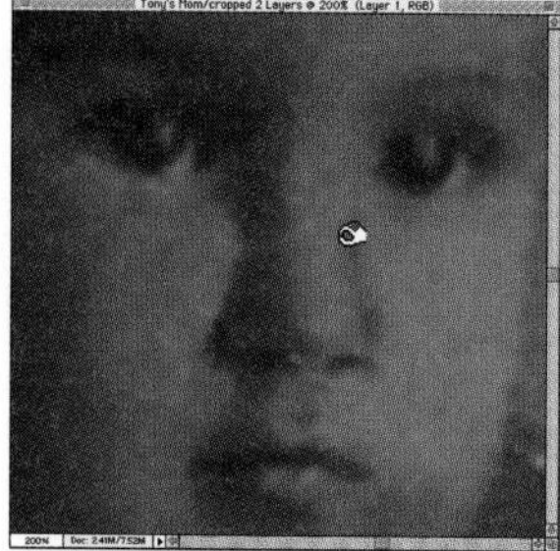

6. You may occasionally have to use painting tools (Airbrush, Paintbrush, Dodge, and Burn) to reproduce an area of an image. In the photograph on the left, we used the Burn tool to add a little shadow to the line of the nose, enhancing the depth of the image along the nose.

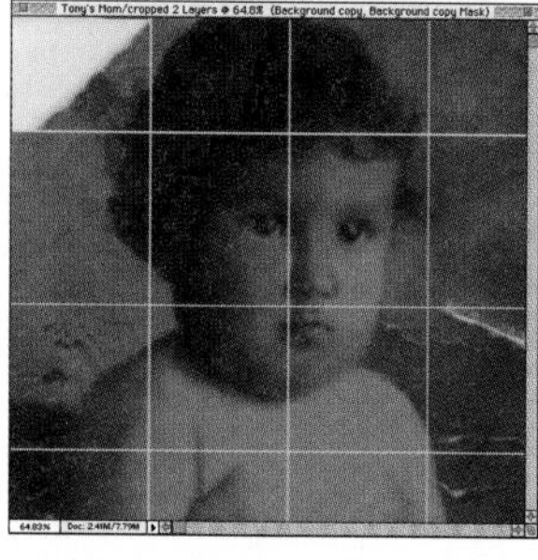

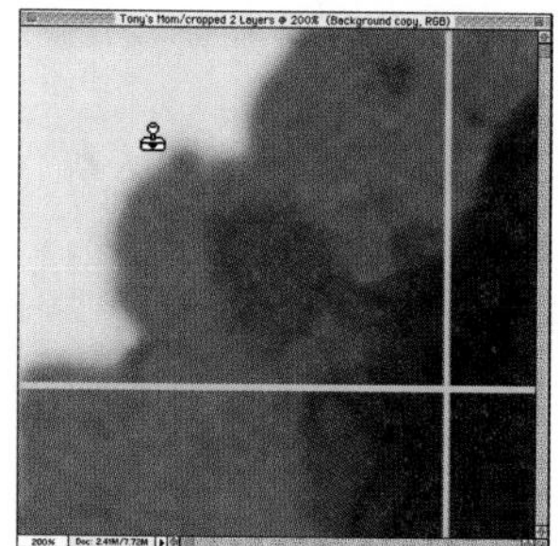

7. For images that require a lot of repair, it is helpful to do one area at a time. With this image, we first laid a grid over it (C) and progressively worked on individual grid squares (D). This technique enabled us to make sure we had done repairs on the entire image when we finished our work session.

8. You may also have to restore photographs that are ripped or have pieces missing. Often, the best tactic is to try to borrow from one portion of the image. In this case, the area above the baby's face was missing. To reproduce that section of the photograph, we increased the canvas size and then added the texture and color of the background into that new image area.

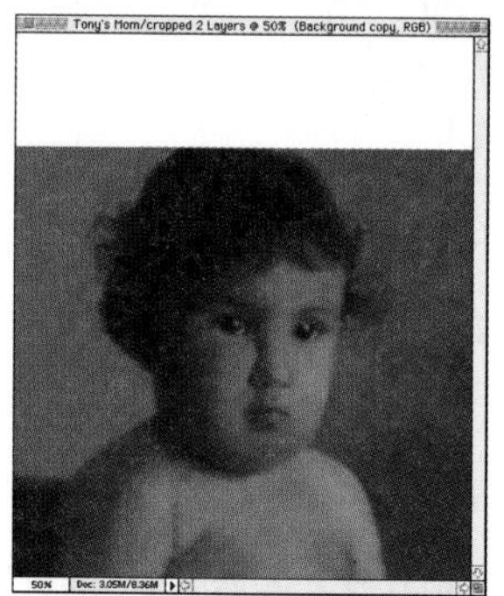

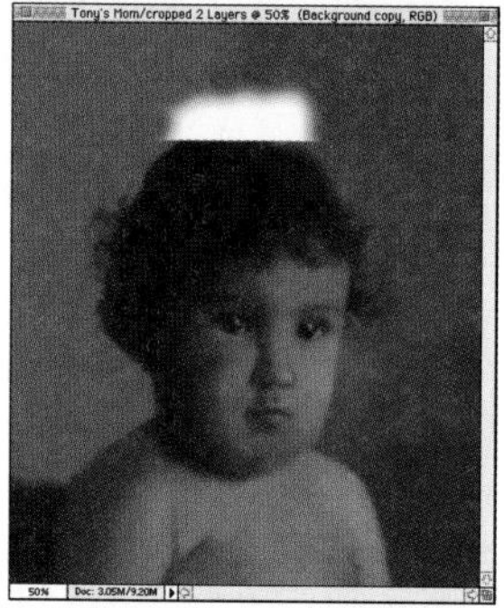

9. We selected a portion of the hair on the left of the baby's head and then copied and pasted it into a new layer. We rotated the layer 90 degrees clockwise and used the Eraser tool to blend the hair into the background.

10. To finish the photograph, we blurred it and created an oval selection. We inverted the selection and filled it with white, creating a vignette effect.

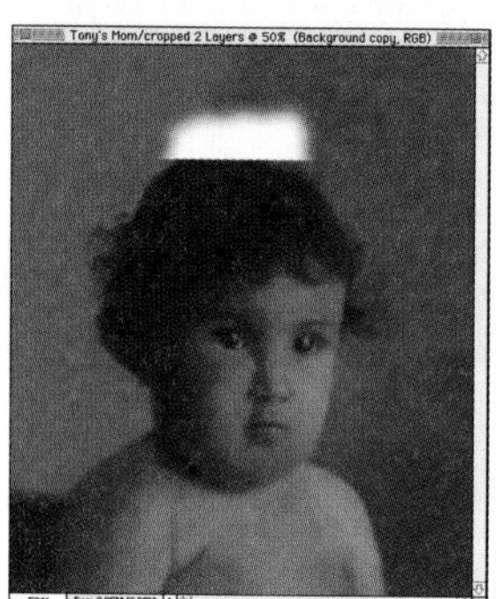

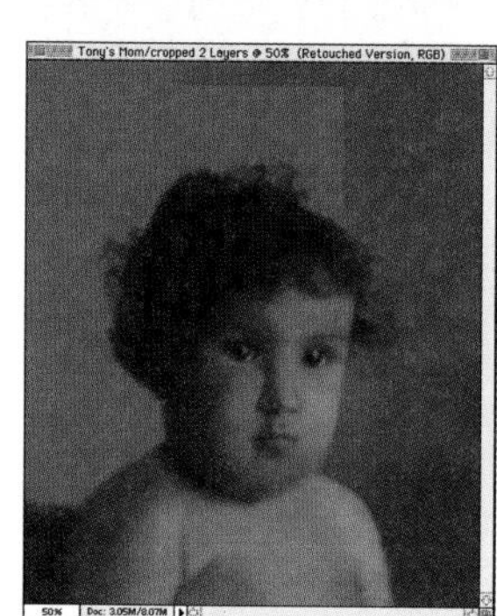

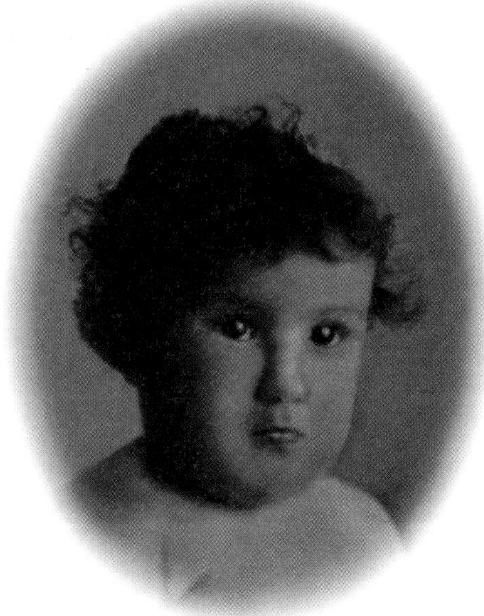

chapter 4

Scanning Photograph Originals

04 1

Scanner Designs and Mechanisms

Scanner Designs

Scanners can be grouped into three types—drum scanners, flatbed scanners, and film scanners.

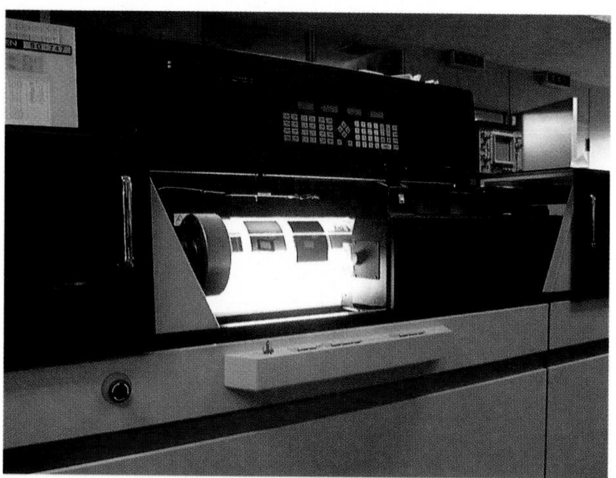

Dainippon Screen SG-747 drum scanner.

Courtesy of Shashin Kagaku Co., Ltd.

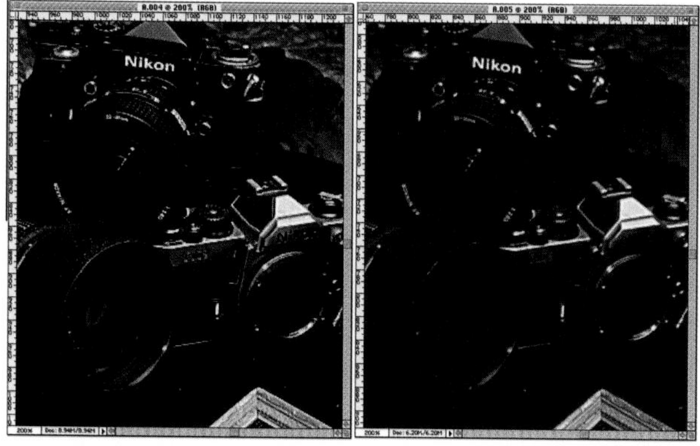

Left: Drum scanner Right: CCD scanner

Drum Scanners

Originals (reflective or transparent) are mounted on an optically clear, acrylic, cylindrical drum. The drum rotates at a high speed during scanning while the light source and light sensor move along the length of the drum. The light sensors used are *photomultipliers*. A single drum scanner can range in price from $25,000 to several hundred thousand dollars, which is as expensive as it sounds.

From the standpoint of performance, however, these scanners have many capabilities that flatbed scanners do not. In particular, their wide dynamic range is important for digital photography. The *dynamic range* is the range of difference between light and dark that the device can capture.

Imagine the black areas (shadows) of a photograph, for example, on color-reversal film that has been underexposed by one stop. These areas are almost pure black, approaching the same density as the non-exposed area of the film (maximum density). Even minute detail in these dark areas can be captured by drum scanners, enabling you to achieve the same result as if you had used the correct exposure (see left). This capability to capture detail in the darkest shadows, even on underexposed originals, is a particular strength of the drum scanner. Except for the capability of capturing detail in shadows of underexposed originals (and, of course, a much higher resolution capability), drum scanners are not significantly different from other scanners. (The one significant difference is resolution; drum scanners are generally capable of much higher optical resolution than flatbed scanners.)

Although the differences in the small printed result here are not as dramatic, the differences are significant when viewed at a zoomed-in view on the monitor. The scan on the right was scanned using an expensive, floor-standing CCD scanner.

Epson GT9500.

Blooming in an image scanned by a flatbed scanner.

Image scanned on a drum scanner.

Flatbed Scanners

In contrast to drum scanners, in which the original is mounted on a cylindrical drum, the original artwork (reflective or transparent) is kept flat when it is scanned on a flatbed scanner. Some exceptions do exist, but most flatbed scanners use CCD light sensors. Flatbed scanners are easy to use and are available in a wide range of prices from several hundred to several thousand dollars.

As far as flatbed scanning performance is concerned, if you scan a color-reversal film that has been underexposed by about one stop, it is very difficult to distinguish between the shadow areas and the maximum-density area of the black frame surrounding the image because flatbeds do not have the same dynamic range as drum scanners.

Even if a flatbed scanner is capable of capturing shadows on underexposed originals, the quality will be poor, especially compared to a drum scanner. Upon close inspection, the shadows will likely include graininess caused by electronic noise or exhibit a flared, ghost-like image called *blooming*.

Still, the progress and effort being made to improve flatbed scanner performance is impressive. Increasingly, top-of-the-line scanners from all manufacturers are able to achieve results for correctly exposed (particularly bright) originals that are virtually indistinguishable to drum scanners. For scanning reflective originals such as color prints, there is absolutely no difference in image quality when compared to drum scanners. In fact, when taking ease of mounting originals into consideration, we can say that flatbed scanners surpass drum scanners in many areas.

NOTE

Flatbed scanners do not scan shadow areas as well as drum scanners, but for reflective originals such as silver halide color or monochrome prints, they are perfectly adequate. This is because the maximum density of reflective originals is lower than that of color-reversal film, so the CCDs can easily capture the shadow areas. If you are scanning only reflective originals, some flatbed scanners can actually acquire much higher-quality images than drum scanners.

Nikon LS-1000.

Image scanned on a film scanner.

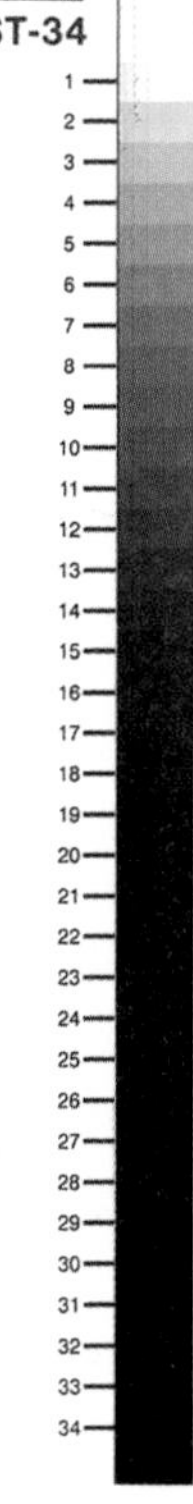

The Kodak Scanner Step Tablet ST-34: A scanner that can differentiate around 30 steps is an excellent scanner.

Film Scanners

Structurally, film scanners are similar to flatbed scanners, but they are designed specifically for scanning 35 mm or 4×5 color-reversal film or color-negative film.

The number of these scanners available on the market has rapidly increased as digital photography and advanced photo system cameras have gained popularity. They are the same as flatbed scanners in that they use CCD light sensors. However, because their design is optimized for exposing small areas on film surfaces and they are equipped with special optical lenses, their performance is superior to flatbed scanners, which are designed specifically for scanning reflective originals.

The dynamic range of film scanners is slightly better than that of flatbed scanners. More importantly, because the optics are designed specifically for scanning film, the film holder doesn't use glass. Several characteristics of CCD electronics solve the difficulties of scanning dark areas, and some film scanners approach the capabilities of drum scanners for scan-image quality. (They are not exactly the same, but are very close....)

The bottom line is that if you are seriously considering adding digital photography to your studio capabilities, we recommend that you invest in as good a film scanner as your budget allows.

NOTE

■ A scanner's dynamic density range is expressed numerically, as in D = 3.3. This number represents the range, from the film's lightest to darkest optical densities, that the scanner is capable of capturing.

For example, the maximum density difference on Kodachrome (KPR25) reversal film, from the area in which the whites are blown out (base density) to the maximum density area (meaning sufficiently deep blacks), is D = 3.3–3.5.

An easy way to understand a density difference of D = 3.5 is to imagine the difference between the combined density of three 1.0 neutral-density filters plus one 0.5 neutral-density filter stacked on top of each other on a lightbox, and the density on the lightbox with no filters.

Many drum scanners have the capability to capture a dynamic range of D = 3.5 or higher. With the exception of a few top-quality devices, the actual use (versus manufacturer claims) dynamic range of flatbed scanners is D = 2.8–3.0.

■ Most scanner manufacturers make public what the density dynamic ranges are for their scanners. Depending on the densitometer used, however, the optical density values can vary greatly. We measure our scanner density values by scanning the Kodak Scanner Step Tablet ST-34 and seeing how many steps the scanner can actually differentiate, as shown on the left.

We would like to request that manufacturers decide on one practical method of expressing density dynamic range that can be used on all scanners and can be easily understood by a range of skill levels.

Scanner Signal Generation

Technically speaking, a scanner generates electrical signals corresponding to the densities of the original photograph. To the typical scanner user, the technology of signal generation is complicated and seemingly irrelevant. Knowing at least a little bit about it, however, can help you understand what is important for maintaining optimal scan-image quality.

Analog to Digital Conversion

The continuously changing electrical signals sent out directly from the scanner's light sensors are *analog signals*. All scanners are slightly different, but most use amplifiers to boost the analog signals and apply logarithmic compression to them.

After that, the signals undergo analog-to-digital conversion (A / D conversion) and are sent to the computer (see the bottom illustration on the next page).

NOTE

A stable precision circuit is required to control the analog electrical signal before it is converted to a digital signal. If you can effectively control this analog electrical signal, you can acquire extremely high-quality images. Most high-end scanners are designed so that you can control basic scan-image signals by manipulating them at the analog signal stage. This is another reason why these scanners fall into the several hundred thousand dollar price range.

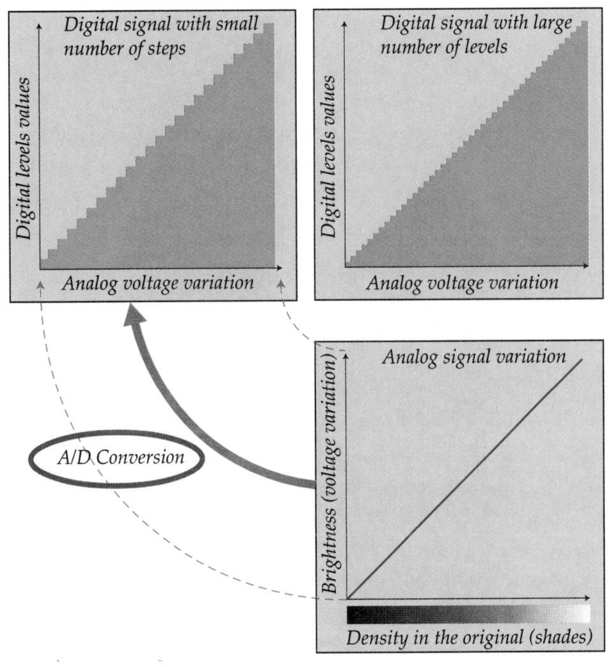

Number of Digital Levels

When the analog signal is converted into a digital signal, the differences in brightness from the lightest area to the darkest area (variations in voltage) are divided into 256, 1,024, or 4,096 levels, as shown in the illustration on the left.

The terms "8-bit," "10-bit," or "12-bit" internal processing refer to the internal number of bit depth that you find described in scanner brochures. The greater the number of bits, the greater the number of levels and thus the better the scanner.

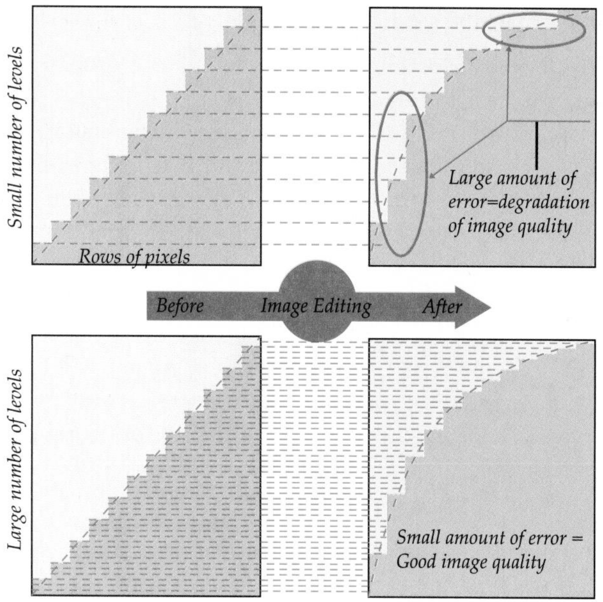

High end scanners that allow adjustment at the analog stage.

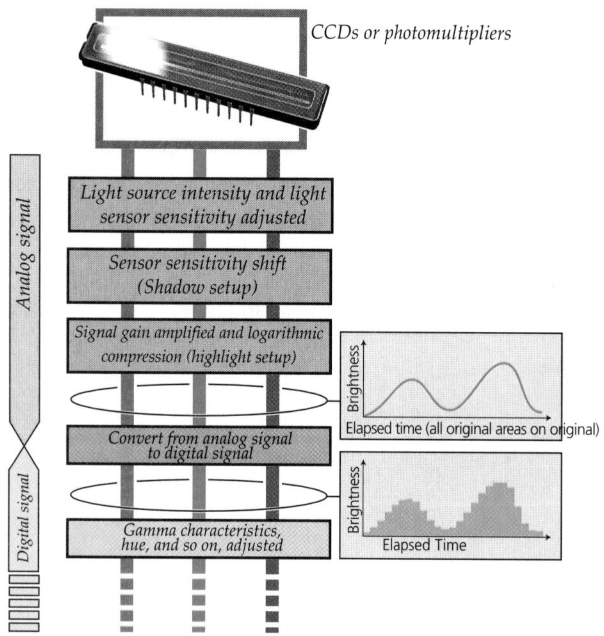

Overview of scanner signal generation.

Number of Steps and Image Quality

Scanners all come equipped with software called *scanner drivers*. This software enables you to view a preview scan and make a variety of adjustments on it, including lightening or darkening the image, or increasing or decreasing the feeling of depth in the image. After you are finished with your adjustments based on the preview, you can make the main scan.

Although an image typically ends up with 256 levels per channel after it's scanned, if the internal bit depth of the scanner is not sufficient then problems in the quality of the scan will occur. These problems, which are due to "quantization error," usually appear when you make post scan adjustments to the image. Problems related to quantization error typically appear in the image as perceptible tone jumps, called "banding," or as unevenness (graininess) in smooth tones such as flesh tones. These problems can be avoided by using scanners with greater bit depth.

The more bit depth, or tone levels, you have available when you're adjusting the preview scan before making the final scan, the more you will be able to maintain image quality. However, if you make no adjustments at all during the pre-final scan stage then you're not taking advantage of the high bit capability of your scanner. If you only use the default settings in the scanner driver, there is little difference in image quality between 8-bit and 12-bit color scanners.

As noted earlier, some high-end scanners enable a user to make a variety of adjustments after the preview scan has been made, but before the analog signal to digital signal conversion takes place. This means the amount of quantization error will be so small that it can virtually be ignored. Unfortunately, scanner manufacturers do not make public exactly which adjustments can be made to the analog signal on which scanners.

Most high-end models from all manufacturers, however, should allow some kind of signal adjustment at the analog stage. In our experience, high-end devices such as the Nikon LS series, the Epson GT9500, PFU Corporation's PS4800, and the Micronix Scanmaker allow some basic adjustments at the analog stage, usually at least to the highlight.

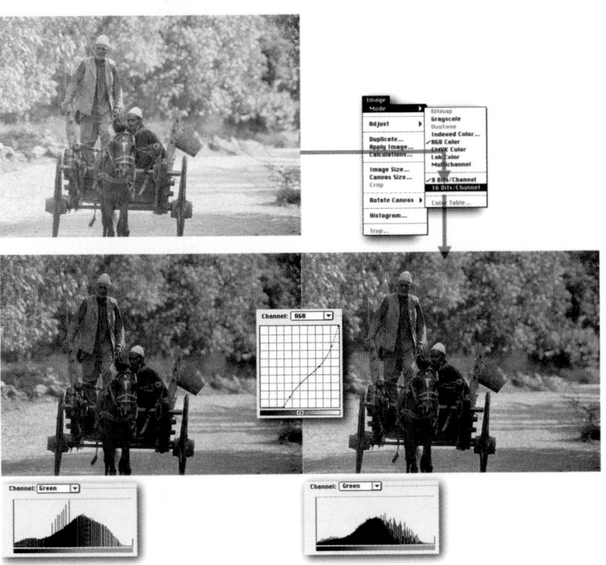

Scanners Capable of Generating 36-bit Color

Some scanners can generate more than 8 bits per channel (8-bit×3 color channels = 24-bit color images). By using a 12-bit (12 bits×3 color channels = 36-bit color images) or a 16-bit (16 bits×3 color channels = 48-bit color images) scanner, you have more information, or levels of tone, to adjust during the scanning stage. Take advantage of this information by making many adjustments and corrections to the image during the scanning stage. All images, however, regardless of the scanner's original bit level, are distilled back down into 8-bit per channel when acquired in Photoshop (as well as most imaging applications). What's important is that even if you only make minor adjustments or corrections while scanning with the 12- or 16-bit devices, you are still able to achieve better results than if you'd originally scanned the image with only an 8-bit device. The benefit of initially scanning at a higher bit level extends to later adjustments of the image in Photoshop, too.

The most critical errors to avoid with these scanners are letting the highlights become blown out and letting the shadows become too open.

In Photoshop 4.0, images with 8 bits per channel (24-bit RGB) can be converted into images with 16 bits per channel (48-bit RGB). This is a recommended step to take, especially when making adjustments such as Curves, Levels, or Selective Color, because it provides an increased range of tones to work with. The difference between making these adjustments in 16-bit versus 8-bit color is a difference in image quality. A Curves adjustment, for example, was applied to two copies of the image to the left, first in 8-bit/channel mode for one copy and then in 16-bit/channel mode for the other copy. By comparing the histograms of the two images, you can see that the 8-bit/channel took an initially smaller range of tones and distributed them widely, resulting in gaps in the histogram that resemble the teeth of a comb. The 16-bit adjustment, however, used an initially wider range of tones to distribute throughout the image, resulting in a more solid histogram. In terms of image quality, this translates into smoother tonal gradations in the version that was adjusted in 16-bit/channel mode. After you have adjusted the color and tone in 16-bit/channel mode, you must return the image to 8-bit mode (very few Photoshop functions are available in 16-bit mode).

04 2

Scanning Preparation

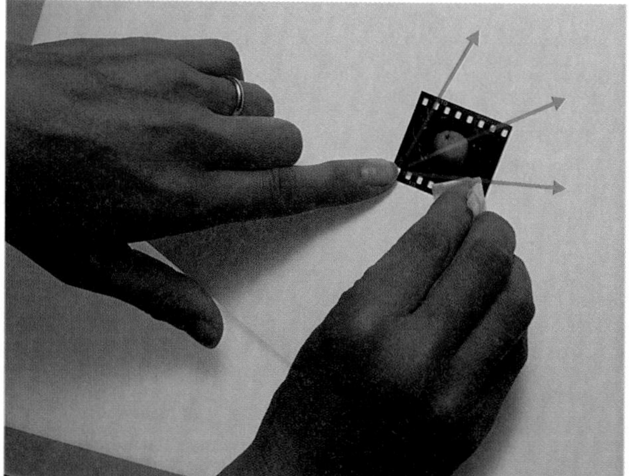

Some Considerations Before Scanning

Just as there are limits to how much you can save an incorrectly exposed photograph in the chemical darkroom, there are limits to how much you can save a poor scan in the digital lightroom. To ensure optimum quality from your scanner, take the following preparatory steps before scanning.

Watch for Dust

Make sure there is no dust on your photographs, just as you would if you were using an enlarger. Darkroom blowers and brushes are effective for removing dust. Also, for places with a lot of static electricity, a static eliminator is useful.

If the surface of your photograph is dirty, lay the photograph on a sheet of clean, lint-free paper (such as copier paper) and use a soft tissue with a small amount of film cleaner to wipe it. The trick is to move the tissue all the way across the film and past the outside edge onto the paper, as shown to the left. Also, make sure not to use the same tissue to wipe the same area again. Otherwise, you end up putting the contaminants right back onto the photograph.

Oil from your fingers is a great enemy. Wash your hands with soap and use lint-free white gloves before handling film. If lint-free gloves are not available, try using a small amount of film cleaner on your fingertips to remove excess oils.

NOTE

Another method to lift dust from the film and the scanner glass surface is with the adhesive from memo pads.

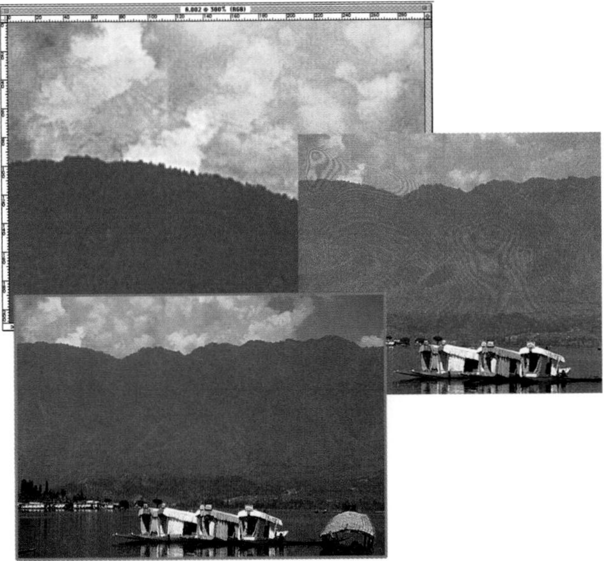

Even Newton's rings that you cannot distinguish at first glance (bottom) become obvious on the entire image surface if the image is enlarged or if the saturation is significantly increased.

Newton's Rings

When you mount glossy photobromide paper or film on the glass surface of a scanner, Newton's rings might occur. If you scan the photograph as is, Newton's rings appear on the digital image as well, and no amount of image editing (cloning, and so on) can adequately remove them. The time taken to remove them after scanning is far greater than the time needed to prevent the problem in the first place.

Several methods for preventing Newton's rings are described in the following:

■ The use of anti-Newton's rings powder is standard practice on prepress scanners. A small amount of powder is applied to the surface of the original. This powder is available from prepress suppliers, so inquire about obtaining it at a local prepress shop. In a pinch, you also can use desiccating powder, such as baby powder, instead.

A small amount of anti-Newton's rings powder is sprayed into the air and settles on the surface of the photograph.

To coat the original surface with a small amount of powder, spray the powder into a box about the size of a monitor. Then, when the powder is just about settled, slowly place the original inside the box. After a while, gently take the original out and it should be coated with powder. Experiment a number of times to find the correct amount of powder, as shown on the left.

After scanning, be sure to remove the powder using first a blower, then a brush, and then cleaner. Avoid spraying and removing powder near scanners or computers.

■ If you are using a drum scanner, it is becoming more common to use paraffin filling oil instead of anti-Newton's rings powder. This is also available at prepress supply shops. It is slightly complicated to use, and we will not go into details here. Your scanner dealer, however, or a high-end scanner operator should be able to show you how to use it (see left).

Use a fiberglass brush to coat the surface of the film with paraffin filling oil.

■ If you are using a flatbed scanner with single-side glass original holders, place the emulsion side of the film down on the glass side of the holder. This should control Newton's rings in most cases. Because the photograph becomes a flopped image, however, you have to use mirroring to reverse the orientation afterwards.

Watch for light
leaking through!

Area around the film is masked with black tape (for photographic studios). Be careful to prevent light from leaking along the edges.

Focus

If you are using a flatbed scanner, particularly one with an optical resolution over 1,000 dpi, the depth of focus at the original scanning surface tends to be shallow. If the original bows on the flatbed, the image will be blurred; so set the original in place precisely, using something like low-tack adhesive tape. It is not unusual for the large glass cover to be inadequate for securing strongly curled originals—35 mm in particular—in place.

Furthermore, if you are using a film scanner to scan color-reversal film that has already been mounted, if the mounts are bent, a focus shift might occur in one area only. When this happens, you should remove the mounts and use the film holder that came with the scanner. Yes, this often seems like a lot of trouble, but it is the only solution.

Nikon

When the Scanner is Not in Use

To prevent dust from getting into the scanning optics, use a plastic cover of some kind to protect your scanner when it is not in use. For film scanners in particular, dust on some internal mechanisms can cause miscalibration of the scanner or streaking on scanned images.

04 3

Basic Scanner Operations

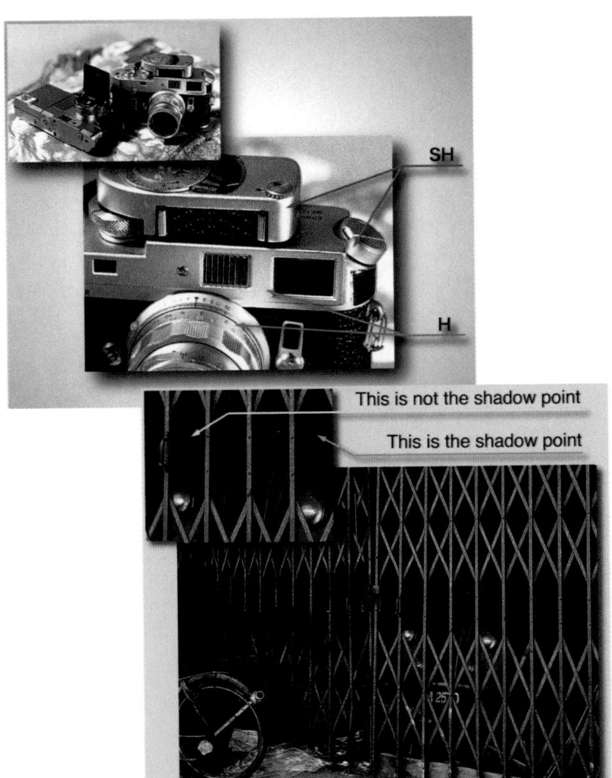
SH
H
This is not the shadow point
This is the shadow point

First check the highlights and the shadows.

Use a high quality loupe.

Look at the Original Carefully Before Mounting It

As we discussed in the Chapter 3 section about tone curve adjustment, the first thing to consider during scanning is the highlight and shadow setup. The highlight scanning setup in particular affects the overall quality of the image. This might seem repetitious, but let's review this material again.

Highlights

When you use something like a color printer, a press, or a monitor to print or display an image, the purest possible white areas of the image are the color of the paper or the monitor signal at maximum. Image highlights are not these pure whites, however, but slightly darker whites. Highlights are tones that create just-barely-visible detail on paper or other media, and they come in different forms (see "H" on the left).

Shadows

You can think about shadows similarly to the way you think about highlights. They are not simply the pure black areas (just as highlights are not purely white areas). Pure blacks are created by laying down 100-percent printing ink or color printer colorant so that you cannot distinguish any tonality. Shadows in photographs are not this pure black, but slightly lighter blacks. Shadows are color that create just-barely-visible detail against pure black.

Before mounting your original on the scanner, always carefully check it. If the original is on color-reversal film, use a large loupe that has about 5× magnification to carefully scrutinize it. Then determine where the highlights, specular highlights, and shadows are, and as a precaution, make a sketch of the photograph marking those areas and how bright they are.

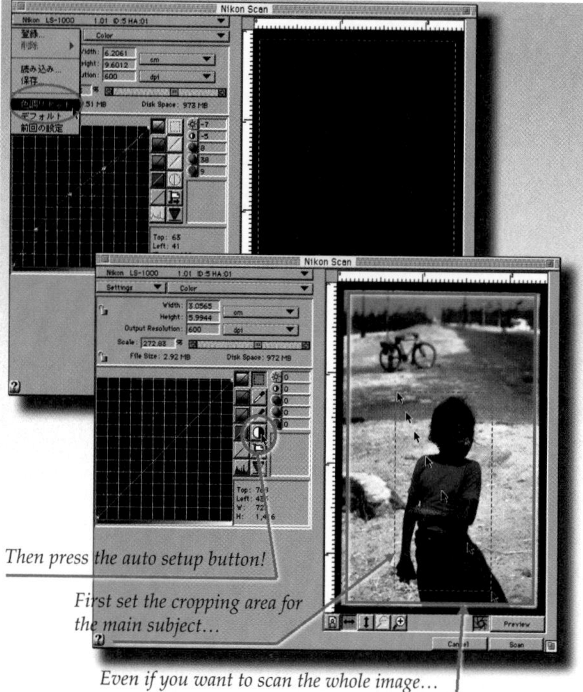

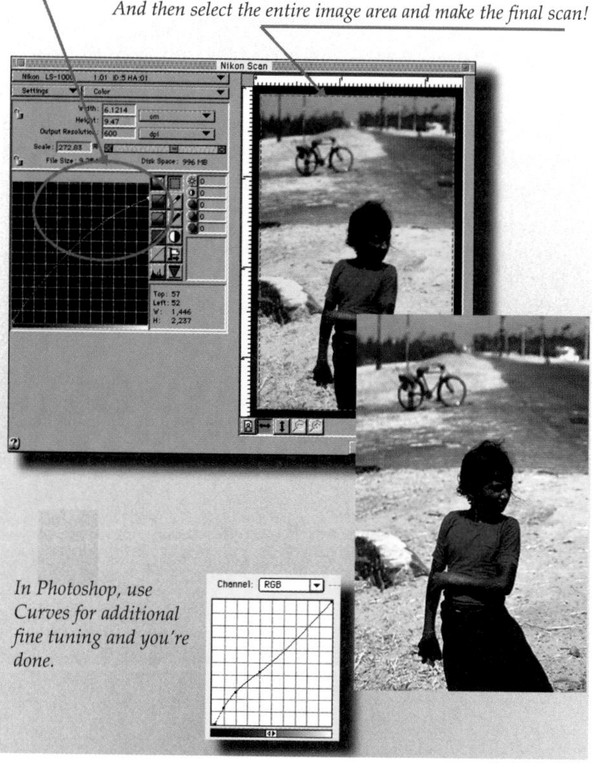

And then select the entire image area and make the final scan!
Nikon Scan
Even if you want to scan the whole image…
Next, make the manual fine tune adjustments…
In Photoshop, use Curves for additional fine tuning and you're done.
Channel: RGB

An example of the Nikon LS-1000 scanner software.

Scanner Setup and Scanning

Scanner operation consists of the following procedures and factors that you should consider when you scan. No matter which scanner you use, these basic operations and personal judgments about your photograph's characteristics will be the same.

Preview Scan

After you have carefully studied your photograph and have decided how you want the final scan to look, insert or mount the original into the scanner.

Scanner driver software varies greatly from scanner to scanner, but on the majority of scanners the first task is to make a preview scan. Before making the preview scan, reset all scan settings (if they've been changed) back to their default settings. There might be times, however, when you are scanning more than one of the same type of original. If the characteristics of the originals are the same (same highlights, shadows, and so on), then you can save time by applying settings from previous scans (such as using the same aperture, exposure, and developing times for making prints from similar negatives). If the characteristics are different, you should return to the default settings and start over. Some scanners also require focus adjustment at this stage.

Determining the Scan Area for the Main Scan

After making the preview scan, crop (or select) the image in the preview window to specify the area of the main scan. You should do this even if you plan to scan the entire image for the final scan. In order to use the scanner's auto setup, for example, it is best to designate a portion (for example, the main subject) of the image as a reference for the function to base optimum settings on.

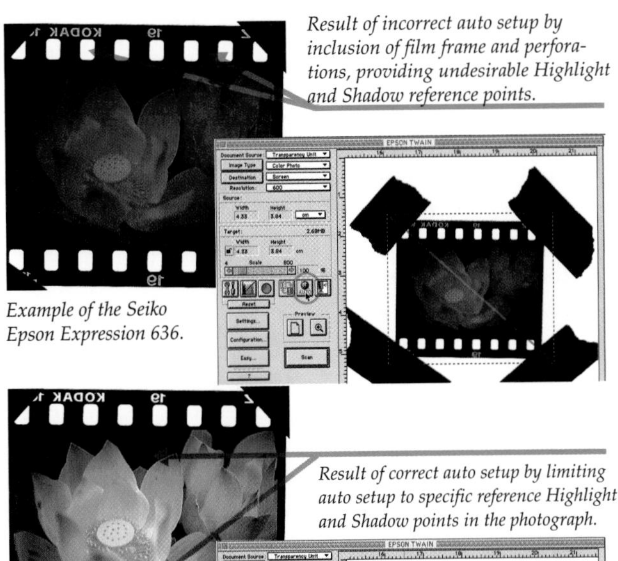

Result of incorrect auto setup by inclusion of film frame and perforations, providing undesirable Highlight and Shadow reference points.

Example of the Seiko Epson Expression 636.

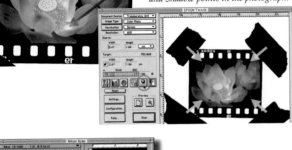

Result of correct auto setup by limiting auto setup to specific reference Highlight and Shadow points in the photograph.

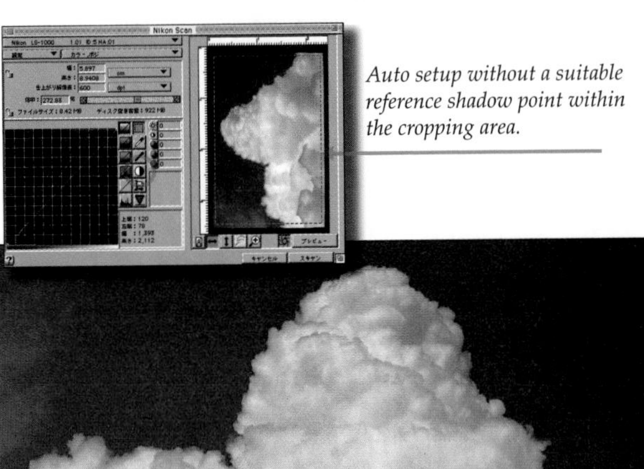

Auto setup without a suitable reference shadow point within the cropping area.

If you try to use auto setup when there is no pure black shadow point, the darkest area of the photograph will end up set to pure black. In this case, the darkest blue of the sky became black (above). If you widen the cropping area, however, so it includes all or a portion of the black frame (avoid including film perforations, though), the scanner bases the black on the border. In this case, the sky is accurately scanned as blue (right).

Auto Setup

Although the name of this function differs from scanner to scanner, most devices have a way to automatically set the highlight and shadow points (auto setup).

The best way to use this function is to analyze the highlight and shadow points of your image, then make a small enough crop or selection to include only those areas. This forces the auto setup to base its highlight and shadow values on areas that you determine need optimal values.

Most auto setup functions set the RGB value for the brightest pixel in the cropping area to 255 and the RGB value for the darkest pixel to 0. This means that the only time you can effectively use a scanner's auto setup function (without further manual adjustment) is when you have a photograph with suitable specular highlights and suitable deep shadows within the cropped area.

One pitfall to avoid is the inadvertent inclusion of the black frame around color-reversal film, or the perforated frame of 35 mm film, in your auto setup scan. In the latter case, for example, the auto setup function will determine that your photograph has very bright highlights and very dark shadows. The result is that the density of the actual highlight point of your image (which should be darker than the perforation) will be *too* dark in the final scan, and the actual shadow point (which should be lighter than the black frame area) will become too light. (See the caption below for a tip on when to intentionally use the black border to set a shadow density).

This is essentially the same thing as when certain lighting situations fool a TTL averaging light meter. Backlit subjects result in an underexposed foreground, or a person in black clothing standing against a black background ends up overexposed.

The finished image.

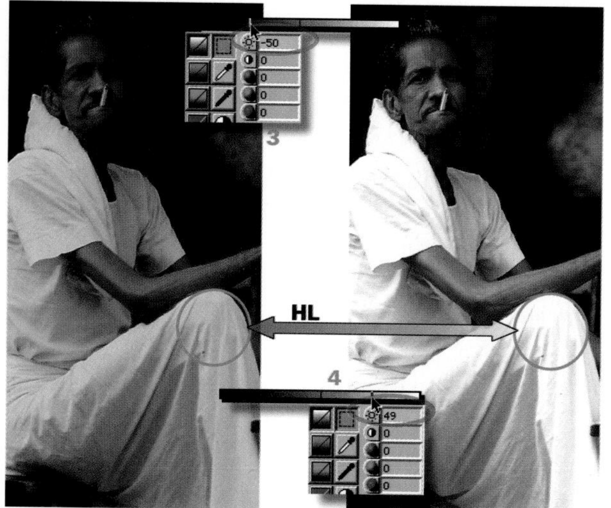

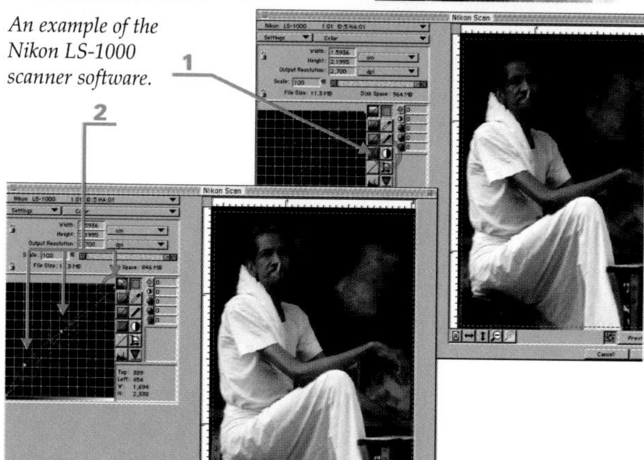

An example of the Nikon LS-1000 scanner software.

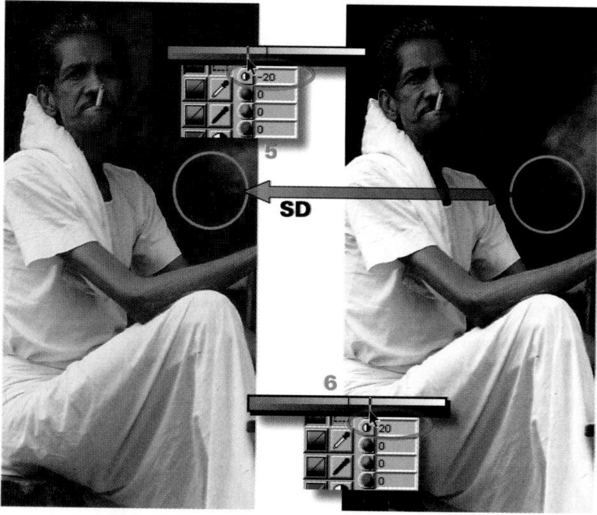

1: Auto setup, 2: Tone curve setup, 3: Results of negative highlight setting, 4: Results of positive highlight setting, 5: Results of negative shadow setting, 6: Results of positive shadow setting.

Manual Setup

Exposure setup for silver halide cameras uses a single control (for example, the camera's lightmeter) that makes the entire photograph uniformly lighter or darker. With manual exposure setup on a scanner, however, you can have "exposure" control over specific tonal regions of the image. Separate adjustments of the areas discussed in the following give precise control over the quality of your final scan.

■ Highlight setup (top left)

This sets the original highlight area to a desired brightness level. On some scanners, this is called *contrast setup* rather than highlight setup. But because this is actually a function that sets the lightness of the highlight, it is not meant to be used as a contrast adjustment. Even if this is called a contrast adjustment on your scanner, the area it is concerned with is really only the highlight area.

■ Shadow setup (bottom left)

This sets the original shadow area to the desired brightness level. On some scanners, this is called *brightness setup*. This name gives the impression that the function somehow adjusts the brightness for the entire image, but in reality, this function is used only to adjust the density of the shadows.

On most scanners, when you use shadow setup, the highlight changes again, too. When this happens, you can use the auto setup function described in the preceding to readjust the highlight, or you can readjust the highlight manually.

Optimal scan result.

Gamma = 200
Gamma = 150
Gamma = 100
Tone curve (Gamma = around 200)

An example of the Seiko Epson Expression 636 scanner software.

■ Gamma or tone curve setup

This sets the original midtone area to the desired level of brightness. The essential elements of tone curve adjustment are described in Chapter 3-5, "Tone Curve Adjustment." You can make tone curve adjustments on images in Photoshop after scanning, but if possible, use the built-in gamma and tone curve adjustments in your scanner software to create an image that has characteristics approximate to what you need. Refer to Chapter 3, "Correcting Photographs," for a discussion of tone curve adjustments.

An example of the Seiko Epson Expression 636 scanner software.

■ Gray balance

On some scanners, there is also a control for adjusting the neutral gray point in the preview image. Use this function when you have a spot on the original that you want to set as neutral gray.

■ Color vividness

Some scanners also enable you to adjust the vividness of the colors. If you use this function, it does not affect the gray balance and only affects the vividness of specific colors, such as red or green. You can adjust the colors so they are more pure or closer to gray (less pure) and then make your scan. For slightly overexposed photographs, one trick for creating a useful scan is to adjust the colors so they are more gray.

Taking Levels Readings

Most scanner driver software includes a function for moving the cursor about the preview image so you can take readings of individual RGB levels. Using this function, you can manually adjust the highlights or shadows incrementally by taking a reading, then readjusting the highlights or shadows, then taking another reading and readjusting, and so on, until you achieve your desired highlight or shadow level.

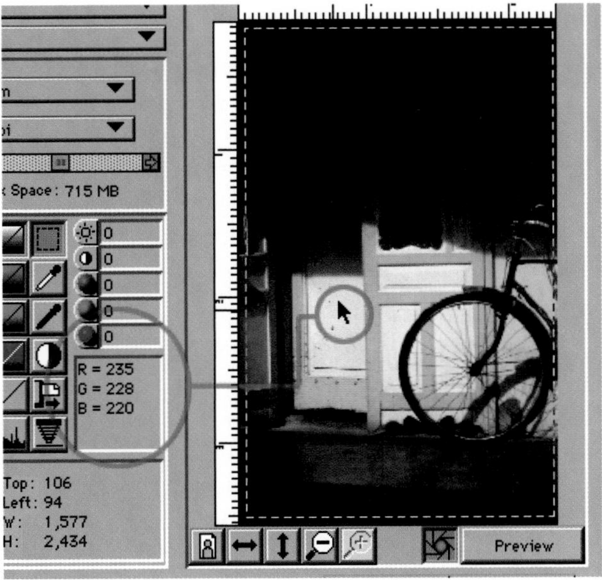

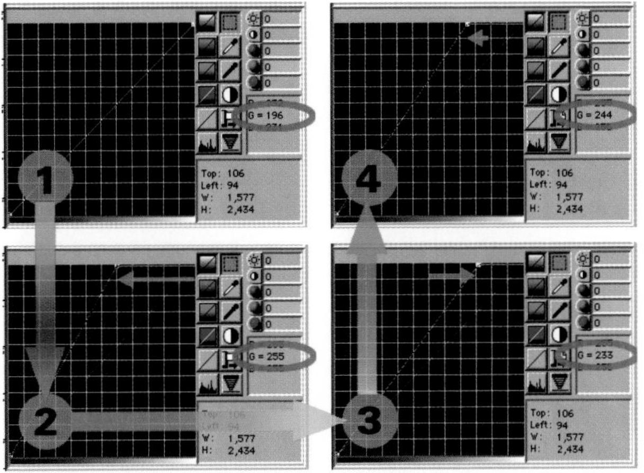

An example of the Nikon LS-1000 scanner software.

Let's say you make a preview scan, for example, and by viewing the RGB levels, you see that the Green channel has a high of 196 pixels (see #1, lower-left illustration). In order to set a value of approximately 245 for the highlight based on this reading, you slide the white point of the graph to the left to brighten the image. After a second preview scan, you measure the white point and discover that you've overcorrected, pushing the highlight value up to 255 (#2). Next, you return to the curve, pull the slider back to the right about a third, and preview again. This time, you overcorrected in the opposite direction, decreasing the values for the white to 233 (#3).

At this point, you've made two previews—one that was a little too light and one that was a little too dark. So, by sliding the white point of the graph to the left just a little bit, you end up at a position on the graph in between the two previous positions and succeed in getting the right highlight (#4). The principle behind this is exactly the same as trying to determine the best print exposure in the darkroom. In the darkroom, the exposure times for the first print might turn out too light and for the second print might be too dark. As a result, you can easily pinpoint the correct exposure time as an exposure time in between the first two.

Unfortunately, there can be times when the levels values in the preview image do not accurately represent the levels values you'll end up with in the final, full-resolution scan. When you discover this happening, you have to think of the levels values in the preview image as general guides or approximate reference points only. In the event that the preview measurements are way off, or you don't have this function at all, there are methods for determining and setting proper highlights.

Standard Targets

Every original is different, but the following should provide guidelines for designating the highlight, shadow, and midpoint targets for the average photograph.

■ Highlight areas

Highlight RGB levels should all be set to approximately 250 for bright or shiny areas with little to no detail. This includes highlight (Specular Highlight) areas that are so bright that you suspect they'll blow out in print if you were to make them any lighter. For white areas in which you know you want to hold detail—such as a white shirt on a sunny day—you should try to set RGB values to at least 240 but no higher than 245.

Detailess white areas.

An area in which you want to leave some white detail.

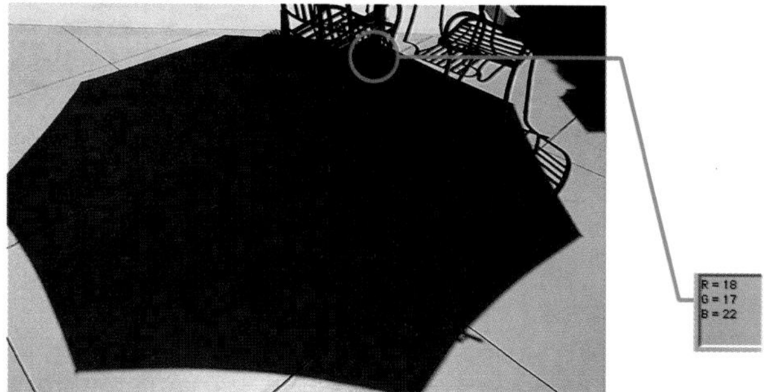

An area in which you want to leave some black detail.

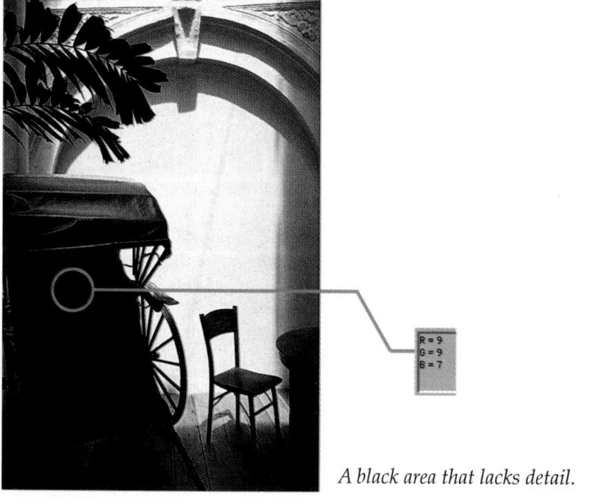

A black area that lacks detail.

■ Shadow areas

Shadow RGB levels should all be set to a minimum of 8 for areas so dark that, if you make them any darker, all the detail in the black areas will be lost on the hard copy. If you have very dark areas in which you know you want to hold detail—such as a black poodle sitting in the shade—set those RGB values to approximately 20.

Also, if your original does not have a standard black and you can't decide what to use, set the shadows so the values for the black frame around the color reversal film are around 3–5. If it is an underexposed original, set the shadows so the frame area will be 5–8; and if it is overexposed, set them so the frame area will be 0. Adjusting shadow settings with the black frame is similar to Zone System exposure, in which basing the exposure on a particular Zone lightens or darkens the overall exposure.

■ Midtone gray areas

Because there are many levels of middle gray tone, from bright gray to dark gray, we cannot definitively say which level of gray is correct for every situation. If you consider, however, that an 18 percent gray reflection card (such as the Kodak Gray Card) is a standard for determining exposure, then you can consider this an accurate guide for determining scanner midtone settings. A standard 18 percent gray reflection card included in a scanned photograph should have levels between around 100–110. If you regularly use a Kodak Gray Scale Q-13 (or Q-14), the M section on the scale is the same as an 18 percent gray card.

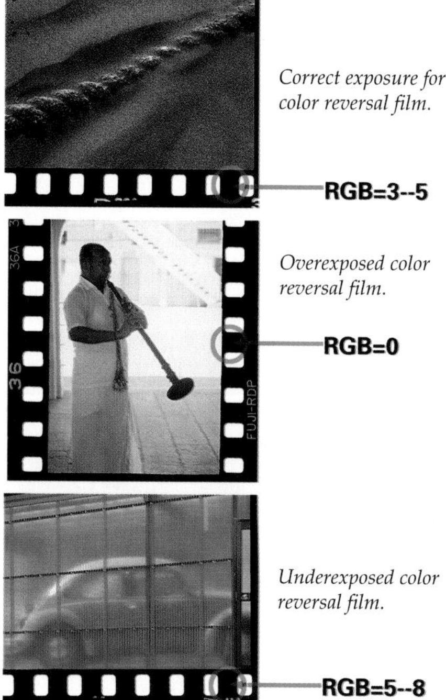

Correct exposure for color reversal film.

Overexposed color reversal film.

Underexposed color reversal film.

RGB=125---135

RGB=100---110

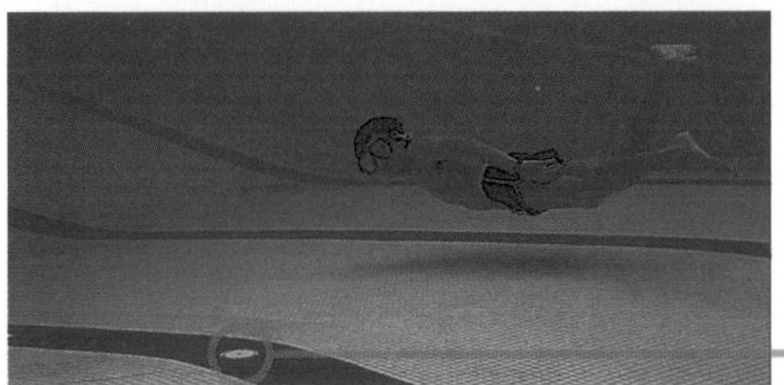

NOTE

■ It is possible to create scanner settings for specific film, camera, and exposure combinations by including a grayscale in film tests. Using a particular brand of film and a camera we frequently use, for example, we take a series of photographs of a Kodak Q-13 Gray Scale, plus and minus 2 ½ stops in ½ stop brackets. Then, for specific brackets (such as +0.5EV, +/-0EV, and –0.5EV), we set up our scanner so the levels value for the A section of the gray scale is 245, the levels value for the 6th section of the gray scale is 128, and the levels value for the B section is 20. (For prints scanned on a flatbed scanner the B point is 10.) We then save these settings labeled with the type of the film and particular exposure. Then, whenever we have to scan a particular exposure on that type of film, a saved scanner setting based on the grayscale can quickly be applied. Similarly, the same method can be used to establish ideal digital camera settings.

■ Ideally, the individual R, G, and B levels would always be exactly the same for highlight, shadow, and midtones. Very rarely, however, will highlights and shadows have the exact same values. Shadows, particularly in color-reversal film and silver halide prints, almost always have a color cast. In situations in which the values are not all the same, and you want to adjust the highlight or shadow without changing the color cast, try the following. For a highlight, determine which of the RGB values on the scanner shows the highest level. This channel is your point of reference as you make the tone curve adjustment to the scan. While you make the adjustment, watch the reference point channel as it approaches a highlight value, such as 245. Although the value of the other channels changes too, the original ratio of the channel values to each other remains the same. You end up with a brighter scan that is true to the original color cast. The opposite is true for maintaining a color cast in the shadow values. Select the channel with the lowest level as your point of reference, and adjust the curve until that value reaches the desired shadow point value.

■ A similar approach applies to setting the midtone gray. If the gray balance is not right, you can adjust the RGB values with the tone curve on the scanner (gamma) to set a general target value (such as 128). Or, if there is a strong color cast, you can lessen while still leaving a slight cast by adjusting only the curve for that color, as shown in the bottom left. The most neutral midtone setting is one in which the average of the three different channels is approximately 128. If you want to keep the nuance of a color cast intact, adjust the midtones so at least one channel is close to 128; a slight difference between this channel and the other channels results in a color cast in the midtones of the image.

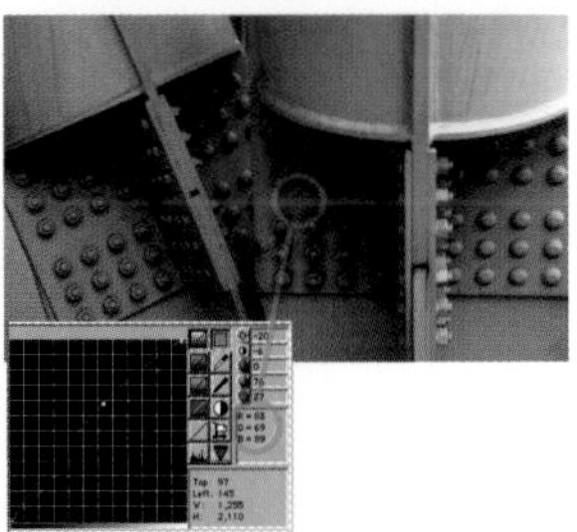

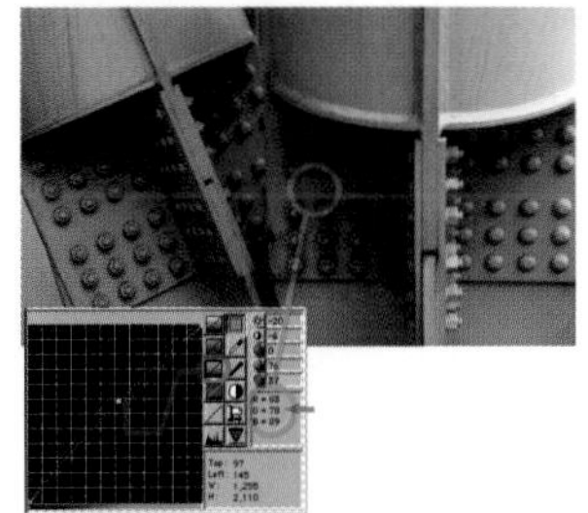

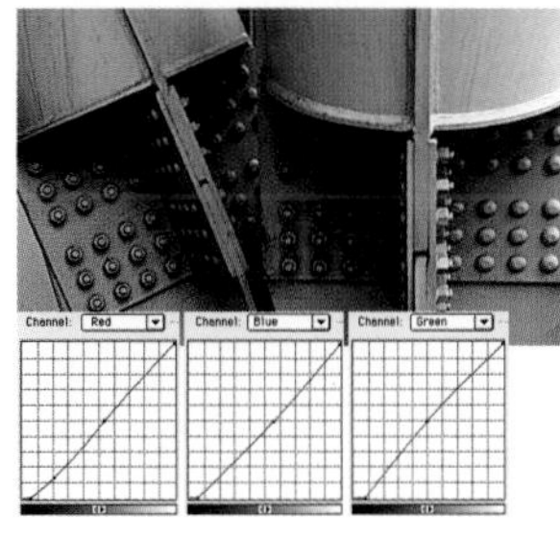

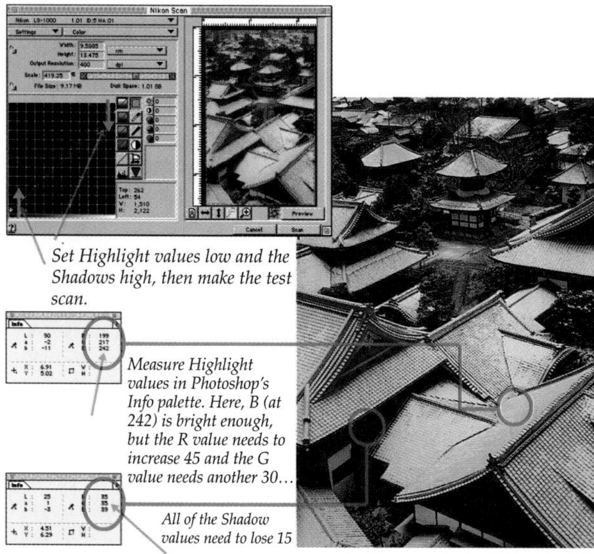

Nikon Scan
Set Highlight values low and the Shadows high, then make the test scan.
Measure Highlight values in Photoshop's Info palette. Here, B (at 242) is bright enough, but the R value needs to increase 45 and the G value needs another 30…
All of the Shadow values need to lose 15

In the scanner software, brighten the R and G values by adjusting the R and G curves separately. Then, set the shadows on the RGB composite curve to the default setting. Make final scan. In this case overall contrast was improved by making the snow whiter and the shadows a bit darker.

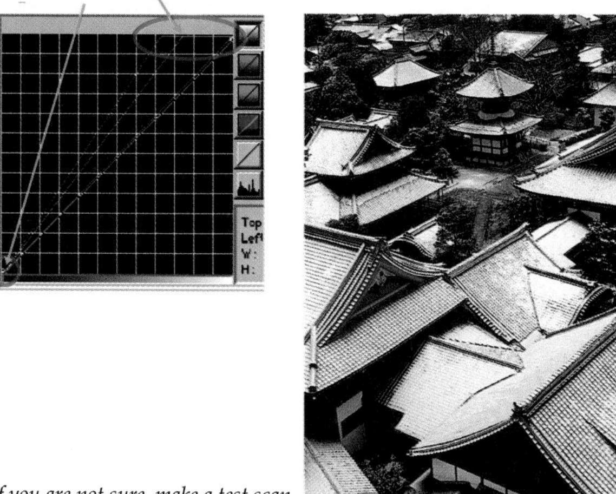

If you are not sure, make a test scan.

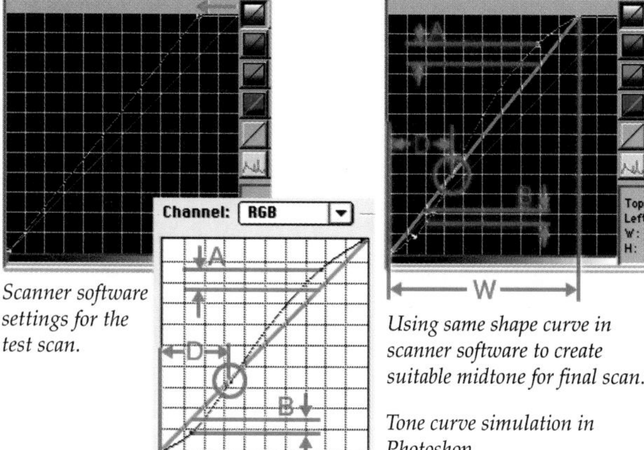

Scanner software settings for the test scan.

Using same shape curve in scanner software to create suitable midtone for final scan.

Tone curve simulation in Photoshop.

Remember the characteristics of A, B, D and W in the Photoshop Curve's function so that you can duplicate them in the scanner tone curve adjustment function.

When you can't check fine areas on the preview image but need a precise scan, skip the preview scan altogether and base your judgments on a series of medium-resolution test scans. To minimize test scan time and file size, set the test scan size to half the size (in pixels) of the final scan size. Also, select or crop only the most important parts (a highlight, a midtone, a shadow) of the image you need in order to determine scanner settings.

Start with settings that keep your highlights slightly dark, your shadows slightly light, and your midtones fairly neutral (a setting you usually use or the default setting). Your goal through testing is to determine what the optimum settings will be. These settings provide certain advantages:

■ If the highlights are scanned slightly dark (about 235–240), you'll prevent the problem of causing the highlights to blow out through further adjustments of the tone curve.

■ Similarly, if the shadows are scanned slightly light, you can prevent the problem of causing details in the shadows to block up through further adjustments of the tone curve.

■ To determine midtone settings with test scans, use the highlight and shadow values determined through previous steps and make the scan. Then in Photoshop, simulate different midtone brightness levels using the gray slider in Photoshop's Levels dialog box. Use this as the basis for determining how to set the gamma control in the scanner's software, either visually or numerically (+ or – values). On some scanners, midtone brightness is set with a tone curve and not with a gamma slider. In this case, use Photoshop's Curves dialog box on your test scan to determine a tone curve shape for midtone brightness. Then duplicate the shape of that curve in the scanner software's tone curve function (as in the example shown on the bottom left) and make a final scan.

NOTE

This trial-and-error method is useful when you are learning the characteristics of a new scanner or when you are learning scanning basics. It's not recommended, however, that you go through this process every time. For professionals concerned with productivity, it is best to learn how to interpret your scanner's software so that you can make good scans based on previews.

Scan setup notes *Date / /*

Original: ________

Film: ________

Comments: ....

Make a sketch of the picture here.

Scanner:

☐ *L5-1000* ☐ *PS4800* ☐ *GT9500*

☐ *F-TS700* ☐ *Other (* *)*

☼ ________ ◑ ________ *Gamma* ________

Resolution: ________ *dpi*

x pixel: ________

y pixel: ________

HL R: ________ *SD R:* ________

G: ________ *G:* ________

B: ________ *B:* ________

Draw the shape of the tone curve here.

Main Scan

After you've adjusted all the scanner settings, as described in previous pages, you make the main scan. Double-check all your parameters carefully and make notes if necessary. You might have to scan the same original at some later date, and using the same settings will save time. We use a data sheet like the one shown on the left to keep records of important scans. Some scanner driver software enables you to save files containing setup parameters. If this is the case with your scanner, it is a good idea to save the setups.

Tips for Choosing a Scanner

As we've mentioned before, if you are buying a scanner for digital photography, the first thing you should check is the shadow-scanning characteristics, particularly if you think you'll be scanning mostly color-reversal film (for negative film, highlights are the important area to check).

Your original test photograph should include shadows nearly as dark (dense) as the black frame along the edges of color-reversal film. The most important point to check is whether you can control noise or ghosted images in the shadows, as shown below. Another potential trouble spot is RGB registration; thin lines of color are visible if the RGB channels are not aligned after scanning. There are other points as well, such as ease of use, preview size, and so on, but your main concern should be the shadow characteristics.

Left: An example of a scan of a 6×7 positive original on a flatbed scanner, which we gave passing marks for performance. Right: An example of a scan we were allowed to make at a retail shop using an unacceptable quality scanner. A noticeable type of flare (blooming) occurs at the edges where the highlights and shadows meet, and there is a lot of streaking. This scanner was fine for reflective originals, but we cannot recommend it for scanning color-reversal film, which is a central task in digital photography.

04 4

Practical Scanning Operations

Using Your Scanner

In the past, whether a prepress business succeeded or failed depended largely on the quality of their scanning services. That is a clear indication of how important the scanning stage is to high-quality image reproduction.

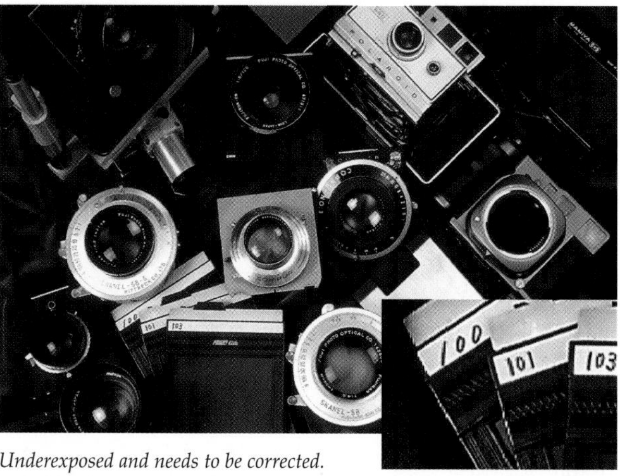

Underexposed and needs to be corrected.

Scan result from a correctly exposed frame.

Fortunately, in recent years, scanners have become more "intelligent," and we don't need to rely as much on highly skilled scanner operators. Also, software applications such as Photoshop enable us to make high-quality adjustments to images after the scan is done. These factors make it easy for desktop computer users to learn how to scan their own images with high-quality results, a situation that is very different from the way it used to be.

As a result, more and more digital photography studios are concerned with scanning productivity and are becoming interested in high-end prepress scanners that are fully automated and robotic. Such systems enable you to set scanning parameters on a dedicated preview station and then leave the scanner running all day unattended, scanning hundreds of images.

Unfortunately, not many high-performance scanners offer ease of operability, high-quality, and productivity in a desktop size at a cost-effective price. The only scanner we know that comes close to meeting these needs is the DT-S1015 from Dainippon Screen. Even the DT-S series of scanners, however, is increasingly designed to meet the needs of high-productivity shops and, as such, is getting bigger and more expensive.

But as we've discussed in this chapter, knowing how to scan can make all the difference when it comes to quality. In many instances, it's not the type or cost of the scanner but how you use it that makes all the difference. The following tips should help anyone using any available desktop scanner to acquire excellent quality images.

Underexposed Originals are Taboo

There is a myth among professional photographers that color-reversal originals intended for print should be slightly underexposed. Another common myth is that slightly underexposed frames in a series of bracketed color-reversal film exposures viewed on a lightbox (where the illuminant is relatively bright) have higher color saturation and more visible highlight detail than correctly exposed frames or overexposed frames.

Photographers have been led to believe this because, up until now, their photos have usually been scanned on high-end drum scanners using photomultiplier light sensors. These systems don't normally generate any visible deterioration in image quality due to scanning, such as noise in shadows.

But if you consider the mostly CCD-based scanners that we use in our own digital photo studios, underexposed photographs are more trouble than they are worth. For example, if you compare a CCD scan of a slightly underexposed photograph with a CCD scan of a correctly—or even slightly overexposed—photograph, you'll see that the former resulted in a significant loss of detail in the shadow areas. Some CCD scanners might even yield better results from slightly overexposed frames than from correctly exposed frames.

Because this photograph is underexposed, it is difficult to remove the muddiness of the colors or to effectively bring out the detail in the shadows.

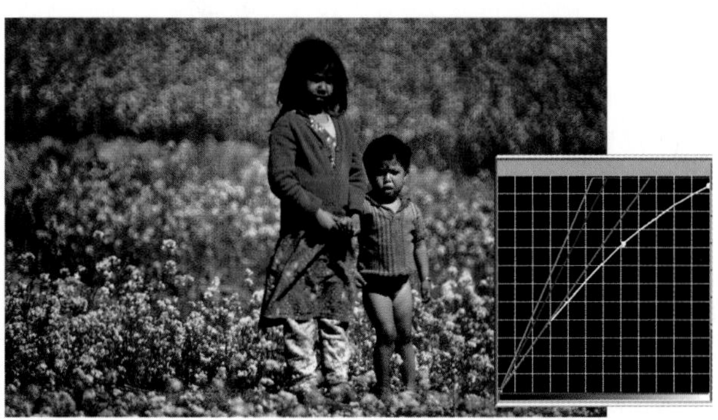

Scanning Underexposed Color Reversal Film

As noted, underexposed frames scanned on flatbed scanners or CCD film scanners often generate noticeable graininess (noise) and don't usually yield enough detail from the shadow to the dark midtone levels. This is even a problem on the Nikon LS-1000, which we like very much and consider to be one of the best scanners in its class.

This isn't meant to suggest, however, that all is lost if you need to scan an underexposed photograph. By using a scanning technique called *double scanning*, you can hold shadow detail and limit noise when scanning an underexposed transparency.

Double Scanning

Double scanning is an unconventional scanning method made possible by powerful imaging applications such as Photoshop. In this technique, two or three scans of the same original with varying scanner settings are merged together with Photoshop's blending modes. This method partially solves the problem of the lack of shadow detail and considerably decreases the amount of noise in the areas from the shadows to the midtones.

STEPS

1. For the first scan, set optimal target RGB values for the highlights and the bright midtones. If the blacks in the shadows appear too open or light, ignore it.

2. On the second scan, use a straight line curve (or a combination of brightness and contrast values) to dramatically lighten the contrast in the shadows. Areas from the highlights to the bright midtones will be blown out, but don't worry about it.

NOTE

For this technique to work successfully, it is important to leave the cropping area unchanged between the first and the second scan.

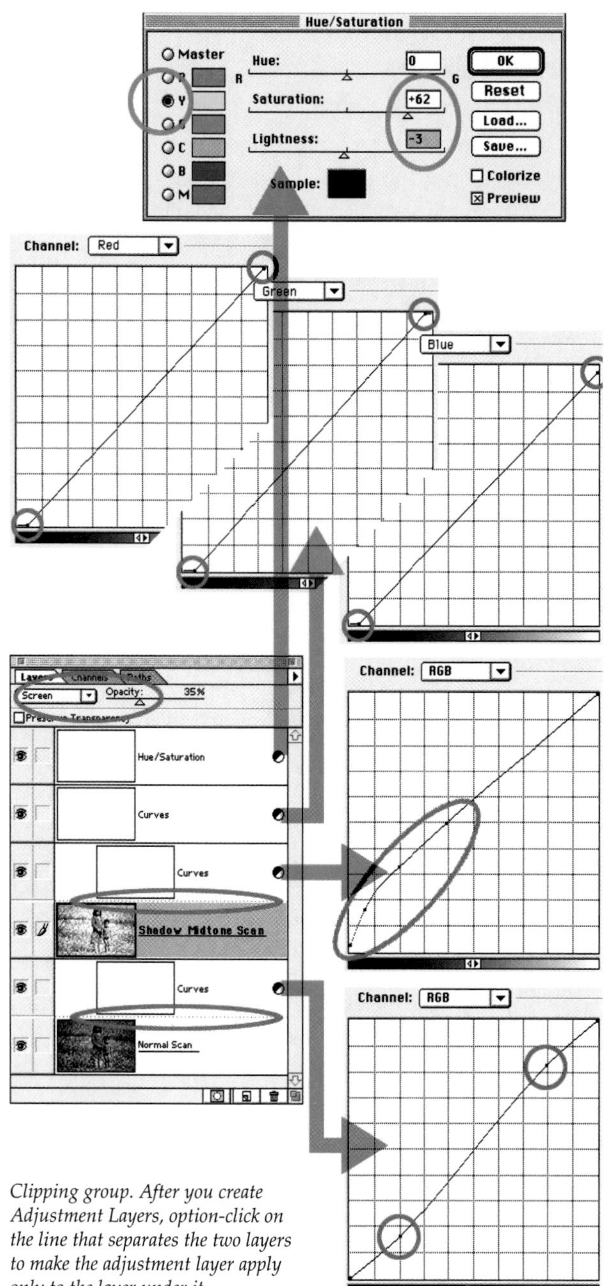

Clipping group. After you create Adjustment Layers, option-click on the line that separates the two layers to make the adjustment layer apply only to the layer under it.

3. Open both scans in Photoshop. Select the Move tool and, while holding the Shift key, drag one image onto the other to make a two-layer file (if the files are the exact same dimensions, the Shift key assures that they line up with one another, pixel for pixel).

NOTE

To check whether the two scans are perfectly aligned, blend the top layer with the bottom layer using the Difference blend mode. If the two images are perfectly aligned, the image turns black. If there's a difference in the alignment, however, it will show as thin lines of color relief against black. To align the two files, shift one layer a pixel at a time using the up, down, left, and right arrows on the keyboard. When you see only black (or worst case, a tiny amount of color relief), the two layers are aligned.

4. Make the top layer active and select Screen from the pull-down menu in the Layers palette. Move the Opacity slider to around 30–40 percent. The combination of adjustments creates a result in which both the shadows and highlights have close to ideal levels.

5. In Photoshop 4.0, you can add Adjustment Layers to both the top and the bottom layers and make fine adjustments using the Adjustment Layer, Curves command or the Adjustment Layer, Levels command.

NOTE

Because you selected optimal values for the highlight and midtone settings when you made the first scan, you should adjust the area of the curve for this scan that corresponds to the area from the highlights to the midtones. The second scan was concerned with the shadows, so you should adjust the area of the curve for the second scan that corresponds to the area from the shadows to the midtones.

6. After you have finished fine adjustments, select Flatten Image from the Options menu in the Layers palette to blend the layers into one image.

7. Adjust the brightness and gray balance for the image one more time as necessary, and your work is finished (see the top photograph on the next page).

Other Examples of Double Scanning

In this section we would like to introduce you to a few other things you can do with double scanning. Also refer to Chapter 3-7, "Practical Correction Techniques," and Chapter 9-5, "Image Layers," for a different perspective on double-layering methods.

Local Color Cast Correction

Color casts often appear in the shadow areas of photographs taken on sunny days and can be removed by using double scanning. You often see these casts in architectural photographs and everyday strobe photography.

In this case, the dinosaur has a bluish cast we'd like to eliminate. We made the first scan using normal settings (bottom left). The second scan settings made the dinosaur slightly yellowish (top left). We then combined the two layers into a single image file with the yellowish scan on top and added a layer mask of the dinosaur to this layer. Then we added a Curves Adjustment Layer (clipped to the yellowish layer) and adjusted the color of the yellow dinosaur to make it more neutral gray.

Of course, it is possible to do this kind of adjustment during the scanning stage, without going to the trouble of double scanning. For photographs like this one, however, in which there are smooth tonal transitions for blue sky (or for flesh tones), large corrections during the scanning stage could cause tone jumps. This technique of double scanning and layers blending is a good workaround for controlling that kind of image degradation.

Even if a single scan gives you the result you want, there may still be considerable noise.

Use double scanning to control noise as much as possible. Triple scanning might be even more effective.

Controlling Scanner Noise

Some scanners generate a tremendous amount of noise in the shadows. Although most of the scanners we used didn't generate as much noise as appears in these samples, one scanner did. If you look carefully, the place in which the noise appears differs on each scan. In these examples, we used double scanning (middle left) to control the intolerable amount of noise in the top left photograph.

The technique was to make two scans with slightly brighter settings than we wanted the original to be, using exactly the same settings for both scans. We combined the two images into a two-layered file and chose Overlay from the Layers palette pull-down menu (bottom left). It isn't always clear which option in the pull-down menu produces the best result, but trial and error usually leads to what works best. With this technique, noise was fairly easy to control because the noise that appeared in the first scan was canceled out by different noise in the second scan. This type of noise control function is normally built into high-end scanner electronic circuits.

chapter 5

Digital Exposures and Follow-Up Processing

05 1

Digital Camera Test Exposures

Digital Cameras Today

If you look back through camera history, revolutionary changes in camera design and photographic technology occurred in every era, always the cause for surprise, and even consternation. Familiar examples of such change include the debut of the M type Leica, half-frame type cameras, 110 mm format film, and autofocus mechanisms. Even as this book was being produced, an entirely new format of film known as APS (Advanced Photo System) was released on the market.

The first production models of digital cameras began to appear in the early '90s, such as the Kodak DCS 100, a B&W only camera that was tethered to a small computer suspended from the photographer's shoulder like a camera bag. One of the first digital cameras we ever used was an early version of the Scitex Leaf DCB in 1992. At that time, the DCB took nearly 90 seconds after releasing the shutter to take three exposures. During that 90 seconds, the turret-style RGB filter mounted on the front of the lens rotated three times for three separate strobe-synched exposures. Obviously, one of the limitations of this camera was its incapability to photograph moving subjects.

Using digital cameras involves other limitations as well. Slow ISOs meant that Tungsten lighting didn't provide adequate light for many types of photographers, and computers were very slow compared to their speed now. The time it took images to appear on the screen seemed agonizingly long (seems silly, of course, when compared to the minimum one day wait we endured without complaint while film was processed). Anyway, sometimes we had to stop and appreciate the irony that some digital camera's limitations at the end of the 20th century were similar to the limitations that users of daguerrotype cameras experienced in the 19th Century.

We weren't particularly intimidated by experimenting with digital cameras, however, because we had experimented with various silver halide cameras, from the tiny Minox to 8×10-inch view cameras. What suprised us was how much we enjoyed using the new cameras. Ultimately, what began as curiousity quickly grew into a conviction that digital cameras, and digital photography, would definitely become important tools for the amateur and professional photographer.

As of October 1996, 46 manufacturers were offering over 112 dedicated still digital cameras. Considering that in September 1995 only 30 manufacturers were offering 70 different devices, there is no question that the transition marks a boom in the industry.

For your reference, a chart of current digital camera specifications published by the *Future Image Report* appears in Chapter 11.

NOTE

The *Future Image Report* is a newsletter focusing on issues related to digital photography. It has been in circulation for years and is published by Future Image Inc. in the U.S.A. For subscription information, please contact Future Image Inc., Burlingame, CA 94010. The phone number is 415-579-0493; the fax number is 415-579-0566; e-mail is `AGFUTURE@aol.com`; the URL is `www.futureimage.com`.

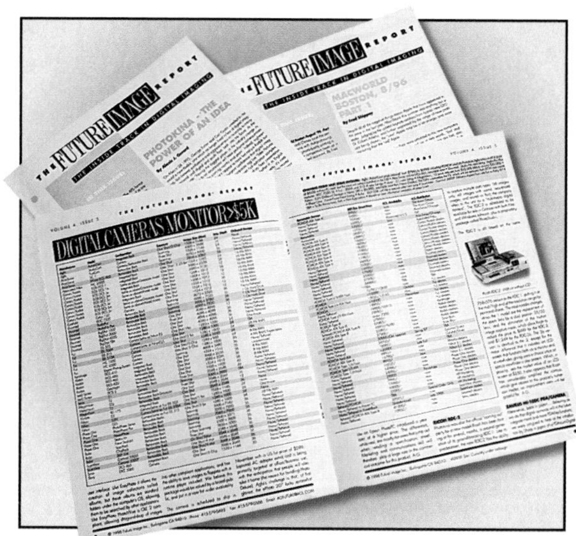

The Future Image Report

Test Exposures

Just as you would take test exposures for a new emulsion color film, we recommend that you make test exposures under a variety of conditions when you use a digital camera for the first time. The following are some tips for testing your camera.

- At the same time you make your test exposures on the digital camera, make exposures using the silver halide color reversal film you are most familiar with.

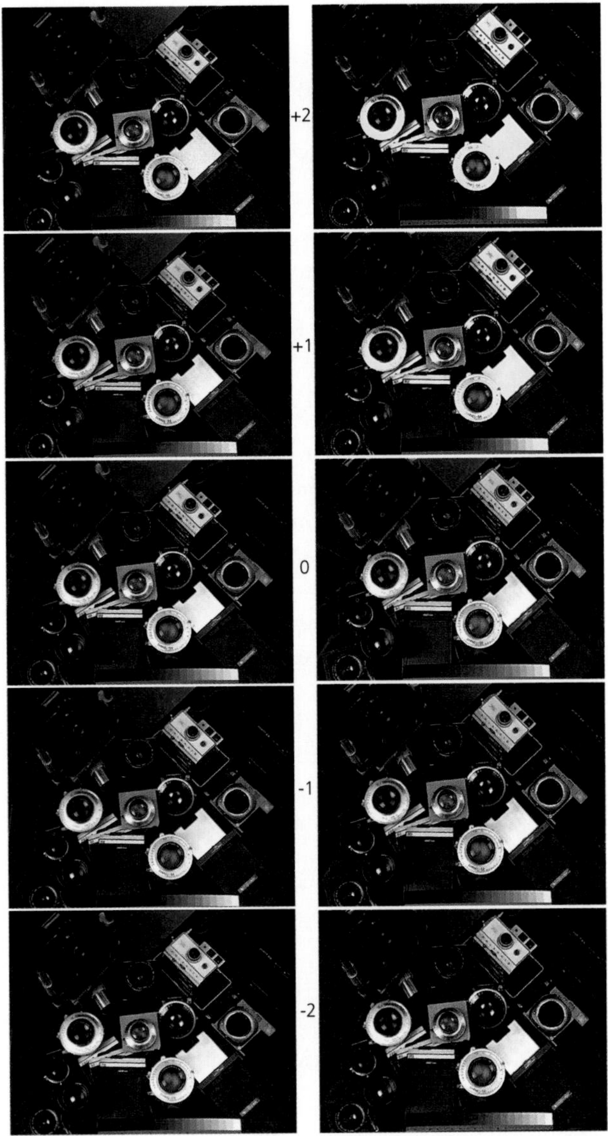

Left: Corrected 35 mm color reversal film. Right: Corrected Nikon E2 digital camera image.

■ Always include a gray scale in your test exposures. Whenever possible, control your exposures in $^1/_3$-stop increments. On cameras with a minimum of $^1/_2$-stop increments, use 0.1 and 0.2 neutral density filters to make your exposures respectively $^1/_3$-stop and $^2/_3$-stop darker in order to control the amount of light in $^1/_3$-stop increments.

■ Take steps to minimize unnecessary influences. Minimize flare, for instance, by using as long a lens hood as possible (this applies to the film photography as well). For example, three-shot cameras—such as the Scitex Leaf DCB II with its turret-style filter mounted in front of the lens—benefit greatly from the use of a lens hood (depending on the camera, a lens hood may have to be attached with tape).

■ [Test 1]. Take a series of exposures that include a broad range of subject luminance, from specular highlights where the light is directly reflected off something such as a metal surface, to deep shadows that are areas almost as dark as when the lens cap is on (left). Use a spot meter to measure the EV values for each of these areas and make notes of them.

■ [Test 2]. Make exposures that include a series of dull colors such as greens, oranges, and browns, which are made of either two or three CMY color components. This can be important for analyzing the quality of reproduction from digital camera data.

■ [Test 3]. Take still life exposures, which include a KODAK Gray Scale Q-13 (or 14) (bottom right).

■ [Test 4]. When relevant to the camera model, make exposures of the same subject using tungsten, sunlight, or strobes for your lighting (we recommend a dark still life).

Color reversal film that was not corrected after exposure.

A gray scale—an essential for digital photography (KODAK Q-13/Q-14).

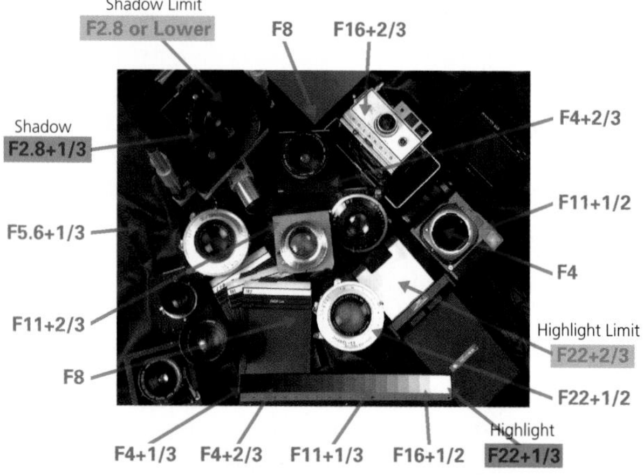

Top: Konica SRS color reversal film scanned on an Epson FS1200S.

Bottom: Nikon E2. We adjusted the tone curve so the gray scale in the two photographs would look the same.

In the case of scanned color reversal film, we were able to hold detail in the highlights even when we overexposed and underexposed by 2 stops. But on the digital camera, the highlights were blown out when overexposed 1 stop, and the shadows blocked up when underexposed 1 stop.

[Test 1]: Basic Latitude

The purpose of Test 1 is to evaluate the range of subject luminance that your digital camera is capable of capturing. First, make notes of a range of subject EV values with a spot meter, from deepest shadow to brightest highlight. Then take a series of bracketed exposures with the digital camera. Study the data carefully for bracketed exposures of the image, and find a frame with a highlight RGB levels value of 240–250, and a frame that has a shadow RGB levels value of 8–15 (see Chapter 4-3, "Basic Scanner Operations," for a technical definition of the word *highlight*). Refer to your notes of EV values and calculate the difference between these two places in stops. This will give you the dynamic range that the digital camera is capable of capturing. We often use the Nikon E2, for example, and have determined by using this method, that it can consistently capture detail within a dynamic range of around 5 stops. Halation often occurs in the highlights of exposures taken with digital cameras, and this test will also help you understand this characteristic of your camera (see Chapter 5-3, "The CCD as Film").

[Test 2]: Color Saturation

Use this test to see how photographs taken with film compare with photographs taken with your digital camera.

With both a digital camera and a film camera (use a color reversal film you're familiar with), photograph a still life subject containing earth tones. Be sure to include a gray scale in both so that you can make similar highlight, midtone, and shadow adjustments. After scanning and adjusting the film based exposure, compare the RGB levels of the same areas in both images.

In most cases, the image data for the exposure taken on color reversal film will have fewer low saturation colors (or unwanted color components (see Chapter 3-6, "Selective Color Correction"). Overall, the colors in the film version will be brighter and more saturated, even in the earth tones. This is because more recent color films have been manufactured with an emphasis on reproducing vivid colors. Comparatively, digital camera images reproduce color more faithful to the color of the photographic subject without imparting a bias built into the film emulsion.

Step No.	RGB Level
A	245
1	229
2	213
3	196
4	173
5	148
6	128
M	107
8	91
9	78
10	65
11	56
12	45
13	35
14	30
15	24
B	20
17	16
18	10
19	8

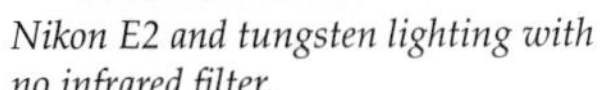

Nikon E2 and tungsten lighting with no infrared filter.

Nikon E2 and tungsten lighting with infrared filter attached.

Infrared filters

Notice that the colors in the film version are more vivid, whereas the colors from the Nikon E2 are less saturated. Because this saturation can be easily enhanced in post processing, this isn't considered a negative characteristic of a digital camera (see page 5-7, "Comparing Color Reproduction").

[Test 3]: Gray Imbalance

This test helps you determine how well a digital camera can reproduce a neutral gray.

Start by photographing a still life that includes a KODAK Q-13 or Q-14 Gray Scale. In Photoshop, use the Eyedropper tool and the Info to find Step No. A with RGB levels between 240 and 250. Then open the Curves dialog box and use the White Point eyedropper to set Step No. A to exactly 245. Similarly, set Step No. B point to RGB = 20 using the Black Point eyedropper. Finally, use the Midtone eyedropper to set the sixth step in the gray scale to a neutral gray using 128 for all three RGB levels (see page 3-18).

At this point all the RGB levels' values should be about the same on all steps of the gray scale. On some digital cameras, however, a color cast may still appear in some steps. This is a minor concern that shouldn't appear in most cameras. If it does, knowing how to identify this characteristic of a digital camera means that you can correct it using Curves, save the tone curve setting, and apply it to images taken by the camera.

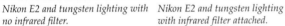

[Test 4]: The Effects of Infrared Light

To test how your camera responds to infrared light, photograph a subject, including a grayscale, under tungsten lights, sunlight, or strobes (gray material or a print like the one from this book are good subjects for this test). Do this without an infrared filter attached. After adjusting for proper contrast and gray balance (see Test 3) you may still find that the image suffers from poor color balance or noise. This will be particularly noticeable when you use light sources that emit a lot of radiant heat, such as tungsten lighting and sunlight. To correct this adverse effect, use the infrared filters that either came with the camera or purchase a set through a professional photo supplier. Although these filters can be expensive, they are essential for acheiving optimum quality.

Kenko DR filters, or similar infrared filters, can be used to correct problems caused by infrared light.

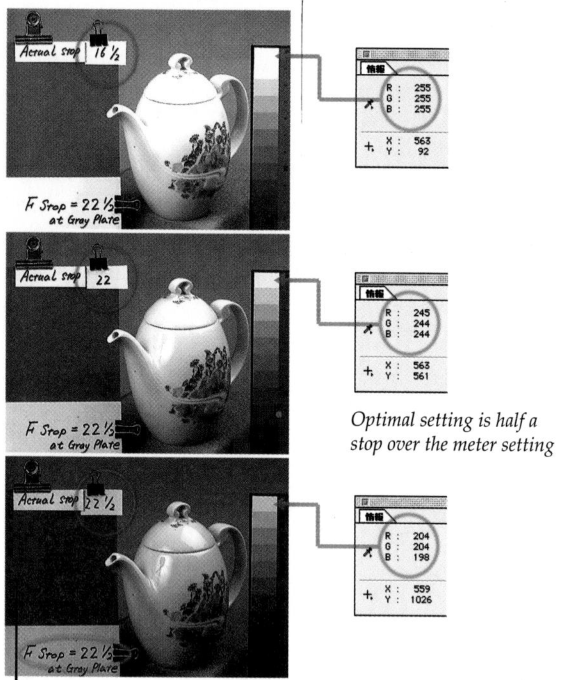

Optimal setting is half a stop over the meter setting

Optimal setting indicated on the meter

Sekonic spot meter with custom-made hood attached

On silver halide film, even if the photograph is more or less overexposed and the whites are almost blown out, you can often do something at the scanning stage to preserve some highlight detail. Using a steep tone curve in Photoshop, or special techniques involving blending layers together (see page 3-37), even more detail can be brought out.

With digital cameras, this is impossible. One of the most prominent characteristics of digital cameras to keep in mind is that you can do nothing to save highlights once they've blown out during exposure.

Therefore, an important technique with digital camera photography is using a spot meter to calculate exposures based on a highlight (the concept is the same as exposing for highlights with transparency film).You can use the spot meter, for example, to determine an ISO to use that will always give you an exposure that limits the white point to 245.

First, use a digital camera to take a series of bracketed exposures of pure white paper using your typical lighting set up. Determine which exposure is the optimum exposure based on the combination of aperture and shutter speed that makes the RGB levels of the white paper 245. Then, starting with the camera's recommended ISO setting, calculate an ISO setting to use on your spot meter that gives you this same combination of aperture and shutter speeds (for example, ISO 800 may become ISO 400). Using this specially calculated ISO will ensure that exposures based on a spot meter reading of white won't result in blown out highlights.

NOTE

■ Because published ISO sensitivity values for digital cameras are not established for when RGB = 245, always check for yourself.

■ If you don't have a spot meter and are photographing subjects with many highlights, always take a series of bracketed exposures.

■ Be especially careful when using lenses such as zoom lenses, where the largest aperture f value is variable.

■ To avoid spot meter error, attach a hood to the spot meter as well. Depending on the meter, a hood can make a difference of $^1/_2$–1 $^1/_2$ stops when measuring the shadow areas.

(A) DCB II and Hasselblad ELX

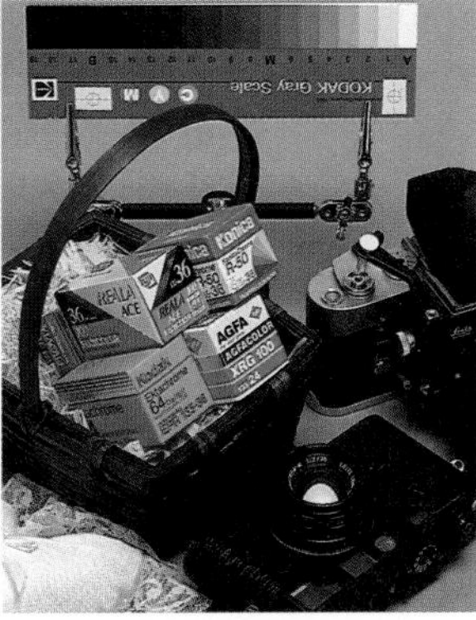

(B) Nikon E2

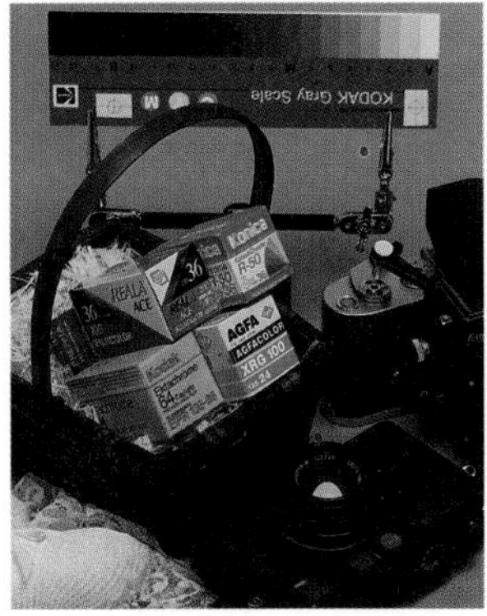

(C) DCS 460

(D) DCS 460 after correction

(E) Ektachrome PRP

(F) Fujichrome Velvia

(G) Konica SRS color reversal film

(H) Nikon E2

Comparing Color Reproduction

A popular misconception is that the color and contrast of the image you get right off of the digital camera should be perfect without any further adjustment. This isn't true. The relationship of capturing an image with a digital camera and then doing image processing is similar (conceptually) to exposing a color negative, then finding the right filter pack to make a correct print from it. This means that an evaluation about whether a digital camera can reproduce color adequately should not be based solely on the results immediately after exposure. This judgment should be made only after you've made tone curve adjustments to values ranging from highlights to the shadows.

To demonstrate this, we created a still life consisting of Kodak yellow, Agfa orange, Fuji green, and Konica blue—colors that are familiar to photographers anywhere in the world.

Photograph A was taken using a Scitex leaf DCB II camera back on a Hasselblad 553ELX and was adjusted in Photoshop, based on the grayscale, to look as though it had been taken on silver halide film. Photograph B was taken with a Nikon E2, and a similar adjustment was made to the image in Photoshop. Photograph C was taken with a DCS 460, and because the software with this camera required that we select either preset daylight, tungsten, or flash color correction curves, we transferred the data into the computer using the "flash" exposure setting. Photograph D is the same data as photograph C, taken with the Kodak DCS 460, but we adjusted it with a tone curve to make the gray scale match the others.

With the exception of photograph C, which didn't receive special tone curve adjustments, the color reproduction in all of these digital camera images is very similar. This means that it was possible, after exposure, to adjust the data from three different types of digital cameras very closely, even though the differences between them after the initial exposure may have been wide.

Interpreting the Feel of a Photograph

Photograph E was taken on Ektachrome, photograph F was taken on Fujichrome Velvia, and photograph G was taken on Konica SRS color reversal film. Photograph H was taken using a Nikon E2 digital camera.

All of the color reversal films were scanned on the Epson FS1200S film scanner and adjusted in Photoshop so their gray scales would look the same (meaning they were adjusted to have the same highlight, shadow, and midtone values). When compared to the film photographs, the

Straight exposure from digital camera

Interpretation #1

To create a more familiar, film-like version, we used a tone curve to darken the shadows and brighten the highlights so they were slightly blown out. Then we used the Hue/Saturation command to increase the intensity of the yellow, red, and green.

digital photograph is duller and the colors are less saturated. At the same time, the film photographs all look identical—homogenized—without any trace of the original film emulsions's characteristics (although they look very different on the lightbox). Why is this?

Digital cameras, as well as film / scanner combinations, give photographers personal control over expression of color in ways that haven't been possible in traditional chemistry-based photography.

In human terms, digital cameras are impartial and emotionless, for example. They don't have built-in characteristics like silver halide films have. So a photograph taken with a digital camera can be made to express a whole range of feelings or moods according to the individual's (or client's) taste. If you consider the range of interpretations that a photographer can make with a black and white negative in a home darkroom, you can understand the range of possibilities for interpreting a color image made possible by the digital camera (see the examples to the left).

Film emulsions, on the other hand, have expressive and emotional "personalities" capable of conveying messages such as warmth and coolness, depending on light source, emulsion, and so on. Although these characteristics can be held in the image through scanning, they can also be removed. The photographs at the bottom of the previous page, for example, were stripped of their "personalities" by setting the same grayscale highlight, shadow, and midtones values for each, in which case they became almost identical.

Interpretation #2

Hue/Saturation adjustments were made to the reds, particularly the apples. By adding blue to the greens, they resemble a green more typical of color reversal film reproduction. Compared to Interpretation #1, this is a more toned down, natural looking version.

Comparing Amounts of Information

We began serious discussions about this book in September 1995, and it took a while to decide on our approach as to what kind of book to write. One big reason for this was that we didn't know how much emphasis we should put on compact digital cameras. New digital cameras were appearing on the market so fast that the more we tried to choose between them, the more we questioned our approach.

In the meantime, a variety of different publications were appearing in bookstores about digital cameras, most of which were special issues on compact digital cameras. This confirmed that we could avoid deep discussions about point and shoot type digital cameras. We chose to include only one of these cameras, the Kodak DC50, which, at the time we were writing, was one of the best compact digital cameras available. In the discussion that follows, we will compare the amount of information captured by four cameras: the Kodak DC50, the Nikon E2, the Scitex Leaf DCB II, and the Kodak DCS 460.

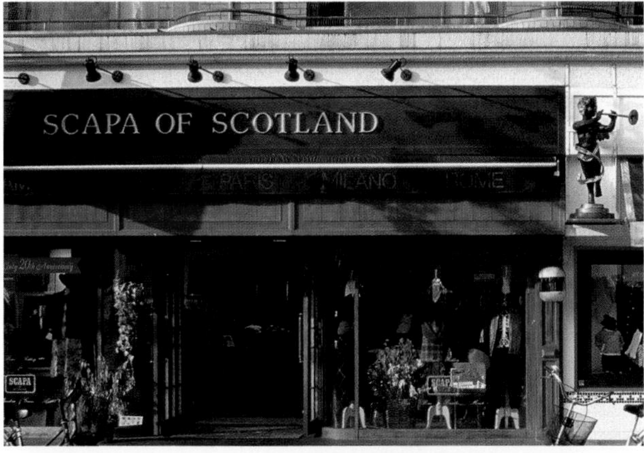

Top: 35 mm color reversal film scanned at 2,800 dpi. The central 2,000×1,300-pixel area was output at an image resolution of 600 ppi.

Bottom: Same area shot with a Kodak DCS460. The central 2,000×1,300-pixel area was output at an image resolution of 600 ppi. Characteristics in the detailed areas are about the same, but the film shows noticeable graininess.

The Amount of Information in a Photograph

The amount of information captured by a digital camera means the total number of pixels immediately after a photograph has been taken. This is expressed as the number of horizontal pixels times the number of vertical pixels.

The Kodak DCS460 and the DCS465, for example, each have a 3,000×2,000 pixel matrix, so the total number of pixels they can capture is six million. The Kodak DC50 compact digital camera has 756×504 pixels, making a total of 380,000 pixels. The DCS460 and the DCS465 are therefore capable of capturing about 16 times more information than the DC50.

This difference, if we consider just surface area, is comparable to the difference between 35 mm film, which has a total surface of 860 mm^2, and 4×5 film, which has a surface area of approximately 13,000 mm^2. That is a difference of about 15 times. Comparatively, in terms of image size at least, we could consider that the DC50 is to the DCS 460 what 35 mm is to 4×5-inch film.

In order to compare the information capable of being captured by a digital camera to information capable of being captured on film, it's necessary to calculate a pixel count that equals the information contained in film (meaning enough resolution to hold the finest details). This is extremely difficult to do.

We consulted a number of academic references, finding many different interpretations, both high and low, so we decided to do our own rough test. On an ISO 100 35 mm color reversal original, we located a medium contrast area where we could just make out the finest details with a 10X loupe. We determined that in order to hold this detail on a 300 dpi color printer we needed a scanning resolution (or scanning pitch) of 3700 dpi (this reproduced the finest line as a 2-pixel wide pitch). We then scanned the entire surface area of the 35 mm original, which generated a scan of around 3,500×5,200 pixels, for a total volume of 18.2 million pixels. At this level of magnification (or resolution), however, grain in the 35 mm original becomes very noticeable. If we take the adverse effect of increased grain on image quality into consideration, then about 20 percent less in pixel volume—or 14.5 million pixels—represents the practical resolution limit for quality image reproduction from ISO 100 35 mm film (this is our own personal assessment). Since this is equal to about twice the amount of information captured by the Kodak DCS460, we can say that the DCS460 generates the equivalent of a "half-frame" ISO 100 color reversal photograph.

Comparing Silver Halide Film and Digital Cameras—Silver Halide Film

Photograph taken using a Nikon F90 camera with a Nikkor 80mm lens at f2 on Ektachrome PRP film. Same camera position as the DCS460 digital camera. The red outline corresponds to the area captured by the DCS460, shown on the next page. Output at 400 ppi.

Comparing Silver Halide Film and Digital Cameras—Digital Cameras

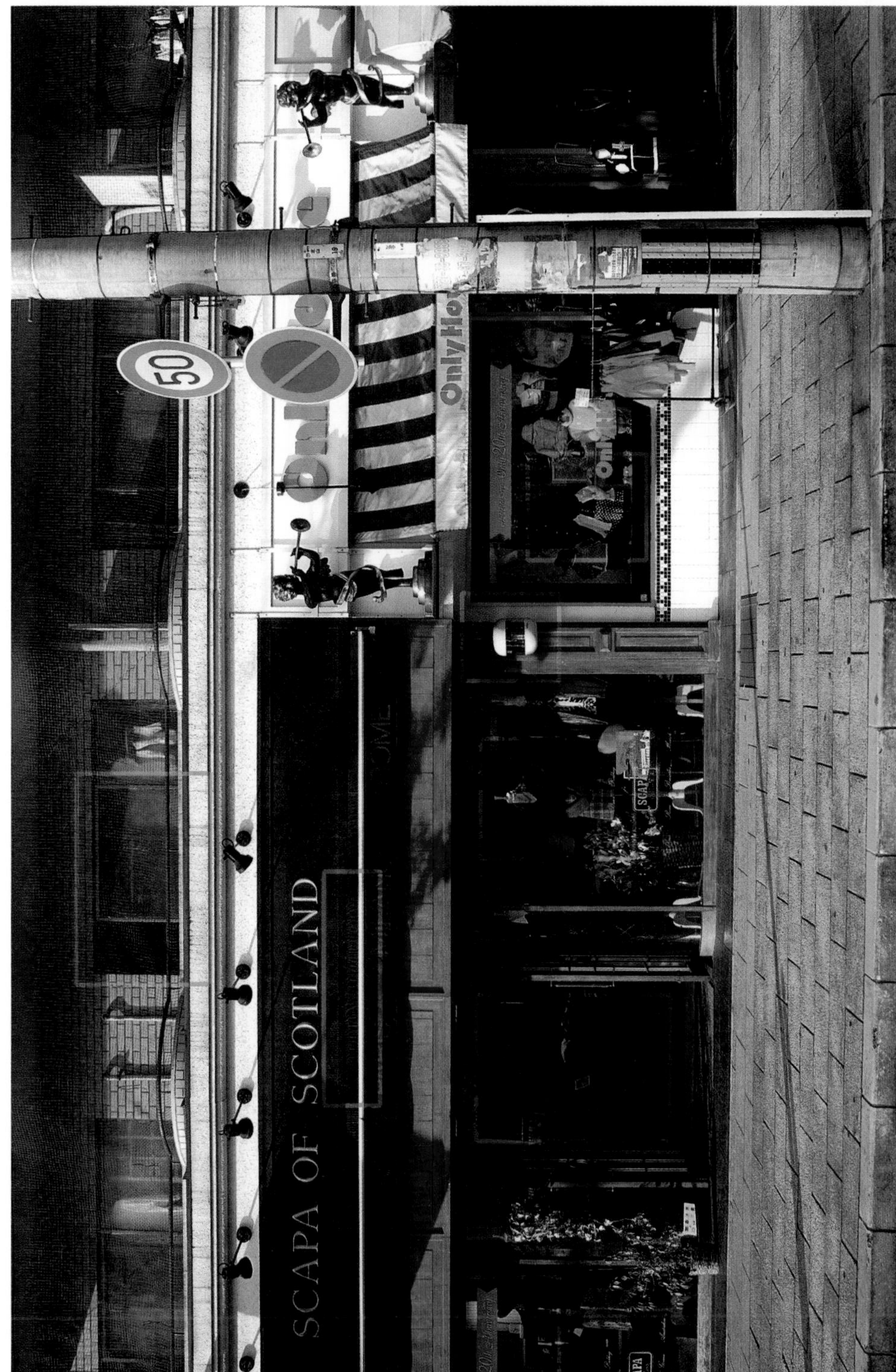

Kodak DCS460, Nikkor 80 mm lens, f2

The camera position is the same as the film photo on the previous page, but the CCD area is about half the size of 35 mm film, so the actual result is an enlarged image. Overall, the DCS460 reproduced better detail on printed paper than the scanned film. Output at 400 ppi.

Compare the blue outlined areas in this image with the same areas in the image on the previous page.

Image Sizes From A Variety of Digital Cameras

*Kodak DCS460/465.
Image resolution:
350 ppi.
2,036×3,060 pixels.*

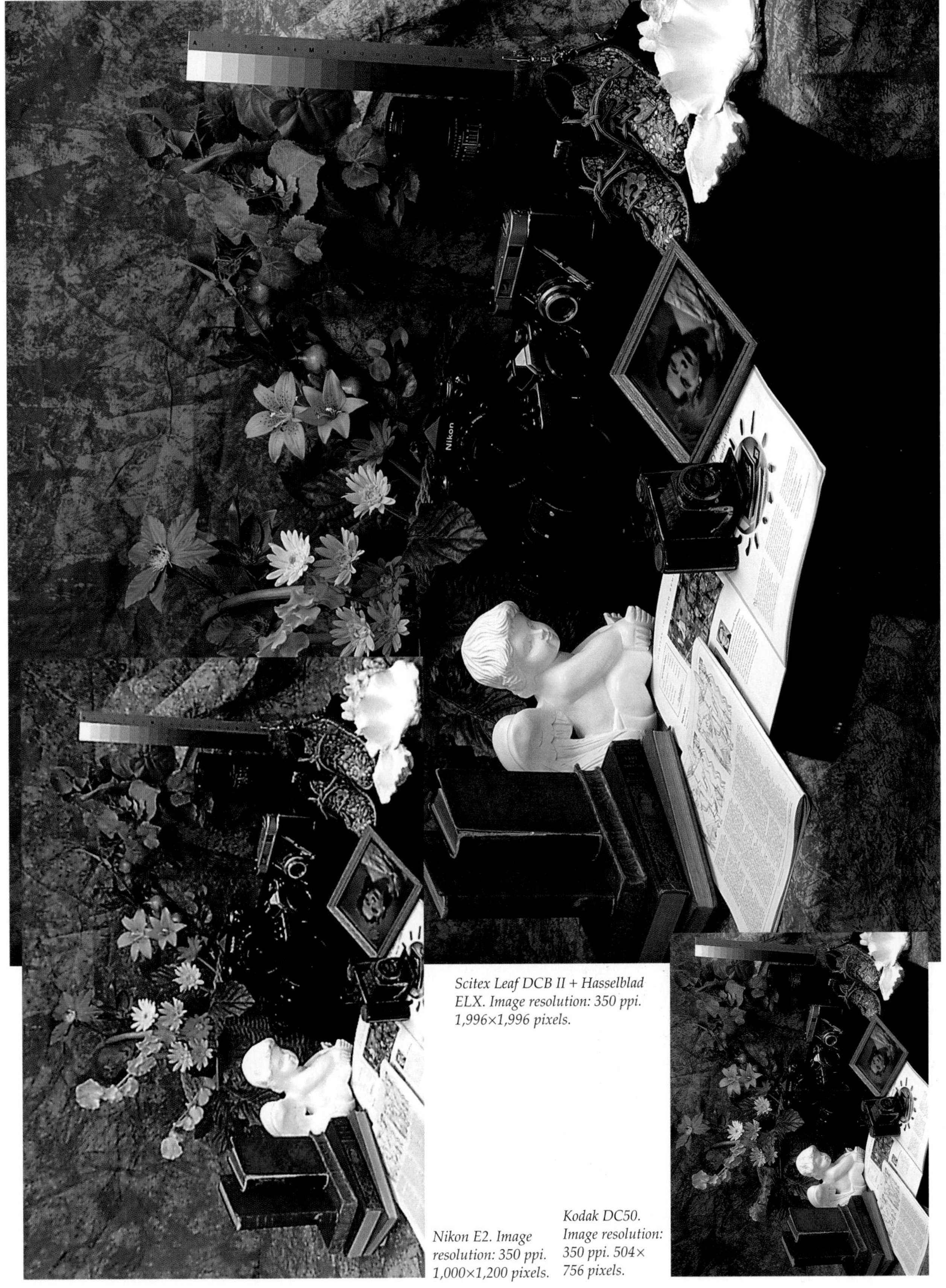

Scitex Leaf DCB II + Hasselblad ELX. Image resolution: 350 ppi. 1,996×1,996 pixels.

Nikon E2. Image resolution: 350 ppi. 1,000×1,200 pixels.

Kodak DC50. Image resolution: 350 ppi. 504×756 pixels.

Limits on Magnification

Although very expensive models of digital cameras are sometimes lacking in image size (pixel volume), it doesn't have to limit their usefulness. As we explain in Chapter 7-2, "Image Processing for Output," if you effectively interpolate and add sharpness, you can output images that are as good as scans from large format silver halide film images.

This is due to the fact that digital camera images have no grain, which means there is none of the noticeable graininess that appears on enlarged silver halide film. You can interpolate an image captured with a scan-type digital camera, for example, and print it as a large format poster (for example 33×37 inches) and it will be sharp without any noticeable side effects of enlarged grain.

The photographs on this page are test exposures taken by Hiroyuki Hayakawa of ABC Studios, Tokyo.

Still life photographed using a Mamiya RZ67 on Ektachrome film. A portion of the film was enlarged 1,850 percent on a high end scanner.

Image shot using a Phase One digital camera back on a 4×5-inch view camera. The original data was interpolated and enlarged 300 percent. This area was cropped and output at 400 ppi (the untrimmed image file was 1.3 GB!). Compared with the enlarged film version, there is a significant lack of grain in the digital camera version.

05 2

Digital Camera Lighting

Maintaining Tonal Information in the Shadows

Photos captured by a digital camera tend to lose detail in the shadow areas when the exposure is set to preserve detail in the highlights. This is especially true when compared to silver halide films. It is due to inherent limits on the dynamic range of the CCDs themselves. Therefore, compared with lighting techniques for film photography, you have to be extra careful to add adequate lighting into shadow areas.

Film Original.

Shadows brightened on scan of film in Photoshop. Shadow detail recoverable.

Photographed with Kodak DCS460 using same light setup as Film Original.

Kodak DCS 460 photo with shadows brightened in Photoshop. Shadow detail cannot be recovered.

Photographed with Kodak DCS460 using reflectors to open shadows.

Kodak DCS460 photo with open shadows. Shadows are further adjusted in Photoshop and detail is adequately maintained.

Can't Get Something from Nothing

Compare the sample photographs on the previous page. Photographs from film-based cameras show adequate detail on the bellows, the plates, and the lenses, and the detail is brought out with correction (previous page, top row).

Notice that when the same subject was photographed using the Kodak DCS460 digital camera under the same lighting conditions, there wasn't enough shadow detail. Even an attempt to open the shadows with a tone curve fails because the detail doesn't exist in the first place—you can't get something from nothing (previous page, middle row).

The logical step is to try to work with the lighting to open the shadows. Just increasing the amount of lighting, however, isn't sufficient. Small reflectors were used to open the shadows in the Kodak DCS460. Then, in Photoshop, the shadows were opened even more with a tone curve and details were preserved similar to the film original (previous page, bottom row).

Silver Bounce Cards

The digital camera lighting technique used in the previous example involved the use of several mini polished bounce cards (in this case, mirror mylar and/or aluminum foil attached to foamcore). When shooting digitally, anywhere you'd normally use a white bounce card to open shadows, you should use a silver bounce card. Large silver reflectors brighten everything, however, even where there are no shadows, so it's better to take the time to make small reflectors focused only on the shadows, as shown on the left. Obviously, if you overuse silver bounce cards it can cause the lighting to look unnatural. But the objective is to ensure that detail is held in the shadows during the initial exposure. After that, in Photoshop, you can easily adjust the shadows to make them look more natural.

05 3

The CCD as Film

Rainbow moiré artifacts

Photograph taken using a Kodak DCS460, immediately after exposure

Rainbow Moiré on Area Array CCDs

Digital cameras that use dye filter area CCD arrays, for example the Kodak DCS series, the Nikon E2, and other compact digital cameras, often have a type of rainbow colored moiré that appears in detailed pattern areas of an image, particularly in the neutral gray areas and white background areas that have highly saturated neighboring colors, as shown on the left.

This happens because each of the sensors on the CCD array has either an R, G, or B coating on it that acts as a filter. A single sensor (one pixel) can only pick up information for a single color component. The camera, or software, fills in the information the other two colors of the pixel afterwards, when the image is opened.

A small number of cameras try to solve this problem using optical filters called low pass filters. These cameras suffer a slight loss in sharpness.

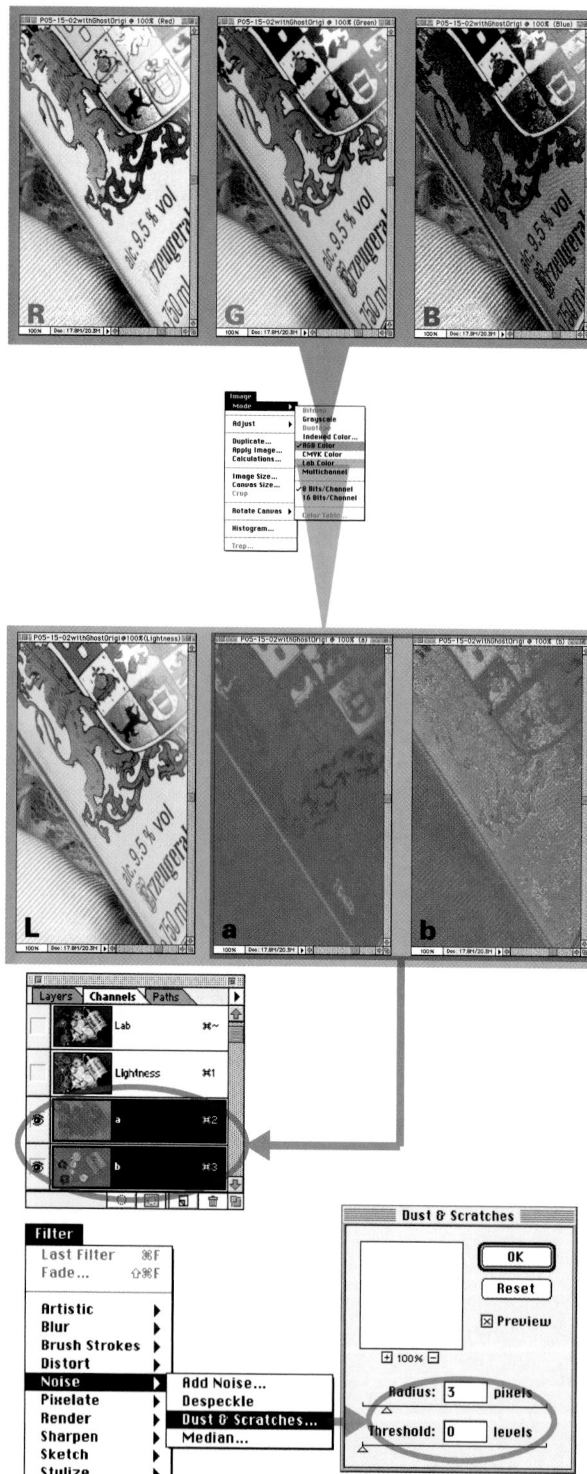

At any rate, whether you enlarge or reduce for output, or even if you leave the dimensions as they are, the rainbow artifacts will appear in areas with detailed patterning.

NOTE

With three-shot scan-type digital cameras, this problem theoretically does not occur.

Two Solutions for Rainbow Artifact Problems

This type of problem can be controlled in two ways.

The first way is to convert the RGB image into a L*a*b* image and use the Dust & Scratches command in Photoshop on the a and b channels only. We'll call this the "Soften a*b*" technique.

The second way to solve this problem is to take either a neutral gray or a single color channel area only, copy that single channel, and then paste it into the other two channels. We'll call this the "Magic Channel Swap" technique.

*The Soften a*b* Technique*

We initially tried the Soften a*b* technique when the Apple QuickTake 100 first appeared, trying to find some way to improve the image quality. The technique turned out to be quite effective and should be built into the software that comes with compact digital cameras (see the trial version of Quantum Mechanics plug-in, which does this basic technique, on the CD-ROM). Here is how to do it (see illustrations on the left).

STEPS

1. Open an RGB image taken with a digital camera in Photoshop.

2. Choose L*a*b* Color from the Mode menu and convert the image into L*a*b* mode.

3. Zoom into the area of the image with rainbow moiré more than 1:1 to check it.

4. Display the Channels palette and click on the a* channel and then the b* channel icons while holding down the Shift key. This selects both the a* and b* channels as the active channels.

5. Choose the Dust & Scratches command from Noise in the Filters menu, and make the settings in the dialog box as shown on the left.

6. Click OK in the dialog box, and then you are finished. Convert the L*a*b* image back into an RGB image.

NOTE

■ When you change the parameters in the Dust & Scratches dialog box, you can see the results in the Preview and adjust the image until it is the way you want it. If you increase the Radius value, the effect is stronger; if you increase it too much, finely detailed areas become blurred, creating a halo effect around small details in the image. If you increase the Threshold value, the effect will be stronger only in high contrast areas.

■ If you use this technique too much, fine artifact lines will occur along the borders of vivid color areas. In this case, take an uncorrected version of the same area and layer it on top. Then apply Saturation blend mode or adjust the opacity to solve the problem.

Before processing *After processing*

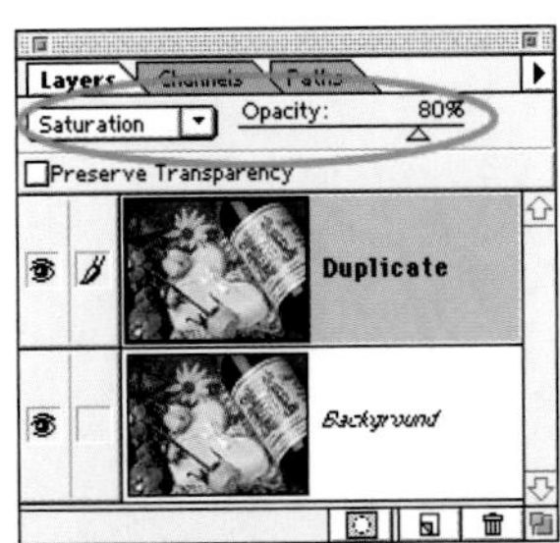

After processing, many of the rainbow artifacts disappear. If you add too much noise using Dust & Scratches, however, the vividness of some colors in finely detailed areas will become dulled, as shown on the left (both reds and blues have become dulled in the processed image).

*After using the Soften a*b* technique. Compare the satin pillow and yellow flower here with the original on page 5-17.*

Booklet related to digital photography distributed by Kodak in Japan.

Magic Channel Swap Technique

A technique similar to the magic channel swap technique has been in use for some time—since around 1985—as an image processing technique on high end prepress systems. It was used as a way of preventing subject moiré, as well as for special effects such as changing the color of a car. Recently, a similar technique was introduced in the Kodak Digital Camera Prepress Reference.

STEPS

1. Open an RGB image taken with a digital camera in Photoshop.

2. The magic of the magic channel swap only works on detailed areas that are either neutral gray or nearly colorless. First locate those places on the image.

3. Use Marquee selection tool to define a representative color area, as shown on the left.

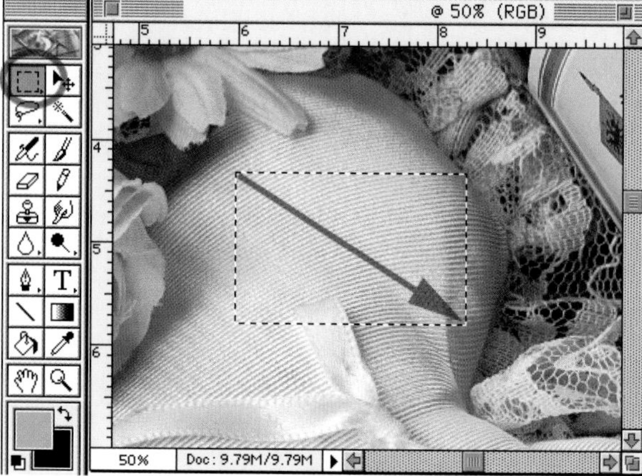

4. Select the Median command under Noise in the Filters menu. Adjust the settings as shown to the left and click OK. Do not deselect the selection.

5. The Median filter averages out all the colors in the selected area. Use the Info palette to take a reading of the RGB levels in the area, as shown on the left, and make a note of them.

6. Cancel the Median command by using the Undo command (⌘+Z).

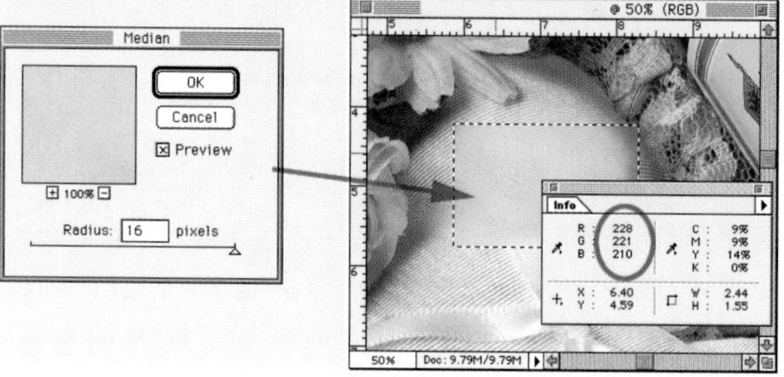

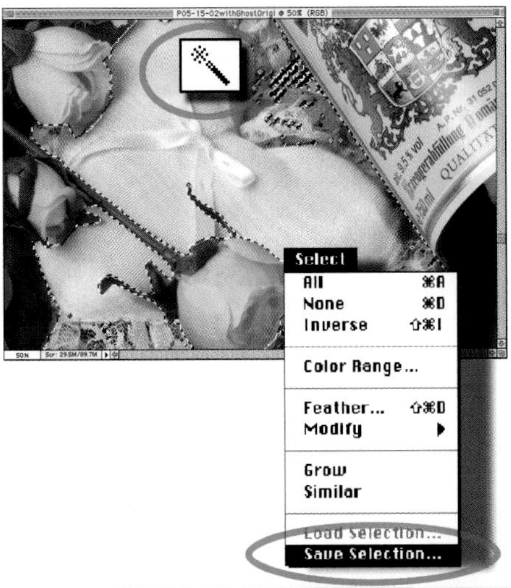

7. Use the Magic Wand selection tool in Photoshop to select the area you want to adjust.

8. After you have made the selection, choose Save Selection.

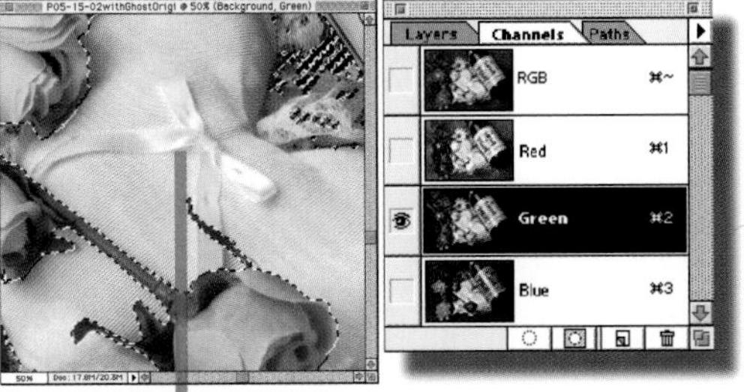

9. Make only the Green channel in the Channels palette active and use ⌘+C to copy it.

10. Without dropping the selection, make the R and B channels in the Channels palette active (Shift-click on each of the channels) and use the Paste Into command to paste the copy from the Green channel simultaneously into the same place in the Red and the Blue channel.

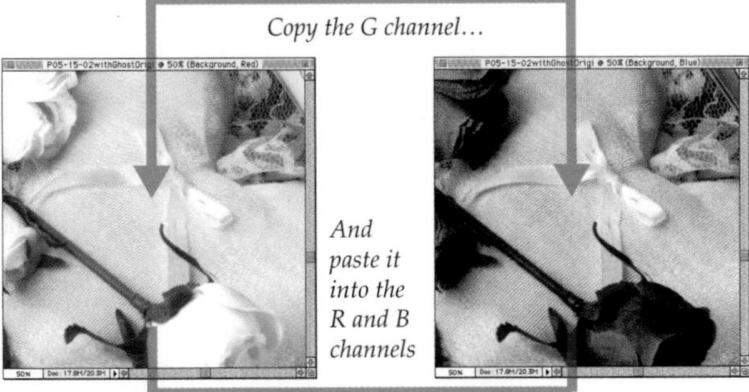

Copy the G channel…
And paste it into the R and B channels

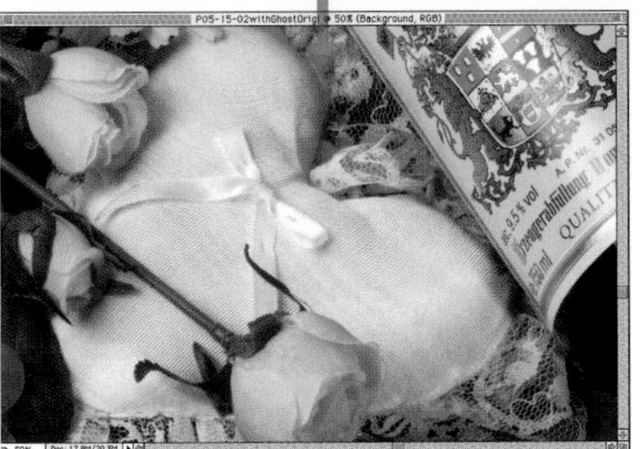

11. Select the composite RGB channel in the Channels palette and the selected should have become a neutral gray. Do not delete the selection yet. If you should delete it by mistake, you can load the selection from the alpha channel saved in step 8.

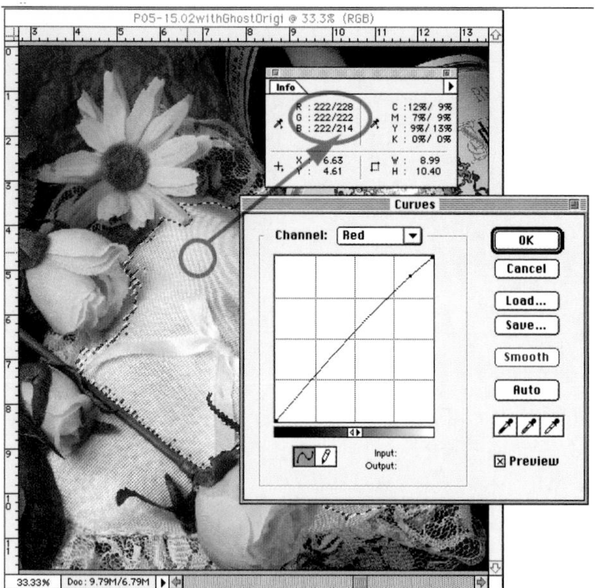

12. Using the Curves command, the Color Balance command, or other color correction commands, correct the color so that it matches the number you noted earlier. The magic is done!

After using the Magic channel swap technique results. Compare the white pillow here with the white pillow at the beginning of this section.

Top: Blooming on the Leaf DCB II. The spoon surfaces converge the light the way a lens does, so that the light that hits that region of the digital camera sensors causes an enormous amount of blooming.

Halation in the Specular Highlights

A type of halation (or flare, often called *blooming*) occurs in digital camera specular highlights that is caused by the structure and principle of CCDs. It occurs because light sensors hit by an enormous amount of light pass the effect of that light to the surrounding sensors. It is easy to think of this as a CCD version of irradiation, a type of halation that occurs on silver halide film.

On digital cameras, information is stored in digital values of either zeros or ones. Therefore, unlike silver halide film halation where the density gradually lightens and finally disappears altogether, on digital cameras, the starting point for halation is clear. This is often particularly noticeable on three-shot scanning digital cameras.

Preventing Halation

Unfortunately, no simple way to prevent or control this blooming problem is built into the cameras.

What is difficult about this is that you cannot know where or how it will appear until you take the photograph. Fortunately, most digital cameras for studio photography are set up next to a computer, so you can check your test exposures and images as if you were taking a digital Polaroid. The important point is to zoom in on any areas of the image that you think are prone to blooming—such as very reflective objects—and if you think blooming has occurred, adjust the subject or the lighting.

You have two possibilities for adjusting the subject or the lighting. Either spray the problem areas of the subject with matte spray, or use a larger, diffused lighting source.

The result after the spoons and the insides of the cups were selectively sprayed with matte spray.

05 4

Photographs for Compositing

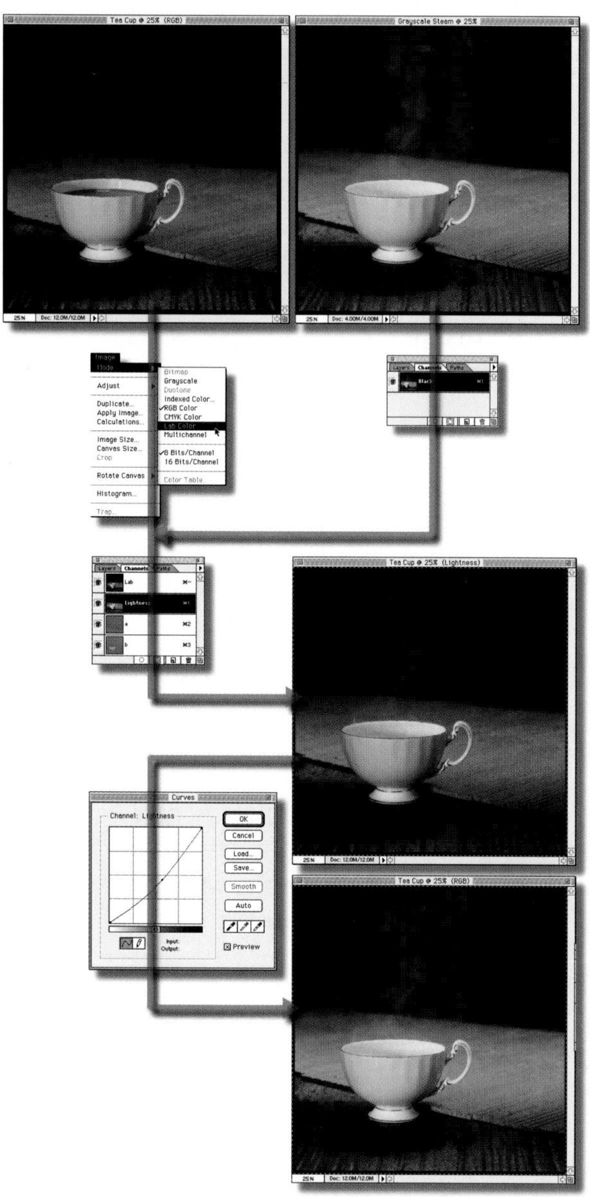

Photographing Moving Subjects

A limitation on three-shot digital cameras is that you cannot photograph moving subjects. In monochrome (grayscale) mode, however, you can shoot moving subjects the way you would with any other camera. Here we shot a teacup in color mode, and then again in monochrome mode to capture the steam rising from the cup. Then we blended the two photographs together in Photoshop.

Preparation

First, we made sure to select a tripod that firmly fixed the camera in place. We were careful not to move the camera or the subject between takes of the two different photos.

Shooting the Color Mode Photograph

Depending on what blend mode you use, the color of the main image may become either lighter or darker. Gradations of tone may change, too. In anticipation of this, we made several shots, changing the ratio between the key and the fill lighting.

Shooting the Monochrome Photograph

Because the final monochrome shot is going to be merged with the color shot, shoot the monochrome shot in a way that will make blending easier afterwards. In this case, we made sure the background was dark and that the incense smoke curling up out of the cup was backlit.

Blending the Color and the Monochrome Images

After shooting both photographs, blend the steam from the monochrome image with the color image.

First, convert the color image into an L*a*b* mode image. Then make the L* channel active in the Channels palette and paste the monochrome image into it or drag the monochrome image on top of it. What this does is replace only the L* channel with the monochrome image with the steam.

By doing only this the color image may become darker or lighter, so you need to use a tone curve to adjust the L* channel only. In this case, it became darker so we used the Curves dialog box to attempt to return the color image to its original brightness.

At this point, the steam was included in the color image. If you look carefully, however, you'll notice that the tea that was supposed to be in the cup has disappeared, as shown on the bottom left. This is because when we took the monochrome photograph, we placed incense inside the cup instead of pouring tea into it.

We therefore made the original color image (without the steam) into a layer on top of the version with the steam. To this layer, we added a layer mask and then used a black Paintbrush on the top layer to mask out all the layer except for the tea. The end result was a photograph of steam rising out of a cup of tea.

NOTE

This may seem like a lot of trouble for a photograph that could've been done in one shot with a film camera. The point not to be missed, however, is the creative flexibility provided by having a digital camera in the studio.

Photographing a moving subject using a three-shot camera. We did it!

Multiple Exposure Photographs

You often see photographers making multiple exposure photographs in commercial advertising studios or on location, for including things such as LED displays. No concept exists in digital cameras, however, of exposing the same film surface two or three times without advancing it. So, with digital photography, we achieve the same result by blending together multiple exposures afterwards in Photoshop to create the same effect.

■ Be careful about the same things you would if you were taking multiple exposures on film. Make sure the camera is fixed firmly in place so it can't move.

■ Set your lighting so that it'll make the job of blending several layers together in Photoshop easier.

■ If you change the aperture, the subject depth of field will change, causing the image to look unnatural when the exposures are blended. Therefore do not change the aperture. Adjust the brightness with lighting and/or neutral density (ND) filters.

■ See the previous section, "Photographing Moving Subjects," as well as "Double Scanning" in Chapter 4-4, "Practical Scanning Operations," for more information about blending techniques.

This Piece of Artwork

Here we photographed a Broncolor strobe power supply. On the first exposure we set subdued lighting so the unit would look realistic, as if in a darkened studio.

On the second exposure, we completely eliminated the lighting in order to make an exposure of just the red characters on the LED control panel.

We blended the images using the Screen blending mode.

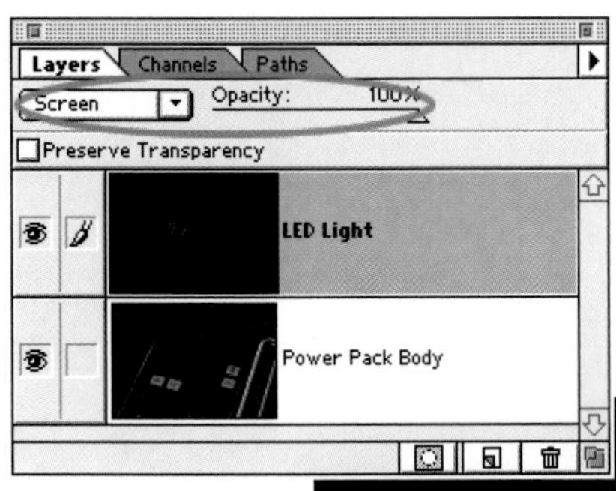

05 5

Browsing

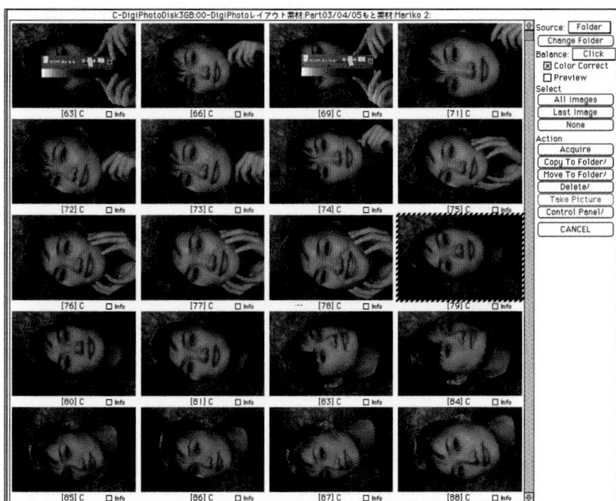

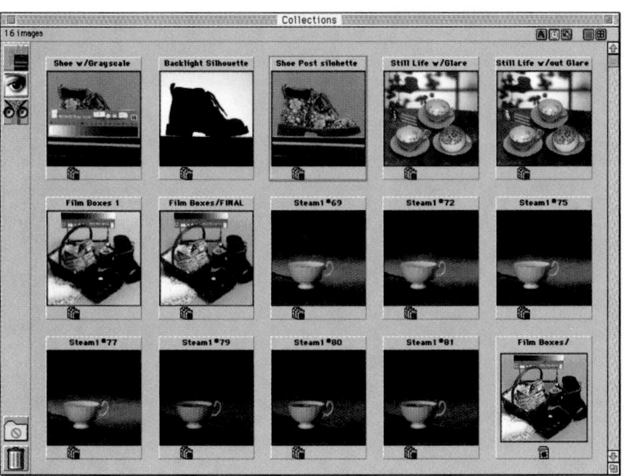

Selecting Your Photographs

It is important to be able to select the best frame from a series of exposures by digital cameras, particularly when you are photographing people in the studio or if you are trying out different techniques in situations like taking outdoor snapshots.

Digital cameras have limitations as to how extensively you can view all of your frames at one time (we call this "browsing") and compare the best candidates, the way you can by spreading transparencies out on a light box.

Nikon E2

The Nikon E2 digital camera comes with Nikon E2 Browser software. This enables you to view 80×62-pixel sample images of your frames to see the effects of different apertures, shutter speeds, and so on. It is a separate application and has a built-in function for exporting selected frames to Photoshop.

Kodak DCS Series

The Kodak DCS series software is a Photoshop plug-in with a built-in browser. It enables you to view all your frames at one time, zoom in on one frame only, or save subsets of photos from a shooting session into different folders. You can also select from a number of different types of lighting correction curves, including daylight, fluorescent, tungsten, and flash, before transferring the data to the computer. You can then export the images to Photoshop with a preliminary color correction already done.

Scitex Leaf DCB II

The Scitex Leaf DCB II comes with two different software applications. The first is called DCB/CatchLight 3.3.3 and is used as you are taking your photographs. The software provides a "postview" image (the opposite of a preview, in that you can see the image immediately after you have taken it) and enables you to adjust the brightness, contrast, and color right on the spot.

The second software application, "Contact Sheet," provides a browser for viewing a lot of stored frames at one time, as shown on the left.

The majority of digital cameras come with some type of browser software that enables you to select the best frames, but all of them are lacking functionality and we have found them mostly unsatisfactory. This is an area that needs development as more and more digital cameras move into the hands of amateurs and pros alike.

In the past, when we scanned silver halide film, this image selection process was already completed before the scanning. Therefore, the only data we had to manage was the digital scan data. But now, with all the information from digital cameras and the Internet, our digital data includes a lot of unnecessary information (this is actually a fundamental problem everywhere in our digital society!). Because of this, we need browsing tools that will enable us to do very detailed viewing, comparison, and measuring, so we can sift through and decide what are necessary and unnecessary photographs.

chapter 6

Digital Photomontages

06 1

Types of Digital Photomontage

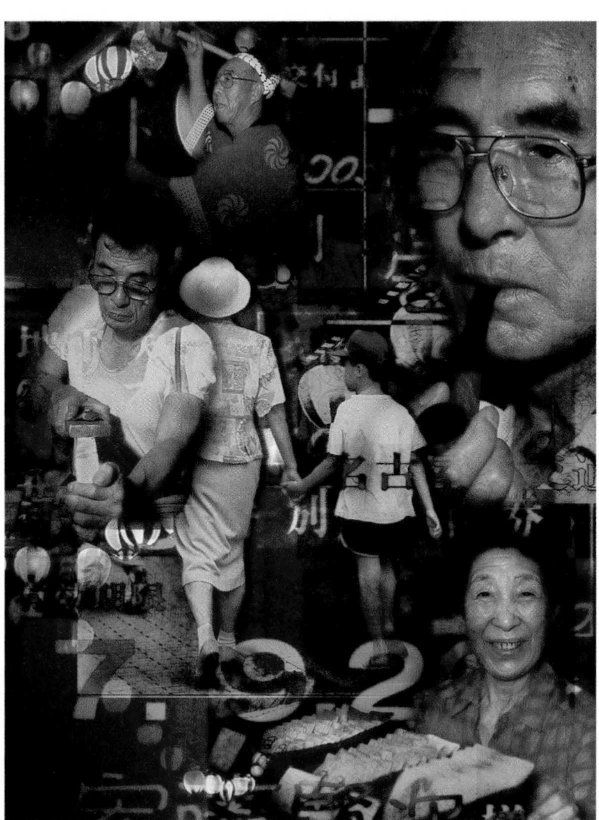

Nagoya Elderly. This is a digital photo collage combining 10–15 different photographs and scanned objects. The final plan for the work, as well as individual image sizes and positions, was not decided beforehand. The final artwork emerged through experimentation with composition and blending of image layers in Photoshop.

Digital Photomontage

Like traditional photomontage, a digital photomontage is created by combining several photographs into one composite image. And like the traditional method, you need lighting, color, and composition skills, as well as a variety of tools, including cameras, film, and lighting equipment. What makes digital photomontage different from traditional photomontage is that the composite image is created using digital tools such as computers, scanners, digital cameras, and image processing software. The addition of these tools to the photomontage process provides us with unlimited freedom for creative expression.

Digital Photomontage can be classified into three groups

- Photo collage
- Photo illustration
- Photorealism

Photo Collage

A digital photo collage is a composite image created by layering several separate photographs or scanned images. The artist has a tremendous amount of creative freedom because images can be combined and enhanced in whatever way desired. Thematically, these separate images can be connected in some way or might have no connection to each other at all. As a result, this method lends itself to spontaneity, experimentation, and a willingness to let "happy accidents" determine the compositional relationships of elements to one another. Because Photoshop and other image processing applications make it relatively easy to seamlessly blend various images together, photo collage is often the first photomontage technique photographers explore (see the artwork of Ann Cutting in Chapter 1).

Digital photo illustration. The size and the relationship between photographic elements were determined in advance, according to a preconceived plan.

Photo Illustration

Unlike photo collage, in which the final effect is often achieved through experimentation, digital photo illustration projects begin with careful determination of the specific subject matter, image sizes, and composition. Compared to the typically looser approach of photo collage, digital photo illustration is intended to communicate a very specific idea or concept (see the artwork of John Lund and Jeff Schewe in Part 1).

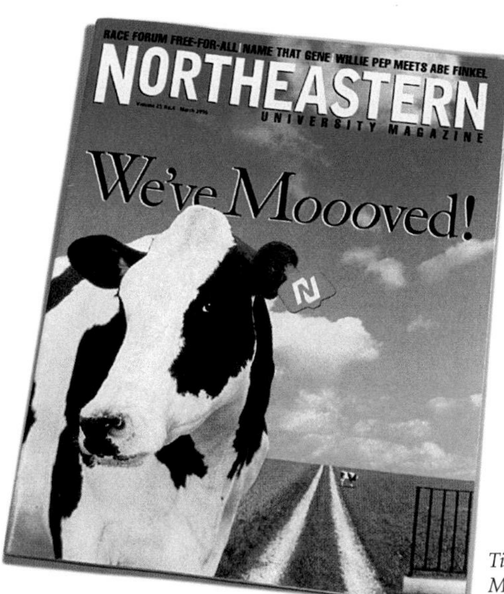

Title: We've Moooved!

Magazine cover using digital photorealism techniques. This work is a composite of six separate images, including separate photos of cows, sky, road, grass, and even a separate photo of a cow's ear tag.

Photorealism

Digital photorealism describes images created to look like real or imaginary worlds. What characterizes photorealism is the careful attention given to details such as highlights, reflections, shadows, and even depth of field. Masking and compositing of source images are so precise, viewers are made to think the work is actually a photo of a real scene and are led to wonder where such a scene might actually exist.

Digital photorealism requires careful planning—from shooting the photographs all the way to scanning and compositing them—and is the most challenging type of photomontage (see the artwork of Michael Brown in Part 1).

The information in this part—as well as the whole book—applies to all the types of photomontage introduced in the preceding sections. We particularly emphasize, however, the skills and techniques necessary to create photorealistic artwork. This is because most of the basic techniques necessary to plan and create photorealistic images can be used when creating other types of photomontage as well.

062

The Digital Photomontage Process

The term *imaging chain* refers to the three processes—image capture, image manipulation, and image output—that comprise digital photography. Let's look at these processes as we move step by step through the creation of an image called "Imaging Chain."

Title: Imaging Chain

Let's briefly look at the basic steps of the digital photo-montage process.

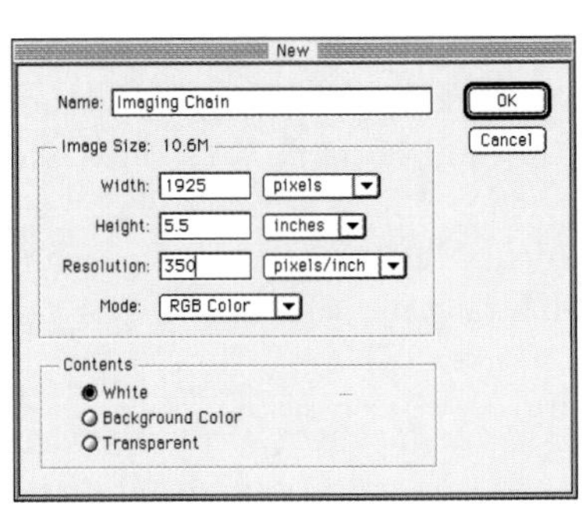

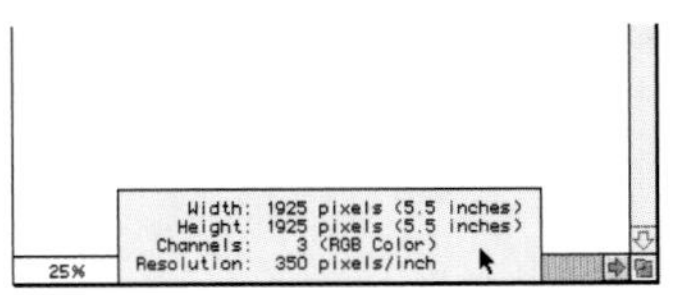

STEPS

1. Defining the image size

We began by defining the final image output size. The pixel dimensions for the image were calculated based on this intended output size. "Imaging Chain" was created for this book, and we knew we wanted a 5 ½×5 ½-inch final image. Because the book was to be printed at a screen ruling of 175 lpi, we doubled the screen-ruling value to arrive at an image resolution of 350 ppi. The final number of pixels came to 1,925×1,925 pixels.

NOTE

Image resolution is calculated using the following formula: screen ruling (lpi)×2 = image resolution

In the case of this book, 175 lpi×2 = 350 ppi. For more information about final output size, image resolution, and final pixel dimensions, see Chapter 2-5, "Recording and Reproduction Devices" and Chapter 7, "Digital Photography Output."

Photograph objects in front of bluescreen to facilitate mask creation.

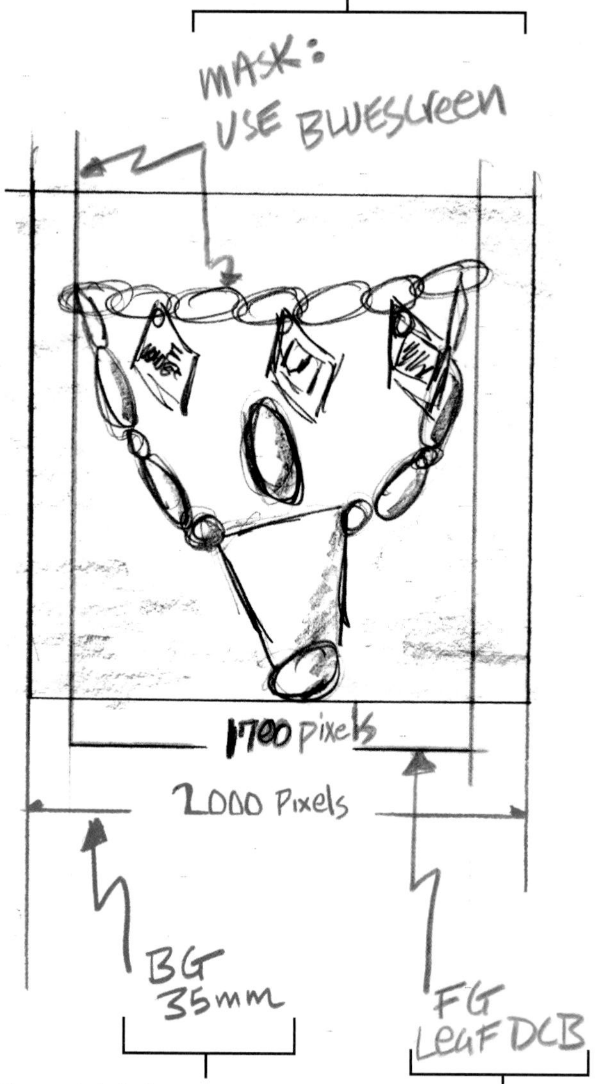

MASK: USE BLUESCREEN

1700 pixels

2000 Pixels

BG 35MM

FG LEAF DCB

Photograph the background texture using a 35 mm camera; make the scan large enough to cover 2,000 pixel width.

Photograph the foreground subject matter with a Scitex Leaf DCBII. Fill the frame/viewfinder of the DCBII enough to give an approximate width of 1,700 pixels to the subject matter.

"Imaging Chain" is an example of digital photo illustration. We sketched the image and determined the size and relationships of the different elements before doing the actual photography.

2. Sketching and Planning

After the image size was set, we drew a sketch of the image. Because digital photomontages use multiple source images, a project can quickly become very complicated. A sketch can provide a vital navigational tool throughout the project. After we made the sketch, we were able to break the image down into its component parts to determine masking techniques, lighting, source image sizes, camera type, and perspective, as detailed below.

■ Masking techniques: If you decide in advance which masking technique to use, you can photograph your original images in ways that make subsequent masking processes easier, such as placing your subjects against plain, neutral-colored backgrounds.

■ Lighting: see step 3.

■ Source image size: Source image sizes are determined based on the final image size. Knowing source image sizes ahead of time helps determine which formats of film, or which type of digital camera, need to be used.

■ Camera type: see step 4.

■ Perspective: Factors such as perspective and depth of field determine camera placement and angle in relationship to all subject matter. They also determine the type of lens to use.

We selected a soft box as the light source for both the metallic chain and the wooden mannequin. Because we used the same lighting for both subjects, we were able to make the degree of light diffusion, the lighting angle, the highlights, and the shadows consistent for both images.

We used a Scitex Leaf DCBII camera back on a Hasselblad 553elx camera body to take the photographs. To simplify masking, we photographed against a blue paper background so we would be able to use a bluescreen masking technique later on (see Chapter 9-9, "Plug-ins").

3. Lighting

Many decisions about lighting are the same for digital photomontage as they are for non-montage photography. This means you use lighting to add mood or atmosphere to the image, or to accentuate or subdue details in the subject matter. Several other points need consideration, however, when you are setting up lighting for digital montage (especially photorealism), including:

- The reflections, highlights, and shadows must be consistent for all the source images.
- To simplify masking processes later on, the background and the subject must be easily distinguishable from one another.

4. Photography

We used a Scitex DCBII to photograph the subjects in this image because the subjects were inanimate and because the camera CCD had an appropriate range of pixels to reproduce the necessary image size. We decided whether to use digital cameras based on the following considerations.

■ Digital cameras

Several factors determine whether you should use a digital camera for a particular photograph: camera availability, whether the camera CCD can produce an image with appropriate pixel dimensions for the source images, and whether it is appropriate for a given animate or inanimate subject. Other types of limitations you have to consider include the fact that some cameras cannot be used with strobe lights and, on others, the lens focal length is too short.

The advantage of using a digital camera is the immediacy of being able to view the photographs right away. In this case, after looking at initial drafts of the composites of the mannequin and chain, we decided to photograph the mannequin directly under the chain (left). This was done so we would be able to capture the actual reflection of the mannequin on the chain (right). Of course, it would have been possible to add reflections to the chain in Photoshop as we composited the images, but photographing the actual reflections was easier and promised a more realistic result (see also the description of the Hip Hog illustration by Jeff Schewe in Part 10).

The Scitex Leaf DCBII is a studio camera that must be connected to a computer when it is used. Therefore, it could not be used outdoors to photograph the side of the corroding dumpster that provided the texture for the composite background. A film-based camera became necessary. When both digital and film-based cameras are used to make the same composite image, we call it hybrid imaging.

Film-Based Cameras

Film-based cameras are very important tools for taking source images for digital photomontage. They are easy to use; photographers are already familiar with them; their images can be easily compared, sorted, and stored; and they generally are less costly than digital cameras. There are times, however, when a composite of photographs originally taken on film can look unnatural. If you shoot multiple photographs on different format films, or even on the same format film, the graininess might vary because of the differences in scaling when the images were digitally scanned.

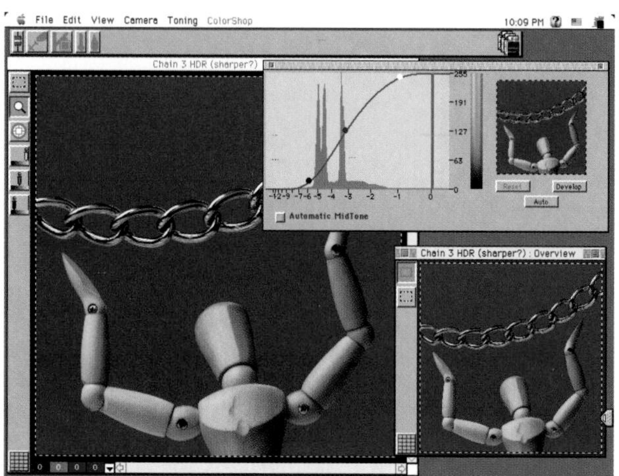

5. Image acquisition/image input

If you shoot your source images with a digital camera, the images are immediately available in digital data form. The next step is simply to acquire and open them in your image-editing application. Silver halide film photographs, in contrast, have to be scanned after they come back from the processing lab and then loaded into the computer.

We used the software accompanying the Scitex Leaf DCBII to transfer the images from the camera into the computer (see Chapter 5, "Digital Exposures and Follow-up Processing").

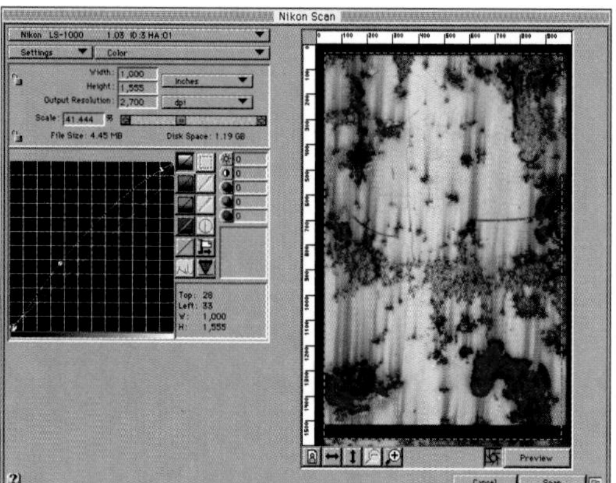

The color-reversal film containing the background texture was scanned on a Nikon LS 1000 35 mm film scanner (see Chapter 4, "Scanning Original Photographs").

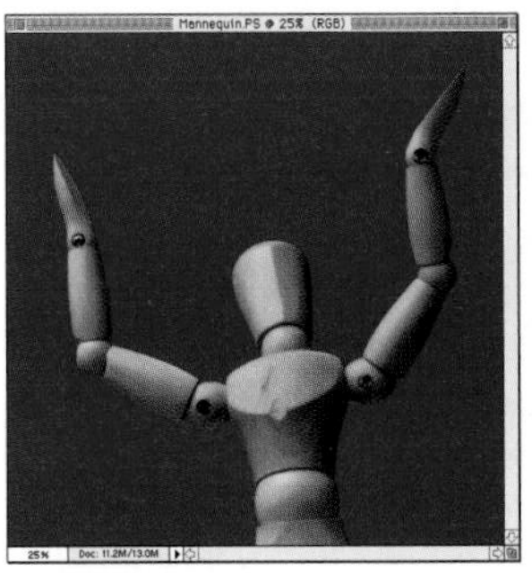

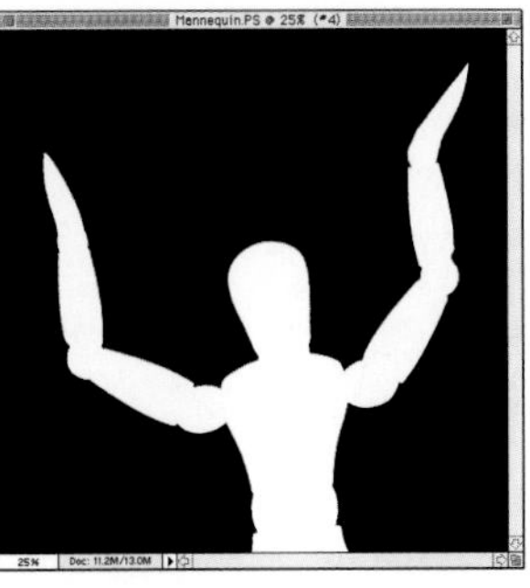

After all the source images were taken, we created an 8-bit alpha channel mask for the foreground image (see Chapter 9-6, "Masking").

6. Masking

Masking is the process of selecting which parts of the image will be altered or copied into other images. The basic concept of how a digital mask works is similar to using high-contrast film to do traditional photomontage in the darkroom (see Chapter 9-6, "Masking").

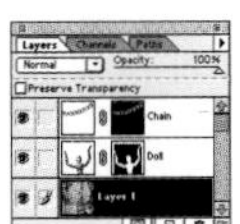

We placed the background texture, mannequin, and chain into three separate layers using the Layers function in Photoshop. Then we composited them.

7. Compositing

After planning, shooting, scanning, and masking are all complete, you can move to compositing. This is when the fun really begins. The sensation of watching your digital photomontage come together on the monitor is very similar to seeing a photograph develop in the developing tray.

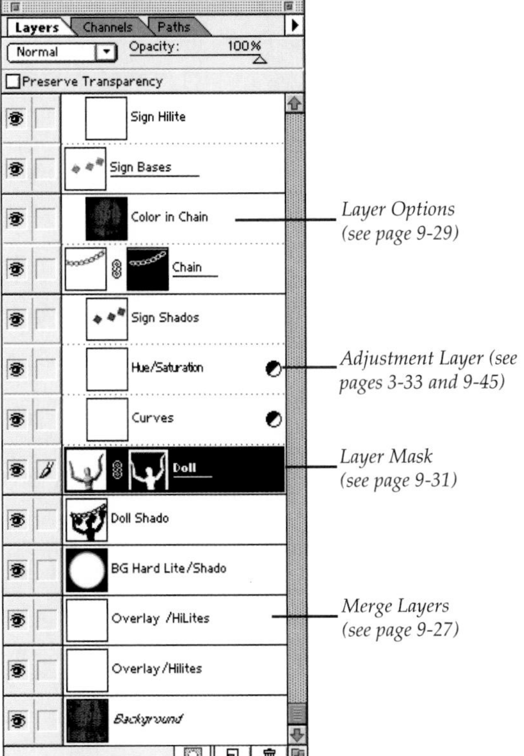

By the time the image was complete, the number of layers had grown considerably. We used both the Adjustment Layer function, used to change the image brightness, and the Merge Layers function many times. All these techniques are discussed in more detail elsewhere in this book.

8. Finishing touches

Many types of artwork can be incorporated into digital photomontage images. For "Imaging Chain," three illustrations that represent the three stages of digital imaging—image capture, image manipulation, and image output—were made using a combination of flat art scans and screen captures.

The final image was completed using a variety of Photoshop image-processing tools (see the completed "Imaging Chain" in the Tutorial Images folder on the CD-ROM accompanying this book). These tools are discussed in more detail elsewhere in this book.

06 3

Types of Source Images

Three Types of Source Images

Digital photomontage contains basically three types of source images: film-based images; images captured with digital cameras; and hybrid images—images captured using both film-based cameras and digital cameras.

Film-Based Source Images

Film is still one of the best methods of creating original photographs for use in digital photomontage. The advantages of using film include the following:

- Film is familiar to the photographer.
- Film is readily available and affordable.
- Film is easily and inexpensively stored.
- Film can be used inside or outside the studio.
- Film is available in many types, which adds to creative freedom.
- Film can be scaled to a wide range of sizes during scanning.

Film's Wide Range of Formats

Because film is available in a wide range of formats, it is particularly useful for creating the range of source images needed for photomontage. The following two case studies illustrate how a wide range of film formats—from 35 mm color negative film to 4×5-inch color reversal film—are used.

Case Study 1

For this magazine cover, we determined how to create our source images based on four factors—time, budget, final image size, and availability of imaging tools. For this image, time was short and the budget was limited. An added complication was that the digital collage images that inspired the client to call us had been taken with a Nikon E2 digital still camera. For this assignment, the client's request was for the same "gritty," low-resolution look. We did not have the same camera at the time, however, so we chose instead to use film.

Image Capture

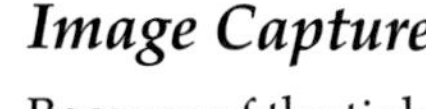

Because of the tight deadline and low budget, we selected negative film for the source images. We exposed several rolls in an afternoon and brought them to a nearby one-hour lab for processing. Before dinner, we had the printed photos in our hands.

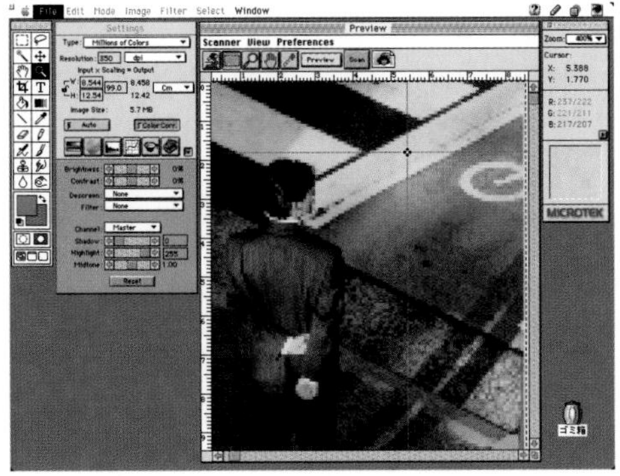

Scanning

We selected the prints we wanted to use and scanned them on a Microtek ScanMaker IIsp scanner. We scanned the prints rather than the film because a film scanner was not available, and we did not have time to have the film scanned using Kodak's PhotoCD process.

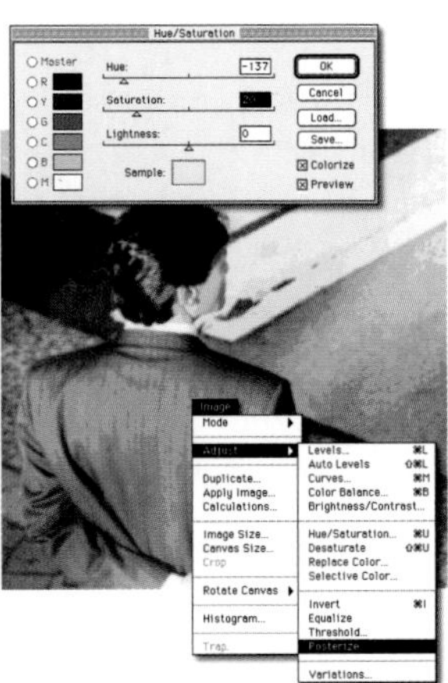

Image Compositing

The image was composited entirely in Photoshop. From the beginning, we wanted an image that looked painterly, not something that looked like a straight, continuous-tone photograph. To give it more of the painted look of an illustration, we used the Colorize function in Photoshop's Hue/Saturation dialog box to tone the individual scans. Then we used the Posterize command to give the continuous-tone photographs a grittier look.

The final image (17 MB) was output on a Kodak XL8300 dye sublimation printer. We submitted this to the client as the finished artwork.

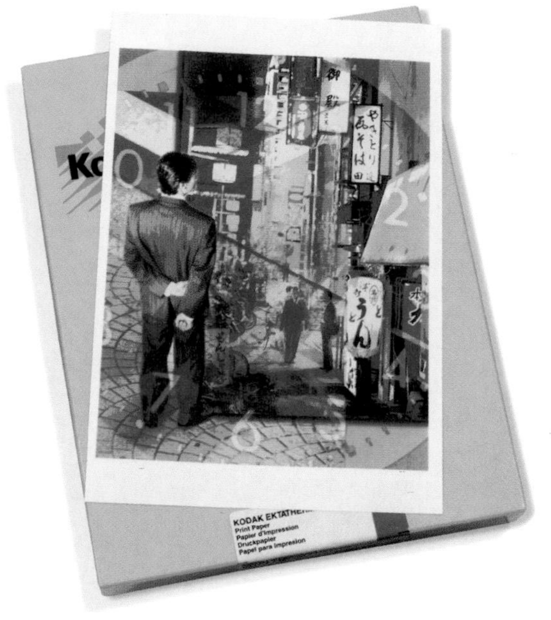

NOTE

Photographers just starting out in digital photography might not have the resources necessary to purchase high-end imaging systems. Because the file sizes you can work with efficiently on average-sized systems are limited, you might experience the frustration of not being able to create images large enough for transparency output (usually a minimum of 4,000 pixels or more on the long dimension of an image, with a minimum file size of approximately 34 MBs).

This limitation, however, can be transformed into a creative opportunity for the thoughtful photographer. By exploring alternative methods of digital output, photographers can offer clients creative output options, such as color copiers, dye-sublimation printers, and Iris inkjet printers. The advantage of this approach is that perfectly acceptable final art can be made from file sizes in the low to medium size range (4–18 MB).

Case Study 2

The quality and file-size requirements for this image were exactly the opposite of those for Case Study 1. The scans were made on a high-resolution film scanner, and output was made using a high-resolution film recorder.

To make this composite image of a car, photographer Michael Brown shot the original scenery and the car on 4×5 film and then scanned the photos on a drum scanner. The average scan size for the 4×5 transparency films was 75–80 MB. Using Photoshop to composite the images, Brown's photomontages normally have 3–4 layers and average 200 MB in size.

He sent the composited image file (approximately 75 MB after all layers had been flattened into a single layer) to a service bureau for 5×7 transparency output on an LVT film recorder (the bottom piece of film on the lightbox at left). The result of using such high-resolution input and output methods is the creation of a digital "original," which meets the clients' demands for quality equivalent to that of an original 4×5 sheet of film exposed using conventional film-based methods.

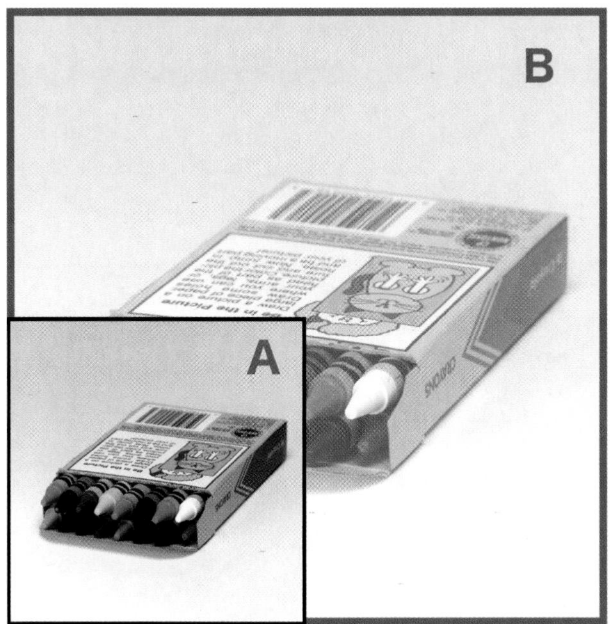

Assume that your final image size must be 4,000×4,000 pixels (B). But you have a camera that can capture only 2,048×2,048 pixels (A). Unless you enlarge the image by interpolating, you cannot use this camera. Interpolation can cause image quality to deteriorate, so you have to decide whether your method of output will have the quality you want after interpolation. Generally speaking, an increase in size of 200 percent, with appropriate image manipulation steps, can produce acceptable quality for most offset printed output.

Digital Camera Source Images

Particularly with respect to image size and quality, digital camera technology has been rapidly developing and improving. This makes a digital camera in the studio not only useful, but almost essential for creating source images for photomontage. The primary advantage of using a digital camera over a film-based camera is the unprecedented level of creative spontaneity afforded by having immediate access to the photographs.

Using Digital Cameras

The decision to use a digital camera depends on whether you have the right camera for the subject and whether your camera CCD can capture the number of pixels required for your source image size.

If your studio has a digital camera with a 2,048×2,048-pixel imager, for example, and you need to create a source image with 4,000×4,000 pixels, your camera's image size is not large enough. (Additional factors, such as whether your studio's lighting is compatible or whether the subject matter is animate or inanimate, also can have an impact on whether you can use the camera for the assignment. For the moment, though, this discussion deals only with size of the camera's imager.)

If your final image size is 3,000×3,000 pixels, however, and you are creating a photomontage, you can easily use the 2,048×2,048-pixel camera and shoot multiple source images. These images can then be composited to build a final image size that is close to 3,000×3,000 pixels.

This illustration shows how a single 3,000×3,000-pixel photomontage (red outline) can be created using a 2,048×2,048 Scitex Leaf DCBII. No interpolation was necessary with this technique, and the first-generation quality of the original photographs was maintained. The important point is that a digital camera is a wonderful tool for a photography studio to own for quickly creating high-quality source images for photomontage work.

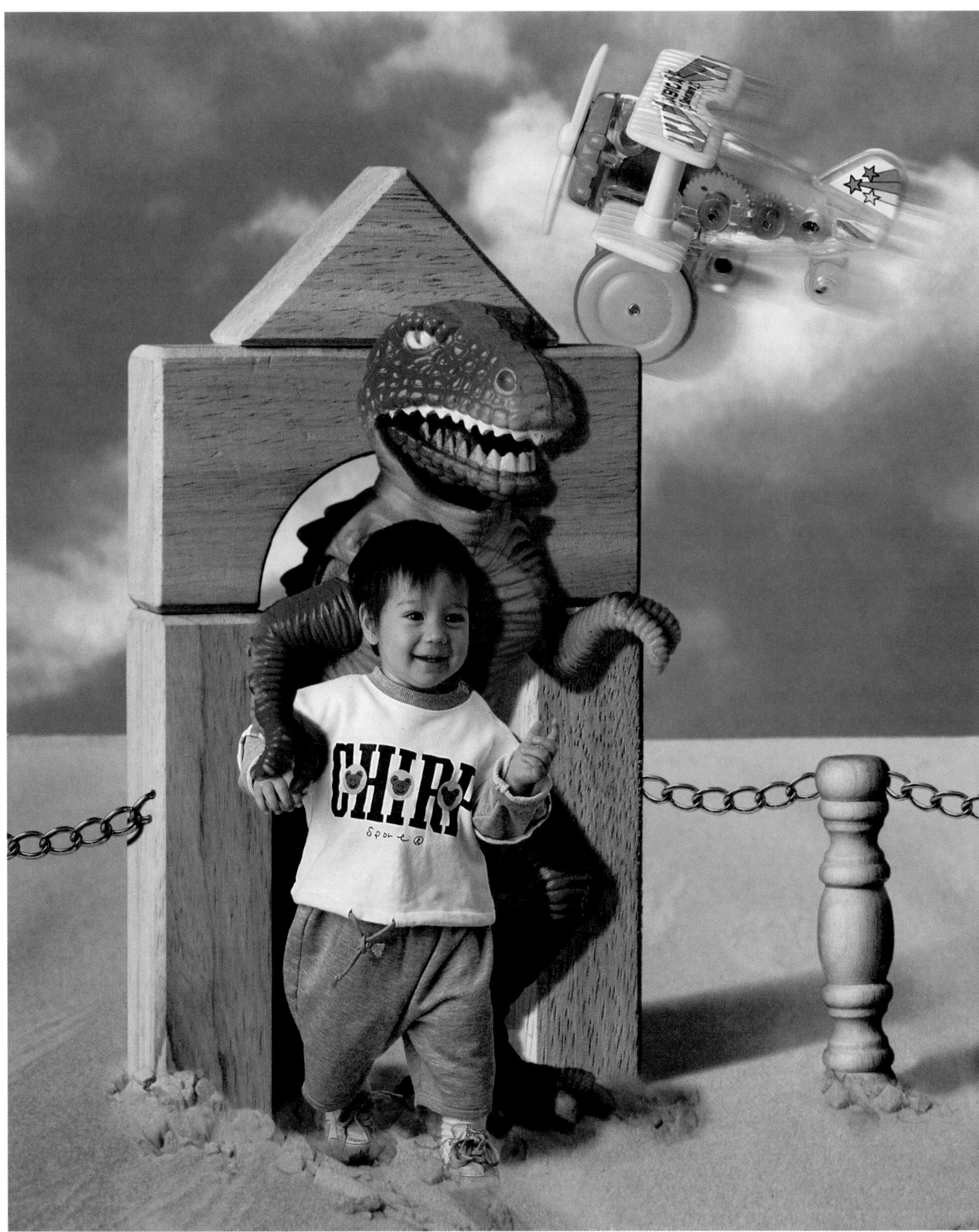

Title: Just T/Rex and Me

Digital Camera Case Study

"Just T/Rex & Me" is an example of how a photomontage can be created using source images from a variety of digital cameras with varying pixel dimensions.

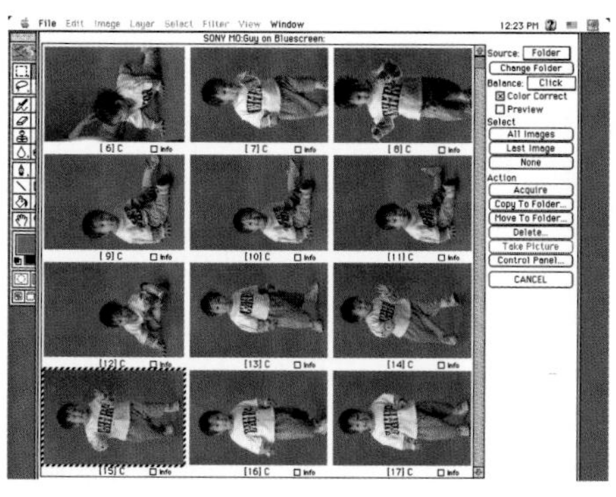

■ Kodak DCS 460

An action photograph of a child taken with the one-shot Kodak DCS 460 formed the basis of this fantasy image of a child with his larger-than-life toys. A number of photos for this project were shot against blue background paper to simplify a masking technique called bluescreen.

■ Scitex Leaf DCBII

We gathered toys from the child's playroom and photographed them in the studio using a Scitex Leaf DCBII 3-shot camera. The wood blocks and the dinosaur were photographed to fill the frame as much as possible, making them approximately 2,000 pixels in height. The camera was kept in a fixed position in order to maintain 1:1 size relationships between the blocks, the dinosaur, and the airplane.

The camera was kept in a fixed position in order to maintain the 1:1 relationships between the blocks, the dinosaur, and the airplane. This was done in order to avoid resizing any of the images when compositing them, an important consideration when using digital cameras.

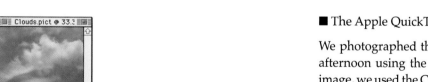

■ The Apple QuickTake 150

We photographed the clouds on the way to lunch one afternoon using the QuickTake 150. After resizing the image, we used the Curves and the Hue/Saturation commands in Photoshop to enhance the low-resolution file. The image was interpolated and enlarged nearly four times its original size, so we used the Gaussian Blur filter to soften the artifacts that resulted from the resizing.

Hybrid Source Images

Hybrid imaging enables us to take advantage of the strong points of both types of cameras—the affordability, high quality, and mobility of film-based cameras on the one hand, and the immediacy and creative freedom of digital cameras on the other.

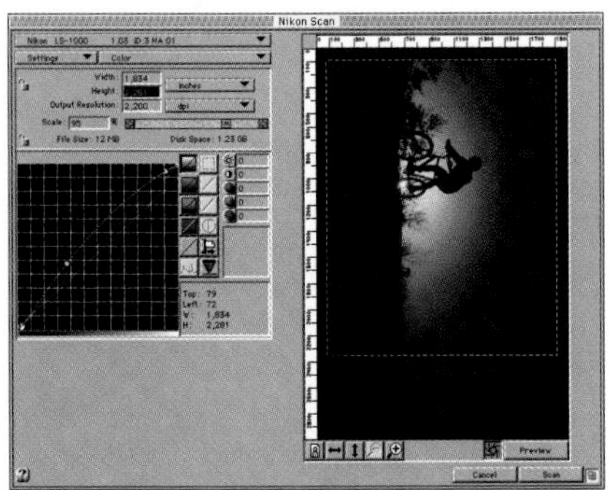

We used both film-based cameras and digital cameras, for example, to create a simulated ad for a bicycle helmet. First we pulled an image of a mountain bike from our stock library and scanned it on a Nikon LS 1000 scanner at 2,000×1,500 pixels.

Then we photographed the helmet using the Scitex Leaf DCBII. The width of the helmet came to approximately 2,000 pixels when the helmet filled the entire frame—just the right size for compositing the mountain bike image without having to resize.

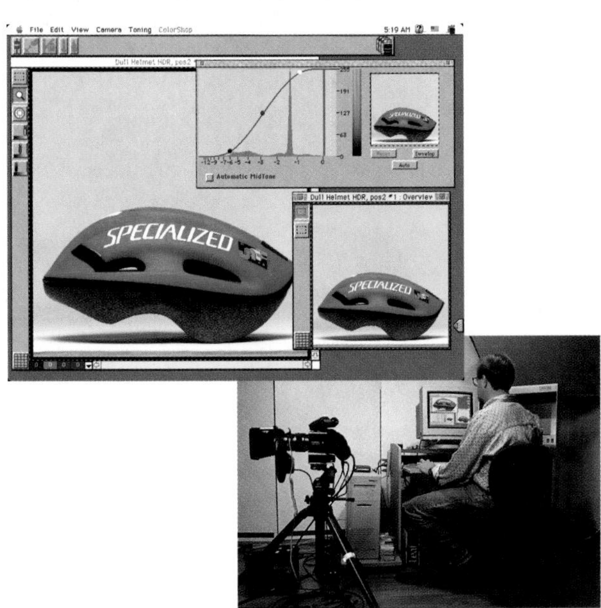

We composited the final image in Photoshop. From start to finish, this project was ready to hand off to the client in only two hours and six minutes! This is not a fantasy, but a realistic example of the impact of digital photography on the studio workflow. This is how the time broke down:

- Stock library search: 10 minutes
- Scanning: 10 minutes
- Lighting, setup: 30 minutes
- Shooting with the Scitex Leaf DCBII: 15 minutes
- Image compositing: 1 hour
- Storage onto portable media (230 MB MO disk): 1 minute

(For another example of digital photography and studio workflow, see the biography about Andy Darlow in Chapter 10.)

SPECIALIZED

06 4

The Characteristics of Film and Digital Photomontage

Grain

In traditional photography, film selection is often based on film grain. A photographer doing a product shoot, for example, usually selects a fine-grain film for maximum clarity and sharpness, while a fashion photographer might choose a high-speed film or push a slower film to evoke a particular atmosphere or mood through the use of exaggerated grain. The same principles apply when selecting film for digital photomontage. The digital photo environment, however, introduces some other variables—such as the effects of scanning upon grain—that must be understood if you want to create predictable results.

Fine Grain

One characteristic of fine grain film is that it can be made coarser through processing. The reverse, however, is not true. A coarse grain film cannot be made finer through processing. This same principle applies in digital photography.

Standard processing

Push processing

A scan of a grainy photo cannot be made any less grainy without incurring unwanted side effects. It is possible to soften the grain with a Blur filter, for example, and then use a Sharpen filter to add sharpness back to the image. But unless you're trying to create a special-textured effect, the results will be blotchy and disappointing.

Coarse grain original photo

Blur and Sharpen filters added

In contrast, a photo originally taken using a fine-grain film can be modified on the computer to have a coarser grain texture through the use of a Noise filter. The Noise filter can be used to control a range of simulated grain effects, including multicolored noise, monochrome noise, or even different amounts or intensities of noise within the same image. This is an important consideration for many types of imaging and retouching tasks in which careful attention to the film grain must be taken to ensure consistency of grain in the final image.

Fine Grain Original

Noise filter added

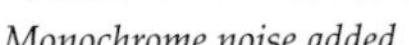
Monochrome noise added

Amount of noise increased

The quality of photos used in photomontage can range from high-quality, first-generation film or digital camera originals to low-quality film dupes. If you end up having to use both in the same image, subtle use of the Noise filter can be one way to unify the quality of the varying source images.

Film Grain and Scanning

In a traditional darkroom, film grain in a photographic print becomes more noticeable the higher the magnification of the enlargement. The same is true for scanning. The more the magnification of the scan is increased, the more noticeable the film grain becomes.

The section of the sky inside the white outline was scanned at 512×768 pixels, resulting in a 1.5 MB image file. The part of the sky outside of the white outline was scanned from the same slide at a higher magnification, resulting in an 18 MB image file (2,048×3,072 pixels). When composited together and compared, the piece of the 18 MB file looks considerably softer and grainier than the 1.5 MB scan.

This becomes a problem if you attempt to take a small section of one photograph and scan it as large as possible to composite with another photograph. The grain and sharpness of the magnified image looks unnatural and out of place when composited with the other image.

NOTE

That said, it is still sometimes necessary to composite source images of varying quality. In these cases, you must do what you can to improve the look of the image. Adding noise is one method, as previously mentioned. But when image quality is radically different, you might need to take another approach. You can blur a soft and grainy image, for example, and use it as a background for a sharp, fine grain foreground subject instead of trying to make both images look the same. Other possibilities include applying hue changes and special effects filters to all your source images in order to give them the same color and texture.

Two different photographs of a tomato were scanned to the same size. On film, the tomato on the left took up a smaller piece of film than the tomato on the right. To make the scans the same size, we had to enlarge the tomato on the left during scanning, which softened details and increased graininess.

Combining Different Film Formats

In digital photography, it is not uncommon to have to composite source images that originate from different film formats—typically 35 mm, 120 mm, and 4×5. The success of these composites, especially photorealistic images, depends on how well you understand the concept of resolution and how carefully you have planned your shoot ahead of time.

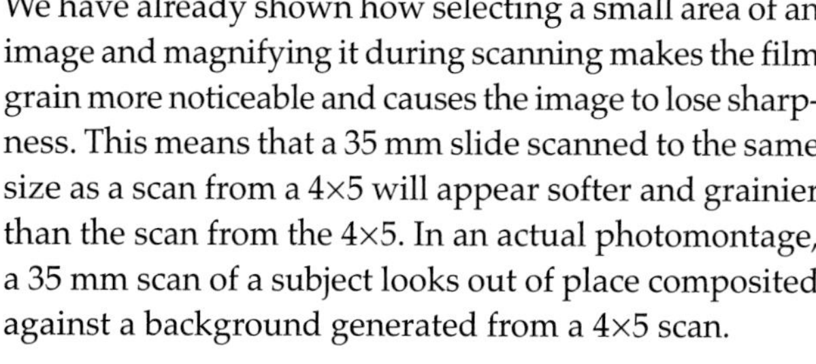

We have already shown how selecting a small area of an image and magnifying it during scanning makes the film grain more noticeable and causes the image to lose sharpness. This means that a 35 mm slide scanned to the same size as a scan from a 4×5 will appear softer and grainier than the scan from the 4×5. In an actual photomontage, a 35 mm scan of a subject looks out of place composited against a background generated from a 4×5 scan.

Another way to think of this is to imagine that the image area of a 4×5 is actually 3½ inches by 4½ inches, and the image area of a 35 mm slide is 1 inch by 1½ inches (we are using rounded numbers to make the math easier). A 1,000 ppi scan of the 4×5 image would generate an image that is 3,500×4,500 pixels. Similarly, a 1,000 ppi scan of the 35 mm slide would generate 1,000×1,500 pixels.

If we assume that the emulsion and the film speed were the same for both images, when the two scans are composited, they should have similar qualities of grain and sharpness (the match might not be 100 percent given differences in lenses and scanner types, but it would be very close).

Photos of both the watch and the orange were scanned at the same resolution, 1,000 dpi, in order to maintain the original film size relationships of the two objects. When composited, the qualities of grain and sharpness were essentially the same.

Next, imagine scanning the 35 mm slide at a resolution of 3,000 ppi. The final scan size becomes 3,000 pixels by 4,500 pixels, close to the pixel dimensions of the 4×5 scan.

Because the scan resolution of the slide was increased to 3,000 ppi, you might believe that the higher resolution scan would equal the quality of the 4×5 high resolution scan (after all, there's more information per inch).

Unfortunately, this is not the case. More pixels per inch were generated from scanning at the higher resolution, but the result is that a smaller piece of the film was magnified to the same size as the scan of the 4×5 film. Increased resolution translates into increased magnification, and this means that the same type of image degradation that occurs when you make traditional photographic enlargements will occur when you scan at higher resolutions. Think of it this way—if you photograph the same subject with a 35 mm slide and a 4×5 transparency and enlarge both to a 16×20 inch print, the print from the 4×5 will be much sharper and less grainy than the print from the 35 mm slide. The same result occurs in scanning.

When we increase the scanning resolution of a 35 mm transparency to 3,000 dpi, the original size is considerably enlarged. Because the percentage of enlargement is high, the grain is more noticeable and there is an overall loss of sharpness (compare the sharpness of the orange stem with the example on the previous page). When we composite the orange with the watch, the differences are obvious and the result feels unnatural.

NOTE

Most commercial photographers have had their photographs scanned electronically for color separations and have seen the results. This experience should make it easy to understand that the grain and sharpness of a magazine cover printed from a 35 mm slide and a magazine cover printed from 4×5 film are entirely different.

A good rule of thumb for maintaining image quality when creating composites from source photographs taken on multiple film formats is to maintain the same size ratios during the scanning stage. For instance, if a 35 mm slide (approximately 1×1½ inches) and 4×5 film are going to be used in the same project, the 35 mm slide should not be scanned any larger than one third the size of the scan from a 4×5.

Of course, there are exceptions. A good example is when an image with little detail, such as a 35 mm slide of soft, puffy clouds, is used as a background for an object shot with a 4×5 camera.

NOTE

When planning a digital image, especially a photorealistic image, that will use different film formats from start to finish, it is best to use the same film type and film speed. This is the most effective way to ensure consistencies in grain, color saturation, and contrast.

On the other hand, if you scan a 35 mm Kodachrome 25 ultra-fine-grain slide to be the same size as a scan from a slightly grainy 6×7 ISO 400 film, the increased magnification of the slide scan will more or less even out the grain characteristics between both images, and there will be little noticeable difference between them.

Compositing with Different Film Formats

Let's look at one other example of a composite that combines several different film formats. The images were a 35 mm film of the clouds as a background texture, a 6×6 format image of a computer, and a 35 mm film containing the image of the tomato that appears on the monitor screen.

Because the background was already soft (clouds), without sharp details, it was possible to scan it larger than the medium format original without worrying about the image quality. Any additional softness through magnification would only help. The 35 mm tomato and the monitor screen were close in size, in terms of film space. Using the same basic input resolution for both (and assuming same film type) meant that the tomato could be composited inside the monitor without looking out of place.

If we compare these two still-life photos, we see that the left photo is flatter and less saturated but has a greater tonal range than the image on the right (for example, the shadow detail of the lower right portion of the basket is more open in the left-hand version than the right).

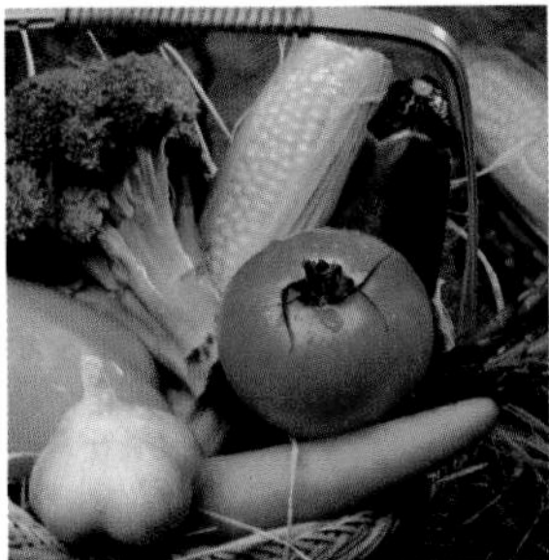

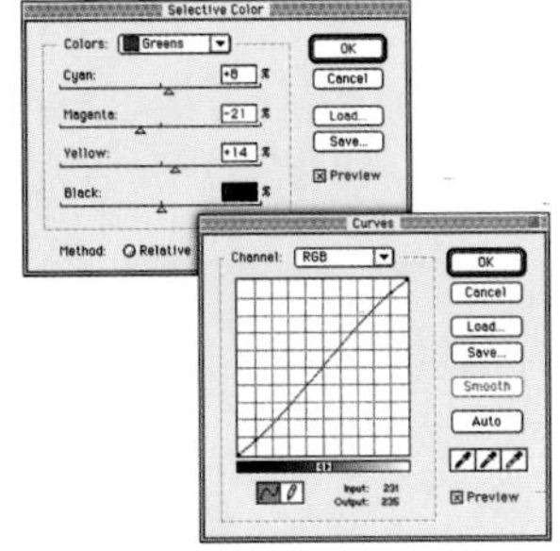

We adjusted the top left image with Selective Color and Curves in Photoshop to increase the color saturation of the greens and to darken the shadow tones.

Color Saturation and Tonal Range

Two other factors, aside from film grain, that you need to consider when you are selecting film for photomontage are the color saturation and tonal range of the film. Traditionally, photographers have made film selections based on personal style, assignment, or specialty. A film with punchier colors and high contrast, for example, might be right for one photographer or assignment but not for another.

In digital photomontage, we select film based on how well the dynamic range of tones in the film can be captured during the scanning process. With the exception of expensive high-end scanners, the film scanners most often used by photographers have difficulty holding details in the D-max areas—the shadows—of a photo.

Therefore, it is important to have as wide a range of tones as possible in the original photograph (for example, a film that can hold detail in deep shadows). This generally means that a less saturated film with a wider tonal range (just slightly) makes a better source for scanning than a punchier film with more contrast. Any lack of color saturation or contrast in the original film can be easily compensated for in your imaging application.

If the image has no detail in the shadows to begin with, no detail will be captured in the scan. Even if the shadow areas of the film have sufficient detail, the dynamic range of the film might be wider than the scanner can record. In either case, trying to open shadow detail where there is none using a tone curve adjustment in an imaging application might lighten the shadow areas, but the adjustment is likely to generate noise in the shadows (for more information, see Chapters 3 and 4).

06 5

Determining Scan Sizes for Source Images

To Adjust Size During Scanning or to Resize After Scanning?

For most digital photomontage work, it is best to scan source images at the size they will be used at in the final image. Although it is always possible to resize images in Photoshop or Live Picture, the process of resampling involves either downsampling (making an image smaller by removing data) or interpolation (making an image larger by adding pixels where none existed). Both processes can affect the quality of the image. Therefore, as a rule of thumb, the material in this chapter emphasizes the importance of sizing images correctly at the scanning stage as the best starting point.

Image scanned at proper size for offset reproduction.

Image scanned at a small size, then resized up. Notice the softening of details.

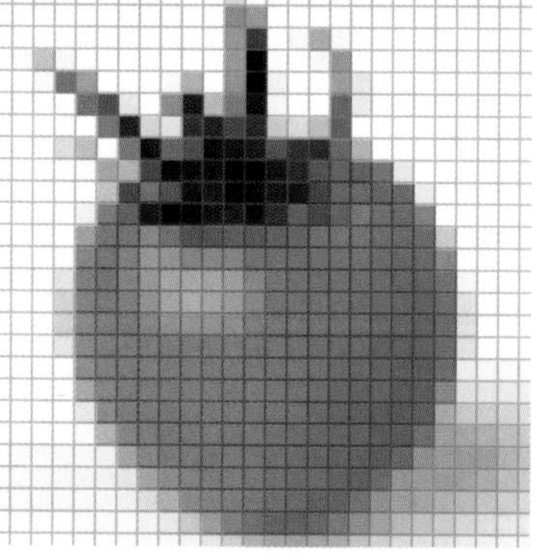

NOTE

When it is difficult to determine scan sizes in advance because the sizes of source images for the final piece change as you are working on a project, you can consider the following methods:

- First, scan all the photos at the same low resolution and do a rough composite. From those results, you can calculate how much each of the source photos has been enlarged or reduced during the image-editing process and then rescan the images at the final, correct size and make a high-resolution version of the image.
- Scan all the source images larger than what you imagine their maximum pixel dimensions will be in the final image and then downsample them as necessary. This produces better results than going in the opposite direction and interpolating (or upsampling) all the images.

Resolution

No other image processing term is more vague or misused than resolution. Refer to Chapter 2-6 for thorough explanations of resolution, resolving power, input resolution, image resolution, output resolution scanning density, ppi, and dpi.

Pictures as Pixels

When a photograph is scanned or captured with a digital camera, the image is displayed on the computer monitor as rows and columns of pixels. In most cases, you determine the number of pixels you need to scan the image horizontally and vertically by multiplying the input resolution by the final output size of the final image. With digital cameras, the pixel dimensions of the input image are determined by the number of light sensors on the camera's CCD (with some exceptions, such as scan-type cameras that are capable of capturing several different resolutions).

Fundamentally, all images are handled as pixels in all imaging applications. Therefore, when we refer to image size in our discussion of image compositing, it is better to use the pixel dimensions, expressed in the number of horizontal pixels (rows) and the number of vertical pixels (columns), rather than inches or millimeters.

500 pixels

500 pixels

Calculating Scan Sizes

After you have determined the overall pixel dimensions for an image, it is relatively simple to calculate the scan sizes for each of the individual source images. For example, the width of the grid to the left is 1,000 pixels and the height is also 1,000 pixels (one grid subtile represents 100 pixels). We wanted the object in the image (a golf ball) to occupy one fourth of the image, so we needed to scan the golf ball so it had a diameter of 500 pixels.

We used pencil and paper to make a rough sketch, calculated the total pixel dimensions of the scan, and then made the scan.

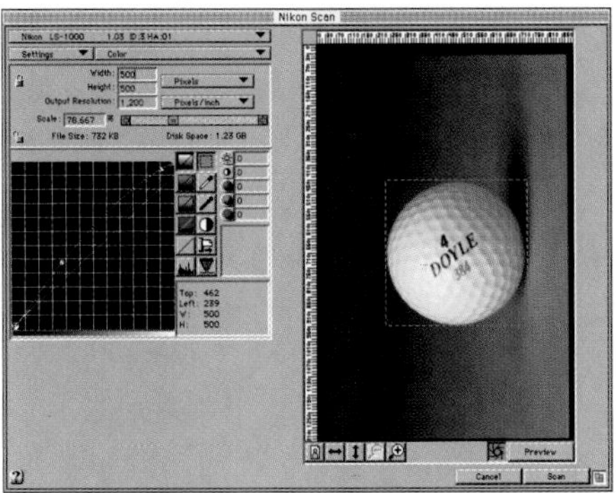

We created a cropping frame around the golf ball in the LS 1000 software preview window. We adjusted and locked the pixel dimensions of the frame to approximately 500×500 pixels and then entered 500 into the Width and Height fields (you can unlock the size of the cropping frame later to scan at a slightly larger size if you need to).

We composited the scanned image of the golf ball (500×500 pixels) into the 1,000×1,000-pixel grid, and the golf ball fit neatly into one fourth of the image space, as planned.

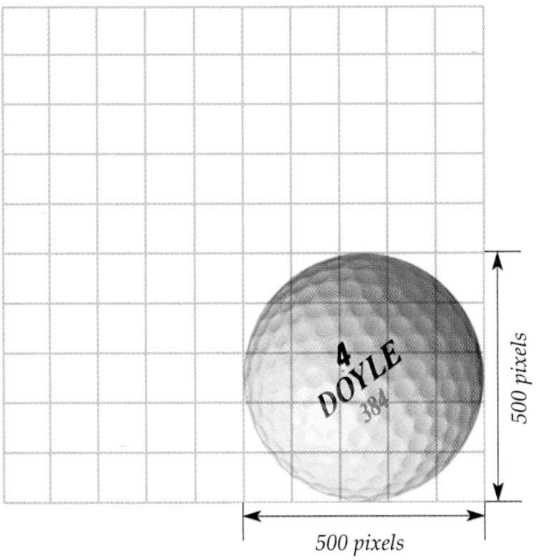

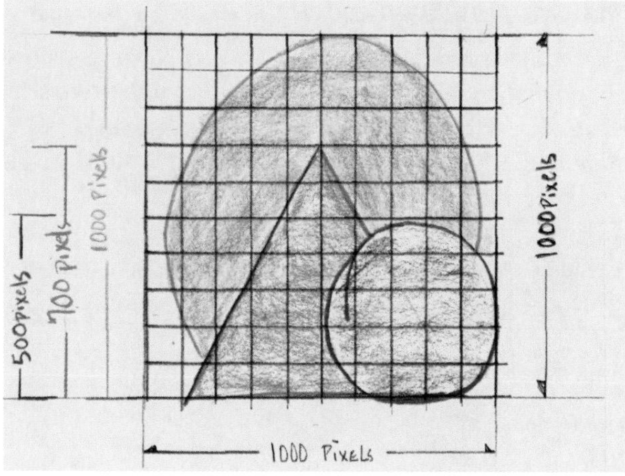

Calculating Scan Sizes—A Case Study

In this section, we provide an actual example of one method for calculating scan sizes.

STEPS

1. We began by deciding we wanted an image 1,000×1,000 pixels in size. Then we made a sketch of these overall image dimensions and added a grid to that, subdividing the sketch into units of 100 pixels.

2. Next we added shapes representing an orange, a wood cone, and a golf ball to the sketch. Once the shapes were drawn, it was easy to determine what their scan sizes should be, by referring to the grid. We could immediately see, for example, that the cone needed a pixel height of approximately 700 pixels.

3. We scanned all the elements based on the calculations in step 2 and composited these images into a 1,000×1,000-pixel file. As you can see, the scanned and composited objects match the sizes planned for in the initial sketch.

NOTE

When you need more precise scan sizes, first sketch the dimensions of the final image (let's say, 8×10) or a reduced size that maintains the aspect ratio (say, half of 8×10, which is 4×5). Then use a ruler and measure the components of the sketch in inches. Multiply these dimensions by the output image resolution (for example, 350 ppi) to determine the necessary pixel dimensions of the scan. For example, a component that occupies 2×3 inches of a final 8×10-inch, 350 ppi image requires a scan size of 700×1050 (350×2 inches, 350×3 inches).

Set these dimensions for the cropping frame in the scanner driver software preview window and make the scan. If the input resolution is defined in terms of pixels rather than dpi from the start, it eliminates a lot of unnecessary, complicated calculations.

06 6

Shooting Original Images

Shooting Using the Same Size Ratio

The easiest way to manage sizes of different objects for photomontage is to shoot each of the objects on the same format film at the same size ratio to each other. This way, the actual size ratios between the objects will be maintained on the film.

NOTE

It is particularly important to maintain size ratios between objects when you are using digital cameras to shoot source images for compositing. To maintain first generation quality (without resizing or rotating), source images have to be photographed in the proper size ratio to one another.

Fixed Camera Position—A Case Study

Fixing the position of the camera and the focal length of the lens is the easiest way to photograph objects so that the size ratio is carried over onto film. In this case study, we photographed a baseball and a golf ball. Because we kept the actual size ratio between the two balls the same when we photographed them, the same ratio was easily maintained when the images were scanned.

Scanning the Baseball

We scanned the full-frame, 852×1,271-pixel transparency of the baseball at 1,300 ppi.

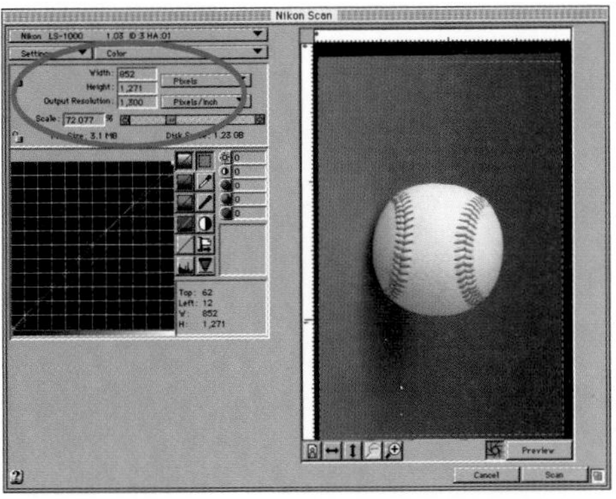

Scanning the Golf Ball

Next, we scanned the full-frame transparency of the golf ball using the same scanner settings we used for the baseball.

NOTE

We made full-frame scans of both transparencies in order to maintain scan size consistency.

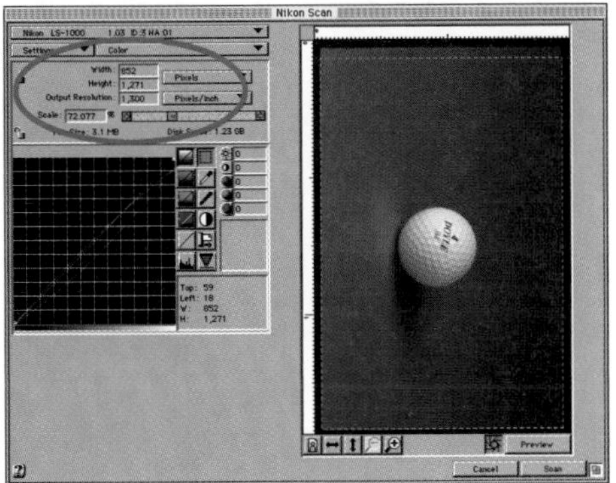

Compositing the Baseball and the Golf Ball

Because we scanned the slides of the baseball and the golf ball using the same settings, the actual size ratios between them were maintained when we composited them into one file.

Using the Entire Film Space

Although photographing multiple objects at the same size ratio to one another helps to simplify size relationships at the scanning stage, it limits the range of possible scan sizes and uses for the photographs. The small area of the film that the golf ball occupies when it is photographed in proportion to the baseball, for example, limits how large it can be magnified at the scanning stage. As we previously saw with the image of the tomato, if you magnify a small area of film too much, the result can be a relatively soft and grainy image.

To maximize the usefulness of photographs for digital photo compositing, it is best to photograph source images to take up as much of the film space as possible. As we see to the left, for example, the golf ball was photographed at the same size as the baseball by moving the camera forward.

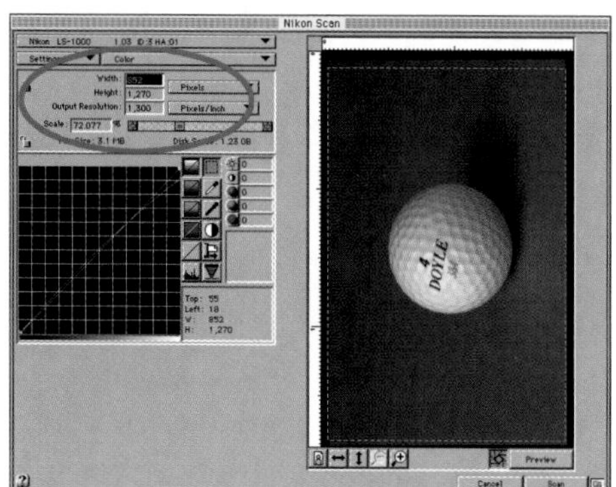

Scanning the Golf Ball

We scanned the full frame of the larger golf ball photograph using the same settings we used on the original baseball slide.

Compositing

Because the two balls were the same size on film, and they were scanned using the same size settings, they were the same size when composited together.

Using the Scanner to Adjust Size

When objects that are the same size on film need to be different sizes in the composite, we adjust their sizes at the scanning stage. In order to composite the large photograph of the golf ball with the photograph of the baseball that represents their real world size relationship, for example, we have to reduce the size of the golf ball when we make the scans.

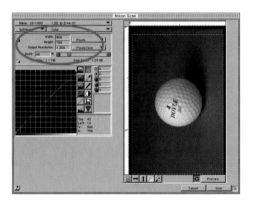

First, we determined that the actual size of the golf ball is about 60 percent of the size of the baseball. Sixty percent of the baseball's original scan size is 510×760 pixels, so we scanned the golf ball at those dimensions.

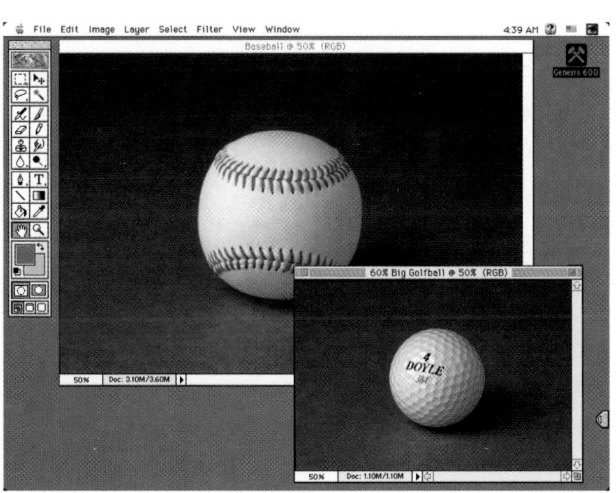

When we display both these scans on the monitor at a zoom ratio of 1:1, the golf ball is clearly smaller than the baseball. If we were to composite the two balls together in the same image, the size relationship between them would be realistic.

Manipulating Size Relationships

One of the most fun aspects of digital photo compositing is that you can create realistic renditions of improbable scenes. Because both the baseball and the golf ball were photographed at the same size, for example, it was possible to reverse their actual size relationship by changing the scanning resolution. We were able to make a small baseball and a large golf ball. Imagine the possibilities, such as large mice harassing small elephants…?

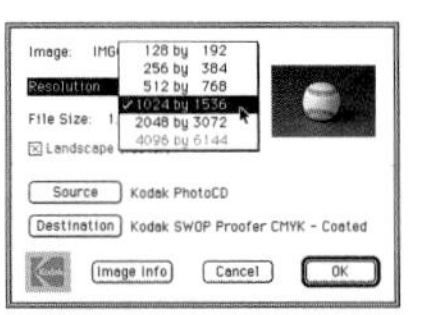

PhotoCD Resolutions

PhotoCD-scanned images automatically come in either five (Master PhotoCD) or six (Pro PhotoCD) different resolutions. You can select which resolution you need from the PhotoCD dialog box.

PhotoCD Scans of Same Size Photographs

If the images scanned onto the PhotoCD were the same size on film and need to be the same size in the photomontage, select the same resolution in the PhotoCD dialog box in order to maintain that relationship. When the baseball and the golf ball were both acquired from the PhotoCD at a resolution of 1,024×1,536 pixels, both balls appeared the same size when the two images were composited into the same image.

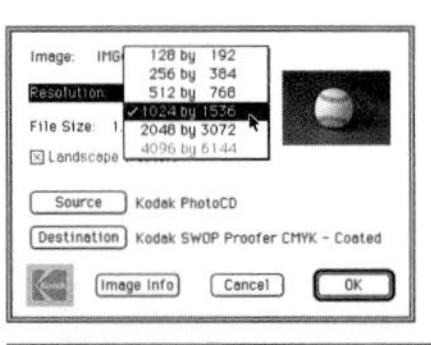

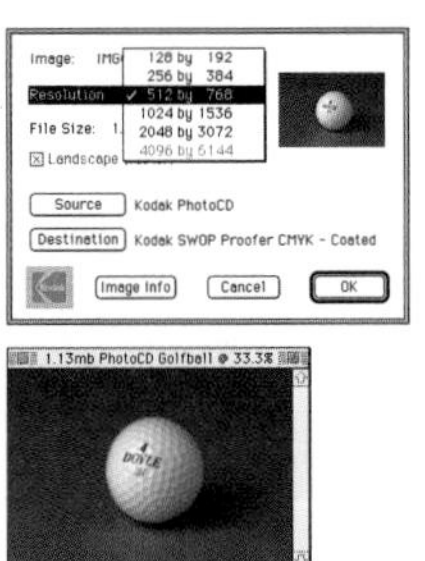

PhotoCD Scans of Different Size Photographs

If the original photographs of the objects were the same size on film but need to be different sizes in the photomontage, we must choose different resolutions for each of the objects. When the baseball is acquired at a resolution of 1,024×1,536 pixels and the golf ball is acquired at a resolution of 512×768 pixels, the golf ball appeared smaller than the baseball when the two images were composited into the same image.

06 7

Camera Position and Lighting

Considerations for Photomontage

Three important factors must remain consistent when you are shooting source images:

- Highlight and shadow direction
- Camera angle and perspective
- Depth of field

Highlight and Shadow Direction

If you are creating all the source images for a project yourself, it is a good idea to plan your lighting so that the direction of the highlights and shadows is consistent for all the source images. When you plan to use an existing image, or have rented an image from a stock agency, study the lighting characteristics of the image and use that as the basis for determining lighting and so on for other images.

The Lighting for "Just T/Rex and Me"

We had the picture of the little boy on hand, and it became the basis of this artwork. The lighting direction, diffusion, strength, and coverage in this photo determined the lighting for all of the other photographs.

The original photograph of the little boy, for example, was done using a special 190×90 cm diffusion lightbox, placed 85 cm from the subject and to the left of the camera.

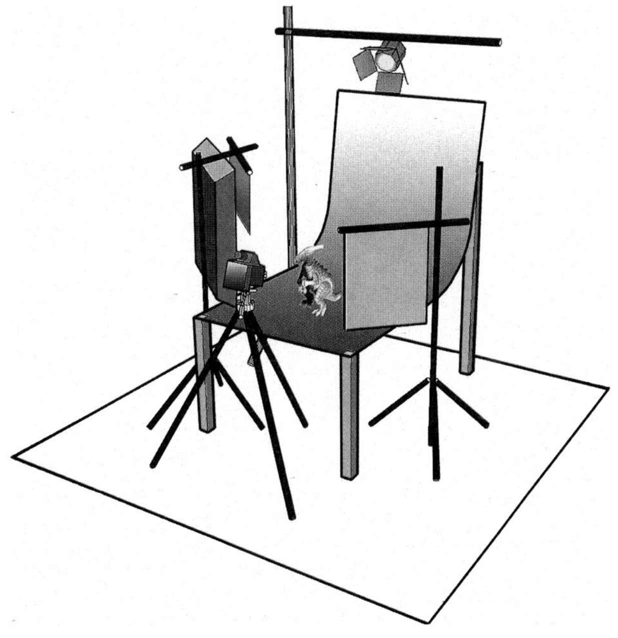

The Light for the Toys

The toys were approximately 20 percent the size of the child. Based on that size ratio, we photographed the toys using a 40×40 cm light source placed 16 cm away from them in order to make the light diffusion and direction consistent. The smallest softbox we had on hand was 80×80 cm, so we masked it with black cloth to shoot the photograph. These steps created a light source that was the same size and distance ratio to the toys as the large light source was to the child.

Camera Angle and Perspective

As with lighting, on projects in which you are creating all the photographs yourself, you must plan so that the camera angle and perspective are the same for all of the source images. Other times, you might have a photograph on hand that will be the basis of the photomontage and will dictate the camera angle and perspective for all the other photographs.

The photo of the photographer hiking up the face of a sand dune, for example, was taken using a 28 mm lens with the camera angle pointed upward. This photo became the starting point for a photomontage idea.

Downward camera angle

Camera Angle: Downward

In this composite image, the mannequin and the wood block tower were photographed with the camera aimed down toward the objects. The perspective of the two images obviously does not match.

Straight on camera angle

Camera Angle: Straight On

When the mannequin and the wood block tower were photographed with a level camera, there is some improvement over the previous example. Because the vertical lines of the wood block tower are parallel, however, we know that the perspective is still not correct.

Upward camera angle

Camera Angle: Upward

A wide angle lens aimed upward toward a tall object, such as a building, will create keystoning (in which two vertical lines are no longer parallel and would eventually cross). By placing the camera at a low angle and pointing the 28 mm lens up at the mannequin and wood blocks, the camera angle used matched the camera angle of the original scene. This produced a more realistic perspective. We know the camera angle is correct because there is visible keystoning in the vertical lines of the wood block tower. Also, by shooting from a lower angle, the top of the wood block tower shifted below the mannequin's shoulder, making the doll seem more powerful.

Depth of Field

Whether you are shooting new source images or selecting images from a stock library, to create a photorealistic photomontage, you must pay careful attention to depth of field.

Incorrect depth of field

Incorrect Depth of Field

In this composite image, both the mannequin and the tomato are in focus. Because the mannequin and the wood blocks were photographed together using a Nikkor 180 mm lens with a wide aperture of f2.8, however, the wood blocks are out of focus. The resulting composite—an out-of-focus subject between a foreground object and a background object that are both in focus—is an impossible "real world" effect.

Correct depth of field

Correct Depth of Field

In this example, the mannequin and the wood blocks are clearly in focus. The resulting composite of the images is more natural and realistic.

06 8

Masking

In general, imaging applications are capable of manipulating images through the use of masks. Although the implementation varies from application to application, the basic principle for all masking is the same: you use masks to control what you want to happen where in an image.

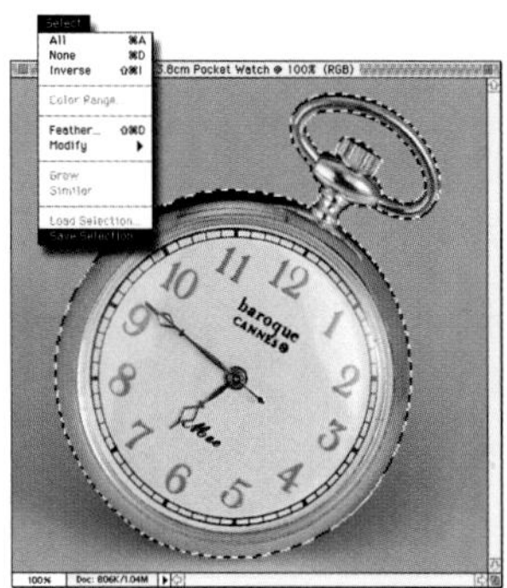

No matter which imaging application you use, masking is the single most important digital imaging skill to learn. Masking skills are as fundamental to digital photomontage as shutter speeds and apertures are to photography.

Masking Basics

A mask limits the effect of an image editing function to a specified area of an image and has parallels to similar methods used in traditional photography. For example, sandwiching a high-contrast black-and-white negative with a color negative or slide is one form of masking. Even the act of using a piece of cardboard with a hole in it to burn in parts of a print is a form of masking.

Selection Area

In digital photography, a selection border is a type of mask that is usually displayed on the monitor as a black-and-white dashed line and is often referred to as a selection. If you are using a paint brush tool, for example, the area inside the selection can be painted, but any area outside the selection is protected from the paint. An important feature of selection borders is that they are temporary, and when they are dropped (or deselected), they disappear forever.

8-bit Channel Masks

An 8-bit channel mask is grayscale masking data that can be saved with the image you are working on. It has two important features.

■ 8-bit channel masks can be used to save selections. In Photoshop, after you make selections, you can use the Save Selection command to convert them into 8-bit channel masks.

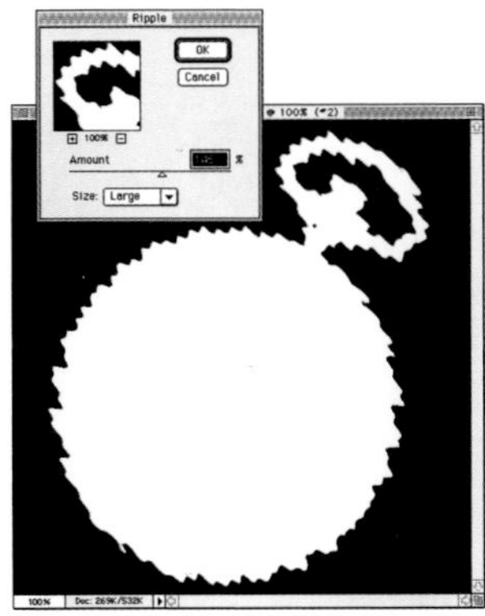

■ 8-bit channel masks are fundamentally the same as grayscale images. This means any image manipulation function that can be performed on a grayscale image can be used on a mask.

Image Object Edges

Any time you select or mask an object in a digital image, you have to pay special attention to accurately reproduce the differences in edge characteristics between the edges of the object and the background. This is especially true for photorealistic photomontage. Factors that determine the characteristics of the object edges include the focal distance and aperture of the lens at the time of exposure, qualities of the subject itself, and the lighting.

Other factors include whether you applied anti-aliasing when you made your selection area and whether you intentionally shifted the selection area away from the actual edges of the object when you made the selection. When you make the final composite, these factors affect whether or not the edges look natural.

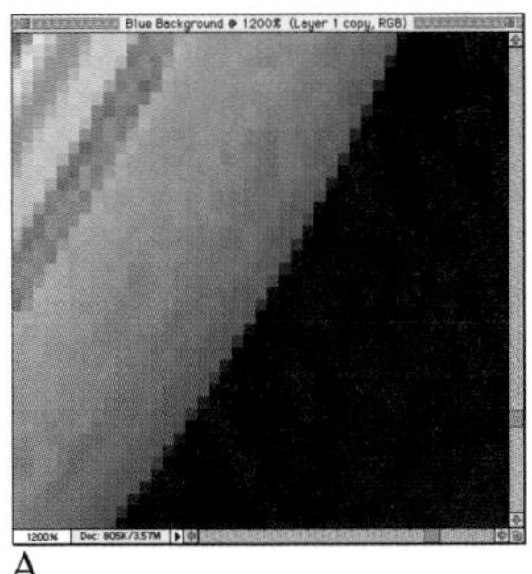

A

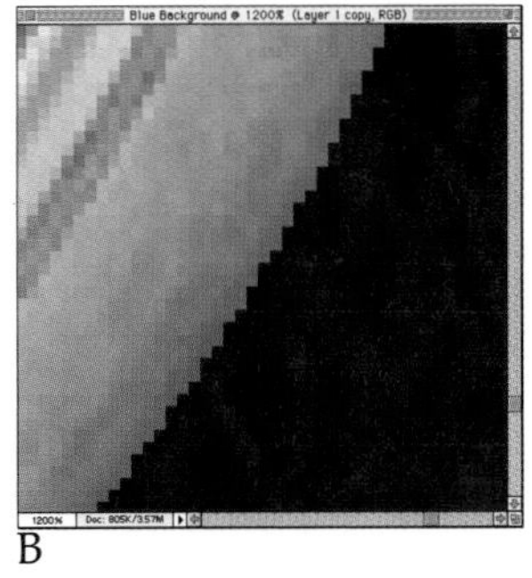

B

Anti-Aliasing

Anti-aliasing is a way to create smooth edges between different colors or gray tones by including transitional shades of color or gray tones between different color or tone regions. With most selection tools and brushes, anti-aliasing is performed automatically by the computer (although there are exceptions).

Picture A shows a composite image in which an anti-aliased selection was used. The edge where the subject and the background meet is made up of a mixture of the subject and the background colors. If you do not have these transitional colors between the subject and the background colors, the edges appear jagged (or "staircased"), as shown in picture B.

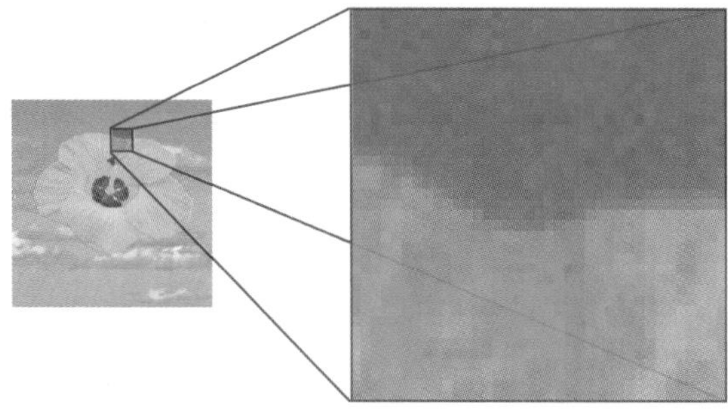

Continuous-Tone Images and Anti-Aliasing

All borders between regions of color or grayscale tones in a continuous-tone image (such as a scanned photograph) are anti-aliased. Without anti-aliasing, continuous-tone photographs would not look natural when composited into one image. Thanks to anti-aliasing, digital images can look photographic on the computer. The drawback, however, is that the intermediate shades along object edges create several problems for digital photomontage.

Fringe Pixels and Matte Lines

When you select an object then copy and paste it from one background to another, the selection often includes pixels from the original background. These pixels, known as *fringe pixels* or *matte lines*, are problems that occur any time anti-aliased borders of color or tone are selected or masked. They can occur no matter which masking technique or tool you use, and in most cases, they need to be corrected.

Masking and Edge Characteristics

The characteristics of an object's edge determine what type of mask is needed. In the illustrations to the left, for example, the edges of the pocket watch are very smooth and hard, whereas the edges of the teddy bear are irregular and soft. Different techniques are needed in order to make masks that accurately duplicate these edge characteristics.

Masking Strategies

Masking strategies basically consist of tools and techniques for accurately defining the edges of a subject without including fringe pixels and matte lines. Depending on which tools you use, the mask characteristics will be hard and well-defined or soft and irregular, or combinations of both.

Selection Tools

The Lasso tool, the Pen tool, and the Magic Wand tool are the standard selection tools used to create freeform outlines around objects (these are specifically Photoshop tools, but similar tools exist in other applications).

A B

The Lasso tool and the Pen tool are appropriate for selecting objects with very smooth edge definitions. The Magic Wand is more useful for selecting more irregular objects, based on differences in contrast and tone. It is very tedious to try to make a mask for an irregular object using the Lasso tool or Pen tool.

Although both the Lasso and Pen tools can be used to select soft objects, such as the teddy bear, they do not accurately define the edges. The bear in picture A on the left was masked using a technique that maintained the soft edges. The bear in picture B was masked using the Lasso tool. The Lasso tool version looks as if it were cut out with a pair of scissors and is neither realistic nor attractive.

NOTE

The bear in picture A was masked using a technique called grayscale masking, described later in this chapter.

Feathering

A

B

Feathering is a method of softening the edge characteristics of a selection by gradually increasing the width of the selection along the object's edge. This is easiest to see when selections are saved as masks. The hard-edged mask in picture A, for example, was created using a selection area with no feathering, while the mask in picture B was created using a selection with a four-pixel feather.

C

D

Feathered selections increase the likelihood of including fringe pixels or matte lines. When the pocket watch was selected with the Lasso tool using a feather setting of 2 pixels (picture D), for example, it included more of the background image than the version selected without the feather setting (picture C).

Next we use a feathered selection tool to select the teddy bear. Although the outline does not perfectly match the edges of the teddy bear, the soft stuffed animal look is maintained. (Compare this with the teddy bear selected with the grayscale masking technique on the previous page).

High feather settings are useful for creating extremely soft edges for translucent blends of images. In the example on the left, a highly feathered circular selection tool was used to select the watch face, then the images were composited into the same file several different times. This is a simple method for quickly blending source photos together in digital photo collage images.

8-bit Channel Masks

Most image-editing applications have channel masks that can be viewed and manipulated without affecting the image. This is very important because the capability to manipulate the mask directly not only enables you to control edge characteristics, but it provides unique opportunities for creating compositing effects (see also Chapter 9-6, "Masking").

Creating Channel Masks

There are basically three methods of creating channel masks. Although the functions and methods introduced here are based on Photoshop, the basic concepts also apply to Painter and xRes.

■ Save Selection command

After making a selection, choose Select, Save Selection.

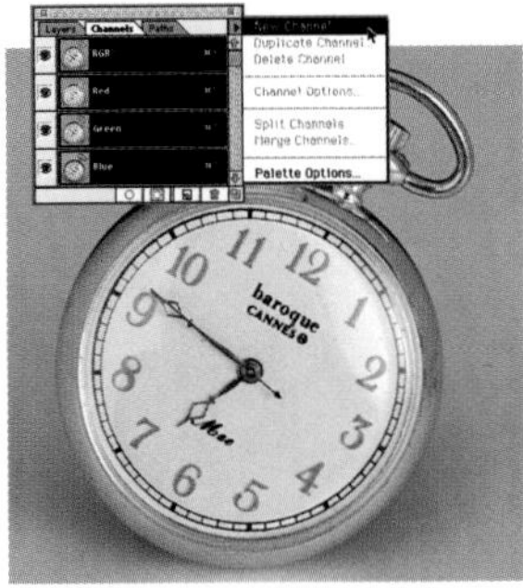

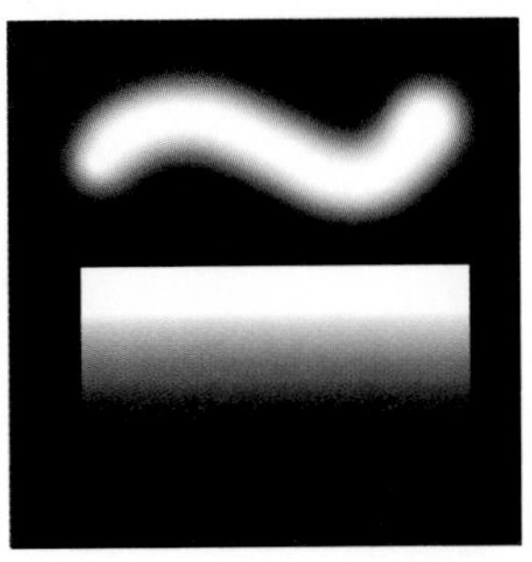

■ New Channel and Paint tools

Choose the New Channel command from the Channel palette and use the Paintbrush tool or Gradient tool to add grayscale tones to the mask.

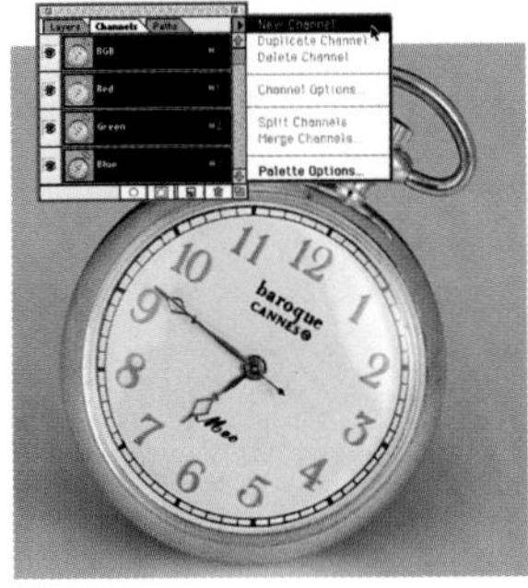

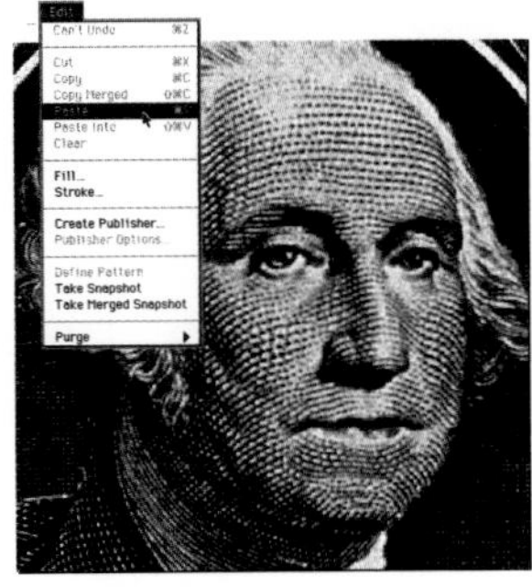

■ New Channel and Paste Command

Choose the New Channel command, then copy and paste grayscale images into the new channel.

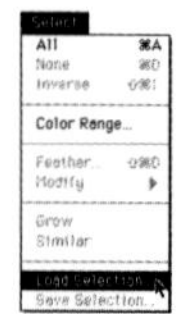

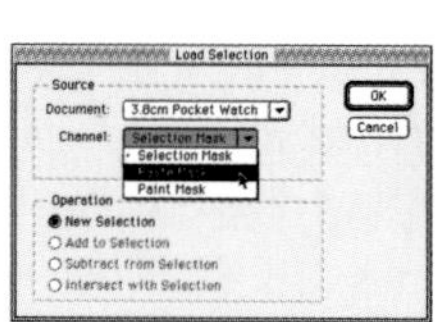

Loading Selections

A channel mask is used by loading the selection from the mask. We loaded the selections from the previous three masks and used the Fill command to fill them with red. Compare the results.

In each case, the effect of the mask is greatest where the mask is 100 percent white and least where the mask is 100 percent black. Where there are intermediate tones of gray in the mask, the effect of the mask is lessened. Where the gray value is 50 percent, for example, the result of the Fill command is 50 percent opaque.

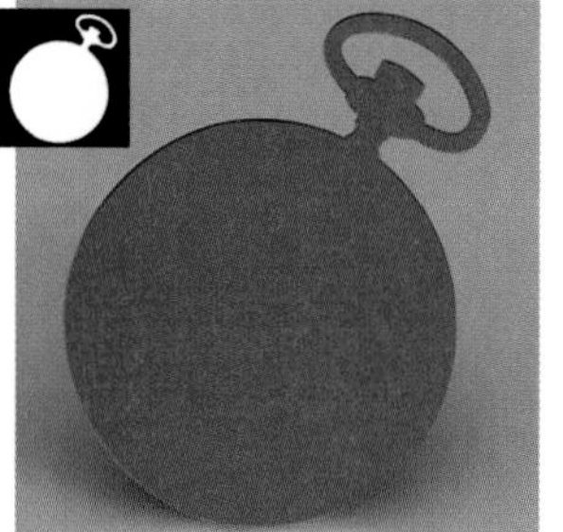

Editing 8-bit Channel Masks

When you save a selection as a mask using the Save Selection command, the shape of the subject of the mask image appears white and the area surrounding it is black, making a distinct delineation between the two. This channel can be edited and modified using Photoshop's tools to change the shape of the mask. You can do this in several ways.

Adding a Gradation

A gradation can be added to the mask with the Gradient tool. The effect of this mask is to gradually blend the object into the background.

Blurring the Mask

An effect similar to applying feathering to a selection tool can be achieved by applying a filter, such as the Gaussian Blur filter, to a mask.

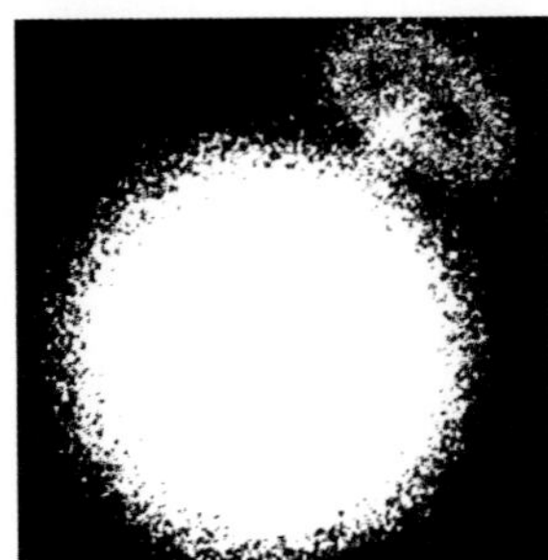

Special Effect Filter in the Mask

The shape of a mask can be altered with most of the filters in the Filter menu. Here, the Spatter filter was used to alter the mask's edge.

Mixed Edge Characteristics

It is very seldom that a subject's edges are all the same. Needless to say, a photograph almost always has a variety of different edge characteristics—some caused by camera factors such as focus and depth-of-field, and some caused by the subject itself, for example, hair or a blurred movement of the subject. To mask these characteristics accurately, the mask must include both hard and soft edges.

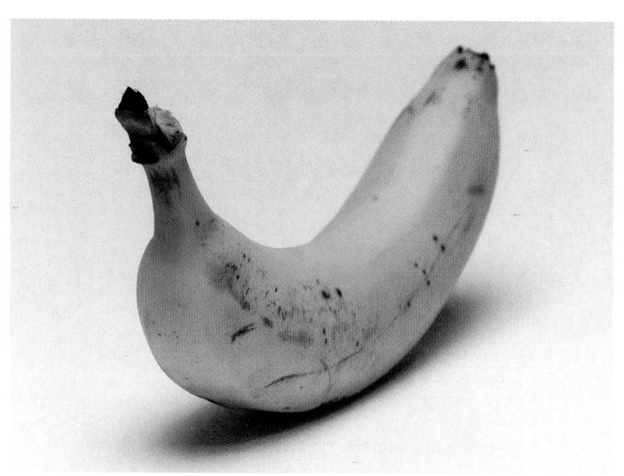

Blended Edges—A Case Study

In this photograph of a banana, taken with the Leaf DCBII, the foreground of the object is in focus and the background is softened due to depth of field. If the goal is to move the banana from this image into a different background as realistically as possible, then the mask has to precisely reproduce both the hard foreground and the soft background edge characteristics.

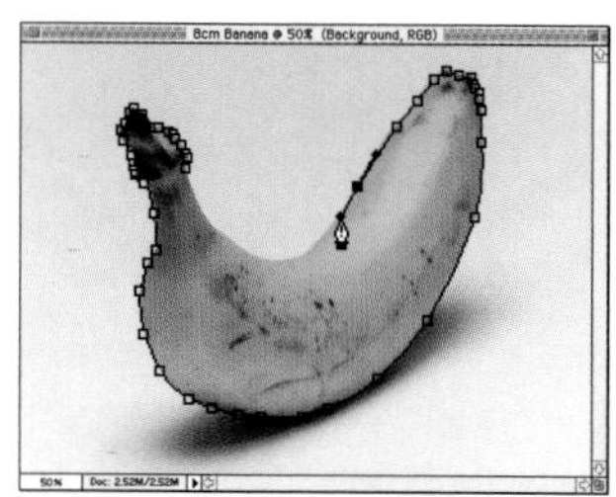

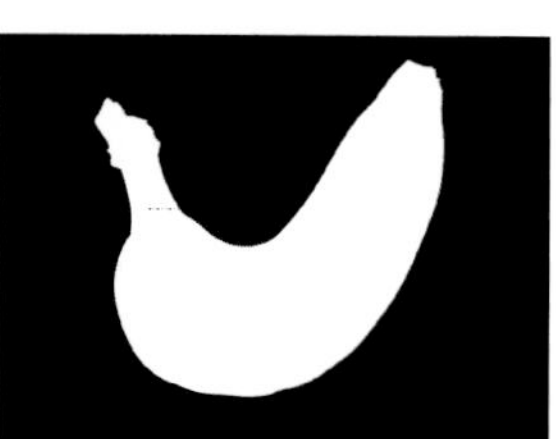

Pen Tool

To stress the importance of creating masks with both hard and soft edges, we first selected the entire banana with the Pen tool, converted it into a selection, and saved it as a channel mask. The result was a uniformly smooth mask edge, from the banana's foreground to the background.

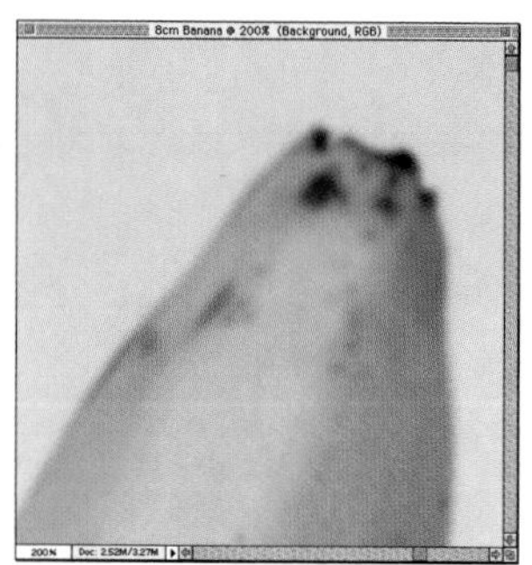

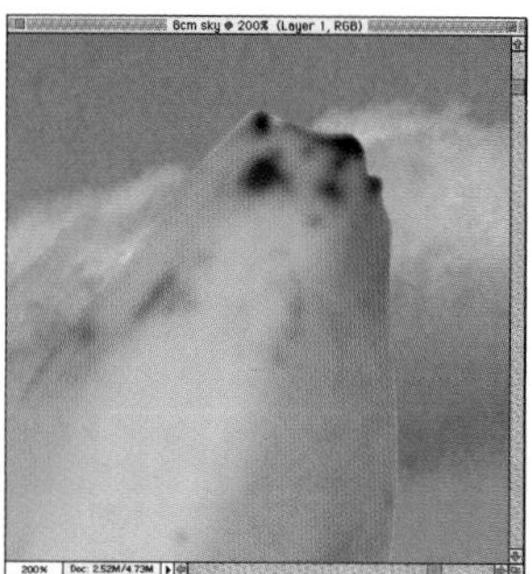

When the mask was used to copy and paste the banana onto a new background, it looked unnatural, as if it had been cut out of the original background with a pair of scissors. It was particularly noticeable in the rear tip of the banana, which softly blended into the background in the original but had a hard edge in the new version.

Blended Edge Strategies

The solution to this problem is to use a channel mask to blend a hard edge together with a soft edge. You can do this in several different ways.

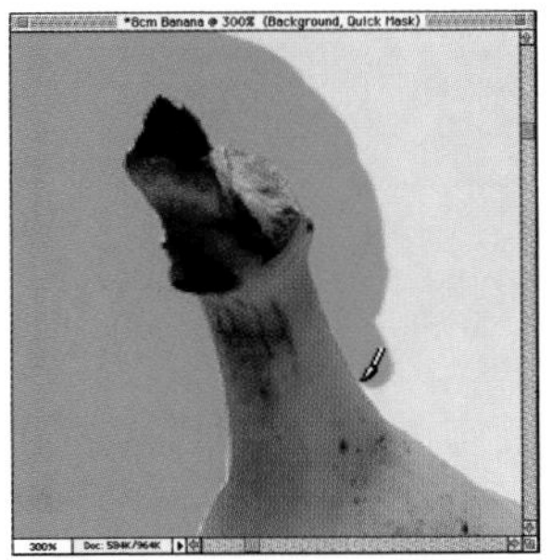

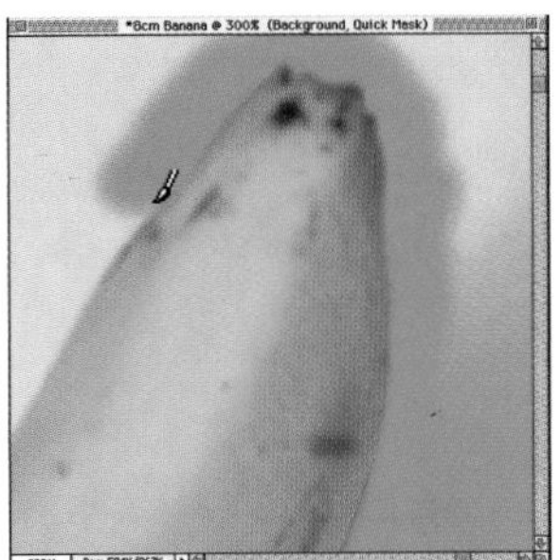

Painting the Mask

In Photoshop's Quick Mask mode, you can use a variety of different brushes to paint a mask that has both hard and soft edges.

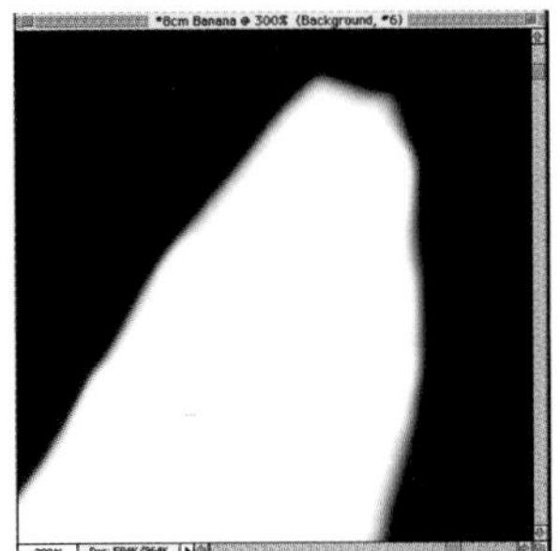

If you save the Quick Mask as a channel mask, you can clearly see the differences between the hard and soft edges.

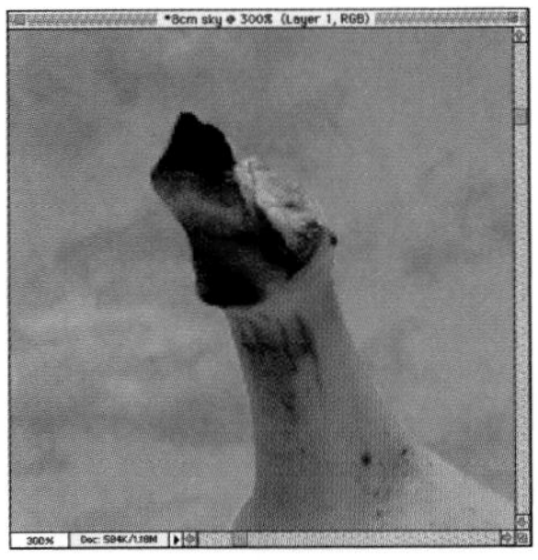

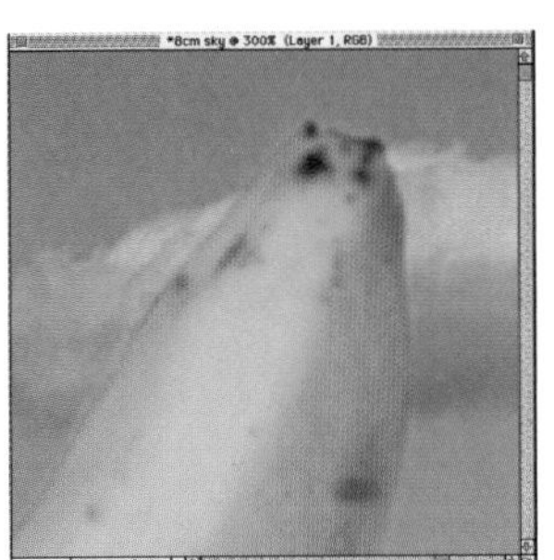

When you use this mask to copy and paste the banana into a new file, it accurately duplicates the edge characteristics of the original banana.

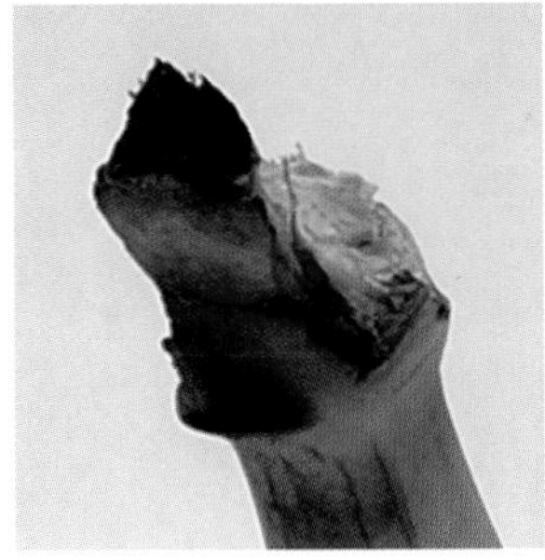

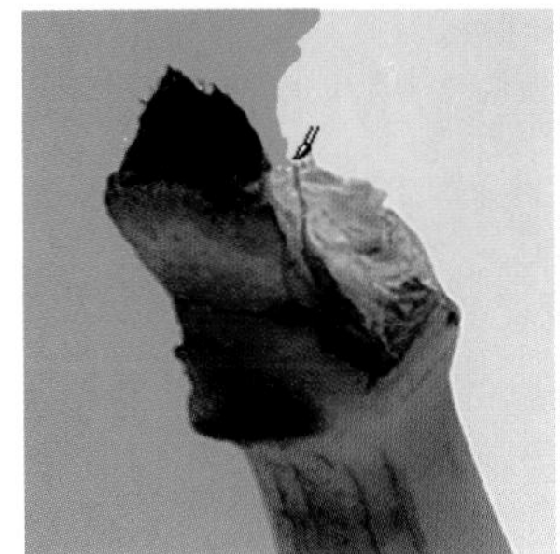

Although painting masks is an effective technique for combining edge characteristics, painting around small details can be tedious and time consuming. These details are often best masked using a grayscale masking technique.

Grayscale Masking Technique

A grayscale mask uses the differences in contrast between an object's foreground and background to create the mask. At first glance, the procedure might seem complicated. But if you photograph your objects knowing you are going to use this technique, it is a quick way to make complex masks that include a mixture of finely detailed, soft and hard edges.

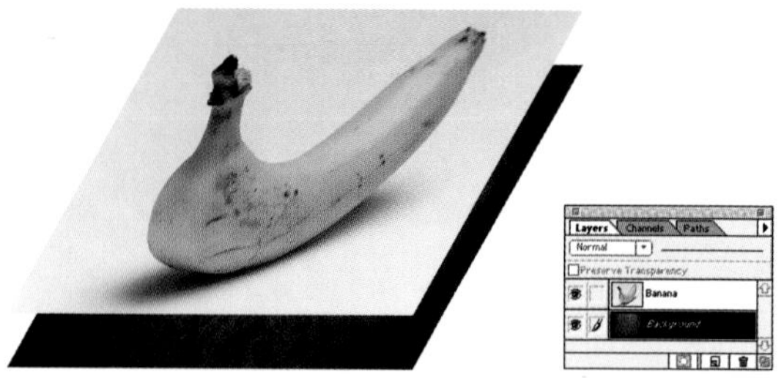

STEPS

This is a bit complicated, so some experience with Photoshop masking is a prerequisite for grasping how this technique works.

1. Open the file labeled Banana.PSD from the Tutorial Images folder on the CD-ROM accompanying this book. This is a two layer file, with the banana photograph in a layer above the background.

NOTE

This file, called Banana.PSD, can be found in the Tutorial Images folder on the CD-ROM accompanying this book. Use it to follow these steps using Photoshop 4.0. If you are using Photoshop 3.0, note that several of the steps are different. Also note that this file is already a two layer file, with the banana layer already placed over a background layer

2. To create a grayscale mask, start by comparing the contrast in the Red, Green, and Blue channels. In this image, the blue channel shows the most contrast between the object and the background.

NOTE

To view the banana's channels only, you must turn off the Background view by clicking on the Eye icon. Press ⌘ (Command key) + 3 to see the R channel, ⌘ + 2 to see the G channel, and ⌘ + 1 to see the B channel. Press ⌘ + ~ to see the RGB composited image.

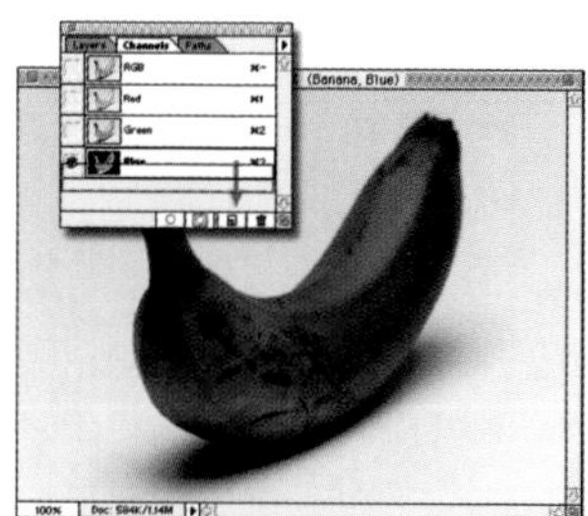

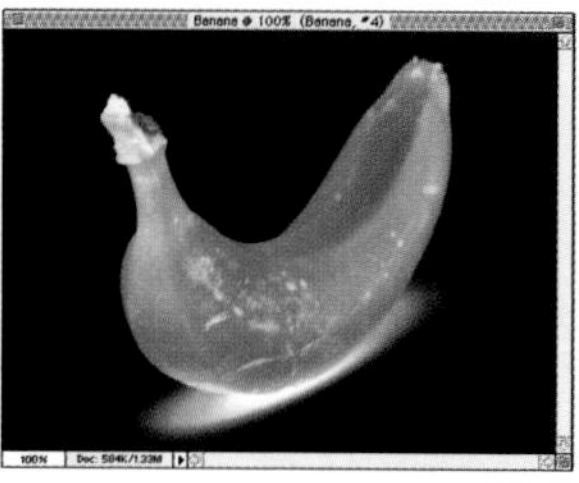

3. Make a copy of the Blue channel by dragging it onto the New Channel icon at the bottom right of the Channels palette. Then invert the duplicated channel by choosing Image, Adjust, Invert.

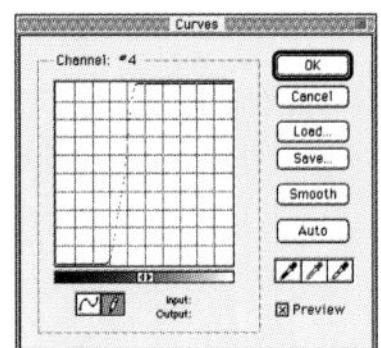

4. Open the Curves dialog box by choosing Image, Adjust, Curves. Select the Pencil icon and draw a horizontal line across the top of the graph and a horizontal line across the bottom of the graph, referring to the Curves screencapture at left to determine the starting and ending points. This shifts the light pixels to white and the darker pixels to black. Next, click on the Smooth button to smooth the curve. This maintains anti-aliasing along the edge between black and white regions of the mask.

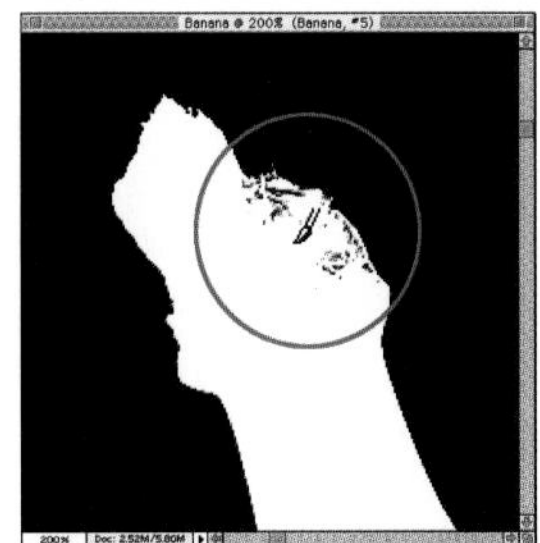

5. Modify portions of the mask using the Paintbrush tool. For example, remove the parts of the banana stem that didn't shift to white with the Curves adjustment by painting over those areas with white. Also, if you add a small amount of Gaussian by choosing Filter, Blur, Gaussian Blur at this stage, this helps to smooth the mask.

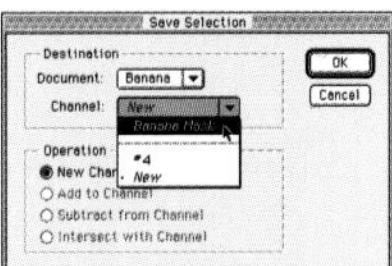

6. Choose Select, Load Selection to display the Load Selection dialog box, and select 4 from the Channel pop-up menu. This activates a selection based on the Channel 4 mask.

Then choose Select, Save Selection and choose Banana Mask from the Destination Channel pop-up menu in the Save Selection dialog box. This creates a layer mask that hides the white background of the banana layer, revealing the underlying gray background image layer.

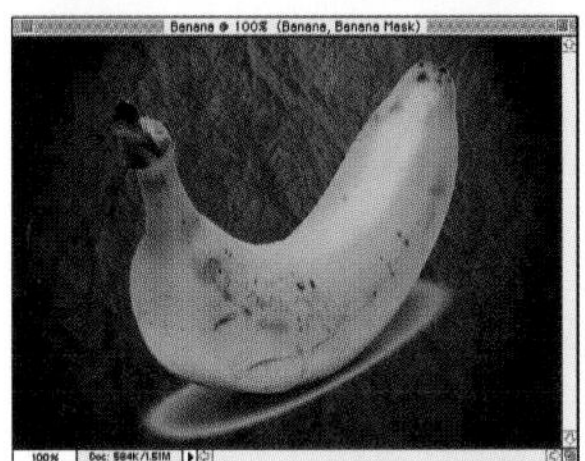

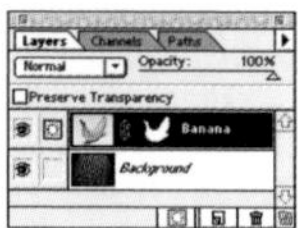

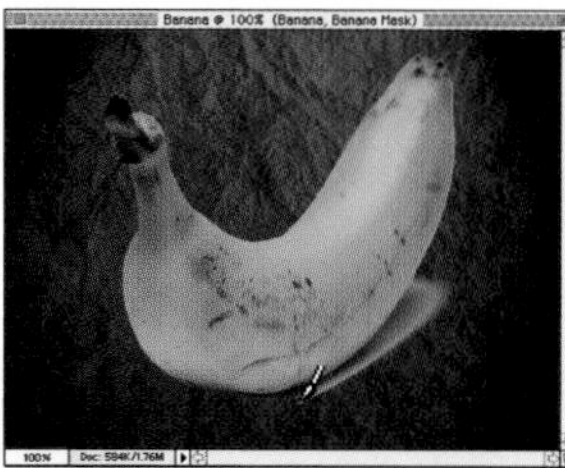

7. While viewing the RGB image, select the layer mask you want to edit by clicking on it. While watching the RGB view, remove the shadow portion of the mask by painting with black in the layer mask. As you paint with black, the shadow under the banana will be hidden.

At this point, the mask does not have the soft edge characteristic of the part of the banana that is out of focus. The fine details of the stem, however, have been nicely preserved.

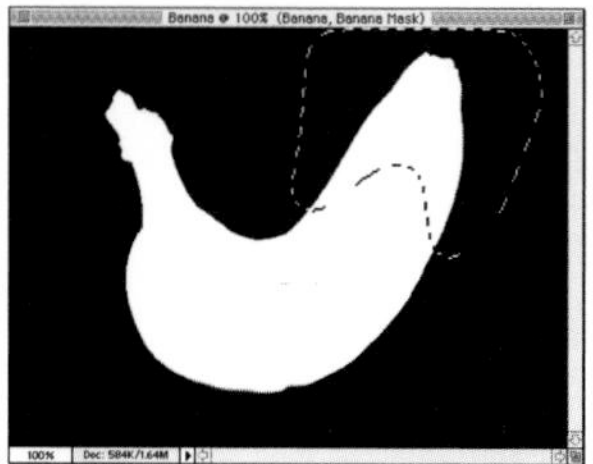

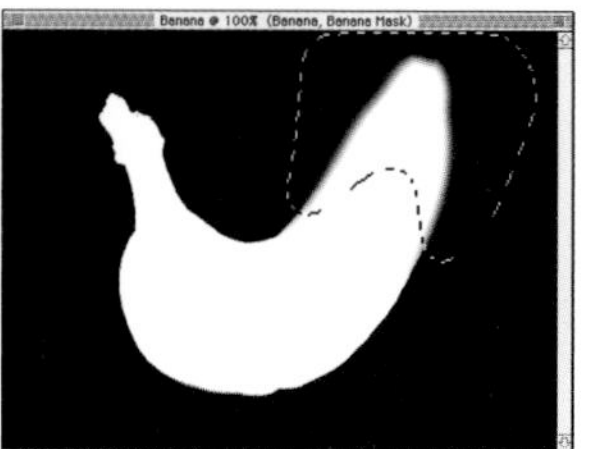

8. To duplicate the soft, out-of-focus edge of the banana, begin by selecting that area of the mask with a feathered Lasso tool. Use a feather setting of 15 and then apply the Gaussian Blur filter with a setting of 6 to the selection. This significantly softens the mask edge.

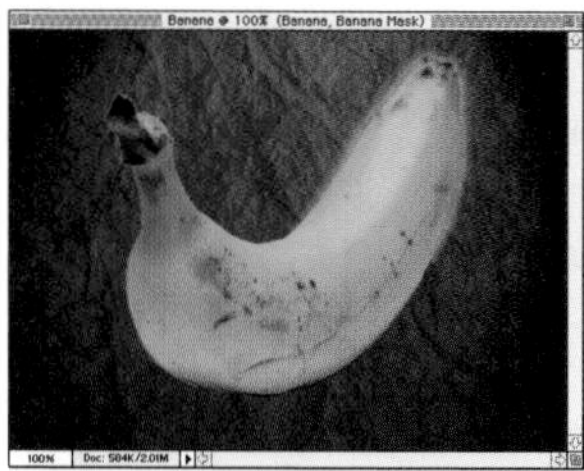

9. The RGB composite view of the two layers together reveals that blurring the mask edge created a soft halo—a type of matte line—around the rear tip of the banana. This is the result of the Gaussian Blur filter expanding the mask and revealing some of the banana's original white background.

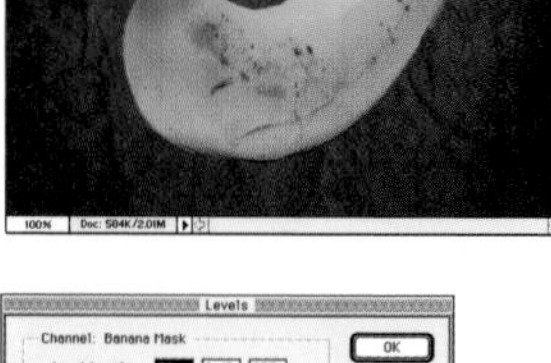

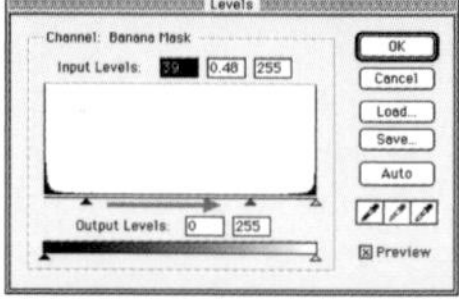

10. Next, with the layer mask still selected and the RGB composite view displayed, open the Levels dialog box. Slide the mid-point slider to the right. This contracts the mask (and eliminates some of the matte line), while maintaining the blurred edge characteristics. Make minor adjustments with the black, gray, and white sliders to get the result you want, which is to eliminate the matte line while maintaining the softness of the mask.

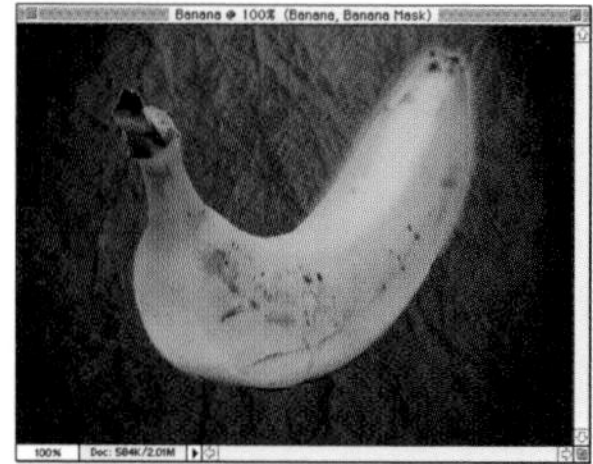

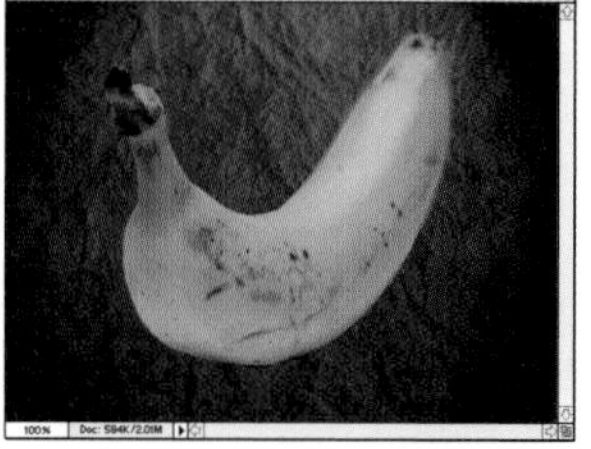

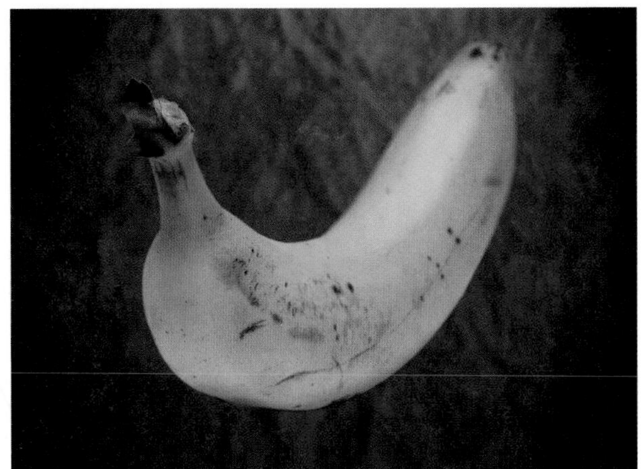

11. The final result is that the in-focus portion of the banana is masked by a sharp, detailed mask, while the out-of-focus portion is masked by a soft-edged mask. The edge differences are even further enhanced by blurring the background layer.

Shooting Strategies for Masking

After you understand masking concepts such as the grayscale masking technique just introduced, you can plan how to shoot your original images in ways that simplify the masking process.

Outdoors

When you start shooting with digital imaging in mind, a clear blue sky above a row of trees or a city skyline no longer means just a sunny day. Instead, with your new digital vision, you will only see the solid field of blue sky as an easily selected region. In the picture to the left, you can mask the blue sky quickly using the Magic Wand and replace it with a puffy cloud sky.

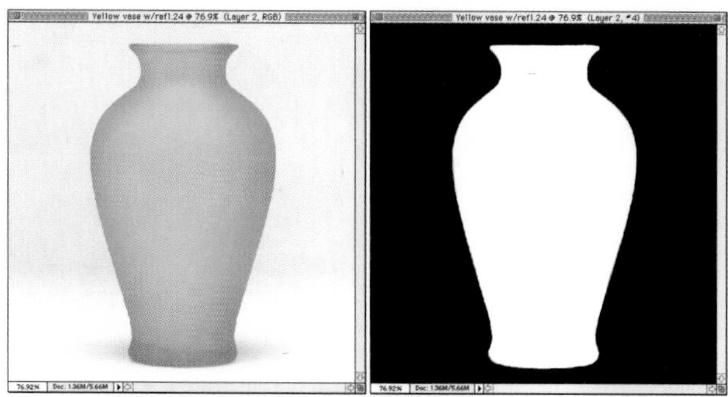

In the Studio: Contrasting Brightness Values

Photos of source images taken in the studio can be prepared for masking by shooting them against neutral color, uniform backgrounds. It is important to choose a background with a brightness value that is in contrast to the brightness of the object you are photographing. A light-toned uniform background behind dark objects, for example, or dark-toned uniform background behind light objects are appropriate. In the photos to the left, the vase was photographed against a neutral background and the grayscale mask technique was used to make the mask (see Chapter 5, "Digital Exposures and Follow-up Processing," for actual masking procedures).

In the Studio: Bluescreen

Bluescreen is an advanced photography technique for shooting source images with intricate details that require masks for things such as hair, smoke, or glass (see Chapter 9-9, "Plug-ins").

chapter 7

Digital Photography Output

07 1

Output Devices for Digital Photography

Output Devices Classified by Purpose

Since you can use almost any printer that you can connect to your computer there are many ways to output hard copies for digital photography. For example, if you just want a quick check of your photos, you can do so on inexpensive monochrome printers. However, for purposes of this discussion, we assume that you want to output color hard copies of your artwork.

Output Devices for Photographic Quality Reproduction

If you want to output your artwork with photographic quality, in your studio or at home, we recommend dye sublimation or silver halide color printers. Because these devices produce continuous tone output, you can make hard copies similar in look and feel (that is, paper weight) to traditional photographic prints. Another feature of these continuous tone hard copies is that they can also be used as original art to hand to a client.

Dye sublimation printers can generate output up to approximately 11.5×16.5-inch size (several are also capable of approximately 16×24-inch size or larger for commercial reproduction use). The maximum output size for silver halide system color printers is 16×24-inch, but larger output sizes should become available in the future.

The Kodak XLS is a popular dye sublimation printer for digital photography.

The Pictrography 4000 on display at the Seybold Seminars exhibition in Tokyo in December, 1996.

Prices for dye sublimation printers range from as low as $1,000 to $20,000, or higher. If you work in digital photography, and want to create fine art quality prints or second generation originals (the first generation original is the digital file itself) as final art for commercial art purposes, a device in the $15,000 or higher range is recommended. These devices have the larger print size capability and allow you to directly output from RGB data.

NOTE

An example of using a print from a dye sublimation printer as final commercial artwork is discussed in Chapter 6-3 (page 6-10).

High-end dye sublimation printers over $20,000 tend to be PostScript compatible devices. Because these are designed as proofing tools for DTP work they can make less than optimal output for digital photography. This is particularly true for PostScript dye sublimation printers that can authentically simulate offset printing (color, gray balance, and so on). These become unsuitable for digital photography output, especially for exhibition or commercial art prints, because the color gamut of their dye ribbons, like the gamut of printing inks, is narrow, and you lose the ability to generate vivid colors. In addition, a certain amount of streaking that can occur in these devices may be acceptable for proofing, but not when the print is to be displayed or used as second generation original art.

PostScript-compatible devices capable of generating the vivid colors used in fine art are increasingly available, but they are expensive. If your budget allows it, purchase a printer that will enable you to output the wide color gamut required for high quality artwork (be sure there is no streaking from the device)—for example, as final artwork for advertising-related digital photography—and at the same time have the capability of simulating offset printing with PostScript.

Devices such as the Kodak XLS 8600 dye sublimation printer, as well as the Fujix Pictrography 3000 and Pictrography 4000 (both of which are silver halide printers) have become well known for their high quality output of digital photography.

The Fujix Pictrography 4000 silver halide printer, in particular, is an excellent printer capable of approximately 12×18-inch output and can be considered a good output device option for both commercial and portrait studios, as well as for fine art photographers. Its output quality is even better than the Pictrography 3000's and the size of the machine itself is nearly the same as its predecessor's, which only outputs approximately 8.5×11-inch prints.

Output Devices for Photo Albums and Portfolios

When you want to give snapshots as gifts or when you want to create your own portfolio to organize your artwork, inkjet printers are a viable option. Devices with an output resolution of 600 dpi or higher in particular provide output that looks roughly equivalent to conventional color prints. Recently a variety of heavier weight inkjet papers have become available. This means that, in addition to the standard thin inkjet printer paper, you can use glossy papers that look and feel like photographic paper.

If you purchase an inkjet printer specifically for digital photography purposes, you should select a device with a fine output resolution of at least 720 dpi (even though the print speed tends to be a little slow). Color inkjet printers can be purchased for as low as several hundred dollars to a bit over $2,000. The more expensive printers tend to offer faster printing speeds, higher quality, and larger paper sizes than the lower priced models.

NOTE

■ Dye sublimation printers under $1,000 capable of postcard size output at around 150 dpi have recently become very popular. They are not adequate for producing second generation original artwork, but since they output continuous tone images, they've become popular "snapshot" printers, especially for users of low resolution, point-and-shoot type digital cameras.

■ Another group of printers widely used for design and office work are color laser printers. However, these aren't recommended if you need a printer for high quality, continuous tone output. At best, the quality is adequate for personal photo albums or 'disposable' portfolios (that is, prints of artwork which you don't need returned and are intended primarily for reference use only).

■ Wax thermal transfer color printers, such as those made by Alps Electronics, are becoming popular. These use hard wax-like pigments which are melted with heat and then transferred onto the paper. For photographers, these can be adequate for creating personal photo albums or portfolios.

■ The Seiko Epson StylusPhoto printer uses a total of six inks by adding light magenta and light cyan to the 4 CMYK printer inks, making it capable of reproducing RGB originals. The output from this printer approaches the quality of a dye sublimation device. However, because of a perceivable dot pattern, it can't be used as an output device of second generation originals for offset press reproduction. The quality is very high, though, and is adequate for digital photography portfolios and even for short term exhibition prints (prints will fade under prolonged exposure to light).

NOTE

Archivability of digital artwork output is an important issue worthy of deep discussion. However, ongoing efforts to improve dye and pigment stability of printing devices make this a rapidly changing topic. For now, it's sufficient to summarize the current situation like this:

■ Among desktop printers, output from the silver halide category has the longest archivability, and can be considered as having characteristics similar to a traditional photographic C-print (such as Kodak Ektacolor).

■ Output from the dye sublimation category of desktop printers is more susceptible to fading when exposed to light than the silver halide printer output. The dyes are fairly stable in dark storage, though. However, the dyes will adhere to vinyl sleeves of portfolios if left in the sleeves for extended periods of time.

■ Output from the inkjet category of desktop printers has virtually no archival qualities and will fade within weeks when displayed.

■ Output from film recorders onto transparency or negative film assumes the archival qualities of whatever film type was used. Likewise, photographic prints made from the film output have the archival quality of the print material.

■ The original digital file is always the most archival version of your image, so keep multiple copies of your most important artwork stored on several types of removable media. In order of stability these include compact disk (CD), magneto optical, and magnetic storage (such as floppies, hard drives, Jaz drives, etc).

This photograph has been reproduced on the following pages to provide a comparison of a variety of different color printers. The image on this page was output directly as separation films for offset printing.

Various types of A4 hard copy output of a photo, taken with a Nikon E2 digital still camera, are displayed in entirety (left) and in a magnified view of the print (right). While the magnified view of the output from the Fujix and Kodak printers looks continuous in tone, some graininess from ink dots is evident in the output from the Seiko Epson inkjet printer.

Fujix Pictrography 3000 silver halide print.

Kodak XLS8300 dye sublimation print.

Seiko Epson StylusPro inkjet print.

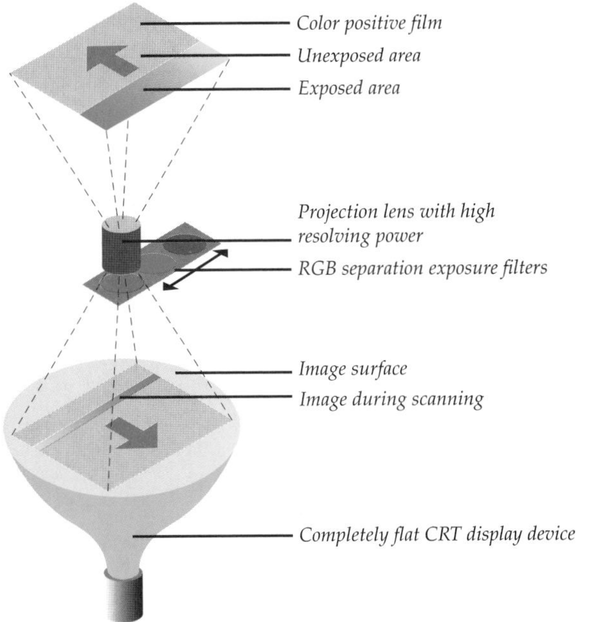

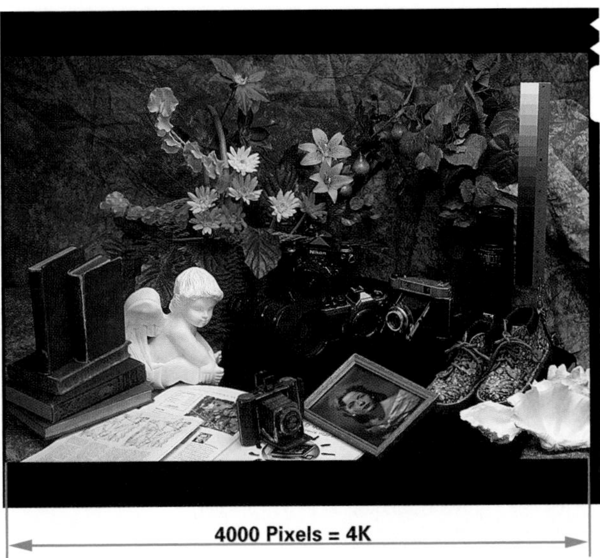

On what is called "4K" output, there are approximately 4,000 pixels across the long dimension of 4×5-inch color positive film. The photographs on the following pages are output samples of this image.

Output Devices for Stock Photos

When you want to output your digital photography artwork as color reversal film and create a stock photo library of your artwork, you should use what is commonly known as a "film recorder." Film recorders are available in a wide variety of configurations and are typically very high performance devices. Many of these systems display the image on a completely flat color picture tube (CRT) and duplicate it onto normal color film (either color negative or color transparency) using internal optics.

There are also film recorders that expose images onto color film by scanning with laser beams or special tungsten light sources. Dedicated output devices for 35 mm film are available, as well as devices that expose 4×5-inch and up to 8×10-inch color film.

Film recorders typically have "2K," "4K," or "8K" output resolution options. This nomenclature is based on the number of image pixels of the long side of the image that can be used to create the film output. For example, an image made for 4K output has approximately 4,000 pixels along the long dimension and is reproduced onto color film using approximately 4,000 scan lines. The larger the number of scan lines, the more detail that can be resolved when you look at the film, especially through a loupe. In some situations, because the resolution is already so high, the perceived quality differences between 4K and 8K film output may be slight, depending on the image. However, the difference between the file size of the image, as well as the cost of the output, can be substantial. Therefore, as long as your reproduction magnifications (either through scanning or photographic output) don't exceed 5× the original film size, you can use 4K output without an appreciable quality difference.

For purposes of creating final artwork for clients, stock libraries from digital photography, archival portfolios, and exhibition prints, film recorder output is ideal. Because film recorders allow you to create second generation originals (remember, your first original is the digital image file) you can have high quality, stable photo enlargements made from either the color negative or color transparency output of a film recorder. Since 1996, a number of excellent film recorders capable of providing film output for this purpose have appeared on the market in the $10,000 price range.

Lower-cost film recorders are also available. These are basically cameras mounted with a macro lens to a box housing a 10-inch, high-resolution monitor. The camera photographs the screen. You can achieve presentation slide quality film output as long as you appropriately adjust the brightness and the contrast of the displayed image. These devices run between $2,000 – $5,000.

Evaluating a 16×20-inch print made by an Iris Inkjet printer on Rives BFK White water color paper, using only a 9MB image file. Output by The Digital Pond, San Francisco.

Devices for Exhibition Quality Output

Another attractive alternative for large format output is to have a printer or specialized output service create large prints for you via large format inkjet printers. A number of such devices, the most well-known being the Iris Inkjet printer, are capable of creating up to 40×50-inch output. A feature of these systems is that high quality, large format output can be made on unusual substrates such as water color paper, using only low to medium file sized originals. Furthermore, the absence of any dot in the final print makes this an appealing option to photographers, since it looks like a continuous tone photograph.

Because ownership of this type of output device is out of the price range of most digital imaging artists, prints are typically ordered through outside services. In many major U.S. cities, businesses offering this service are tailored to making fine art output by offering test strips for evaluation, and so on. Some of these services will take orders by mail, returning test strips for client approval before making a final print. Companies such as Ilford are working on creating archival inks for these printers, with claims that such media can last almost twice as long as traditional photographic C-print material.

Left example: A portion of an image from a file originally created for 4K color transparency output, but instead upsampled 200 percent for a finished size of 20 x 24 inches, and output as separation films for (150 lpi) offset printing. This process of reproducing a digital photo is not unusual.

Middle example: The same portion of the original image after making 4K color transparency output, and then scanning the transparency to the same size and resolution as the output in Example #1. These steps are becoming more common because stock photo agencies are beginning to offer images made digitally, in which case the original being shipped to the customer is usually film recorder output.

Right example: The same portion of an image after making 4K color positive image output, then having a 20×24-inch photographic C-print made. This portion of the C-print was scanned on a flatbed scanner. Not a common scenario, but one that could possibly arise. The point is to be aware of the image quality degradation between one method and the other.

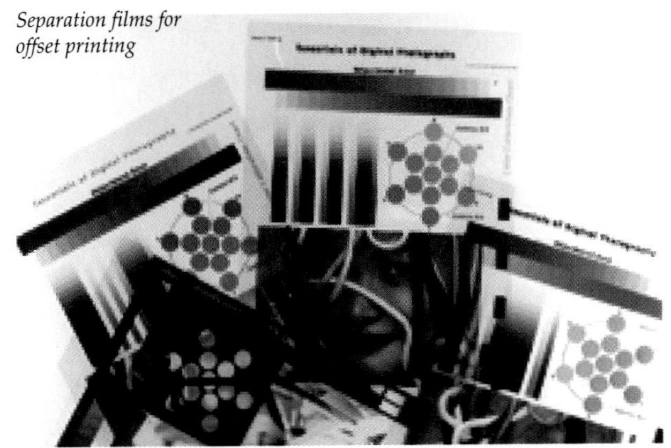

Separation films for offset printing

Output Devices for Color Printing

When you think of output devices for color printing, you may think simply of imagesetters — devices that output color separation film. In reality, you really need to think of prepress and printing companies as a whole as if they were one large output device.

Imagesetters do in fact output digital photography artwork as four CMYK color separation films, but these films are only intermediate products, not the final color print. Of the many factors that can affect the quality of the final color print, the impact on quality from imagesetters is comparatively small (imagesetter quality concerns, such as quality of screening methods, exist but are best debated in specialized books about electronic prepress). This is because imagesetters are capable of separation film output which is relatively stable and consistent in quality compared to other types of output devices.

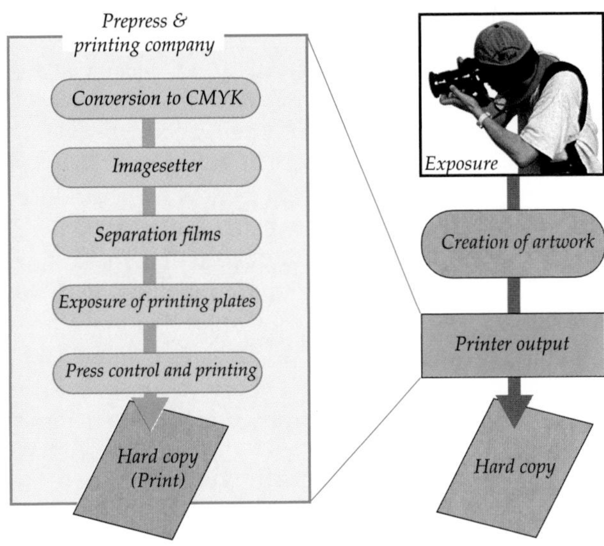

Two factors affect the quality of your printing more than the imagesetter. The first is the quality of the conversion of the data from RGB to CMYK before it goes to the imagesetter, the second is the fidelity of the halftone dot reproduction from separation through platemaking through the actual printing.

Output Devices for Offset Print Color Proofing

Before we output color separation films from the imagesetter, we often make a color proof to simulate the quality of the final offset print result.

We call this type of output device a "DDCP" (Direct Digital Color Proofer) device. A variety of DDCP devices are currently available, such as the Kodak Approval system, as well as systems from Dainippon Screen, and Fuji Photo Film. Many of these are capable of output (or transfer) onto the actual printing stock that will be used in the final printing, an invaluable element when evaluating quality during the proofing stage.

Fuji Photo Film compact First Proof DDCP system. This device works differently than DDCP systems from other manufacturers but is suitable as a digital photography output device.

If you are creating artwork for an exhibition and are not satisfied with the quality of output from large format inkjet printers (especially in terms of image crispness), you can ask a printer to output your work on a DDCP proofing device instead. Color proofers are capable of large format output up to approximately 16 × 20 inches, and while they are generally not used for final exhibition-quality output, the quality is generally very high, so it is an option. However, the CMYK dot pattern is evident and may not be acceptable to some photographers.

07 2

Image Processing for Output

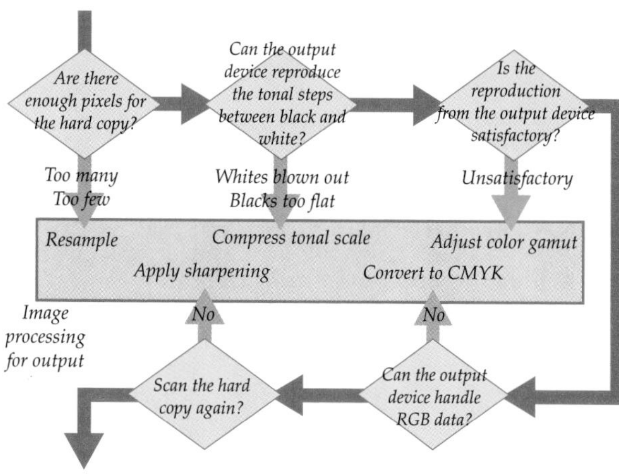

Optimizing Image Data for Output

To output hard copies of your image data, the following basic image processing must be done.

- Interpolate the data to generate the required image resolution for the output device.
- Increase the sharpness to make the image look sharper.
- When necessary, convert the image to CMYK data for the output device.
- Compress the original's tonal scale to a scale that can be reproduced by the output device.
- Convert the color into a gamut that can be reproduced on the output device.

These image processing steps differ depending on the characteristics of the output devices described earlier. While not always taken into consideration when doing the creative aspects of digital photography, if you suspect that your artwork will be printed by color offset printing methods (CMYK) at any time, it's a good thing to use the above steps. If you don't follow these steps correctly, you'll usually end up disappointed with the results of your CMYK hard copy output. In the following pages, we look at these various steps in more detail and explain the different types of processing that are required for different types of output.

Interpolating to Generate the Required Image Resolution for the Output Device

Every output device has an optimal image resolution for output. The illustration below provides a summary of the discussion of resolution presented in Chapter 2-6, "The Language of Digital Imaging."

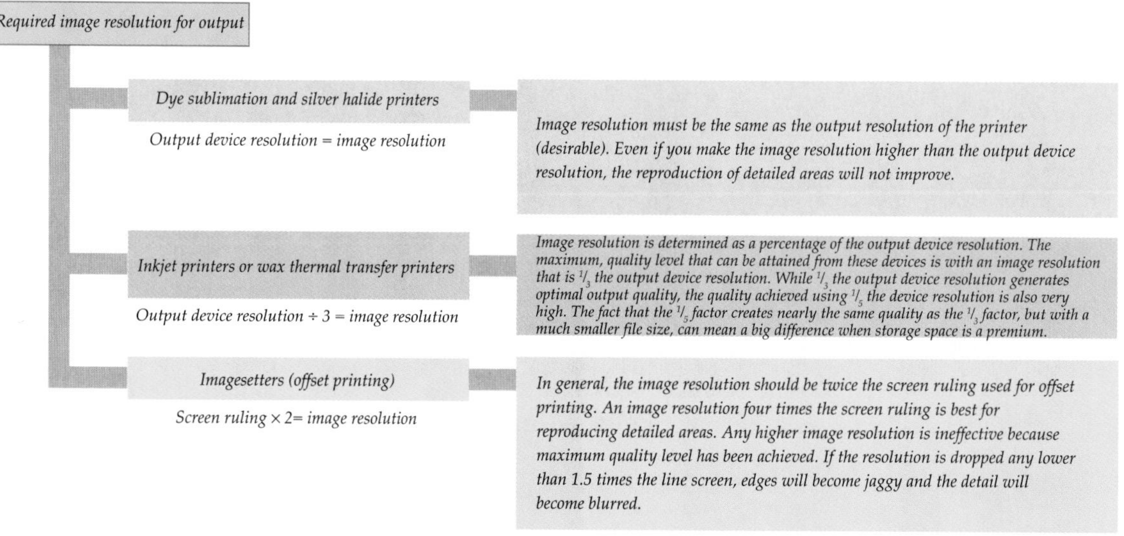

Required image resolution for output
Dye sublimation and silver halide printers
Output device resolution = image resolution
Image resolution must be the same as the output resolution of the printer (desirable). Even if you make the image resolution higher than the output device resolution, the reproduction of detailed areas will not improve.
Inkjet printers or wax thermal transfer printers
Output device resolution ÷ 3 = image resolution
Image resolution is determined as a percentage of the output device resolution. The maximum, quality level that can be attained from these devices is with an image resolution that is 1/3 the output device resolution. While 1/3 the output device resolution generates optimal output quality, the quality achieved using 1/5 the device resolution is also very high. The fact that the 1/5 factor creates nearly the same quality as the 1/3 factor, but with a much smaller file size, can mean a big difference when storage space is a premium.
Imagesetters (offset printing)
Screen ruling × 2= image resolution
In general, the image resolution should be twice the screen ruling used for offset printing. An image resolution four times the screen ruling is best for reproducing detailed areas. Any higher image resolution is ineffective because maximum quality level has been achieved. If the resolution is dropped any lower than 1.5 times the line screen, edges will become jaggy and the detail will become blurred.

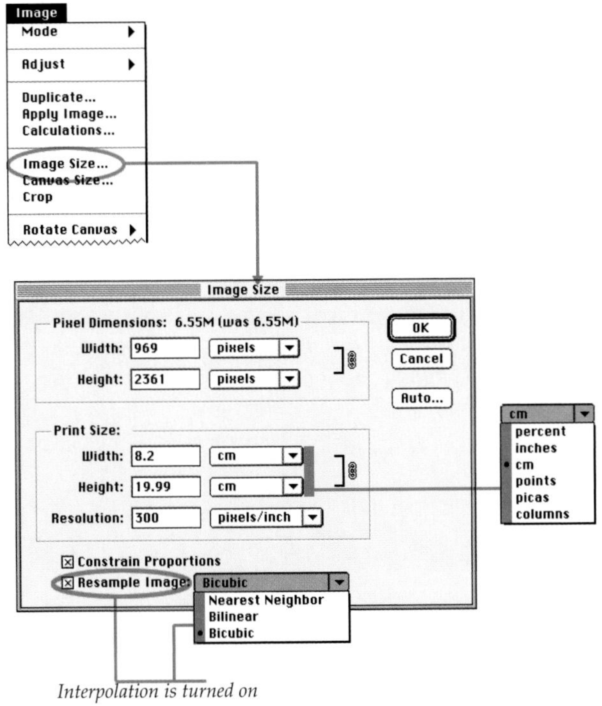

Interpolation is turned on

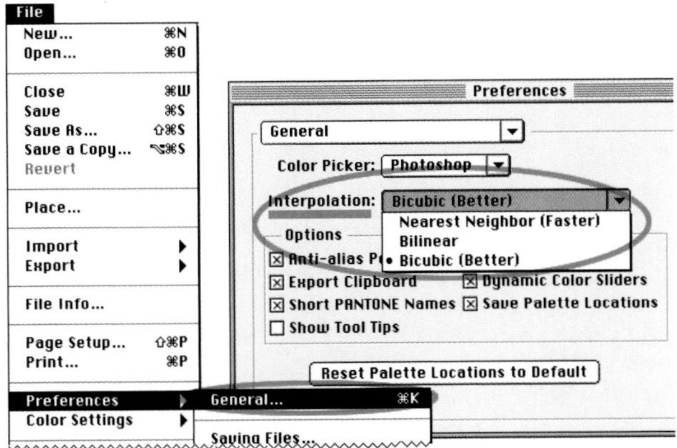

Determining the Output Size

After you have determined what the required image resolution is for your output device, open the piece of digital photography artwork that you wish to output in Photoshop and select the Image Size command.

Uncheck the Resample Image checkbox in the Image Size dialog box (Photoshop 4.0), and change the value in the Resolution field to the image resolution required for your output device.

Then select either inches or cm from the units pop-up menu for the locked Width and Height fields, and you will be able to see what the output size for your hard copy artwork will be.

If this output size is larger or smaller than you want, you will have to resize (by either downsampling or upsampling) in order to obtain the correct image size.

NOTE

There are other ways to output without interpolating. For example, the image resolution for imagesetter output does not always have to be exactly twice the line screen. You can send the data to the imagesetter as is, and the imagesetter will perform its own internal image processing to create a new size—a type of interpolation—for output. Keep in mind, however, that this takes place without the benefit of previewing the quality of a resized image on the monitor and that it's not valid to assume that there will not be a loss of quality.

Also, most printers have settings that allow you to output at image resolutions other than the recommended or specified resolutions (that is, images that are too big or too small for the paper). It is possible to output using options in the Page Setup dialog box such as Scale or Fit to Page.

Because these settings vary widely, we do not discuss these options in detail in this book. Please consult your output device manuals or other resources for more information.

Some Generalizations About Interpolation

The following generalizations about interpolation are useful for digital photography artwork output.

■ Whether you are upsampling or downsampling, you should not sharpen your image before doing the interpolation (see next page).

■ If you interpolate an image that has already been sharpened, very noticeable jagged edges and unattractive lines will appear in the image.

■ There are three types of interpolation in Photoshop, "Nearest Neighbor," "Bilinear" and "Bicubic."

■ You can upsample images using Photoshop's Bicubic interpolation up to 200 percent before major image degradation becomes noticeable. However, some image processing steps are usually required to repair or minimize any side effects of resizing.

■ If you have to upsample more than 200 percent, you can compromise up to 300 percent.

■ If you upsample more than 300 percent, degradation in image quality will become very noticeable to the eye. However, based on variables such as quality of original, subject matter, and so on, it's possible to resize an image as high as 400 percent with proper application of image editing techniques such as Unsharp Masking.

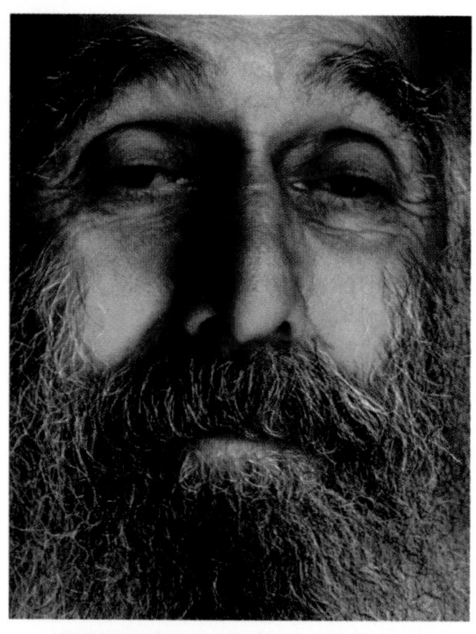

Comparison of an image which was sharpened first and then upsampled and the same image upsampled first and then sharpened. The image that was sharpened first looks unnatural and unattractive because the edges that were emphasized with the sharpening were enlarged.

■ Slightly better results can be achieved by rounding off the percentage of enlargement to even numbers which end with a 0. For instance, a 120 percent enlargement is better than either a 117 percent or a 122 percent enlargement.

■ You can successfully downsample to about 25 percent the original image size.

■ Even if you downsample to less than 25 percent the original image size, you will not see the same amount of image degradation as you see with upsampling.

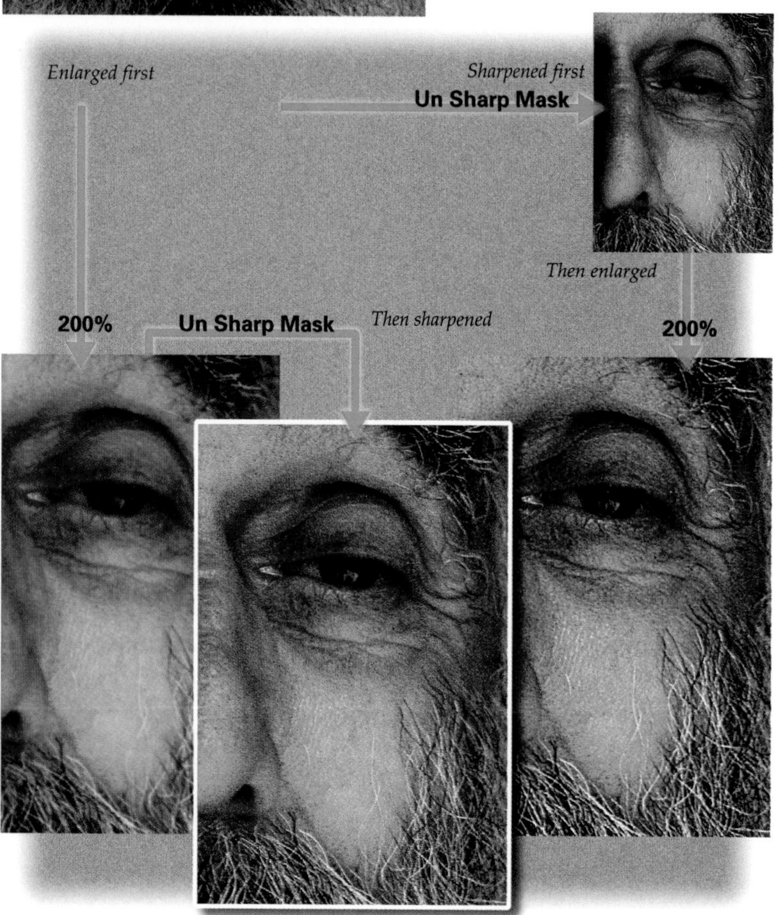

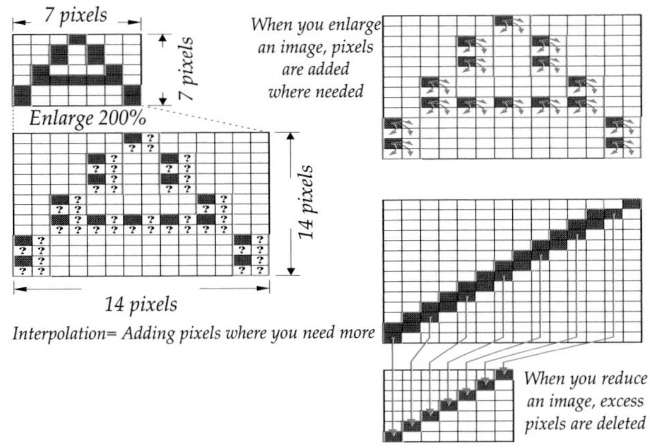

How Interpolation Works

Interpolation is the process of either increasing or decreasing the number of pixels in an image. Depending on how many pixels are needed, new pixels are created from the original pixels to obtain the new number of pixels.

For upsampling (increasing the number of pixels) in particular, new pixels have to be inserted between existing pixels, so some type of computation must be used to generate the new pixels. New pixels are entirely fabricated, so this type of processing usually results in some loss of image quality.

The illustration on the left provides an overview of the simplest type of interpolation, "Nearest Neighbor" interpolation.

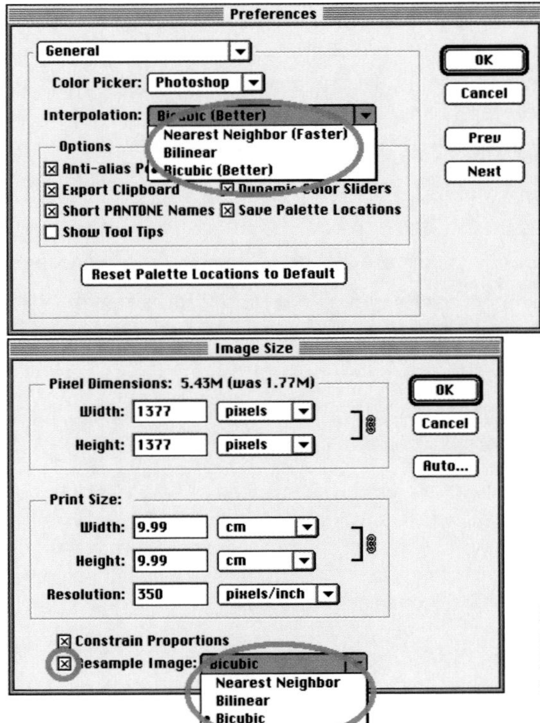

In Photoshop 4.0, in addition to being able to select the method of interpolation in the Preferences dialog box, you can also select it in the Image Size dialog box.

Original: Top left is the original. Top right is the same image enlarged 300 percent. Images below: charts for checking sharpness.

Photoshop offers three different methods of interpolation. Select General under the Preferences command, and choose the method you wish to use from the Interpolation pop-up menu in the Interpolation field within the Preferences dialog box. In Photoshop 4.0 you can make this selection in the Image Size dialog box.

Enlarged 300 percent using Bicubic interpolation

Bicubic Interpolation

This is the default setting in Photoshop, and it allows you to reduce the amount of image degradation associated with interpolation. The disadvantage of this method is that it takes a long time. It works by sampling the levels values of either the eight pixels surrounding a given pixel or the levels values of a larger area around a particular group of pixels and then using algorithms to calculate the levels for the newly generated pixels.

Enlarged 300 percent using Bilinear interpolation

Bilinear Interpolation

This method takes about half as much time as the Bicubic method. It works the same way as the Bicubic method but samples a much smaller number of surrounding pixels. After interpolation, the image will look blurry and considerably lower in quality than images interpolated with the Bicubic method.

Enlarged 300 percent using Nearest Neighbor interpolation

Nearest Neighbor Interpolation

With this method, existing pixels are simply copied to create the new pixels when the image is enlarged and unnecessary pixels are simply deleted when the image is reduced. This can also be called, "simple upsampling and downsampling interpolation."

After interpolation the image will look very jagged, and edges that were already pixelated will remain that way.

NOTE

■ Interpolation is also used when you reshape or rotate images. Bicubic, Bilinear, and Nearest Neighbor methods are used in these processes as well. In Photoshop, the method used when reshaping or rotating images is determined by the Interpolation setting in the File-Preferences-General dialog box.

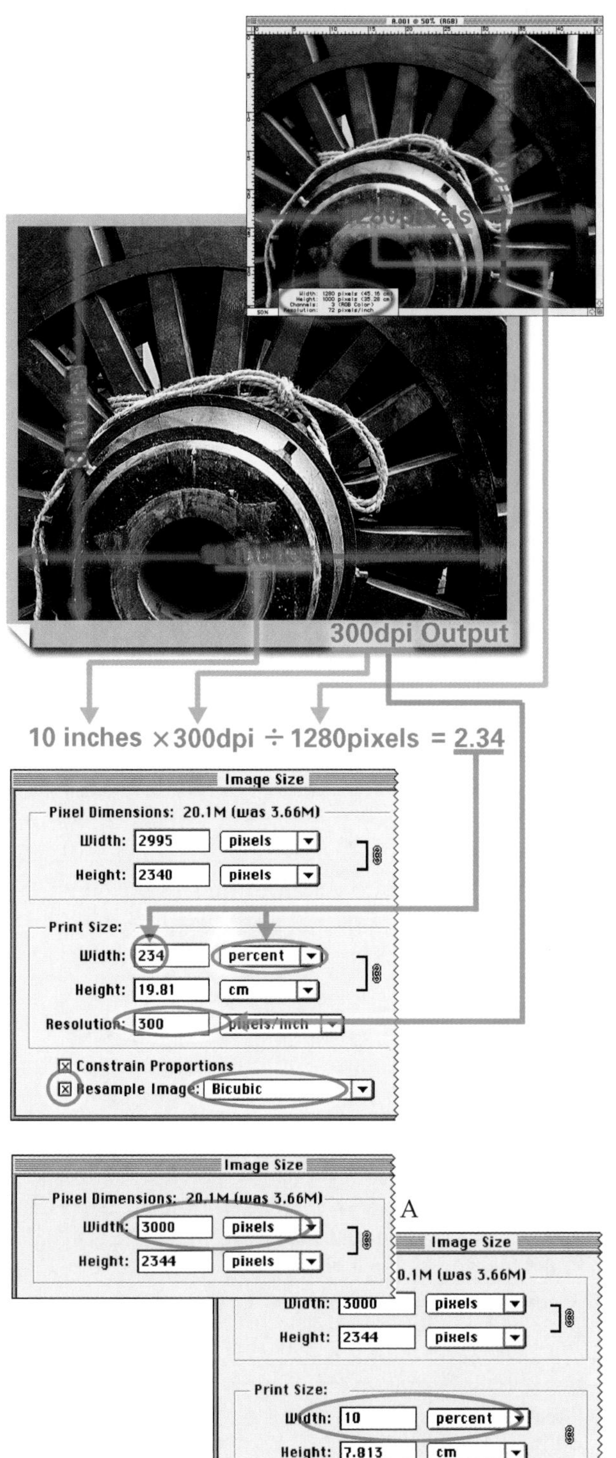

Practical Interpolation Techniques

Imagine you have taken a picture with a Nikon E2 (1,280 × 1,000 pixels) and you want to output it as an 8×10-inch image from a 300 dpi dye sublimation printer.

■ To output an 8×10-inch image on a device capable of 300 pixels per inch output, you need 2,400 pixels for the short dimension (8×300 pixels) and 3,000 pixels for the long dimension (10×300 pixels).

■ The image taken with the Nikon E2 that you want to output is 1,280×1,000 pixels.

■ If you divide the desired finished size of 3,000 pixels for the long dimension by the 1,280 pixels you actually have, you will see that you have to increase the number of pixels by 234 percent.

■ The short dimension requires 2,400 pixels, so if you multiply the number of pixels in the short dimension (1,000) by 2.34, you arrive at 2,340 pixels, approximately the number you need. If you enlarge the short and long dimensions of an image by different amounts, the image will be distorted, so you have to decide the percentage of enlargement based on either the short or the long dimension. In this situation it means that you have to upsample and increase the pixel count for both dimensions of the image equally by 234 percent (you can round off to 230).

■ Next you have to decide which method of interpolation to use. Normally you would select Bicubic since it causes the least amount of image degradation.

■ After you have decided which method to use, turn on image sampling by checking the box in the Resample Image field in the Image Size dialog box.

■ Select "percent" in the units pop-up menu in the Width field and enter "234" for the percentage.

■ Enter "300" in the Resolution field to change the image resolution required for the output device, and click on the OK button.

■ After some processing time, the image will be upsampled to a new pixel count of 3,000×2,340 pixels.

■ It is also possible to directly enter the pixel count you want without calculating the percentage of enlargement, as shown in (A) on the left. You can also directly enter the desired output size.

Original

After sharpening

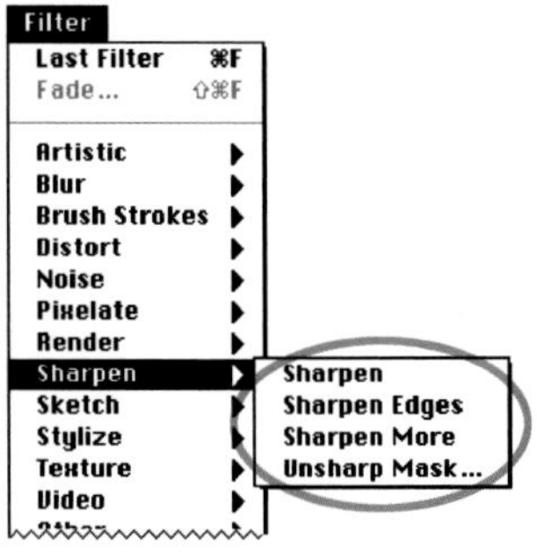

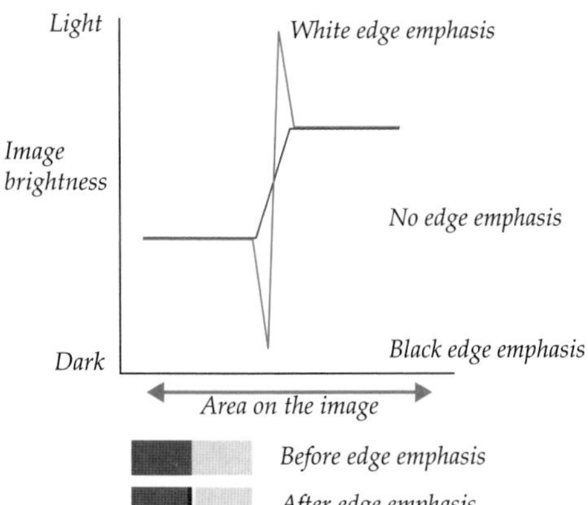

Study the bottom right photograph along the A to B line. These tones are represented in the graph (below the photo) along the horizontal axis. The vertical axis represents the Image Brightness. The blue line in the graph represents the range of tones on the left photo before the application of Unsharp Mask filter. The red line represents the effects of applying Unsharp Mask filter, as seen in the image on the right. The peaks of the red line are an indication that the difference between the light and dark regions of the borders have been emphasized. A real world example of what the graph is illustrating is given in the black bars below the graph. The top two-tone gray bar has no Unsharp Mask filter applied; the bottom shows the results after applying the filter. Notice that a black-and-white line has been created along the border.

Increasing Image Sharpness

Sharpening works by drawing barely perceptible lines along the edges in areas of the image that have clearly defined edges. Sharpness effects are also called "edge emphasis." If you emphasize the edges in an image, for example between a light gray area and a dark gray area, you will be able to see thin whitish and blackish lines ("black edges" and "white edges") on the border between the two areas. The intensity of the sharpening effect depends on three variables — the darkness of the lines (Amount), the thickness of the lines (Radius), and the threshold gradation.

NOTE

This effect is not an unusual phenomenon in normal, film based photography. For example, a similar edge emphasis happens when you develop Black-and-White film using a weak, diluted developer. Prints made from such a negative will look sharper than prints made from a normally processed negative. Also, color negative film manufacturers have been creating dye couplers that are designed to produce emphasized edges.

Photoshop Sharpness Effects

The commands in Photoshop related to sharpening are found in the Filters menu under Sharpen. There are four commands, "Sharpen," "Sharpen Edges," "Sharpen More," and "Unsharp Mask." The "Unsharp Mask" command is used most often in professional environments for achieving optimal sharpness effects because it offers the most control over the three variables that affect sharpness.

NOTE

■ Photographers new to digital imaging don't have to feel ashamed or embarrassed about using sharpen filters! Providing a way of correcting photographers' mis-focused photos is not the intention of an Unsharp Mask filter (although it does come in useful for that sometimes). Instead, Unsharp Masking is a natural part of the pre-press process. The reality is that all photos, no matter how sharp and crisp the original film image is, need some Unsharp Masking after the image has been scanned.

■ Sharpness effects are indispensable for viewing monitor or hard copy images, but if you are going to output images as second generation originals on a film recorder that are likely to be rescanned, you don't need to use sharpening. Film recorder output that's likely to be rescanned is artwork for a client who can't accept or handle a digital file, stock digital photography that's delivered on film or when a piece of hard copy output must serve as the basis for agreement on approved color.

■ On the other hand, if you are going to make photographic (darkroom) enlargements from your film recorder output, you should apply Unsharp Masking to the file before outputting the image to film. However, use only enough to enhance the sharpness on the final print. This means providing just enough sharpness without being able to distinguish the physical symptoms (that is, thin black and white lines) of the filter itself.

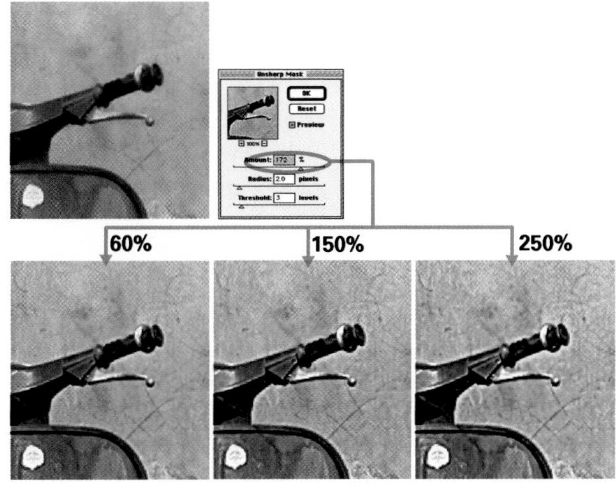

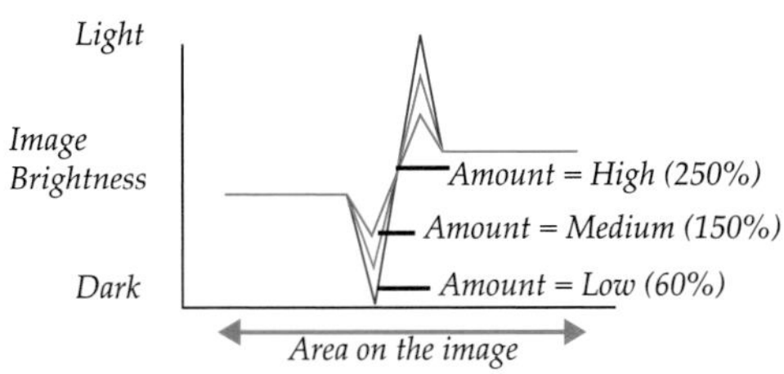

■ Because the way you apply sharpening differs depending on the output device, it's best to leave the Unsharp Mask filter as the last step before output. If you suspect that you will use the same image for several different types of output (for example, film recorder and CMYK), it's best to save a copy of the corrected image prior to applying Unsharp Mask so that you can sharpen it differently later.

■ If you want to keep the feel of a realistic photograph, be careful not to overdue Unsharp Masking. For example, a global application of the Unsharp Mask filter to a landscape will give the same sharpening effect to the near foreground (such as trees, flowers) as to the far background (such as mountains, clouds). This has an overall effect of killing any sense of depth perception in the image.

Unsharp Mask Command

There are three entry fields in the Unsharp Mask dialog box in Photoshop.

■ Amount: This setting determines the darkness of the lines that are drawn along the edges. The larger the number, the more distinct the black edges and white edges will become. The blue line in the graph to the left represents a high setting for amount (250 percent), the red line represents a medium setting for amount (150 percent), and the blue green line represents a low setting for amount (60 percent). For dye sublimation printer output, we typically use 80 percent on pictures of people or pictures with a soft focus. For scenery or still subjects that have a hard feel, we use around 180 percent.

If you use too high a value, lines that originally exist in the image (for example, the mesh on audio speakers) will look unrealistic, and moiré and jaggies are likely to occur.

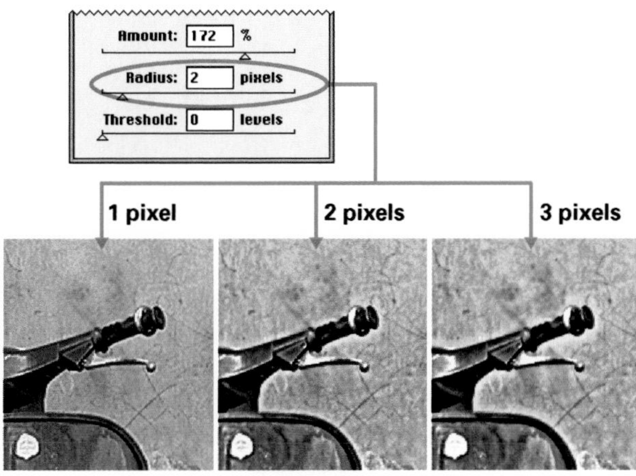

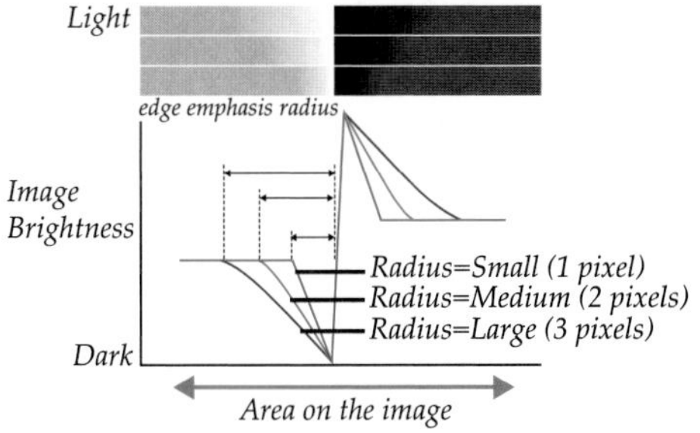

■ Radius: This determines the width of the lines that are drawn along the edges, in tenths of pixels. The radius value is generally related to the image resolution required for a particular output device.

The optimal edge width makes the lines just barely perceptible to the human eye. Of course this is also dependent upon viewing conditions, such as distance and lighting.

Strict definitions of optimal values should be determined by testing, but in general we have found the optimum values to be 0.6 pixels at 150 ppi, 1 pixel at 300 ppi, 1.2 pixels at 350 ppi, and 1.5 pixels at 400 ppi.

Also, for images that have very fine texture, particularly images taken with digital cameras, always keep the radius set to 1 pixel and adjust only the amount of the sharpening. This is because when you have texture (such as fine lines in a pattern) that is only described by a single pixel, a setting higher than 1 pixel will average the values, resulting in a loss of detail.

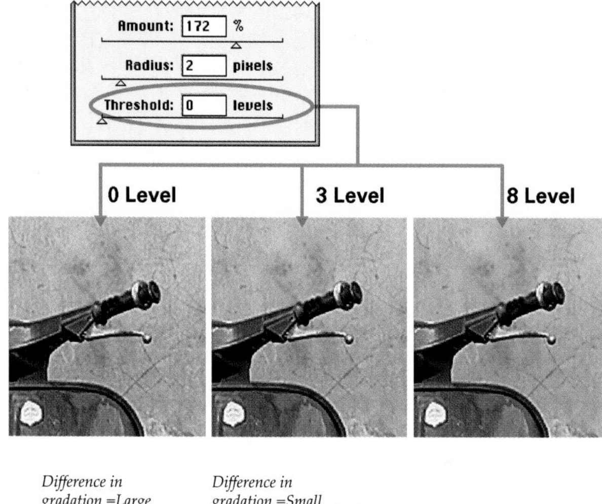

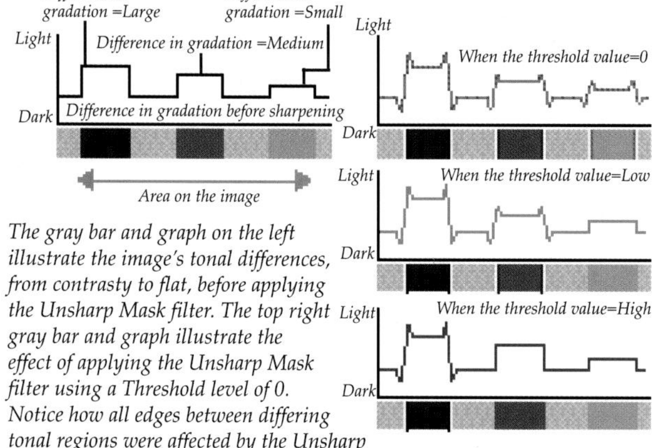

The gray bar and graph on the left illustrate the image's tonal differences, from contrasty to flat, before applying the Unsharp Mask filter. The top right gray bar and graph illustrate the effect of applying the Unsharp Mask filter using a Threshold level of 0. Notice how all edges between differing tonal regions were affected by the Unsharp Mask. In the middle bar and graph, a low Threshold setting was applied (3 levels); the borders between the areas of least tonal difference received no Unsharp Mask effect. Finally, on the bottom gray bar and graph, a high Threshold setting was applied (8 levels) and the effect took place only between the borders with the greatest tonal difference.

■ Threshold: The Threshold setting controls where sharpening will take place based on differences in tonal gradation. A low Threshold setting will affect all differences in tonal gradation in an image, from low contrast to high contrast. A high Threshold will only affect edges with the largest difference in tonal gradation. This means that the Unsharp Mask effect would only be applied to edges with the highest contrast difference. It's possible, therefore, to limit the application of the Unsharp Mask to higher contrast regions of the image, leaving lower contrast regions untouched, by using a higher setting.

Since graininess in an image appears as subtle differences in tonal gradation, a higher Threshold setting should be used for very grainy images to avoid accentuating, or overemphasizing, the grain. In contrast, a low setting should be used for images that are not very grainy.

In general, for a scanned 4 × 5 color reversal film with a pixel count of up to around 4,000 × 5,000 pixels, the threshold setting should be "0." For 35 mm film with a pixel count up to 4,000 × 5,000 pixels, the threshold setting should be around "3" due to the magnified grain. Since digital camera images do not have grain you can keep the Threshold setting at "0."

NOTE

■ To make the effect of unsharp masking that you see on your monitor similar to the effect that is reproduced in your final output, it is helpful to use a 17-inch multiscan monitor that can simulate a 21-inch monitor area (1,024 × 768 dots).

■ It's best to check Unsharp Masking effects by looking at actual hard copy output. However, although any output device can be used to give you a sense of the sharpening effect, one output device is not an indicator of how the effect will look on another output device. Effects of sharpness on one device can only serve as a general indication of sharpness on another device. Different devices will require different settings, and optimum settings can only be determined through testing.

Original

Amount: 200 %
Radius: 2 pixels
Threshold: 0 levels

After sharpening

Machines, Buildings, and Scenery with Clear Blue Skies

A lot of unsharp masking should be applied to images of machines, buildings and scenery with clear blue skies. The three settings should be: Amount = 180–220, Radius = 1.5–2 (at resolutions between 300 and 400 ppi), and Threshold = 0–3. Be aware that photographs of machines, as well as other subject matter, are apt to have a lot of very fine detail. A result of incorrectly using these settings can result in over sharpening, leading to the opposite effect of what was intended, such as a loss of detail.

Controlling Blotchiness in Flesh Tones

You can reduce blotchiness in flesh tones by applying unsharp masking to each of the individual RGB channels. Do this by making the channels where you wish to apply the unsharp masking active in the Channels palette (you can make multiple channels active by clicking them as you hold down the Shift key).

To sharpen while still maintaining the smoothness of the skin, set the unsharp masking settings as follows. The amount should be low (80–120), the radius should be large (1.8–2.5) when the resolution is between 300 and 400 ppi, and the threshold should set individually for each RGB channel depending on how grainy the image is.

The same amount of unsharp masking was applied in each of the RGB channels.

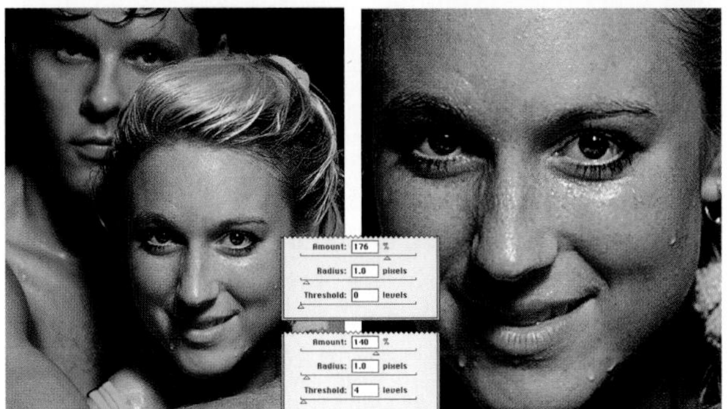

Different amounts of unsharp masking were applied in each of the RGB channels.

From the PhotoDisc image library.

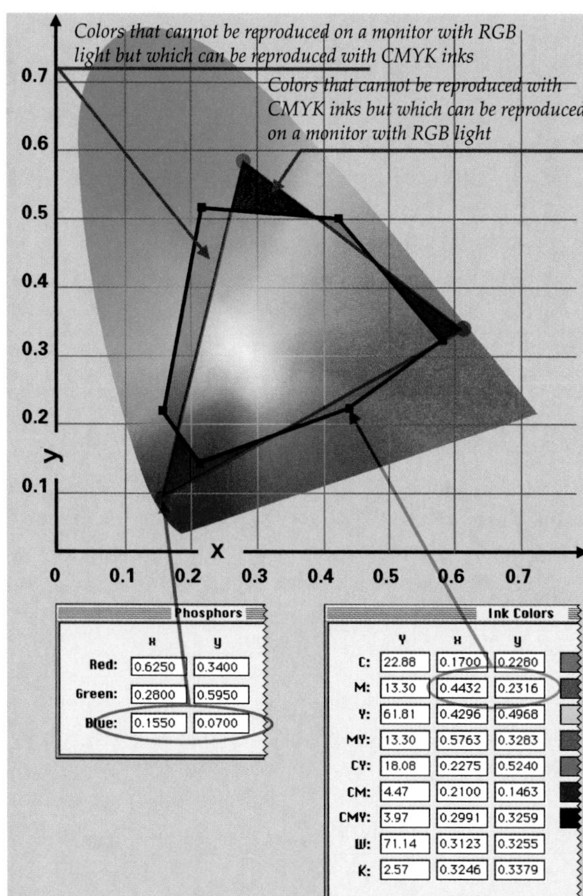

Phosphors

	x	y
Red:	0.6250	0.3400
Green:	0.2800	0.5950
Blue:	0.1550	0.0700

Ink Colors

	Y	x	y
C:	22.88	0.1700	0.2280
M:	13.30	0.4432	0.2316
Y:	61.81	0.4296	0.4968
MY:	13.30	0.5763	0.3283
CY:	18.08	0.2275	0.5240
CM:	4.47	0.2100	0.1463
CMY:	3.97	0.2991	0.3259
W:	71.14	0.3123	0.3255
K:	2.57	0.3246	0.3379

Conversion to CMYK

Because printing inks and color printer ribbons cannot reproduce the color range of RGB color components on paper, RGB colors have to be remapped to CMYK colorant components. This RGB to CMYK conversion is called "color mode conversion." CMYK to RGB conversion is also a color mode conversion. There are several fundamentals about color mode conversion that are useful to know.

Limitations on Color Gamut

When you convert RGB images with beautiful bright oranges, clear blues or fire engine reds into CMYK, the colors often become disappointingly dull compared to the RGB colors displayed on the monitor. This is because the range of colors (called color gamut) that can be printed on paper using CMYK inks is narrower than the range of colors that can be displayed by an RGB mode image on a monitor. When RGB to CMYK conversions are made, Photoshop (as well as other image editing applications) remaps the vivid RGB colors into colors that can be reproduced with printing inks on paper. We express this inability to print such vivid colors as a limitation on color gamut.

Gray Balance and the K Channel

In an RGB image, if the levels values for all of the channels are the same, the color will be gray. However, if you make the halftone percentage values for the CMY channels all the same, the color will not be gray.

In order to obtain gray in print, you have to experiment with combining different amounts of CMY halftone percentages. This is called the *gray balance*. However, even after you do this, you may find that while you can obtain a neutral gray from the highlights to the midtones, you cannot, at the same time, hold a neutral gray in the shadows. No matter what you do, the grays become reddish or yellowish. Therefore, in order to hold neutral grays in the darker tones of the print, as well as to be able to create a true black, a fourth ink — black — is used. There are basically two black generation methods used to create a black (K) plate during the separation process — Under Color Removal (UCR) and Gray Component Replacement (GCR).

K Y M C
100%
C
M & Y
BK
0%
100%
Y + M + C
K + Y + M + C

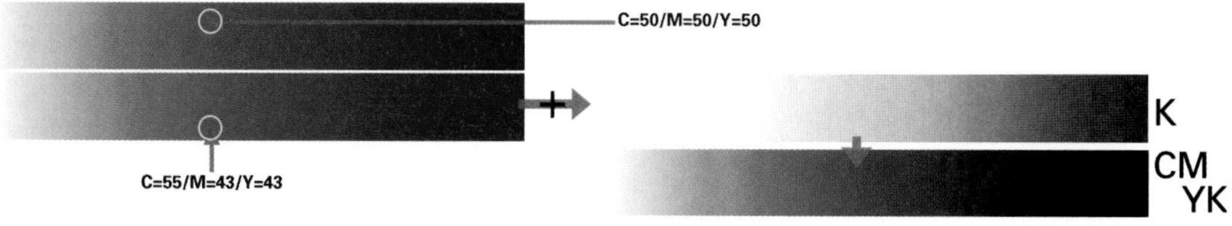

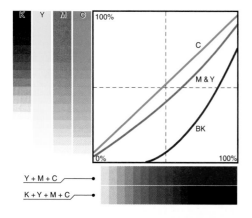

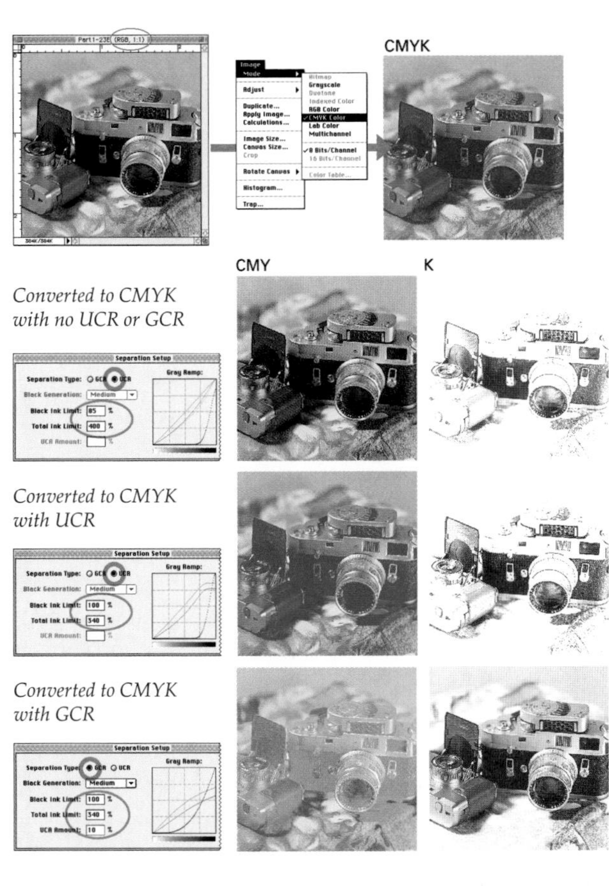

Converted to CMYK with no UCR or GCR

Converted to CMYK with UCR

Converted to CMYK with GCR

UCR and GCR

When Gray Component Replacement (GCR) method is used, areas of the image where all three inks print (not just neutral gray areas, but also chromatic tertiary colors) are removed and replaced with black ink. In their place, black ink is added. When Gray Component Replacement (GCR) method is used, areas of the image where all three inks print (not just gray component areas, but also from tertiary colors) are removed and replaced with black ink. Especially with GCR, the black plate generates most of the image's tonal range, while a combination of one or two CMY inks make up the secondary colors.

In addition to providing the benefit of creating neutral shadows and true blacks, the use of either UCR or GCR reduces the total amount of ink required, which means that there's more control over the process, the inks dry faster (important for high speed, Web press printing) and, especially over long print runs, less ink means lower printing costs.

Although GCR is a bit more complicated than UCR, Photoshop's GCR computation is very precise and provides excellent color reproduction. If you are doing your own RGB to CMYK conversions you should always check with your printer, or your client's printer, about which of the two settings to use. However, when in doubt, use Photoshop's default GCR setting, being sure to change the black generation setting from medium to light.

Simulations of how different levels of dot gain would appear in an image. Basically, as the dots become larger, the image becomes darker. (Dot gain characteristics in these samples are simulated since differing amounts of dot gain cannot be reproduced on the same sheet of paper.)

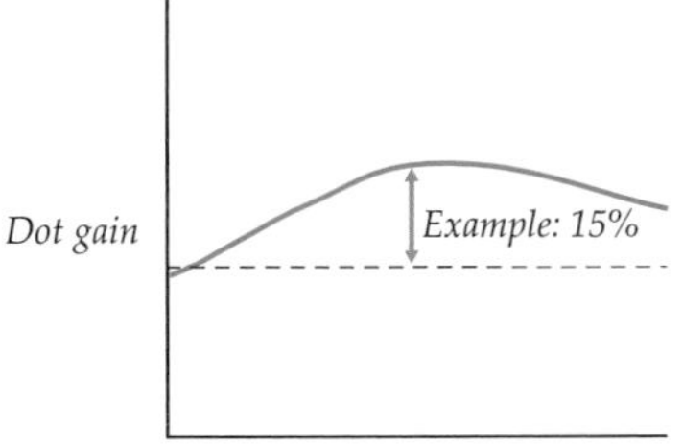

Dot Gain

Before a digital photograph can be printed on an offset printer, it has to go through a number of prepress steps. First, the CMYK data is output as separation films using an imagesetter. Then, these films are used to expose the image onto photosensitive aluminum sheets to create printing plates. The printing plates are mounted onto the press and then the print run begins.

A variety of factors, including the pressure from the press, viscosity, the temperature of the ink, the ink supply, and the type of paper can cause the diameter of the halftone dots printed on the paper to be larger than the dots on the plates. This spreading of the dot size is known as dot gain. If not compensated for, dot gain can cause an image to print darker and muddier than expected.

For the press operator, controlling dot gain on the press is one of the most important aspects for controlling print quality. Fortunately, the amount of dot gain can be accurately measured as a percentage growth in the dot size.

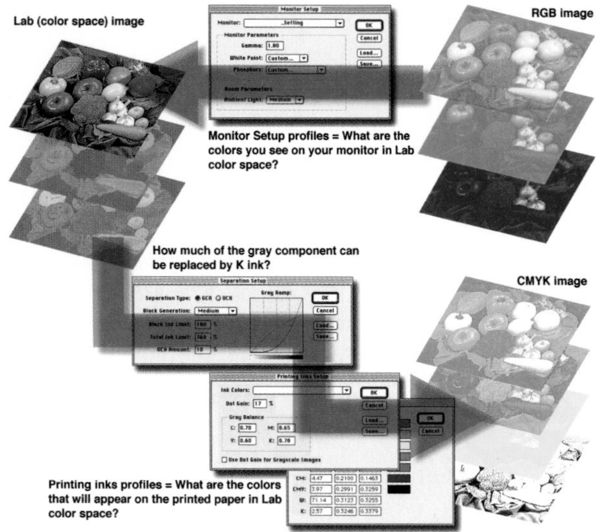

*This figure shows the process of color mode conversion from RGB to CMYK in Photoshop. When the Mode, CMYK Color command is used, Photoshop takes the RGB data (top right) and remaps it to L*a*b* color space (top left) based on settings in the Monitor Profile; then, Photoshop refers to the settings in the Separation Setup and the Printing Inks Setup to convert the L*a*b* color space into CMYK data. For additional explanation of this process, please refer to page 2-15.*

This percentage of dot gain can be provided to you by your (or your client's) printer. This percentage, when entered into the Dot Gain setting of the Printing Inks Setup dialog box, causes the monitor display to simulate the effect of dot gain on a CMYK image. The amount of dot gain that occurs varies depending on where you have your artwork printed, but you can expect at least 11 percent – 18 percent for artwork printed on coated paper on a modern sheetfed press. However, it's always best to check with the printer to find out what the dot gain will be for specific paper stocks.

Color Settings Setup for CMYK Conversion

In Photoshop, the color you see on your monitor display when in CMYK mode or when CMYK Preview is turned on is meant to be as close as possible to the colors that can be reproduced with CMYK inks. This is controlled through adjustment of settings in the Monitor Setup and Printing Inks Setup functions found in the File, Color Settings menu option. When you use these settings to provide Photoshop with information about the image color you are seeing on your monitor and information about the color (the color profiles) in that same image when it is reproduced on paper, Photoshop can adjust the gray balance and color gamut, as well as perform processing such as UCR or GCR (Separation Setup), to give you the best CMYK reproduction possible. Steps for adjusting Monitor Setup and Printing Ink Setup are discussed in Chapter 2-2, "The First Step—Monitor Calibration."

NOTE

One related command that was not discussed in Chapter 2 was the Separation Setup command. The settings in the Separation Setup dialog box are greatly affected by the type of press, the thickness of the ink layers, the viscosity of the ink, and the environmental conditions at the time of printing. Unless told otherwise by your printer, use Photoshop's Default setting in the Separation Setup dialog box (see the comment in the previous section about GCR and UCR).

Actual CMYK Conversion

After you have carefully calibrated your monitor in Photoshop, made your color settings in the Monitor Setup, Printing Inks Setup and Separation Setup dialog boxes, converting an image from RGB to CMYK mode is very simple. Select CMYK Color from Mode in the Image menu, and your image will be converted into a CMYK image.

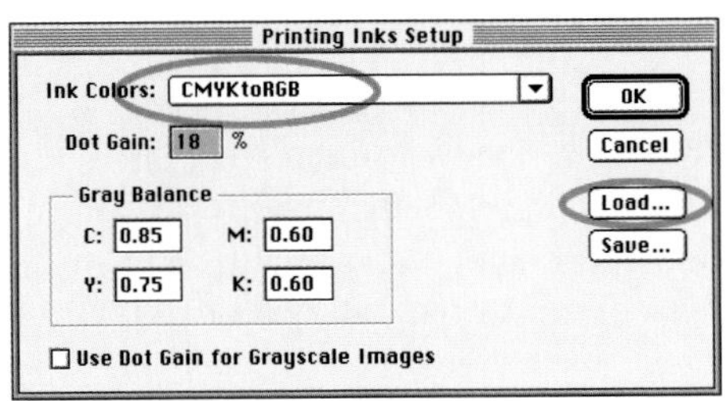

Converting Back to RGB

After you've converted an image from RGB color space to CMYK color space you won't be able to recover the vividness of the colors in the original RGB image if you try to convert the image back to RGB. This is a problem if you intend to use the same image for various types of output, such as film recorders, or on Web pages. In such a case, it's best to always keep an original RGB version of your image, and make RGB to CMYK conversions on an 'as needed' basis.

If you've converted and saved only a CMYK version of an image, but want to use it as an RGB file for other output or for a Web page, you can do the CMYK to RGB file conversion using a special set of Printing Inks Setup settings we've created. This can be found in the Others folder located on the CD-ROM that came with the book. Use the Load button in the Printing Inks Setup dialog box to load this set of settings. While you won't obtain the exact same colors as the original RGB image, you will be able to recover much of the vividness of the RGB original. Remember to return to your original Printing Ink Setup settings after the CMYK to RGB conversion is done, or else you will have incorrect results the next time you do an RGB to CMYK conversion.

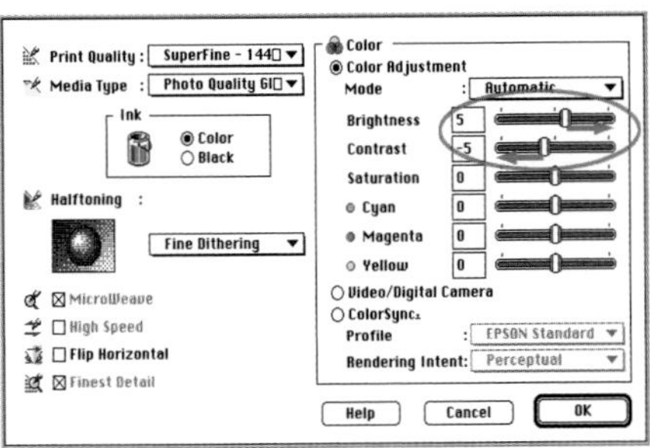

Compressing Image Tonality

The task of matching tonality in a digital image to an output device is similar to matching the contrast of an original negative with the appropriate contrast grade of black-and-white photographic printing paper (you can also think of this as similar to Ansel Adam's Zone System for controlling the relationship of subject values, density values (the negative) and print values (the print). In digital imaging, if the range of brightness values (levels) in an image matches the range of levels an output device can reproduce, then the output should be perfect. When the range of levels in a digital image and an output device don't match, then images may reproduce flatter or with more contrast than expected.

Original data

Output result after tonal compression

In most cases, the printer driver software (like that shown on the left) on your output device will convert the levels values so that this does not occur. However, when your output does not turn out as expected, you can make levels adjustments, in Photoshop or other image editing software, to improve the quality. This process of forcing output devices to reproduce an optimal tonal range is called "tonal compression."

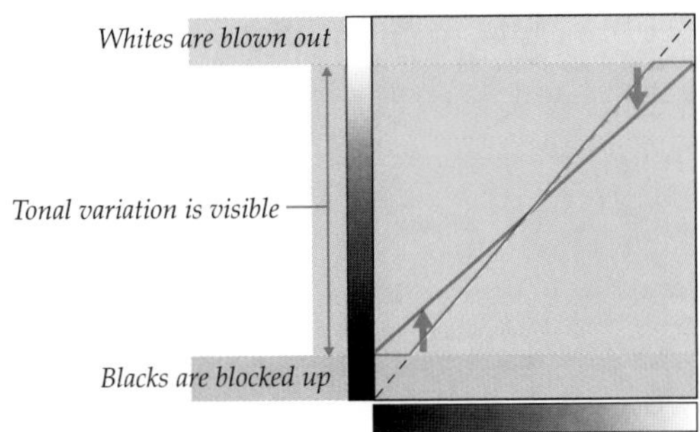

A technique for compressing image tonality for optimum output is explained starting on the next page.

When you make RGB to CMYK conversions for offset printing, tonal compression automatically takes place during the conversion process (transparent to the user) based on the settings used in the Printing Inks Setup and the Separation Setup dialog boxes in Photoshop. However, if you are using a non-PostScript dye sublimation printer, film recorder or inkjet printer to output RGB image data directly, you will usually have to make these adjustments in tonal compression yourself. Here's how it works...

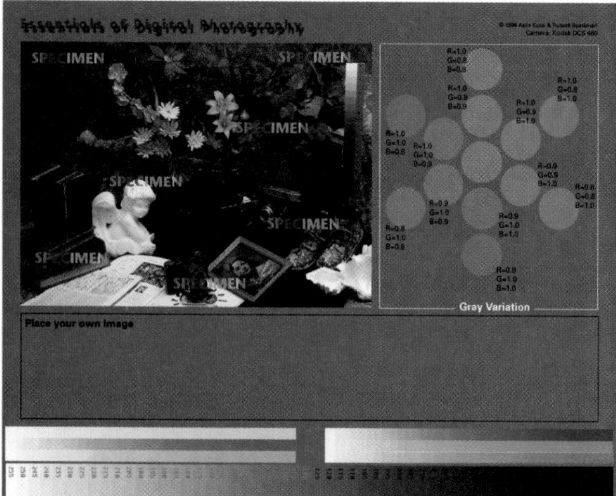

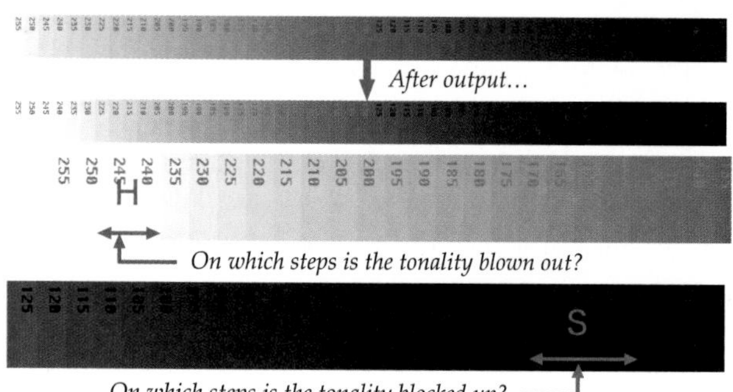

Compressing Tonality for Optimum Output

STEPS

1. Open the ToneCompRGB.tif file in the PrintTest folder on the accompanying CD-ROM. (Please note: this is a 32 MB file).

2. This test chart image has 4,000 pixels on the long dimension and was created for optimal 4K film recorder output. You may have to resize the image for your output device. If you do, use the Nearest Neighbor method of interpolation (although we've previously advised against using Nearest Neighbor, in this case it should be used to maintain the distinctions between tones in the grayscale).

Before you begin this test...

■ This test only applies to printers and film recorders that directly output RGB image data (this means anytime you can output an image without first converting it into CMYK mode).

■ Some printer drivers internally remap RGB image data into CMYK data for controlling the printer, in which case the procedures described on this page may not work.

■ Photoshop's File, Color Settings options do not affect the display of images in RGB mode like they do the display of images in CMYK mode. In order to closely match the RGB display of your image to the more limited color gamut of your RGB output device, without actually converting the image to CMYK, you can use the View, CMYK Preview menu option. For this to work correctly, you need to adjust the monitor display to match a sample output from the RGB output device using the Printing Inks Setup dialog box, following the steps described in Chapter 2 (be sure to save the setting with a name like RGB Output Profile). Then, whenever the CMYK Preview option is on, the display of your RGB image should approximate what the results from your RGB output device will be like.

■ If you follow the directions here and the CMYK Preview display still doesn't look close to your hard copy you should base your decisions about color adjustment solely on the actual hard copy output you're getting for the best results.

■ We are only presenting the concepts here. Please understand that this will take some experimentation on your own to understand the relationships between your monitor and your printer more clearly.

3. Output the test chart on your printer using the printer driver's default settings (using the default settings of the printer driver is similar to starting a film test using the manufacturer's suggested ISO; it eliminates variables and provides a baseline against which you can make adjustments). If you are having the chart output on a film recorder, give the previous instructions to the photo lab or service bureau doing the output.

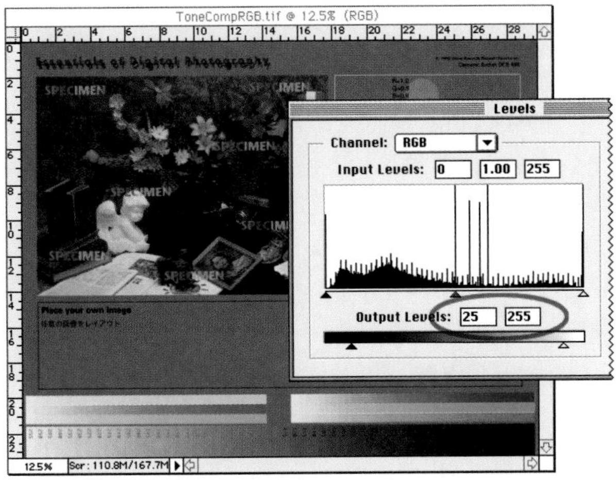

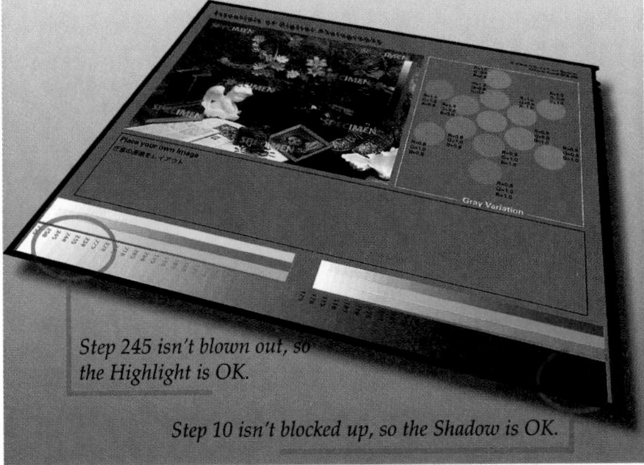

NOTE

If you intend to output color film from a film recorder and then enlarge it photographically, provide some printing instructions by using a simple black-and-white hard copy (laser print is fine) of the test chart. On the hard copy, indicate that you'd like the center circle of the Gray Comparison chart as a target for neutral gray reproduction. For consistent results, ask the photo lab making the print to note the exposure time, correction filter values and other conditions for enlarging the print on this hard copy and save it for later reference. You'll want these as guidelines for the second output in this test process.

4. View the print under standard lighting conditions (5000°K is recommended). Look at the gray scale and locate the step where the tonality first blows out. Then note the number of that step (see H in the chart on the previous page).

5. In the same way, look at the grayscale on the print and locate the step where the tonality first blocks up. Note the number of that step (see S in the chart on the previous page).

NOTE

If you look at the test chart and see that steps 250–255 in the grayscale are blown out and you can't see any tonality, plus steps 0 – 5 are blocked up and also show no tonality, but all other steps are discernible, it means that you are getting the optimal range of tones for that image data on that output device. Since it won't be necessary to go through the trouble of doing tonal compression for that printer, your work is finished after step 5 .

NOTE

If you are able to see tonality in steps 255 or 0 in the gray scale, the printer's output is too flat. It is possible that something is adjusted incorrectly in the hardware or that incorrect settings were made in the printer driver setup. These problems existed prior to this test, so check them carefully, make adjustments and then make another print.

6. Select the Levels command in Photoshop and enter the numbers you noted for the highlight and the shadow on the gray scale in the highlight and shadow fields in Output Levels for the composite RGB channel in the Levels dialog box (the defaults are 0 and 255). Save this setting.

7. Click on OK in the Levels dialog box and look at the test chart. This step has compressed the tonality in the chart so the highlights are not blown out and the shadows aren't blocked up (you'll notice that the image contrast looks flatter on the monitor, compared to the original before the adjustment). Output the adjusted image using the same conditions you used in step 3. If you output film from a film recorder or a silver halide print, be sure to request the same parameters that were used when the first test was made.

8. Look at your result. Check that step 245 on the gray scale is not blown out and shows tonality, and that step 255 is blown out. Check also that you can see a clear difference between step 10 and step 5 on the gray scale, and that you cannot see any difference between step 5 and step 0.

NOTE

If your results do not match those above, increase or decrease the values entered in the Levels dialog box and try again. However, be sure to adjust the original image and not the image to which you've already applied tonal compression.

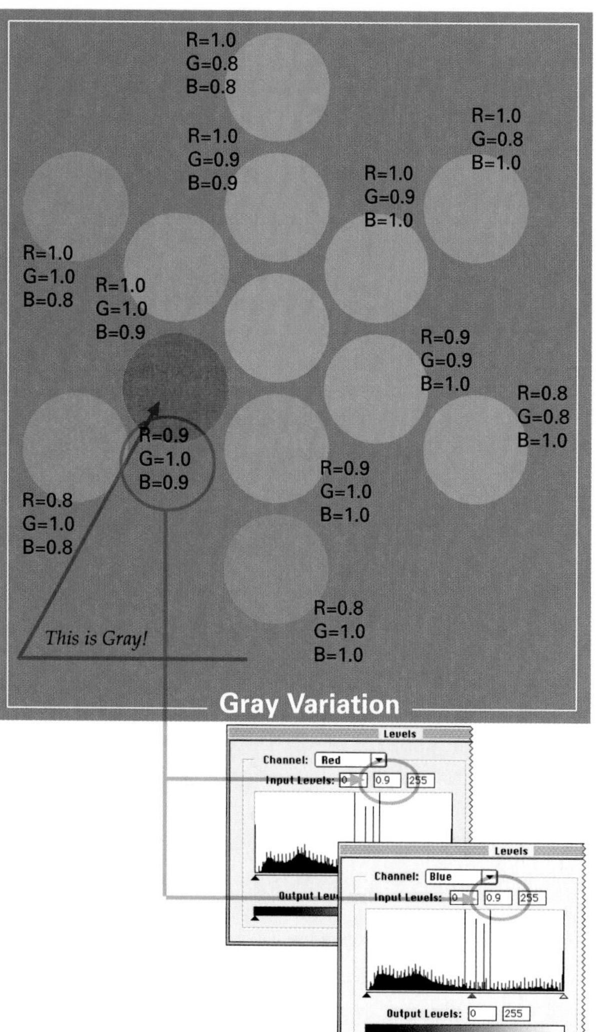

9. This completes tonal compression. However, it's possible that your gray scale doesn't look gray, but has a particular color cast to it. If so, refer to the Gray Comparison chart (the circles) in your output and locate the circle that looks most like an ideal neutral gray (if the image were perfectly neutral, the circle in the center would be the neutral gray. Unfortunately, due to printing variables of your output device (as was the case with the reproduction of this book) the center circle may not be an ideal gray (as is the case on this page).

10. With an unadjusted version of the image, open the Levels dialog box and in the Gamma field for each of the R, G, and B channels (center setting of the Input Levels function) enter the RGB values printed next to the gray circle you have chosen. At the same time, enter the highlight and shadow values you used in Step 6 into the Output Levels fields. Output this file. You should have a print that has a proper tonal range without a color cast.

NOTE

■ If none of the circles appears to be a neutral gray, locate the closest one and increase or decrease the gamma values by 0.1. Decreasing the gamma value will make a large adjustment while increasing the gamma value will make a small adjustment.

■ If you find a color cast in the bright areas that is different from the color cast in the very dark areas of the grayscale, use a tone curve instead of the Gray Comparison chart to correct the gray. However, this test chart is not designed specifically to correct this problem, so please refer to the discussion about tone curves starting on page 3-13 of Chapter 3-5.

11. Click on the Save button in the Levels dialog box to save your settings. It is a good idea to save the file with a name like, "Tonal Adjustment for XX Printer."

12. Later, any time you are doing final output to a printer you've created a Levels tone compression setting for, load and apply the saved Levels to the image before output. The adjusted image data is only for output purposes, so you can close it without saving it or, if an adjusted copy was saved specifically for output, delete that copy after output (be sure you don't delete your original, unadjusted copy, a mistake that could really ruin your day).

NOTE

■ The results of the gamma adjustment in step 10 may make the printed output slightly brighter than you want. To adjust for this, enter a slightly lower value (by about 0.05 as a starting point) in the Input Levels Gamma field of the composite RGB channel in the Levels dialog box. This should make up for any lightening of the image that occurred in step 10.

Simulating Offset Printing Results

If you try to use an RGB output device to give you an idea of how an image will look when it is converted to CMYK and printed on an offset press, there will be a difference between the RGB hard copy output and the CMYK results, primarily because the RGB image data is not converted into the CMYK data required for offset printing.

Also, these printers are mainly focused upon maximizing their individual output capabilities from RGB color (that is, bright, vivid colors), so this is natural. It is possible, however, to simulate the results of CMYK output in your RGB printer, which we explain here. For this example, we used the Seiko Epson Stylus Pro XL inkjet printer, but the same steps can be applied to any RGB output device.

NOTE

Parts of this process rely on subjective image evaluation and a lot of trial and error. Expect the process to take some time to complete. Along the way, however, you'll gain a greater understanding of the interaction between Photoshop's Printing Inks Setup settings and RGB to CMYK conversion.

STEP

1. We are going to ask you to change your Monitor Setup and Printing Ink Setup settings, so if you aren't using standard Photoshop default settings, be sure to save your custom settings now.

2. Open the CompColorRGB.tif file in the PrintTest folder on the accompanying CD-ROM. Output this RGB image on your RGB color printer (dye sublimation, silver halide, or inkjet printer). If the output looks similar to the offset printed version of the file in the back of the book (or to your own CMYK proof converted from CompColorRGB), you don't need to proceed with the following steps.

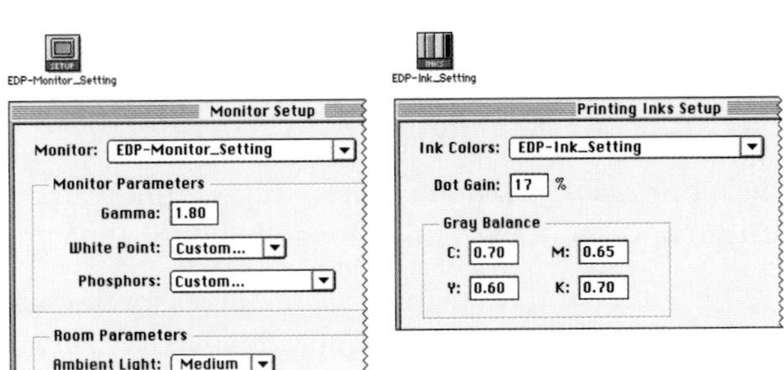

NOTE

You can can begin step 2 by comparing your output to a CMYK proof of the CompColorRGB data made by your or your client's offset printer (instead of comparing it to the version in the back of the book). This means you will be creating an environment for comparing your RGB printer output to the CMYK output from your offset printer. However, for the rest of this explanation, we base the comparisons on the copy of the chart printed in the back of the book.

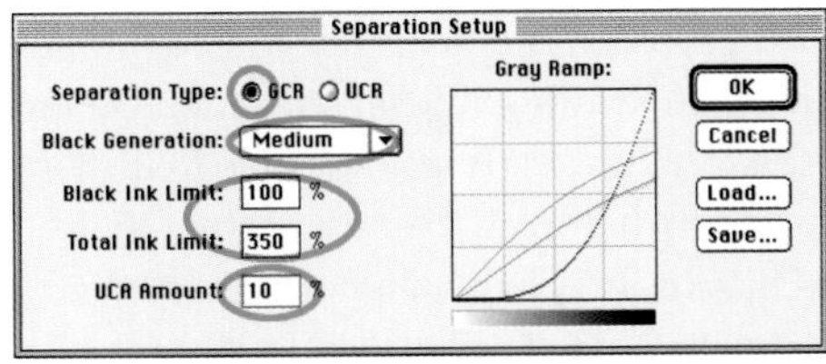

3. Open the File, Color Settings, Monitor Setup dialog box in Photoshop and click on the Load button, and then load the EDP Monitor Setting file from the PrintTest folder on the CD-ROM. Click on OK and close the dialog box.

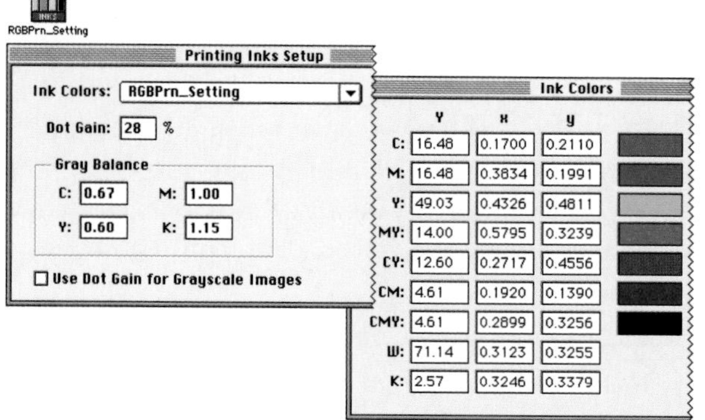

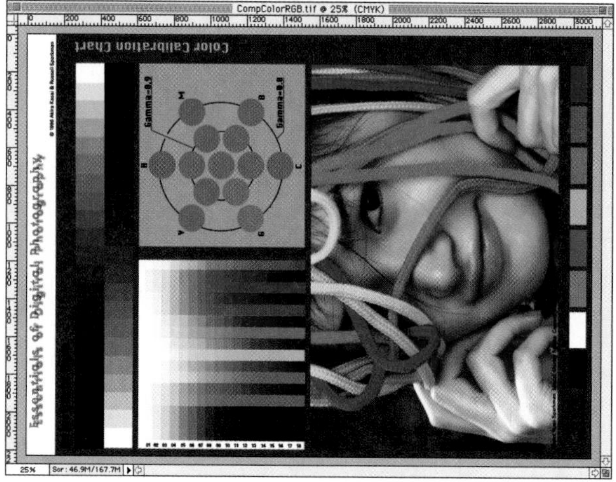

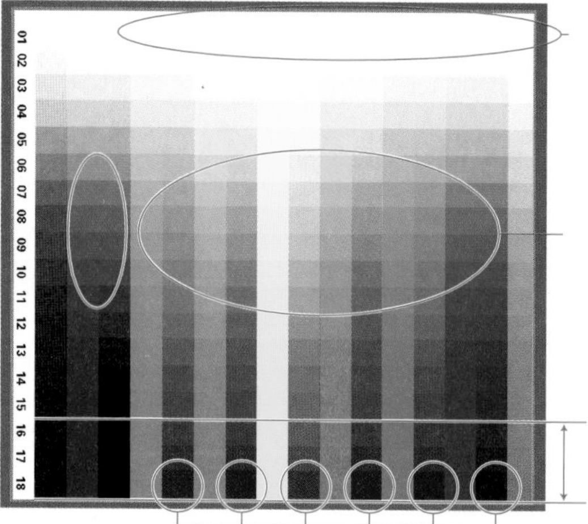

1. Can you make out very slight color in the 01 steps for each color (can you see the line between step 01 and the white paper)?
2. Do the steps in the midtones of the three types of gray blend into each other similarly to the way they do on the color chart in the back of the book?
3. Are the differences between the midtones in the colored steps (not the accuracy of each individual color) similar to the differences on the color chart in the back of the book?
4. Do the differences in saturation between steps 16, 17, and 18 (you can't see the dividing lines) look similar to those on the color chart in the back of the book?
5. Does the muddiness of step 18 for all the colors stand out (this step alone should be fairly noticeable) similarly to the color chart in the back of the book?

4. Similarly, open the File, Color Settings, Printing Inks Setup dialog box and click on the Load button. Then load the EDP Ink Setting file from the PrintTest folder on the CD-ROM. If you wish, you can use the Separation Setup command to make the settings shown in the dialog box on the left.

NOTE

■ If you've made your own Monitor Setup and Printing Ink Setup settings according to the steps in Chapter 2, then convert the image from RGB to CMYK with your own settings. This is especially true if you have made these settings based on having your printer provide a CMYK proof from the MonitorCalibCMYK file, as suggested on page 2-14, and if it's to this printer's output that you want to try to calibrate the output from your RGB printer. If you haven't made these settings, then change them to the settings as described in steps 3 and 4.

■ Normally, when you make adjustments for RGB to CMYK conversion in Photoshop, you adjust Monitor Setup and Printing Inks Setup at the same time, and these should be considered a set to be used together. We have done this in steps 3 and 4 above. The values we suggest you use in steps 3 and 4 are a set of ideal values we made for the offset printing of this book.

5. Convert the CompColor RGB.tif image into a CMYK image using Image, Mode, CMYK Color. The conversion from RGB mode to CMYK mode changes the color gamut and as a result the colors should look muddier and the blacks should look lighter than the RGB mode file. Later in the technique, you'll repeatedly convert this file between CMYK Color mode and RGB Color mode, so make a "Save As" version to your hard drive, using a name indicating that it's the CMYK version of the CompColor file.

6. Once again, open the Printing Inks Setup dialog box and this time load the RGBPrn_Setting file from the PrintTest folder on the accompanying CD-ROM. Don't be alarmed to see the CMYK image display become darker. This new RGB Prn_Setting Printing Ink Setup is not changing the data itself, only the display of the data to simulate CMYK output on the RGB monitor.

Then, before the next step, make a duplicate of this file using the Image, Duplicate command.

7. Convert the duplicate into RGB mode using the Image, Mode, RGB Color command. The purpose of the procedure up to this point has been to shift the color gamut of the original RGB file into the color gamut of a CMYK file, by first converting the image to CMYK and then back to RGB. The Printing Ink Setup loaded in step 6 was designed to intentionally darken the RGB data during this conversion, based on the settings that darken the monitor display of the CMYK data. If you compare the RGB file with the CMYK duplicate, they should look

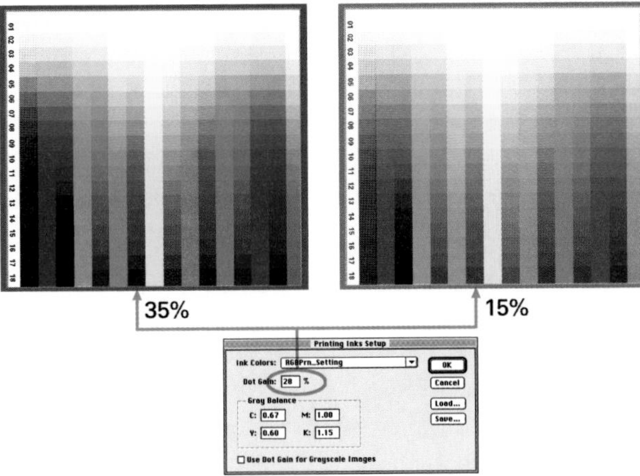

Notice steps 8–14 in all the color charts.

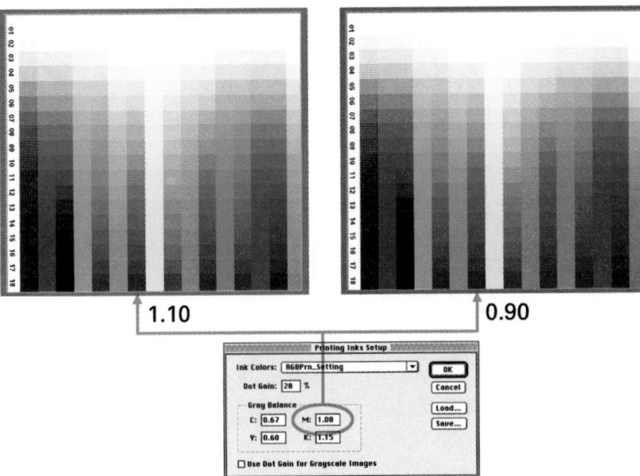

Notice the difference in grayscale between the two.

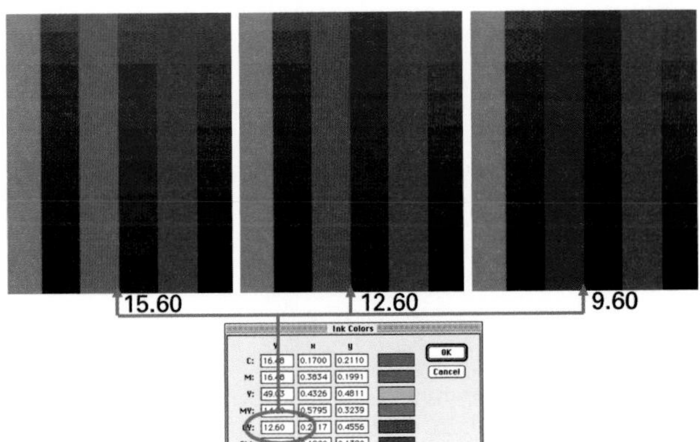

Notice the muddiness in the greens.

the same. The RGB file has intentionally been made darker because when most CMYK images are reconverted to an RGB image, they print lighter on the RGB output device than the actual CMYK data would reproduce on press.

8. Output the RGB image from your color printer and compare the print with the offset print in the back of this book. Check the areas circled in the illustration on the left. If the answers to the questions in the caption at left are all yes, then see step 9. If the answers are no, proceed to step 10.

9. If the characteristics of the areas of your output are close, or if the differences are small enough to be acceptable, then you can use the RGBPrn_Setting to convert CMYK files to RGB for test output on your RGB output device. This means that you can make a rough proof on your RGB printer to give you a general idea of how your CMYK image will print. It is, of course, no substitute for a CMYK color proof from your printing company.

If all of the areas do not match, make the following adjustments to the RGBPrn_Setting parameters according to step 10.

NOTE

The following steps are based on using the RGBPrn_Setting file and the CMYK version of the CompColor file you saved in step 6.

10. Compare the overall brightness of your hard copy to the book copy and decide if it is too light or too dark by looking at the darker midtone steps (steps 8–14) in the three gray scales. If you think it is too light, increase the Dot Gain setting in the Printing Inks Setup dialog box by 4–7, then convert the image from CMYK back to RGB. If it is too dark, decrease the Dot Gain setting and convert back to RGB. Use the Undo command each time to undo the Printing Inks Setup until you settle on a Dot Gain that gives you an accepted brightness.

11. After you're satisfied with the overall brightness in step 10, revert the RGB file back to CMYK mode. Next, adjust the gray balance by looking at the grayscales (particularly the second or third from the left) and determine what color cast you see. Increase or decrease the Gray Balance settings for C, M, Y, and K in the Printing Inks Setup dialog box by increments of 0.05 (that is, if too green, lower the magenta (M) setting by .05). Then convert the file back to RGB and output.

Up to this point, you've adjusted the brightness of your output with the Printing Inks Setup Dot Gain and the gray balance with the Gray Balance setting.

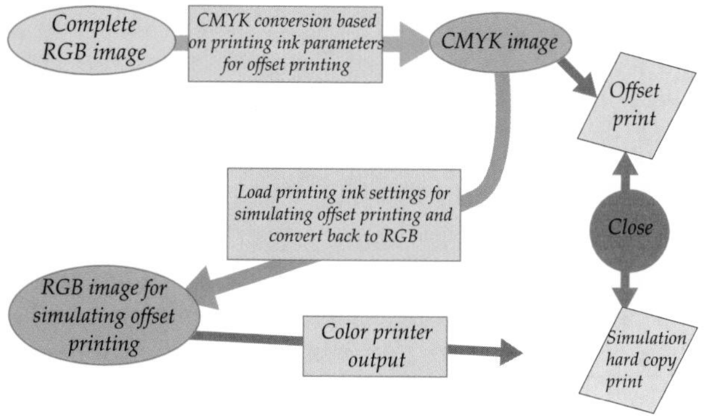

12. This final step is to selectively adjust the reproduction of the three bottom color steps (steps 15–18) of the C, M, Y, MY (red), CY (green) and CM (blue), and CMY scales in the color chart. Open the Ink Colors dialog box by selecting Custom in the Ink Colors Pop-up menu in the Printing Inks Setup dialog box. If, for example, not enough gradation in steps 15–18 of the Cyan (C) scale on your hard copy is visible (you need it lighter), increase the Y value of the Yxy field by 2.00–3.00. If, for example, too much gradation in the Cyan (C) scale is visible (you need it darker), decrease the Y value of the Yxy field by 2.00–3.00. Test the result of your adjustments by converting from CMYK to RGB and print again. Adjust the other colors as necessary.

13. Save the Printing Ink Setup settings you have acquired through steps 10–12 (give the setting a name such as "CMYK to RGB Output"). Then, when you want to simulate offset printing output on your RGB printer, convert the RGB image to CMYK using your standard Printing Ink Setup settings for offset printing. Then load your specially saved CMYK to RGB Output Printing Ink Setup settings, convert the CMYK file back to RGB, and print.

Because the only purpose of this particular RGB file is for test output, you can delete it after printing it out. Also, don't forget to return to your normal Printing Inks Setup settings after this test is over.

Left: Offset print. Right: print from the Seiko Epson Stylus Pro XL using the "Simulating Offset Printing Results" technique discussed in preceeding pages.

The Epson printer's output matches fairly closely that of the offset print version. In order to duplicate the relationship of these hard copy samples here in the book, the two prints were photographed using a Nikon E2 digital camera, with a Kodak Gray Scale Q-13 included in the photo. Highlight, shadow and midtone levels were established based on the Q-13 grayscale. (The difference in the Gray Comparison portion of the chart is due to a change in the design of the chart during production of the book. The data on the CD-ROM, however, matches the Color Calibration Chart in the back of the book).

chapter 8

System Setup for Digital Photography: Hardware

08 1

Digital Photography Systems

What is a Photography System?

Ask a number of different photographers to describe a "conventional photography system" and they'll probably list cameras, lenses, lighting, and so on. But is this all there is to a conventional photography system? Consider the following:

A conventional photography system includes not only individual photographers with their cameras, lenses, and lighting equipment, but also services such as processing labs. With few exceptions, after you take your color photos, the rest is left up to processing labs.

A benefit of this system is that all you really need for photography is a camera. If you're using color reversal film, however, it's critical to perfectly expose photographs at the time you shoot them. With color negatives, you can relax a bit more than you can with color reversal film because of color negative's wider exposure latitude. Printable negatives can be made without worrying about slight differences in color temperature, controlling exposures within $^1/_2$ stop, and so on.

Either way, you have to rely on an outside lab for most, if not all, processing of color photography after exposure. This is especially true in professional photography where post-exposure tasks are divided into very specialized processes.

Whether amateur or pro, after you've ordered color prints or processed your slides, you may find yourself wishing they were different in a variety of ways. You might like to brighten them or remove color casts, or in other cases, you might like to darken specific areas that are overexposed.

The price you pay for the convenience of the photo lab, however, is little to no control over correcting color photos after they're returned (except in the case of ordering slide dupes or reprints). The reality is that in a conventional photography system the only part of the photographic process you can actively participate in—in a hands on way—is the exposure stage.

Most people don't stop to think of conventional photography as being a "system." But once you begin digital photography, you have to be keenly aware of the fact that creating a piece of photographic artwork is not just a matter of using a camera, but also consists of a variety of processes that occur after exposure. Compared with conventional photography systems, however, fewer of these processes rely on outside services. In digital photography, invididuals can control the entire input-manipulation-output of color artwork process in their own homes or studios. The physical components of computers, scanners, software, and so on, used in this process, along with the knowledge and skills it takes to operate it, comprise the digital photography system.

Throughout much of this book we've concentrated on the knowledge and software parts of the system. Here we'll look at the part of the digital photography system that involves hardware.

Digital Photography Systems

The first question is, what kind of equipment is required for doing digital photography? In other words, is there a clearly defined system for it?

Unfortunately, since digital photography systems are fairly new and in a very fluid state of development, we can only offer general guidelines about what to consider standard. One thing that can be said for certain is that a digital photography system involves three processes—input, processing, and output—and that separate pieces of equipment are required for each of these three processes. No matter how large or small your system, you should have equipment for capturing images (exposure), equipment for manipulating those images, and equipment for the output of those images. You must also have equipment for storing (saving) the data between each of these processing steps.

We have looked at input devices—scanners and digital cameras—from a number of perspectives in Chapters 2, 4, and 5. We have also explored output devices, such as printers, in Chapter 7, so please refer back to those chapters as necessary.

What we will focus on here is the essential equipment required for image manipulation—that is, computers themselves, as well as other equipment for data storage, such as hard disks. In addition, because individual devices alone do not make a system, we will also look at how devices are connected and combined to make a complete system.

08 2

Digital Photography System Configurations

1: Power Macintosh 8500 series computer with at least 32 MB RAM and at least 1 GB internal hard disk space. 2: 17 inch or larger color monitor (with VRAM capable of displaying 16 million colors). 3: Digital camera with at least 500×700 pixels. 4: Photographic quality color printer.

A Variety of System Configurations

There are numerous possible system configurations. Your own system configuration will differ depending on whether you are doing hybrid photography or 100 percent digital photography. It will also vary depending upon whether you intend to create and output individual pieces of fine art or whether you need to move large volumes of digital photos through a production environment.

NOTE

The industry being as fast-moving as it is, computer models that we used as examples may be discontinued, or newer, similar priced models may supercede them in features. Use our suggestions as the basis for asking intelligent questions when shopping for your own system.

Minimal Systems

First let's look at what could be considered a minimal system configuration. As shown on the left, four types of hardware are required for a minimal system: a computer with hard disk storage space, a monitor, a digital camera, and a color printer. With this amount of equipment, you have just enough of a system for doing digital photography as it is defined at the beginning of the book in Chapter 2-1, "What is Digital Photography?" This means it's big enough to serve as a compact digital camera system, as well to study applications such as Photoshop.

The photograph to the left shows a minimum system for doing hybrid photography. A hybrid system means that part of the process depends on film, so this system includes a slide scanner. We don't show a color printer, but you would need to add one to create a total system, from input to processing to output. While at this system level you could begin to create commercial artwork, limitations on efficiently working with larger file sizes might make it frustrating.

NOTE

RAM requirements listed are, in our opinion, the minimum for each configuration. If you can afford more, buy more.

1: Power Macintosh 8500 series computer with at least 64 MB RAM and at least 1 GB internal hard disk space. 2: 17 inch or larger color monitor (with VRAM capable of displaying 16 million colors). 3: Jaz drive or other removable storage media. 4a: 35 mm film scanner with at least 1,500 dpi optical resolution, or 4b: Flatbed scanner with transparency adaptor with an optical resolution of at least 600 dpi. Other: Photographic quality color printer as necessary.

Minimal Systems for Professional Use

We are often asked what should comprise a minimum system for a professional photographer. Our usual response is to ask the photographer what is his or her own attitude about digital photography. Then, based on the individual's attitude, we can recommend a system configuration.

What, you might wonder, does attitude have to do with buying a digital photography system? The answer is this: a minimum system is whatever it takes for a photographer to achieve his or her goals in digital photography—and attitudes about goals will vary widely from individual to individual than attitudes about budgets will.

Many professional photographers, if not already involved, are starting to show some interest in digital photography. Perhaps they recognized that what happened to design when it first went digital is going to happen to photography. They might also suspect that there will be limitations on how their businesses can grow based on conventional photography alone. If their attitude about this change is positive, then we can recommend either full blown systems they can grow into or lesser systems that they can grow with over time.

On the other hand, some professional photographers feel, either consciously or subconsiously, that photography will no longer be photography if they go digital. In addition they may experience fear about computers, steepness of learning curves, new methods, and so on. In such cases, we suggest taking small steps, getting only enough of a system to begin learning on.

In any case, the time to get started is now. The following examples are basic configurations that a professional photographer can consider as starting points for professional level systems.

The sample configuration on the left shows the basic system for creating high enough resolution digital photography for commercial offset print output up to approximately 8 $^1/_2$ × 11 inch size. In this case, creating data and creating the final print are not exactly the same thing because this work is based on using outside services for prepress and printing the digital data.

The photo on the left shows a digital camera system configuration for a portrait studio. The purpose of this system is to provide enough speed and storage capacity to take process and output portrait photography as big as 8×10 on dye sublimation or silver halide printers (not shown). Note that scanners are not needed on this particular configuration.

1: Power Macintosh 8500 series computer with at least 128 MB RAM and at least 1 GB internal hard disk space. 2: 17–20 inch color monitor (with VRAM capable of displaying 16 million colors). 3: At least 2 GB external or internal additional hard disk space. 4a: 35 mm film scanner with at least 2,500 dpi optical resolution, or 4b: Flatbed scanner with transparency adaptor with an optical resolution of at least 600 dpi. 5: Jaz drives or other removable storage media.

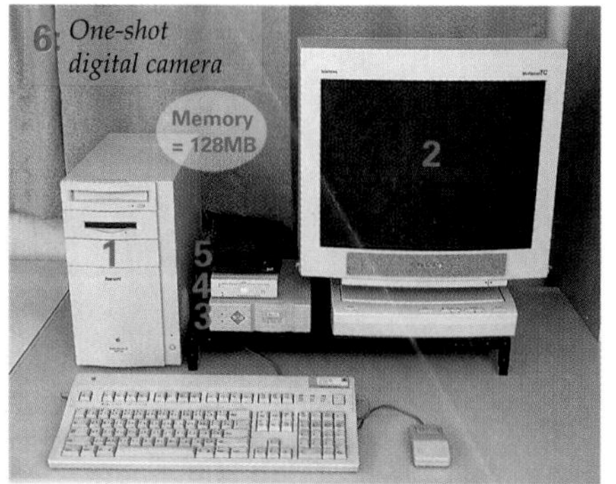

1: Power Macintosh 8500 series computer with at least 128 MB RAM and at least 1 GB internal hard disk space. 2: 17–20 inch color monitor (with VRAM capable of displaying 16 million colors). 3: At least 2 GB external or internal additional hard disk space. 4: Optical disk drive (MO) for long term storage. 5: Jaz drives or other removable storage media for managing your data as you work. 6. One-shot digital camera with at least 2,000×2,000 pixels (not shown).

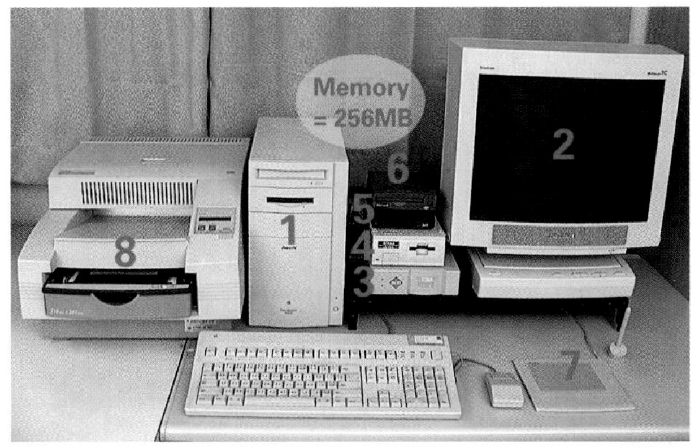

1: Power Macintosh 8500 series computer or higher with at least 256 MB RAM and at least 1 GB internal hard disk space. 2: 17–20 inch color monitor (with VRAM capable of displaying 16 million colors). 3: At least 2 GB external or internal additional hard disk space. 4: 35 mm film scanner with at least 2,500 dpi optical resolution. 5: Jaz drives or other removable storage media for managing your data as you work. 6: Zip drives or other removable storage media for using a service bureau for output. 7: drawing tablet. 8: Dye sublimation printer or silver halide color printer.

FT-S700 scanner, capable of scanning originals up to 5×5 inches

Creating Artwork with Hybrid Digital Photography Systems

Many commercial and fine art applications of digital photography benefit from the use of film and film scanners. For photographers who fear losing touch with their darkroom techniques, this can actually be encouraging because the opposite occurs. Compared to conventional color photography, where most color work is processed by a lab, the digital lightroom provides an unprecedented amount of personal control over color photography.

In the photo on the left, we show a sample configuration for the photographer who wants to scan his or her own 35 mm color reversal film or color negative film and output the final artwork as A4 hard copies or as film transparencies. In addition to, or instead of, a 35 mm film scanner is a 4×5 film scanner, as shown on the left. Because higher resolutions are likely to be used, this system calls for more RAM than the previous systems.

Commercial Photography Studio Systems

Because there are many different commercial photography studios, large and small, it is difficult to define a single system configuration for studios. The illustration below was reproduced with permission by Mr. Hayakawa from the Hayakawa Studio. It shows a large scale digital photography system used by the Hayakawa studio within ABC Studios.

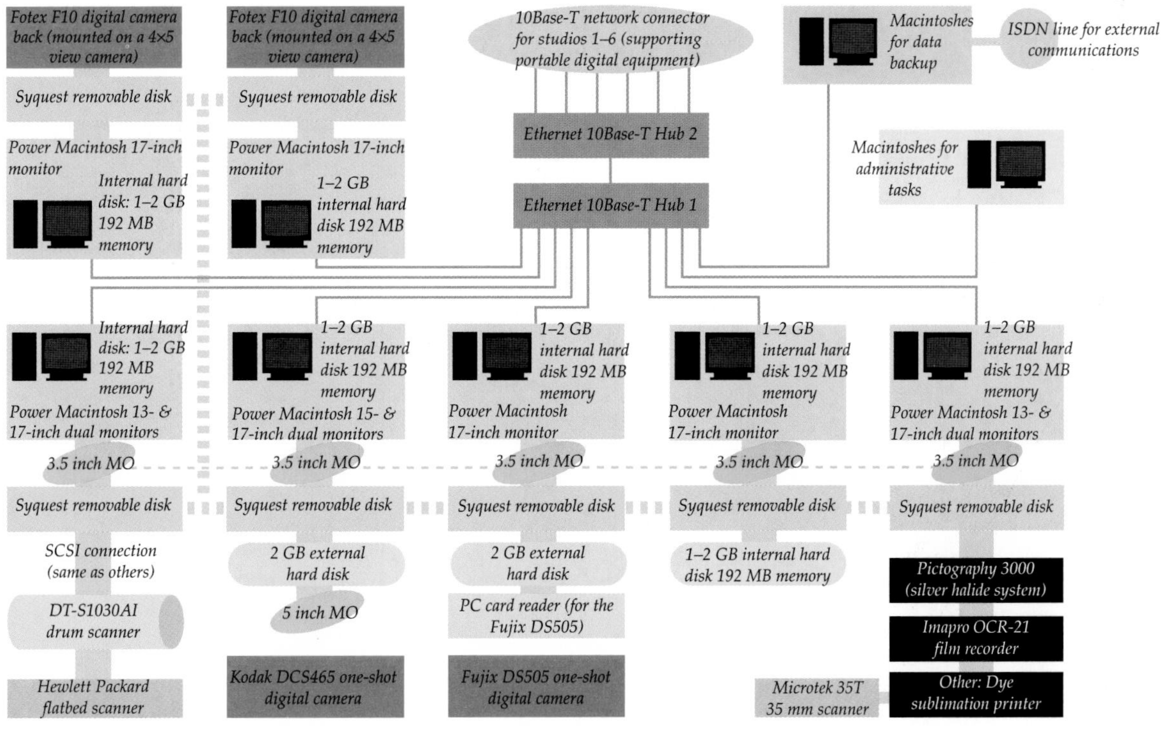

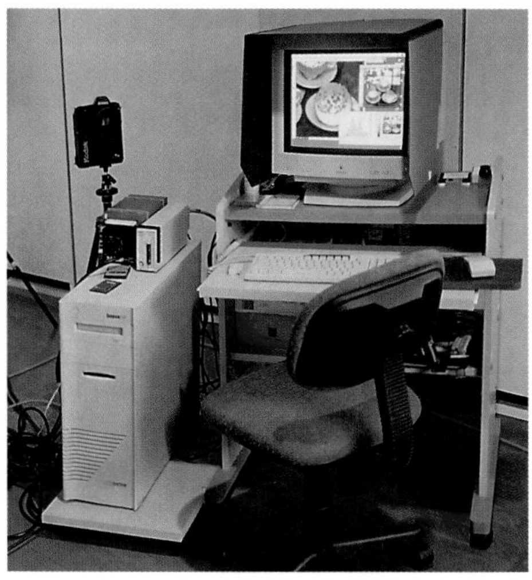

Digital Camera Capture Station

Digital photography studios often have mobile computer workstations for their studio cameras. By mobile it means that the entire system—computer, monitor, storage devices, and so on—is placed on a cart that can be moved about the studio. In our studio, we use an office computer desk with wheels, which are relatively inexpensive and easy to find. If you design your own custom cart, consider making it tall enough to view the monitor at eye level while standing.

Basic Considerations for Configuring a Professional System

If you take a conventional photograph, whether you create a snapshot for a family photo album, a contest entry, or an independent professional artwork, you can repurpose it for mass distribution at some later date if you wish. You can do this because all of these photographs are continuous-tone hard copies, regardless of whether they are transparencies or prints.

With digital photography, however, it is often impossible to repurpose artwork that has been output on inkjet printers or dye sublimation printers for high quality offset printing. If you bring a standard size color snapshot to a printer, you can enlarge it and still get a sharp offset print from it, but if you bring a print that has been output on an inkjet printer, it may appear blurry, show moiré, and not be of good quality. If you want to output digital photography pieces as offset prints later on, consider the following two options.

■ Bring image data that has been prepared for offset printing to the printer.

■ Bring a continuous-tone hard copy of the piece to the printer.

For the first option, because it will be necessary to convert your finished RGB data into CMYK data for offset printing, you should check how well the printer can handle this process.

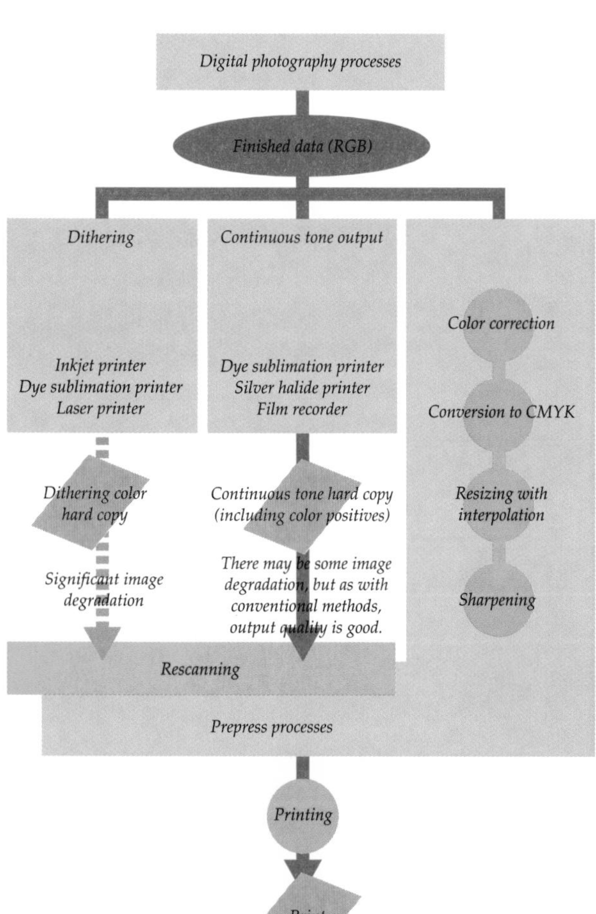

Many printers, however, are still not accustomed to printing digital photography artwork to the satisfaction of a photographer (which is to say, they aren't used to doing conversion to CMYK, sharpening, and color correction). Therefore photographers themselves must increasingly be armed with sufficient technological knowledge to see the process through all the way to offset printing.

The second option—creating continuous-tone output and bringing it to the printer—gives you three output choices. You can use a dye sublimation printer, a silver halide color printer, or a color positive film recorder.

Of these three choices, silver halide color printers are overwhelmingly becoming the most popular because they provide high quality reflective 8×10 originals. Film recorders also offer excellent quality, but because they are expensive, you may have to send your work out to a service bureau or print shop instead of buying one.

We usually provide image data when we need offset printing, and we output our work on a dye sublimation printer only when we need to check it. When we submit data, we do the conversion to CMYK ourselves, but we would prefer to have this done at the printer's as well.

Below: Co-author Akira Kasai's digital photography system configuration. On the right is his assistant's desk. On the left is his main imaging workstation. In the center are a variety of scanners, Jaz drives, a lightbox, and other equipment. The SCSI devices can easily be switched between the two systems as needed.

08 3

The Language of Computers

The Language of Photography and the Language of Computers

We expect that most of our readers are either relatively high-level conventional photographers or people who have considerable experience with digital image processing or DTP (desktop publishing).

Here we would like to provide a relatively non-technical introduction to the language of computers and related hardware for those of you who are well versed in conventional photography but who have less experience with computers and digital technology.

PC machine running Windows 95

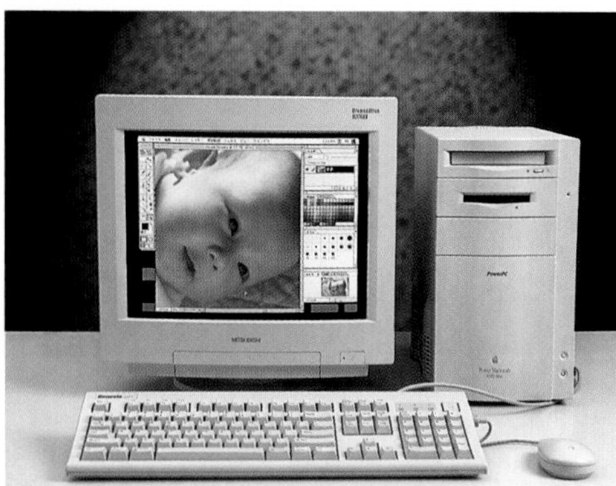

Macintosh

Computers and PCs

We'll start with the word "computer." When individuals like ourselves, who are not part of enormous organizations, use the word "computer," we are referring to personal computers (PCs). The abbreviation "PC," however, has other nuances of meaning.

A *PC* generally refers to a particular type of personal computer, a computer whose internal configuration and basic operating system is based on an IBM computer. PCs based on the IBM are the most widespread in the world.

The NEC PC98 series machines fall into this group of PC machines (even though differences between them do exist). These PCs are extremely popular and range from inexpensive, compact units for home use, through machines for administrative and general purpose office use in large industries. Recently we have come to call them either DOS-V (*doss-vee*) machines or Windows machines.

Strictly speaking, the terms PC, DOS-V, and Windows all represent different types of technology. Engineers and manufacturers need to strictly differentiate between these, but for those of us using computers for digital photography, we can think of the three terms as relatively synonymous.

Computers and Macs

In the world of digital photography, everywhere you go you hear the word "Mac." Macintosh computers differ from PCs in configuration (such as built-in monitor support) and operating system (such as ease of installation and maintenance, as well as compatibility with a wide range of peripheral devices, especially for imaging).

Most of the material in this book was written based on the Mac because the percentage of people like us involved in the digital image processing business who use Macs is much higher than those using PCs (nearly 90 percent in related industries for both Japan and North America).

If you are considering purchasing a computer for the first time and you plan to use it for digital photography and for business, we highly recommend an Apple Macintosh, or Macintosh clone (discussed next).

The Macintosh is well designed for optimal display and manipulation of images, and therefore is more suitable for our type of work than the PC. Perhaps more importantly, the Macintosh is very easy to learn, use, and maintain compared to a PC. This means that, as an artist's tool, it provides a higher ratio of creative time to training and maintenance time than other computer systems.

NOTE

Arguments about which is better, Windows (PC) or the Mac, are common. For the type of clearly defined use we discuss in this book, we don't think there is any question that the Macintosh is the wiser investment between the two. If you already have an investment in a PC, however, and are familiar with its use, then try to maximize its usefulness. If your primary purpose for a computer is other than digital photography, choose the platform that is best for you, provided that it gives you at least the minimum ability to acquire, manipulate, and print images (for example, a PC and compact digital camera combination).

Until very recently, unlike the PC, nobody manufactured clones for the Mac. This is probably why the Mac is called by its trademark name, Macintosh, rather than having the more all-purpose name, PC. Since the second half of 1996, however, other manufacturers have been developing machines that use Apple's operating system, such as Daystar's Genesis, the UMAX Super Mac, Motorola's StarMax, or Power Computing's Power Tower. These are "Mac clones," and they are synonymous with Macs. If you need to handle large amounts of image data, particularly for business, the Genesis machine is currently the most popular. We have been very satisfied with its performance.

The Genesis MP in use at the authors' photography studio

The OS

As we have seen, many different types of computers are called by many different names, such as PC (Windows) and Macintosh. Other types exist as well, such as super computers, mini computers, office computers, and workstations. These are all names for general categories of computer configurations.

Behind all these different configurations is an OS, or operating system. This can also be called *fundamental software*. It would require many volumes as large as this book and very specialized knowledge to explain what an operating system is. Although this may be familiar territory to many readers, we include this explanation here to help those just getting started out.

The functions of the computer you see with your eyes (basically a box) can sometimes be best understood by considering them in human terms. The moment a human is born, for instance, it has a biological instinct to cry. When a manufacturer creates a computer, it isn't capable of performing any kind of data processing the instant after the last screw is put into place. It has no instincts to work from. The computer's instincts, or capability to function, have to be supplied to the computer from the outside.

Basic functions on the computer that correspond to human instincts are performed by the operating system software. Not too long ago it was perfectly normal on both PCs and Macs for this operating system to be stored on a floppy (the startup disk), and for this floppy to have to be inserted into the machine for it to run. This provided the basic instincts for the machine to operate.

With the improvement of hard drives, it became normal for computers to have internal hard drives onto which the operating system is installed. When you turn the computer on, the operating system is automatically loaded from the hard drive into RAM.

On PC machines, the operating system is called *DOS* (more accurately *MS-DOS*, which stands for Microsoft Disk OS). On Macs, the meaning of the term "OS" is slightly different and it hasn't been given a special name. The term MacOS, however, has recently become the most popular term to describe the operating systems that drive both Apple Macintoshes and Macintosh clones. When speaking of a particular version of the MacOS, the Macintosh community generally express it as system/ version number, as in System 7.6.

Operating systems have been under development over many years. Just as human beings have evolved over tens of thousands of years from primitive creatures to present-day modern man, computers have also been evolving, particularly in terms of memory capabilities and computation power. Unlike human evolution, however, the evolution of computers has been extremely rapid, accomplishing in 1–2 years the equivalent of what took humans thousands of years. One example of such rapid change is the appearance of Windows 95 in 1995. With Windows 95, PC machines were said to become nearly as easy to use as Macs.

A similar type of evolutionary change has been announced for the Mac and should be taking place toward the end of 1997 and the beginning of 1998. This is the change from the current MacOS to the OpenStep OS, which Apple acquired in early 1997 when it bought NeXt, a computer company started by Apple co-founder Steve Jobs.

At left, installation and support materials for System 7 (actually, the Japanese version called Kanjitalk) for the Mac. At right, installation and support materials for Windows 95 for the PC.

CPU and Memory

When you put together the computer (body) and the OS (instincts), the computer will run, but that operation also depends on the computer equivalent of organs such as the brain, the heart, and vascular system. Because any level of digital photography might require you to do exploratory surgery inside your computer from time to time, it's a good idea to familiarize yourself with some of the innards, such as the CPU and the memory.

A CPU (central processing unit) is similar to the human brain. From the time we're born until the time we die, we accumulate learning, memories, and experiences from the outside. In computers, the CPU brain is not designed to acquire and store stimulation (information) from the outside. All operations and instructions coming from the CPU were put there when it was made.

This is where RAM comes in. RAM provides short term memory for the computer, the first task of which is to store basic operating functions after the computer is turned on. The operating system stored on the hard disk is read into a fixed part of the RAM (memory address) after the power is turned on, and then a variety of messages tell the user that the computer is ready for operation.

Depending on the computer, a number of slots are available for placing RAM. You can increase the amount of RAM in your computer by filling in empty slots, as shown on the bottom left. As discussed in many places in this book, digital photography is RAM-intensive work, and you will eventually need more than what you have. This is a fairly easy task, albeit a little hard on the bank account.

It is also possible, depending on the type of computer you are using, to increase the number of CPUs in order to create a more efficient brain. Computers that use more than one CPU are called *multiprocessor systems* and have become popular only recently. Inside the Daystar Genesis described earlier, for example, four CPUs are attached to a card that's attached to the computer's motherboard. It seems like this would make the computer run four times faster, but that's not the case. Computations are shared between the four CPUs, although not necessarily equally, resulting in a computer that's faster than a single CPU computer, but not four times faster.

Whether a computer has one or four CPUs, the processing performance of the CPU depends upon its internal structure and what is called *clock speed*. The faster the clock speed of the CPU, the faster the computer is able to carry out processing. Currently, PC and Mac clock speeds average from 80 MHz to 200 MHz (and faster ones are on the horizon). This means that the CPU has the ability to distinguish 80 million to 200 million bits of digital information per second. Clock speeds generally increase 1.5 times on new machines every year.

The RAM is in chips about 10 cm wide by 2 cm high that sit on small printed circuit boards. On average, one circuit board holds 16–128 MB of memory. This photograph shows the inside of the Genesis with four 64 MB DIMMs, or RAM cards.

The four CPUs on the Genesis MP600. In 1997, Apple Computer, as well as other Macintosh clone manufacturers, also started shipping a multiprocessor computer. Computers with multiple CPUs are excellent choices for the processing intensive demands of digital photography.

Application programs, also called "software packages."

Application Programs

We called the operating system the fundamental program because other programs run on top of the operating system. We call these *application programs*. Elsewhere in this book, we simply call these programs "software."

Although the operating system supplies the CPU with instincts and basic functions for living, application programs provide the computer with more adult knowledge and skills. Similar to human beings, computers are not immediately capable of writing, doing math, drawing lines, playing music, or editing images without education. In the computer world, application programs teach these skills.

Application programs themselves have been developed over a long period of education and research. They are stored on the hard disk in the computer (discussed next) and are loaded into memory as necessary.

Floppy disk cartridge (left) and a hard disk. Both store information on a magnetic disk, but as you can see, the hard disk drive contains several platters and a read-write head in one unit.

Hard Disks

When you turn your computer off, anything that was stored in the RAM disappears. Each time you turn it on again, you start out with the memory of a newborn child. Memory like this that depends on the flow of electricity and disappears as soon as the electricity is off is called *volatile memory*.

Because computers frequently suffer memory losses of this type, it was necessary to develop devices where important learning and results could be stored. We call memory that is not lost when the electricity is turned off *non-volatile memory*.

Many types of non-volatile memory exist, but the type most people are familiar with is the floppy disk. If you look inside the disk you'll see that it contains a flexible plastic disk, as shown on the left. Disks that are not flexible like this are classified as *hard disks*.

Hard disks can be either inside the computer, known as internal drives (upper right), or outside the computer connected via a SCSI cable, external drives (foreground).

Hard disks are similar in structure to floppy disks but are made of a very different material. Inside the disk drive is a platter which spins at high speed. The surface of the platter has a magnetic coating, whose characteristics change depending on whether it receives a positive or a negative charge from an electromagnet on the read / write head. The computer reads the magnetic characteristics and moves the data in and out of RAM as necessary. Hard disks can store 500–8,000 times as much information as floppy disks. In addition, unlike floppy disks, which spin very slowly, hard disks spin at very high speeds and are capable of very fast information transfer rates.

If you knock or shake a hard disk while it is spinning at high speed, the read / write head may momentarily come in contact with the magnetic surface of the platter. This can damage the surface of the platter as well as the read-write head, making the disk unusable. This is called a hard disk *crash* and is one of the most frightening things that can happen to you as a computer artist because it's usually impossible to successfully recover all data from a crashed disk.

Macintosh SCSI connector.

Windows machine SCSI connector.

SCSI *(pronounced* skuzzy*)*

If you look at the back of a computer, you will see a variety of connection ports. One connector is for sending out the signal to the monitor. Another connector is for receiving signals from the keyboard. In addition, connectors for printers, modems, and network connectors are available.

The biggest of these connectors, and the one that stands out the most, is called the *SCSI* connector. SCSI stands for Small Computer System Interface.

SCSI is an international standard agreed upon by computer manufacturers. You can connect a variety of SCSI devices, based on the SCSI standard, using SCSI connectors. SCSI devices include hard disks, scanners, printers, magneto optical disks (MOs), memory card readers, and other peripheral equipment.

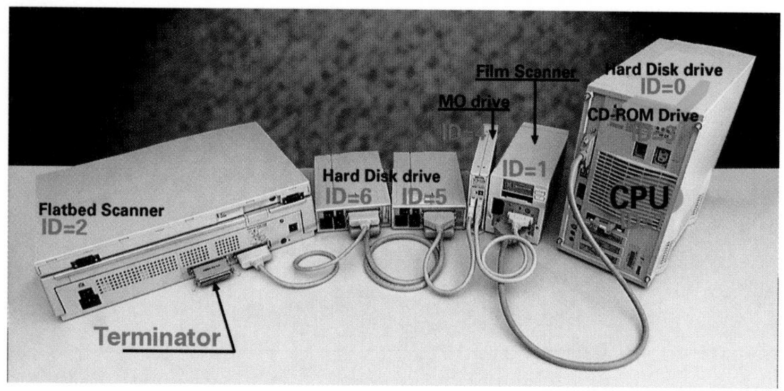

In general, you can connect up to eight SCSI devices to a computer, though it may look like you can only connect five or six. This is because inside the computer, the CPU, the internal CD-ROM, and the internal hard disk already use two or three of the available SCSI device ID numbers.

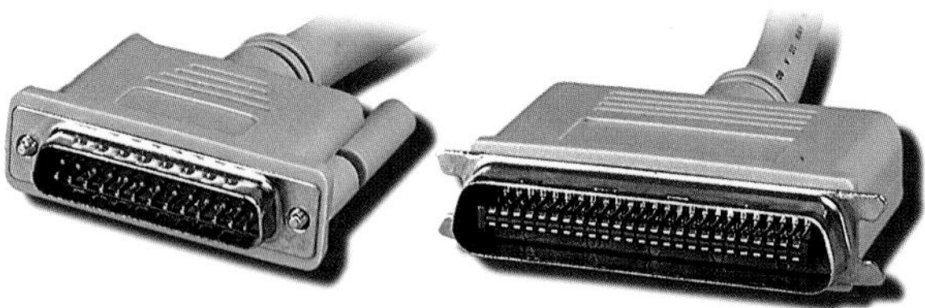

D-Sub 25-pin connector *Full-pitch 50-pin connector*

Half-pitch 50-pin connector *D-Sub half-pitch 50-pin connector*

SCSI address switch

You may wonder how six SCSI devices can be connected to the single connector on the back of the computer. You do it by making a SCSI chain. We call a SCSI chain a *daisychain*. To connect devices on a SCSI chain, each device has to have two connectors that look like the connectors on the back of the computer. The four types of SCSI connectors are full-pitch 50-pin connectors, D-Sub 25-pin connectors, half-pitch 50-pin connectors, and D-Sub half-pitch 50-pin connectors, as shown on the left.

They all look slightly different, but their internal specifications, such as the number of internal signal lines and the types of signals that travel along each line, are strictly standardized.

The CPU must be capable of distinguishing between all the different SCSI devices that are connected to it, so each device is assigned an ID number from 0 to 7 that the user can specify, as shown on the left. Each device in a SCSI chain must have its own individual ID number, commonly referred to as a SCSI address. Usually the CPU itself is given the ID number of 0, and after that you can assign numbers to your devices as you wish. The method for assigning the numbers differs for every manufacturer, but on the back of most devices you will find a small dial, button, or dipswitch that will allow you to set the ID.

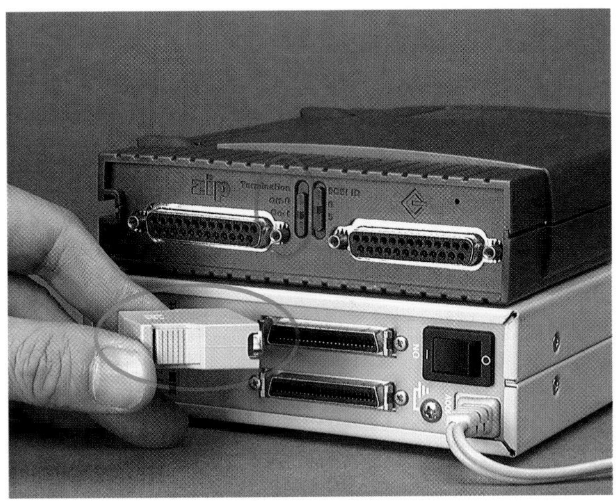

Some terminators are put on the connectors, while others can be turned on and off using a dipswitch, as shown on the top device.

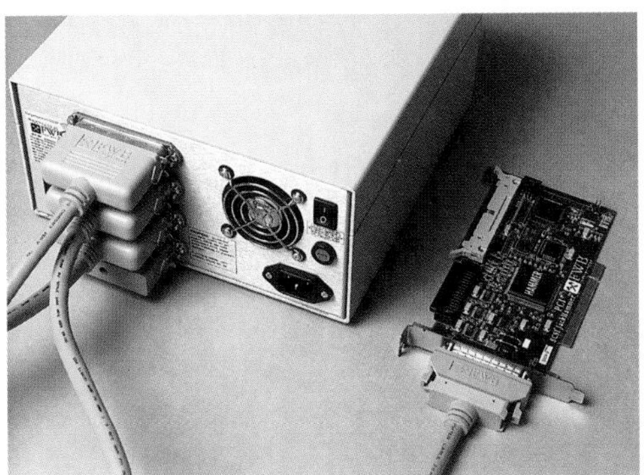

Jackhammer SCSI expansion card

Another important component of the SCSI chain is a terminal resistor, or *terminator*. A terminator is put onto the last SCSI device in the daisychain, as shown on the left. Its function is to prevent the signal that's traveling through the SCSI cable from straying (*reflecting*, which generates noise) when it reaches the last SCSI device in the chain.

Terminators can be either internal or external. An external terminator looks like a cable connector that connects to the back of a SCSI device, except that it doesn't have a cable. When the terminator is internal, you can't see it, so it either has a dipswitch or is checked automatically, meaning that it is automatically turned on when the device is last in the chain (that is, when only one connector is attached at the back of the device).

NOTE

We have said that you can connect up to eight SCSI devices to a computer including the CPU, but if the computer has an additional SCSI port, you can add additional SCSI devices from there as needed.

A SCSI expansion card inside a Daystar Genesis. This card drives additional internal 2 GB and 4 GB hard disks, as shown on the right. It also has a cable to connect an external scanner or hard disk, as shown on the left.

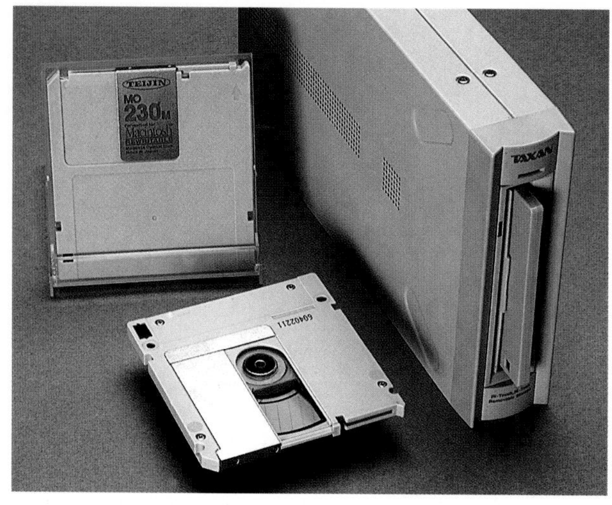

MO Disks

We discussed hard disks earlier, and here we look at another typical device that has the same amount of storage space as a hard disk, the MO.

As we mentioned earlier, the word "MO" is an abbreviation for "magneto-optical" disk. An MO drive reads and writes information using the heat from a laser beam and a magnetic head.

MO disks come in a variety of sizes from 128 MB and 230 MB to 540–640 MB of storage. The most common MO disks are the 230 MB type shown on the left, although the fast 640 MB disks are also becoming increasingly popular.

If you have 640 MB of storage space, you can store CMYK image data for 8–10 fairly high resolution (400 ppi) A4 offset prints. The only problem with these disks is that the data transfer rates are considerably slower than for hard disks.

Jaz Disks

Jaz is a name for a particular type of removable hard disk. On these disks, the platter is inside a plastic cartridge that snaps into a drive, as shown on the left. A few years ago similar removable hard disks, Syquest disks, were known as Syquest removables, and the current Jaz disks are like these.

Jaz disks hold 1 GB of data. The data transfer rate is about the same as a hard disk and therefore faster than average removable media, making these excellent devices for high volume image processing.

We used Jaz disks to exchange data throughout the process of creating this book. Because one of us lives in Kyoto and the other in Nagoya, we needed a convenient way to send data back and forth. In total, the data for this book came to 12 disks of RGB backup image data and 9 disks of CMYK image data for offset printing, making 21 disks (21 GB) in all.

One Jaz disk costs about $100, but they should become less expensive as they gain popularity. Because they are expensive, we now use Jaz disks when a project is still in progress, and when the project is complete we move all the data onto a less expensive medium, such as CD-R, and use the empty Jaz disks for another project. We call disks used for transferring data from point A to point B in a project such as this book *shuttle disks*.

Zip Disks

Zip disks are floppy disks that are like the younger sibling of Jaz disks. One disk can hold around 100 MB. They can't hold all of the data for a book over 300 pages like this one, but they are convenient for storing images and illustrations for large catalogs or a few thousand images taken with a compact digital camera.

RAID Disks

The acronym, RAID, stands for Redundant Array of Independent Disks and is a type of hard disk assembly. It's also often referred to as a *disk array* because it is comprised of a group of linked hard disks. Depending on the RAID level of formatting used, you can increase storage space and data access speeds while protecting your data should an accident occur. In the event that one disk is damaged, for example, the data on that disk can be recovered from the other disks. The many different levels of RAID systems are described on the right.

Artist's conceptualization of the structure of a disk array.

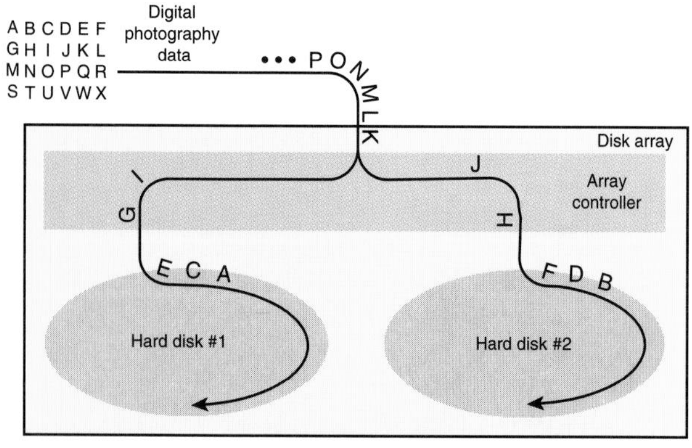

RAID Level 0

A Level 0 RAID is a very effective type of RAID for doing digital photography because data transfer is extremely fast. A single file is divided and recorded on multiple hard disks in parallel (data striping). As a result, in theory, if you have an array with two hard disks, the data transfer rate is halved. If you have three disks, the transfer rate is reduced to one third.

A professional digital photographer may have files over 100 MB in size for a single piece of artwork. Files this size take several minutes to save or load. In addition, as described in the section on virtual memory in Chapter 9-3, when there isn't enough RAM, the hard disk is used to process files in virtual memory. If you use Level 0 RAID, you can dramatically speed up these types of processes. We use a Hammer RAID disk array by StreamLogic.

RAID Level 1 and RAID Level 2

RAID Level 1 and RAID Level 2 use a recording system called disk mirroring. As the name implies, when a file is written onto one hard disk, the information is immediately written onto a second disk as if it were being reflected off a mirror. These types of RAIDs are used on computers or vital database servers, such as Internet servers, that must run 24 hours a day. RAID Level 2 has slightly slower transfer rates but is more secure.

RAID Level 3, RAID Level 4, and RAID Level 5

These RAIDs distribute one file onto multiple hard disks. They are used for the same purposes as disk mirroring RAIDs. We do not discuss these in any detail here because they don't have an application for most digital photography studios.

NOTE

If you have multiple disks this does not mean they can become a RAID. You must have special array drives with a circuit inside them called an array controller.

Hammer 4x CD-R drive (above) and the setup screen for "Toast," the data recording software.

CD-R Disks

CD-R disks are similar to, but not exactly the same as, CD-ROM disks. The *R* in CD-R stands for "record," indicating that you can record data onto these disks. They look the same as CD-ROM disks (which only allow you to read data), but you can actually write data onto them.

The amount of storage space on these disks varies, but on average you can store 640 MB, which means data for around 10 A4 images for commercial printing. You can save 35 images taken with the DCS460 that were opened in Photoshop and saved in Photoshop's native format.

You cannot, however, delete data files that have been written onto a CD-R, so CD-Rs should be used for permanent data storage. For example, we have stored the approximately 21 GB of CMYK data and original RGB image data for this book on these disks. You need a special CD-R drive and software to write ("burn") data onto CD-R disks.

Ethernet

Many different ways to transfer files from one computer to another are available when you are using multiple computers.

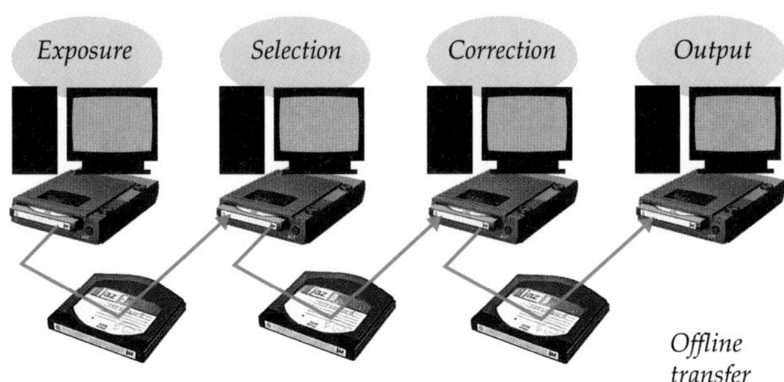

Offline transfer

The first way is to use removable storage media such as floppy disks or Jaz disks. This is called *offline transfer*. A second approach is to connect the computers via cables and electronically transfer the files from one computer to another. This is called *online transfer*. An expanded method of online transfer is called *networking*.

Currently the most popular method of networking is via Ethernet, though many methods exist. Several subtypes of Ethernet networking are also available. Currently the most popular is *10Base-T* networking, named for a type of cable. 10Base-T connectors look like regular telephone connectors, and they connect a computer on one end to a hub (splitting device) on the other end.

Ethernet connector

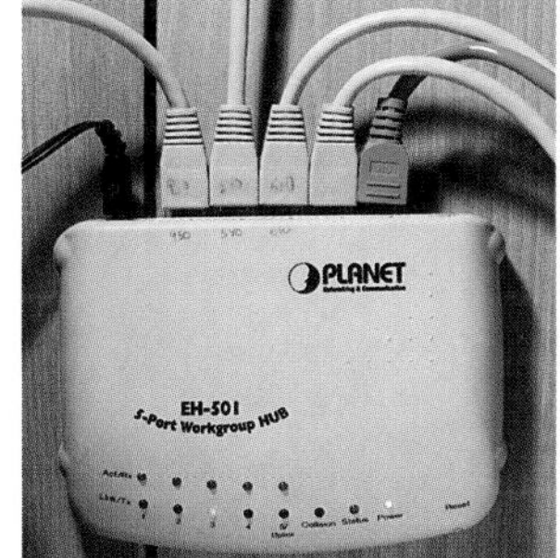

10Base-T hub

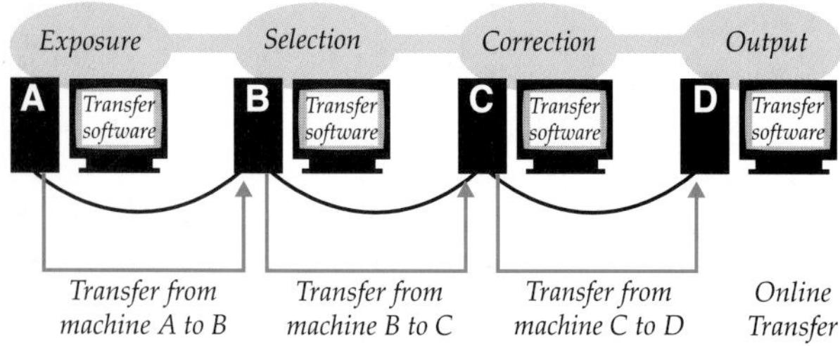

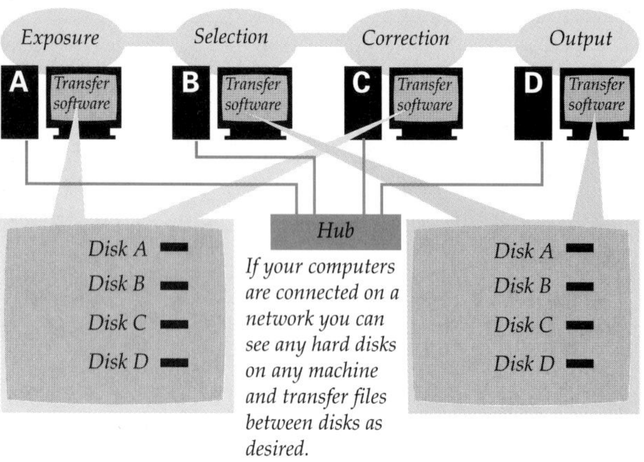

If you connect two, three, or even several hundred computers on this type of network, all the computers are able to exchange files as well as do many other kinds of tasks.

The data transfer rate for Ethernet is adequate for average office work, but for the tasks required for digital photography, it is fairly slow. For high volumes of data that would take forever to transfer via Ethernet, offline transfer (nicknamed *sneaker net*) is still the most convenient.

In the future digital photographers will use other types of fast networking solutions such as CDDI and FDDI, but currently this requires a lot of technical knowledge and the devices and cables are still too expensive for them to be widely used.

Digitizing stylus and drawing tablet

Drawing Tablets

Usually, when we do image editing on a computer, we use the mouse to specify particular positions on the screen. Because the mouse doesn't feel like a pen, however, it isn't always the best tool for drawing smooth lines or entering a lot of small points, the way you do when you draw a picture.

Drawing tablets and digitizing stylus' were developed to solve this problem. Because they have the feel of drawing with a pen on paper, they are very convenient for drawing corrections when you are using techniques such as those described in Chapters 3-9, "Techniques for Retouching Portraits," and 3-10, "Restoring Damaged Photographs."

Drawing tablets are available in a variety of sizes from small postcard size up to large newspaper size. For digital photographers, the A5 postcard size is adequate to give you the feel of working on a 4×5 piece of film.

chapter 9

System Setup for Digital Photography: Software

09 1

The Digital Lightroom

Image-editing software is the key tool in the digital lightroom. Here, Chicago-based photographer Jeff Schewe uses Adobe Photoshop on two monitors as he works. One monitor is for the image while the other monitor displays only the Photoshop tool palettes. (Photo Courtesy of Jeff Schewe).

Just as photochemical methods are a necessary step for turning film negatives into print photographs, image manipulation applications are a necessary step for turning digital image data into some type of hard copy image. As a result, digital imaging takes place on an easel called a *monitor* rather than in a darkroom amidst chemical fumes and wet trays. The image is always clearly displayed on the monitor in a room with lights turned on—hence the term *digital lightroom.*

Major Imaging Applications

At the core of the digital lightroom is a suite of applications we use for manipulating and managing images. For convenience, we have grouped these applications into three categories:

- Full-featured editing applications
- Special effects applications
- Utility applications

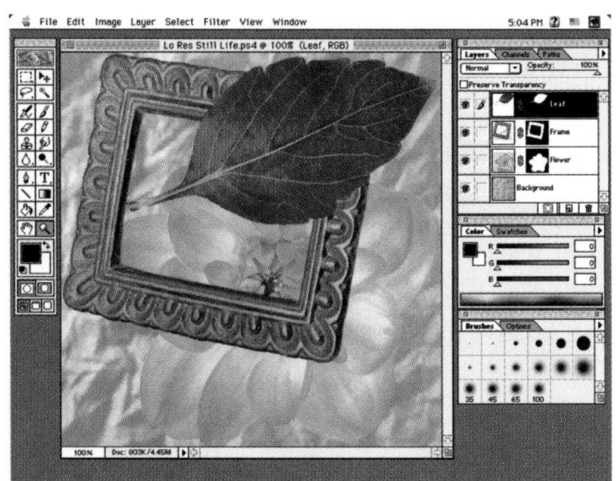

The interface in Adobe Photoshop's full-featured editing application provides a work window, a menu bar for selecting editing functions, and tool palettes.

From left to right, these icons represent Adobe Photoshop, Live Picture, Fractal Design Painter, and Macromedia xRes. The icons are used throughout this chapter to indicate which software application is being discussed.

Full-Featured Editing Applications

Full-featured editing applications provide a wide range of functions for manipulating images, including paint tools, layering capabilities, and masking tools. Currently, the main image-editing applications of interest to the digital photographer are

- Adobe Photoshop
- Live Picture
- Fractal Design Painter
- Macromedia xRes

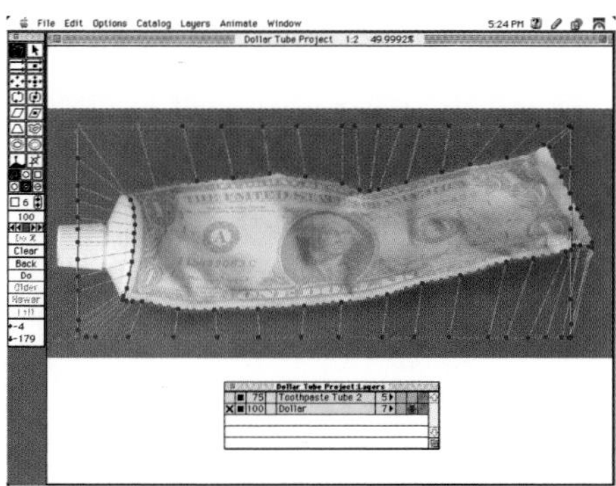

Metaflo special effects software. The interface provides a tool palette and a work window for distorting bitmap images.

Special Effect Applications

Special effect applications have specialized purposes, such as distorting images, creating backgrounds, or altering photographs to make them look like paintings.

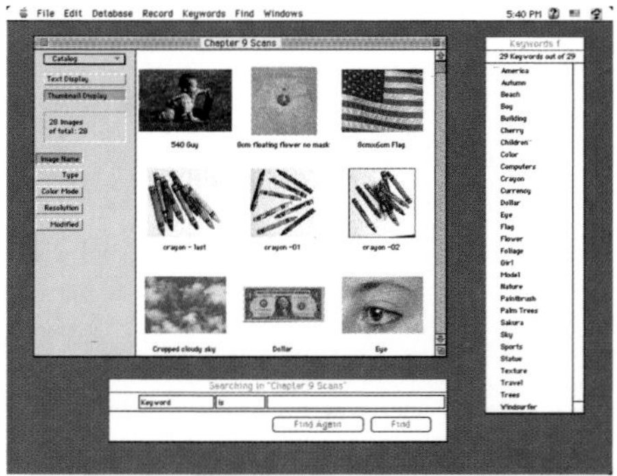

The interface on the Cumulus image-viewing database software.

Utility Applications

Utility applications are designed to ease specific tasks, such as automating repetitive imaging tasks (DeBabelizer), creating databases for cataloging and managing large amounts of image data (Cumulus), or automatically converting large amounts of RGB images into CMYK images.

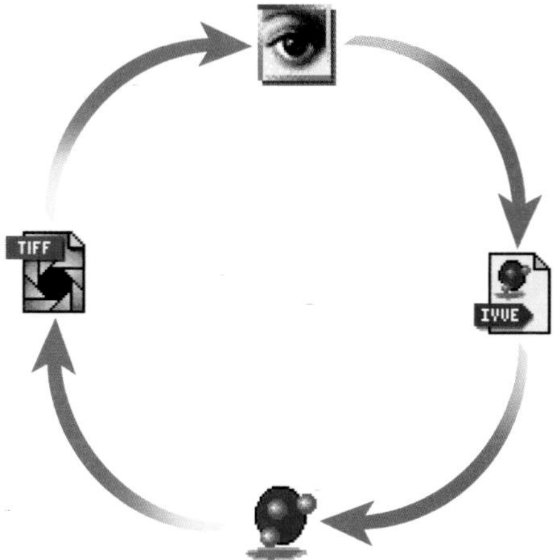

By saving image files in different file formats, you can pass them between multiple image-editing applications. In Photoshop, you can export an image in Live Picture's IVUE format and then insert it into Live Picture to composite it with other images. You can then save the composite as a TIFF-format file in Live Picture, so you can open it again in Photoshop to do further editing. Using multiple applications to edit images is a normal part of digital photography work.

Using Multiple Applications

At first, using more than one image-editing application might seem complicated and slightly intimidating. But just as traditional photographers use more than one type of camera, different focal length lenses, and different types of film, the versatile digital photographer employs more than one image-editing application.

It is not uncommon, for example, to begin editing an image in Photoshop, open Painter to add some special effects, use Live Picture to composite the image with other images, and then reopen it in Photoshop for a final touchup. To achieve the final image, each application is used because it performs a specific task more effectively than the others.

Similarities and Differences

We don't have enough space in this chapter to present dozens of specific tips and techniques available in each of the imaging applications mentioned. Instead, we would like to use this chapter to focus on basic functions and concepts shared by them all. We chose to do this because, if you understand the basic concepts, the skills learned in one application can be applied easily in another.

For example, if you know that a Floater mask in Painter functions very similarly to a Layer Mask in Photoshop, which you already understand, you will be able to easily learn the Painter function. In addition to learning specific techniques, you need to learn the reasoning behind them. With time and experience, you should be able to switch between applications as easily as switching between different films or adjusting your lighting to match different lens characteristics.

The illustration on the left, for example, shows the same image opened in Photoshop, Live Picture, Painter, and xRes. These imaging applications are similar in that each enables you to manipulate scanned images and create digital photomontages. The differences between them lie in how they implement certain fundamental imaging features and functions.

Some of these basic features and functions include:

- How image data is processed
- How multiple layers in one image are handled
- How different masking functions apply effects to one portion of an image
- How multiple levels of undos are implemented

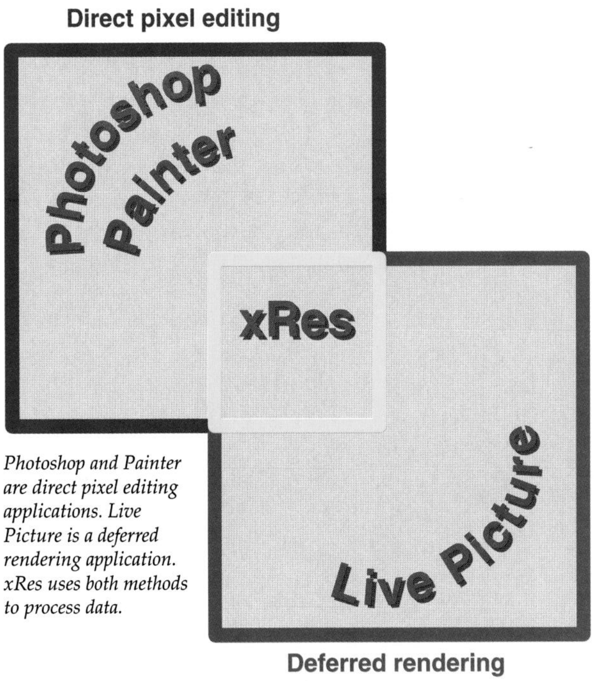

Photoshop and Painter are direct pixel editing applications. Live Picture is a deferred rendering application. xRes uses both methods to process data.

Categories of Image Processing

Because digital photographs are made up of many millions of pixels, applications have to manage vast amounts of data. The full-featured image-editing applications mentioned earlier can be divided into two categories, based on how they process digital image data. These categories are.

- Direct Pixel Editing

Applications that use what we call *direct pixel editing* hold all the actual pixel data for an image in the computer's memory (or RAM) and apply changes directly to that data when you use a specific function. This can also be called *direct mode*.

- Deferred Rendering

Applications that use what we call *deferred rendering* create lower-resolution, subsampled versions of your high-resolution scans and use these subsampled versions to display the image on the monitor screen. These applications then record what changes have been made based on the screen resolution files and apply them to the original image data later on in a post-processing step commonly referred to as *rendering*. This process is also called a *proxy method* or the *building method.*

09 2

Direct Pixel Editing

Is Image Processing the Same as Word Processing?

Imaging applications handle image data in binary code—the same kind of code used to create text documents on the computer. The primary difference between imaging applications and word processing applications is the amount of data being handled. Image files can have from a few hundred to several thousand times more data than the average text document.

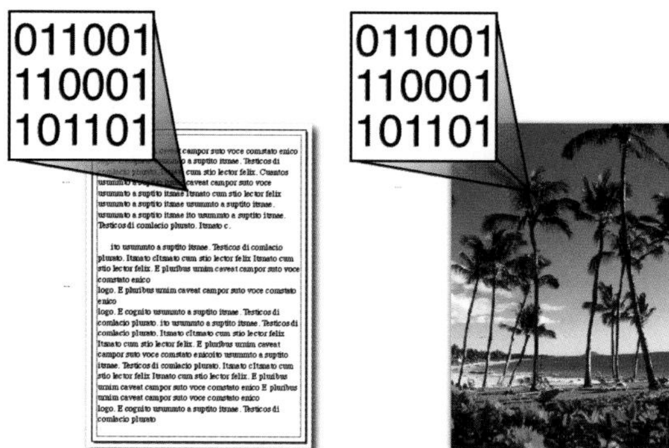

Bitmap Images

Images that have been input with a scanner or photographed with a digital camera are called *bitmap* or *raster* images, and they are made up of rows and columns of pixels. The size of a digital image is described in terms of horizontal and vertical pixels, for example 3,000×3,000 pixels. The total number of pixels for that image is 9 million pixels.

Original: small image

Original: large image

Small brush stroke

Large brush stroke

Small selected area

Large selected area

When direct pixel editing was done on these images, work was always faster on the left-side images. When compared to the right-side images, the required processing time is shorter for the top left image because the file is smaller, for the middle left image because the brush stroke is smaller, and for the bottom left image because the area where the filter is applied is smaller.

Direct Pixel Editing

An important point to keep in mind when using direct pixel editing applications is that they perform computations on the actual pixels in the image data at the time of the edit. The greater the number of pixels affected by the edit, the longer the effect takes to compute. The number of pixels affected depends on three factors:

- The size of the image (total number of pixels)
- The type of edit, such as a filter or a brush stroke
- The size of the area covered by the edit (the number of pixels in a selected area)

Direct pixel editing applications use random access memory (RAM) as a temporary workspace for holding the image and for performing image-editing computations. Therefore, you need a sufficient quantity of RAM to speed up these computations as much as possible. A computer processor with fast clock speed and software accelerator boards also can improve speed with respect to the preceding three factors.

NOTE

- Although the clock speed of the computer is important, a system with fast clock speed and a small amount of RAM is slower than a computer with slower clock speed but a lot of RAM.
- Having a lot of RAM also means that you can run several applications at the same time. For example, it is faster to be able to keep both Photoshop and Live Picture open simultaneously than it is to close Photoshop before you can open Live Picture.

Image Size and Processing Speed

A 2,000 × 3,000-pixel image has a total matrix area of six million pixels.

If we compare a grayscale version of a six-million-pixel image with an RGB version of the same image, the total number of pixels is the same. The RGB image, however, contains three different channels of 8-bit grayscale information (in which each pixel can represent as many as 256 shades of gray), so the RGB file size is three times larger than the grayscale image.

Unsharp Mask: 3.8 seconds

Unsharp Mask: 8.4 seconds

When an editing function is applied to the 2,000×3,000-pixel grayscale image, the computation is done on six million pixels. When the same edit is applied to the RGB image, the computation is done on the six million pixels in each of the three grayscale channels. Effectively, this means that the computation for this edit is being performed on 18 million pixels.

Because direct pixel editing applications perform computation directly on the pixels at the time of the edit, the greater the number of pixels, the longer the computation time. A direct correlation exists between file size and processing speed. It takes 3.8 seconds to apply an unsharp mask filter to a grayscale version of an image, for example, but it takes 8.4 seconds to apply the same filter to an RGB version. (These times vary greatly depending on factors such as file size, computer, and memory.)

Edit Size and Type

Because direct pixel editing applications compute all edits at the moment you apply the function or immediately afterward, the size of the area affected by the edit (either a local or a global area) and the type of edit affects the speed of the computation.

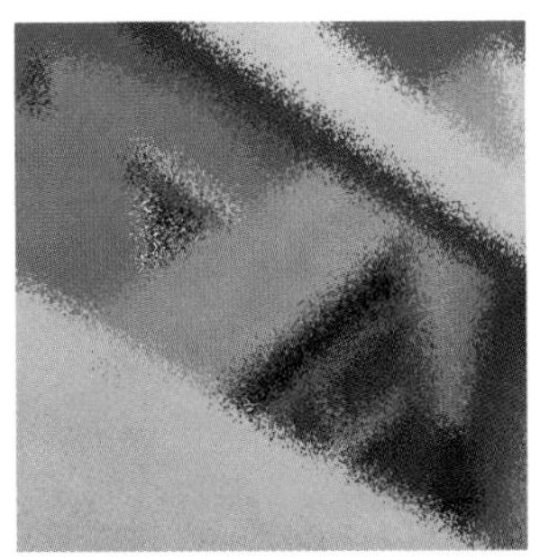

A

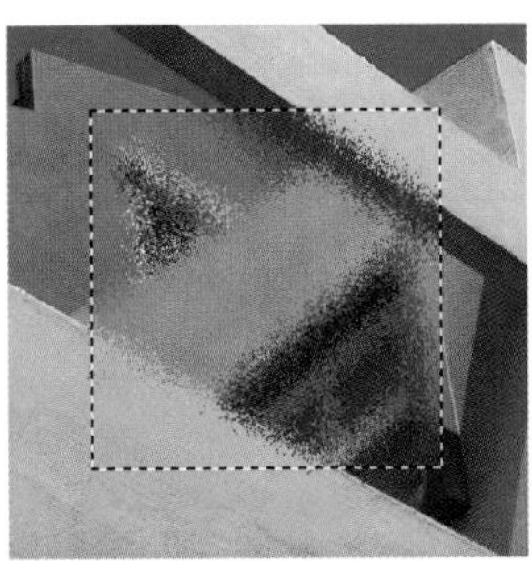

B

Global and Local Edits

A *global edit* is an operation that affects all the pixels in the image, such as brightening the entire image or applying a sharpness filter to it. In example A on the left, a filter is applied to the entire image.

Local edits are operations or effects that are isolated to specific areas within a selection or a mask, as shown in example B on the left. Given the same file size, the edit on the local area will be computed more quickly than the edit on the global area because the local area contains fewer pixels.

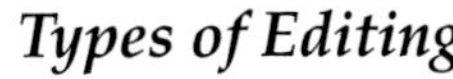

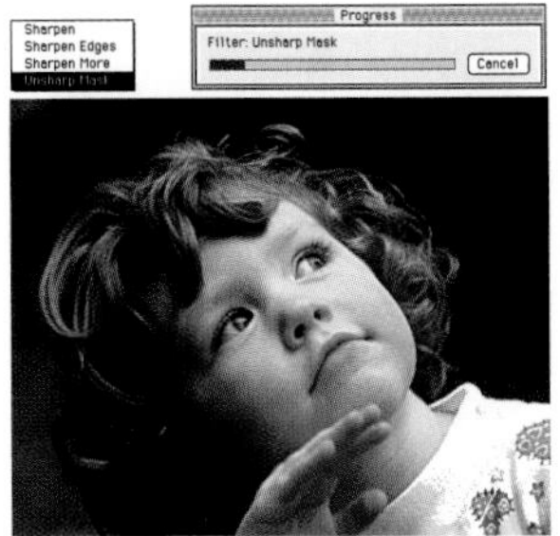

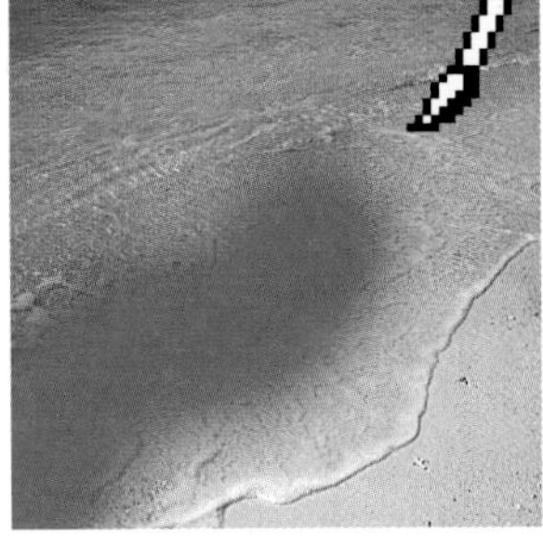

Types of Editing

■ Filters

Some filters require more computation than others. In a direct pixel editing application such as Photoshop, for example, the Unsharp Mask filter takes longer to complete computation than the Add Noise filter.

■ Paintbrushes

In a direct pixel editing application, you can apply a 25-pixel brush stroke quickly and smoothly, but the display of a 200-pixel brush stroke will lag behind the movement of the cursor. The computer can keep up with a brush with a smaller-diameter stroke, but the time it takes to apply the larger stroke to the image in memory and display it causes a time lag with a larger brush.

NOTE

The Spacing setting for brush strokes, set in Photoshop's Brush Options dialog box, can affect the speed of the stroke. The default 25 percent Spacing can be much faster than a 12 percent Spacing setting, for example, especially when using larger brush sizes.

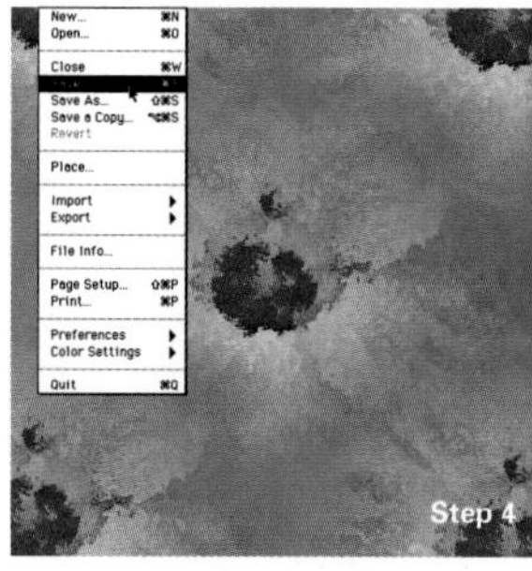

First, we opened the image of the flower (step 1) and applied a filter (step 2). After this, we changed the color (step 3). Finally, we copied the flower, pasted it many times into the same file, and then saved the file (step 4). Because all image edits were computed at the time they were applied, all edits became permanent after the file was saved.

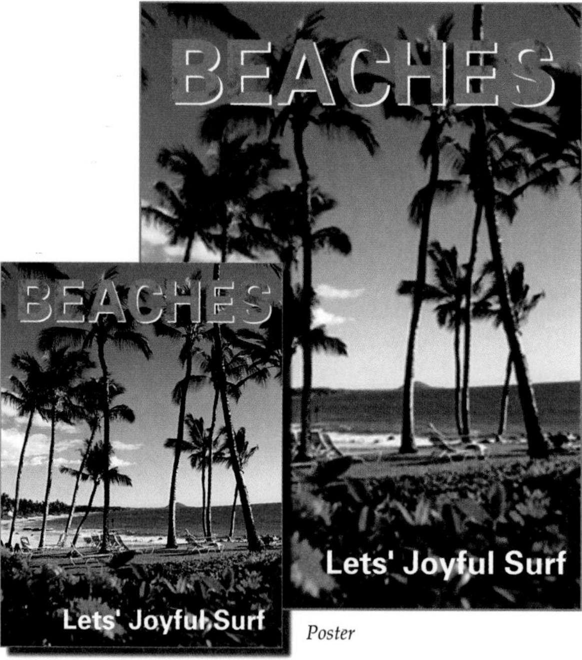

Poster

Magazine

Last Saved Version

All edits in direct pixel-based applications are computed at the time the command or function is applied to a version of the image that resides in memory. This means that all edits applied following the last time the image was saved exist only in RAM, not on the hard disk. After the image has been saved to the hard disk, these edits become a permanent part of the image and cannot be undone. An exception to this involves some edits done in layers, which are introduced later (see Section 9-7, "Single and Multiple Undos").

Fixed Resolution

Images created in direct pixel editing applications have a fixed amount of image information. This is because the number of pixels is fixed. Of course, this does not mean that you can't resize the image; but because resizing in this type of application requires resampling, the image quality might be affected.

If you are asked to make an 8×10-inch magazine cover for a client, for example, the dimensions of the image will be approximately 3,000×4,000 pixels. If the client likes the image so much that he wants a 20×24-inch poster of the same design, you would need to either recreate the image at the new size or use interpolation to enlarge the original size. If you increase the size using interpolation, the image will be approximately 7,500×10,000 pixels. This would greatly degrade the image quality.

Pixel-Level Editing

Theoretically, it is possible to manipulate each individual pixel independently of all the others; but in reality, no one is going to manipulate millions of pixels one at a time. Even so, it is actually very significant that you can do pixel-level editing. If you zoom in on an image on your monitor, you can make out individual image pixels. Editing done at this level is called *pixel-level editing* and is possible in direct pixel editing applications such as Photoshop and Painter.

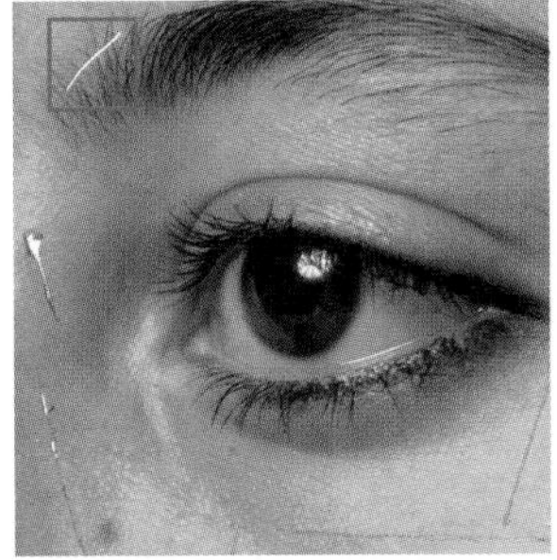

A

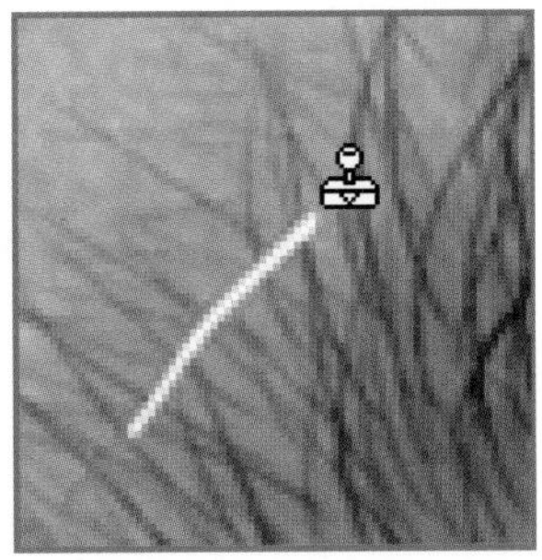

B

Two advantages of pixel-level editing are that it enables you to do both photo retouching and precise masking. In image A on the left, for example, you can easily repair the scratch in the eyebrow by zooming in on the area and using the Rubber Stamp tool to make the repair pixel by pixel (B).

Direct editing of pixels is also useful for making masks using the Paintbrush tool. If you zoom in far enough to see individual pixels, you can modify a mask with the precision of a brain surgeon.

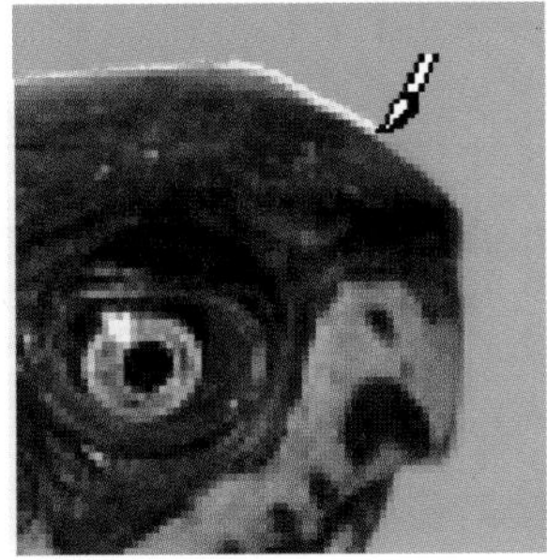

09 3

Direct Pixel Editing and RAM

Direct Pixel Editing Requirements

Up to this point, our discussion of direct pixel editing applications has emphasized that computation-intensive tasks take time, that saving files makes most changes permanent, and that a fixed resolution can limit uses of a single image. This is not meant to suggest, however, that direct pixel editing applications—especially Photoshop or Painter—are slow or ponderous. On the contrary, the following information will help you better understand the system requirements for working more efficiently with direct pixel editing applications. At the same time, this information provides a backdrop for a comparative description of deferred rendering applications.

32 MB RAM

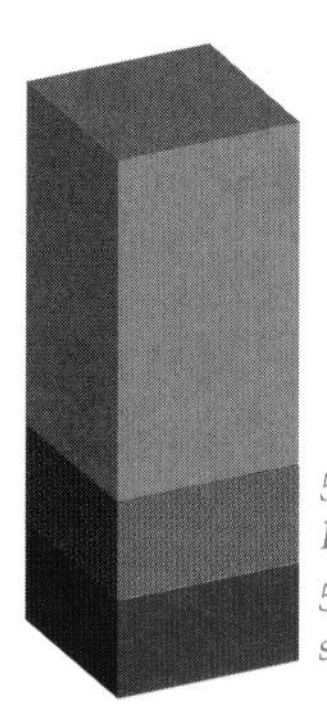

32 MB RAM

32 MB RAM

Dependence on RAM

Direct pixel editing applications depend on an abundance of RAM for efficient processing. Because scanned images or digital camera photographs are typically very large, the digital photographer needs to clearly understand why and how RAM is used during the image-editing process.

64 MB DIMM chip.

Direct Pixel Editing Relies on RAM

As soon as you start up your computer, the operating system (OS) uses a portion of the RAM. Then, when you launch an application such as Photoshop, another chunk of RAM is used by that software application. This means that the total amount of RAM in the system is not the total amount of RAM available for image processing.

Imagine you have a computer with 32 megabytes (MB) of RAM. As soon as you turn the computer on, the operating system immediately uses 5 MB of the RAM. Next you launch Photoshop, which consumes another 5 MB of RAM. That leaves 22 MB of RAM available for opening, displaying, and editing an image file.

NOTE

The system values used in this example are simplified for purpose of explanation. While the relationships are true, the actual values vary widely in the real world.

Now suppose you want to work on a 10 MB image (sufficiently large for a high quality 6×6-inch print of an approximately 2,000×2,000-pixel file). As soon as you open it, it uses up almost half of the remaining 22 MB of RAM.

NOTE

For readers who are fairly new to computers, see a basic description of operation systems in Chapter 8.

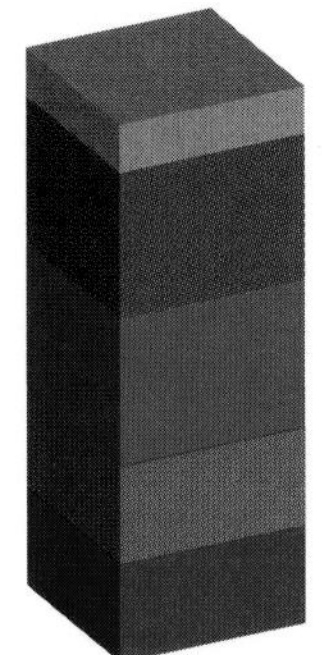

32 MB RAM

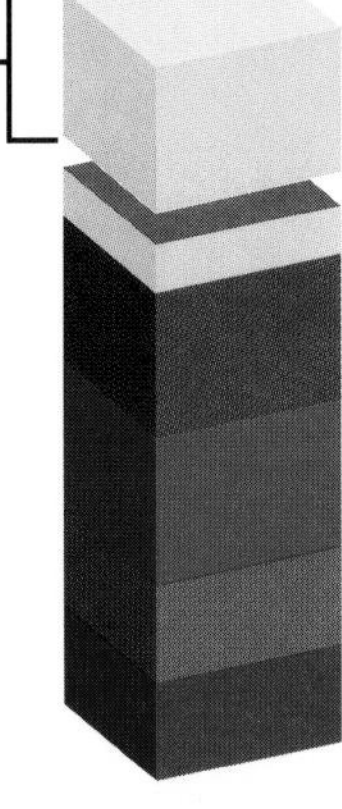

32 MB RAM

In order to efficiently edit an 8 MB image, we need a minimum of 24 MB of RAM.

Next, you make a change to the image. No matter how small the change—such as a short paint stroke—a copy of the image is created in the RAM to provide a single level of Undo. At this stage, you have only 2 MB of free RAM left.

Operations that use the Clipboard, such as Cut or Copy, also use up RAM space. So if you copy the entire image, for example, another 10 MB of RAM are used to hold the duplicate.

At this stage, 30 MB of data are stored for just the one image—10 MB for the original image, 10 MB to copy the image for editing, and 10 MB to copy the image into the Clipboard. At this point, however, the amount of image data exceeds the amount of available RAM.

When all available RAM is used up, Photoshop begins using *virtual memory* or *scratch disk space* as additional processing work space. When free RAM is used up, virtual memory uses free space on the hard disk and manages it as if it were RAM. Because a hard disk is much slower than RAM, work efficiency seriously diminishes.

Determining the RAM Configuration

As the number of pixels increases, the file size, as expressed in megabytes, increases. The more the image files increase in size, the more RAM is required to process them efficiently. The basic rule of thumb for managing this data in a direct pixel editing application is that you should have at least three times the amount of RAM as the size of the file you are opening. Having more—5 times the file size—is even better.

Bitmap Images and RAM

For a multimedia artist who designs interactive interfaces or Internet home pages that are not bigger than a few megabytes in size, the relationship between RAM and processing speed is not an issue. These days, most systems are sold with enough RAM to handle these small image sizes. But for the photographer whose work is going to be output to film recorders or as offset printing, it is very important because these output directions typically require very large file sizes.

For example, an RGB image created for an average 8.5×11-inch hard copy is approximately 24 MB. This means that at least 72 MB of RAM are necessary.

NOTE

In reality, the Macintosh operating system uses approximately 10 MB and Photoshop uses approximately 15 MB (22 MB in the case of Photoshop 4.0), so if you add this to the 72 MB required to process the 24 MB image discussed above, the total RAM required is approximately 100 MB.

If a photographer wants to create "4K" or "8K" second-generation images for high-resolution output, such as 4×5 transparencies, the base file size can be 200 MB or higher. This means that a minimum of 600 MB of RAM is needed for efficient imaging.

In our work, we create high-resolution works like these; but because this is only several times a year, we manage the inevitable drop in speed with only 256 MB of RAM by relying on virtual memory (scratch disks), which we discuss next, to make up for the insufficient memory.

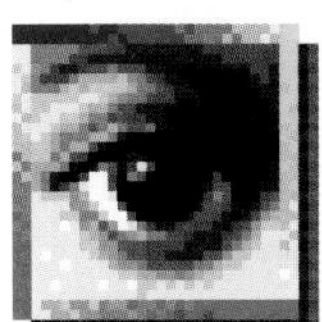

Virtual memory (scratch disk).

Swap disk.

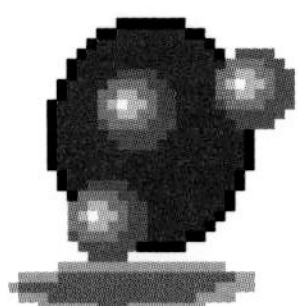

Virtual memory.

Temporary file.

The name differs depending on the software, but all imaging applications have a function for using hard disk space as a scratch disk.

Scratch Disk Space

No matter how much RAM you have invested in, you can never have enough. Using multiple layers or adding channel masks makes the file size grow larger and larger. So even if you start out with a system properly configured for working with a certain large image size, the growth of the image during the editing process often exceeds the amount of available RAM. Inevitably, you'll frequently find yourself pushing the capability of your system.

When an image exceeds the amount of available RAM, the overflow spills into something called virtual memory. *Virtual memory* is hard disk space that functions as a backup workspace for RAM. We call the part of the disk used for virtual memory *the virtual memory disk* or *scratch disk.*

If you use virtual memory, the data handling is slower than RAM, so it is only a partial fix at best. Any time an imaging application has to swap data between memory and hard disk space, it slows the imaging process down.

NOTE

If you have a hard disk with fast access speed, virtual memory works many times faster. The most efficient hard disks are RAID disk arrays. RAID arrays are multiple hard disks that handle data in parallel as if they were a single disk. Handling data in parallel on multiple disks is faster than using a single disk. For more information about RAID arrays, see Chapter 8.

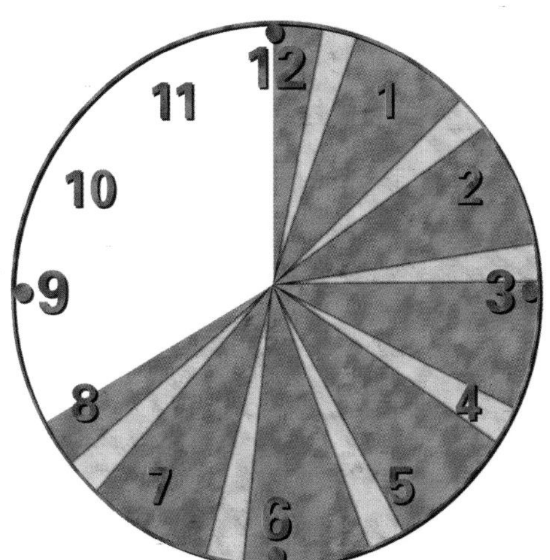

This clock illustration represents, conceptually, the time spent working in a direct pixel editing application (blue) and the time spent waiting for each of the edits (yellow) to be computed. Because you cannot move to the next edit until the computation on the previous edit is complete, the accumulative amount of time spent waiting during an image editing session can become considerable.

Direct Pixel Editing and Your Time

Even if you are working on an optimally configured system and have a lot of RAM and a RAID array, your system still requires time to compute your edits. This means there is a lot of waiting time as the computer completes its computation (for more information, see Chapter 8, "System Setup for Digital Photography: Hardware.")

09 4

Deferred Rendering

Direct Pixel Editing and Deferred Rendering

The most important difference between direct pixel editing applications and deferred rendering applications is how they manage image data. As previously discussed, direct pixel editing applications perform computation-intensive tasks at the time the edit function is applied. Computation efficiency depends on a delicate balance between image size and available RAM. In deferred rendering applications, the relationship between editing and computation efficiency is slightly different.

A computer monitor has a fixed number of display pixels, horizontally and vertically. If your image is larger than the pixel size of your monitor, you will only be able to display part of that image on the monitor at a 1:1 ratio (one monitor pixel per image pixel).

In deferred rendering applications, edits are not applied directly to the original image files during an image-editing session. Instead, the actual edits are recorded in a separate file as a series of instructions through the use of low-resolution previews containing the minimum amount of data necessary to display the image on the monitor. The result is that most editing functions take place much faster than they would in direct pixel editing applications. After all editing is done, the edit instructions are applied to the high-resolution files and a separate, final image is rendered.

Features of Deferred Rendering

There are two key components of deferred rendering applications.

- Pyramid-style image format
- Edit recording document

Two of the four image editing applications discussed in this chapter are deferred rendering applications—Live Picture and xRes.

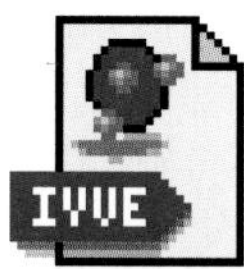

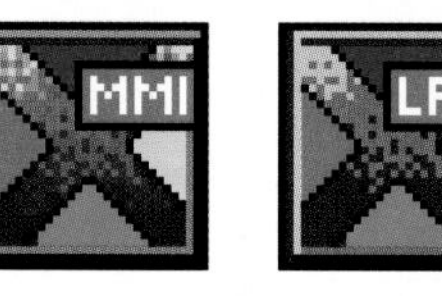

NOTE

This explanation is based on Live Picture's FITS file and IVUE format images. However, the same principles apply to MMI file and LRG image format in xRes.

Pyramid-Style Image Format

The pyramid-style image format is based on the principle that it is unnecessary to load into RAM more of an image than can be displayed on the monitor (only 4 MB on a 17-inch monitor).

At a 1:1 view ratio, the monitor would have to be twice as large as it is in order to display the entire scan of this colorful building on the monitor.

Understanding Monitor Display

Generally speaking, a monitor has a fixed number of pixels (multiscan monitors are an exception, in that they let you choose between several resolutions). Let's say we're using a monitor with 832×624 pixels (an average 17-inch monitor). When you open a 1,500×2,000-pixel image on this monitor at a 1:1 ratio (that means 1 monitor pixel per image pixel), only a 832×624 portion of the overall image can be viewed. The underlying premise of deferred rendering applications is that if this is the most you can see at this zoom view, there is no need to load any more image data than this into RAM.

Pyramid Image Structure

In order to display only the amount of data necessary for viewing an image on the monitor, a pyramid-style file format, such as Live Picture's IVUE, is used to save progressively smaller versions of the image within the original image file. Starting with the original image, each smaller version contains half the number of horizontal and vertical pixels than the previous size image. Each of the subsampled display images is further divided into tiles.

Because the data for the additional subsamples is stored in the same file as the original image file, the file size for the image grows. If you convert a 10 MB TIFF file into IVUE format, for example, it expands to approximately 13 MB.

Images for monitor display only

Actual image

Pyramid Format Image Structure

Zooming In and Out

Only the tiles for the zoom view of the image area you are working on are loaded into RAM and displayed on the monitor.

When the view is zoomed out (reduced) to display the entire image on the monitor, for example, the application goes to the hard drive, retrieves a subsampled image from the pyramid, and loads the necessary tiles into RAM for display on the monitor.

When the image is zoomed in (enlarged) to a 1:1 view, only a portion of the tiles from the largest of the pyramid subsamples is displayed on the monitor.

The same amount of image data is loaded into the RAM regardless of the image view. It doesn't matter whether the image is zoomed in or out, or scrolled to a different view. Even if the original image is 100 MB, no more than a few megabytes are loaded into RAM to display the image. The actual amount of data is dependent on the number of pixels on the monitor—a 640×480-pixel monitor requires around 1 MB, a 1,024×678-pixel monitor requires around 2 MB of RAM.

Advantages of Deferred Rendering

Both direct pixel editing applications and deferred rendering applications take data stored on the hard drive and load it into RAM. The difference between them is how much data they load. Let's assume you have 64 MB of available RAM, for example, which you can use to composite three 30 MB files into a three-layer image on a computer with a 640×480 monitor.

In Live Picture, for example, approximately 1 MB of data per layer is brought into RAM from the hard drive for each image. That is all that is necessary to display the image on the monitor at any zoom ratio. This amounts to about 3 MB of data out of 64 MB of RAM.

In contrast, the same composite assembled in Photoshop requires that all the data for all three images be brought into RAM. That means 90 MB of image data. In this scenario, Live Picture has plenty of RAM overhead for imaging tasks while in Photoshop, we've exceeded the "3 times the file size" formula for working efficiently—even before any edits have begun. The editing and computation in Photoshop takes time because overflow data has to be processed on a virtual memory disk.

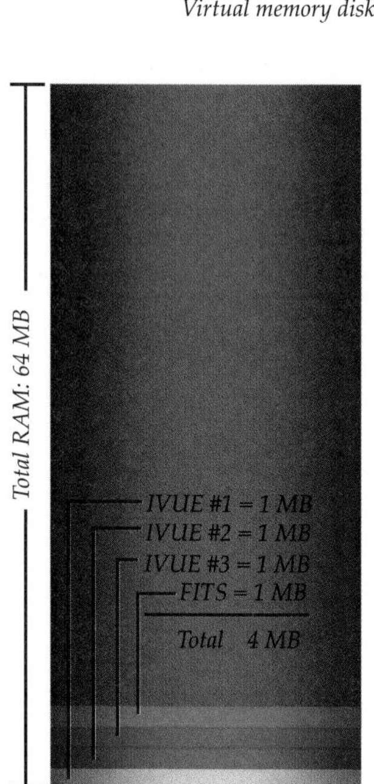

Memory usage in Live Picture (when compositing a 3-layer image).

Memory usage in Photoshop (when compositing a three-layer image).

NOTE

The FITS file in Live Picture that records the edits also takes up some RAM space, but seldom more than a few megabytes. The FITS file size increases depending on factors such as the number of layers, the complexity of the masks, and the type of edits. FITS is explained in more detail in the next section.

In Live Picture, to save a piece of work, a FITS edit recording file (A) is created completely separate from the IVUE format image files (B).

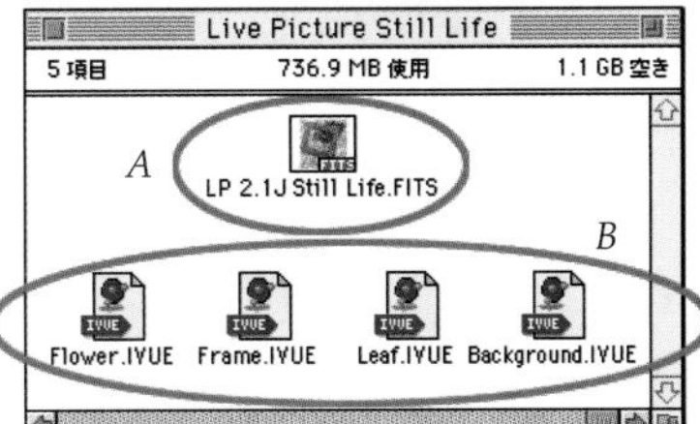

It is easy to think of the FITS file as a set of instructions, on the left above, for assembling the IVUE parts, shown on the right.

The final image is rendered by "building" the file using the FITS file instructions and the IVUE images. The final build does not alter the IVUE image files, instead it creates a new separate file.

Edit Recording Document

In addition to the pyramid file structure previously described, deferred rendering applications also have edit recording documents.

In deferred rendering applications like Live Picture and xRes, edits are not computed on the original high-resolution image data at the time of the edit, as occurs with direct pixel applications. Instead, all edits are recorded and saved in a special document as mathematical expressions of the edits. This document is called the FITS file in Live Picture and the MMI file in xRes.

The Relationship Between FITS and IVUE

Conceptually, the relationship between the FITS document and the IVUE-format image files is similar to the relationship between assembly instructions and the actual parts to be assembled for a model. The instructions (the FITS file) describe the procedure, and the computer reads those instructions in order to correctly assemble the parts (the IVUE image files) into the finished piece. The same principle applies LRG/MMI files in xRes.

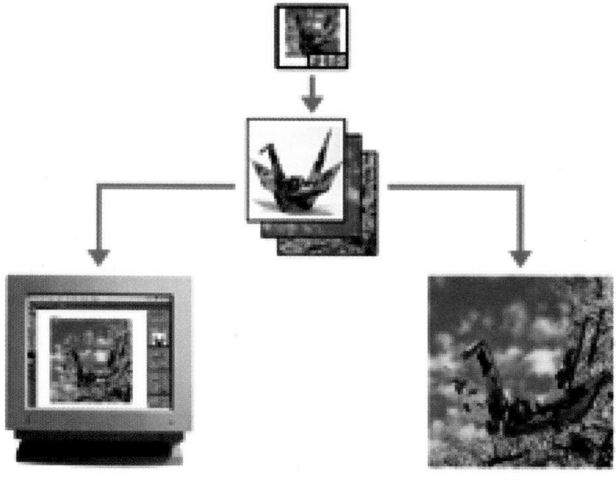

The FITS and IVUE Combination

In a deferred rendering application, the recorded edit instructions, such as in Live Picture's FITS file, use the image data in two ways:

- To display the image on the monitor using the pyramid structure of the IVUE format images.
- To build a separate, final image based on the IVUE format images.

Live Picture Build Command

When you use the Build command, Live Picture applies the instructions saved in the FITS file to the original IVUE files and creates a separate final image. At no point are the original IVUE format images directly changed or altered. Using the Build command, you can render and save various sizes, crops, or versions of the image based on the FITS and IVUE files. *To render* means to automatically apply the necessary changes to the image.

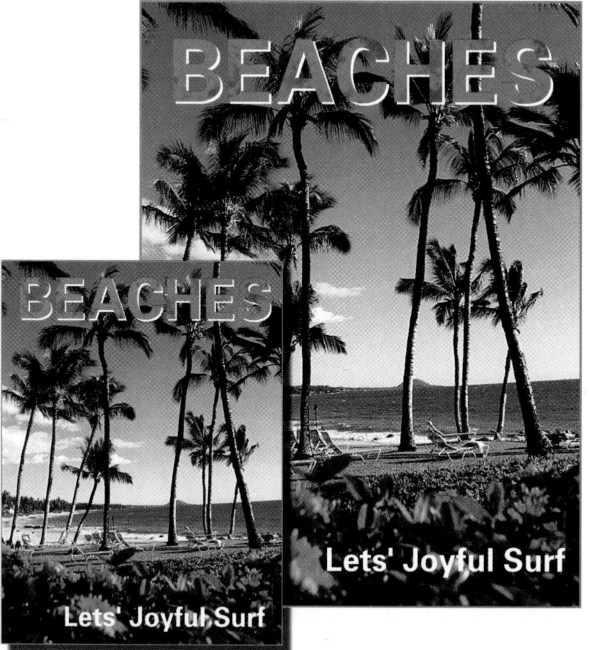

Deferred rendering applications like Live Picture enable you to create any number of different-sized final images. You can create a magazine cover or a poster using the same FITS file and IVUE format images. The condition is that the original IVUE format images, however, must be scanned at a high enough resolution (meaning number of pixels) to render the poster without interpolating the data.

Resolution Independence

The instructions stored in the FITS edit recording document are mathematical expressions of your edits and are independent of the image resolution. This means if you apply paint to an image, the information recorded in the FITS file is information that describes only the color of the paint, the size of the stroke, and the path of the mouse or stylus. Then, when the image is rendered at different sizes, the mathematical expressions of the edits are scaled up or down to become proportional to the resolution of the final image. This is called *resolution-independent* processing.

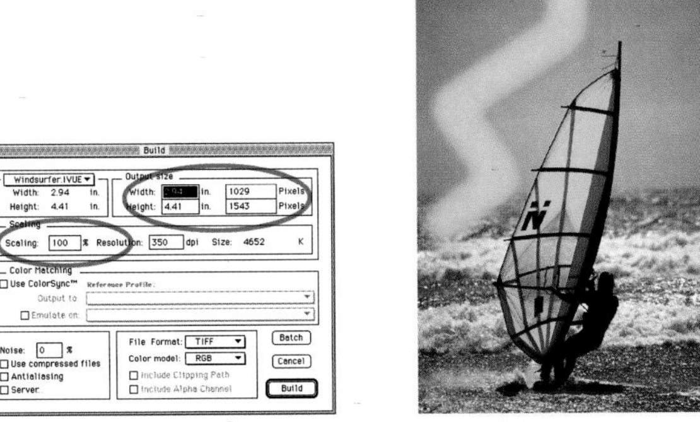

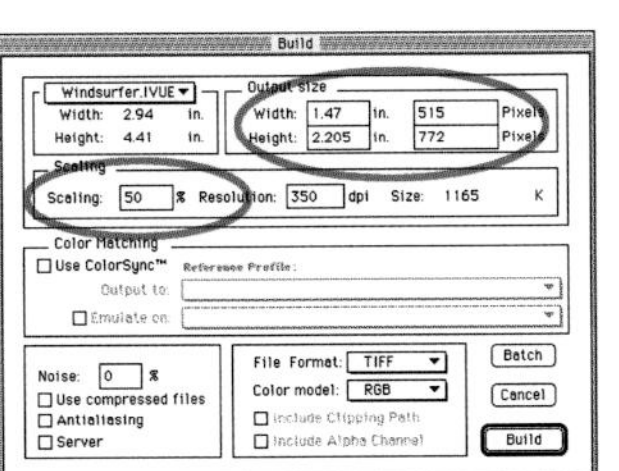

Let's say you are working on a 1,000×1,500-pixel image in Live Picture. First you apply a 200-pixel brush stroke (about one fifth the width of the short dimension of the image) and save the record of the edits.

When you build (render) the same file at 50 percent of the original size, the finished image size is 500×750 pixels. Because the brush stroke exists as a mathematical expression of a brush stroke, it is scaled to the new image size. It remains one fifth of the short dimension of the image, which means it becomes 100 pixels wide.

Resolution Independence and Pixels

In an application such as Live Picture, it is important to understand which edits are resolution-independent and which are pixel-based. As mentioned earlier, a digital image consists of a matrix of pixels arranged in rows and columns. This is as much true for an image in IVUE format as it is for an image in Photoshop format. In Live Picture, however, most edits, special effects, masks, and stencils can be created without concern for how many pixels there are. Using the edit record, they can all be applied in scale to the build size of the final image.

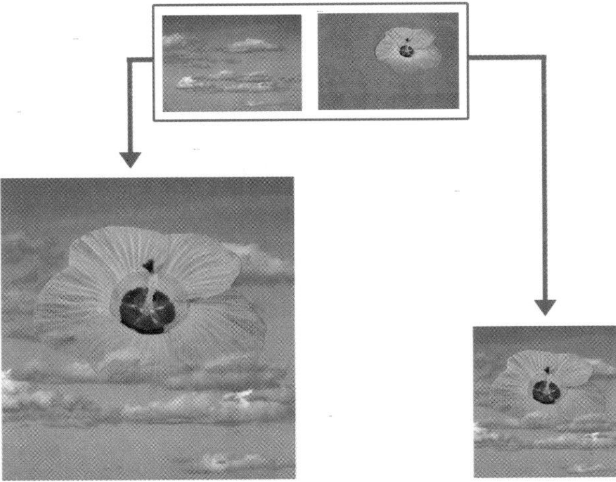

The masks for the image of the flower (outlined in red) are defined in resolution-independent FITS files, so even when rendered at different sizes, you still achieve the same result.

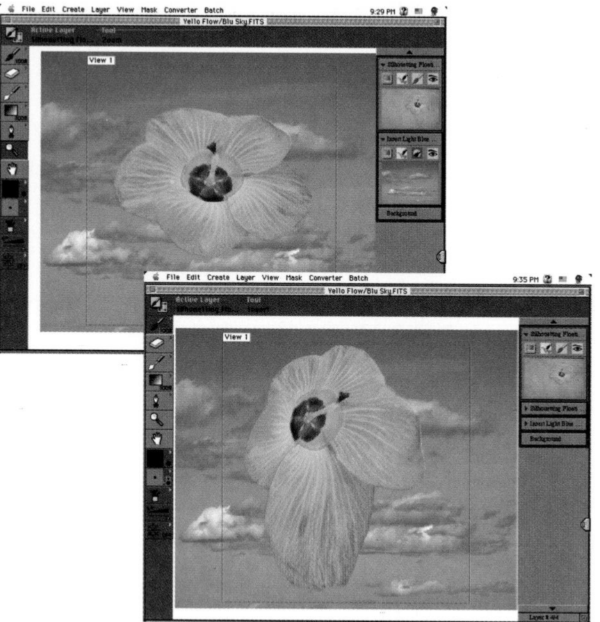

In Live Picture, just as in direct pixel editing applications, interpolation is necessary for scaling, rotation, and reshaping. Because multiple transforms are processed at one time when you build the final image, however, interpolation is kept to a minimum. In this case, the flower was distorted in several different steps, but the distortions were applied in one step during the rendering process.

Live Picture also includes image edits that require interpolation. Functions that change the number or orientation of the pixels—scaling, rotating, or reshaping the image—are similar to direct-editing programs in that the data has to be interpolated in order to achieve the final result. The benefit of the deferred rendering method is that accumulated transformations are calculated as a single transformation when the final image is rendered.

In Live Picture, the larger you scan your original images, the more you can vary the rendered (build) sizes. Because rendering large scans into smaller images does not cause serious image degradation, generally you should scan your images as large as possible and then reduce them (for more on interpolation, see Chapter 7-9). However, the reverse—making small scans larger—requires upsampling. Live Picture has to fabricate pixels that don't exist. From experience we know that enlarging more than 200 percent in either direct pixel rendering or deferred rendering applications will begin to diminish image quality (please see Section 9-8, "Multiple Transforms").

NOTE

A common misconception about deferred rendering applications such as Live Picture is that they maintain image quality because they do not handle pixels. This is not entirely accurate. Although you are not directly accessing the images pixels, the images themselves (for example, Live Picture IVUE format images) do have pixels and can be prone to some of the same types of image degradation that occurs in direct pixel applications.

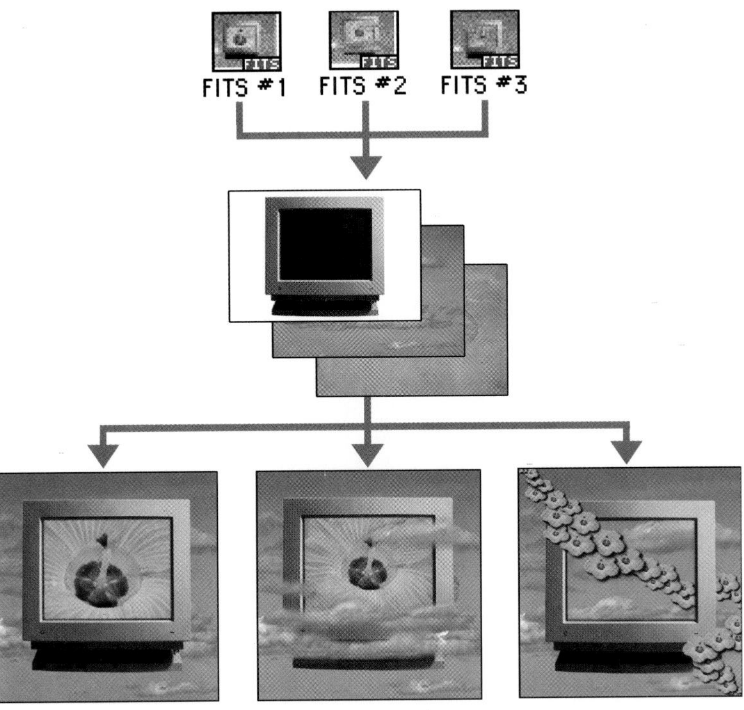

Three different images were created using these IVUE format images of a computer, the sky, and a flower. They were each saved as FITS format files and were rendered into final images by selecting the Build command. This shows that the same image files can be used to create many variations of an image.

Deferred Rendering

The expression *deferred rendering,* used throughout this section, actually refers to the last step in the imaging process in Live Picture or xRes Mode in xRes.

In this final step, all the edit instructions compiled in the edit recording document are used to assemble a new file based on the original high-resolution files, in order to build the final image. Because a new image file is created when you choose the Build command, the original high-resolution files are not changed. As a consequence, any number of different sizes or variations of an image can be created from the same IVUE files.

NOTE

It is easy to understand the basic concept of deferring the rendering process if you have had the experience of doing test strip exposures for determining exposure times for silver halide prints in a darkroom. In this case, you are deferring the printing of the large, final print by taking intermediate steps using smaller pieces of paper and making notes of each step. After you've worked out your basic exposure time, in addition to your burning and dodging times, and so on, then you can make the final print.

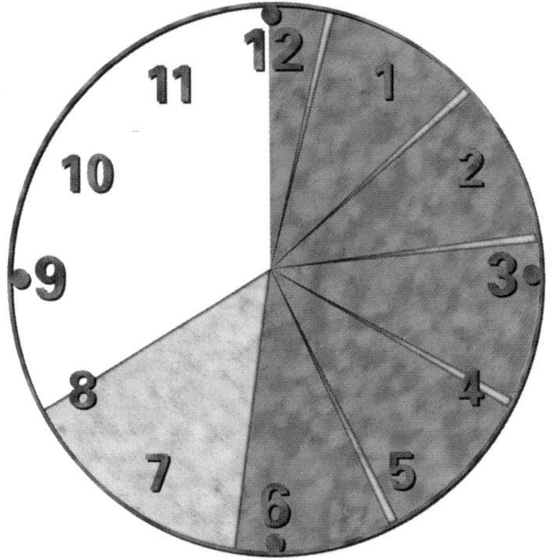

Compared to direct pixel editing applications, deferred rendering applications use less time during image editing for screen redraws and processing. Computation-intensive processes, such as loading large amounts of data, are saved until the final rendering stage, during which it is possible to work on other projects, spend time with the family, and so on....

... or you can play with your cat while your images are rendering!

Deferred Rendering Time Use

Because all edits are recorded and stored as mathematical expressions and computed later during rendering, all the computation-intensive tasks are reserved until the end. The artist can work quickly because the waiting time for screen redraws and edits is short. After image editing is complete, rendering might take a long time—as much as several hours—during which you can work on other projects, play with your cat, or enjoy some free time.

NOTE

In early 1996, a consortium of Microsoft, Kodak, Hewlett Packard, and Live Picture announced the establishment of a deferred rendering file format called FlashPix. This will be an indispensable file format for applications that use deferred rendering and will be offered by both software and hardware makers alike. (In 1997, Apple Computers announced it would incorporate FlashPix compatibility as a system-level function.) FlashPix is an open format, which means that the numbers of deferred rendering applications should increase in the future. FlashPix does not require a lot of RAM, so photographic-quality imaging is becoming increasingly available to a wider range of users from amateur photographers at home to office personnel.

09 5

Image Layers

Three Sheets of Transparency Film

If you sandwich three transparencies together, place them in a stack on top of a light table, and look down at them, you will be able to make out a fourth image that is the sum of the three originals blended together. Conceptually, this is similar to working with image layers in digital imaging applications.

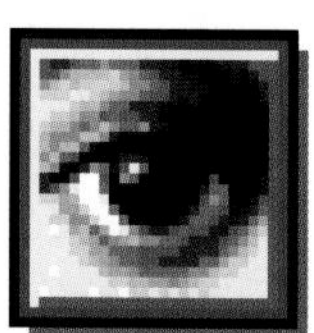

Layer

Layer

Floater

Object

NOTE
The image used in the following discussion can be found on the accompanying CD-ROM in the Still Life folder within the Tutorial Images folder. It has been saved in each of the native file formats for Photoshop, Live Picture, and Painter.

Common Features of Imaging Applications

All four of the full-featured imaging applications introduced in this chapter use a multi-layered method for compositing images, though each uses different terminology and different methods of implementing it. Common layer properties that most of the applications share include:

■ Perpetual compositing freedom: Individual image layers are preserved even after saving.

■ Vertical movement of layers: The front-to-back order of multiple layers can be changed at any time.

■ Lateral movement of layers: Relative positions among image layers can be freely changed at any time.

■ Blending: Various opacity and blending method options between layers can be explored.

■ Masking: Visible and hidden areas of images can be defined.

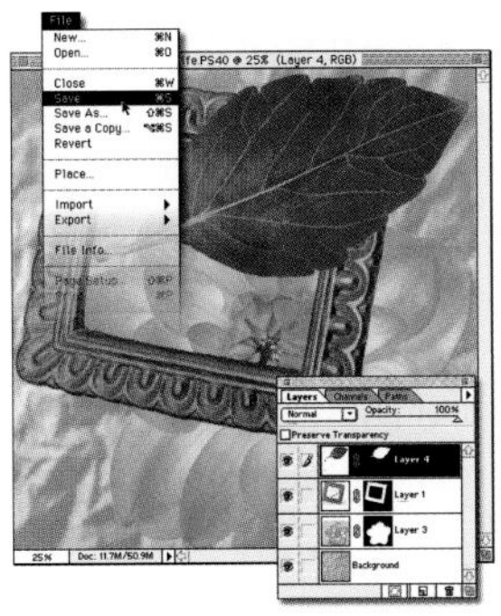

First, open the four-layer image called "Still Life.PSD" in Photoshop and save it to your hard disk.

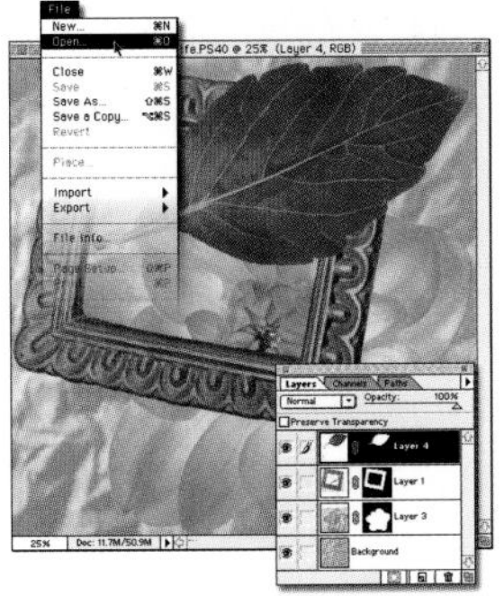

Open the same image again, and the four-layer structure is preserved and the layers can still be edited separately.

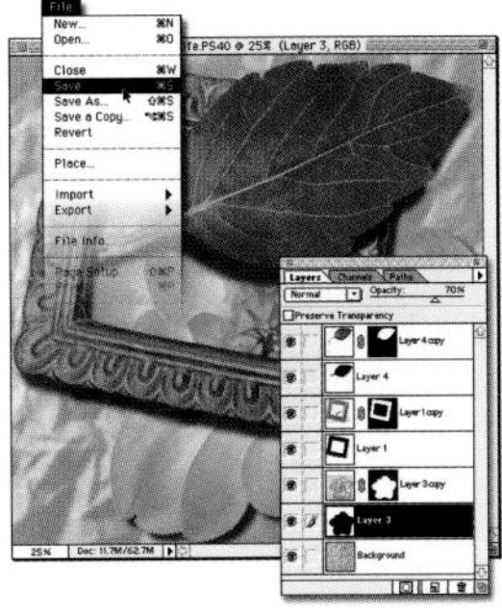

Make a drop shadow for each of the layers and save the file again in Photoshop format. As long as the layer structure is preserved as is, the layers can be edited separately even after the file has been saved.

Photoshop Files

5 項目 1.8 GB 使用 210.2 MB 空き

名前	容量
Background.ps40	16.6 MB
Flower.ps40	17.5 MB
Frame.ps40	18.6 MB
Leaf.ps40	7.7 MB
Still Life w/ Shadow.ps40	45.2 MB

Approximately 105 MB of disk space was used to store and edit this Photoshop image, including the original scans and the multi-layered project.

Live Picture Files

5 項目 1.8 GB 使用 208.6 MB 空き

名前	容量
Background.IVUE	15.4 MB
Flower.IVUE	19.3 MB
Frame.IVUE	17 MB
Leaf.IVUE	10.3 MB
Still Life.FITS	98K

In Live Picture, approximately 62 MB of disk space were used for the IVUE format files and the FITS file. Even if you add new layers, the FITS file does not get that much bigger. If you add new IVUE format scans to your project, however, the amount of data saved to the hard drive for a given project will increase.

Perpetual Compositing Freedom

Perpetual compositing freedom means that at any time in the creation of the final composite image, multiple layers can be added, replaced, or deleted. As long as the image is saved in the native format of the application (that is, Photoshop's Photoshop format, Painter's RIFF format, and so on) during editing or after the image is complete, all layers are preserved.

The Price of Freedom

A cost associated is with maintaining images in an "any-time" editable condition. That cost is measured not in terms of money paid to Adobe or Fractal Design, but in terms of hard disk space. In a period of six months, for example, we have created and saved over 1,000 multi-layered composite images for this book. In that time, we have used at least 15 1-GB Jaz disks to back up the data. If we were to flatten all these illustrations into a single layered file, it would save a minimum of one third the amount of disks needed for backup.

In your own work, if you add up the file sizes of your original image files and the file sizes of the multilayered composite files, the quantity of data for an imaging project can become gargantuan. In deferred rendering applications such as Live Picture, the edit-recording FITS document is never very large. (The size of the FITS document can grow depending on the number of images, masks, and stencils, but it is rare for it to be more than a few megabytes.) The individual image files can be quite large, however, ranging from hundreds of megabytes to even a gigabyte of data stored on a hard disk per imaging project.

NOTE

Live Picture's IVUE format enables JPEG compression. Because the actual IVUE data is not directly altered by Live Picture during the editing or rendering stage, there is no need to worry about the JPEG files being repeatedly opened and recompressed, which can lead to image-quality degradation.

A

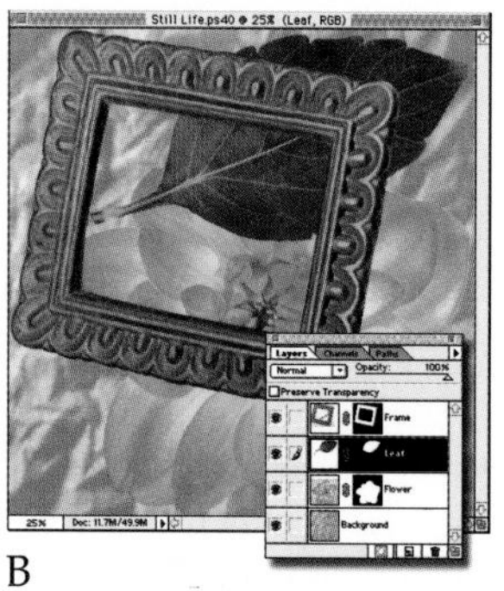

B

Hierarchical Movement of Layers

Vertical movement of layers means that the "in front of" and "in back of" relationships of image layers can be changed. This adjustment is usually made by changing the layer order in the Layers palette or in a layer stack. In the image on the left, for example, the leaf was moved to a position behind the frame by clicking and dragging it (A) to a new position in the Layers palette (B).

Vertical/Lateral Movement of Layers

Vertical and lateral element movement means that the relative positions between elements in image layers can be freely shifted up, down, left, or right within the image window, individually or in groups. This is frequently done as a click-and-drag operation within the window. Some applications include options for positioning elements with numerical controls as well.

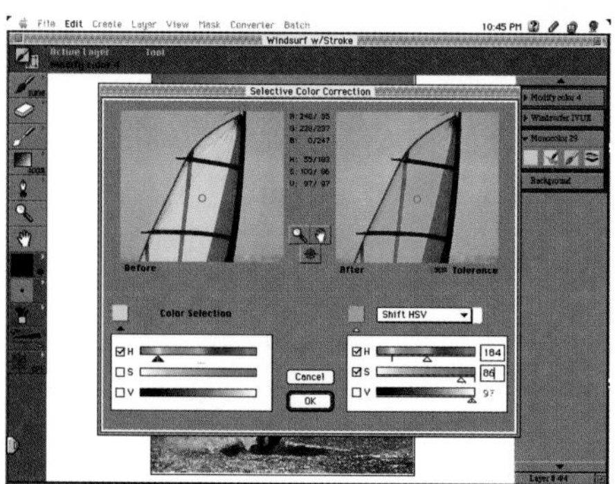

Layer Specific Effects

Some layer functions are specifically related to creating special effects or adjustments, such as brightness adjustment. Many of the image-editing functions in Live Picture, such as for adjusting color and tone or for distorting images, take place using specific layers. In Photoshop 4.0, an Adjustment Layer function can be used to alter the brightness or tone of particular layers. These particular layering functions in both applications enable you to undo changes at any time (see the section in this chapter, "Single and Multiple Undos").

Blending

The example at the beginning of this section (page 9-24) describes the effects of creating a single image by sandwiching several transparencies together. The example on this page shows the result of making three image layers opaque and compositing them together. In digital imaging, you can blend layers into each other using many controls that simply do not exist in traditional photography. In Photoshop, these include Layer Opacity, Blending Modes, and Layer Mask.

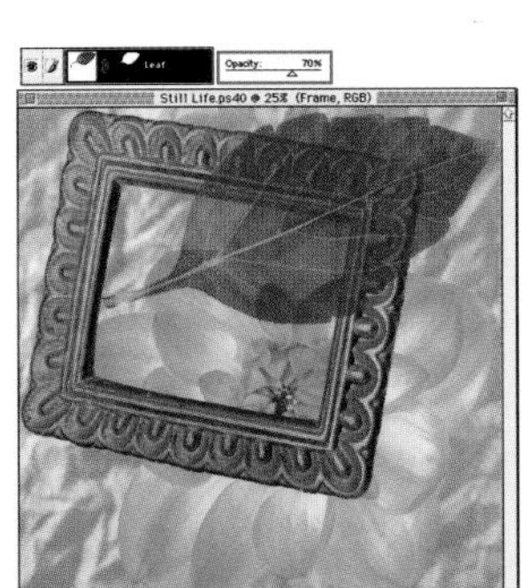

A

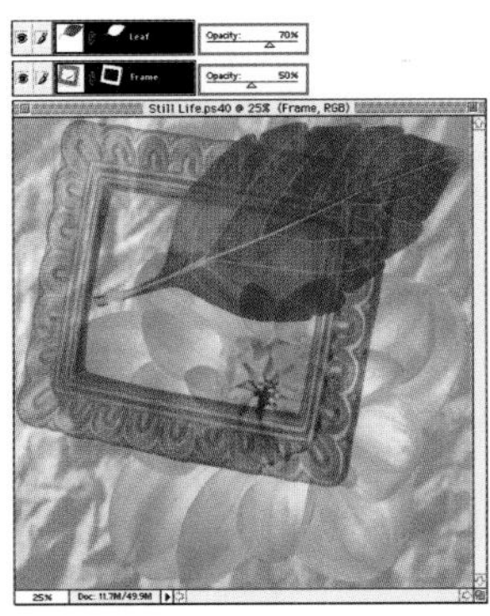

B

Layer Opacity

Changing opacity levels is the easiest method to understand for blending image layers together. As an upper layer's opacity is set below 100 percent using the opacity slider, more of the underlying layers show through. The opacity for each layer can be controlled separately. In the image to the left, for example, the opacity of the Leaf layer has been reduced to 70 percent (A) and the opacity of the Frame layer was adjusted to 50 percent (B).

NOTE

Of the four full-featured imaging applications we introduce, Live Picture is the only one that does not use a slider to adjust opacity. In Live Picture, opacity is controlled through masks. (See Section 9-6, "Masking.")

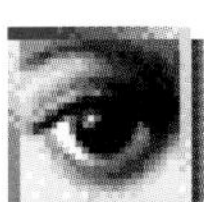

Blend Modes

Blending Modes

Composite Methods

Blend Modes

Blending modes in Photoshop takes the brightness or color values of the pixels in one layer and, through mathematical computation, blend them with the brightness or color values of underlying layers. The results vary widely, depending on the mode selected in the Layers pop-up menu in the Layers palette.

There are basically two ways to approach the use of blending modes. The first is to experiment with several different blend modes until you arrive at a desired or interesting effect.

The second approach is to select modes with predictable effects in order to perform specific tasks. To better understand and predict the results of the different blend modes, try experimenting with the Blend Test image found in the Blend Mode Study folder in the Tutorial Images folder on the accompanying CD-ROM.

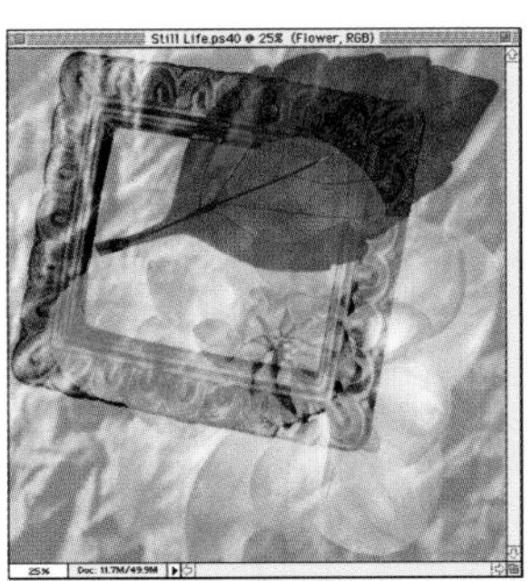

In this image, the Leaf is blended with Photoshop's Difference mode, the Frame is blended with the Color Burn mode (added in Photoshop 4.0), and the Flower is blended with the Hard Light mode. To achieve the result we wanted, we finally settled on this blend after experimenting with various mode combinations.

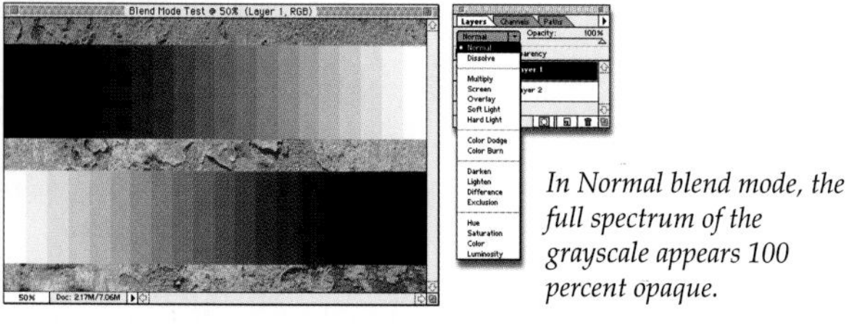

In Normal blend mode, the full spectrum of the grayscale appears 100 percent opaque.

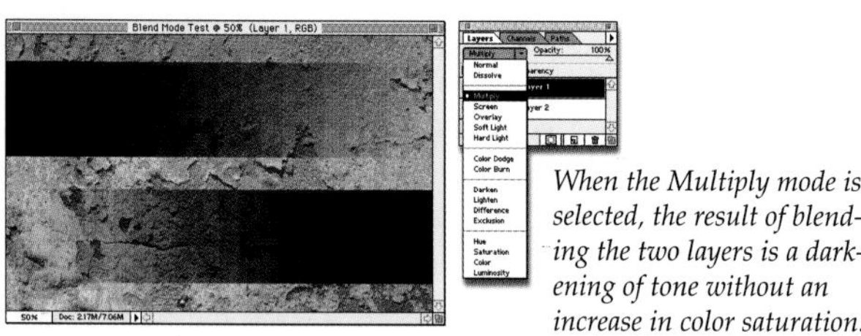

When the Multiply mode is selected, the result of blending the two layers is a darkening of tone without an increase in color saturation.

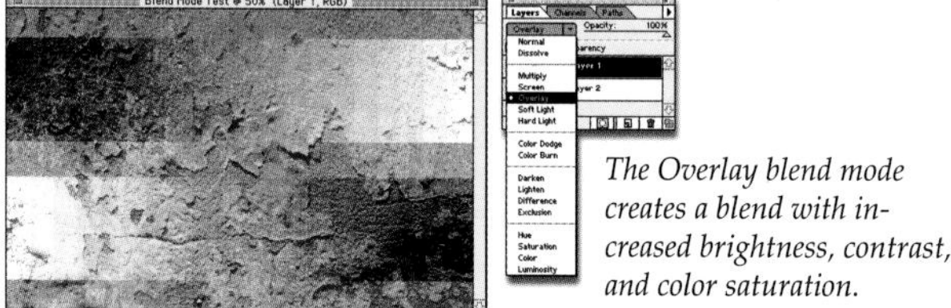

The Overlay blend mode creates a blend with increased brightness, contrast, and color saturation.

If you actually experiment with the Blend Test file, you will see that you can quickly toggle between different blending modes in the Layers palette and analyze the results of blending the upper grayscale layer with the lower texture layer. Although this test omits the use of color in the upper blend layer, it provides a reference point for understanding how brightness values affect the blend results. In particular, the Multiply, Screen, and Overlay blends enable you to achieve effects similar to darkroom techniques like dodging and burning.

Multiply

The overall effect of the Multiply command is a darkening of the image. This effect is easy to imagine if you recall the layering of the three transparencies on the light table at the beginning of this chapter. Multiply can be used as you would use burn-in techniques to darken parts of a print in the darkroom. Graphics designers and prepress specialists can think of it as creating the effect of overprinting.

Overlay

The Overlay mode blends the highlight and shadow tones of the blend layer into the underlying layer and has little to no effect on the middle range of tones. The result is increased shadow and highlight contrast, as well as an increase in color saturation where the two layers overlap.

Screen

Screen mode produces the effect of projecting two images on top of each other using a slide projector (similar to sandwiching two negatives together in an enlarger and exposing them onto photographic paper). The result is that the projected bright areas of each transparency that overlap darker areas of the other transparency lighten these darker areas—cancelling them out.

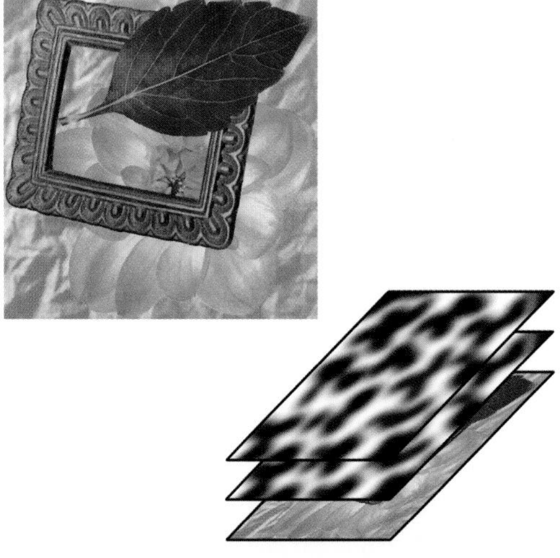

Simulating Light Using Blend Modes

As you have seen, the Multiply and Overlay blend modes affect the levels of darkness and brightness in the blended layers. This means, for example, that you can use these modes to create shadows and highlights.

The lighting in the original image for Still Life.PSD is very flat, for example, without shadows or highlights.

To create a visual sensation of highlights and shadows, we started by creating a new layer with soft, irregular black shapes on a white background (the objective was to make the layer resemble a type of light scrim frequently used to modify light in a photo studio). We duplicated this layer to create two layers above the original Still Life.PSD image. Then the top layer was set to Overlay mode, and the middle layer was set to Multiply mode. Both layers were set to 25 percent opacity. The result of the blends is the image you see.

NOTE

In Live Picture, the Colorize layer offers the capability to paint with Lighten and Darken tools to simulate the same effect we show here.

Brightness Value Blends

Photoshop has a unique blending function found in the Layer Options dialog box that enables you to adjust opacity in the layer based on brightness values. This means that, by using the slider controls of the Layer Options dialog box, you can selectively make dark or light regions of the image transparent. Unlike Blend Modes, only opacity is affected while hue and saturation are not.

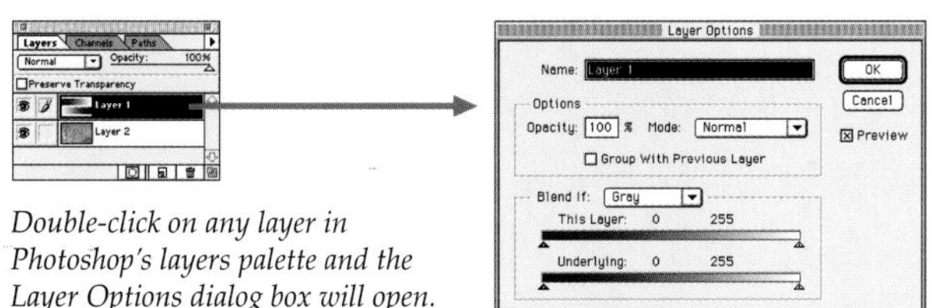

Double-click on any layer in Photoshop's layers palette and the Layer Options dialog box will open.

NOTE

You can use the BlendTest file on the accompanying CD-ROM to experiment with the Layer Options Blend If feature by double-clicking on Layer 1 in the Layers palette.

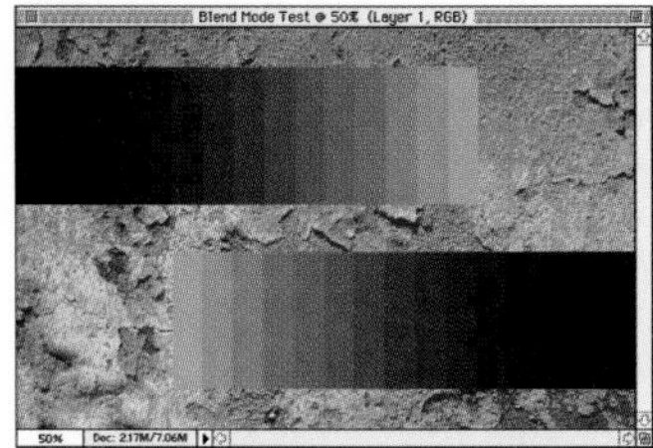

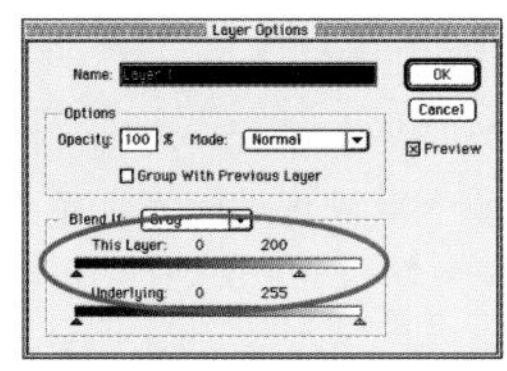

The Layer Slider of the Layer Options Dialog Box

By adjusting the control points of this slider, you can make specific ranges of tones in a layer transparent. For example, slide the white slider from right to left from 255 to 200. Notice how this has made some of the grayscale transparent. In effect, the slider is saying "Take the range of tones in this layer that are between 200 and 255 and make them transparent."

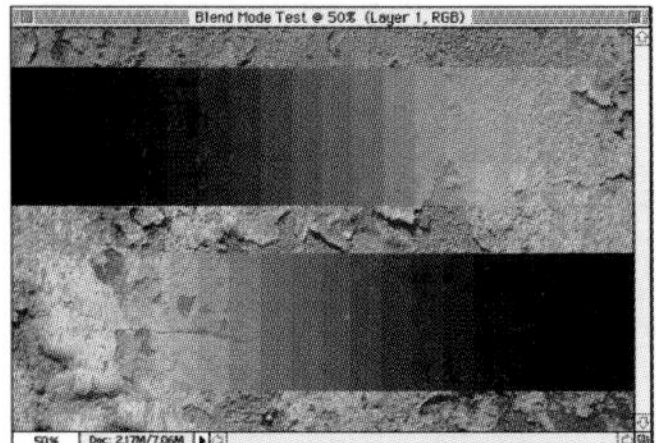

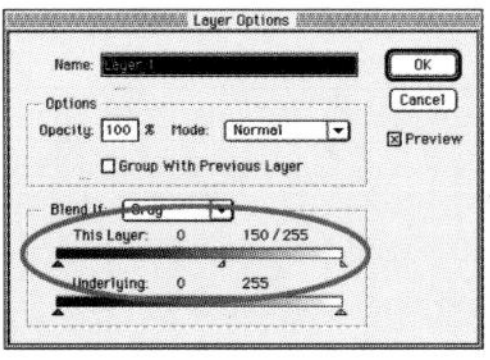

Next, by option-clicking the slider, the slider points can be split in two. Try sliding the left half of the slider to 150 and keep the right half at 255. Notice how this has gradually made some of the grayscale transparent. In effect, this slider is saying "Take the range of tones in this layer that are between 150 and 255 and make them gradually transparent."

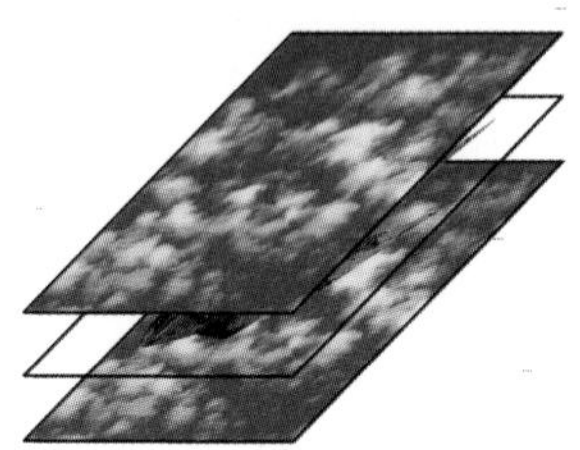

NOTE

The slider titled Underlying lets a range of tones from an underlying layer become visible in the upper layer. This time, however, the slider is effectively saying "Make a range of tones between X and Y from the underlying layer visible in the upper layer."

At times, this blend function in the Layer Options dialog box can be easier and more effective than creating selections or masks to blend images together.

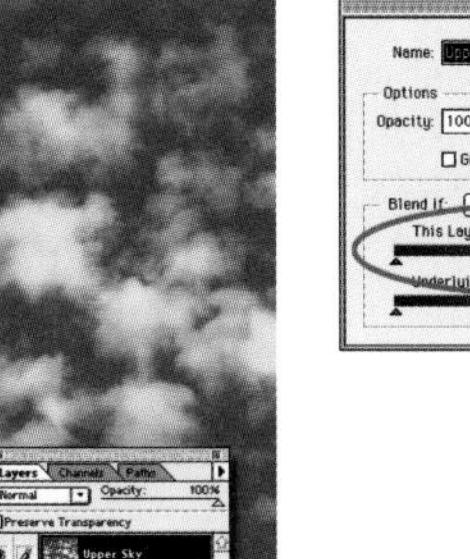

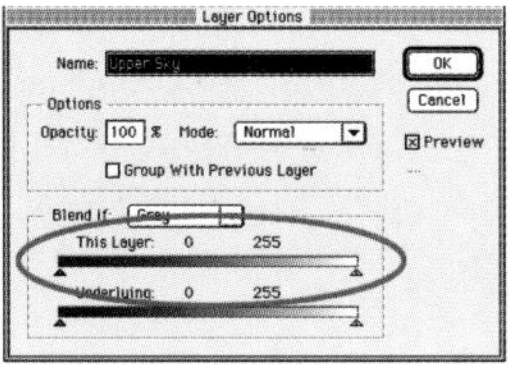

For example, we sandwiched the origami crane in the photo to the left between two layers of the same sky photograph.

By double-clicking on the Upper Sky layer in the Layers palette, we opened the Layer Options dialog box.

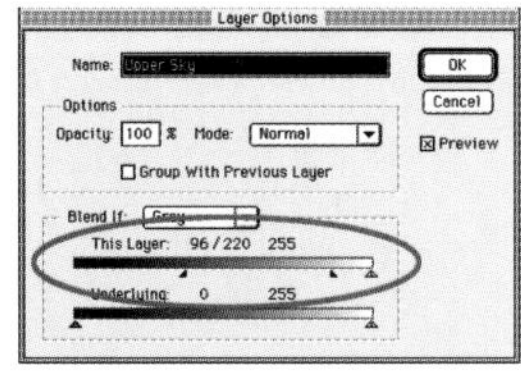

Then we option-clicked on the dark slider point on the This Layer slider in the Blend If field and moved the split slider so that the darker blue tones of the sky became gradually transparent, leaving only the fluffy clouds to show over the origami crane. By splitting the slider and gradually making the blue tones transparent, soft translucent edge characteristics of the clouds were maintained.

Layer mask

Floater mask

Channel mask

If the concept of masks is completely new to you, see the next section and Chapter 6, "Digital Photomontages," for more information about masks.

Layer Masks

Photoshop, Painter, and xRes are all capable of masking layers in order to make some areas less transparent and to eliminate transparency in others. Each layer is essentially an individual image, and each can have at least one 8-bit, grayscale channel mask attached to it. The layer mask is used to control what appears where on a layer.

NOTE
The images here are included on the CD-ROM in multi-layer formats for Photoshop, xRes, and Painter.

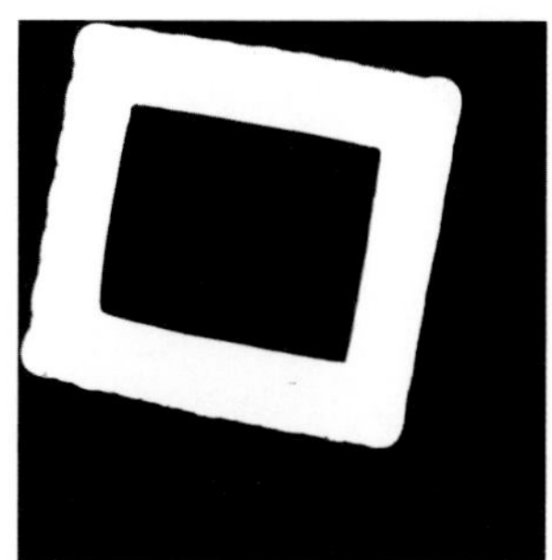

Basic Layer Mask Functions

Layer masks hide or reveal the image in layers according to the values of the grays in the layer mask. There are four layers in the image Still Life.PSD, for example, each with its own layer mask (shown here in Photoshop). The view of the Frame layer is controlled by a frame-shaped layer mask.

An important feature of layer masks such as these is that they do not permanently alter the contents of the images in the layers. This means that you can change the masks to create different effects.

To see how this works, Shift-click the Layer Mask thumbnails in the Layers palette of each layer of Still Life to temporarily turn off the layer masks. The images in those layers will be displayed as they were originally scanned, before the application of the Layer Masks, with backgrounds intact.

This means that if a particular layer mask is not accomplishing what you want it to, all you need to do is modify it or replace it with a new one.

NOTE
A Photoshop Layer Mask can be removed by dragging it to the trash can icon on the layers palette. The resulting dialog box offers a choice to either Apply or Discard the mask. By selecting the Discard option, you remove the mask without applying it; if you select Apply, the pixels originally hidden from view by the mask are replaced in the layer with transparency. In this case, the original background pixels are removed and lost entirely.

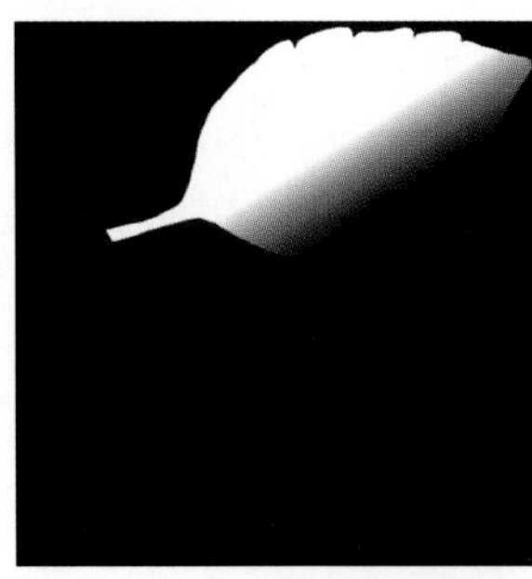

By adding shades of grayscale tone (from black to white) into layer masks, you can further modify the blend of the image. Here, for example, a white to black gradation has been added to the white portion of the leaf layer mask.

NOTE

Using the Multiply mode in either the Paintbrush tool or the Gradient tool is an effective method of adding tone to the white portion of a mask without altering the overall shape of the mask.

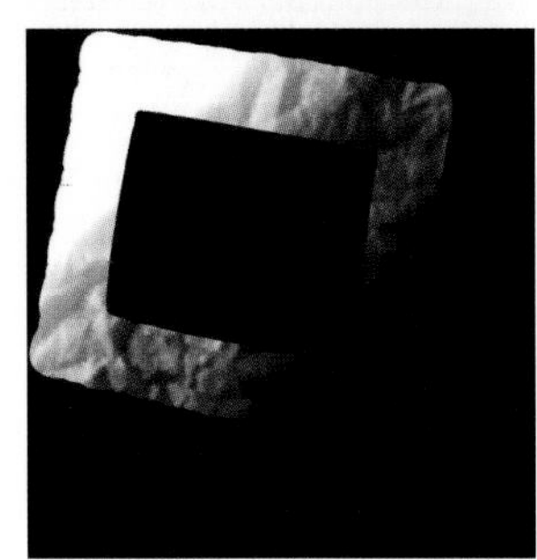

Next, we added a texture and a gradation to the Frame layer mask to blend the Frame into the image.

NOTE

A separate gradation and a separate texture channel were combined with the Frame layer mask using the Multiply blend mode in the Calculations dialog box accessed from the Image menu. Although this dialog box looks complicated at first, it is worthwhile to take the time to understand it. This technique of blending masks together is frequently referred to as Channel Operations in various tips and techniques books about Photoshop.

Live Picture and Layer Masks

Live Picture also has a way of creating layer masks. The implementation is so different from Photoshop, Painter, and xRes, however, that it is discussed separately.

xRes Channel Masks

The xRes version of a layer mask is called a Channel. xRes provides up to 32 Channels per layer. With this many mask channels, you can create a variety of combinations of masks quickly and interactively using the Channels palette. The image at the left, for example, contains a green background and a flower. Although the Flower layer contains three channel masks, no mask functions are yet in use.

Clicking in the Mask column of Channel #4 in the Channels palette turns on a mask that silhouettes the flower layer against the background.

A gradation mask in Channel #5 is turned on next. Now two masks are active at the same time, and the silhouetted flower begins to partially fade into the background.

Finally, the Channel #6 mask, which has a textured border around the perimeter of the flower shape, is turned on. Now three masks are controlling how the flower blends into the background. Any combination of these three masks could be used.

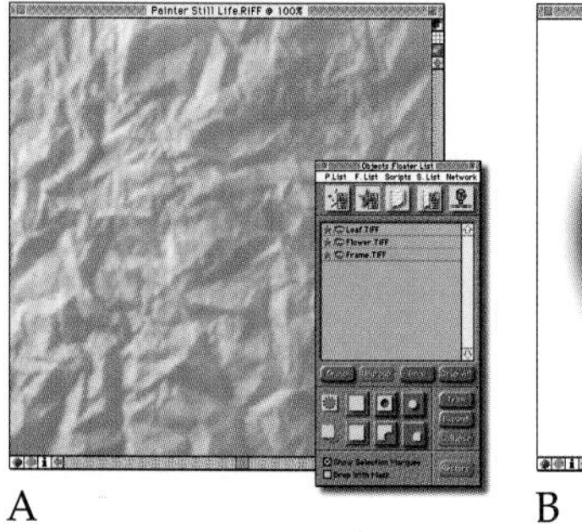
A

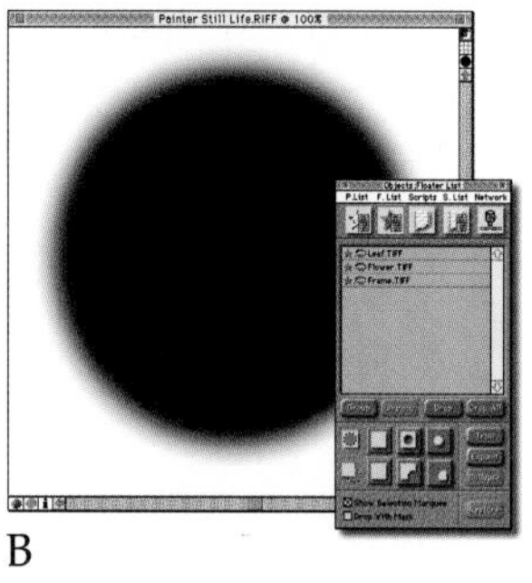
B

You can toggle between displaying Canvas Mode and Canvas Mask Mode by turning the Mask Edit Mode button in the upper-right corner of the image window on and off.

Painter Floater Masks

Painter's version of a layer mask is called a Floater mask. Floater masks are turned on and off with the Mask Modes buttons located at the bottom of the Floaters List Palette. The Mask Modes control the interaction between the Floater mask (a Floater in Painter is the basically the same as a layer in Photoshop) and the mask that belongs to the Canvas, or base layer. For instance, the Canvas layer (A) contains a feathered, circular-shaped mask (B).

C

D

In the Floater List Palette, the view of the flower image (Flower.TIFF) Floater is turned on (C). Then in the Mask Mode, the Masked Outside button is turned on for the flower Floater (D). This silhouettes the Flower against the background.

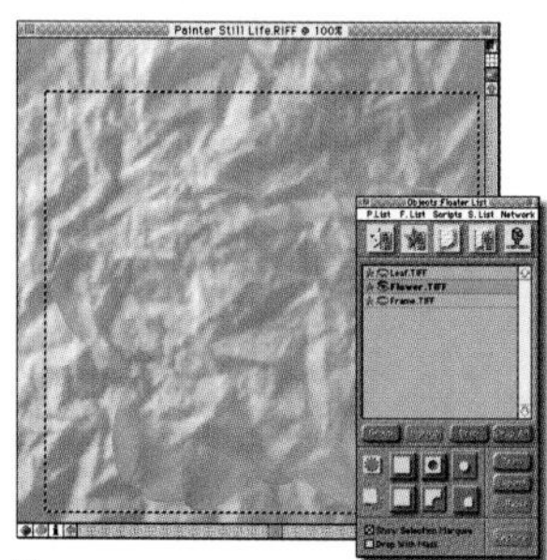
E

F

The buttons in the second row of Mask Mode buttons on the Floater List Palette control the Floater's interaction with the Canvas mask. First the Mask Inside button is turned on, and the center of the flower disappears (E). Then the Mask Outside button is turned on, and the flower is masked as a soft, circular shape (F).

NOTE

The file for this example, Still Life.RIFF, is on the accompanying CD-ROM in the Painter folder within the Still Life folder inside the Tutorial Images folder. You can open the image using the demo version of Painter 4.0 that is included on the CD-ROM.

09 6 Masking

In Section 9-5, "Image Layers," we looked at how Photoshop and other imaging applications use layers for blending images, and on numerous occasions we used the term 8-bit, or grayscale, channel masks. In this section, we introduce the fundamentals of using 8-bit channel masks to blend images.

What is a Mask?

A *mask* is a function used to separate the part of the image where an edit is applied from the part of the image where the edit is not applied. This is similar to when you paint a car and use tape and paper to protect the areas you don't want painted. From compositing multiple elements together to adjusting the brightness in particular image areas to creating complex special effects, masking skills are the cornerstone of the digital photography craft.

Traditional Masks

Masking is not a new concept to photographic technology. Film-based optical methods of masking have been in use almost since the beginning of photography. Masks have been used for everything from increasing or reducing contrast to making complex photo composites.

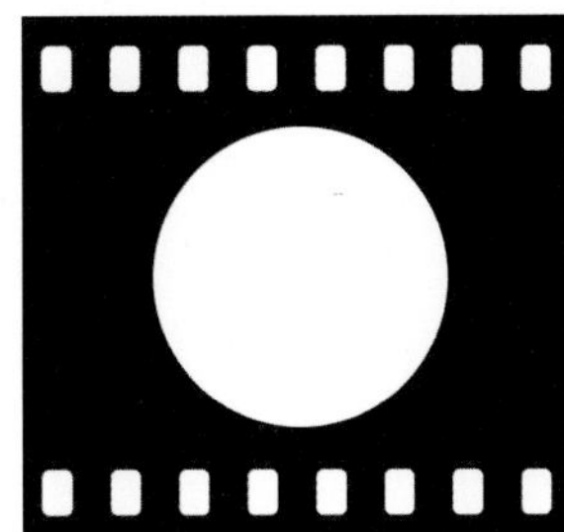

The illustration on the left, for example, represents a 35 mm color negative and a high-contrast lithographic (Kodalith) film. The circle represents the clear portion of the lithographic film, and the black represents the opaque part of the lithographic film.

When the two pieces of film are sandwiched together and viewed on a light table, only a circular portion of the color negative is visible. The portion that is not visible (the area where the light has been completely blocked out) has been masked, or protected.

When these two pieces of film are placed into an enlarger to expose photographic paper, the result is a circular-shaped print. In this case, light from the enlarger was able to pass through the clear portion of the lithographic film negative, while the paper was protected from the light by the black part of the lithographic film.

Digital Masks

In Photoshop, Painter, and xRes, the digital equivalent of lithographic film is an 8-bit grayscale channel referred to variously as a mask, layer mask, a channel, an alpha channel, or a masking channel, depending on where it is being used and in which application.

An alpha channel contains 256 shades of gray and is therefore a *grayscale* channel. While the high-contrast lithographic film previously mentioned can only control whether the image is visible, a digital mask is capable of making an image partially visible—the "partially" being a function of the 256 shades of gray that digital masks can contain. Although each of the applications we discuss has a different implementation of the 8-bit alpha channel (see Section 9-5, "Image Layers"), the fundamental concept is the same. (Masking in Live Picture is quite different and will be discussed further on.)

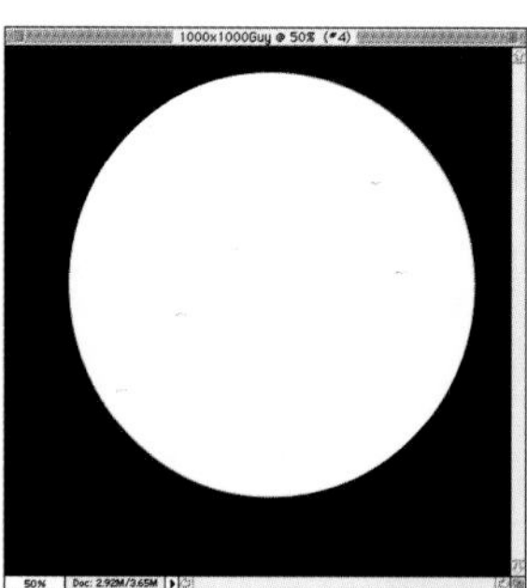

8-bit Alpha Channel Operations

We use Photoshop for purposes of explanation here, but similar concepts apply to Painter and xRes.

The image on the left is an RGB Photoshop image. Therefore, the first channel contains the R, the second channel contains the G, and the third channel contains the B color elements in monochrome images. Channel #4 contains a mask image of a white circle surrounded by a field of black.

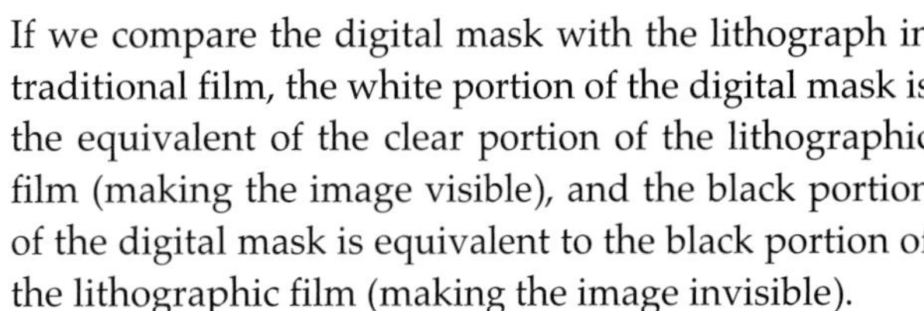

If we compare the digital mask with the lithograph in traditional film, the white portion of the digital mask is the equivalent of the clear portion of the lithographic film (making the image visible), and the black portion of the digital mask is equivalent to the black portion of the lithographic film (making the image invisible).

Depending on the application, there are a variety of ways to use this digital mask. The most basic method is to load a selection based on the grayscale data in the mask. In Photoshop, the Select, Load Selection command is used to load (make active) the selection. After a selection has been loaded, the boundaries of the black-and-white mask become the boundaries of the selected ares. Edit operations can be carried out only within the boundaries of the selected region of the image.

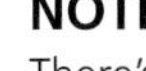

NOTE

There's a lot more to saving and loading selections than what we introduce here. Please refer to the Adobe Photoshop User Guide, or third-party Photoshop books, if you're uncertain how to save selections as channel masks.

In the example to the left, we created a selection in the photograph of the child in Photoshop, and then opened an image of the sky. We then copied and pasted the selection containing the child into the image of the sky to create a new image file of the child in the sky.

Almost every step in digital imaging uses some form of a mask. The round mask used above and its inverse, for instance, were used to make local edits of the hue and the saturation of the image.

Traditional Luminance Masks

In the first example of a traditional mask, a high-contrast lithographic film was used as the mask. In traditional darkrooms, a normal continuous-tone negative could also be used as a mask.

If the color negative on the left, for example, is sandwiched with the black-and-white negative on the right, the negative creates a luminance mask.

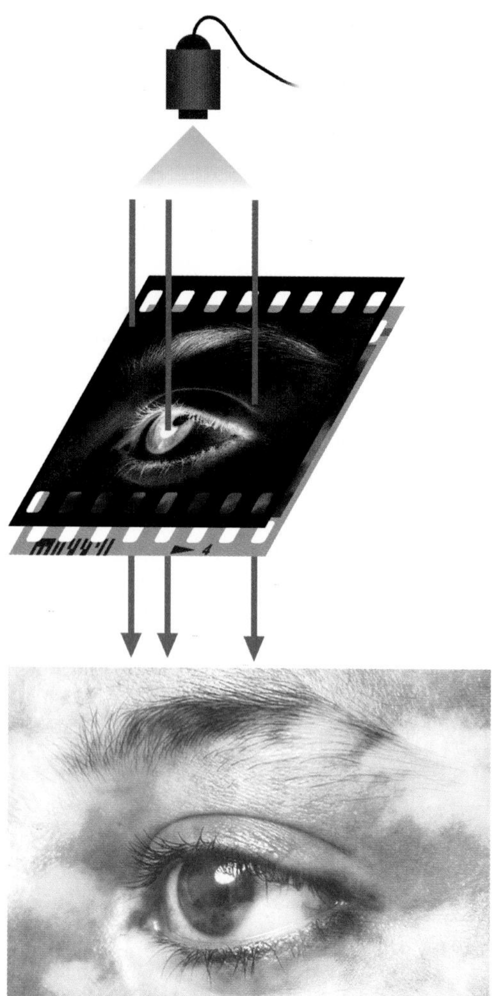

When this sandwiched pair is exposed in an enlarger, the parts of the color negative that overlap the clear parts of the black-and-white negative print at 100 percent. But where the tone in the black-and-white negative is 50 percent transparent (in the midtones), the color image prints at only 50 percent opacity. It fades into the white background. At the 100 percent black portion of the negative, 0 percent of the image printed.

This means that the color negative was simply not made visible or invisible. We could say it was "slightly visible" or "very visible," depending on the opacity of the black-and-white negative. We call this black-and-white negative a *luminance mask*.

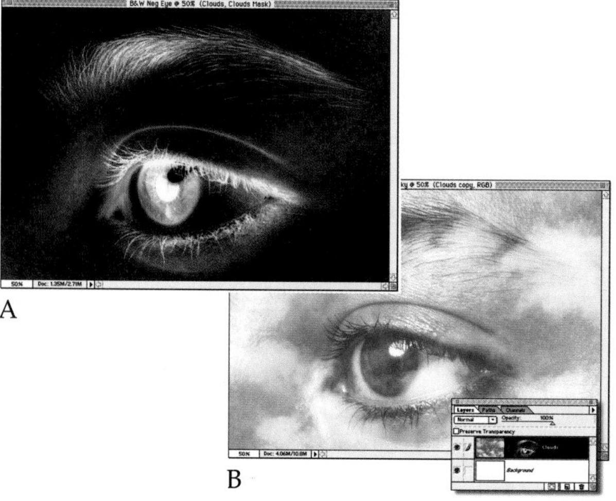

A

B

Digital Grayscale Masks

Alpha channel masks in imaging applications can be used the same way as the traditional film-based luminance mask described above. Let's say, for example, the image of the sky has an alpha channel that includes a full range of tones, as shown in (A) on the left. When this mask is used to select, copy, and paste the image into a white background, the results are similar to the traditional method using an enlarger (B). This time, where the mask is 100 percent white, 100 percent of the image was copied and pasted. In the intermediate midtone areas of the alpha channel, those areas of the copied image were translucent. And where the mask was 100 percent black, none of the image was copied and pasted.

The word MASK in this image symbolizes the concept in Live Picture that the mask is an integral part of the layer. As long as you can see the word, it means the mask is opaque. Here the entire mask is 100 percent opaque, so the image is 100 percent visible and any underlying images are blocked from view.

Fundamentals of Live Picture Masking

Basically two tools control which parts of an image are visible in Live Picture—one is called *masks* and the other is called *stencils*. Live Picture masking operations are quite different from that of the other applications. Photoshop, Painter, and xRes, for example, have grayscale mask channels that can be separately viewed (from the RGB image) and directly manipulated with brushes, filters, and other tools. Live Picture's masks are not visible. The effects of the masks can be seen, but the actual masks themselves cannot be seen.

100-Percent Opaque Masks

A mask in Live Picture can be *imagined* as an opaque mask film that is an integral part of the layer. As long as this mask is opaque, the image on the layer can be seen, and images on lower layers are blocked from view. A 100-percent opaque mask means that the source image is 100-percent visible, and underlying layers are 100-percent invisible.

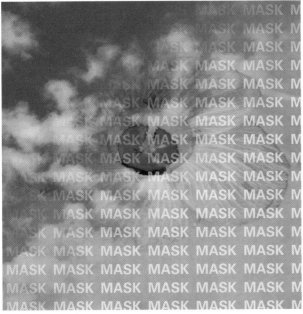

We used the Eraser tool in Live Picture to remove mask opacity in the Flower layer, revealing a portion of the underlying Sky layer. Notice the relationship between the opacity of the word MASK and the opacity of the Flower layer. Where the word MASK is fading, it means that the mask is becoming less opaque.

0-Percent Opaque Masks

You can use tools such as the Eraser tool to make the mask less opaque. As the mask becomes less opaque, the underlying image is revealed. If the mask is 0-percent opaque, the source image is 0-percent visible and the underlying layer becomes 100-percent visible.

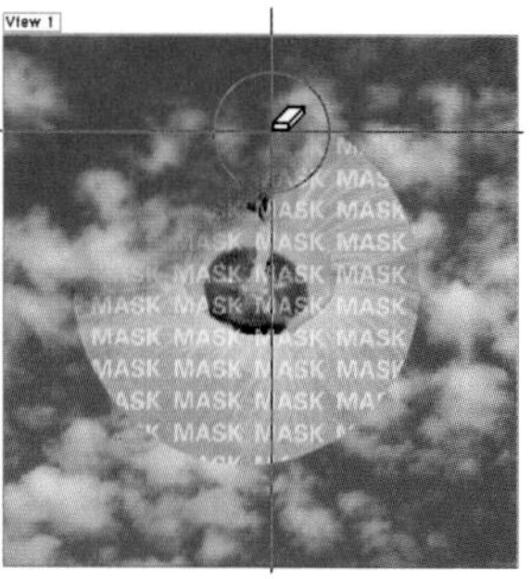

A

B

Stencils

Stencils in Live Picture are used to create boundary shapes within which the opacity of masks can be controlled.

To illustrate this idea, we created a circular path in the layer containing the Flower image, as shown on the left.

Then we converted the path into a stencil using the Path to Stencil command. This trimmed the Flower image layer into the circular shape we created in the previous step.

Next we changed the opacity of the mask within the stencil. First, using the Eraser tool, we removed portions of the mask, making the layer less opaque (A). Then, using the Insert function of the Paintbrush tool, we increased the opacity in portions of the mask, which reinserted some of the mask. By making the mask opaque again, we made the image reappear (B). An important point to note is that the stencil creates a border that can't be altered by any of the mask editing tools.

Stencils and Masks Compared

You can define the shape of an image in a Live Picture layer using either a mask or a stencil. The difference between them is the malleability of their edges. The edges of a shape generated by a mask have *malleable* borders, meaning that they can be affected by the Erase or Paintbrush-Insert tools. Borders created using a stencil, however, are unmalleable. As we saw in the previous example, the edge of the stencil was not affected by the Erase or Insert tools. To demonstrate this, we will create a mask using the same path we used to create the Stencil.

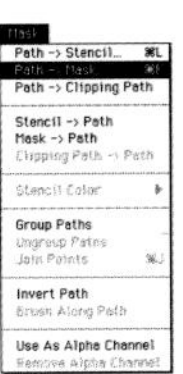

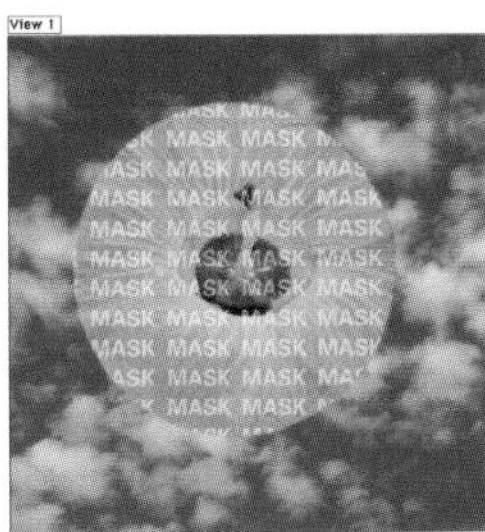

STEPS

1. We made a circular path in the Flower layer, but this time we used the Path to Mask command to convert the path.

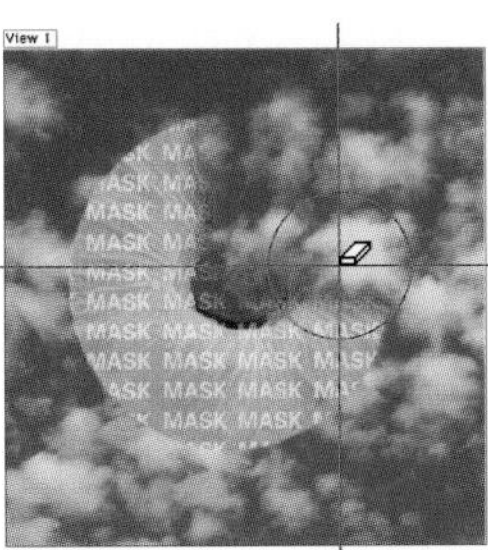

2. Then we used the Eraser tool to remove a portion of the circular mask. At this point, the result looks very similar to the result achieved from using the Path to Stencil command.

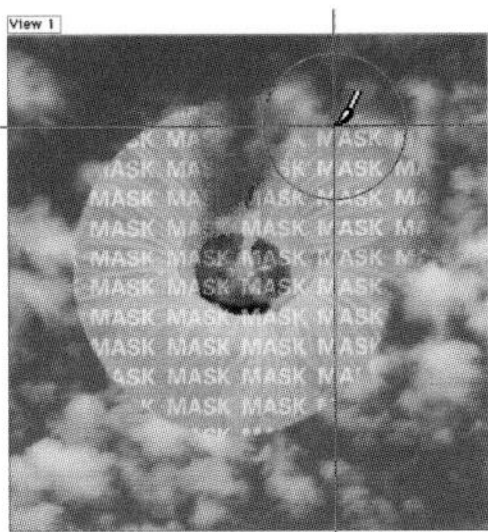

3. Next, the Paintbrush-Insert tool was used to reinsert portions of the erased circle. This time, however, portions of the image beyond the border of the circle were also reinserted. This is due to the fact that the Path to Mask function removes mask opacity just like the Eraser tool does, so any Insert option that touches outside the border of the original shape will reinsert mask opacity.

09 7

Single and Multiple Undos

Single Undos

Undo commands are a measure of flexibility in imaging applications. They can range from a single undo to a specified number of undos to an infinite number of undos. Generally speaking, all four of the full-featured applications we are introducing have one basic undo command, located in the Edit menu. The single undo function operates like a toggle, enabling the artist to flip between undoing and redoing a function. The single undo command always applies to the last edit step taken.

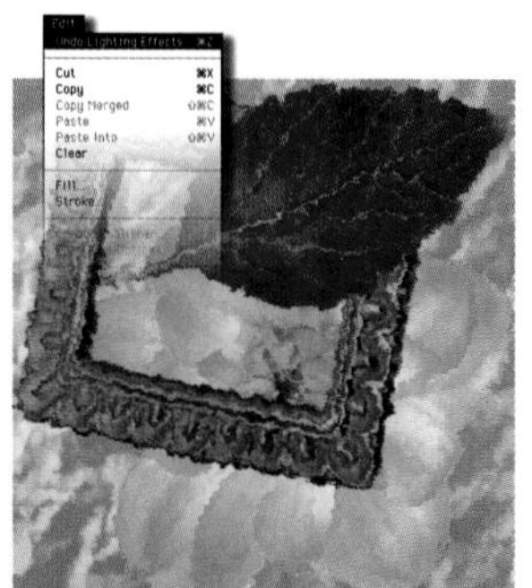

In the example on the left, we applied two filters to the image Still Life.PSD in Photoshop—the Spatter filter (new in Photoshop 4.0) and the Lighting Effects filter. Before we used another function, we selected the Undo command and the image returned to the state it was in right after the Spatter filter had been applied. Undo erased only the effect of the Lighting Effects filter. At this point, the Undo command turns into a Redo command. If used, the previous Undo would be canceled, returning the image to the state it was in after the Lighting Effects filter had been applied.

Multiple Undos

Multiple undos means that more than one editing step can be changed, corrected, or removed. Multiple undos come in several forms, including work session-specific undos and perpetual undos.

Work Session-Specific Multiple Undos

The term *work session-specific multiple undos* refers to more than one level of undo that can be performed before an image is closed. After the image is saved and closed, the ability to undo changes is lost.

In the course of an imaging session, you can add many types of effects, brush strokes, and filters to an image. With a multiple undo capability, you can reverse edits sequentially if you decide you don't like the accumulated results. xRes and Painter enable you to set the total number of undos—xRes can be set as high as 20, and Painter can be set as high as 32.

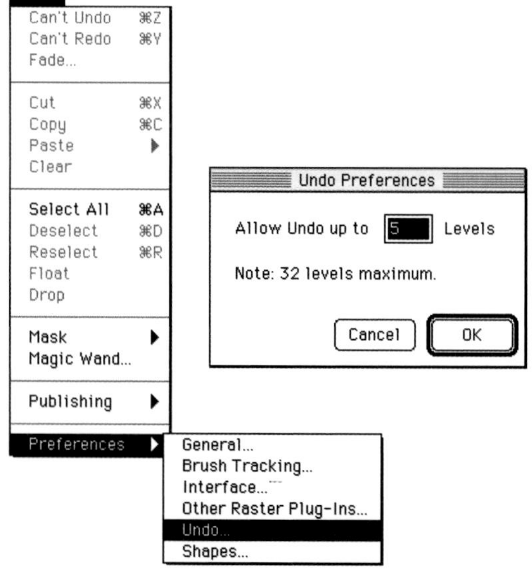

Painter's multiple undo levels are set by selecting Edit, Preferences, Undo and then entering a level of undos in the dialog box. You can set up to 32 undos, but if you actually allow that many undos in a large image file, it will slow your work speed, so it is better to leave it at the default setting of 5 (you do not actually have to use the undos for things to slow down).

A B

We applied a sequence of five image editing steps to the image Still Life.PSD (A). In clockwise order starting from the upper left, these included Glass Distortion, Flip Horizontal, Express Texture, Apply Surface Texture, and Apply Marbling. Next, we used the Undo command 3 times, removing in reverse order, the Apply Marbling, Apply Surface Texture, and Express Texture effects (B).

Multiple undos are saved in a special memory area usually referred to as an Undo buffer, either in RAM or on the virtual memory scratch disk. Each of the processing steps must be stored in the Undo buffer. This means that if the edit is a global edit—applied to the entire image—the entire image has to be copied into the buffer. An image that starts out at 10 MB, for example, will add an additional 10 MB to the undo buffer each time an edit is applied to the entire image. In Painter, for example, if all 32 levels of undo are used for a 10 MB image, over 300 MB of disk space is needed for the Undo buffer.

NOTE

To take advantage of multiple work session undos, you have to have a fast hard disk dedicated for use as virtual memory. xRes, for example, requires 20 times the file size of free hard disk space to take full advantage of its 20 levels of undo. A 50 MB image would therefore need almost 1 GB of free disk space.

Perpetual Edits

The term *perpetual edits* refers to edits that can be changed or modified even after the file has been saved and closed. If you open the file again, you can remove or change any edits that were made.

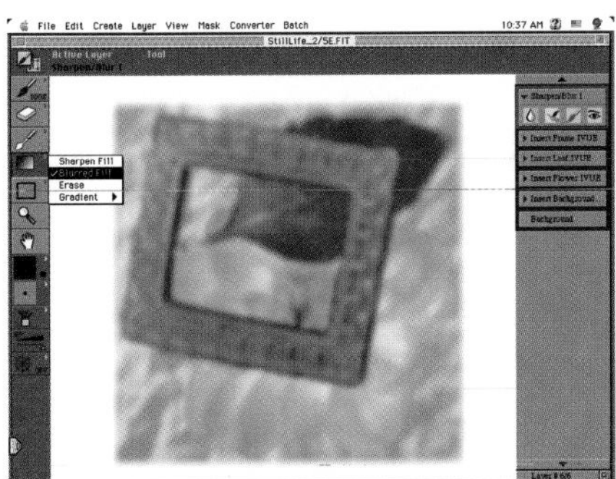

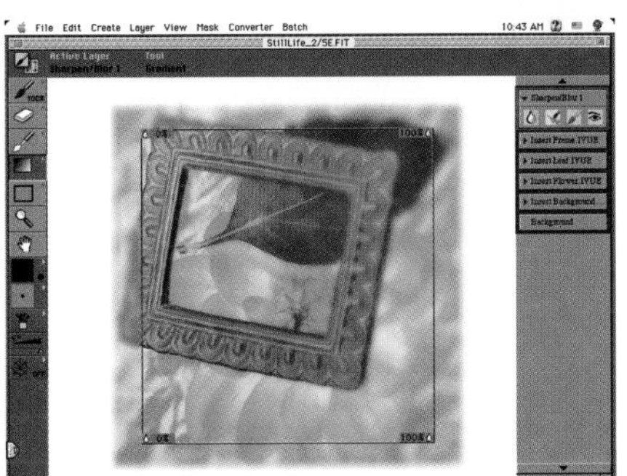

Live Picture

In Live Picture, most image editing tasks are done using special layers. A Sharpen/Blur layer, for example, was added to the Still Life.PSD image on the left in order to apply a heavy blur. Because the blur effect is caused by the Sharpen/Blur layer, only that layer, not the image itself, needs to be changed in order to alter the effect. This is similar, conceptually, to coating a sheet of glass placed over a sharp photograph with Vaseline. The Vaseline would blur the view of the image without actually blurring the image itself. To change the blur would involve adding or removing the Vaseline.

The characteristics of the Blur effect were changed by using the 4-Point Gradient option of the Marquee tool. Because the images themselves are never actually blurred, this type of adjustment can continue endlessly, even after the file has been repeatedly saved, closed, and reopened.

To demonstrate the concept of multiple undos, we applied a sequence of five image-editing steps to the image Still Life in Painter (A). In clockwise order starting from the upper left, these included Glass Distortion, Flip Horizontal, Express Texture, Apply Surface Texture, and Apply Marbling. Next, we used the Undo command three times, removing in reverse order the Apply Marbling, Apply Surface Texture, and Express Texture effects (B).

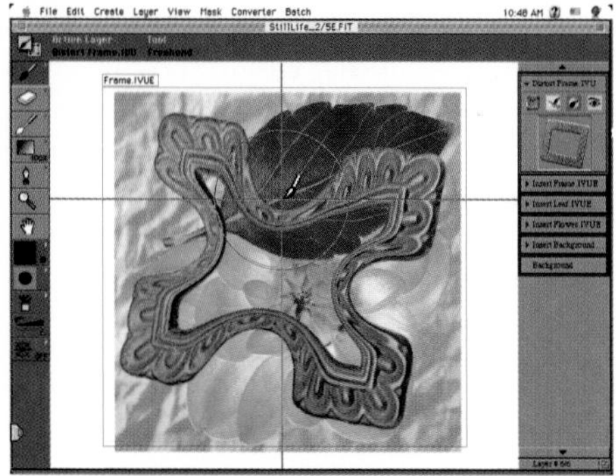

The Image Distortion layer is another example of how flexible the editing process is in Live Picture. Images on an Image Distortion layer can be distorted and undistorted indefinitely. For example, the frame was inserted as an Image Distortion layer and distorted heavily with the Freehand distortion paintbrush.

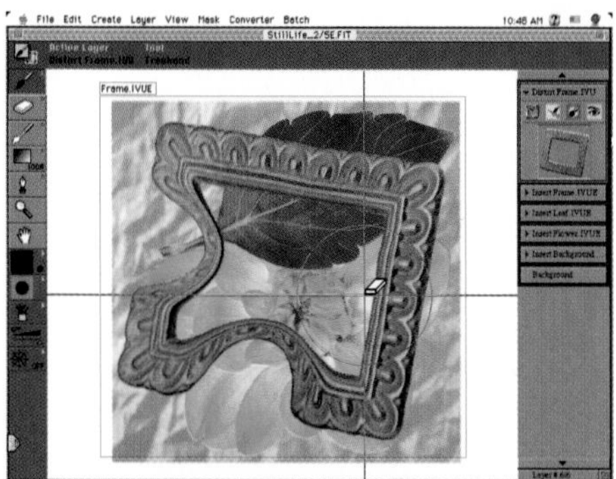

Then, the distortions were gradually undone using the Eraser tool.

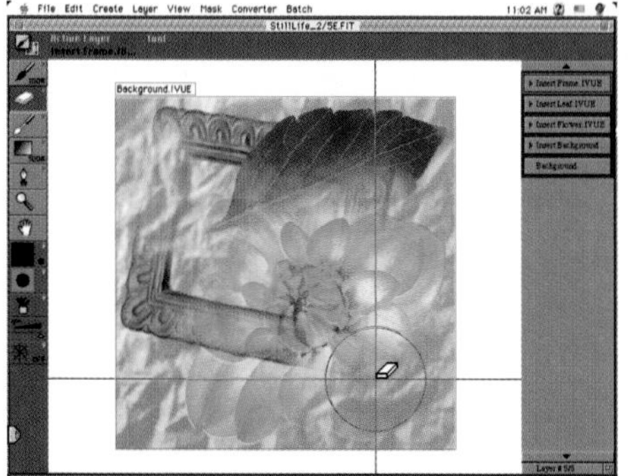

A

Masking in Live Picture is another type of perpetual editing function. If you toggle back and forth between the Eraser and the Paintbrush tool, you can continuously remove (A) or reinsert (B) mask opacity. Other perpetual edit functions in Live Picture include paint layers and IVUE Corrections (color corrections and adjustments).

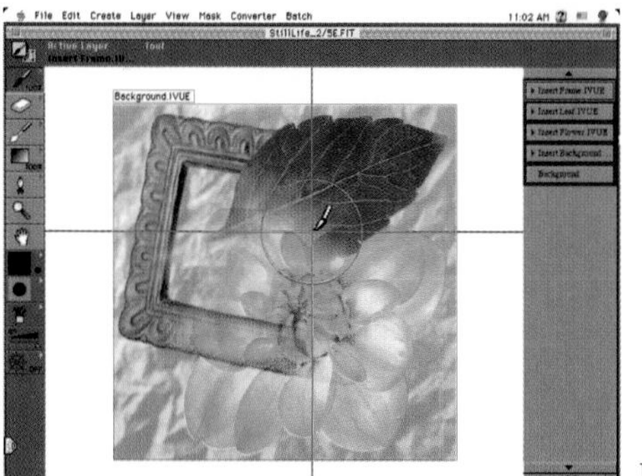

B

Perpetual Undos in Photoshop 4.0 (Perpetual Editing)

We have seen how layer masks in Photoshop enable you to modify what appears on a layer without permanently changing the image in that layer. In Photoshop 4.0, the Adjustment Layer function is another method of manipulating images without permanently altering the image.

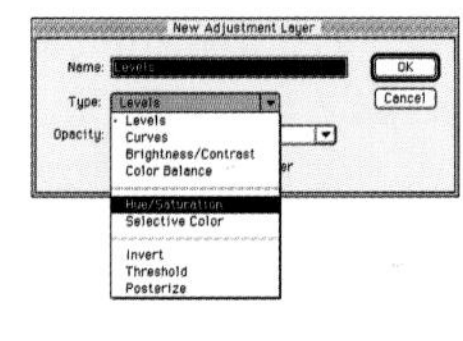

When you select the Adjustment Layer command, the New Adjustment Layer dialog box appears and enables you to select one of nine different image adjustment functions. After you select the adjustment you want to use and click on OK, a special image adjustment layer is added to the image in the Layers palette. Although the Adjustment Layer remains in the Layers palette, the result of the adjustment can be seen in the image below it.

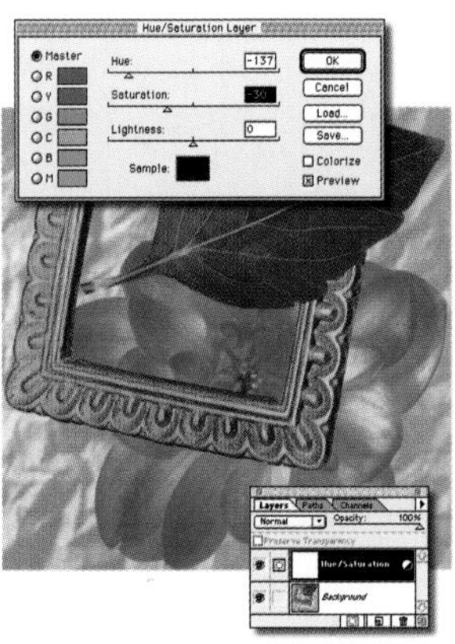

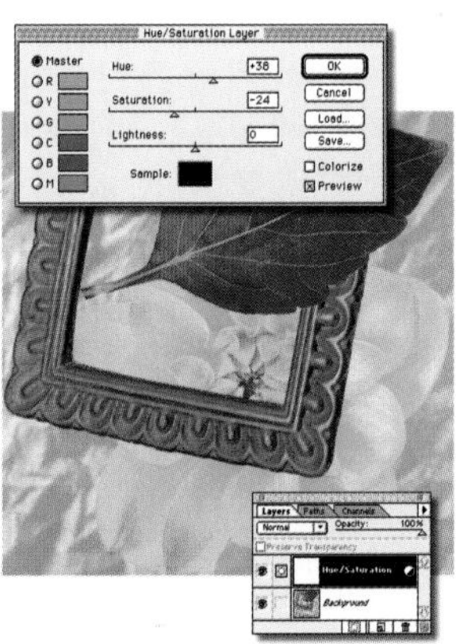

We added a Hue/Saturation Adjustment Layer to the image Still Life.PSD shown on the left, for example, in order to adjust the hue and saturation. Then by double-clicking on the Adjustment Layer in the Layers palette, we opened the Hue/Saturation dialog box for that layer to change the hue and saturation values. You can also turn off or delete an Adjustment Layer if you don't like its effect without permanently altering the image data.

These adjustments do not affect the hue and saturation of the original pixels of the image itself. This is very similar to adding gels to a light source to alter the appearance of a still life object, but not alter the color of the still life object itself.

09 8

Multiple Transforms

Image Degradation

Photographers are familiar with the effect successively duplicating a photograph has on image quality. Each time a dupe or internegative is made from an original color reversal film, there is degradation in the quality of the photograph. In the same way, transforms (such as resizing and reshaping) or adjustments (such as tone curves and color corrections) can degrade digital image quality.

A

B

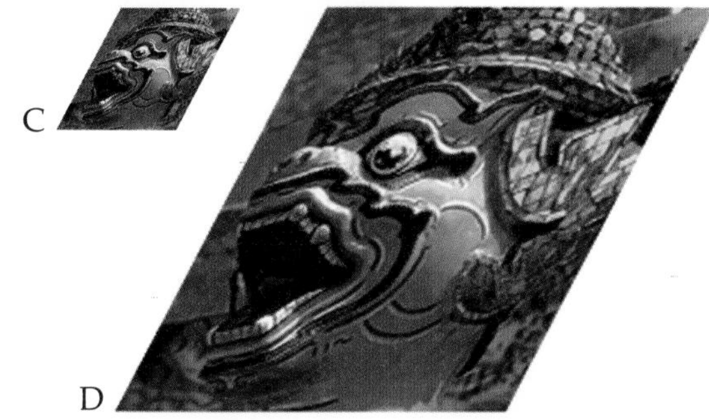

C

D

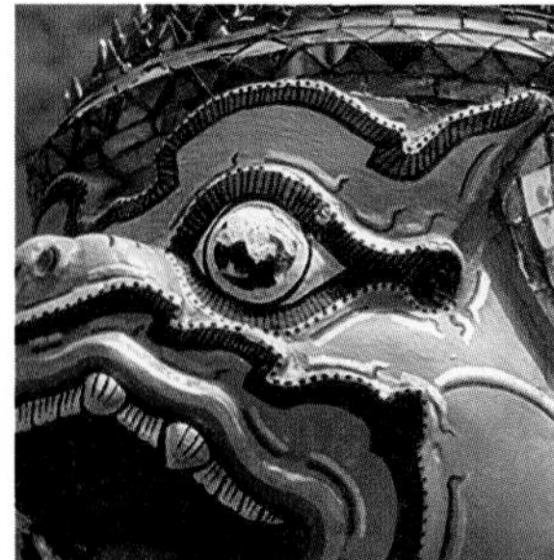

E

Transforms is a term that describes the manipulation of the shape or size of a digital image—this includes resizing, skewing, and rotating. Any time a shape is transformed in an imaging application, the new shape or size is interpolated, or resampled, resulting in a loss of image quality. If you make successive, multiple transformations such as enlarging an image 1.5 times and then rotating it 30 degrees, for example, careful steps need to be taken to maintain the quality of the image. The amount of care depends on whether you are using a direct pixel editing application or a deferred rendering application (please refer back in this chapter to descriptions of these terms).

Direct Pixel Editing Transforms

Each time the shape of an element is changed in a direct pixel editing application, the new shape is created through interpolation, which changes the number and arrangement of the image pixels. This can cause problems when you try to reshape or resize an image in several separate steps.

We reduced the image of the Thai deity (A), for example, to 25 percent of its original size (B). To do this, the data had to be interpolated so that of every four pixels, three were eliminated from each four-pixel group. The original tonal values assigned were averaged and assigned to the remaining pixel. Next, the image was skewed to form a rhombus. This required another interpolation of the image data to change the pixels in the horizontal plane (C).

Finally, the whole image was resized to about 80 percent of its original size (D). If you compare a detail from the final image with a detail of the original (E), you can clearly see how changing the shape and size of the image in three separate steps degraded the image quality.

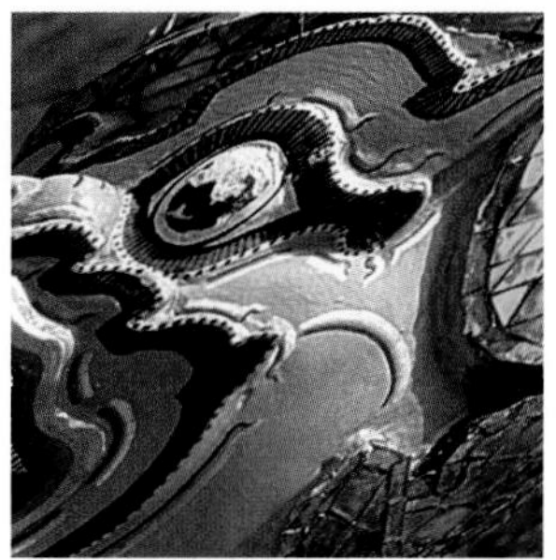

Free Transform in Photoshop 4.0

By using the Free Transform command added in Photoshop 4.0, the three transforms made in the last example can all be done in one step. Using Photoshop's Numeric Transform dialog box, for example, you can scale the image down to 80 percent of its original size and then skew it 40 degrees.

If you compare the detail between the original image and the transformed version, you can see that the quality of the image changed very little. If you were to go one step further, however, and alter the shape of this already transformed version, it would begin to exhibit the same loss of image quality as the image that was transformed in separate steps. The effect of multiple transforms is cumulative.

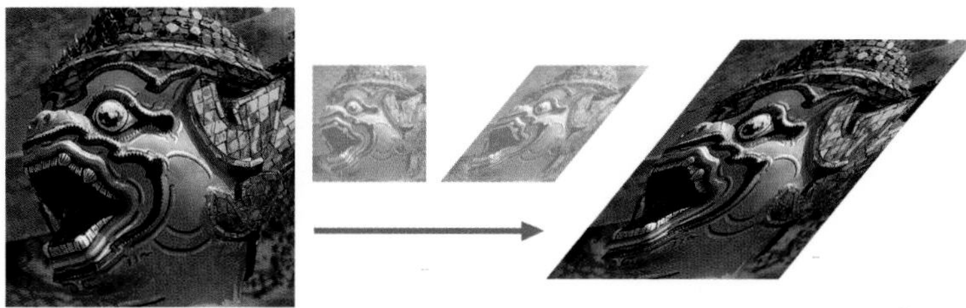

In a deferred rendering application such as Live Picture, the final transformed shape is the sum of all the steps taken to get there. During the rendering stage, these steps are bypassed and the final shape is calculated directly from the original image file.

Deferred Rendering Transforms

Multiple transforms and interpolation in deferred rendering applications are not done on the actual image data until the build, or rendering, stage. More importantly, because all transformations are saved in the edit-recording document, interpolation takes place only once. This means you can change your transforms as many times as you like without fear of serious degradation of image quality.

09 9

Plug-Ins

Plug-in modules are accessory pieces of software that expand the capabilities of your primary imaging application. Some plug-ins are supplied with an imaging application, some are supplied with peripherals such as scanners, and some are available as products developed by third parties. Plug-in functions range from special effects filters to special purpose production modules for automating or batch processing particular tasks.

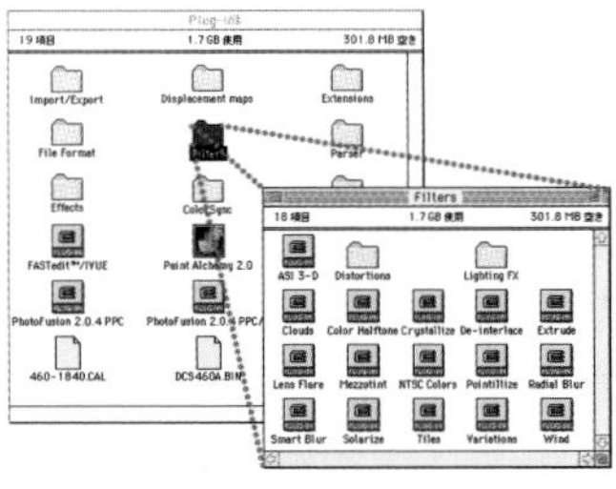

Plug-ins are usually placed inside a plug-in folder inside the application folder. Depending on the type of plug-in, it might be placed in a special folder, such as the Filters folder in Photoshop, which contains all of the special effects filters.

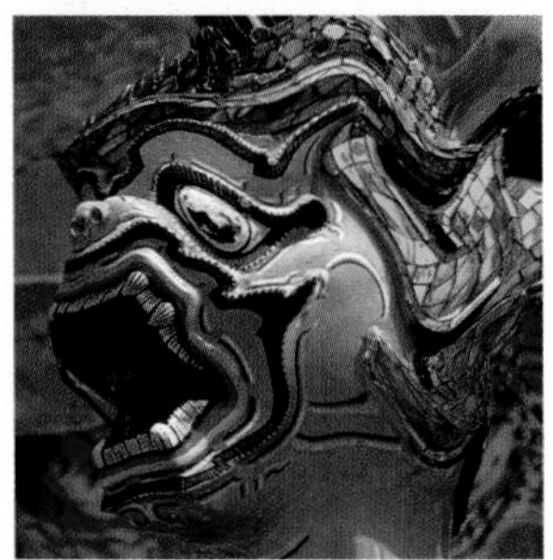

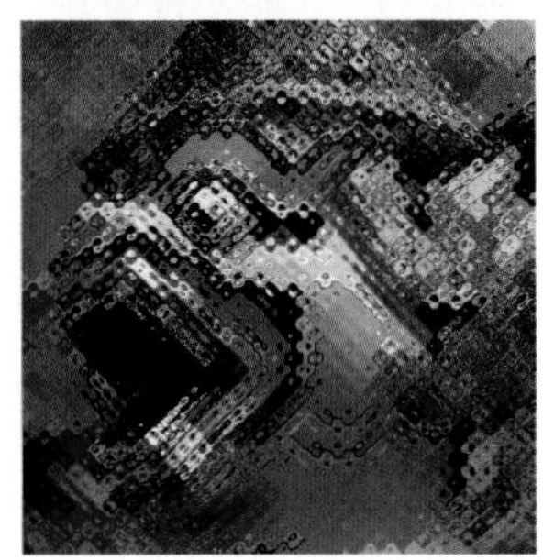

Photoshop special effects filters applied to the image of the Thai deity. Clockwise starting from the top left, the Lighting Effects, Rough Pastel, Wave, and Glass Distortion filters.

Special Effects Plug-Ins

Special effects filters can be used for everything from making a picture look painterly to adding lens flare, ghosting, or pond ripples. When a single special effects filter is simply applied to an image, the result often looks cheap and gimmicky. When multiple filters are used in specific, sequential combinations, however, you can achieve amazing results. Because there are numerous books about special effects filters, especially for Photoshop, we don't cover this in depth here.

Utility and Compatibility Plug-Ins

Utility plug-ins are used to add functions to image editing applications. This can include adding scanner drivers for scanner input or creating file format compatibility between one imaging application and another.

Input Device Drivers

Input devices, such as scanners and digital cameras, often rely on full-featured applications such as Photoshop as a host for acquiring images.

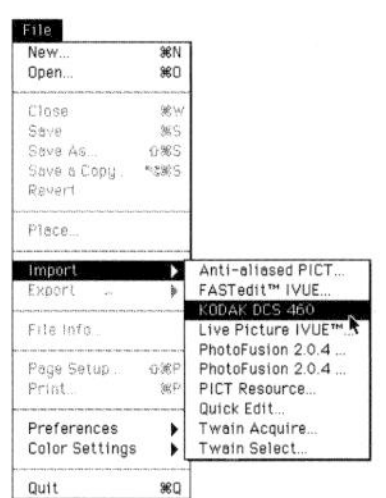

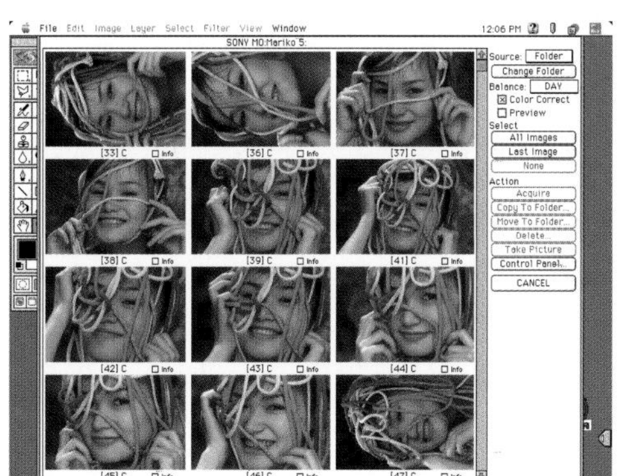

An example of an input device driver plug-in is the acquire plug-in for the Kodak DCS 460 digital still camera. When you select the File, Import, Kodak DCS 460 command, an interface appears that enables you to directly open images stored in the camera or to copy images from the camera to a hard disk.

Compatibility Plug-Ins

Compatibility plug-ins facilitate the transfer of images between applications that use different image formats or applications that have functions that are complementary to image editing applications.

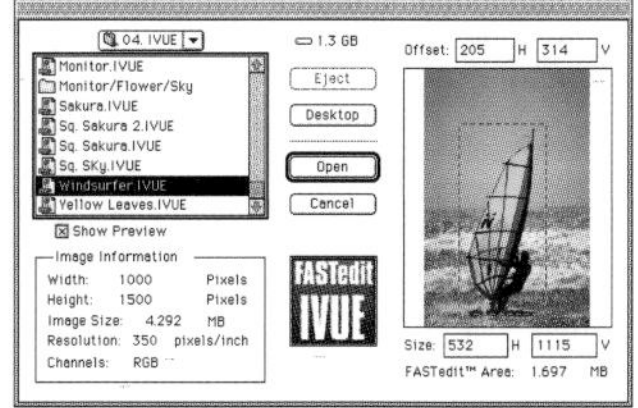

The FASTedit plug-in is used to select a portion of the IVUE format Windsurfer image.

The FASTedit / IVUE plug-in from Total Integration, Inc., for example, makes it possible to select and open a portion of a Live Picture IVUE format image for editing in Photoshop. Some edits, such as filters, can be done faster in Photoshop than in Live Picture. (To filter an image in Live Picture, you have to filter the entire layer, even if you only want the filter applied in a limited area.) Because it is possible to open only a portion of the Live Picture image in Photoshop, you can edit the portion in Photoshop and then reinsert it back into the IVUE image using the same plug-in.

The portion of the Windsurfer image selected using the FASTedit plug-in is opened and edited in Photoshop and then reinserted into the original IVUE file.

Another example is the Cumulus plug-in for Photoshop, which is described later in this chapter.

Third Party Plug-In Filters

Third party plug-ins are developed and distributed by software companies or individuals to enhance the operation of primary imaging applications such as Photoshop. Because many of the third party plug-ins have been designed to be used with Photoshop, newer applications such as Live Picture, Painter, and xRes have adopted the Photoshop plug-in structure so these third party plug-ins will be compatible. Numerous special effects plug-ins are available, ranging from texture-generating plug-ins to plug-ins dedicated to creating 3D shapes.

A

B

Texture Generating Plug-Ins

An example of a texture-generating plug-in is Xaos Tools Paint Alchemy 2. Paint Alchemy takes any scanned photograph and gives it a painterly texture. Paint Alchemy uses a 128×128-pixel grayscale "brush" (A) in conjunction with controls over brush coverage, stroke size, and color (B) to create painterly illustrations. You can select from a number of default grayscale images for brushes or use your own grayscale images for customized brushes.

3D Object Plug-Ins

3D modeling (creating 3D objects) and rendering (adding color and texture to shapes) applications are highly specialized tools. To use them well, you need extremely specialized knowledge and a wide range of skills. The time required to learn 3D applications is at least the same, if not more, than the time required to learn about digital photography. Most photographers might not have the time or desire to learn these 3D applications, but they might still occasionally want to add a 3D effect to an image.

The Series 2 3D plug-in filter from Andromeda Software operates in Photoshop and is used to wrap a Photoshop image around a basic 3D shape, such as a sphere, a box, a cylinder, or a plane.

These shapes are very basic and practical uses for them are limited. But if used in combination with separate programs capable of image distortion, these shapes can be used to create more complex 3D shapes.

As a step for distorting the dollar in Valis Group's Metaflo', the dollar was mapped to a cylindrical shape using the Series 2 3D plug-in. See the discussion of Metaflo' later in this chapter for more details.

Images created in 3D applications often look very synthetic. If you combine the Andromeda 3D filter and Metaflo' software (discussed later), however, you can create very realistic looking, imaginative 3D special effects.

Bluescreen Plug-In

The original photograph was taken in natural outdoor light against a blue backdrop using the Kodak DCS 460. There were three reasons for shooting the photograph outdoors—to assure uniform lighting against the backdrop, because the weather was wonderful, and because digital photographers are always looking for an excuse to get away from their computers...

Ultimatte's PhotoFusion plug-in is a dedicated plug-in for generating bluescreen (background cutout) masks for still photographs.

Photoshop's Color Range command or Live Picture's Image Silhouette command can be used to quickly generate masks that separate foreground objects from their backgrounds. The advantage of using a product such as PhotoFusion, however, is that it more accurately generates masks for difficult-to-mask areas, such as fine details (hair) or transparent objects (glass). This is especially true when these areas exist together in the same image. In Photoshop or Live Picture, for example, it would be nearly impossible to automatically mask all the levels of detail and transparency that exist in the photograph on the left with the glass vase and the wispy plant.

The controls in PhotoFusion use special algorithms to quickly generate a mask based on selected areas of the blue background, as shown to the left. This is exactly the same technology used in the movie and TV industry. In fact, PhotoFusion is likely the only piece of Macintosh software ever to be awarded an Oscar.

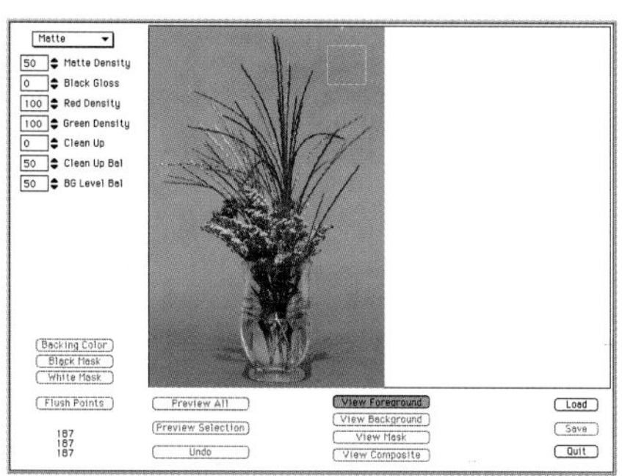

The first step in PhotoFusion is to extract the blue background (shown in the yellow square). The mask is created based on the average RGB values in this extraction area.

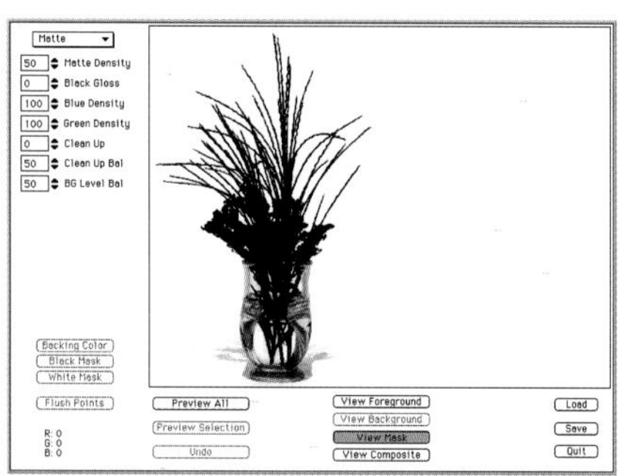

After the initial mask is generated, controls are used to tweak the mask, as shown on the left. The Matte and Black Gloss controls affect the density of the mask, for example, while the various Flare controls help suppress the amount of blue spill (fringe) that exists along the edges of the foreground object.

After fine-tuning the adjustments, we saved the image with the mask created in PhotoFusion. Next, we placed the image against a white background to judge the quality of the mask. If you look at the magnified view shown on the left, you can see that almost no matte lines, fringe pixels, or blue spill were copied from the original blue background.

The final image, with the mask created in PhotoFusion, was composited against a new blue sky background.

PhotoFusion won't necessarily generate a perfect mask every time with a single click of the mouse. Many potential problems can be avoided, however, if you plan the shoot carefully, making sure the bluescreen background is properly lit. This is because the more even the blue background, the easier the masking task.

In order to achieve the best results, you need to understand how the light will hit your subject as well as understand the effect of flare and shadow. You also need to know how to do touch-ups on the image and the mask before and after using PhotoFusion.

The glass vase was touched up prior to using PhotoFusion, for example, to make sure there were enough highlights in the glass to prevent it from becoming totally invisible. Also, after we made the mask in PhotoFusion, we enhanced the glass further in the composite by using Hue/Saturation in Adjustment Layer to remove even more blue from the glass and the shadow. We also used the Multiply blend mode to make two layers of the same image, which created the effect of "thickening" the look of the glass.

09 10

Special Effect Modules

Up to now we have focused upon the standard image editing capabilities of our four full-featured image editing applications, but each of them also offers its own special effects capabilities.

Photoshop has a very complete set of special effects filters, many of which are unique to Photoshop (such as the Distort-Displace filter, about which an entire book could be written). Live Picture has the Image Distortion layer, which could be said to be the most powerful means of altering the shape of an image in the world. And xRes includes a Texture Palette for painting in the image or the mask with special textures.

A

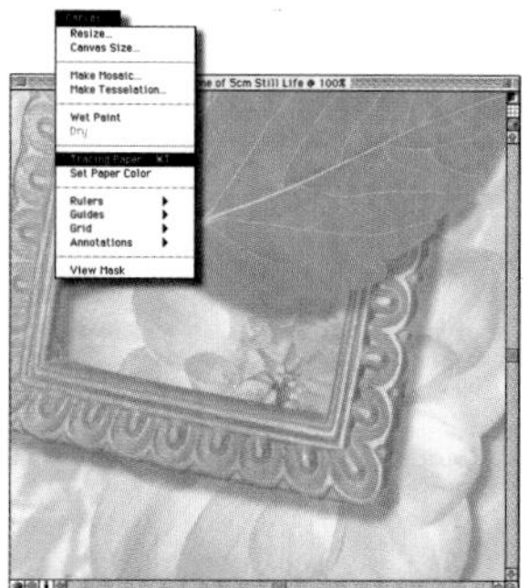

B

In addition to the standard image-editing applications, it is a good idea to add special effects applications such as Painter and Metaflo' to your digital photography repertoire.

NOTE

In addition to the variety of editing applications for photographic images, there is an entire realm of related applications—2D vector-based drawing programs, 3D modeling and rendering programs, and animation programs—which can be integrated into the photographer's digital toolbox. Most of the data created in these applications can be converted into all-purpose file formats such as TIFF, EPS, or PICT and edited in all the applications we discuss in this book. Information concerning how to incorporate artwork from these applications is available in User Guides or other third-party books on the market.

Painter

In the beginning of this chapter, we grouped Painter among the other full-featured image-editing applications because it has the standard features needed to manipulate digital photographs—layers, masking, blending modes, and transform tools. Painter makes a special appearance here in the Special Effects section, however, because it contains dozens of unique special effects tools that a photographer might find useful. These include Clone and Tracing Paper, Apply Surface Texture, and the Image Hose.

Clone with Tracing Paper

Painter provides the capability to create a version of the photograph that looks hand-painted, using the tracing paper function.

For example, we turned the StillLife.RIF photomontage (A) into an impressionistic painting. First we use the File, Clone command to create a separate cloning file from the original. After selecting the entire image and deleting it, we turned on the Tracing Paper command to display a ghosted view of the original image (B).

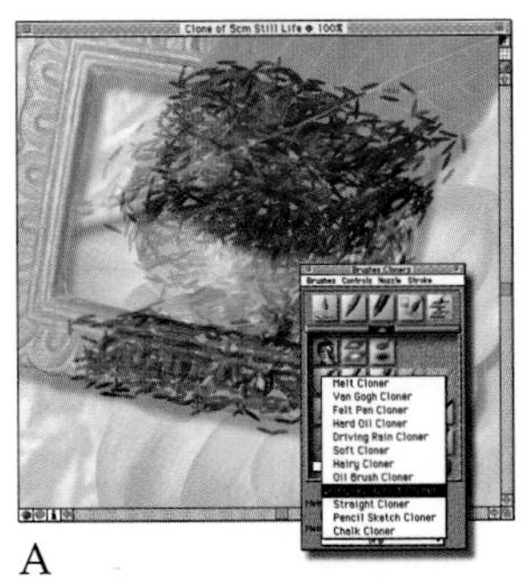

A

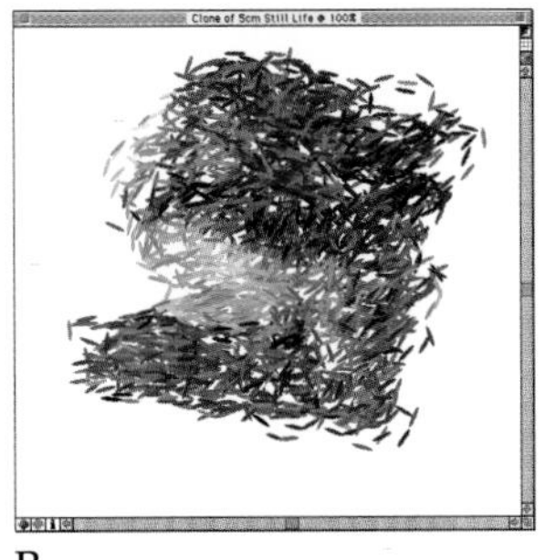
B

Using the ghosted image as a reference, we added paint strokes by hand using the Brush Palette, Cloners, Impressionist Cloner tool (A). When the tracing paper view was turned off, only the paint strokes were visible (B).

We could have completed this painted image by hand, stroke by stroke. In this case, however, we automated the strokes using the Record Stroke and Auto Playback functions from the Brush Palette to paint the final image.

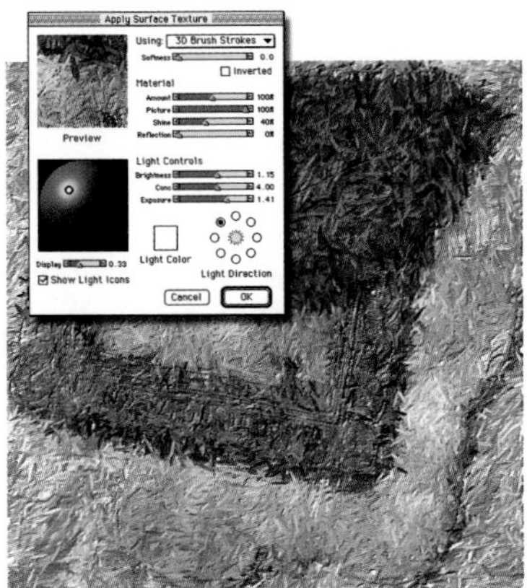

Apply Surface Texture

A surface texture can be added to images using Painter's Apply Surface Texture effect. We used the Apply Surface Texture command on the painted image created in the previous explanation, shown on the left. This simulated the application of realistic, three-dimensional brush strokes on a canvas.

Image Hose

In addition to standard paint brushes, Painter also has the Image Hose, which is a special effect function that sprays a portion of an image over the canvas like water.

The Image Hose paints with images, meaning that any photograph, or series of photographs, can be made into a paint brush style. The pattern of flowers on this pair of Dr. Martins children's boots, for example, became the basis for an all-digital photographic project.

First, we photographed the boot using a Leaf DCB II digital camera back. Then we masked the boot out of the background using Photoshop.

Next, we selected individual flowers from the boot (see left), copied each of them into a new file, and created a mask for each in Channel #4. These masks are used to mask the flower in Painter.

NOTE

In Painter's default setting for mask effects, the black portion of the mask indicates the visible, unmasked portion of the image, and the white portion represents the protected portion of the image. This is the reverse of Photoshop.

Then we created a new file and laid the flowers and their masks out in a grid. We saved this file in Photoshop format and then opened it in Painter.

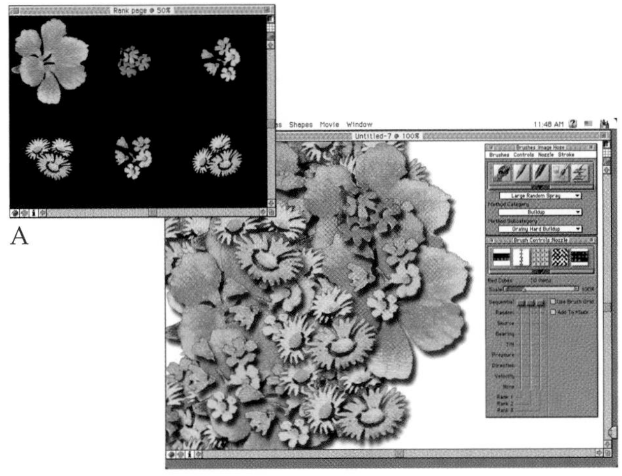

In Painter, the grid of flowers was defined and then loaded as a Nozzle for the Image Hose (A). Then, when we made strokes inside the image window with the Image Hose, the "spray" of flowers from the Nozzle created a background on the canvas (B).

NOTE

This is a very simplified explanation of a process that involves a number of intricate steps. Refer to "Image Hose" in the Painter User Guide for more information.

We returned to Photoshop and composited the boot in a layer over the flower background. Additional steps included adding dappled light and blur, as well as the table shadow, to give the image dimension.

Valis Group's Metaflo'

Metaflo' performs a specific task, which is to stretch, bend, warp, twist, squeeze, and morph images in every imaginable way. The most straightforward use of Metaflo' is to shape or contort a single object. But the real strength—and exciting potential—of Metaflo' is how it can be used to warp one photograph to the shape and size of an object in another photograph. To demonstrate the basic concept, we shaped a dollar bill and then composited it onto a toothpaste tube.

We began the project by painting the toothpaste tube white and photographing it with a Kodak DCS 460 digital camera.

In Photoshop, we opened the dollar from a Photo CD scan and saved it as a PICT file. Next, we opened the dollar in Metaflo'. Then, using the Place command, we placed the toothpaste tube in a layer above the dollar. The view of the toothpaste tube was changed to 50 percent opacity in the layers palette so that the relationship between the two objects to each other could be easily seen.

NOTE

Had the toothpaste tube been more rounded instead of flattened, it would've been necessary to give the dollar a more cylindrical shape to give it the appearance of wrapping around the tube. For this purpose, first wrapping the dollar around a cylinder in Andromeda 3D would help.

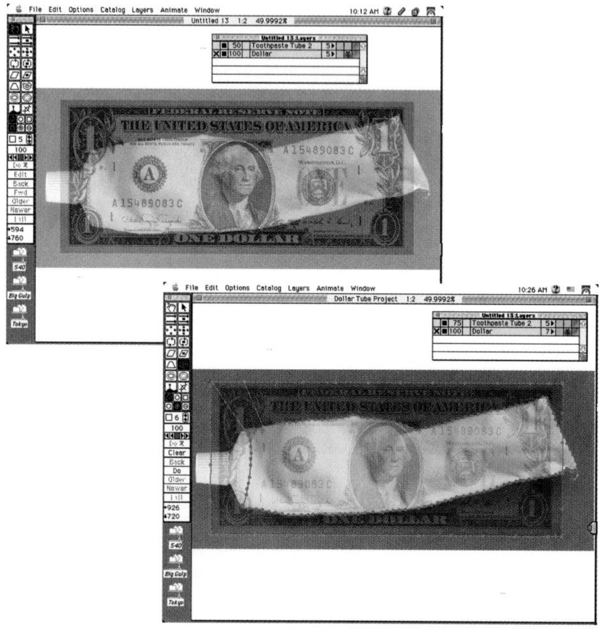

Preparing an image to warp to the shape and size of another image is done in two stages. First, we outlined the image to be distorted using the Reshape tool. This appears here as a red outline of the dollar. Next, we outlined the image that served as the basis for the distortion shape. This appears as a magenta outline of the toothpaste tube.

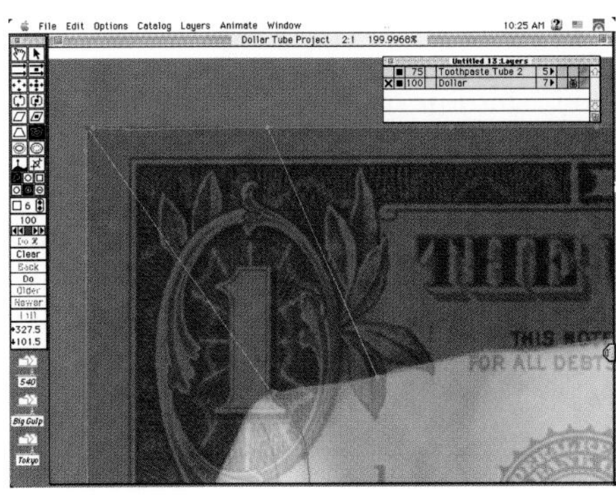

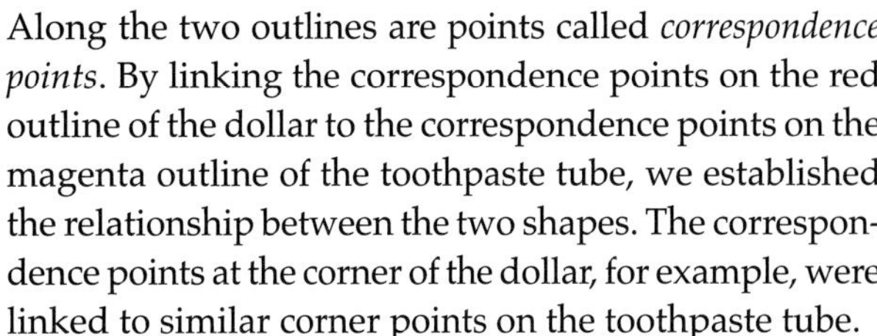

Along the two outlines are points called *correspondence points*. By linking the correspondence points on the red outline of the dollar to the correspondence points on the magenta outline of the toothpaste tube, we established the relationship between the two shapes. The correspondence points at the corner of the dollar, for example, were linked to similar corner points on the toothpaste tube.

We maintained precise control over which points of the dollar were warped to specific parts of the toothpaste tube by using many points along the lines. The accuracy of the distortion improved as the number of correspondence points increased.

NOTE

For purposes of explanation, the number of points have been exagerrated in order to illustrate why certain parts of one shape will conform to parts of another shape. In reality, Metaflo' does an excellent job by adjusting the shape of the red line to the shape of the magenta line using a minimum number of correspondence points

Next, we clicked on the Go command on the Tool Palette, and Metaflo' displayed a preview of the distortion. At this point, the distortion settings and points can be edited and tweaked until you have the desired results. Finally, the image was rendered and saved in TIFF format for use in Photoshop.

We made the final composite in Photoshop. Because the toothpaste tube was painted white, it was possible to use its highlights and shadows to give dimension to the composite. This was done in a multi-layered composite of the dollar, using a combination of Multiply and Overlay modes. The Multiply mode made the shadows of the toothpaste tube visible on the dollar surface, but the overall composite was too dark. So we made a duplicate layer of the dollar in Screen mode to help lighten the effects of the Multiply blend mode. Then we adjusted the overall contrast using Curves in an Adjustment Layer.

09 11 Utility Applications

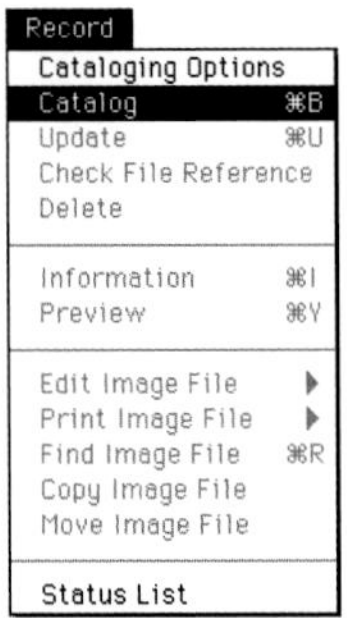

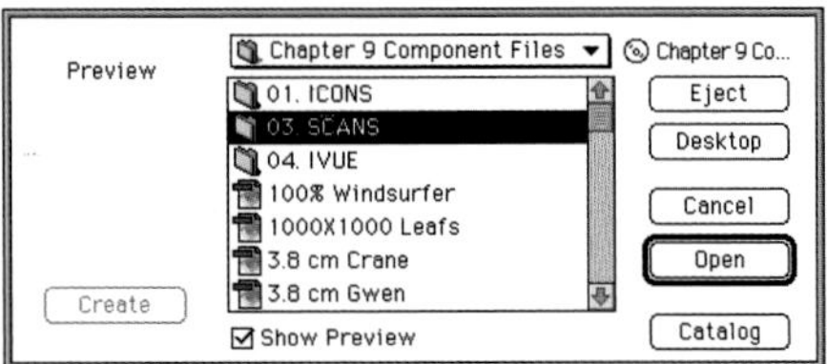

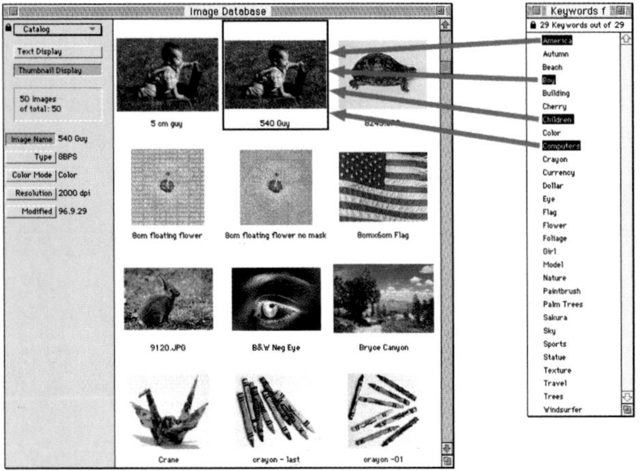

Image Management

For most photographers, image management means storing slides in slide sleeves and tucking them away in file drawers. More meticulous photographers might have ways of cataloging and keeping track of thousands of photographs for quick retrieval.

In digital photography, the need for a way to manage image data is equally, if not more, crucial than in traditional photography.

Cumulus Image Database

Without organizational software, digital images can't be as easily or quickly searched and viewed as slides or negatives. Therefore, image management applications, such as Cumulus from Canto, have been designed to assist in this task.

You can create a new image database in Cumulus by first selecting the File, New command. Then enter a Catalog into the new database by using the Record, Catalog command and select the folder that contains your images.

In Cumulus, groups of images in the database are called a *catalog*. As you create the catalog, Cumulus builds a low resolution file of each image called a *thumbnail*. The thumbnails can be viewed in the administration window.

The next step is to add keywords to the database to assist searching for images. First, you enter a list of keywords specific to the catalog that is open. Then you assign the keywords to the images by clicking and dragging them onto the image thumbnail.

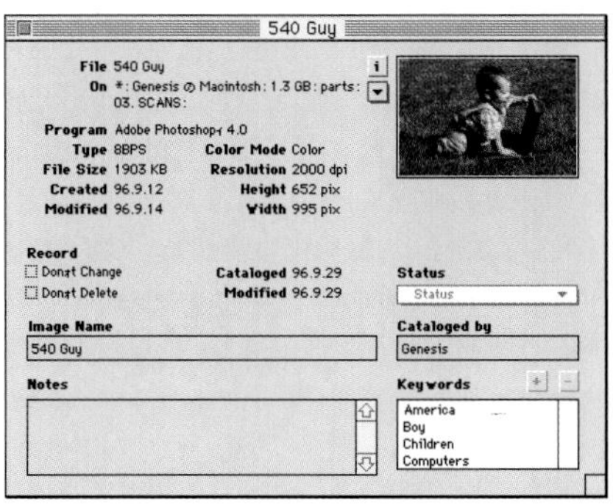

Select a thumbnail and use the Record, Info command to open a dialog box containing information about that image. This information includes the keywords assigned to the image, the file size, the name of the software the image was created in, as well as the name of the disk and folder where the image is located.

After you have created image catalogs, you can search for images using a wide range of criteria, from keyword searches to creation date to file size.

Databases can be created for image catalogs that are located not only on internal drives, but also on remote servers or removable media (MOs, Jaz disks, or CD-ROMs). A catalog, for example, can be created for a group of several hundred scans that have been recorded onto a CD-ROM. If you conduct a search later on and Cumulus finds an image that is stored on the CD-ROM, it will instruct you to insert the necessary disk.

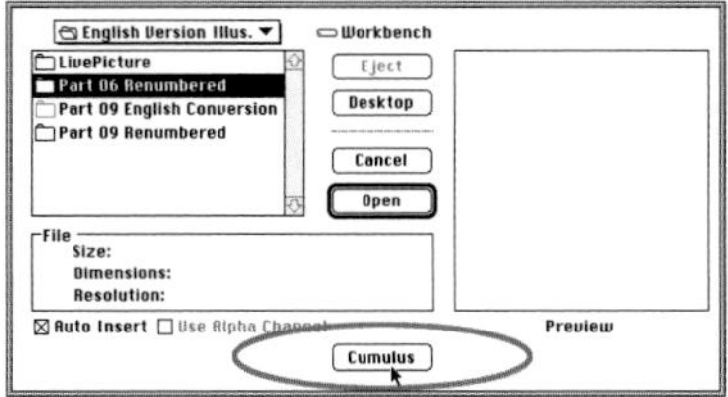

Cumulus Compatibility

Cumulus is very compatible with applications such as Photoshop and Live Picture. For example, Cumulus can be opened through Photoshop's Import menu or Live Picture's Image Insertion command. Images found as the result of a search can then be opened directly in either Photoshop or Live picture.

NOTE

Cumulus is available in two versions, one for single computer use (Cumulus) and another for multiple computers connected on a network (Cumulus Network). Cumulus Network makes it very easy to take large image files stored on the computer connected to a studio digital camera and view them on different computers for tasks such as selecting cuts for a particular project.

Automated Image Processing Software

As you proceed with your image editing, you will discover that you do some tasks repeatedly. You might have 120 frames taken with a digital camera that all need to be rotated 90 degrees clockwise, for example, or you might need to convert all your composited images from RGB to CMYK. These are repetitive tasks that can be carried out by the computer in the absence of a human life form.

Many software modules are available to automate tasks like this. Here we introduce a few of them, all of which run on the Macintosh.

Automated Hue and Saturation Adjustment

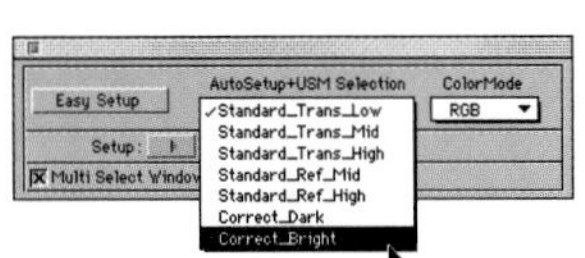

Left: The ColorScope Pro work window.
Top: You can achieve the desired correction by selecting standard specifications from the pop-up menu, such as brighten or leave as is. Finer adjustment is possible with tone curve and sharpness controls.

Commercial photographers shooting product photos for inserts or mail-order catalogs might shoot hundreds of frames and need to keep the hue and saturation for all of them consistent for output on a printed page. In this situation, if each photograph had to be adjusted one at a time in Photoshop or another full-featured application, it would take an enormous amount of time.

Software such as ColorScope Pro from Dainippon Screen or ColorPro from Binuscan enable you to automate basic color correction for specific problems such as slight underexposure or overexposure, color cast, or incorrect gray balance. Because they also perform automatic RGB to CMYK conversion, you can convert large quantities of digital camera RGB data into CMYK data without human intervention.

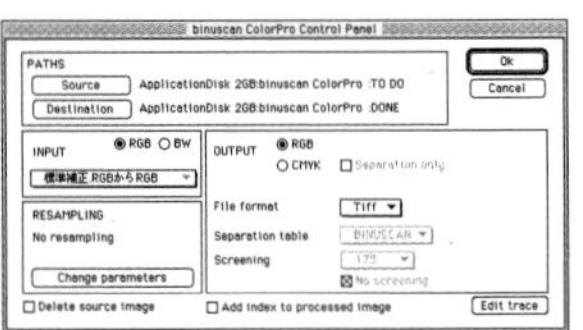

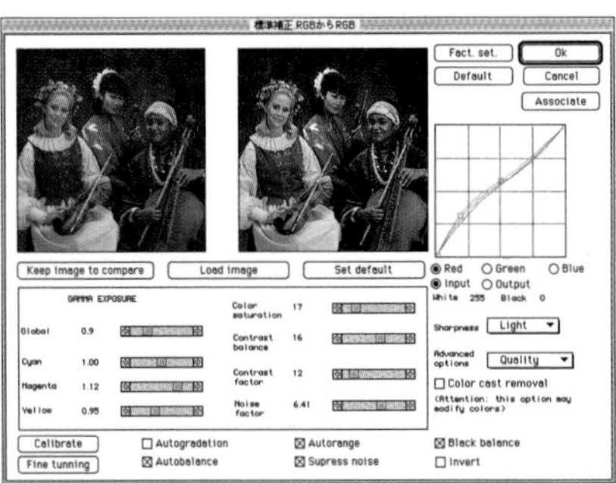

Top: The ColorPro main dialog box. You can call up preset correction parameters, specify folders for saving correction results, and so on.
Right: The Options dialog box. You can set up more finely tuned adjustments. It is necessary to define characteristics of images that are underexposed, and so on.

Left: Original image. Right: Results of automated adjustment. Correction parameters for underexposed images were specified in ColorPro. The orange cast from the sunset was suppressed and the lack of shadow tonality was corrected.

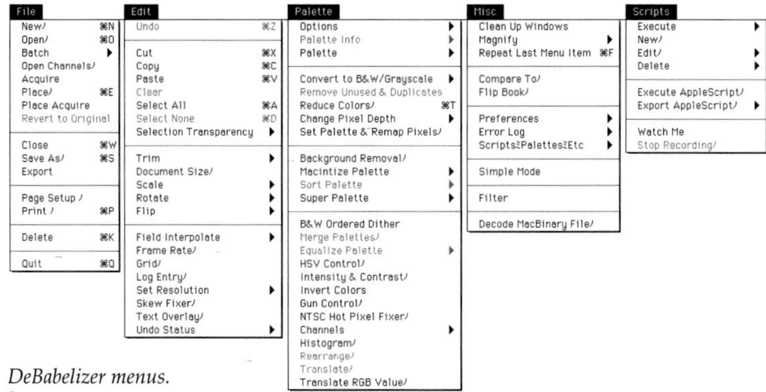

DeBabelizer menus.

DeBabelizer offers almost all of the available specialized image-correction functions, as shown in the slightly intimidating technical terminology in its menus. After you press Record, all operations are recorded in a log file. Debabelizer is also capable of batch processing, which applies the exact same set of operations to each file.

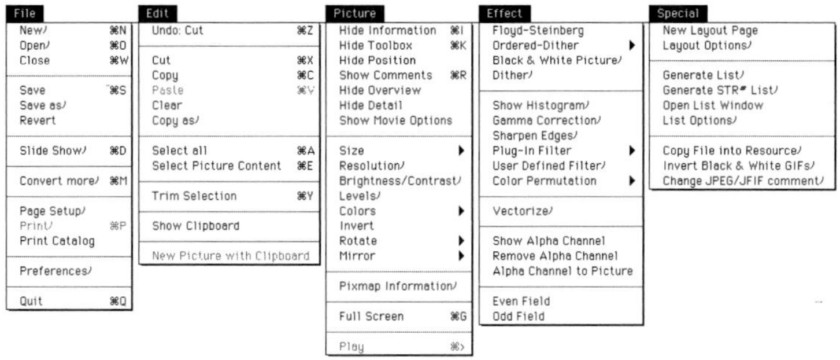

Graphic Converter menus.

Graphic Converter, like DeBabelizer, is capable of batch processing. It also offers some simple paint functions, color correction for small image files, and a variety of file conversions.

Automated File Format Conversion

Most images posted on Internet home pages are small—only around 300×300 pixels—but the same images created for printed output are very large—often more than thousands of pixels square. Graphic Converter, shareware created by Thorsten Lemke, and DeBabelizer from Equilibrium Technologies, are two applications capable of interpolating images created for printed output so that they can be posted on the Internet. They are also capable of automatically converting files into the GIF or JPEG file formats most often used on Internet pages, and they can perform a wide range of color corrections as well. Images placed in a specified folder are converted and then saved in another folder.

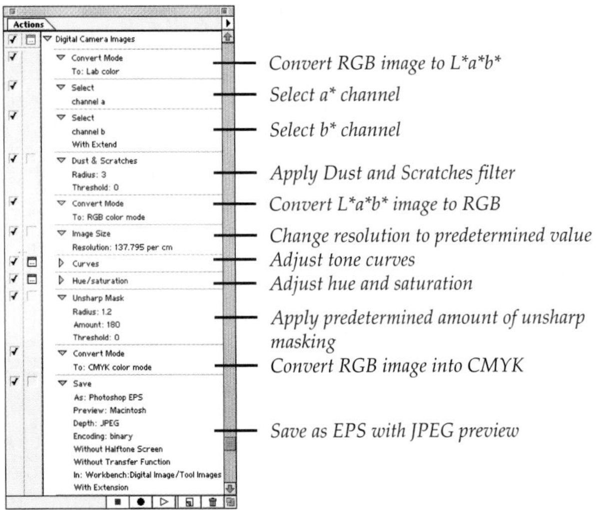

An example of an Actions (automated processing) palette called "Optimized for Digital Cameras."

Automated Processing in Photoshop 4.0

Photoshop 4.0 offers automated processing through its Actions palette, which enables you to freely set up sequences of automated processing.

The Actions palette enables you to set up a long sequence of actions so that a group of images in a specified folder will each be automatically processed with exactly the same sequence of operations. A typical sequence might be: "Open 48-bit RGB images taken with the Scitex Leaf DCB II digital camera, apply a tone curve to them to achieve a set amount of brightness, convert them into 24-bit images, trim them, enlarge them by 150 percent, apply unsharp masking, convert them to CMYK, and save them."

Or if you want to be able to see the images during any one of these steps (say, for trimming), you can specify a standby at that point and then work as you need to.

Because most of its commands can be automated and it allows a lot of flexibility, Photoshop is necessary for the prepress industry and others who process large quantities of data.

chapter 10

Contributing Artist Profiles

Katrin Eismann & John McIntosh

Katrin Eismann, a photoimaging artist and educator, founded PRAXIS Digital Solutions in May 1992. PRAXIS offers educational and consulting services for professional photographers, commercial labs, and educational institutions that seek to incorporate digital imaging technology into their businesses, fine art, or curriculum.

Eismann's in-depth knowledge of digital imaging can be traced back to the Rochester Institute of Technology where she graduated with a Bachelor of Fine Arts degree in photography, augmented with a concentration in electronic still imaging. She was one of the first RIT graduates to have completed the program with a concentration in electronic still imaging. Upon graduation, she played a significant role in the development of the Kodak Center for Creative Imaging, where she eventually became Director of Education.

A year later, John McIntosh joined PRAXIS. McIntosh holds a Master of Fine Arts degree in photography from Yale University. John's photography and sculpture has been exhibited throughout the United States, and his work is in the permanent collections of the Corcoran Gallery of Art in Washington, D.C. and the Menil Collection in Houston, Texas. John is an aggressive and distinguished educator, responsible for the design and implementation of degree programs in Photography, Digital Imaging, and most recently in Digital Media Studies. Recently, John was named the Director of Technology Programs at the American Film Institute in Los Angeles, California.

Together, Eismann and McIntosh form an internationally renowned team as educators, consultants, and evangelists in many aspects of digital photography, ranging from fine art digital imaging to the incorporation of digital photography technologies into emerging commercial businesses.

PRAXIS has provided consulting services to the biggest companies in the industry, including Eastman Kodak, Apple Computer, Adobe Systems, and Time-Life, Inc. Eismann and McIntosh are also regular instructors and lecturers for universities and professional associations, such as the Photo Marketing Association, Professional Photography Association, and World Press Photo.

In 1994, Eismann and McIntosh were recruited to create a presentation and printed support materials required to introduce the landmark Kodak Professional DCS 460 digital camera system at Photokina (Cologne, Germany). The presentation, which highlighted the advantages and disadvantages of silver, digital, and hybrid imaging, generated tremendous press attention for Kodak, including numerous German national TV and radio spots.

Additional international programs produced by PRAXIS include presentations and hands-on workshops at Recontre '95 in Arles, France; Digital Photography in Photo Journalism presentations and seminars at the World Press Photo Masters Class in Amsterdam (1995) and Rotterdam (1996); and the Kodak Imaging By All Means Tour in the Asian Pacific region (Eismann was assisted on the Imaging By All Means Tour by Essentials co-author, Russell Sparkman). All photos and illustrations courtesy of Katrin Eismann & John McIntosh.

Katrin Eismann & John McIntosh
PRAXIS Digital Solutions
3400 Ben Lomond Pl. #218
Los Angeles, CA 90027
Tel. 213-663-5626
praxistwo@aol.com

Ann Elliott Cutting

Prior to working with digital photography tools, Ann Cutting had developed a personal style of mostly B&W photography for the various advertising, editorial, and annual report assignments that she was receiving. It was a style she didn't feel she had to let go of simply because she was working digitally.

"I tend to do mostly editorial and annual report assignments with the computer," Cutting explains, "and for the jobs that are done digitally, I'm using layers almost as double exposures and adding wilder colors. Still, I dislike making the images look too digital. I try to keep my style, and I'm happy when people aren't sure whether the image was created in camera or on the computer."

Cutting first began offering a digital version of her style of photography in 1992. At the time, she recalls, the biggest obstacle to convincing clients to accept digital was that they needed to have LVT film output, "which cost a lot of money then." In addition, it took some work to convince clients that the resolution of the image would be what they needed for their projects.

After Cutting was able to overcome these obstacles, she found the task of selling the creative benefits of digital photography too easy. "For example," she adds, "some annual reports that were very conceptual were easier to solve digitally." This ability to solve conceptual image challenges through the use of digital photography has meant that her largest market for digital images has been for editorial and annual report assignments.

Although Cutting has been happy with the style of digital photography that she created based on her traditional style of photography, she says that she's looking forward to enlarging her repertoire by creating new styles to offer clients. "The digital tools are a whole new way to create images that I've hardly tapped," she explains, "this means that I'm still always learning." All photos and illustrations courtesy of Ann Elliott Cutting.

Cutting shares a Pasadena, CA photo studio with another photographer. The 2700-sq.-ft. studio includes a loft and a shooting space.

Cutting keeps her digital imaging workstation, a Quadra 900 with 128 MB RAM, in the loft above the shooting space. She has several gigabytes of hard disk storage, plus Iomega Zip and Jaz drives for removable media. For input, she uses an Agfa Arcus flatbed scanner with transparency adaptor.

Next, in Photoshop, Cutting added a green to blue gradation using the Color blend mode setting for the Gradation tool.

Cutting built up her image layer by layer, using combinations of heavily feathered selections, blurred masks and Photoshop blend modes to create the final image with a look and feel of multiple exposure photograph.

Ann Cutting begins many of her digital photo-illustrations as black and white photographs. For this magazine cover assignment, she started by photographing sheets of paper on Polaroid Type 55 4×5 film. The contrasty lighting and shallow depth of field that Cutting uses for her digital work is very similar to her style of straight, non-digital black and white photography.

Ann Elliott Cutting
188 South Delacey Ave.
Pasadena, CA 91105
Tel. 818-440-1974
http://www.cutting.com/
E-mail: ann@cutting.com

Andy Darlow

The emergence of digital photography, particularly the use of digital cameras, means that two previously distinct components of the graphic arts industry—photography and electronic prepress—are converging. Prepress houses have, in fact, played a leading role in the acceptance of digital cameras for a wide range of photography assignments, ranging from catalogs to advertising.

Many prepress houses are hiring full-time photographers to manage their internal digital photography operations. This is the hat that Andy Darlow wears at Unidigital/Cardinal Corporation in New York, New York.

Darlow was working as a production assistant in the company's Cactus large-format digital printing division at Cardinal Communications Group (now Unidigital/Cardinal Corporation) when the company took on a project that would require the use of a digital camera. They rented a Leaf DCB digital camera, a Hasselblad, and a Macintosh Quadra 950 computer to do the job.

"We completed the entire project in a very short time frame," recalls Darlow, "at a quality level far exceeding our expectations. This cemented my belief that digital photography was truly the best way to capture images for a wide range of photographic projects."

At the same time that Darlow is an enthusiastic proponent of digital photography, he is also pragmatic about the difficulties involved, especially to the part of the work that relates to prepress functions. "Due to the responsibility involved with capturing images without film," he explains, "a photographer must be not just an image maker, but a retoucher and a prepress color expert as well."

For example, he points out, numerous output options contribute to a different visual representation of the same image data. Therefore, "fairly substantial time for proper calibration of monitors to output devices is required." For this reason, Darlow suggests, digital cameras are best used either within a graphic-arts-related company or by a photographer who develops a strong relationship with such a company.

Challenges notwithstanding, Darlow believes that "digital photography can be very profitable if undertaken with a thorough knowledge of photography, digital imaging, prepress and printing." All photos and illustrations courtesy of Andy Darlow.

Andy Darlow shot this original photograph on 4×5 film as a test image for a candy manufacturer's catalog. The client was happy with the photograph, and Unidigital/Cardinal was given the account to produce the catalogs for 15 different categories of chocolates. The client was so satisfied with this particular photograph that they wanted to use it. The problem was that several products had been left out of the test shot.

Darlow discussed solutions with the president of the manufacturer. It was decided that, rather than reshoot the entire photograph, the missing products would be photographed as separate elements and composited into a scan of the original. Darlow shot the plate of candy and the additional boxes of chocolate using the Leaf DCB digital camera, paying careful attention to match the lighting and camera angle used for the original photograph.

The process of shooting the individual elements and compositing them seamlessly into a single image involved considerable trial and error. This process, says Darlow, was made easier by the immediate access to photographs created with the digital camera. In the final composite, it's impossible to tell that the elements were photographed separately.

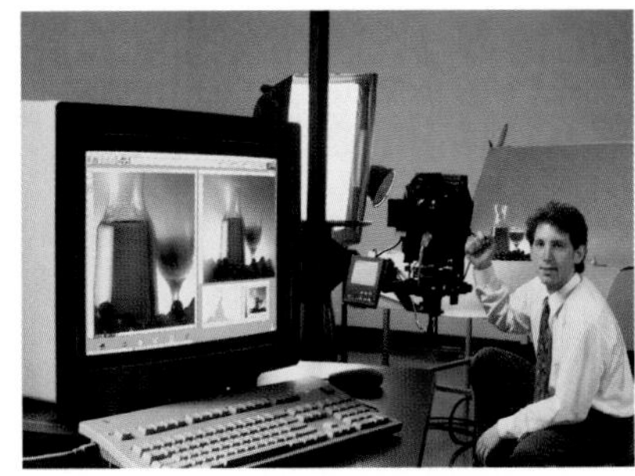

Within the photo studio at Unidigital/Cardinal are two systems. The Leaf DCB, mounted on a Sinar P2 4×5 view camera, is attached to a Macintosh 840AV, with 128 MB RAM and a 2 GB hard drive. The second system, which clients can use to drop photos into a layout during a shooting session, is a Power Mac 7100. According to Darlow, there are at least 10 more Power Macintosh systems within Unidigital/Cardinal, all connected by Ethernet.

Andy Darlow
Unidigital/Cardinal Corporation
545 West 45th Street
NY, NY 10036
(212) 489-1717
andy@andydarlow.com
www.andydarlow.com

John Lund

Like many commercial photographers, John Lund was continually on the watch for some new approach—some new look—to add to his portfolio. For a time, he experimented with creating in-camera montages, and to his later amazement, began to receive assignments based on the work.

"It's one thing to create in-camera montages for yourself, or for your portfolio," he admits. "It's another story to be able to do it for an art director."

At about the same time he was struggling to create in-camera montages on demand, someone recommended he go see a demo of "something called Photoshop." "It must've been in late 1990 when I called Adobe to arrange for a demo," recalls Lund, adding that at the time "they were glad to meet a photographer who wasn't hostile."

Soon after the demo, Lund bought his first Mac, a used Mac II, with 8 MB of RAM, which he immediately upgraded to 32 MB. Almost right away, Lund got work for his computer-based images. "I started taking assignments before I probably should have been doing actual jobs," he says. "The deadlines were on, and I was spending 20 hours a day on the machine."

Dealing with the computers and their idiosyncracies is an unexpected reality of working digitally, Lund admits. "We have five computers," he explains, "so take the number of problems you can have on one system and multiply it by five." Lund is quick to point out, however, that the technical headaches are "counterbalanced by being able to create virtually anything that I want."

Lund and his studio, TeamDigital, have been particularly successful creating imaginative digital photographs for stock sales. "We all sit around the studio and if one person uses an idiom, such as 'money doesn't grow on trees,'" he explains, "another person will suggest we make a stock image of the idea." In stock photo sales alone, Lund confides, "we're now averaging about $20,000 per month in royalties." All photos and illustrations courtesy of John Lund.

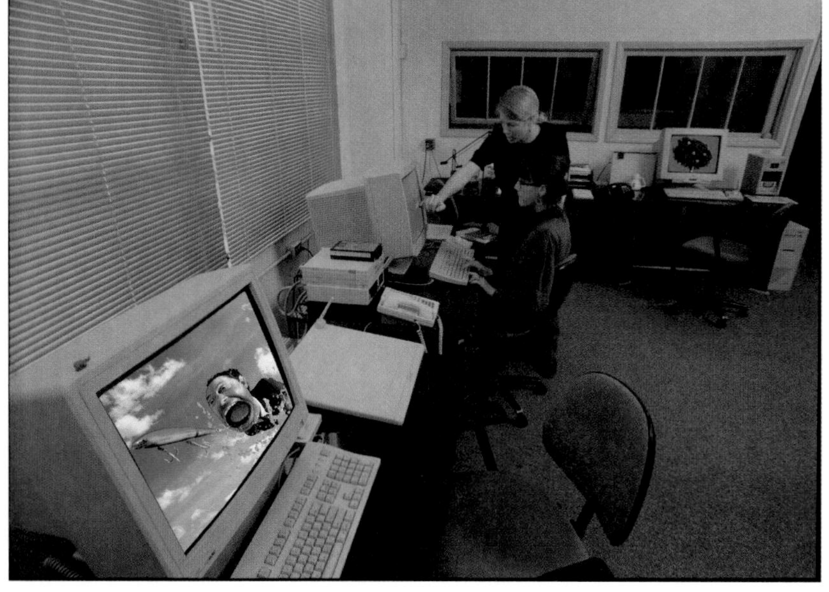

The TeamDigital studio has three full-time employees, including John Lund and his twin brother, Bill. Pictured here is the third employee, Lauren Burke (standing), working with an intern. The studio has four imaging workstations, including a Daystar Genesis 528 and three Quadra 950s, each with a Daystar Power Pro card. To move data between the systems, Lund uses Nomadic modular hard drives that can be moved easily between systems without shutting down and rebooting. For input, TeamDigital uses a Scanmate 5000 drumscanner and a Leaf DCB digital camera back. A Macintosh IIfx, with 80 MB of RAM, is dedicated to the Leaf DCB.

The Lure

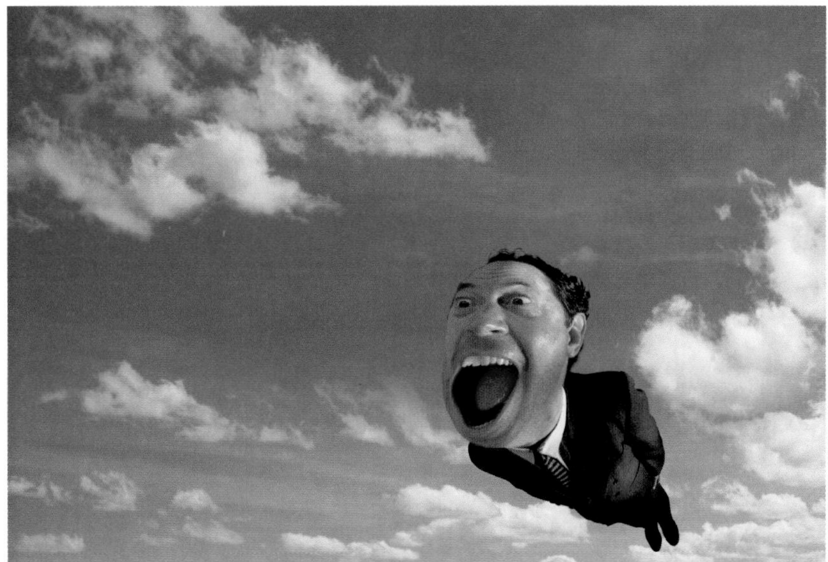

Lund photographed the male model with a Hasselblad on Kodak EPP film. The sky was photographed using a Fuji Panorama Camera on Kodal EPP. After scans were made on a drum scanner, the photo of the man was inserted into Live Picture as an Image Distortion layer. Then, Lund used the Freehand option of the Distortion paintbrush to enlarge the man's mouth.

Lund used a combination of film and digital source images, known as hybrid imaging, to take advantage of each method's strengths. For example, the film-based photos of the man and the sky were scanned at a very high resolution. Digital photographs, created with a Leaf DCB, allowed Lund to experiment quickly and freely with the water and lure elements. After the elements were composited together, the water was turned blue using Live Picture's Colorize layer. As a final step, text was created in Adobe Illustrator and added to the lure as an EPS Insertion layer.

Next, a splash of water was photographed in an aquarium using the Leaf DCB digital camera. The photograph was taken as a single, grayscale photo (because the Leaf DCB is a three-shot type camera, a moving subject like the water can only be taken in grayscale). The grayscale image was inserted into the image in Live Picture. By making the water layer 50-percent opaque, Lund was able to view the underlying man and sky composite as an aid to helping him place the water in just the right spot.

John Lund/Teamdigital
860 Second Street, Suite 3
San Francisco, CA 94107
Tel. (415) 957-1775
Fax. (415) 543-7665
http://www.teamdigital.com
E-mail: Teamdigtal@aol.com

Michael Brown

Ask LA-based car and truck photographer Michael Brown about the day when he first became interested in digital photography, and he describes it like it was an epiphany, an awakening.

"It was on June 4th, 1992 at 2:30 PM," Brown recalls with a laugh, "I'd just lost a huge bid for a Peterbilt job that was going to involve digital imaging. I was mad enough to want to learn more about it."

Soon after, Brown found himself standing in ZZYZX Visual Systems, a division of A & I Color Labs. Bob Goldstein, President of ZZYZX, listened attentively to Brown's explanations about losing the Peterbilt account. Then, as Goldstein led Brown into the lab for a Photoshop demo, he said, "I'm going to change your life."

"And he did," admits Brown. Within 24 hours of his meeting with Goldstein, Brown found himself sitting in Macintosh computer classes—his first lesson being how to use the mouse. Then he began teaching himself about digital imaging, with one goal in mind.

"I wanted to see if I could shoot cars locally, travel to shoot backgrounds and then see if I could composite them together seamlessly," Brown explains.

After investing $17,000 and six months of time in training and self-education, Brown had four or five sample images to show for his efforts. "It was an exhilarating experience," he recalls. And it was enough, he says, to demonstrate that his idea was viable. Soon after, he bought his first Macintosh-based imaging system.

"I've done exactly 305 car strip images since then," says Brown, "and the one thing that I've learned about digital imaging is that you've never learned everything. Every time you sit at the computer, you learn more. And the better you get at using the computer, the more potential you can see. So what's really interesting is that, after creating 305 digital car and truck photographs, they still take me the same amount of time to do—but they are infinitely more complex images." All photos and illustrations courtesy of Michael Brown.

Michael Brown's home-based digital imaging studio includes a Power Macintosh 8100 as his primary work station. This system includes 270 MB RAM and 5 GB of hard disk space, including RAID arrays. His secondary system (which was also his original system) is a Macintosh Quadra 950, with 72 MB of RAM. Brown uses Syquest and MO disks as removable media, and he archives all his data on DAT tape. According to Brown, using all external devices is a way to impress upon clients that because he is serious about his work, he has made considerable investment in professional-level equipment .

Pathfinder-Bryce Canyon

A

B

Brown makes frequent trips to America's wilderness areas to shoot stock images for use as foregrounds and backgrounds in his car photomontages. For this image of the Nissan Pathfinder, Brown selected as a foreground image a photograph he'd taken of a rocky ledge in Zion National Park in the early morning light (A). He selected a similarly lit photograph taken in Bryce Canyon National Park for use as a background image (B). Both photographs were taken with a Toyo 4×5-inch view camera, on Kodak Ektachrome 6117 film.

Based on the camera position used for the foreground and background elements, Brown decided the Nissan Pathfinder needed to be photographed from a low angle. To match the angle of the rock ridge, Brown had the front end of the vehicle raised on blocks. The photograph was taken just before sunrise at an airport, giving the vehicle a soft, unobstructed (no unwanted shadows or reflections) natural side light that matched the light of the foreground and background elements. (See page 6-12 for an explanation about how the images were digitally composited).

Michael Brown
Photographic
Productions, Inc.
P.O. Box 45969
Los Angeles, CA 90045
Tel. 310-379-7254
Fax. 310-379-3306
E-mail:
MBProd@earthlink.net

Jeff Schewe

The path that led Chicago-based photographer, Jeff Schewe, into digital photography was paved by a reputation for being a photographer who could do the impossible. "I evolved as a specialist in difficult shots," Schewe explains, "including in-camera masking, multiple camera set-ups, etc. All that stuff is pretty problematic."

Many of the problem-solving photo assignments that Schewe was hired for involved shooting separate elements for digital compositing on a proprietary, high-end workstation. This experience provided Schewe with an acute understanding of the essential techniques needed for successful digital photomontage.

First of all, says Schewe, "it's important to have a strategy or method of approaching the image." This, he says, "harks back to the Ansel Adams concept of previsualizing the image. You have to have an image in mind; otherwise, it becomes very frustrating to try to do things willy nilly." Secondly, when multiple objects are to be photographed and then composited together, it's crucial that careful attention be paid to lighting, says Schewe.

"If one object is lit with a soft light source, and the other is lit with a hard light source, they just won't blend together. For example, shadows won't match."

Schewe readily admits that his whole style of shooting has changed, due to the influences of working digitally. "I have evolved my photography to the point where I shoot only for the essence of the image," he explains, "which means paying special attention to not only the quality of light, but also the direction of the light and the camera's point of view."

In addition to the importance of shooting correctly for high quality digital imaging, Schewe points out that properly configuring computer hardware, particularly with enough RAM, can also have an effect on image quality. "If a photographer tries to shoot a photograph with less-than-adequate equipment, it's inevitable that it'll affect the quality of the final image. It won't look professional. The same is true of the computer. For example," he continues, "you may never see the RAM itself, but in terms of image quality, you will certainly see the residue of not having enough RAM." All photos and illustrations courtesy of Jeff Schewe.

Jeff Schewe's digital imaging studio is based on two systems. The main imaging system, on the left, is a Daystar Genesis 720 using 4-180mHz 604 processors. The Genesis has 1 GB of RAM, and two RAID array drives that total 16 GB of drive space. The RAID array drives are connected via FWB PCI Jackhammer boards. The system on the right is a Quadra 950 with a Daystar 601/100mHz PPC upgrade card and 256 MB of RAM. This system serves as a scanning and business administration sytem. According to Schewe, Max (right), enjoys sitting at the Quadra and surfing the Net.

Schewe is as adept in a workshop as he is behind the camera or in front of the computer. Here, he uses a welder to create a prop for use in a photograph.

Hip Hog

A

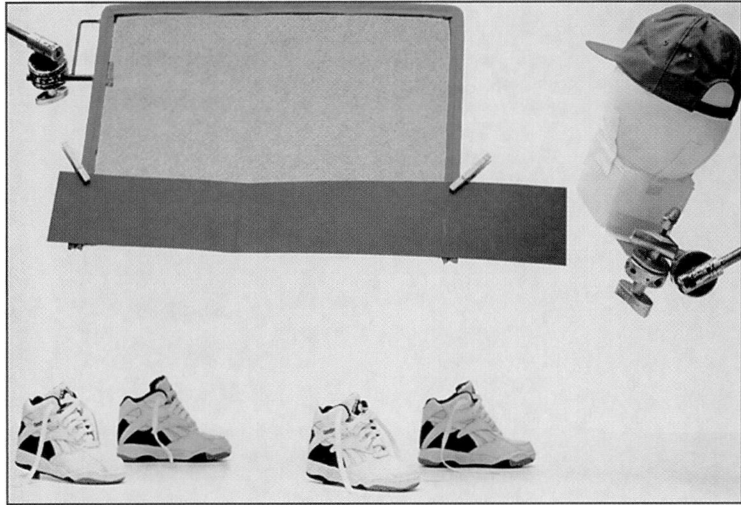

B

Whenever possible, Schewe tries to shoot multiple elements under the exact same lighting conditions. In the case of "Hip Hog," Schewe first got a photograph of the pig standing and smiling (A). Then, under the exact same lighting conditions, he placed the props in the exact position they would be in the final image. To enhance the realism, Schewe used a scrim to place a shadow on the far set of shoes, in much the same way the pig's body would naturally shade the shoes (B). For the final composite, Schewe touched up on the pig, including repairing its ear.

Jeff Schewe
Jeff Schewe Photography
624 West Willow
Chicago, Illinois 60614
T 312-951-6334
F 312-787-6814
Schewe@aol.com

Globe on Hands

A

B

After Schewe scanned the original 4×5-inch photograph of the Globe (A), he prepped it for the composite by increasing the color saturation of the continents and adding blue to the oceans (B).

The natural shape of two hands cupped together was not perfectly round (C). To improve the circular shape of the hands, Schewe used VALIS Groups' Metaflo (D).

Using a combination of Paste functions—including Paste From Snapshot and Paste From Saved—Schewe made an initial version of the image with the globe and hands together. He alternated between these Paste commands and used various blend modes and opacity settings to gradually blend the globe into the hands.

C

D

Akira Kasai

The photos on these pages were created for the contents of an interactive CD-ROM entitled "Cocktail Time," produced by co-author Akira Kasai's company, InfoArts. The photos were taken on location at a bar in Kyoto, Japan, using a minimum of equipment, including a Nikon E2 digital still camera, a tripod, and a three-foot wide roll of white seamless. All that was needed from the photographs were basic "raw" photos that could be manipulated in Photoshop to create the desired result. All photos and illustrations courtesy of Akira Kasai.

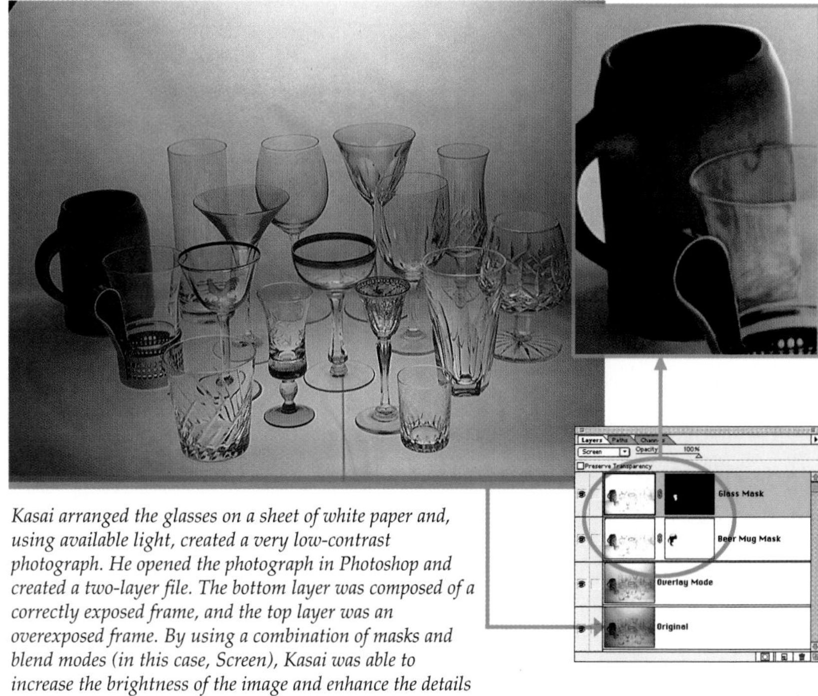

Kasai arranged the glasses on a sheet of white paper and, using available light, created a very low-contrast photograph. He opened the photograph in Photoshop and created a two-layer file. The bottom layer was composed of a correctly exposed frame, and the top layer was an overexposed frame. By using a combination of masks and blend modes (in this case, Screen), Kasai was able to increase the brightness of the image and enhance the details and translucency of the glass.

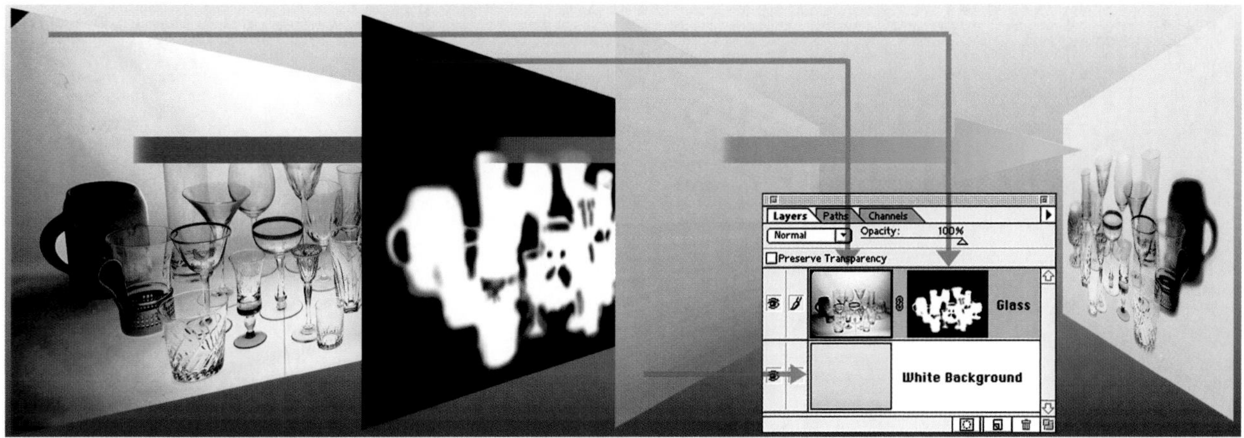

Kasai flattened the two layers. He then created a new file the same size as the photo and created a white to light gray gradation background file. The photo was placed in a layer above the background and silhouetted with a heavily blurred layer mask. The overall effect of the final result was similar to that of glass objects lit from behind by light bounced off a white background.

Because of the Nikon E2's relay lens, the depth of field couldn't be made very shallow (minimum aperture is 6.7), so Kasai used layers to help simulate a photograph taken with a shallow depth of field. First, Kasai blurred the entire image and put that on layer 1. On layer 2 he placed a non-blurred copy of the image and created a mask that revealed only the bottles. He used a third layer, which included a mask, to create a flare effect around the bottles.

This piece is essentially the same as the one above, but here Kasai made a separate "foreground blur" layer of the image, as well as a "background blur" layer of the image. He made the background blur image into layer 1 and the foreground blur image into layer 2. Above these two layers he added a third layer containing a sharp image of the bottles and masked it so that a few bottles would look in focus. He then blended the top layer into the lower layers by using a combination of 50 percent opacity and the Hard Light blend mode.

chapter 11

Appendixes

Degradation of Digital Camera Image Quality After Upsampling

The photos in this section are details of photos taken with the Nikon E2, the Scitex Leaf DCB II and the Kodak DCS460 or DCS 465 digital cameras (uncropped versions appear on pages 5-12 and 5-13). Image processing included eliminating the rainbow moiré from the Nikon E2 and the Kodak DCS images, according to the technique described on page 5-17. Then, copies of the 350 ppi resolution images were enlarged 200, 300, and 400 percent using Bicubic interpolation in Photoshop. Afterward, all images were sharpened with Unsharp Mask. The results show that enlargements up to 200 percent produce minimal quality degradation, and that, depending on usage (such as posters viewed from a distance), the absence of film grain means that enlargements up to 400 percent can be made with acceptable quality.

Nikon

Nikon

Nikon

Nikon

Nikon
AT NIKKOR

Nikon

Nikon

Nikon

Variation in Digital Image Sharpness

Original image: Kodak DCS460, unretouched. Resolution: 300 ppi.

Unsharp masking applied Amount: 190%. Radius: 1 pixel. Threshold: 0 levels.

Unsharp masking applied (minimize grain setting) Amount: 190%. Radius: 1 pixel. Threshold: 6 levels.

Rainbow moiré technique; No unsharp masking. Dust & Scratches Filter: Radius: 3 pixels. Threshold: 0 levels.

Dust & Scratches Filter (same as left) Unsharp Mask: Amount: 230%. Radius:1 pixel. Threshold: 3 levels.

Dust & Scratches Filter (same as left) Unsharp Mask: Amount: 230%. Radius:1 pixel. Threshold: 6 levels.

Dust & Scratches: Radius: 1 pixel. Threshold: 0 levels. Unsharp masking: Amount: 190%. Radius:1 pixel. Threshold: 0 levels.

Dust & Scratches: Radius: 2 pixels. Threshold: 0 levels. Unsharp masking: same as left.

Dust & Scratches: Radius: 3 pixels. Threshold: 0 levels. Unsharp masking: same as left.

Unsharp masking applied (minimize grain setting) Unsharp masking: Amount:190%. Radius:1 pixel. Threshold: 12 levels.

The photographs running across these two pages demonstrate variations in settings of the Unsharp Mask filter. In the middle and bottom rows, the Unsharp Mask filter was used in combination with the Soften a*b* technique described on page 5-18 for removing digital camera rainbow moiré artifacts using the Dust and Scratches filter.

The image at top left on the opposite page is the original, unretouched version. From left to right on the top row, the Threshold setting of the Unsharp Mask was the only setting changed. Higher Threshold settings minimized the amount that grain was accentuated, while still sharpening important features such as the eyes (see page 7-14 for an explanation about the Unsharp Mask filter settings).

In the middle row, the Dust and Scratches settings were kept constant, but the Unsharp Mask settings were varied. In the bottom row, the Unsharp Mask settings were kept constant, but the Dust and Scratches settings were changed. The image labeled Author's "Standard" represents the typical starting point settings authors apply to a 300 ppi image. The image labeled Author's "Optimum" represents the optimum combination of settings for sharpening this image and removing the rainbow moiré artifacts.

Dust & Scratches Filter (same as left) Unsharp masking: Amount: 230%. Radius: 0.5 pixel. Threshold: 0 levels.

Dust & Scratches Filter (same as left) Unsharp masking: Amount: 230%. Radius:1.5 pixel. Threshold: 0 levels.

Dust & Scratches Filter (same as left) Unsharp masking: Amount: 230%. Radius: 2.0 pixels. Threshold: 0 levels.

Dust & Scratches: Radius: 4 pixels. Threshold: 0 levels. Unsharp masking: same as left.

Dust & Scratches: Radius: 5 pixels. Threshold: 0 levels. Unsharp masking: same as left.

Dust & Scratches: Radius: 6 pixels. Threshold: 0 levels. Unsharp masking: Amount: 500%. Radius: 0.5 pixels. Threshold: 0 levels.

Digital Camera Comparison Chart: Cameras Under $5,000

The charts on the following pages appeared in the March 1997 issue of the *Future Image Report,* and are reprinted here with permission from Future Image, Inc. These charts are updated monthly in the *Future Image Report* and represent the most complete list of digital camera type and specifications available (not all specifications listed in the original chart are reproduced here). These charts are copyrighted ©(1997) by Future Image Incorporated and Alexis Gerard.

For more information about the *Future Image Report* and how to subscribe, see page 5-2. Please note that the information here was the most current at the time this book was produced in spring, 1997, and that rapid changes in the market mean that omissions are inevitable. Manufacturer's names have been abbreviated.

Digital Cameras Less Than $5,000

Manufacturer	Model	Configuration	Exposure	Image Size	Img. Depth (Max)	Onboard Storage	Removable Storage
Agfa	E-Photo 307	Camera	One Shot	640x480	24	2 MB RAM	None
Apple	QuickTake 150	Camera	One Shot	640x480	24	1 MB RAM	None
Apple	QuickTake 200	Camera	One Shot	640x480	24	None	SSFDC
Canon	PowerShot 600	Camera	One Shot	832x608	24	1 MB RAM	PCMCIA Type I/II/III
Canon	PowerShot 350	Camera	One Shot	640x480	24	None	CompactFlash 2 MB
Casio	QV-10A Plus	Camera	One Shot	480x240	24	2 MB Flash Memory	None
Casio	QV-11	Camera	One Shot	480x240	24	2 MB Flash Memory	None
Casio	QV-30 Plus	Camera	One Shot	480x240	24	2 MB Flash Memory	None
Casio	QV-10	Camera	One Shot	640x480	24	4 MB Flash Memory	None
Casio	QV-120	Camera	One Shot	640x480	24	2 MB Flash Memory	None
Casio	QV-300	Camera	One Shot	640x480	24	4 MB Flash Memory	None
Chinan	ES 3000	Camera	One Shot	640x480	24	1 MB RAM	PCMCIA Type I/II
Connectix	QuickCam	Camera-Grayscale, Still/Motion	One Shot	320x240	6 bit/4 bit	None/Tethered	None/Tethered
Connectix	Color QuickCam	Camera-Still/Motion	One Shot	640x480	24	None/Tethered	None/Tethered
Connectix	QuickCam 2	Camera-Still/Motion	One Shot	640x480	24	None/Tethered	None/Tethered
Dakota Digital	DCC-9500	Camera	One Shot	640x480	24	1 MB RAM	PCMCIA Type I/II
Dycam	3	Camera-Grayscale	One Shot	496x365	8	1 MB RAM	None
Dycam	10C	Camera	One Shot	640x480	24	1 MB RAM	PCMCIA Type I/II
Epson	PhotoPC	Camera	One Shot	640x480	24	1 MB RAM/Expandable	None
Epson	PhotoPC 500	Camera	One Shot	640x480	24	2 MB RAM/Expandable	None
Epson	Colorio	Camera-Same as PhotoPC	One Shot	640x480	24	1 MB RAM Expandable	None
Fuji	DS-220	Camera	One Shot	640x480	24	None	PCMCIA Type I/II
Fuji	DS-300	Camera	One Shot	1280x1000	24	None	PCMCIA-ATA Type I/II
Fuji	DS 7	Camera	One Shot	640x480	24	None	SSFDC
Hitachi	MPEG Camera	Camera-Motion/Still	One Shot	352x240	24	TBA	PCMCIA Type III
Kaiser	Scando 256	Camera-Grayscale	Scanning	3270x2600	8	None/Tethered	None/Tethered
Kodak	CD20	Camera	One Shot	493x373	24	1 MB RAM	None
Kodak	DC25	Camera	One Shot	493x373	24	2 MB RAM	CompactFlash
Kodak	DC50	Camera	One Shot	756x504	24	1 MB RAM	PCMCIA Type I/II

Manu-facturer	Model	Configur-ation	Exposure	Image Size	Img. Depth (Max)	Onboard Storage	Removable Storage
Kodak	DVC300	Camera	One Shot	640x480	24	None/Tethered	None/Tethered
Konica	Q EZ	Camera	One Shot	640x480	24	None	Miniature Card
Konica	Q-Mini	Camera	One Shot	640x480	24	None	CompactFlash
Leaf/Scitex	Lumina	Camera	Scanning	2700x3400	36	None/Tethered	None/Tethered
Minolta	Dimage V	Camera	One Shot	640x480	24	None	SSFDC
NEC	PC-DC 401	Camera	One Shot	768x494	24	2 MB RAM	None
NEC DCB-J2	Picona	Camera	One Shot	640x480	24	None	Miniature Card
Nikon	Coolpix 100	Camera	One Shot	512x480	24	1 MB RAM	None
Nikon	Coolpix 300	Camera	One Shot	640x480	24	4 MB RAM	None
Obsidian	Obsidian IC/100	Camera	One Shot	768x494	24	None	PCMCIA-ATA Type I/II/III
Olympus	VC-1000/1100	Camera	One Shot	768x480	24	Undetermined	PCMCIA Type I/II
Olympus	D-200L	Camera	One Shot	640x480	24	2 MB RAM	None
Olympus	D-300L	Camera	One Shot	1024x768	24	6 MB RAM	None
Olympus	C-400	Camera	One Shot	640x480	24	2 MB RAM	None
Olympus	C-410L	Camera	One Shot	640x480	24	3 MB RAM	None
Panasonic	Card Shot/NV-DCF1	Camera	One Shot	640x480	24	None	CompactFlash
Panasonic	KXL-600A-N	Camera	One Shot	640x480	24	None	CompactFlash
Pentax	E1-C90	Camera	One Shot	768x560	24	2 MB RAM	PCMCIA Type I/II
Pixera	Pixera Personal	Camera-Still/Motion	One Shot/ Scan	1280x1024	24	None/Tethered	None/Tethered
Pixera	Pixera Professional	Camera-Still/Motion	One Shot/ Scan	1280x1024	24	None/Tethered	None/Tethered
Polaroid	PDC-2000/40	Camera	One Shot	1600x1200	24	40 MB Hard Drive	None
Polaroid	PDC-2000/60	Camera	One Shot	1600x1200	24	60 MB RAM	None
Polaroid	PDC-2000/T	Camera	One Shot	1600x1200	24	None/Tethered	None/Tethered
Ricoh	RDC-1	Camera	One Shot	768x576	24	None	PCMCIA
Ricoh	RDC-2 with LCD	Camera	One Shot	768x576	24	2 MB RAM	PCMCIA Type I/II
Ricoh	RDC-2 no LCD	Camera	One Shot	768x576	24	2 MB RAM	PCMCIA Type I/II
Ricoh	RDC-2E	Camera	One Shot	768x576	24	2 MB RAM	PCMCIA Type I/II
Rhythm Watch	Visimo	Camera	One Shot	737x480	Undetermined	Undetermined	Undetermined
Samsung	SSC-410N	Camera	One Shot	768x494	24	None	CompactFlash
Sanyo	VPC-G1	Camera-Same as PhotoPC	One Shot	640x480	24	1 MB RAM Expandable	None
Schneider Praktica	Color Scan	Camera	Scanning	2700x3600	30	None/Tethered	None/Tethered
Schneider Praktica	Scan	Camera-Grayscale	Scanning	2592x3272	8	None/Tethered	None/Tethered
Sega	DIGIO	Camera	One Shot	320x240	24	None	SSFDC
Sharp	MI 10 DC	Camera/PDA	One Shot	320x240	24	2 MB RAM	Flash Memory Cards
Sharp	MD Data	Camera	One Shot	640x480	24	None	MD Data Disc Camera
Sharp	VE-LS5U	Camera	One Shot	720x480	24	4 MB RAM	None
Sharp	XL-DX1	Camera-Motion/Still	One Shot	720x480	24	2 MB RAM	TBA
Sharp	TBA - equiv. of MI 10 DC	Camera/PDA	One Shot	TBA	24	TBA	TBA
Sierra Imaging	SD 640	Camera-Same as PhotoPC	One Shot	640x480	24	1 MB RAM Expandable	None
Sony	DKC-ID1	Camera	One Shot	768x576	24	None	PCMCIA Type II
Sony	DSC-F1	Camera	One Shot	640x480	24	4 MB RAM	None
StarDot Technologies	WinCam.One	Camera-Still/Motion	One Shot	640x480	24	None/Tethered	None/Tethered
Toshiba	Proshot PDR-100	Camera	One Shot	640x480	24	2 MB RAM	PCMCIA
Toshiba	PDR-2A	Camera	One Shot	640x480	24	None	SSFDC
Vivitar	ViviCam 2000	Camera-Still/Motion	One Shot	640x480	24	1 MB RAM	None
Vivitar	ViviCam 3000	Camera	One Shot	1000x800	TBA	.5 MB RAM	PCMCIA Type I/II
Yashica	DA-1	Camera	One Shot	640x480	24	None	2" Floppy

Digital Camera Comparison: Cameras Over $5,000

The information in these charts is based on specifications appearing in the *Future Image Report*. Please see the previous page for more information.

Digital Cameras More Than $5,000

Manufac-turer	Model	Configur-ation	Exposure	Image Size (Max)	Image Depth	Onboard Storage	Removable Storage
Agfa	ActionCam	Integrated Back	One Shot/ 3 Chip	1528x1148	24	None	PCMCIA ATA Type III
Agfa	StudioCam	Camera	Scanning	4500x3648	36	None/Tethered	None/Tethered
Arca-Swiss	TrueCam	Camera/ Removable Back	Three Shot	1520x1124	24	None/Tethered	None/Tethered
Arca-Swiss	SC1	Removable Back	Scanning	6250x8450	36	None/Tethered	None/Tethered
Arca-Swiss	M-Line DCS 465	Removable Back	One Shot	2036x3060	36	None/Tethered	Removable
Associated Press	NC 2000E	Integrated Back	One Shot/ 2.25 fps	1024x1280	24	16 MB RAM	Removable
Canon/Kodak	EOS DCS 1c	Integrated Back	One Shot	3060x2036	36	16 MB RAM	PCMCIA ATA Type III
Canon/Kodak	EOS DCS 1m	Same as above-Grayscale model	One Shot	3060x2036	12	16 MB RAM	PCMCIA ATA Type III
Canon/Kodak	EOS DCS 3c	Integrated Back	One Shot	1268x1012	36	16 MB RAM	PCMCIA ATA Type III
Canon/Kodak	EOS DCS 3m	Same as above-Grayscale model	One Shot	1268x1012	12	16 MB RAM	PCMCIA ATA Type III
Canon/Kodak	EOS DCS 3ir	Same as above-Infrared model	One Shot	1268x1012	12	16 MB RAM	PCMCIA ATA Type III
Canon/Kodak	EOS DCS 5c	Integrated Back	One Shot	1524x1012	36	16 MB RAM	PCMCIA ATA Type III
Canon/Kodak	EOS DCS 5m	Same as -above Grayscale model	One Shot	1524x1012	12	16 MB RAM	PCMCIA ATA Type III
Canon/Kodak	EOS DCS 5ir	Same as above-Infrared model	One Shot	1524x1012	12	16 MB RAM	PCMCIA ATA Type III
Dicomed	FieldPro	Removable Back	Scanning	6000x7520	36	1 GB Hard Drive	None/Tethered
Dicomed	StudioPro	Removable Back	Scanning	3000x3760	36	1 GB Hard Drive	None/Tethered
Dicomed	Studio Pro XL	Removable Back	Scanning	6000x7520	36	1 GB Hard Drive	None/Tethered
Dicomed	BigShot 1000	Removable Back	One Shot	4096x4096	12	None/Tethered	None/Tethered
Dicomed	BigShot 3000	Removable Back	Three Shot	4096x4096	36	None/Tethered	None/Tethered
Dicomed	BigShot 4000	Removable Back	One Shot	4096x4096	36	None/Tethered	None/Tethered
Dicomed	BigShot TBA	Removable Back	One Shot	4096x4096	36	None/Tethered	None/Tethered
Fuji	DS 515A	Camera	One Shot/ 3 fps	1280x1000	24	None	PCMCIA
Fuji Flash	DS 505A	Camera	One Shot/ 1 fps	1280x1000	24	None	PCMCIA Type I/II ATA
Fuji Flash	HC 2000	Camera	One Shot/ 3 Chip	1280x1000	30	4 MB RAM/Expand.	PCMCIA Type I/II ATA
Kaiser	Scando Color	Camera	Scanning	3600x2700	30	None/Tethered	None/Tethered
KanImage	Digital Photog. System	Camera	Scanning	4608x3480	36	None/Tethered	None/Tethered
Kodak	DCS 410	Integrated Back	One Shot	1524x1012	36	2 MB RAM	PCMCIA Type III
Kodak	DCS 460c	Integrated Back	One Shot	3060x2036	36	8 MB RAM	PCMCIA ATA Type III
Kodak	DCS 460m	Same as above-Grayscale model	One Shot	3060x2036	36	8 MB RAM	PCMCIA ATA Type III
Kodak	DCS 465c	Removable Back	One Shot	3060x2036	36	8 MB RAM	Tethered/PCMCIA ATA Type III
Kodak	DCS 465m	Same as above-Grayscale model	One Shot	3060x2036	36	8 MB RAM	Tethered/PCMCIA ATA Type III

Manufacturer	Model	Configuration	Exposure	Image Size (Max)	Image Depth	Onboard Storage	Removable Storage
Kodak	DCS 420c	Integrated Back	One Shot	1524x1012	36	8 MB RAM	PCMCIA ATA Type III
Kodak	DCS 420m	Same as above-Grayscale model	One Shot	1524x1012	36	8 MB RAM	PCMCIA ATA Type III
Kodak	DCS 420ir	Same as above-Infrared model	One Shot	1524x1012	36	8 MB RAM	PCMCIA ATA Type III
Leaf/Scitex	Catchlight	Removable Back	One Shot	1920x1920	48	None/Tethered	None/Tethered
Leaf/Scitex	DCB II	Removable Back	Three Shot	2048x2048	42	None/Tethered	None/Tethered
Leaf/Scitex	DCB II Live	Removable Back	Three Shot	2048x2048	42	None/Tethered	None/Tethered
Leica	S1	Camera	Scanning	5000x5000	TBA	None/Tethered	None/Tethered
MegaVision	T2	Removable Back	Three Shot	2048x2048	36	None/Tethered	None/Tethered
MegaVision	ST2	Removable Back-Grayscale	One Shot	2048x2048	12	None/Tethered	None/Tethered
MegaVision	T3	Removable Back	One Shot	2048x2048	36	64 MB RAM	PCMCIA hard disk
Minolta	RD 175	Integrated Back-	One Shot	1528x1146	24	None	PCMCIA ATA Type III
Nikon	E2N	Camera-Same as Fuji DS 505A	One Shot/ 1 fps	1280x1000	24	None	PCMCIA Type I/II ATA Flash
Nikon	E2NS	Camera-Same as Fuji DS 515A	One Shot/ 3 fps	1280x1000	24	None	PCMCIA Type I/II ATA Flash
Phase One	PhotoPhase Series	Removable Backs	Scanning	5000x7142	36	None/Tethered	None/Tethered
Phase One	PhotoPhase Plus	Removable Back	Scanning	5000x7200	36	None/Tethered	None/Tethered
Phase One	PowerPhase	Removable Back	Scanning	7000x7000	36	None/Tethered	None/Tethered
Phase One	StudioKit	Removable Back	Scanning	2500x3571	36	None/Tethered	None/Tethered
Phase One	New Studiokit	Removable Back	Scanning	2500x3600	36	None/Tethered	None/Tethered
Phase One	PowerPhase for 4x5	Removable Back	Scanning	6000x8400	36	None/Tethered	None/Tethered
Phase One	PowerPhase for Bronica ETRSi	Removable Back	Scanning	6850x5300	36	None/Tethered	None/Tethered
Rollei	ChipPack	Removable Back	Three Shot	2048x2048	36	None/Tethered	None/Tethered
Rollei	DSP-104	Removable Back	One Shot/ 3 shot	2048x2048	36	None/Tethered	Tethered/PCMCIA
ScanView	Carnival 2000S	Removable Back	One Shot/ 4 shot	2048x2048	36	None/Tethered	None/Tethered to Power PC
Sinar	DCS 465	Camera/ Removable Back	One Shot	3060x2048	36	8 MB RAM	Tethered/PCMCIA ATA Type III
Sony	DKC 5000	Camera	One Shot/ 3 Chip	1520x1144	30	None/Tethered	None/Tethered
Sony	DKC-ST5	Camera	One Shot/ 3 Chip	2560x2048	24	9 Frames	None/Tethered

Index

Symbols

Q-R

S

Color Calibration Chart

The color chart on the right-hand page is used for monitor calibration. A high resolution file of this chart for printed output and a low resolution version for monitor display are included on the CD-ROM.

To use this chart for monitor calibration, cut it out and mount it onto illustration board (neutral gray is based) and place it next to your monitor under a 5,000K light source. Be sure to use a monitor hood, as explained on page 2-6.

The full process of calibrating your monitor is described on pages 2-4 to 2-15. Here we will describe each of the areas of the color chart.

1. Adjustment Base

Refer to this gray scale when adjusting Printing Inks Setup Gray Balance settings, as described on 2-13. When you use this gray scale to evaluate gray balance, we recommend that you cover all other areas on the print with gray paper. This will make it easier for you to evaluate without influence from other colors on the chart.

2. Color Step Chart

This is a color step chart with color steps numbered from 1 through 18.

■ The "K" series of steps is a gray chart printed using black ink only. By not using CMY inks in this grayscale, it will always print neutral and can be used as a reference point for determining color casts that may appear in the other two gray scales.

■ The "CMY" series of steps is a gray printed chart using cyan, magenta and yellow inks. Because of the impurities of printing inks and other influences, the area from the midtones to the shadows is not completely gray on the printed chart. Of the three grayscales, this one is a good reference to use for determining the Printing Inks Setup Gray Balance values, as described on page 2-13 (in addition to the Adjustment Base at the top of the chart).

■ The "CMYK" series of steps is a gray chart printed using all four inks. A lot of black ink was added to the shadow areas while the CMY inks were more controlled. Use this chart as a secondary chart for comparing the gray balance of hard copy output and the monitor.

■ For each color in the color chart, two series of steps have been created: one series, which includes only Wanted Colors (pure colors) and the other, which includes Unwanted Colors (muddy colors). On the series with muddy colors, steps 13 and down in particular have been created to show a dramatic loss in purity. The way these muddy colors change after step 13 (the way they darken) is used as a standard of comparison for a variety of calibration techniques.

■ Step 1 for all of the color step series is the lightest color possible immediately before white. Depending on press or printer conditions, this color may not be reproduced. Whether or not this step is reproduced is another standard of comparison to use during calibration.

See page 7-26 for a related explanation.

3. Gray Circles

The Gray Comparison Chart provides another tool for evaluating the gray point. The center circle was created to appear gray, but because there may be some variation due to the high volume printing of this book, the one that you are looking at may not necessarily be a middle gray.

If the gray balance is off, one of the gray circles around the center circle will be middle gray, and that gray circle will look the same or very similar to the background gray (the background gray was printed using only black ink).

The gray circles in the series closest to the center have been created from either 1 or 2 CMY colors and have been created to display on the monitor as gray when the Printing Inks Setup Gray Balance values are set to 0.9. Similarly, circles in the outermost series have been created from either 1 or 2 CMY colors and have been created to display on the monitor as gray when they have a gamma of 0.8. See page 2-14 for basic information about how to use this part of the chart for monitor calibration.

4. Portrait

This portrait was taken using a Kodak DCS460. It is used for overall evaluation of the monitor and the print after color calibration is complete. Points to look for are bright skin color on the hand at the bottom left, smooth tonal variation in the darker skin between the eye and the nose, and no magenta or yellow casts.

Also, the detail in the red, yellow, light blue, and dark blue cords will look very different depending upon the extent to which Unwanted Color components are included in the colors; the more Unwanted Colors there are, the more detail will be lost.

5. Vertical Color Patches

This color chart shows 100 percent values for all of the color patches in the chart—C, M, Y, M + Y (R), C + Y (G) and C + M (B).

The black patch on the bottom was printed with 100 percent C, M and Y ink. The second patch from the bottom was printed with 100 percent K ink. In order to determine your own L*a*b* values based on sample output from your or your client's printer, use a colorimeter to measure these patches and enter the values into the fields for Custom Ink Colors in Photoshop's Printing Inks Setup dialog box.

6. Horizontal Color Patches

This color chart shows color patches created with combinations of R, G, and B values of either 255 or 0, which are then converted into CMYK mode. As a reference, these patches can show how well particular Printing Inks Setup parameters are converting the RGB colors into CMYK, but they are not intended for use in calibration.

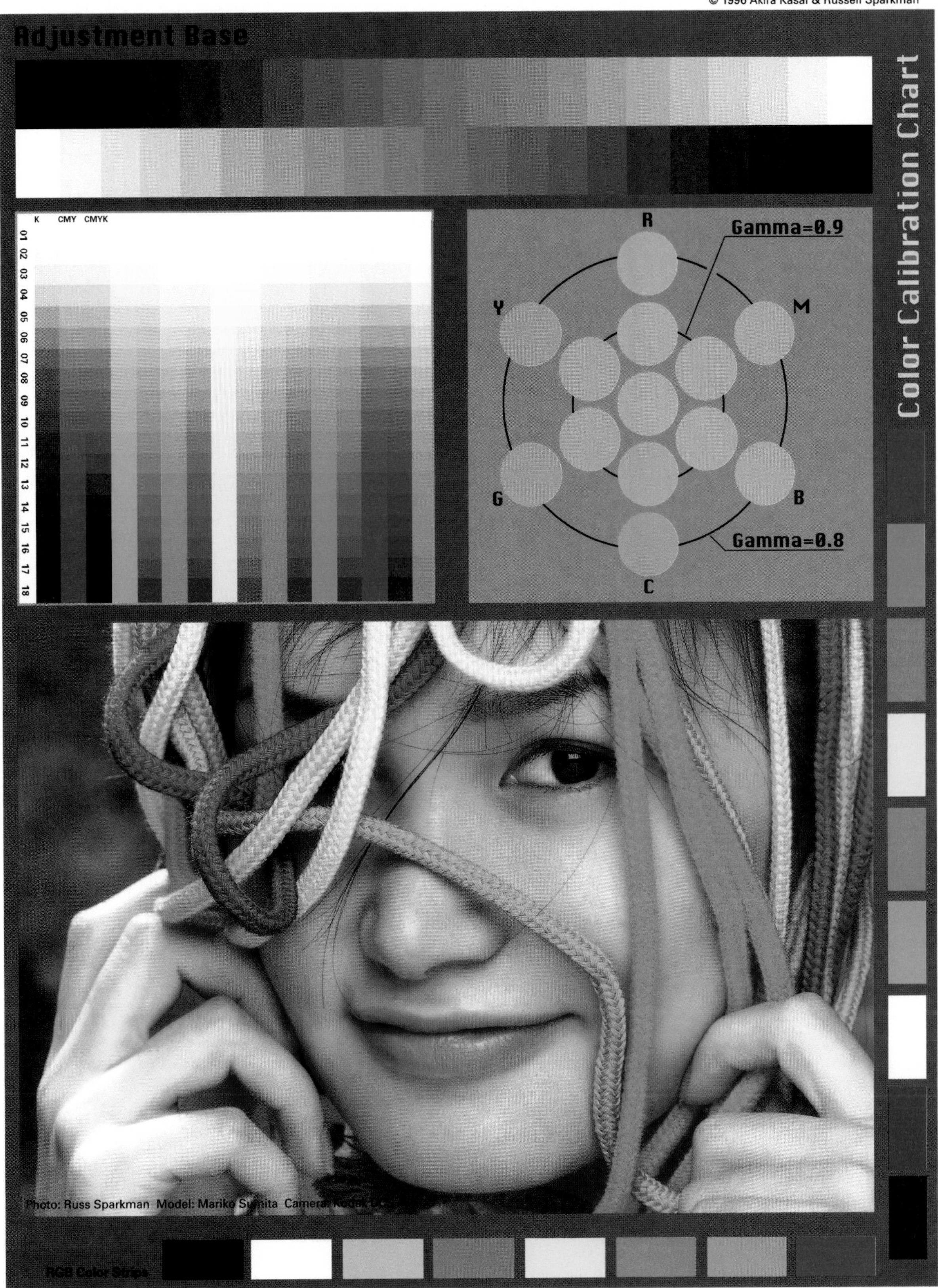
Essentials of Digital Photography
© 1996 Akira Kasai & Russell Sparkman
Adjustment Base
Color Calibration Chart
K CMY CMYK
01 02 03 04 05 06 07 08 09 10 11 12 13 14 15 16 17 18
R
Gamma=0.9
Y
M
G
B
Gamma=0.8
C
Photo: Russ Sparkman Model: Mariko Sumita
RGB Color Strips

Viewing card for comparing monitor white to reference white

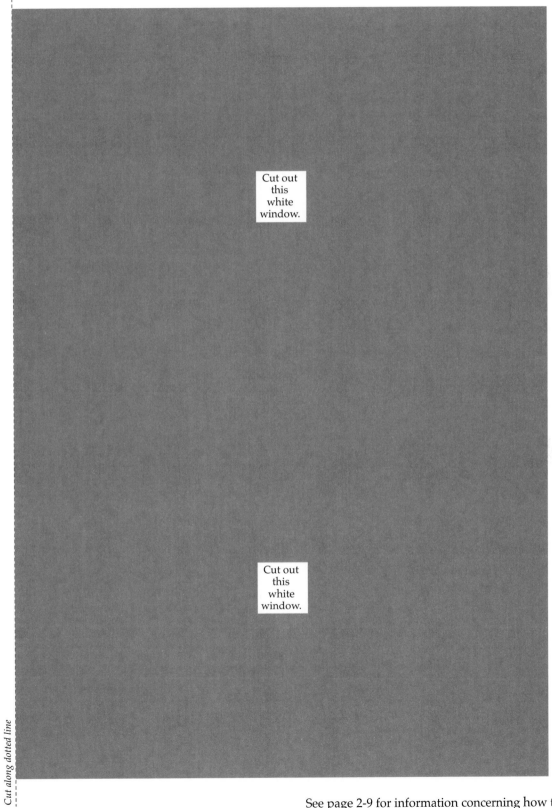

Cut along dotted line

See page 2-9 for information concerning how to use this card.

The Making of This Book

The following equipment, resources, and people contributed to the production of this book.

Equipment and Software

Digital Cameras

Kodak DCS460

Kodak DCS465 + Hasselblad 553ELX

Kodak DC50

Scitex Leaf DCB II + Hasselblad 553ELX

Nikon E2

Film-Based Cameras

Mamiya 7

Hasselblad 500CM

Nikon F2/F90

Nikon FM2

Leica M4/M6

Linhof Kardan

Toyo Field 45

Studio Lighting

Broncolor OPUS A4 (Strobe)

Broncolor HM1575 (metal halide light source)

Computers

Daystar Genesis MP600 (256 MB RAM)

Power Macintosh 8500/120 (128 MB RAM)

Removable media: 1 GB Jaz disks

Scanners

Nikon LS 1000 (35 mm film scanner)

Epson Expression 636 (flatbed scanner)

Epson FS1200S (35 mm film scanner)

Dainippon Screen FT-S700 (reflective scanner with adaptor for transparencies up to 5x5)

Printers

Kodak XLS8300 (artwork proofing)

Seiko Epson Stylus Photo (artwork proofing)

Pictrography 3000 (comparison tests)

Imagesetter

Scitex Dolev 800

The computer hardware and photographic equipment support we received for this book was the result of a coordinated effort that spanned the globe! We would like to thank the following manufacturers and Japanese distributors for their help:

Daystar Genesis MP 528 and Genesis MP 600 Marubeni Electronics/Tokyo, Japan and Daystar Digital/Atlanta, GA

Broncolor studio lighting equipment Agai Trading Corporation/Tokyo, Japan and Bron Elektronik AG/Switzerland

Hasselblad cameras and lenses Shriro Trading Company, Ltd./Tokyo, Japan

Hammer RAID array and CD-R drives Streamlogic/Chatsworth, CA, USA

Kodak DCS 460 & DCS 465 digital cameras Kodak Japan/Tokyo & Osaka

Scitex Leaf DCBII digital camera back Nihon Scitex, Ltd./Tokyo, Japan

DCM-460 Print Viewing StationShashin Kagaku Co., Ltd./Kyoto, Japan

Technical support/photographs of scanners and inkjet printers Seiko Epson Corporation/Nagano, Japan

FT-S700 scanner, photomultiplier and scanner information Dainippon Screen/Kyoto, Japan

Color positive film output experiments Konica Color Kansai/Osaka, Japan

About the CD-ROM

For Windows 95 Users

Because the explanations in this book were written for the Macintosh, using this CD-ROM may be very difficult. Please be aware of the following.

■ Choose the "View" menu rather than the Display menu because filenames do not display properly when you select Icon mode.

■ If the ReadMe and other text files do not display properly onscreen, choose Options from the Display menu and check Display All Files.

■ To open image files in Photoshop whose names do not appear with the Open command, use Open in Specified Format and select "TIFF" (*.TIF) or "Photoshop 3.0" (*.PSD) format.

■ Copy the ink settings files and the monitor setup files onto your hard disk and load them after adding the extension ".api" to the ink settings file and ".ams" to the monitor setup file.

Operating Environment

The CD-ROM for *Essentials of Digital Photography* can be used in the following computer environments.

■ Power Macintosh, 68K Macintosh

■ Windows 95 machine

Contents

■ Both Windows and Macintosh

MonitorCalib Folder (Directory)

The test charts and parameters files necessary for the monitor calibration procedure (for matching monitor display color to hard copy color), described in "The First Step—Monitor Calibration," on pages 2-4–2-15 of Chapter 2, "Digital Photography Basics," are in this folder.

MonitorCalibCMYK.tif

This is the image data file for the Color Calibration Chart which appears on page 11-23 for offset printing use. This file is 27 MB, so make sure to allow enough memory to open it in your image editing application. See page 11-22 for more information about this chart.

MonitorCalibRGB.tif

This is the RGB image file which is the basis of the MonitorCalibCMYK.tif image above. This file should be used for making test output to RGB devices, like dye sublimation printers or film recorders. See page 2-15 for instructions on how to use this RGB data to calibrate your monitor to RGB output devices (This chart is not intended to be used as a CMYK comparison chart for calibration; use only the CMYK version, MonitorCalibCMYK, for that purpose).

MonitorCheck.RGB

This color chart can be opened in Photoshop and used for the monitor black point adjustment, instead of a desktop pattern, as explained on page 2-7. This can be useful particularly for Windows users who cannot make a desktop pattern, as described in the technique.

RGBchart.tif

Use this chart if you want to measure the color coordinates of the three RGB colors on your monitor with a transmissive colorimeter to determine your own custom Phosphors values for Photoshop's Color Setting, Monitor Setup dialog box. See page 2-12.

Other Parameters Files

These parameters files are used throughout the tutorials on pages 2-4–2-15.

ToneCurveStudy Folder (Directory)

The seven image files in this folder are used in the tone curve adjustment discussion on pages 3-18–3-24.

StandardImages Folder (Directory)

This folder contains images that appear in Chapter 5, "Digital Exposures and Follow-Up Processing."

DCS460 Image, Leaf DCBII Image, NikonE2 Image, Kodak DC50 Image

These images were taken with a variety of different digital cameras of the same subject under the same lighting conditions. The images were adjusted, based on the grayscale included in the photo, to have the similar highlight, midtone and shadow values.

Konica SRS Film Photo, Nikon E2 DigiCam Photo

These are photographs of the same subject, taken on Konica SRS 35 mm color reversal film with the Nikon E2 digital camera. We have adjusted both images using the included gray scale. See page 5-4 for more information.

IR-Filter Effect

This image compares exposures using the Nikon E2 digital camera under conventional tungsten lighting conditions and exposure of the same subject using an infrared filter (described in more detail on page 5-5). The left image was taken without an infrared filter and the right image was taken with an infrared filter attached. The color cast caused by not using the infrared filter is particulary noticeable if you compare the gray cloth in both photos.

PrintTest Folder (Directory)

The PrintTest folder contains all the necessary test charts and parameters files for Chapter 7, "Digital Photography Output."

ToneCompRGB.tif

This color chart image is convenient for checking tonal compression when you output from a film recorder or other device. A procedure for doing this appears on page 7-22.

CompColorRGB.tif

Use this file when you want to understand how much the tonal range has been compressed on RGB images output from an inkjet printer or other devices, including offset printing. This is the same image as the MonitorCalibRGB.tif, but the file size has been made smaller. How to use this file to create custom Printing Inks Settings for using an RGB printer as a CMYK proofer is explained starting on page 7-25.

Other Parameters Files

Included in this folder are various parameters files mentioned in Chapter 7.

Others Folder (Directory)

This folder contains a variety of reference images.

CMYKtoRGB

Use this Photoshop Printing Inks Setup preferences file when you wish to recover the vividness of pure colors after you have converted an image to CMYK and you want to convert it back to RGB. See page 7-21.

ColorTemperature Folder

This folder contains images of the same subject taken under different lighting conditions. Use these to experiment with color correction.

DCS-GhostColor

This file shows rainbow moiré artifacts in an image taken with a 1-shot area array CCD digital camera such as the Kodak DCS460. See page 5-17 for an explanation about how to remove these types of artifacts from the image.

Under/Over-Exposure Folder

This folder contains photos of the same scene, ranging in exposure from 2 stops under to 2 stops over 1-stop increments. Use these to help understand the characteristics of over-, under- and properly exposed images on computers, as discussed in Chapter 3.

GrayScale Sample

This image is an optimally corrected Kodak Q-13 gray scale. Please use it as a reference for proper highlight (part A on the scale), midtone (part 6 on the scale, RGB= 128) or part M for the RGB equivalent on an 18 percent gray card), or shadow (part 19 on the scale) values.

Mac Only

Tutorial Images Folder

The Tutorial Images folder contains a variety of images discussed in Chapter 6, "Digital Photomontages," and Chapter 9, "System Setup for Digital Photography: Software." The files are either standard TIFF format files or files saved in native format for use in the demo applications which are included on this CD in the Demo_Appli_ForMacintosh folder. Please see Chapters 6 and 9 for more information.

Demo_Appli_ForMacintosh Folder (Directory)

Demo versions of the following software applications are included in this folder. Installation instructions are included in the ReadMe file in each folder.

- Adobe Photoshop 3.0J
- Adobe Photoshop 3.05E
- Live Picture 2.1J
- Live Picture 2.5E
- xRes 3.0E
- Painter 4J
- Painter 4E
- Quantum Mechanic (see the ReadMe file in the folder)
- Valis Flo' Sampler (sampler of multimedia software)

Windows Only

Tutorial Images Folder

The Tutorial Images folder contains a variety of images used in Chapter 6.

For Windows users, we've only included image files in formats that can be opened on Windows versions of Adobe Photoshop and Painter. Please see Chapters 6 and 9 for more information.

Demo_Apl For Windows Directory

Demo versions of the following software applications are included in this folder. Installation instructions are included in the ReadMe file in each folder.

- Adobe Photoshop 3.0J
- Painter 4E

Users of the Photoshop 3.0 demo software on this CD-ROM will be able to open most of the image files on this CD-ROM. The image file titled "ImageChain," however, was included to show Photoshop 4.0's new feature, Adjustment Layers, in use. If opened in Photoshop 3.0, the Adjustment Layers in this image will appear as layers that are filled with solid white.